Daniel Boone Alone in the Wilderness.
SEE PAGE 259.

OUR WESTERN BORDER
IN
EARLY PIONEER DAYS

Containing the True Account of
Western Frontier Life and Struggle
in the Most Heroic Age of America

THRILLING NARRATIVES OF DARING DEEDS AND MARVELOUS ADVENTURES OF AMERICAN PIONEERS MORE THAN A CENTURY AGO, EMBRACING DESPERATE CONFLICTS WITH INDIANS, TALES OF CAPTIVITY, STORIES OF MASSACRE, MIRACULOUS ESCAPES, ADVENTURES OF FAMOUS SCOUTS, HUNTERS, TRAPPERS, PIONEER WOMEN, BRAVE BOYS, AND INDIAN CHIEFS OF THE EARLY DAYS OF AMERICAN HISTORY

Rare Tales of the Western Border
(Now Out of Print and Otherwise Impossible to Obtain)

Embellished with Many Costly, Rare and
Beautiful Engravings on Wood

Charles McKnight
The Famous Historian of Pioneer America
Author of *Old Fort DuQuesne* and *Simon Girty*

HERITAGE BOOKS
2016

HERITAGE BOOKS
AN IMPRINT OF HERITAGE BOOKS, INC.

Books, CDs, and more—Worldwide

For our listing of thousands of titles see our website
at
www.HeritageBooks.com

A Facsimile Reprint
Published 2016 by
HERITAGE BOOKS, INC.
Publishing Division
5810 Ruatan Street
Berwyn Heights, Md. 20740

Copyright © 1993 Heritage Books, Inc.

Entered according to the act of Congress, in the year 1875, by
Charles McKnight
In the office of the Librarian of Congress, Washington, D.C.

Copyright © 1902 Educational Company, Chicago

— Publisher's Notice —
In reprints such as this, it is often not possible to remove blemishes from the original. We feel the contents of this book warrant its reissue despite these blemishes and hope you will agree and read it with pleasure.

International Standard Book Numbers
Paperbound: 978-1-55613-843-0
Clothbound: 978-0-7884-6360-0

TABLE OF CONTENTS.

Chapter I.

INTRODUCTION—Destruction of the Erie Tribe of Indians—Contrast Drawn between the French Canadian and the English Trader—Washington's First Visit to the Great West—He is hurled into the Allegheny and shot at by a Savage—Washington's First Campaign—The Surrender of Fort Necessity—Remarkable Adventures of Major Robert Stobo—His Escape from Quebec and Daring Exploits—He Captures two Ships with all on Board—Braddock's Expedition against Fort Duquesne—The Character of Braddock and his Army—The Disastrous Battle of Braddocks Fields—Sir Peter Halket's Death—Braddock's Retreat and Death—Capture of Fort Duquesne—Colonel Grant's Defeat—Highland Rage—Strange Discovery by the young Sir Peter Halket of the Skeletons of Father and Brother—The Touching Story of Fanny Braddock—Remarkable Adventures of Colonel James Smith, Five Years a Captive among the Indians—Ducked in the River by three Squaws—Adopted into an Indian Tribe—Cunning of the Catawbas—Smith Lost in the Woods—Odd Ways of Hunting Bears, Foxes, Raccoons, &c.—Attempt to Run Down Horses—Scolded for Helping the Squaws—Habits of the Beaver—Smith Snowed Up and Lost—Singular Indian Customs—An Indian Drinking Frolic—Indian Deer Drive and Ring Hunt—Novel Fishing—Smith's Marriage—A Wilderness Hermit—He takes a British Fort—Captain Jack, the "Wild Hunter of the Juniata"...1–111

Chapter II.

THE CONSPIRACY OF PONTIAC—First Mutterings of the Awful Storm—Pontiac's Subtlety—Machillimackinac Captured through a Game of Ball—The Trader Henry's Narrow Escapes from Death—Obstinate Defence of Presq' Isle Fort—Pontiac's Siege of Detroit—An Ojibwa Maid Reveals the Plot—Officers Captured—Anecdotes of Pontiac—A Thrilling Boat Scene—A Frightful Massacre—Capture of Forts—Fire Rafts—Old Major Campbell Killed—A Fierce Struggle at Bloody Run—A Dreadful Repulse—The Siege Abandoned—Death of the Mighty Pontiac—Guyasutha's Attack on Fort Pitt and Repulse—Ruse with a Stuffed Paddy—Bouquet Comes to the Rescue—His Desperate Battle of Bushy Run—He Penetrates into the Heart of the Indian Country—Touching Scenes on the Delivery of the Captives—The Desperate Battle of Point Pleasant—General Andrew Lewis—The Battle Rages—The Savages Retreat—Atrocious Murder of Cornstalk and his Son—The Murder of the Great Chief, Bald Eagle—Sketch of Logan, the Famous Mingo Chief—Massacre of the Conestoga Indians...112–182

Chapter III.

LIFE ON THE BORDER—Manners and Customs of Western Pioneers—The Titles to Lands and Hardships of Settlers—Hunting and Hunters of the Border—How Marriages were Conducted—Setting up Housekeeping—Strange Frolics—Pioneer Women and Their Duties—Tattling, Shirking and Thieving, and how Punished—Household Furniture and Customs—Indian Tracking and Fighting—Sports and Pastimes on the Border—Captivity of John McCullough and his Adventures among Savages—How he was Made Happy—An Indian Boy Shot and Killed and McCullough Suspected—Captive nearly Drowned—A Squaw Whipped for Abusing Him—Novel Punishment—McCullough Escapes from his Own Father—Captivity and Escape of the Bard Family—Horrible Death of Daniel McManimy by Torture—Wanderings in Search of a Lost Wife—Origin of the Indian Term "Long-Knives"—John Harris, Founder of Harrisburg, Pa.—Dr. Benjamin Franklin as a Commander—Conrade Weiser and the Onondaga Chief—Border Forts, Stations and Block-Houses—A Singular Will Case on the Border—Sir William Johnson, Baronet—"A Fine old Irish Gentleman, all of the Olden Time"—Peculiar Education of Sir William's two Daughters—He Marries the Famous Molly Brant—A Wild Indian Girl—A late Visit to Johnson Hall and Castle............183–252

Chapter IV.

DANIEL BOONE, PIONEER OF KENTUCKY—Kentucky as it was in the Older Time—Boone Captured for the First Time and Escapes—Alone in the Wilderness—He Moves his Family West and Loses a Son—Capture of his Daughter and the Calloway Girls—His Fight with two Savages and Capture—Siege of Boonesborough—Indian Stratagems Foiled—Defeat of Captain Estill—A Well-Fought Action—Simon Girty's Desperate Attack on Bryant's Station—Heroism of the Kentucky Women—Running a Bloody Gauntlet—Girty Chaffed by Reynolds—Disastrous Battle of the Blue Licks—Boone's Son Killed—Thrilling Incidents—Reynolds' Capture—Hugh McGary's Fierce Character and Defence—Boone's Last Days—Touching Scenes—Marks out his own Grave—Two New Anecdotes of Boone—Kentucky Sports—Boone Barking Squirrels—Driving the Nail and Snuffing the Candle by Rifle—General Simon Kenton alias Butler—Thinks he is a Murderer—Herds of Elk and Buffalo—Hendricks Burnt—Kenton's Fight—Kenton Passes Through a Series of Extraordinary Adventures—He Tries a Mazeppa Ride—Escape and Recapture—Girty Intercedes and Saves his Friend—A Savage Axe Blow—Kenton meets Logan—Butler Changes his Name to Kenton—His Last Sorrowful Years—The Wetzel Family, Father and Five Sons—Lewis the Right Arm of the Wheeling Border—Martin Wetzel Captured and Kills three Savages—John Wetzel on a Horse-Stealing Expedition and Captures an Obstinate Savage—Jacob Wetzel and Simon Kenton Attack a Camp—Lewis Wetzel and his Dare-Devil Adventures—He Slays Three Savages in a Running Fight—Shoots a Red Gobbler and Attacks a Camp—Handcuffed by Harmar and Escapes—The Border Rises to his Rescue—Thrilling Adventure...253–349

TABLE OF CONTENTS.

CHAPTER V.

THE ZANE FAMILY WHO SETTLED WHEELING—Shooting Adventures—Major Samuel McColloch and his Famous Leap—Benjamin Logan and his Heroic Deeds—Perilous Journey after Powder—Bowman's Singular Behavior—Murder of Moluntha by the Fierce Hugh McGary—Another Account—A Spirited Lad and how he Became Famous—His Romantic Death—Adventures of Captain Johnny—A Desperate Indian Duel—Captain William Hardin, Pioneer of Kentucky—Captain Bland Ballard and his Adventures—Exciting Adventure of "Big Joe Logston"—Jack Wells' Dream and What Came of It—Major Robert Benham and his Strange Adventure—McConnel's Capture and Signal Revenge—Adventure of the Three Brothers McAfee—Bryant's and Hogan's Parties Assaulted by Indians—A Schoolmaster Attacked by a Wild Cat—David Morgan's Famous Combat with two Savages—Events from Dunmore's War to the Moravian Massacre—The Delaware Chiefs, Captains Pipe and White Eyes—The Tories, Girty, Elliott and McKee, Desert from Fort Pitt—Death of White Eyes—A Horrid Massacre.......................344-896

CHAPTER VI.

GOD'S MIGHTY WORK IN THE WILDERNESS—King Pomoacon Destroys the Moravian Towns and Carries the Inhabitants Captive—Frightful Massacre of Moravians at Gnadenhutten—The Converts told to Prepare for Death—Touching Scenes—Driven into two Slaughter Houses and Inhumanly Butchered—One Little Boy Saved—Slaughter Renewed at Smoky Island—Full Sketch of Simon Girty, the "White Savage"—He Marries the Beautiful Kate Malott—Captain Samuel Brady, the Daring Partisan Leader—His First Bold Scout to the Upper Sandusky—A Conflict at "Brady's Bend"—His Adventure with Phouts—Saves Himself by a Shrewd Device—A Wholesale Kill—Curing a "Sick Gun"—A Line Shot and Three Savages "Bagged"—The Lone Hunter's Revenge—A Dread Holocaust—Tracked by a Dog—An Indian Captured—"Brady's Leap" over the Cuyahoga River—His Trial, Marriage and Death—Andy Poe's Famous Fight with Big Foot—Only Reliable Account yet Published—The Two make a Desperate Effort to Drown Each Other—Poe's Fight with a Young Bull—A Revenge Thwarted—Colonel Crawford's Expedition against Sandusky—A Fight with General Daniel Morgan—Disastrous Defeat and Retreat, and Horrible Death by Torture—Dr. Knight's Escape—Slover's Capture and Mad Ride for Life—The Mysterious Major John Rose turns out to be a Russian Nobleman...397-476

CHAPTER VII.

GENERAL GEORGE ROGERS CLARK—His Heroic Deeds—Character of Border Warfare—Secret Advance on Kaskaskia—Singular Scenes—Big Gate Won Over—Chiefs Thrown into Irons—Extraordinary Scenes at a Council—Vincennes Retaken—In Great Peril—Strangest and Most Daring March on Record—Wading Through Deep Waters—Clark's Stratagems — Kentucky

TABLE OF CONTENTS.

Sharp Shooting—Major Hay Trembles—Curious Incident—Fort Surrenders—Clark's Disappointments and Death—"The War Belt, a Legend of North Bend"—James Harrod, Pioneer Hunter and Indian Slayer—He Nurses a Wounded Indian—Combat and Escape of Peter Kennedy—Adventure of Boone, related by himself...477-515

Chapter VIII.

The Two Sieges of Fort Henry—Mason's and Ogle's Commands Cut to Pieces—Deplorable Ambuscade of Foreman's Party—Second Siege of Wheeling in 1782—A Wooden Monster—Betty Zane's "Gunpowder Exploit"—The Northwestern Campaign—Expedition of General Harmar—Singular Adventure of Johonnet—Desperate Combat—Disastrous Defeat of General St. Clair—General Butler Killed—Prodigious Slaughter and Disgraceful Rout—The Ranger's Race for Life—Colonel Darke's Escape—Mad Anthony Wayne tries it and Wins—Battle of "Fallen Timbers"—Enemy Routed—Captain Wells and Robert McClellan, the Rangers, and their Thrilling Exploits—Singular Recovery of a Brother—Five Rangers Attack a Camp—McClellan Rescued by a Girl—More of McClellan's Adventures—Alone in a Desert and Reduced to Starvation...516-570

Chapter IX.

A Series of Thrilling Events—Adventures of May, Johnston, Flinn and Skyles—A Successful Decoy and Boat Capture—Exciting Chase and Repulse—Johnston Bothered by a Cow—The Game of "Nosey"—Two Children saved by Messhawa—Flinn Tortured—Wonderful Escape of Skyles—Miss Fleming's Sad Plight—Rescued by The Crane—Adventures of Ward, Calvin and Kenton—Ward Finds a Lost Brother—Desperate Attack on Hubbell's Boat—An Obstinate Resistance—A Brave Boy—Savage Boat Attack and Terrible Combat—An Obstinate Defence and Barren Victory—A Fierce Conflict by three Kentuckians—Thomas Marshall and James Girty—Captain Ward and the Fat Dutchman—Exciting Narrative of Van Campen.............571-624

Chapter X.

The Frightful Massacre of Wyoming—Catharine Montour alias Queen Esther—Fierce Attack of Hammond and the Bennetts—Frances Slocum, the Lost Sister—Revenge of Colonel John Moredock—Thrilling Adventure of Audubon, the Naturalist—Ogilvie's Contrary Adventure—Obstinate Combat of Higgins, the Ranger—Colter's Famous Race for Life—An Indian's Sagacity at Trailing—Bell's Conflict with three Savages—Western Emigration—Odd Scenes—Pack-Horses—Boating Life on the Western Waters—Mike Fink, the "Last of the Keelboatmen"—Game and "Deer Drives" of the Olden Time—Captain Minter's Famous Bear Fight—How Muldrow Found his Next Neighbor—A Wild White Man and his Story—How Major Smith Recovered his Sweetheart—Jesse Hughes, the Mountain Hunter—Sad Death of Captain

Van Buskirk—Massacre of the Purdy Family—Massacre of the Tush Family—Massacre of Captain Thomas and Family—Attack upon Kirkwood's Cabin—A "Perfect Devil" Kills Seven Indians—Levi Morgan's Stratagem for Life—Riddled with Bullets and yet Escapes—A Handsome Squaw makes Love to Biggs—Cacasotte throws Fourteen Robbers Overboard..................625-683

Chapter XI.

PIONEER WOMEN—THEIR TRIALS AND HEROISM—Touching Narrative of Massy Harbison—Desperate Attack on Widow Scraggs' Cabins—Mrs. Merrill, the Terrible "Long-Knife" Squaw—Family of Mrs. Daviess Captured—A Rescue—Murder of the Two Misses Crow—Desperate Attack on the Cunningham's—Captivity and Wanderings of Mrs. Frances Scott—Rebecca Boone, and how Daniel Won Her—"Mad Ann Bailey," of West Virginia—The Beautiful and Dashing Louisa St. Clair—Mrs. Mason Kills One and Frightens a Score—Escape of Hannah Dennis—Mrs. Clendenin—Mrs. Cunningham Attacks Two Indians—Heroic Defence by the Two Widows Cook—"That's John's Gun"—A Widow Won at Last—Ruth Sevier marries a Shawnee Chief—The "Isaac and Rebecca" of West Virginia....................684-719

Chapter XII.

PLUCK AND SPIRIT OF THE BORDER BOYS—Remarkable Exploit of the Johnson Boys—A Lad Kills a Red-Crested Gobbler—Capture of Two Boys and the Price Paid—Adventures of Five Kentucky Boys—Jonathan Alder Captured—His Strange Return—The Captivity of Two Little Brothers—Francis Downing Saved by a Bear—Narrative of John Brickell's Captivity—Two Touching Instances of Indian Generosity—Adventures of Young James Ray—Four Hours under Fire and how Saved—How Readily Captive Boys became Indianized—Two Lads save the Life of a Girl—George Bozarth's Ruse and Escape—Two Boys in the Woods all Winter—A Boy Made to Slay Six Indians—Anecdotes of Indians..720-752

LIST OF ILLUSTRATIONS.

DANIEL BOONE ALONE IN THE WILDERNESS, - - Frontispiece.
YOUNG WASHINGTON HURLED INTO THE ICY ALLEGHENY, - - 21
MAJOR HALKET DISCOVERS SKELETONS OF FATHER AND BROTHER, 67
YOUNG SMITH DUCKED IN THE RIVER BY SQUAWS, - - - 76
INDIAN MAID BETRAYING PONTIAC'S PLOT TO GLADWYN, - 128
RECOVERY OF CAPTIVE CHILD BY A MOTHER, - - - - 159
ABDUCTION OF THE BOONE AND CALLOWAY GIRLS, - - 261
SIMON KENTON TAKES A MAZEPPA RIDE, - - - - - 305
LEWIS WETZEL SLAYS THREE IN A RUNNING FIGHT, - - 329
MAJOR SAM. MCCOLLOCH'S FAMOUS PLUNGE, - - - - 350
CAPT. SAM. BRADY, THE DARING PARTISAN LEADER, - - 426
ANDREW POE'S FAMOUS COMBAT WITH BIG FOOT, - - - 445
TWO VICTIMS OFFERED TO APPEASE GEN. CLARK, - - 488
MIKE FINK, THE "LAST OF THE KEELBOATMEN," - - 658
A PIONEER WOMAN MAKES DESPERATE WORK, - - 698
THE LITTLE JOHNSON LADS KILL THEIR CAPTORS, - - 722

PREFACE.

The object of the following work is simple, and may be expressed in few words. We aim to exhibit to the present generation, a faithful and reliable portraiture of Western Frontier Life and Struggle. We confine ourselves chiefly to what may fitly be called the Heroic Age of the Border, embraced between Dunmore's War of 1774 and the Battle of Fallen Timbers, in 1794, when the power of the Western Confederation was forever crushed, and its coherence utterly destroyed by "Mad Anthony Wayne."

Never since, or even including, the feudal times of the Robber Barons of Germany, or of the Moss Troopers of Scotland, has that stormy and turbulent period been excelled for deeds of personal prowess and of dauntless, unrecking courage. It really seems as if the constant environment and familiarity with perils the most instant and appalling, had begotten for them an utter contempt. The iron-hearted and steel-nerved woodsmen of the Border appear absolutely to have known no fear, and to have bidden a grim and unflinching defiance to all danger, come in whatever Protean shape it might. They even seemed to court it and to grow restive at its absence. As with Fitz James—

> If a path were dangerous known,
> The danger's self was lure alone.

The cruel and furious warfare that ever existed between the jealous red possessor and the resolute white invader of the Western soil, was one to the death and to the bitter end. It was, in fierceness and stubbornness, much like—and for the self-same reasons, too—that between God's wandering people and the nations beyond Jordan. Before them lay the promised Canaan—the "land flowing with milk and honey." They were bidden to go in and "possess it," and to smite the inhabitants thereof "hip and thigh." The contest was to be one of extermination to one side or the other—and the Jews won.

We have sought to avoid overloading our work with cumbrous detail, but to connect together chronologically a few only of the more salient and memorable of the Combats, Massacres and Captivities with which that tempestuous period actually bristles; to sketch some of the more prominent actors who best illustrate the spirit of that time, and to group together some representative facts and every-day occurrences, so as to give those of a far different age and occupation some idea of the domestic and social life of the wilderness—the sports, perils and privations of our Western Border, one hundred years ago.

The old and well-thumbed Border books of Pritts, Withers, Doddridge, De-Hass, McClung and McDonald — filled to repletion with the stirring adventures or harrowing sufferings of the exposed and oft-smitten Border—have long been out of print and cannot now be obtained "for love or money." These we have patiently sifted—in many instances corrected—and herein essay to give the very cream of them all, adding much fresh and interesting information gleaned from our researches in this line, or furnished us by the descendants of the Pioneers, or by those who have made Border History a specialty. It gives us pleasure, in this regard, to acknowledge our personal obligations to such enthusiastic and well-posted collectors as Lyman C. Draper, of Wisconsin; Wills DeHass, of West Virginia; Dr. W. A. Irvine, of Pennsylvania; C. W. Butterfield, of Bucyrus, Ohio; General L. V. Bierce, of Akron, Ohio; Messrs. Veech, Hampton, Craig and Schwartz, of Pittsburgh, and others, who have so cheerfully assisted us in our "labor of love."

It is great pity that the simple and unlettered actors in the rude and eventful old Border days recorded so little of their stirring deeds and conflicts, and that, hence, so much is now left to changing and confusing tradition. As one after another Pioneer has passed from the stage, the power of amending all this has been diminished. It is now, alas! almost too late. What can yet be done, however, should speedily be done to rescue from oblivion the evanescent memories of days that are past; to supply existing deficiencies; to correct the many errors which prevail, and to restore some degree of order to the great confusion existing among Border Chronicles and Traditions. This is now so great as to amount, not only to marked discrepancies of fact, date and locality, but, in many instances, almost to positive contradictions. Such disorder rules as to justify, in a measure, the biting remark of that witty scoffer, Voltaire, that "History does not *always* lie."

PREFACE.

We have to do with a time and condition of our nation's progress so strange and of such marked peculiarity, that nothing like unto it can ever again occur. It is said of Sir Walter Raleigh, that when once engaged writing history, he saw a fracas occur just before him, but was so disgusted and discouraged by the different and contradictory accounts brought of it, that he tore his manuscript into fragments, remarking, in effect, that since it was so difficult to record the exact truth about events happening right before one's eye, how impossible it must be to attain accuracy as to occurrences transpiring centuries before. There is a pregnant truth in the anecdote, and each year makes the task of amending and justifying our Border History and Traditions more difficult. In this duty each "picker up of unconsidered trifles" has his value, for it is of such stuff that history is made.

We have striven to contribute *our* share; taking pains to be correct; rejecting all we knew to be false; supplementing, where possible, what was insufficient, and amending what was confusing and disjointed. While our aim is truth, we do not profess infallibility. If we can show through what perils, trials and privations our country has been won, we thereby show—and so attain the object of our work—how dearly prized it should be by all, and how sacred should be the memories of the old Pioneers and their families, who fought so heroically, suffered so patiently and endured so persistently,

INDEX.

	Page.		Page.
Alaquippa, Queen	21	Forces a peace and recovers hundreds of captives	156
Alder, Jonathan, captured	725	Brickell's captivity	736
His strange return	728	Bryant's and Hogan's party attacked	381
Anecdotes of Indians	748		
Audubon, Thrilling adventure of	636	Brothers, Two little, captured	731
		Butler, General Richard, hero of North Bend council	502
Bailey, "Mad Ann," of W. Va	709		
Bard Family, Captivity of	225	Death of, at St. Clair's defeat	539
Bald Eagle, Murder of	168		
Battle of Braddocks Fields	47	Cacasotte, throws fourteen robbers overboard	681
Of Blue Licks	277		
Of Fallen Timbers	550	Canadian, French	13
Of Bushy Run	152	Captivities—Col. James Smith	75
Of Point Pleasant	161	McCullough	204
Of Bloody Run	143	Bard Family	225
Benham, Major, his adventure	374	John Brickell	736
Bell, Sam'l, his deadly conflict	649	Jonathan Alder	725
Biggs, William, made love to by a handsome squaw	680	Mrs. Clendenin	713
		Colonel Crawford	456
Bingaman kills seven Indians	677	Massy Harbison	685
Bloody Run, Battle of	143	Casey, Wm., a lad, saves his sister	744
Blue Licks, Battle of	277	Catawbas, Cherokees and Chickasaws	6
Boating life on Western waters	653		
Boone, Daniel, Sketch of	253	Clark, George Rogers, Sketch of	477
He moves to Kentucky	257	Marches on Kaskaskia	481
Left alone in the wilderness	258	Treatment of Indians	485
Daughter stolen off	261	His strange march	490
Kills two savages	263	Takes Vincennes	495
At Battle of Blue Licks	278	His disappointment and death	498
Son Israel killed	280	At North Bend council	500
Last days of	286	Clendenin, Mrs., Capture of	713
Death and burial of	288	Colter's famous race for life	644
Portrait of	1	Conestoga Indians, Massacre of	177
Anecdotes of	289	Cook, The widows, their heroic defence	715
"Barking squirrels"	290		
Adventure of, related by himself	512	Cornstalk, Chief	166
		Murder of, and son	166
Boone, Rebecca, and how Daniel won her	708	Coureurs des Bois	15
		Crawford, Colonel William	449
Boys of the Border, their pluck and spirit	719	Who he was	451
		Expedition against Sandusky	454
Boy kills an Indian	722	His defeat and capture	456-459
How easily became Indianized	722	Interview with Girty	460
Two remain in the woods all Winter	746	Awful tortures and death of	462
		Crepps and Crist, their desperate boat fight	610
Brady, Captain Sam'l, Sketch of	426		
Brady's Bend	429	Crow, the Misses, Murder of	702
Kills two savages at a shot	433	Cunningham, Mrs., Capture of, and saved by Girty	70
Attacks an Indian camp	435		
Tracked by a dog	437		
His famous "Leap"	439	Cunningham, Mrs. Edward, her valor	714
His trial, marriage and death	441		
Bozarth, Geo., his ruse and escape	745		
Bouquet, Colonel Henry	150	Dalzell, Captain	142
His battle of Bushy Run	152	Death of	145

INDEX

	Page		Page
Darke, Lt. Col., his daring and escape	546	Hammond and the Bennetts, Escape of	629
Daviess, Mrs. Samuel, Courage of	699	Harmar, Gen., his campaign and defeat	530
Davis, Caffree and McClure, their fierce combat with Indians	615	Harris, John, of Harrisburg	234
Deer drives and ring hunts	101	Harbison, Massy, Touching narrative of	685
Delaware Indians	6	Harrod, James, Life and adventures of	505
Dennis, Hannah, Escape of	712	Nurses a wounded Indian	508
Detroit, Siege of	127	Mysterious death of	509
Downing, Francis, saved by a bear	734	Hart, Silas, his son avenges him	745
Dunbar, the Tardy	45-60	Henry, Alexander, the trader	118
Dunmore's War	161	His adventures	121
Duquesne, Fort	22	Higgins, the Ranger, Obstinate combat of	641
Braddock's expedition against	40	Holland, Luke, his sagacity at trailing	647
Capture of	64	Hubbell, Captain, Desperate attack on boat of	604
Elliott, Capt., deserts to the British	392	Obstinate defence	606
Emigration, Western—odd scenes	650	Hughes, Jesse, mountain hunter	669
English traders	13	Hurons, The	6
Eries, Destruction of	7		
Erlewyne, Fred., a lad, captured	723	Indians, Anecdotes of	748
Estill, Captain, his well-fought action and death	269	Introduction	1
		Iroquois or Six Nations	7
Fink, Mike, last of the keelboatmen	655	Jack, Captain, the wild hunter of the Juniata	56-109
His feats and death	666-669	Jesuit Pioneers	14
Fleming, The Misses, adventures	569	Johonnet, Jackson, Singular adventures of	532
Sad plight of, and rescue	594	Johnson Boys, Remarkable exploits of	721
Flinn, the hunter, Sad fate of	589	Johnson, Sir William, Baronet	243
Forts, Presq' Isle	125	Peculiar education of his daughters	245
Detroit	127	Author's late visit to Johnson Hall and Castle	248
Duquesne	22		
Henry	515	Kennan, the Ranger, his race for life	542
Sieges of	523	Gallantry	545
Necessity	23	Kennedy, Peter, Combat and escape of	510
Machillimackinac	117	Kenton, Simon	298
Franklin as a commander	236	Remarkable adventures of	301
French Canadian	13	Saved by Girty	309
Game and deer drives of olden time	659	Meets Logan	312
Girty, James	618	His last years	315
Girty, Simon, before Bryant's station	274	Appearance of	318
Saves Kenton	309	Adventure with Wetzel	325
At Crawford's torture	461	Adventures with Ward and Calvin	598
Not at first siege of Wheeling	517	Kentucky in the olden time	254
But at second	523	Kentucky, Women of	273
Repentant	618	Sports of	290
Saves Mrs. Cunningham	705	Kentucky, Adventures of five boys of	725
Deserts from Fort Pitt	392		
Sketch of	418		
His attack on Bryant's station	271		
Marries Kate Malott	418		
Death of	424		
Halket, Sir Peter	44		
His death	55		
Singular discovery of his remains by his son	66		

INDEX.

	Page.		Page
Kirk, a lad, made to slay six Indians	747	Muldrow, how he found his neighbor	664
Kirkwood, Captain Robert	546-675	Northwestern campaign	529
Knights of Golden Horseshoe	2		
Knight, Dr. John, his wonderful escape	468	Ogilvie, Pleasant adventure of	639
		One hundred years ago	1-8
Lewis, General Andrew	164		
Little Turtle, a chief	546	Pack-horseing	652
Logan, Benjamin	352	Perry, Levi and Reuben, two little boys, in woods all Winter	746
After battle of Blue Licks	284	Pioneers, Life and customs of	183
Logan, the famous Mingo Chief	170	Hardships of	187
Death of	175	Woodcraft and hunting	191
Logan, Captain, a Shawnee chief	360	Weddings, frolics and amusements of	193
His romantic death	363		
Logston, "Big Joe"	369	Pioneer women	4-5
		Of Kentucky	273
Machillimackinac, Fort, captured	117	Their trials and heroism	685
Marshall, Thos., and Jas. Girty	618	Pipe, Captain	389
Mason, Mrs. George, kills one and frightens a score	711	Pitt, Fort, Guyasutha's siege of	148
Massawomee Indians	6	Poe, Andrew and Adam, their famous fight with Bigfoot	445
May, John, Johnston, Flinn and Skyles, Adventures of	571	Andrew's tussle with a bull	447
		His narrow escape	448
Merrill, Mrs. John, the "Long-Knife Squaw"	698	Pontiac, Conspiracy of	112
Messhawa, a noble chief	577-585	Character of	114
Fights with Tecumseh	597	Anecdotes of	134
Miller, The Brothers, and their adventures	555-558	Death of	147
		Point Pleasant, Battle of	161
Minter, Captain John, his famous bear fight	662	Purdy Family, Massacre of	672
McAfee Brothers, Adventure of	379	Ray, James, Adventures of	740
McClellan, Robert, the Ranger	554	Reynolds, Lieut., chaffing Girty	276
His life and extraordinary feats	562	Gallantry of	281
His later exploits	566-571	Rice's Fort, Attack on	528
McCullough, John, Captivity of	204	Rose, Major John, at Crawford's expedition	455
McColloch, Major Samuel, at siege of Fort Henry	520		
McGary, Hugh, at Blue Licks	277	Schoolmaster attacked by wild cat	383
His defence	283	Scarrooyaddy, Chief	18
Kills Moluntha	360	Scott, Frances, Wanderings of	706
McKee, Captain, deserts to the British	392	Scraggs, Widow, fierce attack on her cabin	695
McManimy, Torture of	227	Sevier, Ruth, marries a Shawnee Chief	717
McConnel's capture and revenge	377	Shawnees	6
Mills, Thos., riddled with bullets	679	Six Nations	7
Moluntha, Murder of	358	Slocum, Frances, the lost sister	639
Montour, Catharine, alias Queen Esther	628	Slover, John, the guide, Capture and adventures of	468
Moravian mission	397	His escape and mad ride	471
Towns destroyed	400	Smith, Col. James, his captivity	75
Massacre of	403	His marriage	105
Moredock, Colonel John, his terrible revenge	633	Takes a British fort	107
Morgan, David, his desperate conflict	385	Smith, Major, how he recovered his sweetheart	667
Morgan, Levi, his stratagem for his life	678	St. Clair, Sir John	46
		St. Clair, General Arthur, his campaign and defeat	537

INDEX.

	Page.
~lair, Louisa, the dashing and beautiful	710
Stobo, Major Robert	26
Remarkable adventures of	29
His escape from Quebec	31
Captures two ships	35
Thomas, Captain John, massacre of family	674
Tush Family, Massacre of	673
Van Buskirk, Sad death of	671
Van Campen, Major, his wonderful combat	621
Vincennes, Capture of	495
Ward, Captain James, and the fat Dutchman	619
Ward, Calvin and Kenton's adventures	598
War Belt, legend of North Bend	500
Washington, George, his first visit to the West	17
To Venango	19
Hurled into the Allegheny and shot at	20
His first campaign	23
Surrenders Fort Necessity	25
Sick on the march	46–49
Conduct at Braddocks Fields	50

	Page.
Wayne, "Mad Anthony," Campaign of	547
Weiser, Conrade	237
Wells, Capt. William, the Ranger, and daring exploits	554–559
Wells, Jack, and his dream	372
Wild white man and his story	665
Wetzel family	319
Martin captured	320
John's adventures	321
As a boy	723
Jacob and Kenton	325
Lewis the most daring and famous	327
Captured when a boy	328
Kills three savages in a running fight	329
Adventures of	330
Death of	342
Widow won at last	716
Williams, The Isaac and Rebecca of West Virginia	718
Williamson, David	403-7-16—450-8
White Eyes, a noble Delaware Chief	389
Will Case on the border	241
Zane, Betty, her famous gunpowder exploit	524

OUR WESTERN BORDER

IN

EARLY PIONEER DAYS

CHAPTER I

THE PIONEERS

> Where are the sturdy yeomen
> Who battled for this land,
> And trod these hoar old forests,
> A brave and gallant band?
> They knew no dread of danger
> When rose the Indian's yell;
> Right gallantly they struggled,
> Right gallantly they fell.
> From Alleghany's summit
> To the farthest western shore,
> These brave men's bones are lying
> Where they perished in their gore.
> Their bones were left to whiten
> The spot where they were slain,
> And were ye now to seek them
> They would be sought in vain.

To learn the lesson of history and profit thereby, it is necessary to learn the first chapters, the early history, for it is upon the work of the pioneers that the future of a nation is built. The most thrilling and heroic period of our country's history was in the latter half of the eighteenth century and the daring deeds of American pioneers have no parallel in any other country. Compared with Egypt, Greece or Rome, our Republic is yet in infancy.

Time, however, is not tested by periods, but by events. "Better," writes Tennyson, "fifty years of Europe than a cycle of Cathay." Of how much value, then, is one year in America, where life is so intensified; where quick-thronging events so crowd and jostle each other, and where rapid developments is such a very marvel that the wild dream of yesterday becomes the sober reality of today; where entire communities rise, as it were, like exhalations from the earth, and where the magic growth of Chicago and St. Louis may soon find parallel in some far city of the Plains or of the Pacific Slope.

A little more than a century ago, the vast and magnificent domain beyond the Alleghenies was an unbroken wilderness—an illimitable ocean of verdure, sweeping over hill and dale in billowy undulations; seamed here and there by dividing ridges, or cut into leafy rifts by abounding streams; intersected only by devious Indian trails or buffalo paths; inhabited by swarthy and subtle savages, or infested by noxious serpents and prowling beasts of prey. Green intervals, dotted with browsing deer; expansive savannas, cumbered with clumsy bison; savage gorges; wild, sunless glens, or matted, luxuriant thickets, here and there broke the monotony of all this sylvan scenery.

What is now the Great West, was then the Unknown West—as mysterious a region and as provocative of daring adventure as are to-day the unexplored wilds of Central Africa. If the hardy hunters who ventured into those vast solitudes brought not back with them stories of "Cannibals that each other eat; Of Anthropophagi and men whose heads Do grow beneath their shoulders," they *did* circulate many wondrous stories of the marvelous fatness and beauty of those vast wastes; of the variety and prodigality of the vegetation—vines, grasses, woods, flowers and exuberant undergrowth; of the plenteous supply of every variety of noble game, and, especially, of the fierce and untamed savages, who threaded the virgin forests; who paddled their birchen barks on the full-banked streams, or who, hideous in paints, encountered them amid woodland glooms with horrid whoop and fierce assault.

Little more than a half century before, Spottswood, the spirited Governor of the Colony of Virginia, had endeavored to stimulate the slumbering Livingstones of his day and district, by establishing what was called the Transmontane Order of the Knights of the Golden Horseshoe, investing each of those who ventured beyond the mountains, with a miniature golden horseshoe bearing the legend, "Sic jurat transcendere montes," or "Thus (or by this) he swears to cross the mountains." Equipping a company of horsemen, the adventurous Governor commenced his march in great pomp from Williamsburg, the then capital of the colony. Pursuing their slow and devious way amid forests of majestic growth; crossing bright streams of sparkling freshness; passing by constant displays of leafy or floral exuberance, they finally climbed to the summit of the Allegheny mountains. But, that was the *ultima thule* of their explorations. They were, it is true, enchanted with the magnificent prospect which, from their rocky perch, burst upon their enraptured vision, but they never reached the thither or sunset slopes of those mountains, but contented themselves with gazing, as did Moses from Mount Pisgah, at the affluent Canaan beyond. Even thirty years later there were but few, and those belonging to the "wild turkey

INTRODUCTION. 3

breed" of whom Boone and Kenton were such conspicuous members, who had advanced as far west as the Shenandoah Valley; but it was not really until about 1760 that the prophetic line of Bishop Berkeley began to be realized :—" Westward the star of empire takes its way."

It is quite foreign from our purpose to present a formal and precise chronicle of the gradual penetration of the pioneers into the western wilderness; nor do we design to cumber and overload our work with details of Indian nations, customs and habits. All this would require whole volumes, and has been done fully and acceptably by others. What may be called the Heroic Age of Western Border Life and Struggle, is embraced in the last half of the 18th century, or to speak more definitely, from about the year 1760, after the capture of Forts Duquesne and Niagara, down to the year 1794, when "Mad Anthony Wayne" forever broke the spirit and crushed the power of the Confederate Western Tribes at the battle of the "Fallen Timbers." Within the period thus limited, we may safely challenge all history, ancient or modern, to exhibit such a constant series of stubborn and desperate struggles. The turbulent times of the Robber Barons of Germany, or the bitter and violent feuds of the Scottish Border, furnish no parallels to the frequent forays and marauds; to the innumerable acts of daring; of cool, reckless courage and adventure; of persistent tenacity of purpose, as are embraced in the chronicles and the unwritten traditions of the Pennsylvania, Virginia, Kentucky and Tennessee frontiers. It was a fierce, dogged, savage and desperate struggle between two brave and jealous races; the whites fighting for room and opportunity to live and thrive, and the reds for what they deemed their own soil and hunting grounds. "When Greek meets Greek, then comes the tug o' war," and every man who went out upon those borders carried his life in his hands; liable, at any time, to be shot or tomahawked from every tree that could cover a lurking foe; his home and family constantly exposed to the merciless attacks of a savage, wily and implacable enemy. Each knew well that it was "war to the knife, and the knife to the hilt," and worked, idled or slept with his trusty blade or rifle within easy grasp. It was generally the young, ardent and the adventurous, who thus boldly made haste to bid grim defiance to perils and to offer a standing challenge to fierce and revengeful foes.

From this incessant exposure to imminent peril, there naturally grew up on the border a race of sturdy, reckless, rough-and-ready frontiersmen to whom fear was absolutely unknown, and to many of whom the most thrilling passion of their lives was long, solitary hunts after Indians whom they would track with the unswerving tenacity of the bloodhound and, when found, grapple with a most marvelous audacity and doggedness. All their senses were on the alert; trained to a wondrous skill and quickness with the keen tomahawk or the unerring rifle; practiced in every variety of wood-craft; they had an eye equal to the savages themselves for detecting the minutest signs of an enemy, and for trailing him through the most bewildering woods and undergrowth to his very lair. We often shudder when, sitting by our quiet firesides, we read of the desperate combats between such mighty hunters as Gerard and Cummings and the ferocious lions, tigers, and other wild beasts, whose jungles they have gone long distances to penetrate; but what are the fiercest and most infuriate of all animals that ever crouched to a leap, compared with the subtle and desperate American savage, perfectly at home in his native wilds; with all his destructive wits, sharpened to an extraordinary acuteness; taught from childhood to find life's highest honors in killing and scalping, and trained in every possible wile to lure or ensnare a foe. How truly the famous Poe, with his quaint and homely hunter's jargon, confessed to a common passion of the Border, when he said, with deepest feeling, " I've fout cats and bar and painter, and every other wild varmint of the woods, but Injuns beats them all ! Yes, Injuns beats them all !"

And think, too, of the heroic women !—the wives and mothers of the pioneers. As one of their own number has said, "A good Providence sent such men and women into the world together. They were made to match." It is said that war, if it lead to havoc, mourning and desolation, has also a tendency to excite the nobler and more heroic passions of the soul. It is, in a measure, true, and the women of the scourged and harassed Border were—under their constant familiarity with danger in its most horrid and appalling forms—perfect paragons of nerve and fortitude. The annals of the West are absolutely brilliant with the most marvelous exhibitions of female heroism. They had not, like the men, the passions and excitements of the chase, but were left in exposed, isolated cabins, with all the cares and anxieties of the family upon them, and when these homes were suddenly invaded by the pitiless savages and themselves carried off into a hopeless captivity, were liable to see the brains of their young babes dashed out against the nearest tree, and their older children either killed or scalped before their eyes or scattered among various captors. How crowded are all our Border chronicles with the sickening horrors of settlers' cabins attacked and the women and children shamefully maltreated !

   The Mothers of our Forest Land,
    Such were their daring deeds.
   Their monument! where does it stand?
    Their epitaph, who reads?
   No braver dames had Sparta,
    No nobler matrons Rome,
   Yet who or lauds or honors them
    E'en in their own green home?

They had no respite from a wearing, consuming anxiety, except in the dead of winter, when the Indians generally lay quiet in their forest towns; as soon, however, as the wild geese were seen steering their way to the north, or the frogs were heard piping in the ponds and marshes, then a great dread came over them. The poet has sung of Autumn, that the "melancholy days have come, the saddest of the year," but with women of the border, it was the Spring whose breezes came freighted with sadness. The customary harbingers of Spring to them were the appalling, blood-curdling yell of the stealthy savage, or the gleam of his thirsting and unsparing tomahawk. They regarded the budding of trees and the opening bloom of flowers with the most gloomy forebodings, and listened to the songs of the woodland birds as but the prelude to the shriek of assault. Then was the bark of the watch-dog at night, especially if their male protectors were absent, far more dismal than the cry of either wolf or panther, since it suggested the probability of lurking redmen, and the fond, anxious mother would start from her troubled slumber, and, with ear attent and head uplifted, would listen, listen, listen for the sound of the distant war-whoop or the rude assault upon her barred, oaken door. Then, perchance, she would fall again into fitful, uneasy slumber, to dream of some murderous deed or horrid scalping. Oh, "we, in these piping times o' peace," may never know— most certainly can never realize, a tithe of the dreads, the privations, the sufferings and the untold and untellable horrors which the noble and heroic women of the West endured for many and many years of their lives. Surely, had not a constant familiarity with danger bred indifference to it, their lives would have been inexpressibly hard and intolerable.

It would be clearly impossible, as indeed it would be undesirable, to publish a full and detailed chronicle of all that was done or suffered by the pioneers and their families. We can only hope to give readers a true and impressive idea of border life and struggle, by carefully selecting salient events and personal adventures, each differing from the other in character and incident, but all, together, furnishing, as it were, a historical panorama of a half century of forays, marauds, massacres and adventures, and narrated, so far as may be, in the chronologic order of occurrence, and connected together by a running commentary of explanation. By thus retaining only the *cream* of the various border books—most of which have long been out of print, and are exceedingly rare and costly; by adding many new sketches and adventures, known to a comparative few; by correcting the errors of the old, staple histories, and furnishing much new and original matter, we hope, within the compass of a portable book, to give a faithful idea of our western border as it was one hundred years ago.

And, first, it is a great but common error to suppose that the vast domain stretching west of the Alleghenies was thickly settled and occupied with Indians. The whole of Kentucky had not a single tribe resident within its ample borders, but was used by the Catawbas, Cherokees and Chickasaws to the south, and by the Delawares, Shawnees and Hurons to the north, as one common hunting and skirmishing ground. It was about the same with the western half of Virginia and eastern half of Ohio. Immense tracks of woodland—a very paradise for hunters—were left an utter solitude. Large parts of Michigan, Illinois and Tennessee were tenanted by wild beasts alone. In the whole vast region lying between the Atlantic and Mississippi, the Cumberland and Lake Superior, the entire Indian population, at the opening of the Revolution, scarce exceeded ten thousand warriors, of which the Six Nations of New York numbered about two thousand, the Delawares six hundred, the Shawnees five hundred, the Hurons or Wyandots about the same, the Miami tribes eight hundred, &c. Most of the Ohio Indians, too, were but late comers, the Delawares and Shawnees having emigrated from Pennsylvania from 1730 to 1750, and the Hurons having moved down from the neighborhood of Detroit and the upper lakes.

The Shawnee villages which Christian Post found in the upper Ohio valley were soon after abandoned, and the majestic Ohio, "strong without rage; without o'erflowing, full," swept onward from its head to its mouth, with scarce a hamlet along its woody margins to denote the abodes of human beings. On interior streams, however, as the Sciota, Muskingum, Wabash, Miami, &c., the villages of the redmen were more numerous. A significant reason is given for this. It is said that the same beautiful and abounding stream which the French so appropriately called La Belle Riviere, was long previously known to some of the tribes which lived along its borders under the dread name of the River of Blood. It was no idle title. Tradition tells of many a sanguinary battle along the picturesque shores of this grand old river, over whose sylvan banks has so often trickled the crimson stream of Indian massacre.

When Virginia was first known to the whites, the Massawomees—so called by the Indians of East Virginia, to whom they were a constant source of alarm—were the most powerful confederacy of western tribes, and many a fierce and bloody fight are they reported to have had with the then Five Nations of New York, the most powerful combination of eastern tribes. It had, in the early times, been the fashion of these Iroquois, settled about the York lakes, to come down the Allegheny and Ohio in flotillas of canoes, and, moving thus swiftly and secretly, having few *impedimenta* and little or no trouble about provisions, and leaving no trail either to betray their presence or indicate their line of retreat, they could thus swoop down like a tempest upon towns and villages within striking distances of the Ohio. For this reason the regions on both margins of that stream had long been unoccupied, and were only roamed over by hunting parties of various nations, the tribal villages generally lying from fifty to a hundred miles back, and being located at the forks of some tributary stream allowing easy canoe navigation in all directions.

These Six Nations, called Iroquois by the French and Mingoes or Mengwe by the Dutch, merit a somewhat more extended notice at our hands, since of all the savage tribes in America they stood foremost in war, in eloquence, in primitive virtues, and in all the arts of policy. They were the Romans of America, and were the proud conquerors of an immense extent of country, including even Canada itself, and it was through actual or alleged purchase from them that the English asserted title to all the land west of the Allegheny Mountains, the French claiming the same magnificent domain by right of discovery and prior possession. They consisted originally of five nations: the Mohawks, the Oneidas, the Onondagos, the Cayugas, and the Senecas, to whom a sixth, the Tuscaroras, from the south, were admitted in. The confederacy thus formed was strong, close and harmonious, their ambition and ferocious valor adding one domain after another, and subjecting to their dominion every tribe in the whole country worth contending with.

As De Witt Clinton truly remarked: "They are the Romans of America," and through the magic potency of union and concerted action, were able to accomplish wonders. It was among them, and at the time when they had arrived at the height of their power, that we must look for the highest type of the American Indian, such as he was before debauched and degraded by the contaminating influences of the debased trader and rum-seller. To give only one instance of the success of the Iroquois in the subjugation of other nations, we subjoin their traditional account of the total

DESTRUCTION OF THE ERIE TRIBE OF INDIANS.

The Eries were famed as the most powerful and warlike of all the Indian tribes. They resided at the foot of the great lake of the same name, at a place called Tu-shu-way, now the opulent city of Buffalo.

When the Eries heard of the close confederation formed between the Mohawks, Oneidas, Onondagos, Cayugas and Senecas, which went under the name of the Five Nations, they imagined it must be for some mischievous purpose. Although confident of their superiority over any one of the tribes inhabiting the countries within the bounds of their knowledge, they dreaded the power of such combined forces. In order to satisfy themselves regarding the character, disposition and power of those they considered their natural enemies, the Eries resorted to the following means.

They sent a friendly message to the Senecas, who were their nearest western neighbors and styled the Warders of the Threshold of the Long House, inviting them to select one hundred of their most active and athletic young men to play a game of ball against the same number to be selected by the Eries, for a wager which should be considered worthy of the occasion and the character of the great nation in whose behalf the offer was made.

The message was received and entertained in the most respectful manner. A council of the Five Nations was called, and the proposition fully discussed and a messenger in due time dispatched with the decision of the council, respectfully declining the challenge. This emboldened the proud and warlike Eries, and the next year the offer was renewed, and, after being again considered, was again formally declined. This was far from satisfying the proud Lords of the Lake, and the challenge was renewed a third time. The young "braves" of the Iroquois now became greatly excited. They clamored for the acceptance of the audacious *defi*, and, finally, the wise councils which had hitherto prevailed at last gave way and the challenge was accepted.

Nothing could exceed the enthusiasm with which each tribe sent forth its chosen champions for the contest. The only difficulty seemed to be to make a selection where all were so worthy. After much delay, one hundred of the flower of all the tribes were finally designated, and the day for their departure was fixed. An experienced chief was chosen as the leader of the party, whose orders the young men were strictly enjoined to obey. A grand council was called, and in the presence of the assembled multitude the party was charged in the most solemn manner to observe a pacific course of conduct towards their competitors and the nation whose guests they were about to become and to allow no provocation, however great, to be resented by an act of aggression on their part, but in all respects to acquit themselves worthy the representatives of a great and powerful people, anxious to cultivate peace and friendship with their neighbors.

Under these solemn injunctions, the party took up its long wilderness march for Tu-shu-way. When the chosen band had arrived near their their destination, a messenger was sent forward to notify the Eries of their arrival and the next day was set apart for their entree.

The graceful and athletic forms, the tasteful yet not cumbrous dress, the noble, dignified bearing of their chief, and, more than all, the modest demeanor of the young warriors of the Iroquois party won the admiration of all beholders. They brought no arms. Each one bore a bat, used to throw or strike a ball, tastefully ornamented, being a hickory stick about five feet long, bent round at one end and a deer-thong netting woven across the bow.

After a day of repose and refreshment all things were arranged for the contest. The Chief of the Iroquois brought forward and deposited upon the ground, a large pile of elegantly-wrought belts of wampum, costly robes, silver and copper bands, beautifully ornamented moccasins and other articles of great value in the eyes of the swarthy sons of the forest, as the stake and wager on the part of his people. They were abundantly matched by the Eries with stakes of equal value—article by article, tied together and again deposited on the pile.

The game began and although contested with desperation and marvelous skill by the Eries, was finally won by the Iroquois, who bore off the prizes in triumph. Thus ended the first day.

The Iroquois having now accomplished the object of their visit, prepared to take their leave, but the Chief of the Eries, addressing himself to their leader, said their young men, though fairly beaten in the game of ball, would not be satisfied unless they could have, also, a foot race, and proposed to match ten of their number against ten of the Iroquois party, which was finally assented to by the Iroquois, who were again victorious.

The Kauk-waus, who resided on the Eighteen Mile Creek, being present as the friends and allies of the Eries, now invited the Iroquois to visit them before their return home and thither the whole party repaired. The Chief of the Eries, as a last trial of the courage and prowess of his guests, proposed to select ten men, to be matched with a like number from the Iroquois, to wrestle, and that each victor should dispatch his adversary on the spot by braining him with a tomahawk and bearing off the scalp as a trophy.

This savage proposition was not pleasing to the Iroquois; they, however, concluded to accept the challenge with a determination, should they be victorious, not to execute the bloody part of the proposition. The champions were accordingly chosen. A Seneca was the first to step into the ring, who threw his adversary amid the shouts of the excited multitude. The victor, however, stepped back and declined to slay the victim lying passive at his feet. As quick as thought, however, the Chief of the Eries cast his tomahawk and at a single blow scattered the brains of the vanquished warrior over the sod. His body was dragged out of the way and another champion of the Eries presented himself, who was as quickly thrown by his adversary and as quickly dispatched by the infuriated Chief of the Eries. A third met the same fate.

The Chief of the Iroquois seeing now the terrible excitement that agitated the swaying assemblage, quietly gave the signal for retiring.

This visit and astounding victory of the Iroquois only served to increase the alarm and jealousy of the Eries and to profoundly convince them that they had most powerful and formidable rivals to contend with. It was no part of their policy to cultivate friendship with tribes growing daily stronger by union. They knew of no better mode of securing peace by themselves but by exterminating all who might oppose them, and concluded that their only chance of success against this growing confederation would be to attack each tribe singly. They were far more than a match with any one of the confederate tribes. Should they wait to be invaded and cope with the whole united force of their adversaries, or should they make a sudden and secret movement and destroy them in detail? The question was urgent and the decision was prompt, and a powerful war party was organized to attack first the Senecas, residing at the foot of the lake of the same name.

It happened that at this time there resided among the Eries a Seneca woman, who in early life had been taken prisoner and had married an Erie "brave." He had died and left her a widow without children, a stranger in a strange land. Seeing the terrible preparation for a bloody onslaught upon her kindred and friends, she formed the resolution of at once apprising them of their danger. At the first nightfall, therefore, taking the course of the Niagara river, she traveled all night, and early next morning reached the shores of Ontario. Jumping into a canoe which she found fastened to a tree, she boldly pushed out into the open lake and coasted along to the mouth of the Oswego, where was located a village of her nation. She directed her steps to the lodge of the third chief and disclosed her fateful news. She was secreted by this chief, and fleet runners were at once dispatched to all the tribes, summoning them to meet in grand council at Onondago. When all were assembled the chief arose and in the most solemn manner rehearsed a vision, in which he said a beautiful bird had appeared to him and asserted that a great war party of the Eries was preparing to descend upon them, and that nothing could save them but an immediate rally of all their warriors to meet the foe before he could be able to strike.

This solemn announcement was heard in breathless silence. When the chief had sat down there arose one fierce yell of rage and madness, and the earth fairly trembled as the mighty mass stamped upon the ground with fury, brandishing on high their war clubs and tomahawks.

No time was to be lost. A body of five thousand warriors was speedily organized and, also, a corps of reserve, consisting of one thousand young men who had never yet been in battle. The bravest and most experienced chiefs from all the tribes were placed in command; the spies immediately set out in search of the hated foe, and the whole body stealthily took up its line of march in the direction of the expected attack.

For several days they continued to advance. They had scarcely, however, passed the foot of the Can-an-da-gua Lake, when their scouts brought back news of the advance of the Eries, who had already crossed the Ce-nis-se-u (Genesee) river in great force. The Eries had not the slightest intimation of the approach of their foes. They relied upon the secrecy and celerity of their movements to surprise and subdue the Senecas almost without resistance.

The two parties met at a point about half way from Canandagua Lake and the Genesee river, and it was just at the outlet of the little lake Honeoye that the struggle took place. This small stream alone divided the two hostile arrays. The entire strength of the Confederates was not in view of the Eries. The reserve force of young men did not appear at all, being carefully kept concealed.

Nothing could resist the fierceness and impetuosity of the Eries at the first view of their hated foes. They rushed through the intervening stream and fell upon them with shrill yells and incredible fury. The undaunted courage and desperate valor of the Iroquois could not avail against such a terrible and irresistible onslaught and the first ranks were compelled to yield ground. The entire force, the Iroquois reserve only excepted, now became engaged. The shock of battle was terrible! Hand to hand, foot to foot, they struggled long and desperately. No quarter was asked or given on either side.

As the fight thickened and became more obstinate and destructive, the Eries, for the first time, appeared sensible of their true situation. What they had long feared had now become a terrible reality. *Their enemies had combined for their destruction* and they now found themselves engaged in a desperate struggle, not only for the glory, but for the very existence of their nation.

Too late to falter now! They were proud and valorous and knew how to conquer, but not to yield. The combat grew from that instant more bloody and obstinate. The Iroquois feeling strong in numbers; fired with zeal and ambition; acting for the first time in concert and led on by their bravest and mightiest chiefs, felt themselves to be invincible. Though staggered at first by the fierce and repeated rushes of their opponents, they manfully rallied and returned yell for yell and blow for blow.

And now the awful din of battle rises higher and higher. The war club, the tomahawk, the scalping knife do terrible deeds of death and havoc. During the very hottest of this savage and bloody battle, the corps of reserve of one thousand eager and wrathful young Iroquois were secretly led across the stream and placed in ambush in the rear of the Eries.

Seven times had the brave and heroic Eries been driven across the crimson stream, and as often regained their ground and now when exhausted and hardest pressed by this appalling and unequal contest, the shrill, blood-curdling yells of the Iroquois' reserve are heard in their startled ears. Unblenched; disdaining to yield but ready to die, they turn to confront this fresh and formidable foe. In vain! In vain! What could valor, however heroic, avail against this fresh swarm whose onset was so terrible and irresistible. The battle was lost and all that remained was to meet the death they courted like true warriors. Hundreds were cut down and trampled over. Only a comparative few of the Eries escaped to carry the sad news of their utter overthrow to their wives, old men and children. But the victors gave them no rest but pursued with the fierceness and tenacity of savage sleuth-hounds. Few were left to tell the tale of disaster.

Tradition adds that many years after a powerful war party of the descendants of the Eries, who had fled beyond the Mississippi, ascended the Ohio and Allegheny and made a last desperate assault upon their hereditary foes, the Senecas, at Tu-shu-way. A great battle was again fought, but with a like result. The Eries were not alone defeated, but were slain to a man. The places that once knew them, now knew them no more, and nothing at this late day but the *name* of Erie remains to tell that such a nation ever existed.

We find among the records of the Jesuit Missions another episode of this international contest which, although known but to few, is yet full of romantic interest. Twelve years before the date of the great battle at the foot of Honeoye, the Jesuit missionaries were at work among the Iroquois, but with scarcely any appreciable results. When the news of the advance of the Eries was blazoned abroad among the tribes, Father Le Moyne was zealously serving at Onondago, where was stationed the

Long House of the Five Nations. Of those who gathered at the call of the council to meet the invasion, was an influential chief, Achiongeras by name. On the eve of his departure he called on the faithful priest—pictured to him the perils he was about to encounter, wished to put himself under the protection of the Great Spirit and was finally baptized. The converted chief, with the dews of baptism yet damp upon his brow, then started, at the head of his savage legion, on the war path.

The opposing forces came together, as we have related, with a dreadful shock. When the lines of the Iroquois were slowly retreating before the victorious Eries, Achiongeras, whose intrepid bearing had made him conspicuous in the fight, suddenly paused amid the deadly conflict and beckoned to the braves who supported him. They gathered about him at the signal. Dropping upon his knee, the Christian convert lifted his crimsoned hands towards heaven, the group of encircling savages imitating the action, when with a solemn vow they unitedly plighted their faith in the God of prayer if He would only give them aid in this crisis of their peril. The vow was honored from above. Animated afresh, the wavering band regained its footing, won back its lost ground and paused not until the field was won.

Achiongeras and his followers were true to their pledge. After the return of the victors a general council was called, when, by solemn decree, Christianity was proclaimed in the capital of the confederacy. The French were invited over from Canada to plant a Mission. Fathers Menard, Dablon, Broar and Boursier, attended by a numerous escort of savages, launched their fleet of canoes at Quebec, ascended the St. Lawrence, the banner of the Cross waving its silken folds at the head, and amid the roar of cannon and the ringing cheers of waiting multitudes, landed, after a tedious but prosperous voyage, on the shores of Onondago, and soon after erected a house of worship; and so was founded the great central Mission of St. Marys, which, for a long time, grew and prospered, having its branch missions among the other four nations of the confederacy.

THE FRENCH CANADIAN AND THE ENGLISH TRADER.

We have already stated that the French claimed all the country watered by the Mississippi and its tributaries by right of discovery and prior occupation. This last fact was owing to a most marked and notable difference of character between the French and the English colonists. The latter were not at first fond of roaming, but confined themselves to the narrow belt of settlements along the eastern sea-coast. They were toilers and moilers; slow, patient, contented and industrious as compared with their French neighbors; less ambitious to make explorations than to wrest from the soil a comfortable living. The French Canadian, however, was his very antithesis; gay, buoyant, restless and roaming, he had an invincible longing for vagabondizing and a marvelous faculty of adaptation to any and all circumstances. As Parkman has so truthfully remarked, he was a rightful heir to French bravery and restlessness. He had an eager love for wandering and adventure, and this propensity found ample scope in the service of the fur-trade.

When the priest had shrived him of his sins; when, after the parting carousal, he embarked with his gun and merry *compagnons du voyage* in the deep-laden canoe; when their oars kept time to the measured cadence of their song, and the blue, sunny bosom of the Ottowa opened before them; when their frail bark quivered among the milky foam and black rocks of the rapids, and when, around their camp-fire, they lightly wasted half the night with jests and laughter—then the Canadian was in his element. His footsteps explored the farthest hiding-places of the wilderness. In the evening dance, his red cap mingled with the scalp-locks and feathers of the Indian braves, or, stretched on a bear-skin by the side of his dusky mistress, he watched the gambols of his hybrid offspring, in happy oblivion of the partner whom he left unnumbered leagues behind.

This spirit for far-reaching exploration lay not alone in the peculiar genius and temperament of the people, but was greatly enhanced by a fervent religious zeal—a regular devoteeism of the intense, engrossing kind which nerved Cortez and Pizarro to perform miracles of valor and endurance that they might win whole peoples to the "true faith." Canada was a loyal child of the Catholic faith. The church, the convent and the shrine were seen at every turn; over every cluster of the small white houses of the Canadians glittered the sacred emblem of the cross, and in the towns and villages could everywhere be met the black robe of the Jesuit, the gray garb of the Recollect priest, and the austere habit of the Ursuline nun. All France was filled with the zeal of proselytism, and the conversion of whole races of American heathen was the line in which their enthusiasm went out.

The Jesuits, with their far-famed and self-sacrificing devotion, were the foremost in carrying their faith to the remotest and most inaccessible regions of the West. Nothing could stay—nothing appall them. Their story is replete with romance—miracles of patient suffering, heroic self-sacrifice and daring enterprise. They were the pioneers of French America. We see them, says Parkman, among the frozen forests of Acadia, struggling in snow-shoes with some wandering Algonquin horde, or crouching in the crowded hunting-lodge, half stifled in the smoky den, and battling with troops of famished dogs for the last morsel of sustenance. Again, we see the black-robed priest wading among the white rapids of the Ottawa, toiling with his savage comrades to drag the canoe against the headlong water. Again, radiant in the vestments of his priestly office, he administers the sacramental bread to kneeling crowds of plumed and painted proselytes in the black forests of the Hurons or, bearing his life in his hand, he carries his sacred mission into the strongholds of the Iroquois, like a man who invades, unarmed, a den of angry tigers. Jesuit explorers traced the St. Lawrence to its source and said masses among the solitudes of Lake Superior, where the boldest fur-trader scarcely dared to follow.

We have already noted the wonderful success the French had for winning the hearts of the untutored redmen of the forest; it was as remarkable, in its way, as the genius of the English in repelling and alienating them. The latter nation appeared to want land; the former to establish empire—hence these showed the savages every honor; lured them with medals and decorations; were prodigal of their gifts, and, with the well-known pliant, plastic temper of the Frenchman, even condescended to hunt, live and marry with them, furnishing another illustration of the truthful border saying, that it is impossible for an Indian to turn "pale-face," but remarkably easy for a pale-face to turn Indian. In order better to show the contrast that existed between the two races in their methods of dealing with the redmen, we again quote Parkman:

"The fur-trade engendered a peculiar class of men, known by the appropriate name of bush-rangers, or *coureurs des bois*—half-civilized vagrants, whose chief vocation was conducting the canoes of the traders along the lakes and rivers of the interior, but many of whom, shaking loose every tie of blood and kindred, identified themselves with the Indians and sank into utter barbarism. In many a squalid camp among the plains and forests of the West, the traveler would have encountered men owning the blood and speaking the language of France, yet in their wild, swarthy visages and barbarous costumes, seeming more akin to those with whom they had cast their lot. He loved to decorate his long hair with eagle feathers; to make his face hideous with soot, ochre or vermilion, and to adorn his greasy hunting frock with horse-hair fringes. His dwelling, if he had one, was a wigwam. He lounged on a bear skin while his squaw boiled his venison and lighted his pipe. In hunting, dancing, singing, lounging, or taking a scalp, he rivaled the genuine Indian. His mind was tinctured with the superstitions of the forest. He had faith in the magic drum of the conjurer; he was not sure that a thunder cloud could not be charmed away by whistling at it through the wing-bone of an eagle; he carried the tail of a rattlesnake in his bullet-pouch by way of amulet, and he placed implicit trust in the prophetic truth of his dreams.

"The English traders and the rude men in their employ showed, it is true, a swift alacrity to throw off the restraints of civilization, but though they became barbarians they did not become Indians. With the British settlers of the frontier, it was much the same. Rude, fierce and contemptuous, they daily encroached upon the hunting grounds of the Indians, and then paid them for the injury in abuse, insult, curses and threats. Thus the native population shrank back from before the English as from before an advancing pestilence, while, on the other hand, in the very heart of Canada, Indian communities sprang up, cherished by the government and favored by an easy-tempered people. The scouts, hunters and traders who ranged the woods beyond the English border, were a distant, peculiar class, many of them coarse and ferocious.

"As for the traders, their goods were packed at Fort Pitt on the backs of horses, and thus distributed among the various Indian villages. More commonly, however, the whole journey was performed by means of trains, or, as they were called, brigades, of pack-horses, which, leaving the frontier settlements, climbed the shadowy heights of the Alleghenies and treaded the forests of the Ohio; diving through thickets and wading over streams. The men employed in this perilous calling were a rough, bold and intractable class, often as fierce and truculent as the savages themselves. A blanket coat, a frock of smoked deer-skin, a rifle on the shoulder and a knife and tomahawk in the belt, formed their ordinary equipment. The principal trader, the owner of the merchandise, would fix his head-quarters at some large Indian town, whence he would dispatch his subordinates to the surrounding villages, with a suitable supply of blankets and red cloth, guns and hatchets, liquor, tobacco, paint, beads and hawks-bells. The wild traffic was liable to every species of disorder—and it is not to be wondered at that, in a region where law was unknown, the jealousies of rival traders should become a fruitful source of broils, robberies and murders.

"It was no easy matter for a novice, embarrassed with his cumbrous gun, to urge his horse through the thick trunks and underbrush, or even to ride at speed along the narrow Indian trails where, at every yard, the impending branches scratched him across the face. At night the camp would be formed by the side of some spring or rivulet, and if the traveler was skillful in the use of his rifle, a haunch of venison would often form his evening meal. If it rained, a shade of elm or basswood bark was the ready work of an hour, a pile of evergreen boughs formed a bed and the saddle or knapsack a pillow. A party of Indian wayfarers would often be met journeying through the forest—a chief or warrior, perhaps, with his squaws and family. The Indians would usually make their camp in the neighborhood of the white men, and at meal time the warrior would seldom fail to seat himself by the trader's fire and gaze with solemn gravity at the viands before him and receive his fragment of bread and cup of coffee with an ejaculation of gratitude."

It was just such traders as these who, from the year 1748 down to 1783, were first stopped by the French and warned off the soil, or, finding that course ineffective, were then seized and sent captives to Canada. The French were then busy erecting a continuous chain of forts from Niagara down to Louisiana, and plainly with the intent of firmly holding all the vast country which they openly claimed as theirs. Alarming reports of their violent and summary proceedings now reached the English colonies.

WASHINGTON'S FIRST VISIT TO THE GREAT WEST.

Gov. Dinwiddie, of Virginia, an official of great energy and determination, was not only startled but indignant at the various rumors which reached him from the Ohio region. He, therefore, appointed Major George Washington,—at that time a young surveyor of about twenty-two years of age, of excellent repute for judgment and bravery, and whom previous life had enured to hardships and instructed in woodcraft,—to proceed immediately into the distant wilds of the west; visit and deliver a letter to the French commandant; ascertain precisely their strength in the Ohio country, the number and location of their forts, and what were their claims and intentions.

The appointment was a good one. The zealous Major set out promptly on the very day he received his commission, and arrived at Wills Creek on Nov. 14th. Engaging horse and servants, and selecting Jacob Van Braam as his French interpreter, and Christopher Gist, who was better acquainted with the western wilderness than any colonist of that day, as his guide, he turned into an old Indian trail and commenced his toilsome way, arriving at Turtle Creek, near the very point where scarce two years after he engaged the French-Indian army in the disastrous battle of Braddocks Fields, on the 22d.

Washington kept a very accurate and interesting journal of his proceedings, which on his return was immediately published, both in the

Colonies and in Great Britain, and was the means of enlightening the English government as to the aggressive designs of the French. Some parts of his journal we will quote; and first, the earliest mention made of the forks of the Ohio—called De-un-da-ga by the Indians, and afterwards the famous site of the French Fort Duquesne, then of the British Fort Pitt, and now of the vast and opulent city of Pittsburgh. We quote:

"The waters were quite impassable without swimming our horses, which obliged us to get the loan of a canoe from Frazier" (an Indian trader who had lately been driven away from Venango by the French, and whose humble log cabin, on the banks of the Monongahela, was the ultima thule of English frontier advance), "and to send Barnaby Currin and Henry Steward down the Monongahela with our baggage, to meet us at the forks of the Ohio, about ten miles below; there to cross the Allegheny.

"As I got down before the canoe did, I spent some time in viewing the rivers and the land in the fork, which I think extremely well situated for a fort, as it has the absolute command of both rivers. The land at the point is twenty-five feet above the common surface of the water; and a considerable 'bottom' of flat, well-timbered land all around it, very convenient for building. The rivers are each a quarter of a mile or more across and run here very nearly at right angles.

"About two miles from this, on the south-east side of the Ohio, at the place where the Ohio Company intended to erect a fort, lives Shingiss, King of the Delawares. We called upon him to invite him to a council at Logstown. Shingiss attended us to Logstown" (an Indian town on the Ohio, about twenty miles below the forks), "where we arrived between sun-setting and dark, the twenty-fifth day after I left Williamsburg.

"As soon as I came to town I went to Monakatoocha" (afterwards a famous chief, generally known as Scarrooyaddy, who accompanied Braddock's Expedition as chief guide, and who was noted for his loyalty and repeated services to the English) "and informed him by John Davidson, my Indian interpreter, that I was sent a messenger to the French General and was ordered to call upon the sachems of the Six Nations to acquaint them with it. I gave him a string of wampum and a twist of tobacco, and desired him to send for Tannacharison, the Half King (who was absent at his hunting cabin at Little Beaver Creek) which he promised to do by a runner early the next morning, as also for other sachems.

"About three o'clock this evening the Half King came to town. I went up and invited him privately to my tent, and desired him to relate some of the particulars of his late journey to the French Commandant, and to give me an account of the ways and the distance. He told me that the nearest and levelest way was now impassable by reason of many large miry savannas; that we must be obliged to go by Venango, and should not get to the fort in less than five or six days' good traveling, &c., &c.

"The Half King then said that he had been received very sternly by the French commander, who abruptly asked him his business, &c. The Half King then made to him a strong protest against the French occupying their lands, building forts, &c., and warned him off the whole territory and menaced him with a rod to drive him away. The French Commandant had answered very haughtily that he was not 'afraid of flies or mosquitoes, and that down that river (the Allegheny) he was sure to go, and that if the river was blocked up he had abundance of force to burst it open; that the Half King talked foolish to call the land Indian land since the French had seen it first,' &c. He also informed the Half King that the French had built two forts, one at Lake Erie (Presq' Isle, now Erie, Pa.,) and another on French Creek (where Waterford, Pa,, now stands.)"

All this was important news to Washington, and after a few days of ceremonious delays, he set out for the French Fort at Venango, situate on the Allegheny at the mouth of French Creek, in company with the Half King, Jeskakake, an old and prominent chief, White Thunder and the Hunter (who after became celebrated by the name of Guyasutha and fought the bloody battle of Bushy Run with Col. Bouquet.)

After much very fatiguing travel they arrived at Venango on the 4th of December, and found the French colors hoisted on the house from which Frazier had been ejected. One of the three officers, Captain Joncaire, famed for his influence among the Indians and his skillful, politic manner of first winning and then managing them, received Washington very politely, but told him he would have to travel further to the fort on French Creek, where there was a superior officer. The French officers later in the day drank copiously, which unloosed their tongues so as to talk freely of French designs. They asserted boldly that it was their absolute design to take possession of the Ohio and by G—d they would do it, for although they knew that the English could raise two men for their one, yet that their motions were too slow and dilatory to prevent any French undertaking. They claimed the whole country watered by the Mississippi and its tributaries, and they were determined to occupy it all the very next Spring and thus prevent the

English settling on the Ohio. Washington further found, by skillful "pumping," that there were then about seven hundred French west of Lake Ontario, scattered in a number of newly-erected forts.

The French now privately coaxed the Major's redskin escort among them, and so liberally plied them with liquor that notwithstanding all his warnings they became quite drunk, but the Half King happily remained firm and constant, and the next day offered Joncaire a belt, (which that wily and politic officer refused to receive,) and warned the French off of the Indian soil. Every stratagem was used to prevent the chiefs from going on with Washington, but in vain, for they finally set off for the French Creek fort, which, on account of excessive rains, snows and frequent swamps, they did not reach until the 11th. The commander was an elderly soldierly gentleman, a Knight of St. Louis, and named Legardeur de St. Pierre. He received Washington very courteously, read Dinwiddie's letter, and he with his brother officers retired to consult as to what answer should be sent it.

Meanwhile the Major used his eyes busily, jotting down the minutest particular and finding in fifty birch and one hundred and seventy-five pine canoes drawn up along the beach, a startling confirmation of Joncaire's boast that a fort was to be built, as soon as Spring opened, at the Forks of the Ohio. The one-eyed Knight of St. Louis, too, had boldly laid claim to all the territory as far east as the Allegheny mountains.

With the important news he had gathered, Washington hastened down the creek by canoe, reaching Joncaire again on December 22d. Here the horses were found so weak and the baggage so heavy, that they were given up, and after going with them three days, Washington and Gist, guns in hand and packs on back, started through the woods on foot, piloted by a bad and treacherous Indian guide. The very next day a party of French Indians lay in wait for them, and one of them, writes Washington, in his journal, " fired at Mr. Gist or me, not fifteen steps off, but fortunately missed. We took this fellow into custody, and kept him until about nine o'clock at night, then let him go, and walked all the remaining part of the night without making any stop. The next day we continued traveling until quite dark, and got to the Allegheny about two miles from Shannopins. We expected to have found the river frozen, but it was not, only about fifty yards from each shore. The ice, I suppose, had broken up above, for it was driving in vast quantities."

WASHINGTON HURLED INTO THE RIVER AND SHOT AT BY A SAVAGE.

"There was no way for getting over," continues the Major's journal, "but on a raft, which we set about with but one poor hatchet, and fin-

Young George Washington Hurled into the Icy Allegheny.
—See page 21.

ished just after sunsetting. This was a *whole day's work!* We next got it launched, then went on board of it and set off, but before we were half way over, we were jammed in the ice in such a manner that we expected every moment our raft to sink, and ourselves to perish. I put out my setting pole to try and stop the raft that the ice might pass by, when the rapidity of the stream threw it with so much violence against the pole, that it jerked me out into ten feet of water; but I fortunately saved myself by catching hold of one of the raft logs.

"Notwithstanding all our efforts, we could not get to either shore, but were obliged, as we were near an island, to quit our raft and make to it. The cold was so extremely severe that Mr. Gist had all his fingers and some of his toes frozen; and the water was shut up so hard that we found no difficulty in getting off the island on the ice in the morning, and went to Mr. Frazier's. As we intended to take horses here, and it required some time to find them, I went up about three miles to the mouth of the Youghiogheny to visit Queen Alaquippa, who had expressed great concern that we passed her in going to the fort. I made her a present of a match-coat and a bottle of rum, which latter was thought much the better present of the two."

This island was Wainwright's Island, now almost completely destroyed, but which lay near Herr's, and is about three miles above the Ohio forks. The former island lay near the eastern bank, and that branch of the river might well freeze over in a night, but the wide channel between Herr's Island and Shannopins could scarcely so easily freeze over. Now, Gist also kept a journal on this memorable expedition. His account of the attempt by the Indian guide at murder is so very creditable to Washington's kind and humane heart that we will quote the passage at length:

"We rose early in the morning, and set out about two o'clock, and got to Murderingtown, on the south-east fork of Beaver Creek. Here we met an Indian whom I thought I had seen at Joncaire's. This fellow called me by my Indian name and pretended to be glad to see me. I thought very ill of the fellow, but did not care to let the Major know I mistrusted him. But he soon mistrusted him as much as I did. The Indian said he could hear a gun from his cabin, and steered us more northwardly. We grew uneasy, and then he said two whoops might be heard from his cabin. We went two miles further. Then the Major said he would stay at the next water, and we desired the Indian to stop at the next water. We came to water; we came to a clear meadow. It was very light, and snow was on the ground.

"The Indian made a stop. The Major saw him point his gun towards us and he fired. Said the Major, 'Are you shot?'

'No!' said I; upon which the Indian ran forward to a big standing white oak, and began loading his gun, but we were soon with him. *I would have killed him, but the Major would not suffer me.* We let him charge his gun; we found he put in ball; then we took care of him; either the Major or I always stood by the guns. We made him make a fire for us by a little run, as if we intended to sleep there. I said to the Major, 'As you will not have him killed, we must get him away, and then we must travel all night;' upon which I said to the Indian: 'I suppose you were lost, and fired your gun.' He said he knew the way to his cabin, and it was but a little way. 'Well,' said I, 'do you go home, and as we are tired, we will follow your track in the morning; and here is a cake of bread for you, and you must give us meal for it in the morning.' He was glad to get away. I followed him and listened until he was fairly out of the way, and then we went about half a mile, when we made a fire, set our compass, fixed our course, and traveled all night. In the morning we were at the head of Piny Creek."

All doubts as to French claims and intentions were removed by Washington's important visit. In order to arouse the Colonies and Britain, Governor Dinwiddie had the Major's journal published far and wide, and reprinted in England, which led to very important and immediate action, since it was the first positive intelligence of the views and designs of the French. Instant steps were taken by Dinwiddie to send troops to the Ohio forks, which were at that time supposed by him to belong to his province. One company, under command of Captain Trent, was soon ready, and early in April Ensign Ward reached the forks, and commenced work on a rude fortification. They had made but little progress, however, before a French-Indian force of a thousand men, with eighteen cannon, suddenly made their appearance on the Allegheny, in sixty batteaux and three hundred canoes, and an immediate summons to surrender their works was made on Ward by Contrecœur. Tannacharison, the Half King, who was present with Ward, in order to gain time, shrewdly urged him to reply that he had no authority to surrender but would send for orders. To this, of course, the French leader would not listen, but gave just one hour to retire, which poor Ward was compelled to do. The French then landed and built there a fort, first giving it the name of "The Assumption of the Holy Virgin," afterwards changing it to Fort Duquesne, in honor of the Marquis Duquesne, the then French Governor of Canada; and this little affair has always been considered as the commencement of that long and memorable "seven years' war," only terminated by the Treaty of Paris, and by which France ceded to England all Canada and almost the whole territory east of the Mississippi.

Washington's First Campaign—Surrender of Fort Necessity.

Washington immediately sent expresses to the Governors of Pennsylvania, Maryland and Virginia, acquainting them with the forced surrender of Ward's company and the erection of a fort in what was then clearly considered to be part of Virginia. He himself proceeded—as soon as he could gather the force—at the head of three companies, to the Monongahela, at the point now occupied by Brownsville, Pa. He soon received a message from his old friend Tannacharison, the Half King, that the French from Fort Duquesne were marching against him. Next day Col. Gist, who had formed a frontier settlement near where Uniontown, Pa., now stands, joined him with the startling news that a French force of fifty men had been at his place the day before. Close on the heels of these tidings arrived another message from the Half King, who was then encamped with his warriors some six miles distant, with information that the French had encamped near him, and urging Washington to "strike" them.

Washington immediately started with forty men to join his faithful ally. The night was pitch dark; the rain fell in torrents; the woods were pathless and tangled with undergrowth, and the soldiers often lost their way groping through the matted bushes and clambering over logs and rocks, but at length they arrived at the Indian camp just before sunrise, May 28, 1754.

A council with the Red Chief was held at once, and a joint attack on the French was resolved upon. Two Indian spies discovered the enemies' position in an obscure place surrounded by rocks and about a half mile from the main trail. Washington was to advance on the right, the Half King on the left. They all then stealthily approached in single file until discovered by the French, who flew to arms. The action commenced by a sharp firing on both sides, but in a very brief time the French had succumbed, with the loss of Monsieur Jumonville, their commandant, and ten of his men. Twenty-two were taken prisoner and sent off to Dinwiddie.

This was the very first "baptism of blood" received by Washington, and the affair was afterwards misrepresented, greatly to his injury. It was also the first overt act in a long war which had not yet been declared, but which for many years after deluged all Europe in blood.

The news of this fateful action stirred up a tremendous hubbub, not only in the American Colonies, but in England and France. War had not yet been generally declared, and it was the policy of each government to throw the blame of commencing hostilities on the other party. It was officially charged by France that Jumonville was leading an embassy of peace, and that while conveying a civil summons to Washington, asserting the French claim to all the country watered by the Ohio and its tributaries, and requesting the English forces to retire, he was waylaid and *assassinated*. Unfortunately some color was given to this charge of *assassination* against Washington afterwards in the articles of capitulation at Fort Necessity, when the word *assassination* instead of *killing* was, through the stupid blundering of Van Braam, the interpreter, allowed to stand, making it appear as if Washington confessed the base charge.

The whole affair has been carefully examined and discussed by English and American historians, and, without entering into the detailed *pros* and *cons* of the controversy, we need only state that the result was a complete and triumphant vindication of Washington.

Among the prisoners taken by Washington was a Mr. La Force, who was known throughout the whole western country as an uncommonly bold and enterprising leader of great subtlety and exercising a potent sway among the Indians.

As Washington knew that the news of this successful assault upon Jumonville would draw on him an attack in overwhelming force from Fort Duquesne, he set his troops at once to prepare an entrenched work at the Great Meadows, which he named Fort Necessity. The Half King, Queen Alaquippa and their friendly Indians began to flock in, and Captain Mackay with a South Carolina company joined him most opportunely. Shortly after a company of nine deserters from Fort Duquesne arrived with the startling tidings that the French, by their artful wiles and bountiful presents, had induced the warlike tribes of Delawares and Shawnees to "dig up the hatchet" against the English and would soon appear in force.

Shortly after friendly Indians brought the news that the French at the forks had been heavily reinforced from Canada, and were preparing to march against him and drive him out of the country. Washington, for many reasons not needful here to enumerate, resolved to abide the issue at Fort Necessity, situated near the Laurel Hill and about fifty miles west of Cumberland, Md. Trees were felled, breast-works were strengthened, and all put in the best possible state of defence.

On the 3d of July, the enemy "put in an appearance." Washington had drawn up his men on the flat outside of the trenches, but finding the foe in superior force and that they refused an open encounter, but were using all their arts to circumvent him, he retired his men and gave them permission to fire at discretion. A brisk fire was maintained all day by an enemy that never dared to emerge from the sheltering cover of the woods. An untimely rain filled the trenches with water, the provisions and ammunition were exhausted, and many of the miserable, worthless arms of the soldiers were out of order; so that, when a very civil summons for a parley came from the French leader, M. de Villiers, a brother of Jumonville, Washington was ready to negotiate.

The result was a capitulation under very favorable terms, the whole garrison being allowed to retire to the east, taking all their effects with them except their artillery, and to march out of the fort with the honors of war, their drums beating and colors flying. Washington agreed on his part, to restore the prisoners who had been taken at the late skirmish with Jumonville, and as a surety for this article, Captain Van Braam and Major Robert Stobo, (of the latter of whom we shall speedily say more and nothing to his discredit,) were delivered to the French as hostages. It was moreover agreed that the English should not attempt to build any more establishments west of the mountains for the space of one year.

Washington accordingly marched forth next day, but had gone but a short distance when a large body of hostile French Indians surrounded them and could hardly be restrained from an attack. They pilfered the baggage and did other mischief. Washington finally, after being compelled to leave much baggage behind, reached Wills Creek in safety. Much dissatisfaction, however, prevailed in the colonies where the terms of this capitulation were published. The war spirit against these overt acts of the French was rising to fever heat. The truth is that Washington had been grossly deceived by the interpreter, Van Braam, either through his ignorance or his design. He was a Dutchman and it is probable erred through his ignorance of the French language. Be this as it may, the Virginia House of Burgesses approved Washington's campaign and he was accorded a vote of thanks. It was ever a matter of mortification to him, however, that Dinwiddie refused to ratify that article of the capitulation regarding the return of the French prisoners who instead were sent to England. Thus it happened that Major Robert Stobo, the hostage given to the French for their return, was for many years kept in confinement, and had a series of remarkable adventures which we shall now proceed to relate.

REMARKABLE ADVENTURES OF MAJOR ROBERT STOBO.

This gallant and indomitable Scotchman had scarce arrived at Fort Duquesne before he began casting about how he should put it into the hands of the English. With a boldness that while it challenges admiration, yet savors much of rashness, he entrusted to the hands of friendly Indians, two highly interesting letters, signed openly with his own name. Had his messengers proved faithless, Stobo's life would at once have paid the forfeit, but the brave Major, as we shall speedily find, was a patriot of the true metal and perfectly willing to take all consequences.

These letters contained a very accurate plan of the fort; an account of the amount and disposition of the forces; gave much news of the savages and of the artful lies which the French had employed to make them hostile to their old friends, the English, and furnished many valuable hints as to how the fort could be easily taken, and urged upon Washington to immediately make an advance and capture it.

They also contained such expressions as these: "If this news is true," (alluding to some Indian defection), "it will make our return very hazardous, but that is not to be considered." "La Force," (the French leader captured by Washington), "is greatly wanted here. No scouting now—he certainly must have been an extraordinary man among them, he is so much regretted and wished for." "When we engaged to serve the country, it was expected we were to do it with our lives. Let the country not be disappointed. Consider the good of the expedition without the least regard to us. For my part I would *die a thousand deaths* to have the pleasure of possessing this fort but for one day. They are so vain of their success at the Meadows, it is worse than death to hear them." "Strike this Fall as soon as possible. Make the Indians ours. Prevent intelligence. Get the best, and 'tis done. One hundred trusty Indians might surprise the fort." "The French manage the Indians with the greatest artifice. La Force is greatly missed here. Let the good of the expedition be considered preferable to our safety. *Haste to strike.*"

The whole spirit breathing through these letters was so bold, manly and self-sacrificing, that the Pittsburgh historian, Neville B. Craig, made repeated efforts to learn more about the gallant Major. The information he gathered was of the most meagre description. Later, he happened to be rummaging over an old book, and the first words that caught his eye were "Captain Stobo," which were included in a letter from one English historian to another—David Hume to Tobias Smollet. It ran thus: "I did not see your friend, Captain Stobo, till the day before I left Civencester, and then only for a little time, but he seemed to be a man of good sense, and has surely had the most extraordinary adventures in the world."

All this only increased Craig's zeal and curiosity to know something more of the mysterious Stobo, and, in answer to a public call for information, he was fortunate enough to obtain from the British Museum a manuscript copy of the "Memoirs of Major Robert Stobo," which he republished in Pittsburgh about twenty years ago.

From these memoirs, written in a quaint, old-fashioned style, we learn that Robert Stobo was born at Glasgow, Scotland, in 1727, and was of a very delicate constitution. He received a good education, but early betrayed a love for arms, employing his play-hours in a constant drum-beating and drilling his comrades. Losing his excellent parents, his friends determined to carry out his own wishes of emigrating to Virginia, in order to serve in a store there.

He soon began business for himself, returning to Glasgow in '47, converting all his property into ready money and merchandise, and returning to America, where his natural goodness of disposition, joined with a turn for gaiety and social pleasure, made his acquaintance much courted by the best people of the province. He kept open house and dispensed his hospitality with such a free and liberal hand, that when his friend, Gov. Dinwiddie, was raising a regiment to oppose French aggression in the Ohio Valley he was glad to receive the commission of captain. He soon became a great favorite and displayed military talents of no mean order. He it was who planned and erected Fort Necessity, the capitulation of which brought him to Fort Duquesne as an hostage.

His bold letters from that fort have been already referred to. They had a curious fate, and in the end worked much damage to the writer. The letters came safely to Washington's hands, were forwarded to Gov. Dinwiddie, went into possession of Gen. Braddock when making his expedition against Fort Duquesne, and then fell into possession of the enemy, having been left behind with the rest of Braddock's baggage after the disastrous defeat of that general at Braddocks Fields.

When the French found that La Force and the other prisoners were not to be returned according to terms of capitulation, Stobo and Van Braam were removed, in September, 1754, from one French fort to another, till at last they reached Quebec. They, however, were treated with great kindness and liberality. Stobo having, on account of his free, jovial manners, been admitted to the society of the French officers, thought it necessary to study French, in which pleasant occupation he was greatly assisted by several French ladies, who taught him how to talk and pronounce and made much of him generally. In fact no company was thought complete unless the gallant and accomplished Monsieur Stobo made one of it. He, at the same time, became very popular among the French Indians, studying their language, customs, sports, &c., and was so much esteemed by them that the honor of the Mississaga Indian nation was conferred upon him, the ceremony of his adoption into the tribe having been pricked by means of sharp fish bones and indelible juices into his two thighs immediately above his garters. "Setting aside," says his biographer, "the gentleness of his manners, there was something in his appearance very engaging; he was nearly six feet tall, of a dark brown complexion, had a penetrating eye, an aqueline nose, round face, a good cheerful countenance, a very genteel person, rather slender than robust, and was graceful in his whole deportment."

But a sudden change was all at once to come over his fortunes. When the Braddock papers came to be published in France, his two famous letters, with his own name attached, came into notoriety, and he was by the press denounced as a dangerous spy. The French officers now began to look frowningly at him, but he still managed to preserve his credit among his many lady friends. It was now concluded to treat him with rigor as a suspect. He was clapped into prison and used with great harshness. Next came an order from France to the Governor of Canada to try him for his life as a spy.

Some time in '56 he effected his escape from prison, but a reward of 6,000 livres, offered to any who would bring him in alive or dead, filled the woods with thousands of eager persons, and he was soon caught and thrust into a black, horrible dungeon. In this damp, dark, dreary, dismal, doleful, damnable dungeon his eyes soon acquired such a power that they could discern a rat running over the floor, and it may be added that they received much exercise in that line.

In November our hero was brought before the military court, arraigned for breach of faith and violating the laws of nations. His condemnation was a foregone conclusion. The vote was put—hang he must. The day was fixed and he was remanded back to prison. But his indomitable heart was yet unshaken, and he busied himself meditating over plans of escape. The judgment of the court, however, was not approved by King Louis, and the dungeon was changed for a jail, with two vigilant sentinels at the door and two below the one window, but *fortuna favet fortibus*. They could not hold a man of his daring spirit.

Many were his plans of escape. The window offered him the best chance. He found it firmly barred with iron up and down, but not across. He must cut a groove in the hard stone, so as to throw one of the bars aside. He had but a sorry knife, round at the point, and as it would imperil all to make a noise, his business must be done by careful, silent rubbing. The work went slowly on. Meanwhile he must gather provisions for his long journey. He managed to secrete a sort of a knapsack, and on the stove he parched grain to carry with him. His room was always open to his jailers, and he had to fill the groove as fast as he made it by stuffing it with chewed bread, which was then covered with sand or ashes.

Sometimes the grating noise would bring in the jailer, but the groove was so neatly concealed and the Major was generally found sitting so calmly, walking, smoking or reading, that, after peering around the room with jealous eye, the jailer was fain to depart with shaking head.

At length the groove was done; the bar had room to play, but being short and fast at top, the Major could not bend it. Tying his handkerchief around the two bars, he inserted a stick and by twisting it about had leverage enough to bring the bars together. The knapsack was now stored with over thirty pounds of various kinds of provisions which he had managed to secrete, and all was ready for the escape.

The 30th of April was a horrible day from wind, rain and hail. The night was no better. The sleepy sentries, suspecting naught, sought favorable shelter from the wretched weather. Stobo's eyes were on guard and soon as he saw the parts deserted he knew his time had come. Hurriedly tying about him his knapsack and applying the handkerchief tourniquet, a passage was soon opened and down he jumped into the mud below, and is off like a shot. Soaked with rain, buffeted by the wind, straight on he flies, certain of his way. Far above the town he took refuge in a farmer's outhouse and anxiously awaited the chance for escape.

His flight was at once detected; again 6,000 livres were offered for his arrest, and out set the whole town in search. For two days, knowing that many would be seeking him, the Major lay snug. At midnight he stealthily stole out and made straight for Charles river, crossed it with knapsack on his head, the water coming up to his chin. Now he gains the friendly covert of the woods, where he remained the next day; towards evening he edges down the river, hoping to secure a canoe wherewith to cross the St. Lawrence. He wandered on and on until he had got below the Falls of Montmorenci, eight miles below Quebec, when just as he had set foot on the great road, he spied some gentlemen riding towards him, who unfortunately were just as quick in spying him and made hard after him. He was caught and dragged back to prison.

Who can imagine the sad, gloomy thoughts of the poor prisoner? That can his biographer, who thus quaintly laments this sad relapse into captivity : "Ill used before, better could not be hoped for; he sickens at the thought of his sad fate; a dreary while for him to linger out in sad despondency, well barred and bolted in with treble vigilance. A long, long Summer and a dismal Winter were to come, and these, for what he knew, might be repeated, if life so long would stay. He could not stand the thought; his spirits failed him; his looks grew pale; corroding, pensive thought sat brooding on his forehead, and left it all in wrinkles; his long, black hair grows like a badger grey; his body to a shadow wastes, and ere the Winter came with her keen edge of hardened cold, his health was gone; yet he must struggle still with the remaining span of life, for out he must not come and he's given up for dead. There dwelt by lucky fate in this strong capital, a lady fair of chaste renown; of manners sweet and gentle soul; long had her heart confessed for this poor prisoner a flame, best suited with the spirit of the times to smother, whose tender heart felt double smart at this his deep affliction which threatened certain death; her kindred was confessed and influence, too, well known with Vaudreuil and, strange speech of love, thus she accosts the proud Canadian Vice Roy," &c.

We need not give this tender love song, but the burden of it was an urgent appeal to change the Major's prison and give him exercise and good air, and so a chance for his life. The prayer prevailed. The wan and wasted prisoner was allowed to walk the ramparts. By the care of this kind lady and her daughter, the Major's health recovers by degrees, and he became very watchful and studious to disarm all suspicion. The months passed on and Stobo made the acquaintance of some English prisoners brought in—among others a Scotchman, by the name of Clarke, a ship carpenter by trade, who, by a facile and timely change of religion, was released and was soon employed at work in the shipyard. With this man and another prisoner by name of Stevenson, he concocts a new scheme. In order to dismiss his kind lady attendant, he feigned illness. Instead of going to bed, however, he dressed in a plain coarse workman's dress he had provided; incased his head in a thick worsted wig and quietly stole down the stairs, past the rooms of the family that had been so kind to him, out into the garden, and leaped the wall.

No sooner out of town than he quickened his pace and made his way to a little windmill on the river, which was fixed as the rendezvous for the whole escaping party. He found them all there, with guns, ammunition and provisions. March was the word, and Stobo, as leader of this gallant little band of five, moved along the river for a couple of miles in hope to find some vessel by which to escape.

Major Stobo's Escape from Quebec and Daring Adventures.

At length they came across a large birch canoe, which they carried to the water, and all safely embarked. With nimble hands they plied the paddles, and flew down the strong current of the St. Lawrence. By daylight Quebec was left far behind, and they sought the protection of the woods, carrying their canoe with them. As before, the Major's flight was early discovered. The whole house was in a terrible uproar. The Governor hears of it, and is moved to a terrible wrath. The old reward is offered, and thousands ransack the woods for the fugitives.

This time in vain! The little party lay by quietly all day, but soon as night came on they launch again their frail bark upon the current, and paddle away like all possessed. By daylight they were, with their fragile canoe, in the woods again. This was their life for ten long days and chilling nights, until they had gotten a long distance below the city, and the river had grown as broad as a firth. Latterly they had taken the risk of hunting game, and encamped by day in order to save their stock of provisions, which was getting low.

On the eleventh night they paddled out into the middle of the broad river, but soon encountered a violent storm. The waves broke over them. The canoe filled with water, and they tried in vain to make the shore, but passed the night, tossed like a cork upon the waters, and only saved from wreck by unintermitting bailing. A piercing cold now set in, freezing their drenched clothes to their backs. By morning they succeeded in again reaching shore, but in a most sorry plight. Their frozen garments rattled like coats of mail; scarce one could lift a limb, and a mother and children, who formed part of their crew, were almost dead. The steel and flint were found wherewith to build a fire, but the tinder was too wet to catch.

At length the poor mother sought in her bosom and found a dry rag; a fire was built, and a couple of days more are spent drying and thawing out. The boat was again trusted to the waves, and by morning had reached a little bay, on whose shores they debarked, the two marksmen going out for game. They soon ran back, frightened by the appearance of two armed savages. Stobo reassured them, and demanded to be led to a sight of them, thinking that if they were scouts for a larger party, it might be necessary to cut them off. They soon came upon the two unsuspecting savages, when Stobo broke out into a French cantata, and saluting the savages in French, seized the gun of one, while Stevenson grappled him and Clarke the other. Stobo then said they were Frenchmen, but in search of English prisoners who had escaped, and that he must be sure who they were. They were much alarmed, and offered to lead the way to their tent and to the fire of which they were the guardians, so that the whole country might be alarmed at the advance up the river of any hostile British fleet. These fires, they said, were placed at regular distances from the mouth of the St. Lawrence to Quebec, so that news could be speedily carried of any hostile invasion.

The wigwam was found full of furs, wild duck and maple sugar, and the Major's party began to rifle it. The Indians now realized their mistake, and the one Stevenson held gave a backward spring and set up a dreadful yell. To prevent any further noise, Stevenson had to shoot his man, and his comrade was soon made to share his fate. The camp again reached, Stobo thought it was imprudent to leave the bodies unburied, and sent Dick Clarke and another to inter them, which they did.

They now saw out in the river a fleet of French transports, with a convoy, ferrying their slow way up to Quebec. One ship in the rear, judged, by her size, to be the commodore of the fleet, was lying to. Stobo concluded that she had seen their smoke and had sent her boat ashore to learn the meaning of it. The fire, therefore, was put out, and the canoe and baggage moved off into the woods, and then a roundabout course taken to the river again. They now espied a large four-oared batteau rowing for the shore and no ship in view. "Courage, my lads!" cried the fearless Stobo. "I hope, by your assistance and God's blessing on our arms, this prize shall be our own; these men our prisoners, too, and they shall lessen your fatigue and row for us; observe but what I order."

Stobo's party now lay closely concealed among some rocks while the boat's crew pulled briskly in. Scarce had the prow bumped the beach when a volley was sent in among them, by which two were wounded. The astonished Frenchmen at once cried out for quarter. The Major and his companions rushed down from the rocks and ordered out the whole five. A reverend old gentleman, who was steering the boat, stepped out with a polite bow of submission, and very naturally asked whose prisoner he was. To this the Major answered in French: "We are British subjects, and, by the fortune of the war which now does rage betwixt that country's mighty King and France, we have been prisoners in Canada, but now," &c., telling them that they and their boat must aid their escape. To this the old Frenchman said he had been a long distance down the river, and was returning with his boat laden with wheat; that he was the Chevalier La Darante, and sole owner of the Camaraski Isles, the first gentlemen of them all doing him vassalage; that the best blood of Canada ran in his veins, as he was kin to the great Duke de Mirepoix and other prominent French nobles, and that, in addition to all this, he was old and feeble, and therefore should well be excused from being compelled to row his enemies.

To all which, in brief, the Major answered that self-preservation was the first law of nature, and that if he were King Louis himself, and each of his crew a peer of the realm, he would have to row now British subjects. This ended the matter. As the shallop was too deep-laden for expedition, much of the wheat was cast out, and, all hands embarking, the boat left the shore, the faithful canoe dragging astern.

To lie by in the day was now impossible, neither did the Major like much to trust his prisoners ashore. About noon they noted a lofty frigate, which had been convoy to the fleet of transports. This sudden and dreadful apparition gave no small alarm, but since they could not stand a fight, a run was resolved upon. So the Major took the tiller and swore that the first man who offered to impede the boat's way should die in the instant, and ordered all to pull hard and to spread the sail, so as to pass the frigate's stern.

The usual signal to heave to came from the frigate, but our party paid it no attention; a second followed, which was likewise disregarded. The third report came accompanied by a shot which whizzed over their heads, uncomfortably near. Then followed shot after shot, as long as the boat was in sight. Rejoicing at their lucky escape, the boat flew along, continuing on its course all night. The old Chevalier's remonstrance as to the hardships and indignities he was compelled to undergo, passed unheeded. "Il est fortune de guerre, Monsieur," was all the reply vouchsafed by the Major.

Days sped on. Capes, islands and mountains were passed, one by one, but no sail was met. At length a boat was found upon the beach, when Stobo promised to the Chevalier that he would let him go if he would promise for him and his party that he would keep secret what had transpired till the Camaraski Isles should be passed; after that he did not care. The Chevalier readily promised. "Then, Monsieur," replied the Major, loftily, "your mast and sail are ours. Our case is desperate, but I'll pay you for them. Here, too, is money for your lost wheat. Go tell all Canada how good the British monarch is!"

All things being ready, the two parties took separate ways. Stobo's boat continued along all night. With the morning they espied abreast of them a ship at anchor and heard the signal to heave to. This they declined, when a swivel, loaded with grape, opened fire and after that another, completely riddling their sail but doing no further damage. On they pushed all that day and the next, but after that they were not quite so fortunate. Towards evening a dreadful storm arose. At the point they now were, the St. Lawrence was very broad and the waves ran as high as upon the ocean, while the surf was quite as loud and dangerous. To beach the boat, however, is the only salvation for them, and straight to shore they let her drive. Near the shore, she came upon a rock with a dreadful shock, bursting open the boat's bows and filling her with water. The waves break over them and all hands, taking with them what they could, make for shore. The boat was completely demolished. Soaking as they were, a wet and dreary night was passed.

Next morning a sober council was held. All other methods of escape except by water are declared impossible, and so the boat's wreck is hauled ashore, and all, under the direction of Clarke the ship carpenter, set to work to make it sea-worthy again. With wistful search they scan the shore for nails, pieces of board and what not to piece the old hulk up. Some eight days are spent in this tedious and disheartening work, and the stock of provisions was, too, getting fearfully low. At length the boat was ready for the first pitch and oakum, carefully gathered from sticks found along many miles of shore. Stockings, handkerchiefs and other articles of dress were used to stuff the joints, and at last the frail cutter was ready for launching.

Just as this interesting ceremony was about to be performed, two sails are seen standing down the river, and finally their anchors are dropped right off the point where the crazy vessel sat upon the stocks. Here was a strange dilemma! All labor stops at once! Down squat the men! The sails of the strange vessels are down, in preparation for riding out the flood tide.

Major Stobo Captures Two Ships with all on Board.

At this crisis, a daring and desperate idea enters Stobo's pate. They were in a terrible strait. Starvation on the one hand; renewed slavery on the other. "Here are two enemy's vessels," he said, "and by their distance one may be attacked; nor by their mean appearance should I think them freight with men or arms; more like some country vessels and so I'll wish and hope and think; and now, could I divide the force of either and calmly, under cloud of night, steal on her by surprise, then might I hope success. The very thought elates my soul. By jove, she's mine! This next is the smallest of the two; on her the project shall immediately be tried."

A council is called; all hear with wonder, and promise to assist. Stobo orders them not to stir, but to keep close to the ground, while he should give a signal. Cutting a long stick he fastens thereon his handkerchief, and with it in one hand and a musket in the other, he coolly marches to the water's edge and fires his gun and waves his extemporized flag. The sun was just setting. His signal is seen from the ship. A boat is observed dropping over the side and two men and a boy came rowing to the shore where the redoubtable Major stands ready to receive them.

Approaching near they yet warily stand off and ask what he wants. Stobo answers in pretty good French that he was on the king's errand, ("under which King, 'Benzonian? speak or die!'") and now he wants a passage down the river, for which he would willingly pay liberally. The night was cold and he had a bottle of rum which they were welcome to if they would fetch it, &c. The boat is driven to shore and hauled upon the beach, and while guzzling down the rum, violent hands are laid upon them, and the three are taken and bound.

All is fair in war, thinks Major Stobo, and he tells his astounded victims that they are in British hands subject to death, but "look here, my lads! you yet may live, if you faithfully declare what hands you left on board and what their arms." They are examined separately and all agree. The boy consents to pilot them aboard, as the Major thought his well-known voice might answer unpleasant questions and disarm all suspicion.

It was now darkest night. The two prisoners were bound each to a tree and the one woman, with drawn tomahawk, left to guard them. The patched-up vessel is then taken off the stocks and launched, the ship's boat being considered too small to carry six. She leaks badly, it is true, but she'll doubtless last to reach the ship. While two row, two more are kept busy bailing, and to this there was no let up. "Off they go, and rowing softly on with silent stroke, came alongside the ship. A light there's in the binnacle, but ne'er a watch on deck; they're all hands down; the sloop rode fair; her buoy was clear ahead, the weather moderate and some turn in to sleep, for yet 'twas not half flood. The rest, at ease, enjoy themselves below."

"Our hero first gets up the side, and as he softly stepped up on the deck, the trusty pistol, which in his belt was stuck, catches the ratlins of the shrouds which pulls it out, and it comes clatter on the deck. This gave the alarm, but woe to him who first came up! So soon as he had shown his face at the companion door and bounding up, so soon the Major let fly a shot in this surprise, and down the fellow tumbled. The shot had hit him right along the back and grazed the bone, but he's not killed, but quarter was the word and now the rest are all upon the deck. The prisoners he orders one by one down to the hold, the master only left and then he locks the hatches, and then he questions freely. 'That schooner there above is my consort, and we are bound to Gaspee to bring provisions for three hundred Indians now assembled at Miramichi and Aristigush, under the command of Monsieur Bohaber, and who, on our return, are to proceed to Quebec to reinforce that garrison.'"

The Major is suddenly fired with the wish to prevent these Indians from joining his country's foes. By further querying he finds the schooner has ten men, but no gun or carriage or a swivel; of this last sort the sloop had six, all on one side. The windlass is now manned, the anchor is apeek, and now she's under way, and steered by Stobo straight for the schooner. "Stand firm, my lads," said Stobo, in low, collected tones, "this is a glorious night, and as for you, Monsieur, if you should once but mutter, your life that moment shall surely pay the cost."

Stobo now laid the sloop right alongside the schooner, and by his stern orders, a dose from all the swivels is poured into her at once. She was then boarded without one instant's delay, her crew instantly calling out for quarter.

This was a most extraordinary deed of Stobo's! How must that little band have been dazed at this daring and unexpected assault! Stobo now stood, with cocked musket, at the companion door; boldly ordered down the prisoners, one by one, from the sloop; removed everything valuable from the latter and smaller vessel; transferred the swivels, and then deliberately set fire to the sloop, which lights up the whole heavens with her funeral pyre.

All this time the poor woman stood trembling on the shore, keeping guard over the first two prisoners. When the thunder of the broadside was heard, the noise went to her heart like death's last summons. She was sure the guns were fired at Stobo and the rest, since she knew they had no guns. She was just about to surrender herself to her own two prisoners, and to entreat them to save her and her children, when she sees the vessel a-fire. She fears and wonders, but keeps her own thoughts. Now Stobo selects two of his best men and two prisoners, and sends them ashore for the company there, and brought all safely on board. The hatches now being closed on no less than eighteen prisoners, which are too many to be safe, they are ordered up by ones, and eight are sent adrift in the small boat, when off sails the schooner under British command.

The small boat's party made straight to shore, and thence to the nearest military post, and told all that had happened. The officer, having heard of Stobo's escape from Quebec and the munificent prize offered for his capture, at once raised every man that could be spared; armed a suitable vessel and made chase after the schooner. Too late! by this time Stobo was too far ahead, and kept steadily on his course for several days, until the Island of St. John's appeared. By scudding along on one side of the isle, they chanced to miss a British fleet which was passing towards the river by the other channel. The armed sloop in pursuit of them, however, had no such good luck, for she was captured by the British.

At length our adventurous party sighted Cape Breton, away across the Gulf of St. Lawrence, and soon gained the British fortified port of Louisburg, having been full thirty-eight days making the voyage from Quebec. The news of this wonderful and gallant escape flew from mouth to mouth, and the whole place was in a ferment of excitement. Stobo was for a time the "observed of all observers." The schooner, with its valuable furs and other goods, was sold, and Stobo gave all his own share of the proceeds to the poor woman and her children.

Two days only passed when behold Stobo on board an armed vessel about to join the expedition against Quebec. No danger in the river now is dreaded, and he is just as anxious to reach Quebec as he was formerly anxious to escape from it. Having arrived safely, Stobo at once waited on the British General Wolfe, told him who he was, and his intimate knowledge of the place where he had been so long confined, and asks for service. The General at once engaged him on reconnoitres, making him one of his own household. Once, when Wolfe was on a vessel closely examining the batteries about Montmorenci, an enemy's ball hit the vessel, causing a splinter to grievously wound Stobo in the thigh. He was daily engaged to lead scouting parties in every direction, and soon became known throughout the whole fleet and army for his activity.

Once, when Stobo was on the Admiral's ship, he was informed there was a French prisoner aboard who knew him, and found him to be the barber who used to dress his hair. Stobo ended the interview by taking him into his own service. The Major's thorough local information was of much use to Wolfe. When the great and successful assault was made, it was Stobo who pointed out the best place for a landing, and was then chosen to proceed to Boston by vessel as a courier, with important dispatches and kind recommendations, to General Amherst. When the Atlantic was reached, the vessel was chased by a French privateer. Stobo, soon as he found the capture of the British vessel was inevitable, committed his dispatches to the deep, and determined to shoot his French valet to preserve his own life, but on the fellow solemnly swearing that he would never betray him, he removed his pistol from his temple and spared his life.

The privateer had taken several British vessels, and had aboard more prisoners than they could well secure. When this new vessel, therefore, was captured, the crew, among whom the Major passed undetected, was packed into a sloop, but his valet was put in irons as a French deserter. The sloop was then sent adrift with one day's provisions, to find the port of Halifax, which they were four days reaching. Stobo had scarce set foot on land before he hastened to reach Amherst by land—a dreary and wonderful journey through almost a total wilderness.

Of Stobo's difficulties and adventures during this tedious journey, we have no information, but we do know that he safely reached Amherst and delivered his dispatches, as, also, that he attended that General as a volunteer in his Lake Champlain Expedition. That being concluded, he proceeded to Williamsburg, Virginia, arriving there in November, 1759.

The Virginia Assembly, soon as they could convene, resolved that a thousand pounds should be presented him, over and above, from the time of his rendering himself a hostage, as a reward for his zeal. The House of Burgesses also made an address to the Governor, desiring that he would take him under his especial favor and would promote him in the service, and passed also a motion of thanks for "singular bravery and courage, and that Messrs. Nicholson, Bland and Washington should wait on the Major to return him their thanks for his invaluable services;" to all which Stobo returned a most graceful answer.

This was not all. The Major was now tendered a twelve months' leave, as Major of his regiment with full pay, if he should choose to go to England, which generous offer was duly accepted, and early in 1760 he took passage for Europe, with many letters of recommendation from Generals Amherst, Monkton and others. His troubles, however, it seems, were not yet quite over, for when the vessel was about entering the English Channel, she was chased and boarded by a French privateer. Stobo had taken the precaution to put himself in disguise, and to sink his letters many fathoms deep over the vessel's sides. The vessel was rummaged, the passengers were rifled of their watches and valuable property and the vessel released by paying the privateer twenty-five hundred pounds. The Major's share of this redemption money was a hundred and twenty-five pounds. Had the French only known who he was (for by this time the fame of his exploits had traveled far and near) no sum could have secured his release.

The English port of Falmouth was now reached, and as Stobo was drawing on his coat to go on shore, he found, to his great surprise, under the arm-pit, a letter from General Monkton to the great Pitt, which had by some means escaped the fate of the others. He learned, however, that the story of his marvelous adventures had preceded him. On arriving at London he drew up a modest narrative of what he had done and suffered and asked to have a command in his country's service. He was well received by Pitt, who held a long conference with him concerning America and gave him a strong letter to General Amherst, stationed at Boston, in which he signified the King's approbation of Stobo's success, and asked that Amherst as "a particular favor" would give him command in his own or Anstruther's regiment. Armed with this, the Major did not long delay, but in two days sailed back for America.

The memoirs of Stobo, published by Craig, end at this point in his history. We can find no further allusion to him. Washington is said to have made mention of Stobo's being alive and probably residing in London as late as 1771. It is most probable he was there in the English service or had retired on half pay. If alive when the American Revolution broke out, he may not have had it in his heart to aid in oppressing a struggling people for whom he had once endured uncommon hardships, and who in turn had paid him graceful honors.

BRADDOCK'S EXPEDITION AGAINST FORT DUQUESNE.

The news of the capitulation of Fort Necessity created a great excitement throughout all the eastern colonies. It came upon them like "thunder from a clear sky." It was truly considered that if the previous collision between Washington and Jumonville had rendered war between France and England possible, this later conflict at Fort Necessity had made it inevitable. In the mother countries the seriousness of the crisis was at once recognized, and both governments, while diplomatically exchanging courteous notes or making mutual explanations, were quietly but busily preparing for war. England, however, at that period was badly governed. She moved slowly, and nothing whatever was done to resent the French aggression in the West during the whole of the year '54. While the French were making good their possessions west of the Allegheny river, building their forts, holding treaties, and plying all their arts with the Indians, the Colonies were doing little but wrangling among themselves or unitedly calling on the mother country for help.

The year 1755, however, marked an ominous change. While both sides professed the most peaceful desires and intentions, preparations for a very vigorous conflict for the vast and rich domain stretching for thousands of miles west of the Allegheny mountains, were constantly going forward. Gen. Braddock, with two regiments, arrived in February as Commander-in-Chief of all His Majesty's forces in America, and the coming campaign contemplated the attack of four key-points of the French: Fort Duquesne, Niagara, Crown Point, and the French posts in Nova Scotia. To Braddock himself was committed the important *role* of reducing Fort Duquesne. It was his belief that the British flag would be floating over it by the 1st of June, and it was his intention then to proceed north and reduce other French posts; but it is "man who proposes but God who disposes."

The French at Fort Duquesne had early news of Braddock's advance against them. They had few regular troops on which to rely, and were obliged to supplement them, as far as possible, by a gathering of the savages. To induce them to fight the English, was now the aim of Contrecœur, the commandant at Fort Duquesne. To this end emissaries were sent to the Mingoes, Delawares and Shawnees, who, by crafty pow-wows, delusive promises and frequent distributions of gifts, succeeded in detaching them from their old allies, the English. Fortunately for their arms, a treaty that had been made with the Six Nations (who claimed the whole boundless West by right of conquest) a short time previous, at Albany, New York, had produced universal rage and disgust among the Ohio tribes. For a few beads, bells, blankets and trinkets, they found the whole territory they claimed and occupied as their own, now given away from under their feet.

The Delawares, too, had never forgotten or forgiven the disgraceful swindle practiced on them in '37, and generally known in history by the Walking Purchase, and which we may describe hereafter. In brief, the Indians had been persuaded to give a very valuable tract of land on the Delaware as "far as a man could walk in a day and a half." Instead of construing this contract as it was evidently meant, the best and most active walkers of the country were hunted up and put in training; at the same time a smooth road was laid out, so that no obstruction might be offered. By this means an incredible distance was gotten over, and the outraged Delawares were justly indignant and refused to move and give up their villages and grain fields until compelled by the Iroquois, their masters. As one of the swindled remarked of the walkers: "White man no walk, no drink, no stop to rest or shoot squirrel, but run, run, run whole time." All this the French leaders, mingling familiarly among them, promised to win back for them, and with faces freshly painted and heads duly shaved and plumed for the war-path, the dusky warriors flocked in to Fort Duquesne.

In fact the poor Indians were very much troubled and confused at this juncture. They were opposed to the encroachments of both French and English. One of their chiefs had, at one of these palavers, shrewdly put the pertinent query, "Since the English claim all the lands on the other side of the Allegheny, and the French all the lands on this side, where, pray, do the Indians' lands lie? Tell me that!"

In addition to the local savages drawn to the fort for its defence against Braddock's formidable army, there were scattered beneath the sombre forest around, Ojibwas and Ottawas, under the lead of the Sieur de Langlade and Nis-so-wa-quet; and Hurons and Cauhnanagas, under the lead of Athanase, the Christianized Chief from Lorette, Canada. Among the prominent chiefs arrayed with them were Pontiac, Shingiss, Beaver and Catahecassa, all cruel as wolves upon the scent of blood.

And now let us stop to consider awhile who Major General Braddock was, and how well he was fitted for the important task before him.

THE CHARACTER OF GEN. BRADDOCK AND HIS ARMY.

Generalissimo of all His Majesty's troops in North America, and favorite of the great Duke of Cumberland, Major General Braddock was now full sixty years of age, over forty of which were passed in active military service with the famous "Cold Stream Guards." It is difficult within the compass of a few brief paragraphs to sketch his life and character. It is generally allowed, even by his bitterest enemies, that he was personally brave, honest, loyal, and well versed in military matters, but a rigid martinet, and too apt to rely on exact drill and discipline exclusively for success. "Desperate in his fortunes, brutal in his behavior, obstinate in his sentiments," writes Walpole, "he was still intrepid and capable." Mr. Shirley, his own military secretary, in a confidential letter written while far on this march to Governor Morris, of Pennsylvania, says, "We have a General most judiciously chosen for being disqualified for the service he is in, in almost every respect. He may be brave for aught I know, and he is honest in pecuniary matters."

In private life, it must be confessed, Braddock was, or rather had been, dissolute and reckless, keeping the low and disreputable company of London actors; given to the debaucheries of his day and class—the bottle and the gaming table. Franklin, that keen observer of human nature, pronounced him a brave man and a good officer, but arrogant, having too much self-confidence, too high an opinion of regular troops, and too mean a one of both Indians and Americans. The old philosopher, when hearing Braddock's account of what was to be done after Duquesne was taken, told him that the only fear he had, was from Indian ambuscades and from the stretch of his attenuated line of march, nearly four miles long, which would be exposed to flank attacks and liable to be cut like a thread into several pieces. The Indian opinion of him was given by Chief Scarrooyaddy to Governor Morris and the Pennsylvania Assembly three months after the defeat, which he attributed to pride and ignorance. "He is now dead," said the Half King, "but he was a bad man when alive: he looked upon us as dogs, and would never hear what we said to him; and that's the reason why a great many of our warriors left him, and would not be under his command."

There are numerous incidents told of Braddock before his arrival on our shores. It is pretty certain, for instance, that he had once made a most unfeeling speech and a cruel pun when he heard of the sad death of his beautiful but unfortunate sister Fanny, who committed suicide under most distressing circumstances; that he was mean and base enough to live on the infamous wages of a notorious Mrs. Upton, in whose eyes he had found favor. He was known to be so needy that in one of his duels—this time with a Col. Gumley—his opponent, on coming on the ground, tossed him his purse, saying, "Braddock, you're a poor dog; there, take my purse; if you kill me, you'll have to run away, and then you'll not have a shilling to support you;" and, finally, that he spent the last evening in London, prior to his departure for America, in the company of that frail actress, Miss Bellamy, then living as the reputed wife of a Mr. Calcraft, whom Braddock afterward made his executor. It is little wonder that the witty and sarcastic Walpole called him a "very Iroquois in disposition."

But these were matters of the past. All authorities, foreign and provincial, unite in stating that since his arrival on our shores, the General had conducted himself with honesty, dignity and diligence, using his utmost energies to push matters forward—and this under the most vexatious and disheartening difficulties—and being anxious to further the king's service.

The worst that could be said of Braddock since his sojourn in America, was that he was impatient, intolerant, and complaining—scolding at everybody and finding fault with everything. But then it must also be admitted he had much reason therefor. The delays, swindles, and outrageous impositions which he and his army had to submit to, in the way of horses, wagons, provisions, and general army supplies, were almost incredible. The General's intercourse, too, with both Washington and Franklin was always pleasant and honorable to all parties; and when the latter had raised a large number of wagons and teams for Braddock, in Pennsylvania, by means of a timely hand-bill circulated among the Dutch farmers, in which the threat was craftily held out that unless the aid was granted, the ferocious Hussar, Sir John St. Clair, would enter the province with a body of horses and forcibly take what he wanted, Braddock expressed his thanks to him in person, and wrote to his government that it was "almost the first instance of integrity, address and ability that he had met with in all these provinces."

During his march, Braddock had gotten rid of many of his

foolish and pompous European notions. He soon discovered that America was a strange, unknown territory for him and his veterans, and that a western wilderness, wih its crowded trees, dense thickets, and bridgeless streams, was a very bad place for high style or display. Thus he started by buying a tawdry and lumbering traveling chariot from General Sharpe, of Maryland; and on the 10th of May, the army was startled by Braddock's rapid transit, on his way to Fort Cumberland, sitting grandly in his chariot, with a body of light-horse galloping on either side. Poor, mistaken old man, he was soon glad to come down to one sorry, attenuated cob, and after, to a rude litter, carried by a few faithful soldiers.

Sir Peter Halket was second in command. He was a wary old Scotchman and a high-born gentleman of the ancient regime. A nobleman by birth, he had married the Lady Amelia Stewart, daughter of the Earl of Moray, two of his sons being then with him. He was a brave, loyal, sagacious and honorable gentleman and an experienced officer, who had risen by merit alone; and had Braddock trusted more in him and in Washington—the two who generally agreed touching all military movements—it would have saved him from defeat as well as disgrace. At the famous battle of Preston Pans—which occurred only ten years before between Sir John Cope and the Highland clans and Jacobitish adherents of Charles Edward, the Pretender—Sir Peter, then lieutenant-colonel, had been captured and released on parole by Charles. This coming to the ears of the Duke of Cumberland, he ordered that officer to disregard his parole and rejoin his regiment, which Sir Peter stoutly and resolutely refused to do, saying that "His Royal Highness was master of his commission but not of his honor." The king approved this proper resolve of an honorable soldier and he retained his rank.

It is not our purpose to give a detailed account of Braddock's ill-fated command, and its tedious, toilsome march, first to Cumberland, and thence to its battle-ground of disastrous defeat. Its nucleus, in the shape of the 44th regiment, Col. Sir Peter Halket, and the 48th, Col. Thomas Dunbar, had arrived from Ireland, disembarking at Alexandria about the middle of March, 1755. Neither regiment numbered five hundred, and these were made up of Irish, Scotch and English, drafted from different commands, and a large proportion of base material. After reaching this country, these two regiments were recruited by raw, provincial levies up to an effective of seven hundred each, and, after innumerable and vexatious delays and immense labor, were joined by independent companies from New York, Virginia, Maryland, South and North Carolina. The trouble, expense and delay in getting the army supplied with wagons, provisions, horses, etc., was almost incredible and entirely disheartening, and it was not until about the 8th of June that the heterogeneous little command was ready to march from Cumberland.

The whole force was divided into two brigades under Colonels Halket and Dunbar, numbering about 2,150 effectives, not counting the usual train of non-militants—women, wagoners and hangers-on. The progress of this ill-sorted command was painfully slow, five miles being considered an excellent day's march, while most frequently it did not reach half that. Bridges had to be built, roads to be cut the whole way, deep and miry marshes to be traversed, and steep and rugged hills to be surmounted. The route chosen was by no means the shortest or the easiest one. The advice of Nemacolin, the Indian guide, was too closely followed. Frequently morasses had to be waded through and savage hills to be climbed, the heavy artillery being let down by the sailors with block and tackle. The number of wagons and pack-horses was strung out in a line of over four miles in length, which was constantly made the object of attack, though happily by small parties. In addition to the natural difficulties of the route, were superadded such as arose from crazy wagons, wretched and inadequate food, most miserable horses, and a general sickness and discontent among the soldiers and officers. It is little wonder, then, that this army had been ten days in reaching the Little Meadows, but twenty-four miles from Cumberland. This fatal tardiness would never do, and reductions of baggage were constantly occurring. Even the officers were compelled to give up their horses to the service.

At the Little Meadows a council of war was held, the result of which was that Washington's advice was taken, and the army was divided. It was daily more evident if Fort Duquesne was to be reached before it was reinforced and in time to allow of subsequent military operations, that a light fighting division must push forward more rapidly, and so about twelve hundred of the best and most reliable troops were sifted out, together with a select train of artillery and pack-horses for the provisions. Colonel Dunbar, with all the heavy wagons, useless artillery and other impedimenta, was left behind with the worst and most unreliable troops, to make his way as best he might. Even with these aids to a more rapid progress, it was not until the 21st of June that Braddock entered Pennsylvania, and not until the

30th, that he crossed the Yough, near where Connellsville, Pa., now stands, and on the 7th of July, Turtle Creek yet remained to be passed.

Had the General waited here for Dunbar's army, as was strongly urged by Sir John St. Clair, the Quartermaster-General, it would probably have been the middle of August before the fort, then but a few miles off, would have been reached, and the whole army would either have starved or fallen into the hands of the enemy, as numbers would have availed little. "Dunbar, the Tardy," as he was called, had lost so many of his wretched draught horses by sickness, by starvation, and by constant stealings, that he could only move half his wagons at a time. After one day's march, the miserable and worn-out old jades were sent back to bring up the remainder, and then two days more before a fresh start could be made. Disputes and jealousies were common, too, among the officers, and Braddock was not even on speaking terms with his two brigade commanders. Even the robust constitution of Major Washington had given away under this state of things, and he had been traveling for ten days in the rear in a covered wagon, and was but just now returning. He had exacted a promise from Braddock that no battle should be fought without him being present.

Turtle Creek, at the point where the army first struck it, was soon found utterly impracticable for artillery and the wagon train, without constructing a very long and costly bridge, and it was decided to abandon this line altogether, turn sharp about and make for the Monongahela, where the Indian guides said there were two excellent fords. The night of July 8th was passed about two miles from the Monongahela. It had been decided that what was known as the river "Narrows"—it being impracticable for artillery and affording for several miles admirable facilities for hostile ambush and attack—should be avoided by crossing the Monongahela at the first ford, and recrossing it at the second ford a few miles below. By eight o'clock on the memorable 9th of July the first passage of the river was made at a point opposite Crooked Run, and even to this day observable by a deep scar in the banks where they were graded down to make a road for the artillery. The army now found itself on a broad bottom, covered with a fine growth of maple, walnut and sycamore, and moved steadily forward in the road cut for them. By eleven o'clock the second ford was reached, nearly opposite the mouth of Turtle Creek, and but a quarter of a mile below what is known now as the "Second Dam."

Here the bottom begins to narrow until it runs into the hills very near the margin of the river. On this grassy savanna, denuded of trees, Braddock, not doubting that the enemy from the opposite bluff were anxiously watching his every motion, resolved to impress them with the size and character of his command. Accordingly, while the banks were being graded down, on that as well as the other side, to allow of the passage of the artillery, baggage wagons, cattle, etc., the troops were ordered to appear as for dress-parade. Now the astonished hills re-echo with the loud beat of drums and the swell of martial music. Every man was attired in his cleanest apparel. The flags and colors were unfurled, and the joyful and well-drilled troops, glittering in scarlet and gold, were rapidly marched and manœuvred and put through all their movements, which they executed with the precision of a piece of machinery.

This plateau, where, for over an hour, all this showy parade was going on, was in full and uninterrupted view from the subsequent battlefield. The officers and soldiers viewed it with undisguised pride and delight. But one belief prevailed—the speedy occupation of the fort. No wonder that Washington, in after life, declared it to be the most beautiful and inspiring spectacle he had ever witnessed. All was now ready and after a brief repast the army had safely passed the river and reformed about one o'clock in a thick walnut grove, several hundred yards below the mouth of Turtle Creek, and hard by Frazier's cabin.

THE DISASTROUS BATTLE OF BRADDOCKS FIELDS.

(Taken from the Historical Novel of "Old Fort Duquesne.")

> The death-shot hissing from afar;
> The shock, the shout, the groan of war,
> Reverberate along that vale,
> More suited to the shepherd's tale.—*Byron's Giaour.*

> One effort—one—to break the circling host;
> They form—unite—charge—waver—all is lost!
> Within a narrow ring compressed, beset,
> Hopeless, not heartless, they strive and struggle yet.
> Oh! now they fight in firmest file no more;
> Hemmed in—cut off—cleft down and trampled o'er.—*Byron's Corsair*

We quote from "Old Fort Duquesne," the subjoined account of the battle of "Braddocks Fields," not alone because unusual pains have been used to make it full and reliable, but because the dialogue form in which it is cast, serves to liven it up and break the monotony. Captain Jack, the Scout, and Scarrooyaddy, the Oneida Chief, are both historical characters. We quote:—

It was now past one o'clock of a sultry afternoon. The rear guard had not entirely crossed the river, before the van had been pushed forward towards the hills; Gage, with his three hundred videttes, engineers, light-horse and pioneers in front, followed at a little interval by Sir John St. Clair's working party, with its two brass six-pounders, and its tumbrels and tool carts. Their business it was to cut and prepare the road marked out for them by the engineers. The march was to continue until three, and then the last bivouac before resting in Fort Duquesne, or, at least, before encamping down about it. On either flank of the advance were thrown out squads of videttes, to guard against surprise.

The distant sound of the ringing axe, and the crash of falling trees, could be distinctly heard as the pioneers rapidly advanced—first over the broad and gently-rising river bottom, and then up the slope which led to another gradually-ascending plain, which, in its turn, rested against a line of bold, wooded hills. This second alluvial slope was more heavily timbered than the flat below, while the undergrowth of vine, thicket, and tall wood grass became at every step more abundant and luxuriant.

Adown this second sloping plain—although at that time, and not until long after known to or even suspected by the British—ran several ravines nearly at right angles to the brow of the hill which the advance had just surmounted. From one on the left trickled a little stream, which as it debouched into the first bottom, lost all distinctive channel, and was so diffused as to cause a sort of marsh. It was to avoid the treacherous footing of this miry bog, and to pass the head of the ravine which gave it birth, that the army was mounting so far towards the hill-sides. The ravine on the extreme right, which sprang from the hills and traversed the whole second plain, was both broad and deep, its sides and bottom thickly covered with huge trees, and having an unusually rampant growth of vines and brambles, and sufficiently ample to conceal an army of ten thousand men.

About two hundred yards from the line of hill and the same distance from the broad ravine just mentioned, commences, right in the middle of the plain, and without any apparent *raison d'etre*, a most singular ditch, with a depth and breadth of a few feet at its head, but increasing soon to ten or twelve, and at that time overhung and completely concealed by a thick growth of vines and bushes; of grasses and trailers and the wild Indian plum. Even to this day it can scarcely be perceived, or, at least, its full capacity cannot be fully appreciated, until one is right upon and then *in* it. It is a most peculiar ditch, and could not be better adapted, either for attack or defence, were engineers to devise and fashion it. It could easily conceal a thousand men.

The main place of action was on the densely-wooded tract between these two ravines, with its fallen trunks, its coverts and thickets of vines and brush and grass. The course of the twelve-foot-wide road cut through these leafy coverts, was not parallel with either, but diagonal and turning the head of the last-described ravine at an angle of about forty-five degrees, the whole face and flanks of the passing army being exposed to a long line of the enemy's fire at an *average* distance of sixty or seventy yards.

This then was the spot so carefully reconnoitred and so admirably chosen by the six French officers and Indian chiefs, whose departure from the fort we described in our last. Here was the slaughter-pen they had so adroitly marked out for their foes. When, or if, beaten by their adversaries at the river crossing, it was to this refuge they would retire, and here would they prepare their ambush. Not a man or officer of the British army ever dreamed of these ravines, and never saw them during the three hours of combat, and it was only long after the disastrous action, when reason resumed its sway, and the beaten, driven mob of fugitives considered how pitilessly they were pelted and mown down by a terrible but unseen *feu d'enfer*, that they concluded their wily foe *must* have fired from hidden ravines.

Pass over these quiet, peaceful "fields" now, as we have but lately done, part of them in grass and part staked out and soon to be occupied by the country seats of Pittsburgh business men, and then imagine them covered with a sombre and luxuriant forest, the ravines choked with vines and brush and undergrowth, and the long rows of deadly rifles resting on their edges and deliberately sighted by hundreds of naked savages, and then see the narrow road choked up with an unsheltered crowd of soldiers and mounted officers, and Braddock's defeat is easily accounted for. Had the French hunted for days, or had their engineers the privilege of selecting a ground for successful combat and arranging artificial ditches for attack and concealment, they could not have found or prepared any place better fitted for a dreadful and successful assault, or one which could so easily have protected the assailants.

As Braddock and his *aide* Washington—still weak and shattered from his fever and unable to sit on his horse without a pillow—were standing on the river's bluff, trying to bring order out of confusion, and to separate the noisy mob of soldiers, wagoners, artillery and cattle, the clear ring of the distant axe was suddenly exchanged for the rapid and continuous discharge of firearms. The crack of rifle, followed by the roll of musketry, appeared to be incessant.

"My God, Major!" cried Braddock, as he leaped to his horse, whose bridle his servant Bishop was holding near him, "the advance is attacked, and sharply, too! What can it mean? Mount on the instant, and bring me back a report of what's going on! Tell St. Clair and Gage to throw well out their flankers! and urge Burton, as you pass, to hurry forward with the vanguard, while I get the artillery in motion. Here! you infernal scoundrels of wagoners and cattle-drivers, get you out of the road with your rubbish into the woods on either side, and let the troops and guns press on! Quick step! Don't dally!"

Washington delayed not an instant, but springing upon his powerful roan, spurred along under the trees and by the side of the road now choked up with artillery and soldiers, all pressing forward with utmost speed and excitement. He soon reached the first slope; a few strides and his horse was over its brow and on the plain beyond. The firing was now straight ahead of him. Officers and men stood huddled in groups in the road; some few had taken to the trees on either side. The two brass pieces had just been unlimbered and the cannoneers were preparing to apply the match. The attack had evidently been sudden and unexpected, and Washington now saw Gage's advance doubled back upon St. Clair's working party, and for a brief space all was confusion. Nothing could be seen in front but the flashes of the enemy's guns and the shadowy forms here and there of French and Indians as they glided from tree to tree; nothing heard but the crack of rifles, the noise of muskets, the piercing yells and whoops of savages, who seemed to fill the woods and to be working around in a semicircle.

"Ho! Sir John," exclaimed Washington, as St. Clair, foaming with rage and mad with excitement, approached to form and urge on the men. "What's all this? The General bids you halt where you are; throw your flankers well out, and hold your own—if hotly pressed—until Burton comes up. What's the nature of the attack?"

"Fierce as furnace fire and hot as d——n," answered the fiery Sir John. "Harry Gordon was in the very front marking out the road when, upon hearing a rushing noise ahead and looking through the trees, he saw a pack of French and Indians on the run, a gaily-dressed officer, with a silver gorget on his bosom, leading the way with long kangaroo leaps. Soon as they got within musket shot, the cursed Frencher stopped short in his tracks, and waving his plumed hat above his head and then stretching his arms to either side, his pack of red devils scattered to right and left, crouched down and slunk away behind trees, trunks, and what-not, until, by heavens, they had completely vanished—not a painted head or hide of one of them to be seen—the skulking cowards! The first we knew, a pitiless hail of bullets rained upon us, amid the most horrible screeches and yells and infernal noises sure ever mortal heard. I'm blessed, Major, if I'm used to this kind of fighting—don't know what to make of it. Our flankers have all run in, and the carpenters, or what's left of them, are huddled down the road like so many sheep worried by wolves, and the troops are fairly appalled by these screeching demons. For God's sake, hurry old Braddock up! tell him we've got the whole French-Indian army in our front, and will have to fight our way to the fort step by step."

Washington, after a few more brief, rapid questions, took in the whole situation and turned his horse's head. He had gone but a few steps when he saw Jack and the Half King a few yards on one side of the road, each peering from behind his tree and trying to catch sight of something to shoot at.

"Halloo! Jack and Scarrooyaddy. *You* there, my braves? Where are the other Indians? They must scatter in the woods and try and find out where those devils are hiding and what's their force. I'll have Braddock here in a flash." Just then a crack was heard and a bullet whizzed by, going through and through the lappel of Washington's coat.

"Aha! Major," cried Jack, quick as thought, as he raised and fired his rifle, "that's just the chance I've been waiting for. I've watched that skulking Shawnee now for over a minute. I knew he wouldn't let you pass without a shot. That's their game, the cunning varmints. Pick off the mounted leaders, and the rest comes, of course. Don't stay to see where I hit him, Major. Old 'Black Rifle' is certain as death. Hurry up the troops! we'll need 'em all, for the savages are in full feather in front; if there's one, there's a thousand, twisting and creeping and gliding about among those trunks. Halloo! there's Yaddy's rifle. Hit him again, by Jupiter! and a Frencher, too! No bark without its bite is the plan we're acting on."

Washington had not far to go. Braddock, finding the uproar not only continuing but even increasing in front, had raged through the whole army like mad, and could not wait for his aid's report. Ordering Burton to detach eight hundred men and hurry forward with all possible speed, he left Sir Peter Halket in the rear with full four hundred to protect the baggage. He then swore and stormed along the whole artillery line, and pushed the guns forward as fast as possible.

Washington met the General, his eyes fairly aflame and with spurs buried deep into his horse's flanks, right on the brow of the hill. Gage's cannon at that moment had just filled the woods with their resounding roar, which was followed with cheer after cheer from the British, who were standing in a confused crowd in the middle and on the sides of the road, loading and firing as fast as they could.

The terrible, leaden hail, which had been so steadily raining on the English and shattering their columns, now slackened for a while. The British then advanced on the French in front, pouring in a hot fire, though very few of the enemy could be seen. As they drew near, another staggering discharge met them, appearing to come, as it were, right out of the ground.

The British rallied again, and opened a dreadful storm of grape and musketry, sweeping away everything living before them, but the grievous misfortune was, that about the *only* living things were the trees of the woods. Beaujeu, the chief leader of the foe, and several others, were seen to fall, while the Indians, unaccustomed to the appalling roar of artillery and the loud huzzas of the soldiery, appeared to waver, and for the moment gave way. A well-pushed bayonet charge just then would have put them to remediless flight. Observing, however, that the French and Canadians still held their ground in the direct front; much exasperated by the fall of their loved Beaujeu, and urged on to revenge by Dumas, Langlade and de Lignery, they took fresh heart, and returned to their trees and ravines, through and along which they extended more and more.

It was just at this critical moment that Braddock's horse leaped into the road, and, struck instantly by a bullet in front, fell on the very leap, throwing the General violently to the ground. The grim and infuriated old warrior staggered to his feet, sword in hand, and glared around like a lioness robbed of her whelps. His eyes fairly shot flames, and his face grew livid with rage as he saw his carefully-drilled veterans standing in groups and without order, all appearing to fire at random, while many were shooting into the trees above them, as if their foes were birds in the branches. To increase his disgustful rage, just at this moment Gage's advance gave way entirely. The unseen enemy had worked themselves along the ravines on both flanks, and, from behind the dense undergrowth and tall grass which fringed them, poured in a most galling fire, coolly and securely picking off officer after officer.

Colonel Burton's command had just come upon the ground, and were forming, as well as could be under such a murderous hail of lead and in such a narrow road, when crowding down upon them came Gage's and St. Clair's shattered columns trying to get into their rear, and mixing the two regiments in inextricable confusion.

Then it was that Braddock stormed around with a rage and an indignation which was almost sublime from its intensity. Turning sharply on Gage:

"How's this, craven sir! would ye so basely dishonor your king and the duke? God's wrath! is *this* the way you've been taught to fight! By the Eternal, but I'll break your disgraced sword where you sit in saddle! Curses on you all for a set of white-livered cowards! You look more like a flock of silly sheep set on by hounds than drilled soldiers. For shame! for shame! Fall in ranks, every mother's son of you, and come out from behind those trees! By the great God above us, men, but I'll cut down with my sword the first soldier, British or American, who *dare* skulk behind a cover! Out with you, cowards!" and suiting the action to the word, Braddock leaped to the road side and actually hit with the flat of his sword several whom he found behind the trees, while others he pushed into the road.

"General," sullenly expostulated Gage, "these insults are undeserved. We can't fight a deadly foe who surrounds us on three sides but whom we can't see. The officers are falling like leaves all about you. The men are plainly panic-stricken. If allowed to get behind whatever cover offers, they can pick up heart and reform when the enemy is found. If not, we'll all be killed, officers and men."

"Killed!" hoarsely roared Braddock, while mounting his second horse. "And why not? Better die with naked front to the foe than blink and skulk like hares in their 'forms.' Get behind trees! Oh, that ever I'd live to hear a British officer and a nobleman's son, too, give voice to such dastard words! Officers, I command you to separate yon frightened mob! Advance the regimental colors! Set up rallying points! Tell the men off into platoons, and hunt up the enemy in that way! Major Washington, bid the rest of the artillery advance and open with grape!"

The word had scarce left his lips before his second horse was laid low with a bullet, and Braddock was again on his feet in the road, which did not go far to improve his temper. Here Washington ventured to observe, quietly and in low tones: "General, since the enemy's evidently in great strength ahead and on each flank, would it not be well to find out exactly where he is, and how he manages to so hide himself? If we could retire the troops a little out of fire, beat up these woods with the bayonet, and reform—"

"Retire! retire out of fire! and before a d—d dastardly foe who dare not uncover himself!" shouted Braddock. "Major Washington, you are my aid-de-camp to *carry* orders, not to *give* them! *Retire* is a round, well-picked word! It may suit your American militia, but, sir, it is a disgraceful word for an officer holding His Majesty's commission, either to speak or to hear! It was by *retiring*, as you well call it, that Forts Duquesne and Necessity were given up by you last year to the French! Dam*m*e, sir, it has been so much retiring that brings me and my army on this field! Here, orderly, bring me another mount!"

Washington's pale face flushed up with indignation at this stinging, but totally undeserved, taunt, the more galling since Braddock had repeatedly given his approval of the '54 campaign. Seeing the General's obstinate temper, and knowing he had no right to offer advice, he put spurs to his horse and was soon over the hill to hurry up the artillery.

"That's right, officers!" hoarsely shouted Braddock, soon as he was again mounted. "Tell off your men into small parties, advance on a double-quick, and drive these d—d skulking vagabonds from their hiding-places!"

It was useless. By this time the confident and whooping savages had enveloped both flanks, while a most galling concentric fire was poured in upon the panic-stricken army, which was particularly severe upon the officers. In vain these officers, with unparalleled bravery, put themselves repeatedly at the head of small parties and advanced with cheers upon the hidden foe. Distinguished by their horses and uniforms, they were simply sacrificed. In the dark and narrow road, surrounded on all sides by gloomy trees and dense thickets, were crowded close together the panic-stricken wretches, appalled at the fatal fire of foes whom they never saw. Many fired away into the air; many more brought down their own men.

Wherever a puff of smoke was seen, off went the soldiers' muskets; while all around, securely hidden in those mysterious, unsuspected ravines, lay a screeching, murderous, insatiate foe, their rifles or muskets loaded with both bullet and buckshot, peering through grass and bushes, resting them on the brinks, gathering more and more confidence with each fatal volley, and making the forest echo with demoniac yells and whoops and savage clamor. Occasionally a naked and hideously-painted savage would break from cover, and rush forward with fearful screech to secure the scalp of some officer he had shot. Then would follow a volley of musketry from the poor soldiers, killing or wounding their own fellows more than damaging the enemy.

SIR PETER HALKET'S DEATH—BRADDOCK'S RETREAT AND DEATH.

What followed deserves not the name of battle; it was simply a horrible slaughter. Once Colonel Burton managed to gather a hundred men and advanced towards a rising ground in front, the very centre of the French position, but upon his being disabled by a rifle ball, the rest retired precipitately. By this time Sir Peter Halket came up with reinforcements, but too late for good. The men were hopelessly disordered and panic-stricken, firing off all their ammunition, quarreling with their brave officers, who threw themselves from their horses and led them repeatedly on foot, but only to be swept into eternity.

The only thing for Braddock to do when he found himself caught in this horrid slaughter-pen, was, manifestly, to retire his forces while he had them yet under control; throw out scouting parties to beat up the enemy's position; bring up his artillery to the ends of the ravines and thoroughly rake them with grape and canister, or to rout out the securely-hidden foe with the bayonet. Indians have never yet been found able to withstand a bayonet charge. The cold steel at close quarters demoralizes. They quiver, break and fly. This was what both Halket and Washington urged him to do, but to no purpose. He raged along the road like a fury; drove back his men by the sword and seemed determined to overcome by mere force of drill and obstinacy. Indeed, it is uncertain whether he now could have executed the manœuvre. No soldiers—not even Cumberland's veterans—could long withstand a deadly and concentrated fire from front and both flanks.

The fact that the fatal flashes and puffs of smoke and volleys seemed to come right out of the ground and from unseen foes, while the whole air and woods around rang full of savage yells and horrible screechings, completed the demoralization. Many afterwards declared that during the whole three hours' contest they had never once seen a foe; while others would not assert that they had seen over half a dozen. It is only wonder that soldiers so wretchedly posted and so badly commanded, could stand it as long as they did. The Provincials suffered as much as the British soldiers. Whenever and wherever they could, they took to the trees. It is even asserted, and we think it probable, that some of the officers who, by Braddock's explicit command, attempted to beat back into the road the men who had thus sought shelter behind trees, were shot by their own men.

In one of the pauses of this one-sided conflict, Washington, who had been kept busy carrying the General's orders—the other aids, Orme and Morris, having been wounded—saw Colonel Halket, grim and weary-looking, standing dismounted under a huge oak, and leaning heavily against its massive trunk. Hastening up and out a little from the fire, he anxiously inquired:

"I trust, Sir Peter, you are not very badly hurt?"

"Na, na, Geordie; but Ise gotten eneuch. 'Tis joost aboon my baldric. Wha culd luke to go thro' siccan an awsome day wi'out scaur or scaith. I ha'e fear Ise ta'en a strong grippit o' death. I am sair, sair forfoughten, but never fear, mon, but wha' the auld Sir Peter will e'er present a heckle to his foes."

"Oh, 'tis not so bad as that, Colonel," said Washington; "but you, like the rest of us, have received your baptism of fire. 'Tis a gory field, and the end's not yet."

"D'ye mind, Major, the 'secon-sight' I tauld ye of yestreen and the vision of bluid? Said I not recht?—but, ha'e ye seen Jamie, laddie?"

"I have, Sir Peter; there he stands, and unhurt."

"'Tis strange, verra strange. 'Tis the bairn Francis, and not James that's hurt and ta'en to the rear, alang wi' Sir John Sinclair, Colonel Burton, Gladwin, and mony ithers. Oh, but this is a sorra day! Braddock's joost lost his fourth horse. The fule carle thinks he's fightin' on the broad plains o' Flanders. 'Tis eneuch amaist to drive one distraught to see him trying to wheel and manœuvre a whail army, shoulther to shoulther, in a twal-fut road. I ha'e beggit him to let his men tak to the woods, but the dour deevil wi' not. He's clean daft, Geordie, clean daft."

"Well, Colonel," said Washington, "no use to discuss the General now. You need immediate attention. I'll send some soldiers to take you to the rear."

Washington had scarce gone a hundred paces before a bullet, sped by an Indian rifle from the ravine, struck Halket straight through the heart. Just as he was falling, his son James rushed forward and caught him in his arms. He, too, was at the same instant mortally struck, and both fell together, locked in each other's embrace, and this was the last of the old Scotch nobleman. The two bodies lay, just where they fell, for years, through Summer's heat and Winter's snow—"'mid all the wreck of the spiteful elements." We will hereafter relate how, three years after, two skeletons were found locked together, and in how singular a manner the young Sir Peter Halket identified them as those of his father and brother. The Provincials—the American militia of whom Braddock was so contemptuous—were among the last to yield the hill. Among them were Jack, Gist, Waggoner, Scarrooyaddy and others of the more cool and collected scouts and rangers, who had, wherever they could obtain a " coign of vantage," kept up a desultory fire upon the foe.

About this time Jack, his face all begrimed with powder, his bullets almost all spent, his eyes glowing and teeth clenched in a sort of bulldog fixedness, was sullenly retiring from tree to tree hotly pushed by some Ottawa Indians, when he noted the approach of our old acquaintance, Captain Waggoner of the Virginia Rangers, with what was left of his men. They were doggedly retreating step by step, casting many an anxious look behind.

"Waggoner," exclaimed Jack, "'tis a crying shame that we should stay here and be butchered for the mad whims of a man, who may be as brave as Julius Cæsar, but who's also as crazy as a loon. Now, I've been studying the lay of these lurking red devils, and from the line of their fire, I feel certain their whole position can be turned from that huge fallen tree yonder, lying just on the rise of the hill. What say you? Can you take your men, and let us run for it?"

"Good! Jack. Give me your hand on't, old hickory! I'm with you till death. I can depend on what is left of my company to a man, and think I can get enough rangers from Dobb's, Dagworthy's, Stevens' and Peyronies' companies to make the attempt. Ho!" he shouted in clear, ringing tones, "American rangers, stay one moment! We've tried fighting Indians on the British plan, and if we go on one short half hour longer, we'll not have a whole scalp left. Captain Jack proposes to run forward and take possession of yonder huge log, which commands the enemy's position and will give us complete protection, and we'll route those cursed, yelping, barking devils down there, quicker'n you could scrunch a nest of rattlesnakes. All who want to redeem this disgraceful day and strike at least *one* stout blow for victory, follow me!"

A hearty cheer rang out, and about eighty American rangers, including, also, Jack, Scarrooyaddy, Alaquippa's two sons, Gist, Fairfax, and two other friendly Indians, agreed to follow.

"Now, lads, all load up, and sling each man of you around his tree and draw their fire."

"So!" as a brisk volley came from the foe. "Now for it!" and Jack and Waggoner leading, they darted rapidly forward, rifles cocked, all ready in trail and losing only three men by the way.

"Now!" shouted Waggoner, "spread yourselves along snug and fire at will, and if we don't have a little to boast of this day, my name's not Tom Waggoner. Look! Jack; look! D'ye see the painted slippery devils wriggling and gliding away! *A-ha!* we've got 'em, every pop! Now for it, boys! Quick! quick! before you lose 'em. Ready! Take aim! *Fire!*"—and a tremendous volley and red line of flame leaped from their rifles.

"Ha!" yelled Jack, springing to his feet with excitement, as he saw a whole raft of Indians break cover. "One more like that and we'll have scalps enough to buy a farm apiece. Hurrah! boys; hur—"

His words were drowned by the roar of guns and a general discharge of musketry behind him, and at least forty of the eighty fell killed and wounded by the fire from the mob of British regulars in their rear, who loaded and fired wherever they saw a flash or smoke.

"My God!" gasped Jack, the first to recover from the dreadful shock which seemed to paralyze and hold speechless all that were left. "Shot by our own men, as I'm a living sinner! Worse than murder, by heavens! Come, Waggoner and Yaddy, it's no use. The day's lost when British soldiers can thus slaughter their betters."

Another volley was poured on their doomed heads, until fifty out of the gallant little band were either killed or wounded, and the rest were put to a hasty flight. Their rage, disgust and indignation can be imagined but not described.* Braddock, almost all his best officers either killed or wounded, and all the ammunition shot away, found it now almost impossible even to effect a safe or orderly retreat. The Indians, having little more to fear from the army on the hill plain, had now worked down the ravines until they appeared on the first "bottom," and commenced to attack the baggage. The flank parties posted for its security all but one ran in. A great number of horses and some drivers were shot down, while the rest, cutting loose the best horses in the teams, mounted and were off. The cannon did some service, and, commanded and sometimes even served by Washington himself, had for some time kept off the foe, but the spot was so woody that very little execution could be done.

Just at this juncture, Braddock himself, who had had five horses killed under him and whose clothes had been riddled with bullets, received a mortal wound while standing beneath a large tree on the brow of the second rise. The ball passed through his right arm, lodging deep in his lungs. The order he was just giving was left unfinished on his lips. Falling from his horse, there the brave but unfortunate General lay, with but a few friends around him and all his drilled veterans flying off in headlong, disgraceful flight. "They ran," wrote Washington in his first letter after the battle, "as sheep pursued by the dogs, and it was impossible to rally them."

It is related by George Croghan, the famous Indian interpreter, that Braddock, unwilling to survive the disgrace of his defeat; disgusted at his desertion by the famous soldiers "who had served with the Duke," and probably tormented by the pains from his wound, refused to be carried from the field, insisted upon being left alone, and finally tried to possess himself of Croghan's pistol, wherewith to make an end of himself. Be this as it may, Captain Orme, wounded as he was, offered sixty guineas to any of the regulars who would carry him off the field,

---

* This awful disaster to Waggoner's volunteer movement, the only one of the day which promised success, is historical; indeed the whole account of this batd. is based on information carefully gathered from every possible source, and can be taken as reliable.

but in vain. It was a *sauve qui peut* rout with the regulars and "devil take the hindmost."

Captain Stewart of Virginia, commander of the body-guard of light horse, and Braddock's own "*aide*," Captain Orme, carried the dying General off the field, put him in a tumbrel, then upon a fresh horse, and thus the old veteran was borne from the scene of his defeat. It was a custom in those days for every officer to carry a sash of scarlet, silken net-work, with which to bear him, if wounded, from the field. The sash in which Braddock was this day carried, the date of its manufacture (1707) and the initials E. B. wrought in the woof, and the blood-red stains upon its netting still visible, is said to be yet preserved in the family of the late President Taylor.

The fall of the General destroyed all semblance of further opposition. Every aid but Washington and every field officer was struck down. About nine hundred out of the fourteen hundred men, and sixty-three out of the eighty-six officers were either killed or wounded, and the rest scarce waited for the drums to sound the retreat. All, all was abandoned! Horses. cattle, wagons, artillery, military chest, personal baggage, *every thing*—and what was worse, almost *every person* who was badly wounded.*

Down, down the fugitive mob rushed to the ford, over which they had passed with such pageantry and enthusiasm in the morning. The whole route was strewn with guns, military trappings, and even clothing—*all* which could impede flight. About fifty Indians pursued even to the Monongahela, tomahawking several in the passage.

It was well that the savages, glutted with blood, ladened down with scalps, or having a wholesome fear of Dunbar's army still in the rear, turned aside from the monotony of slaughter to the work of gathering the rich spoils of the disastrous field. Had they chosen to pursue across the river, or had they gone up the same bank and waited at the other ford, two miles above, for the poor, panting, exhausted and panic-stricken fugitives, as they crossed the stream for the fourth time that day, but few would have been left to tell the sad and disgraceful tale.

But happily, and it is a well-attested historical fact, the French and Indians were about as much frightened as the British. After hastily

---

* There were two exceptions worthy of special note. Captain Treby of the 44th was so desperately wounded as to be unable even to crawl to the nearest bushes to avoid the pursuing Indians. While the herd of fugitives went trooping by, his woeful situation arrested the attention of a gentleman volunteer named Farrel, who placed the sufferer on his own back and so carried him until out of danger. At the first fire, Captain John Conyngham's horse was shot down and he himself very severely wounded. Falling under his horse, and being unable to rescue himself, his soldiers "for the love they bore him," rushed to his rescue and finally carried him in triumph to a place of safety, although many were shot dead in the attempt.

tearing away the scalps from both living and dead lying on the fatal field; after having loaded themselves and the captive beasts with all manner of spoils and killed all the horses they could not take with them, they spiked the British artillery and burst all the shell, and only followed the route of the British fugitives when they learned from deserters that the panic with Dunbar's reserves was even greater than with the army in the field.

Scarcely believing that this disgrace, which was at the time considered throughout the country as far greater, more inexcusable, and more disastrous in its consequences than even the defeat and flight of Braddock's army, could be possible, Dumas—Beaujeu's successor—then sent a force to follow the route, and to destroy all that " Dunbar, the Tardy," in his pusillanimity, had left.

This headlong, disgraceful flight is an unwelcome theme, and not being directly connected with our story, we care not to dwell on it, except to say that about a quarter of a mile on the other side of the river, a hundred men were prevailed upon to make a brief stand at a favorable point. Braddock and some wounded officers remained there an hour or so, but soon all the soldiers sneaked off, and Washington, sick, exhausted and fever-stricken as he was, and having so lately passed through a most terrible ordeal, with two horses shot under him and four bullets through his coat, was dispatched by Braddock to Dunbar to forward wagons, provisions, etc., to the wounded. He rode, sad and oppressed, during the whole of that wet, long and dismal night; through dark, gloomy forests, frequently having to dismount to grope for the path, and reached Dunbar—whose camp was in an incredible state of alarm and confusion from reports brought by the frightened wagoners —by sunrise the next morning. His wretched feelings during that truly doleful ride can better be imagined than described. Thence, being still very feeble, he retired to Mt. Vernon to recruit his shattered health.

It is a well-attested fact, that in 1770—fifteen years after this battle— Washington, when traveling on the Big Kanawha, was visited by an old Indian chief, who stated that he had been present at the battle of Braddocks Fields, and had not only often fired on Washington himself but had instructed his young warriors to fire; but finding it in vain, had come to the conclusion that he was protected by the Great Spirit and was preserved for a great future. So, indeed, he was. We may pause by the way one moment to follow Braddock till death released him. He remained under the faithful care of Captain Stewart; was first carried on horseback and afterwards conveyed by soldiers in his sash, fastened on poles as a "stretcher."

At ten P. M. on the 10th, the day after the battle, he reached Gist's plantation. Next morning he arrived at Dunbar's camp, high up in the Laurel Hill, six miles from the present city of Uniontown, where the half-famished fugitives from the battle-field were constantly coming in and soldiers deserting by the score without ceremony. Braddock's strength was now rapidly ebbing away. He had abandoned all hope of achieving anything; and it is to be supposed that the sufferings of his mind were far greater than those of his body. He still issued his commands, and confidently expecting pursuit and knowing that Dunbar's panic-stricken force was in a most shameful and dangerous state of demoralization, ordered the destruction of the immense stores of arms, wagons, powder and provisions, resuming his march towards Cumberland on the 12th. These orders were not fit for a British officer to give nor for one to obey. Want of horses and demoralization of his army were Dunbar's excuses.

On the 13th Braddock was evidently sinking fast. Ever since the retreat commenced, he had preserved an almost unbroken silence. His dying hours were very much embittered, and it would have been far better had he left his remains on the carnage field. The only allusions he made to the fate of the battle, was to softly repeat to himself once or twice: "Who would have thought it?" Turning to Orme: "We shall better know how to deal with them another time!" and these were his parting words. A few moments later he breathed his last at eight P. M. Sunday, the 13th, and was buried the next morning right in the middle of the road—Washington reading the funeral service over his grave. The troops, wagons and artillery passed over the place to destroy all traces and prevent discovery and mutilation by the enemy, supposed to be in pursuit.

About 1823, some laborers, while working on this road, exposed these last "unwept, unhonored and unsung" remains. They were still distinguishable by their military trappings. It is asserted that some were sent to Peale's Museum, Philadelphia, while the rest were re-interred under a tree near by. This tree has, in these present times, either by "decay's effacing fingers," or by the spoliations of relic-hunters, been reduced to a mere rotten stump. It remained for Josiah King and John Murdock, of Pittsburgh, to rescue the spot from total neglect. In December, 1871, they proceeded to the forsaken grave, situate on the farm of James Dixon, nine miles east of Uniontown, and planted about it a number of elms, spruces, larches and willows.

We scarce deem it worth while to allude to a Pennsylvania tradition, industriously circulated and generally believed throughout the whole country for half a century, that Braddock fell by the hands of one of

his own men. Thomas Fausett, a sort of mountain hermit of Fayette
county, wild, uncouth and gigantic in his appearance, distinctly claimed
for himself that he killed Braddock to save the remnant of the army
from destruction, and to revenge the cutting down of his brother Joseph
by Braddock for taking a position behind a tree. There is not a tittle
of trustworthy evidence to support the story. All cotemporary authorities are totally silent concerning any such feat, and Fausett's own tale
— as well as are the accounts of those who uphold his claim—is bung-
ling, absurd and inconsistent.

It is *now* known, from sundry French accounts, that the French, who
had scouts out following and menacing Braddock's army from the time
it left Fort Cumberland—scarcely expected to give it more than a check
on its way. The French Indians were very much demoralized by the
rumors of the size of the well-equipped English army, and refused to
make a stand. The day before the battle, however, Beaujeu, the commandant of the fort (*not* Contrecœur, as the histories have it), went out
and made an earnest and passionate harangue to the savages, but they
held a council and still refused to stir, alleging that it would be madness for such a small force as theirs to attack Braddock's great army.
Beaujeu, who was very influential with the Indians and much beloved
by them, made now a last appeal: "I am determined to go," he said.
"What! will you suffer your father to go out alone?" He then started
out with his tomahawk and rifle, accompanied by his regulars and Canadians, and was immediately followed by a mob of yelling savages.
Beaujeu was killed almost at the first fire, Dumas then taking the command. The French loss was very trifling, and Langlade, who led the
Indians, stated that some of those who were killed were not hit by the
enemies' bullets, but by the falling limbs cut from the trees by the over-
shooting of the English cannon. As soon as the defeat was sure Langlade had all the English liquors poured out upon the ground for fear of
a savage debauch.

The French-Indian force was not known until lately, but according
to three accounts from their side, is now put down at seventy-five regulars, one hundred and fifty Canadians, and six hundred and thirty Indians.
It is also pretty certain that the French intended making their first stand
at the river, and had selected the ground where the actual battle was
fought as the best place to which to retire in case of defeat. But the
English army was quicker than expected, and they had scarcely time to
take their places about the slaughter-trap that they had so artfully selected, before the hapless Britons were enmeshed. When the French
were first sighted, they were undoubtedly all on the spring, Beaujeu
far in the advance. Smith's interesting narrative (given hereafter) fur-

nishes the only English account of the departure of the French force to the battle, and of its return thence, laden with booty, and of the subsequent horrible torture of prisoners, a barbarous sequel which must forever rest as a foul stain upon the French escutcheon.

Of course this disastrous battle settled for the time the dominion of all the vast territory between the Allegheny and the Mississippi—but more, it left naked and defenceless the whole western half of the provinces of Pennsylvania and Virginia. The disgraceful and panic-stricken retreat to Philadelphia of Dunbar, the "Tardy," was, as we have said, far more deplorable and immediately calamitous than Braddock's defeat itself. All was given up as lost. The whole back country was thereby left naked and unprotected, and its inhabitants, finding themselves deserted, with no money or leaders or organization, became also panic-stricken, and left houses and stock and growing crops, and moved back to and even beyond the Susquehanna. It was some time before the French and their Delaware and Shawnee allies discovered the woeful state of panic and demoralization which followed the great battle; but when small, adventurous parties of scouts and robbers brought back news how their mere presence even put whole communities to flight, and how houses, crops, cattle, and the entire settlements were deserted, both Indians and French entered upon their horrid work with alacrity and with a keen relish for blood and slaughter. Many of the friendly Indians living along both sides of the Allegheny mountains, became at first discouraged, then defiant, and then hostile, joining with the western bands to burn, murder and destroy, until the whole country, from New York down deep into Virginia, became one vast theatre for the most wanton destruction and inhuman barbarities.

The only redeeming feature in that whole period was the successful expedition which Colonel John Armstrong made, September, '56, against Kittanning, at that time occupied by Delaware Indians, headed by the brave but cruel Captain Jacobs, and the point and direction from which most of the forays against the Susquehanna border were made. The village was attacked in the night, a number of houses burned and Indians killed, including Jacobs and some of his wives, and a great many white captives set free. In fine, these were sad and humiliating days for England, both at home and abroad. Everything British was at the very lowest ebb. There was nothing but defeat, disgrace and despair; and so, indeed, it continued until the great man after whom Pittsburgh was named seized the helm of State. His nerve and ability soon put a new complexion on matters. Among his very first resolves was to make a second attempt to take Fort Duquesne, and to recover to the English crown the vast domain given up to the

French at Braddocks Fields; and to this end he ordered the immediate collection, in Eastern Pennsylvania, of a large force, under a brave and skillful general.

Duquesne's Capture—Grant's Defeat—Highland Rage.

The army of the Scotch General John Forbes—the "iron-headed," as he was called—was nearly six thousand strong, composed of about thirteen hundred Highlanders and the rest chiefly Virginia and Pennsylvania troops. At Raystown (now Bedford) he halted, and sent forward Colonel Bouquet with two thousand men, to occupy the Loyal Hanna. The detachment by Bouquet of eight hundred men under Major Grant; the advance, and empty bravado of that officer under the very walls of Fort Duquesne; the subsequent sally of the French and Indians from the fort, by which Grant's army was flanked on both sides of the hill which now bears his name and situate right in the centre of Pittsburgh, and his force only saved from utter annihilation by a stand made by the Provincial troops, are all well-known matters in history and we need not dwell on them. It is sad, however, to be compelled to relate that De Lignery was cowardly enough to deliver five of the prisoners taken at that rout to be burned at the stake, and that the remainder were tomahawked in cold blood on the *parade ground of the fort.*

The triumph at Grant's Hill almost brought the French to ruin, for, as after the battle of Braddocks Fields, so now, the Lake Indians, believing the English army completely defeated, deserted for their distant homes. A most timely visit, just at this time, of the Moravian Missionary, C. Frederick Post, to the Delaware and Shawnee chiefs between Duquesne and Beaver, completed the demoralization of the French. The two tribes were found very sick of the war and most anxious to return to their allegiance, so that when Forbes' army—after innumerable difficulties and disheartening delays—drew near, De Lignery, after firing the buildings, destroying the stores, and all possible of the works, ended by blowing up the magazine, and embarking in boats, some down the Ohio and others up the Allegheny. On the 24th of November, 1758, Forbes' army had encamped at Turtle Creek, his provisions, forage, etc., so nearly exhausted that even from that advanced point a retreat was seriously advised by a council of war.

The sick and emaciated but stout-hearted old General—who was carried on a litter all the way from and back to Philadelphia, where he shortly after died—would not hear of it, but swore he would sleep in the fort the next night.* That very evening a great smoke, in the direction of the fort, was reported, and at midnight the whole camp was startled by the dull, heavy sound of some great explosion. *It was the magazine of the old fort;* and encouraged by these signs, the army pressed on, the Provincials, in their fringed hunting-shirts, leading the way; next came the Royal Americans, their drums beating a lively march, followed by the old iron-headed General, his wasted form reclining in a litter; and last of all came the Highlanders, in a long and picturesque line, in their kilts and plaids—the "petticoat warriors," as the Indians called them.

As they all approached the fort, they passed along a race-path, on either side of which a horrid sight presented itself. A long row of naked stakes were planted, on each of which was impaled the head of a Highlander, killed at Grant's defeat, while beneath was suspended his kilt and accoutrements. Disgusted and provoked at the scene, it is said the Americans quickened pace and hastened on; but not so the Highlanders. One who was present thus relates the exciting scene that followed:

"The first intimation given by the Scots of their discovery of the insulted remains of their butchered brothers, was a subdued, threatening murmur, like the angry buzzing of a swarm of bees. Rapidly swelling in violence, it increased to a fierce, continuous, low shriek of rage and grief, that none who listened to would willingly hear again. In this moment, officers as well as men seemed to have abandoned every sentiment but one of quick and bloody vengeance, and, inspired by a common fury, cast all discipline to the winds. Their muskets were dashed upon the ground, and, bursting from the ranks, the infuriated Gaels, with brandished claymores, rushed madly on with hope to find an enemy on whom to accomplish retribution. Startled at the sound of swiftly tramping feet, the amazed Provincials looked round to see the headlong torrent sweep by, burthening the air with imprecations, and foaming 'like mad boars engaged in battle.'"

Too late! The fort was in flames, and the last boat of the flying Frenchmen was disappearing in the evening mist that hung around

---

*An amusing story—to which, perhaps, the Italian proverb, "si non e vero, bene trovato ," (if it is not true, it ought to be) would well apply—is told of some French chiefs who had secretly approached Forbes, the "iron-headed," when near Fort Duquesne, on a peace mission. The General, as stated, was very sick, and had to be constantly conveyed in a close litter. From this he spoke to the strange chiefs, who were greatly surprised, and asked why he was so carried. The officers told them that he was a desperate fighter, and was so savage and terribly ferocious against the faithless Indians that he had to be closely confined. The chiefs were much impressed, and departed, it is said, both sadder and wiser men. When the fort was found abandoned, no savages were found about.

Smoky Island. In place of old Fort Duquesne—the scene of so many exploits and the bone of contention for so long a time between two great and powerful nations—there was now but a heap of smoking ruins, the stacks of some thirty chimneys only remaining to mark where the houses stood, and sixteen barrels of gunpowder and ball and a cart-load of scalping knives—discovered in the only magazine which had refused to fire—were the only spoils which remained to be gathered. But a small force was left, the main army marching east soon after. A square stockade for two hundred men, under Colonel Hugh Mercer, was built, which was succeeded the next year by the more imposing and much more costly structure, Fort Pitt.

Strange Discovery by the young Sir Peter Halket of the Skeletons of his Father and Brother.

No sooner had General Forbes possession of the fort, or rather its site, than Major Halket, the son of Sir Peter Halket, and successor to his title and estates, resolved to visit the battle-ground of Braddocks Fields with a company of sharpshooters, under command of Captain West, brother of the great painter, Sir Benjamin West. The young Sir Peter had piously accompanied the Highlanders to America mainly to try and discover the remains of his father and brother, whose sad and peculiar death, at Braddocks Fields, we have already described.

By interrogating some of the Indians who had fought with the French at that massacre, he found one who said he had seen an officer, answering the Major's description, fall near a remarkable tree, which he thought he could discover, stating, moreover, that the incident was impressed on his memory by observing a young subaltern, who, in running to the officer's assistance, was shot dead on reaching the spot, and who fell across the other's body. The Major had a mournful conviction on his mind that the two officers were his father and brother, and the expedition, commanded by Captain West, and piloted by the Indians, took up their melancholy march. From Galt's Life of Benjamin West we give this brief account of this remarkable excursion.

"Captain West and his companions proceeded through the woods and along the bank of the river, towards the scene of the battle. The Indians regarded the expedition as a religious rite, and guided the troops with awe and in profound silence. The soldiers were affected with sentiments not less serious, and as they explored the bewildering labyrinths of those vast forests, their hearts were often melted with inexpressible sorrow, for they frequently found skeletons lying across the trunks of fallen trees—a mournful proof to their imaginations, that the men who sat there had perished of hunger, in vainly attempting to find

Major Halket Discovers Skeletons of Father and Brother.

their way to the plantations. Sometimes their feelings were raised to the utmost pitch of horror by the sight of skulls and bones scattered on the ground—a certain indication that the bodies had been devoured by wild beasts; and in other places they saw the blackness of ashes amidst the relics—the tremendous evidence of atrocious rites.

"At length they reached a turn of the river, not far from the principal scene of destruction, and the Indian who remembered the death of the two officers stopped; the detachment also halted. He then looked round in quest of some object which might recall, distinctly, his recollection of the ground, and suddenly darted into the woods. The soldiers rested their arms without speaking. A shrill cry was soon after heard, and the other guides made signs for the troops to follow them towards the spot from which it came.

"In a short time they reached the Indian warrior, who, by his cry, had announced to his companions that he had found the place where he was posted on the day of the battle. As the troops approached, he pointed to the tree under which the officers had fallen. Captain West halted his men around the spot, and with Sir Peter Halket, and other officers, formed a circle, while the Indians removed the leaves which thickly covered the ground. The skeletons were found, as the Indians expected, lying across each other. The officers having looked at them some time, the Major said, that as his father had an artificial tooth, he thought he might be able to ascertain if they were indeed his bones and those of his brother.

"The Indians were, therefore, ordered to remove the skeleton of the youth, and to bring to view that of the old officer. This was done, and after a short examination, Major Halket exclaimed, 'It is my father!' and fell back into the arms of his companions. The pioneers then dug a grave, and the bones being laid in it together, a Highland plaid was spread over them, and they were interred with the customary honors."

NOTE.—Subjoined is a representation of Bouquet's old Block-house, the only existing relic, or rather suggestion of Fort Duquesne. It still stands in Pittsburgh, strong and staunch, and the loop-holes for musketry plainly visible, amid a crowd of shabby, dingy houses near the river junction. It was built over the ruins of the evacuated post by Col. Bouquet. The stone in the facade bears in rude characters the inscription:

"A. D. 1764. COL. BOUQUET."

For the purpose of better preservation, it has lately been removed to the New City Hall, by order of the Councils of Pittsburgh.

THE TOUCHING STORY OF FANNY BRADDOCK.

In our description of General Braddock's character we stated that he "had once made a most unfeeling speech and a cruel pun when he heard of the sad death of his beautiful but unfortunate sister Fanny, who committed suicide under most distressing circumstances." We may here very aptly introduce a brief sketch of this accomplished lady, condensed from an account given by Goldsmith in his Life of Beau Nash:

Mistress Fanny Braddock was left a large fortune at her sister's decease, moved in the very best society, and contracted a passion for elegance. "Whatever the finest poet could conceive of wit, or the most celebrated painter imagine of beauty, were excelled in the perfections of this young lady." Naturally gay, sprightly, generous to a fault, and excelling in conversation, she left writings both in prose and verse which were as witty and brilliant as any in that age. Her chief failing was imprudence in the use of money. Anxious to relieve distress, she was lavish beyond reason; at nineteen she was surrounded by lovers among whom was S——, a talented but unfortunate man, whose love pity, generosity, and even friendship, were all in excess. He was called "the good-natured man," and became Mistress Braddock's favorite. Very soon, his debts becoming overwhelming, he was arrested and thrown into prison, and his lady-love immediately took the fatal resolution of releasing him by discharging all his debts. All the admonitions of Nash and her other friends were disregarded. Her fortune was by this means exhausted, and, with all her attractions, she lost rank and esteem, and accepted Nash's invitation of a return to Bath, where, for a time, she moved in the very first circles, but a settled melancholy now possessed her and nothing could divert her.

Her beauty, simplicity and artlessness finally made her the victim of a designing woman who kept fashionable gambling rooms, and who, by flattery, loans of money, etc., soon gained an entire ascendency over the thoughtless deserted girl, and in 1727, Miss Fanny Braddock, without, as Goldsmith says, "ever transgressing the laws of virtue, had entirely lost her reputation. Whenever a person was wanting to make up a party for play at dame Lindsey's, Sylvia, as she was then familiarly called, was sent for, and was obliged to suffer all those slights which the rich but too often let fall upon their inferiors in point of fortune."

This charming girl struggled hard with adversity, and yielded to every encroachment of contempt with sullen reluctance. Matters soon grew from bad to worse, until her friend Nash induced her to break off all connection with dame Lindsey and to rent part of a house, where she behaved with the utmost complaisance, regularity and virtue; but her detestation of life still grew on her, and about this time she frequently dwelt, and conversed much, on suicide. She soon became so poor that, unable to mix in company for want of the elegancies of dress, she lived a lonely and deserted life, and accepted the position of governess in Mr. Wood's family.

While he and part of his household were absent in London, she conceived the fatal resolution of leaving a life in which she could see no corner for comfort. Thus resolved, she sat down at the dining-room window, and with cool intrepidity wrote the following lines on one of the panes:—

> O death! thou pleasing end of human woe;
> Thou cure for life! thou greatest good below;
> Still mayst thou fly the coward and the slave,
> And thy soft slumbers only bless the brave.

She then went into company with the most cheerful serenity, and ordered supper to be ready in the little library, where she spent the hours before bedtime in dandling two of Mr. Wood's children on her knees. From this point we quote Goldsmith:

"In retiring to her chamber, she went into the nursery to take her leave of another child, as it lay sleeping in her cradle. Struck with the innocence of its looks and the consciousness of her meditated guilt, she could not avoid bursting into tears and hugging it in her arms. She then bid her old servant good-night and went to bed as usual. She soon quitted it, however, and dressed herself in clean linen and white garments of every kind, like a bridesmaid. Her gown was pinned over her breast, just as a nurse pins the swaddling clothes of an infant. A pink silk girdle was the instrument with which she resolved to terminate her misery, and this was lengthened by another made of gold thread. The end of the former was tied with a noose, and the latter with three knots.

"Thus prepared, she sat down and read; for she left the book open at that place, in the story of Olympia, in the 'Orlando Furioso' of Ariosto, where, by the envy and ingratitude of her bosom friend, she was ruined and left to the mercy of an unpitying world. This fatal event gave her fresh spirits to go through her tragical purpose. So, standing upon a stool and flinging the girdle which was tied round her neck over a closet door that opened into her chamber, she remained suspended. Her weight, however, broke the girdle, and the poor despairer fell on the floor with such violence that her fall awakened a workman that lay in the house, about half after two. Recovering herself, she began to walk about the room, as her usual custom was when she wanted sleep, and the workman, imagining it to be only some ordinary accident, again went to sleep.

"She once more, therefore, had recourse to a stronger girdle, made of silver thread, and this kept her suspended till she died. Her old maid waited as usual for the ringing of the bell, hour after hour, until two of the afternoon, when the workman, entering by the window, found her unfortunate mistress still hanging and quite cold. The coroner's jury brought in a verdict of lunacy, and her corpse was next night decently buried in her father's grave.

"Thus ended," concludes Goldsmith, "a female wit, a toast and a gamester; loved, admired and forsaken; formed for the delight of society; fallen by imprudence to be an object of pity. Hundreds in high life lamented her fate, and bought up her effects with the greatest avidity; and she remains the strongest instance to posterity that want of prudence alone almost cancels every other virtue."

When the news of the suicide was told to her brother, Edward Braddock, he is said to have uttered this cruel and unfeeling play upon words: "Poor Fanny, I always thought she would play till she would be forced to *tie herself up.*'" To "tie oneself up from play" was a cant phrase of the day for incurring some obligation, which should act as a restraint upon gambling.

REMARKABLE ADVENTURES OF COL. JAMES SMITH.
Five Years a Captive among Indians.

Among the captives confined at Fort Duquesne during the battle of Braddocks Fields and the subsequent torture of prisoners on the banks of the Allegheny, was a brave and enterprising Pennsylvania lad by the name of James Smith. He was adopted into an Indian tribe and remained a captive five years. After his release he had a series of adventures, and after his removal to Bourbon, Ky., became quite a prominent citizen and legislator, and wrote an exceedingly interesting narrative of his captivity. He furnishes the fullest and most faithful account ever yet published of the habits, customs, sentiments and daily forest life of the American Indian, such as he was before being debauched and contaminated by intercourse with swindling traders and rum traffickers.

Smith has been appropriately called the "untutored Defoe," and there is such a charming quaintness and simplicity in his invaluable narrative that we very much regret we may not give it entire. We cannot refrain, however, from quoting him for as much as we have room. In fact it is to him, as the only English-speaking person in the fort, that history is indebted for the *only* account of the French-Indian departure for the battle, their return from the gory field laden down with scalps and spoils, and the subsequent horrid and inhuman torture of prisoners. We quote :—

In May, 1755, the province of Pennsylvania agreed to send out three hundred men, in order to cut a wagon road from Fort Loudon to join Braddock's road, near the Turkey Foot, or three forks of Yohogania. My brother-in-law, William Smith, Esq., of Conococheague, was appointed commissioner, to have the oversight of these road-cutters. Though I was at that time only eighteen years of age, I had fallen violently in love with a young lady, whom I apprehended was possessed of a large share of both beauty and virtue; but being born between Venus and Mars, I concluded I must also leave my dear fair one, and go out with the company of road-cutters, to see the event of this campaign; but still expecting that some time in the course of this Summer, I should again return to the arms of my beloved.

We went on with the road without interruption until near the Allegheny mountain, when I was sent back in order to hurry up some provision wagons that were on the way after us. I proceeded down the road as far as the crossings of the Juniata, where, finding the wagons were coming on as fast as possible, I returned up the road again toward the Allegheny mountain, in company with one Arnold Vigoras. About four or five miles above Bedford, three Indians had made a blind of bushes, stuck in the ground, as though they had grown naturally, where they concealed themselves, about fifteen yards from the road. When we came opposite to them they fired upon us at this short distance, and killed my fellow-traveler, yet their bullets did not touch me; but my horse making a violent start, threw me, and the Indians immediately ran up and took me prisoner. The one that laid hold on me was a Canasataugua; the other two were Delawares. One of them could speak English, and asked me if there were any more white men coming after. I told them not any near, that I knew of. Two of these Indians stood by me, whilst the other scalped my comrade: they then set off and ran at a smart rate, through the woods, for about fifteen miles, and that night we slept on the Allegheny mountain, without fire.

The next morning they divided the last of their provisions, which they had brought from Fort Duquesne, and gave me an equal share, which was about two or three ounces of mouldy biscuit—this and a young ground-hog, about as large as a rabbit, roasted and also equally divided, was all the provision we had until we came to the Loyal Hanna, which was about fifty miles; and a great part of the way we came through exceeding rocky laurel thickets, without any path. When we came to the west side of Laurel Hill, they gave the scalp halloo, as usual, which is a long yell or halloo for every scalp or prisoner they have in possession; the last of these scalp halloos was followed with quick and sudden shrill shouts of joy and triumph. On their performing this, we were answered by the firing of a number of guns on the Loyal Hanna, one after another, quicker than one could count, by another party of Indians, who were encamped where Ligonier now stands. As we advanced near the party, they increased their repeated shouts of joy and triumph; but I did not share with them in their excessive mirth.

When we came to this camp, we found they had plenty of turkeys and other meat there; and though I never before eat venison without bread or salt, yet as I was hungry, it relished very well. There we lay that night, and the next morning the whole of us marched on our way for Fort Duquesne. The night after we joined another camp of Indians, with nearly the same ceremony, attended with great noise and apparent joy among all except one. The next morning we continued the march, and in the afternoon we came in full view of the fort, which stood on the point, near where Fort Pitt now stands. We then made a halt on the bank of the Allegheny, and repeated the scalp halloo, which was answered by the firing of all the firelocks in the hands of both Indians and French who were in and about the fort, in the aforesaid manner, and also the great guns, which were followed by the continued shouts and yells of the different savage tribes who were then collected there.

As I was at this time unacquainted with this mode of firing and yelling of the savages, I concluded that there were thousands of Indians there ready to receive General Braddock; but what added to my surprise, I saw numbers running towards me, stripped naked, except breech-clouts, and painted in the most hideous manner, of various colors, though the principal color was vermilion, or a bright red; yet there was annexed to this black, brown, blue, &c. As they approached they formed themselves into two long ranks, about two or three rods apart. I was told by an Indian that could speak English that I must run betwixt these ranks, and that they would flog me all the way as I ran, and if I ran quick it would be so much the better, as they would quit when I got to the end of the ranks. There appeared to be a general rejoicing around me, yet I could find nothing like joy in my breast; but I started to the race with all the resolution and vigor I was capable of exercising, and found that it was as I had been told, for I was flogged the whole way. When I had got near the end of the lines, I was struck with something that appeared to me to be a stick, or the handle of a tomahawk, which caused me to fall to the ground. On my recovering my senses, I endeavored to renew my race; but as I arose, some one cast sand in my eyes, which blinded me so that I could not see where to run. They continued beating me most intolerably, until I was at length insensible; but before I lost my senses, I remember my wishing them to strike the fatal blow, for I thought they intended killing me, but apprehended they were too long about it. The first thing I remember was my being in the fort, amidst the French and Indians, and a French doctor standing by me, who had opened a vein in my left arm; after which the interpreter asked me how I did: I told him I felt much pain; the doctor then washed my wounds, and the bruised places of my body, with French brandy. As I felt pain, and the brandy smelt well, I asked for some inwardly, but the doctor told me, by the interpreter, that it did not suit my case.

When they found I could speak, a number of Indians came around me and examined me, with threats of cruel death if I did not tell the truth. The first question they asked me was, how many men were there in the party that were coming from Pennsylvania to join Braddock? I told them the truth, that there were three hundred. The next question was, were they all armed? I told them they *were* all well armed, (meaning the arm of flesh,) for they had only about thirty guns among the whole of them; which, if the Indians had known, they would certainly have gone and cut them all off; therefore, I could not in conscience let them know the defenceless situation of the road-cutters. I was then sent to the hospital, and carefully attended by the doctors, and recovered quicker than what I expected.

Some time after I was there, I was visited by the Delaware Indian already mentioned, who was at the taking of me, and could speak some English. Though he spoke but bad English, yet I found him to be a man of considerable understanding. I asked him if I had done any thing that had offended the Indians, which caused them to treat me so unmercifully? He said no, it was only an old custom the Indians had, and it was like "how do you do;" after that, he said, I would be well used. I asked him if I should be permitted to remain with the French? He said no—and told me, that, as soon as I recovered, I must not only go with the Indians, but must be made an Indian myself. I asked him what news from Braddock's army? He said, the Indians spied them every day, and he showed me by making marks on the ground with a stick, that Braddock's army was advancing in very close order, and that the Indians would surround them, take trees, and (as he expressed it,) *shoot um down all one pigeon.*

Shortly after this, on the 9th day of July, 1755, in the morning, I heard a great stir in the fort. As I could then walk with a staff in my hand, I went out of the door, which was just by the wall of the fort, and stood upon the wall and viewed the Indians in a huddle before the gate, where were barrels of powder, bullets, flints, &c., and every one taking what suited; I saw the Indians also march off in rank entire— likewise the French Canadians, and some regulars. After viewing the Indians and French in different positions, I computed them to be about four hundred, and wondered that they attempted to go out against Braddock with so small a party. I was then in high hopes that I would soon see them fly before the British troops, and that General Braddock would take the fort and rescue me.

I remained anxious to know the advent of this day; and, in the afternoon, I again observed a great noise and commotion in the fort, and though at that time I could not understand French, yet I found that it was the voice of joy and triumph, and feared that they had received what I called bad news.

I had observed some of the old country soldiers speak Dutch; as I spoke Dutch, I went to one of them, and asked him, what was the news? He told me that a runner had just arrived, who said that Braddock would certainly be defeated; that the Indians and French had surrounded him, and were concealed behind trees and in gullies, and kept a constant fire upon the English, and that they saw the English falling in heaps, and if they did not take the river, which was the only gap, and make their escape, there would not be one man left alive before sundown. Some time after this I heard a number of scalp halloos, and saw a company of Indians and French coming in. I observed they had a great many bloody scalps, grenadiers' caps, British canteens, bayonets, &c., with them. They brought the news that Braddock was defeated. After that, another company came in, which appeared to be about one hundred, and chiefly Indians, and it seemed to me that almost every one of this company was carrying scalps; after this came another company with a number of wagon horses, and also a great many scalps. Those that were coming in, and those that had arrived, kept a constant firing of small arms, and also the great guns in the fort, which were accompanied with the most hideous shouts and yells from all quarters; so that it appeared to me as if the infernal regions had broke loose.

About sundown I beheld a small party coming in with about a dozen prisoners, stripped naked, with their hands tied behind their backs, and part of their bodies blackened—these prisoners they burned to death on the bank of the Allegheny river opposite the fort. I stood on the fort wall until I beheld them begin to burn one of these men; they had him tied to a stake, and kept touching him with fire-brands, red-hot irons, &c., and he screaming in the most doleful manner—the Indians in the meantime yelling like infernal spirits. As this scene appeared too shocking for me to behold, I retired to my lodgings both sore and sorry.

When I came into my lodgings I saw Russel's Seven Sermons, which they had brought from the field of battle, which a Frenchman made a present of to me. From the best information I could receive, there were only seven Indians and four French killed in this battle, and five hundred British lay dead in the field, besides what were killed in the river on their retreat. The morning after the battle, I saw Braddock's artillery brought into the fort; the same day I also saw several Indians in British officers' dress, with sash, half moons, laced hats, &c., which the British then wore.

A few days after this the Indians demanded me, and I was obliged to go with them. I was not well able to march, but they took me in a canoe up the Allegheny river, to an Indian town, that was on the north side of the river, about forty miles above Fort Duquesne. Here I remained about three weeks, and was then taken to an Indian town on the west branch of the Muskingum, about twenty miles above the forks, which was called Tullihas, which was inhabited by Delawares, Caughnewagas and Mohicans.

The day after my arrival at the aforesaid town, a number of Indians collected about me, and one of them began to pull the hair out of my head. He had some ashes on a piece of bark, in which he frequently dipped his fingers, in order to take the firmer hold, and so he went on, as if he had been plucking a turkey, until he had all the hair clean out of my head, except a small spot about three or four inches square on my crown; this they cut off with a pair of scissors, excepting three locks, which they dressed up in their own mode. Two of these they wrapped round with a narrow beaded garter made by themselves for that purpose, and the other they plaited at full length, and then stuck it full of silver brooches. After this they bored my nose and ears, and fixed me off with ear-rings and nose jewels; then they ordered me to strip off my clothes and put on a breech-clout, which I did; they then painted my head, face and body, in various colors. They put a large belt of wampum on my neck, and silver bands on my hands and right arm; and so an old chief led me out in the street, and gave the alarm halloo, *coo-wigh*, several times repeated quick; and on this all that were in the town came running and stood round the old chief, who held me by the hand in the midst.

SMITH DUCKED IN THE RIVER BY THREE SQUAWS.

As I at that time knew nothing of their mode of adoption and had seen them put to death all they had taken, and as I never could find that they saved a man alive at Braddock's defeat, I made no doubt but they were about putting me to death in some cruel manner. The old chief, holding me by the hand, made a long speech, very loud, and when he had done, he handed me to three young squaws, who led me by the hand down the bank, into the river, until the water was up to our middle. The squaws then made signs to me to plunge myself into the water, but I did not understand them—I thought that the result of the council was, that I should be drowned, and that these young ladies were to be the executioners. They all three laid violent hold of me, and I for some time opposed them with all my might, which occasioned loud laughter by the multitude that were on the bank of the river. At length one of the squaws made out to speak a little English, (for I believe they began to be afraid of me,) and said *no hurt you;* on this I gave myself up to their ladyships, who were as good as their word; for

Young James Smith Ducked in the River by Squaws.
—*See page 76.*

though they plunged me under the water, and washed and rubbed me severely, yet I could not say they hurt me much.

These young women then led me up to the council house, where some of the tribe were ready with new clothes for me. They gave me a new ruffled shirt, which I put on; also a pair of leggins done off with ribbons and beads; likewise a pair of moccasins, and garters dressed with beads, porcupine quills, and red hair—also a tinsel laced cappo. They again painted my head and face with various colors, and tied a bunch of red feathers to one of those locks they had left on the crown of my head, which stood up five or six inches. They seated me on a bear-skin, and gave me a pipe, tomahawk, and polecat-skin pouch, which had been skinned pocket fashion, and contained tobacco, killikinnick, or dry sumach leaves, which they mix with their tobacco—also spunk, flint and steel. When I was thus seated, the Indians came in dressed and painted in their grandest manner. As they came in they took their seats, and for a considerable time there was a profound silence—every one was smoking—but not a word was spoken among them.

At length one of the chiefs made a speech, which was delivered to me by an interpreter, and was as followeth: "My son, you are now flesh of our flesh, and bone of our bone. By the ceremony which was performed this day, every drop of white blood was washed out of your veins; you are taken into the Caughnewaga nation, and initiated into a warlike tribe; you are adopted into a great family, and now received with great seriousness and solemnity in the room and place of a great man. After what has passed this day, you are now one of us by an old strong law and custom. My son, you have nothing to fear; we are now under the same obligations to love, support and defend you, that we are to love and defend one another; therefore, you are to consider yourself as one of our people." At this time I did not believe this fine speech, especially that of the white blood being washed out of me; but since that time I have found that there was much sincerity in said speech,—for, from that day, I never knew them to make any distinction between me and themselves in any respect whatever until I left them. If they had plenty of clothing I had plenty; if we were scarce, we all shared one fate.

After this ceremony was over, I was introduced to my new kin, and told that I was to attend a feast that evening, which I did. And, as the custom was, they gave me also a bowl and wooden spoon, which I carried with me to the place, where there were a number of large brass kettles full of boiled venison and green corn; every one advanced with his bowl and spoon, and had his share given him. After this one of the chiefs made a short speech, and then we began to eat.

The name of one of the chiefs of this town was Tecanyaterighto, alias

Pluggy, and the other Asallecoa, alias Mohawk Solomon. As Pluggy and his party were to start the next day to war, to the frontiers of Virginia, the next thing to be performed was the war dance, and their war songs. At their war dance they had both vocal and instrumental music —they had a short hollow gum, closed at one end, with water in it, and parchment stretched over the open end thereof, which they beat with one stick, and made a sound nearly like a muffled drum—all those who were going on this expedition collected together and formed. An old Indian then began to sing, and timed the music by beating on this drum, as the ancients formerly timed their music by beating the tabor. On this the warriors began to advance, or move forward in concert, like well-disciplined troops would march to the fife and drum. Each warrior had a tomahawk, spear or war-mallet in his hand, and they all moved regularly towards the east, or the way they intended to go to war. At length they all stretched their tomahawks towards the Potomac, and giving a hideous shout or yell, they wheeled quick about, and danced in the same manner back.

The next was the war song. In performing this, only one sung at a time, in a moving posture, with a tomahawk in his hand, while all the other warriors were engaged in calling aloud *he-uh, he-uh*, which they constantly repeated while the war song was going on. When the warrior that was singing had ended his song, he struck a war-post with his tomahawk, and with a loud voice told what warlike exploits he had done, and what he now intended to do, which were answered by the other warriors with loud shouts of applause. Some who had not before intended to go to war, at this time were so animated by this performance that they took up the tomahawk and sung the war song, which was answered with shouts of joy, as they were then initiated into the present marching company. The next morning this company all collected at one place, with their heads and faces painted with various colors, and packs upon their backs: they marched off, all silent, except the commander, who, in the front, sung the traveling song. Just as the rear passed the end of the town, they began to fire in their slow manner, from the front to the rear, which was accompanied with shouts and yells from all quarters.

This evening I was invited to another sort of dance, which was a kind of promiscuous dance. The young men stood in one rank, and the young women in another, about one rod apart, facing each other. The one that raised the tune, or started the song, held a small gourd or dry shell of a squash in his hand, which contained beads or small stones, which rattled. When he began to sing, he timed the tune with his rattle—both men and women danced and sung together, advancing towards each other, stooping until their heads would be touching together, and then ceased from dancing, with loud shouts, and retreated and formed again, and so repeated the same thing over and over, for three or four hours, without intermission. This exercise appeared to me at first irrational and insipid; but I found that in singing their tunes, they used *ya ne no hoo wa ne*, &c., like our *fa sol la*, and though they have no such thing as jingling verse, yet they can intermix sentences with their notes, and say what they please to each other, and carry on the tune in concert. I found that this was a kind of wooing or courting dance, and as they advanced, stooping with their heads together, they could say what they pleased in each other's ear, without disconcerting their rough music, and the others, or those near, not hear what they said.

Shortly after this I went out to hunt. We traveled about south from this town, and the first night we killed nothing, but we had with us green corn, which we roasted and ate that night. The next day we encamped about twelve o'clock, and the hunters turned out to hunt, and I went down the run that we encamped on, in company with some squaws and boys, to hunt plums, which we found in great plenty. We remained at this camp about eight or ten days, and killed a number of deer. Though we had neither bread nor salt at this time, yet we had both roast and boiled meat in great plenty, and they were frequently inviting me to eat when I had no appetite.

We then moved to the buffalo lick, where we killed several buffalo, and in their small brass kettles they made about half a bushel of salt. I suppose this lick was about thirty or forty miles from the aforesaid town, and somewhere between the Muskingum, Ohio and Scioto. About the lick was clear, open woods, and thin white-oak land, and at that time there were large roads leading to the lick, like wagon roads. We moved from this lick about six or seven miles, and encamped on a creek. Though the Indians had given me a gun, I had not yet been permitted to go out from the camp to hunt. At this place Mohawk Solomon asked me to go out with him to hunt, which I readily agreed to. After some time we came upon some fresh buffalo tracks. I had observed before this that the Indians were upon their guard, and afraid of an enemy; for, until now, they and the southern nations had been at war. As we were following the buffalo tracks, Solomon seemed to be on his guard, went very slow, and would frequently stand and listen, and appeared to be in suspense. We came to where the tracks were very plain in the sand, and I said, it is surely buffalo tracks; he said, *hush, you know nothing—may be buffalo tracks, may be Catawba.* He went very cautious until we found some fresh buffalo dung: he then smiled, and said *Catawba cannot make so.*

CUNNING OF THE CATAWBAS—SMITH LOST IN THE WOODS.

He then stopped and told me an odd story about the Catawbas. He said that formerly the Catawbas came near one of their hunting camps, and at some distance from the camp lay in ambush; and in order to decoy them out, sent two or three Catawbas in the night past their camp, with buffalo hoofs fixed on their feet, so as to make artificial tracks. In the morning those in the camp followed after these tracks, thinking they were buffalo, until they were fired on by the Catawbas, and several of them killed; the others fled, collected a party, and pursued the Catawbas; but they, in their subtlety, brought with them rattlesnake poison, which they had collected from the bladder that lieth at the root of the snake's teeth; this they had corked up in a short piece of a cane stalk; they had also brought with them small cane or reed, about the size of a rye straw, which they made sharp at the end like a pen, and dipped them into the poison, and stuck them into the ground among the grass, along their own tracks, in such a position that they might stick into the legs of the pursuers, which answered the design; and as the Catawbas had runners behind to watch the motion of the pursuers, when they found that a number of them were lame, being artificially snake bit, and that they were all turning back, the Catawbas turned upon the pursuers and defeated them, and killed and scalped all those that were lame. When Solomon had finished his story, and found that I understood him, he concluded by saying, *You don't know, Catawba velly bad Indian, Catawba all one devil, Catawba.*

Some time after this I was told to take the dogs with me and go down the creek, perhaps I might kill a turkey; it being in the afternoon, I was also told not to go far from the creek, and to come up the creek again to the camp, and to take care not to get lost. When I had gone some distance down the creek, I came upon fresh buffalo tracks, and as I had a number of dogs with me to stop the buffalo, I concluded I would follow after and kill one; and as the grass and weeds were rank, I could readily follow the track. A little before sundown I despaired of coming up with them; I was then thinking how I might get into camp before night; I concluded, as the buffalo had made several turns, if I took the track back to the creek it would be dark before I could get to the camp; therefore I thought I would take a nearer way through the hills, and strike the creek a little below the camp; but as it was cloudy weather, and I a very young woodsman, I could find neither creek nor camp. When night came on I fired my gun several times and hallooed, but could hear no answer. The next morning early the Indians were out after me, and as I had with me ten or a dozen dogs, and the grass and weeds rank, they could readily follow my track. When they came up with me, they appeared to be in a very good humor. I asked Solomon if he thought I was running away, he said, *no, no, you go too much crooked.* On my return to camp they took away my gun from me, and for this rash act I was reduced to a bow and arrows for near two years. We were out on this tour for about six weeks.

When we returned to the town, Pluggy and his party had arrived, and brought with them a considerable number of scalps and prisoners from the south branch of the Potomac; they also brought with them an English Bible, which they gave to a Dutch woman who was a prisoner; but as she could not read English, she made a present of it to me, which was very acceptable. I remained in this town until some time in October, when my adopted brother, called Tontileaugo, who had married a Wyandot squaw, took me with him to Lake Erie.

On this route we had no horses with us, and when we started from the town all the pack I carried was a pouch, containing my books, a little dried venison, and my blanket. I had then no gun, but Tontileaugo, who was a first-rate hunter, carried a rifle gun, and every day killed deer, raccoons, or bears. We left the meat, excepting a little for present use, and carried the skins with us until we encamped, and then stretched them with elm bark on a frame made with poles stuck in the ground and tied together with lynn or elm bark; and when the skins were dried by the fire we packed them up and carried them with us the next day. As Tontileaugo could not speak English, I had to make use of all the Caughnewaga I had learned even to talk very imperfectly with him; but I found I learned to talk Indian faster this way than when I had those with me who could speak English. As we proceeded down the Canesadooharie waters, our packs, increased by the skins that were daily killed, became so very heavy that we could not march more than eight or ten miles per day. We came to Lake Erie about six miles west of the mouth of Canesadooharie. As the wind was very high the evening we came to the lake, I was surprised to hear the roaring of the water and see the high waves that dashed against the shore, like the ocean. We encamped on a run near the lake, and as the wind fell that night, the next morning the lake was only in a moderate motion, and we marched on the sand along the side of the water, frequently resting ourselves, as we were heavy laden. I saw on the strand a number of large fish, that had been left in flat or hollow places; as the wind fell and the waves abated, they were left without water or only a small quantity; and numbers of bald and grey eagles, &c., were along the shore devouring them.

Some time in the afternoon we came to a large camp of Wyandots.

at the mouth of Canesadooharie, where Tontileaugo's wife was. Here we were kindly received: they gave us a kind of rough, brown potatoes, which grew spontaneously, and were called by the Caughnewagas, *ohenata*. These potatoes, peeled and dipped in raccoon's fat, taste nearly like our sweet potatoes. They also gave us what they call *caneheanta*, which is a kind of hominy, made of green corn, dried, and beans mixed together. We continued our camp at the mouth of Canesadooharie for some time, where we killed some deer and a great many raccoons; the raccoons here were remarkably large and fat. At length we all embarked in a large birch-bark canoe. This vessel was about four feet wide and three feet deep, and about five and thirty feet long; and though it could carry a heavy burden, it was so artfully and curiously constructed that four men could carry it several miles, or from one landing place to another, or from the waters of the lake to the waters of the Ohio. We proceeded up Canesadooharie a few miles and went on shore to hunt; but to my great surprise they carried the vessel that we all came in up the bank, and inverted it or turned the bottom up, and converted it into a dwelling house, and kindled a fire before us to warm ourselves by and cook. With our baggage and ourselves in this house we were very much crowded, yet our little house turned off the rain very well.

We kept moving and hunting up this river until we came to the falls; here we remained some weeks, and killed a number of deer, several bears, and a great many raccoons. While we remained here, I left my pouch with my books in camp, wrapped up in my blanket, and went out to hunt chestnuts. On my return to camp my books were missing. I inquired after them, and asked the Indians if they knew where they were; they told me that they supposed the puppies had carried them off. I did not believe them, but thought they were displeased at my poring over my books, and concluded to destroy them, or put them out of my way.

After this, I was again out after nuts, and on my return beheld a new erection, composed of two white-oak saplings, that were forked about twelve feet high, and stood about fifteen feet apart. They had cut these saplings at the forks, and laid a strong pole across, which appeared in the form of a gallows, and the posts they had shaved very smooth, and painted in places with vermilion. I could not conceive the use of this piece of work, and at length concluded it was a gallows. I thought that I had displeased them by reading my books, and that they were about putting me to death. The next morning I observed them bringing their skins all to this place, and hanging them over this pole, so as to preserve them from being injured by the weather. This removed my fears. They also buried their large canoe in the ground, which is the way they took to preserve this sort of a canoe in the Winter season.

It was some time in December when we finished our Winter cabin; but when we had got into this comparatively fine lodging, another difficulty arose—we had nothing to eat. While I was traveling with Tontileaugo, as was before mentioned, and had plenty of fat venison, bear's meat and raccoons, I then thought it was hard living without bread or salt; but now I began to conclude, that if I had anything that would banish pinching hunger, and keep soul and body together, I would be content. While the hunters were all out, exerting themselves to the utmost of their ability, the squaws and boys (in which class I was,) were scattered out in the bottoms, hunting red haws, black haws and hickory nuts. As it was too late in the year, we did not succeed in gathering haws; but we had tolerable success in scratching up hickory nuts from under a light snow, which we carried with us lest the hunters should not succeed. After our return the hunters came in, who had killed only two small turkeys, which were but little among eight hunters, and thirteen squaws, boys and children; but they were divided with the greatest equity and justice—every one got their equal share.

The next day the hunters turned out again, and killed one deer and three bears. One of the bears was very large and remarkably fat. The hunters carried in meat sufficient to give us all a hearty supper and breakfast. The squaws, and all that could carry, turned out to bring in meat—every one had their share assigned them, and my load was among the least; yet, not being accustomed to carrying in this way, I got exceeding weary, and told them my load was too heavy, I must leave part of it and come for it again. They made a halt, and only laughed at me, and took part of my load and added it to a young squaw's who had as much before as I carried. This kind of reproof had a greater tendency to excite me to exert myself in carrying without complaining, than if they had whipped me for laziness. After this the hunters held a council, and concluded that they must have horses to carry their loads; and that they would go to war even in this inclement season, in order to bring in horses.

Tontileaugo wished to be one of those who should go to war; but the votes went against him; as he was one of the best hunters, it was thought necessary to leave him at this Winter camp to provide for the squaws and children; it was agreed upon that Tontileaugo and the three others should stay and hunt, and the other four go to war. They then began to go through their common ceremony. They sung their war songs, danced their dances, &c. And when they were equipped, they went off singing their marching song, and firing their guns. Our camp appeared to be rejoicing; but I was grieved to think that some innocent persons would be murdered, not thinking of danger.

After the departure of these warriors we had hard times; and though we were not altogether out of provisions, we were brought to short allowance. At length Tontileaugo had considerable success, and we had meat brought into camp sufficient to last ten days. Tontileaugo then took me with him in order to encamp some distance from this Winter cabin, to try his luck there. We carried no provision with us; he said he would leave what was there for the squaws and children, and that we could shift for ourselves. We steered about a south course up the waters of the creek, and encamped about ten or twelve miles from the Winter cabin. As it was still cold weather and a crust upon the snow, which made a noise as we walked and alarmed the deer, we could kill nothing, and consequently went to sleep without supper. The only chance we had, under these circumstances, was to hunt bear holes, as the bears about Christmas search out a Winter lodging place, where they lie about three or four months without eating or drinking.

Odd Ways of Hunting Bears, Foxes, Raccoons, &c.

The next morning early we proceeded on, and when we found a tree scratched by the bears climbing up, and the hole in the tree sufficiently large for the reception of the bear, we then felled a sapling or small tree, against or near the hole; and it was my business to climb up and drive out the bear, while Tontileaugo stood ready with his gun and bow. We went on in this manner until evening, without success; at length we found a large elm scratched, and a hole in it about forty feet up; but no tree nigh suitable to lodge against the hole. Tontileaugo got a long pole and some dry rotten wood, which he tied in bunches with bark; and as there was a tree that grew near the elm, and extended up near the hole, but leaned the wrong way, so that we could not lodge it to advantage, to remedy this inconvenience, he climbed up this tree and carried with him his rotten wood, fire and pole. The rotten wood he tied to his belt, and to one end of the pole he tied a hook and a piece of rotten wood, which he set fire to, as it would retain fire almost like spunk, and reached this hook from limb to limb as he went up; when he got up, with this pole he put dry wood on fire into the hole; after he put in the fire he heard the bear snuff, and he came speedily down, took his gun in his hand, and waited until the bear would come out; but it was some time before it appeared, and when it did appear, he attempted taking sight with his rifle; but it being then too dark to see the sights he set it down by a tree, and instantly bent his bow, took hold of an arrow, and shot the bear a little behind the shoulder; I was preparing also to shoot an arrow, but he called to me to stop, there was no occasion; and with that the bear fell to the ground.

Being very hungry we kindled a fire, opened the bear, took out the liver, and wrapped some of the caul fat round, and put it on a wooden spit, which we stuck in the ground by the fire to roast; we then skinned the bear, got on our kettle, and had both roast and boiled, and also sauce to our meat, which appeared to me to be delicate fare. After I was fully satisfied I went to sleep; Tontileaugo awoke me saying, "Come! eat hearty! we have got meat plenty now." The next morning we cut down a lynn tree, peeled bark and made a snug little shelter, facing the south-east, with a large log betwixt us and the north-west; we made a good fire before us, and scaffolded up our meat at one side. When we had finished our camp we went out to hunt, searched two trees for bears, but to no purpose. As the snow thawed a little in the afternoon, Tontileaugo killed a deer, which we carried with us to camp.

The next day we turned out to hunt, and near the camp we found a tree well scratched; but the hole was above forty feet high, and no tree that we could lodge against the hole; but finding that it was very hollow, we concluded that we would cut down the tree with our tomahawks, which kept us working a considerable part of the day. When the tree fell we ran up. Tontileaugo with his gun and bow, and I with my bow ready bent. Tontileaugo shot the bear through with his rifle a little behind the shoulders; I also shot, but too far back; and not being then much accustomed to the business, my arrow penetrated only a few inches through the skin. Having killed an old she bear and three cubs, we hauled her on the snow to the camp, and only had time afterwards to get wood, make a fire, cook, &c., before dark. Early next morning we went to business, searched several trees, but found no bears. On our way home we took three raccoons out of a hollow elm, not far from the ground. We remained here about two weeks, and in this time killed four bears, three deer, several turkeys and a number of raccoons. We packed up as much meat as we could carry, and returned to our Winter cabin. On our arrival, there was great joy, as they were all in a starving condition—the three hunters that we had left having killed but very little. All that could carry a pack, repaired to our camp to bring in meat. Some time in February the four warriors returned, who had taken two scalps, and six horses from the frontiers of Pennsylvania. The hunters could then scatter out a considerable distance from the Winter cabin, and encamp, kill meat and bring it in upon horses; so that we commonly after this had plenty of provisions.

The way that we generally used our maple sugar while encamped was by putting it in bear's fat until the fat was almost as sweet as the sugar itself, and in this we dipped our roasted venison. About this time some of the Indian lads and myself were employed in making and attending traps for catching raccoons, foxes, wild cats, &c. As the raccoon is a kind of water animal, that frequents the runs or small water courses, almost the whole night, we made our traps on the runs, by laying one small sapling on another, and driving in posts to keep them from rolling. The upper sapling was raised about eighteen inches, and set so that on the raccoon's touching a string or small piece of bark, the sapling would fall and kill it; and lest the raccoon should pass by, we laid brush on both sides of the run, only leaving the channel open.

The fox traps we made nearly in the same manner, at the end of a hollow log, or opposite to a hole at the root of a tree, and put venison on a stick for bait: we had it so set that when the fox took hold of the meat the trap fell. While the squaws were employed in making sugar, the boys and men were engaged in hunting and trapping. About the latter end of March, we began to prepare for moving into town, in order to plant corn: the squaws were then frying the last of their bear's fat, and making vessels to hold it: the vessels were made of deer skins, which were skinned by pulling the skin off the neck, without ripping. After they had taken off the hair, they gathered it in small plaits round the neck, and, with a string, drew it together like a purse: in the centre a pin was put, below which they tied a string, and while it was wet they blew it up like a bladder, and let it remain in this manner until it was dry, when it appeared nearly in the shape of a sugar loaf, but more rounding at the lower end. One of these vessels would hold about four or five gallons; in these vessels it was they carried their bear's oil.

When all things were ready, we moved back to the falls of Canesadooharie. On our arrival at the falls, (as we had brought with us on horseback about two hundred weight of sugar, a large quantity of bear's oil, skins, &c.,) the canoe we had buried was not sufficient to carry all; therefore we were obliged to make another of elm bark. While we lay here, a young Wyandot found my books: on this they collected together; I was a little way from the camp, and saw the collection, but did not know what it meant. They called me by my Indian name, which was Scoouwa, repeatedly. I ran to see what was the matter; they showed me my books, and said they were glad they had been found, for they knew I was grieved at the loss of them, and that they now rejoiced with me because they were found. As I could then speak some Indian especially Caughnewaga, (for both that and the Wyandot tongue were spoken in this camp,) I told them that I thanked them for the kindness they had always shown to me, and also for finding my books. They asked if the books were damaged. I told them not much. They then showed how they lay, which was in the best manner to turn off the water. In a deer-skin pouch they lay all Winter. The print was not much injured, though the binding was. This was the first time that I felt my heart warm towards the Indians. Though they had been exceedingly kind to me, I still detested them, on account of the barbarity I beheld after Braddock's defeat. Neither had I ever before pretended kindness, or expressed myself in a friendly manner; but I began now to excuse the Indians on account of their want of information.

When we were ready to embark, Tontileaugo would not go to town, but go up the river and take a hunt. He asked me if I choosed to go with him? I told him I did. We then got some sugar, bear's oil bottled up in a bear's gut, and some dry venison, which we packed up and went to Canesadooharie, about thirty miles, and encamped. At this time I did not know either the day of the week or the month; but I supposed it to be about the first of April. We had considerable success in our business. We also found some stray horses, or a horse, mare, and a young colt; and though they had run in the woods all Winter, they were in exceeding good order. There is plenty of grass here all Winter, under the snow, and horses accustomed to the woods can work it out. These horses had run in the woods until they were very wild.

ATTEMPT TO RUN DOWN HORSES—SCOLDED FOR HELPING SQUAWS.

Tontileaugo one night concluded that we must run them down. I told him I thought we could not accomplish it. He said he had run down bears, buffaloes and elks; and in the great plains, with only a small snow on the ground, he had run down a deer; and he thought that in one whole day he could tire or run down any four-footed animal except a wolf. I told him that though a deer was the swiftest animal to run a short distance, yet it would tire sooner than a horse. He said he would at all events try the experiment. He had heard the Wyandots say that I could run well, and now he would see whether I could or not. I told him that I never had run all day, and of course was not accustomed to that way of running. I never had run with the Wyandots more than seven or eight miles at one time. He said that was nothing, we must either catch these horses, or run all day.

In the morning early we left camp, and about sunrise we started after them, stripped naked excepting breech-clout and moccasins. About ten o'clock I lost sight of both Tontileaugo and the horses, and did not see them again until about three o'clock in the afternoon. As the horses run all day, in about three or four miles square, at length they passed where I was, and I fell in close after them. As I then had a long rest, I endeavored to keep ahead of Tontileaugo, and after some time I could hear him after me, calling *chakah, chakoanaugh,* which signifies, "pull away!" or "do your best!" We pursued on, and after some time Tontileaugo passed me, and about an hour before sundown we despaired of catching these horses, and returned to camp, where we had left our clothes. I reminded Tontileaugo of what I had told him: he replied he did not know what horses could do. They are wonderful strong to run; but withal we made them very tired. Tontileaugo then concluded he would do as the Indians did with wild horses when out at war; which is to shoot them through the neck under the mane, and above the bone, which will cause them to fall and lie until they can halter them, and then they recover again. This he attempted to do; but as the mare was very wild, he could not get sufficiently nigh to shoot her in the proper place; however, he shot, the ball passed too low, and killed her. As the horse and colt stayed at this place, we caught the horse and took him and the colt with us to camp.

We stayed at this camp about two weeks, and killed a number of bears, raccoons, and some beavers. We made a canoe of elm bark, and Tontileaugo embarked in it. He arrived at the falls that night; whilst I, mounted on horseback, with a bear-skin saddle and bark stirrups, proceeded by land to the falls: I came there the next morning, and we carried our canoe and loading past the falls. We again proceeded towards the lake, I on horseback, and Tontileaugo by water. Here the land is generally good, but I found some difficulty in getting round swamps and ponds. When we came to the lake, I proceeded along the strand, and Tontileaugo near the shore, sometimes paddling, and sometimes poling his canoe along.

After some time the wind arose, and he went into the mouth of a small creek and disappeared. Here we stayed several days on account of high wind, which raised the lake in great billows. While we were here, Tontileaugo went out to hunt, and when he was gone a Wyandot came to our camp; I gave him a shoulder of venison which I had by the fire, well roasted, and he received it gladly, told me he was hungry, and thanked me for my kindness. When Tontileaugo came home I told him that a Wyandot had been at camp, and that I gave him a shoulder of venison: he said that was very well, and I suppose you gave him also sugar and bear's oil, to eat with his venison. I told him I did not; as the sugar and bear's oil was down in the canoe, I did not go for it. He replied, "you have behaved just like a Dutchman. Do you not know that when strangers come to our camp, we ought always to give them the best we have." I acknowledged that I was wrong. He said that he could excuse this, as I was but young; but I must learn to behave like a warrior, and do great things, and never be found in any such little actions.

After I had got my new clothes, and my head done off like a red-headed wood-pecker, I, in company with a number of small Indians, went down to the corn-field to see the squaws at work. When we came there they asked me to take a hoe, which I did, and hoed for some time. The squaws applauded me as a good hand at the business; but when I returned to the town, the old men, hearing of what I had done, chid me, and said that I was adopted in the place of a great man, and must not hoe corn like a squaw. They never had occasion to reprove me for anything like this again; as I never was extremely fond of work, I readily complied with their orders.

As the Indians, on their return from their Winter hunt, bring in with them large quantities of bear's oil, sugar, dried venison, &c., at this time they have plenty, and do not spare eating or giving—thus they make away with their provisions as quick as possible. They have no such thing as regular meals, breakfast, dinner or supper; but if any one, even the town folks, would go to the same house several times in one day, he would be invited to eat of the best—and with them it is bad manners to refuse to eat when it is offered. If they will not eat, it is interpreted as a symptom of displeasure, or that the persons refusing to eat were angry with those who invited them.

At this time, hominy, plentifully mixed with bear's oil and sugar, is what they offer to every one who comes in any time of the day; and so they go on until their sugar, bear's oil and venison are all gone, and then they have to eat hominy by itself, without bread, salt, or anything else; yet still they invite every one that comes in to eat whilst they have anything to give. It is thought a shame not to invite people to eat while they have anything; but if they can, in truth, only say, we have got nothing to eat, this is accepted as an honorable apology. All the hunters and warriors continued in town about six weeks after we came in; they spent the time in painting, going from house to house, eating, smoking, and playing at a game resembling dice or hustle cap. They put a number of plum stones in a small bowl; one side of each stone is black, and the other white; they then shake or hustle the bowl, calling *hits, hits, hits, honesy, honesy, rego, rego,* which signifies calling for white or black, or what they wish to turn up; they then turn the bowl and count the whites and blacks. Some were beating their kind of drum and singing; others were employed in playing on a sort of flute, made of hollow cane; and others playing on the Jew's harp. Some part of this time was also taken up in attending the council house, where the chiefs, and as many others as chose, attended; and at night they were frequently employed in singing and dancing. Towards the last of this time, which was in June, 1756, they were all engaged in preparing to go to war against the frontiers of Virginia: when they were equipped they went through their ceremonies, sung their war songs, &c. They all marched off, from fifteen to sixteen years of age; and some boys, only twelve years old, were equipped with their bows and arrows, and went to war; so that none were left in town but squaws and children, except myself, one very old man, and another about fifty years of age, who was lame.

When the warriors left the town we had neither meat, sugar or bear's oil left. All that we had then to live on was corn pounded into coarse meal or small hominy—this they boiled in water, which appeared like well thickened soup, without salt or anything else. For some time we had plenty of this kind of hominy; at length we were brought to very short allowance, and as the warriors did not return as soon as they expected, we were in a starving condition, and but one gun in the town, and very little ammunition. The old lame Wyandot concluded that he would go a hunting in the canoe, and take me with him, and try to kill deer in the water, as it was then watering time. We went up the Sandusky a few miles, then turned up a creek and encamped. We had lights prepared, as we were to hunt in the night, and also a piece of bark and some bushes set up in the canoe, in order to conceal ourselves from the deer. A little boy that was with us held the light; I worked the canoe, and the old man, who had his gun loaded with large shot, when we came near the deer, fired, and in this manner killed three deer in part of one night. We went to our fire, ate heartily, and in the morning returned to town, in order to relieve the hungry and distressed.

When we came to town, the children were crying bitterly on account of pinching hunger. We delivered what we had taken; and though it was but little among so many, it was divided according to the strictest rules of justice. We immediately set out for another hunt, but before we returned a party of the warriors had come in, and brought with them, on horseback, a quantity of meat. These warriors had divided into different parties, and all struck at different places in Augusta county. They brought in with them a considerable number of scalps, prisoners, horses, and other plunder. One of the parties brought in with them one Arthur Campbell, that is now Colonel Campbell, who lives on the Holston river, near the Royal Oak. As the Wyandots at Sunyendeand and those at Detroit were connected, Mr. Campbell was taken to Detroit; but he remained some time with me in this town;

his company was very agreeable, and I was sorry when he left me During his stay at Sunyendeand he borrowed my Bible, and made some pertinent remarks on what he had read. One passage where it is said "It is good for a man that he bear the yoke in his youth." He said we ought to be resigned to the will of Providence, as we were now bearing the yoke in our youth. Mr. Campbell appeared to be then about sixteen or seventeen years of age.

There were a number of prisoners brought in by these parties, and when they were to run the gauntlet, I went and told them how they were to act. One John Savage was brought in, a middle-aged man of about forty years old. He was to run the gauntlet. I told him what he had to do; and after this I fell into one of the ranks with the Indians, shouting and yelling like them; and as they were not very severe on him, as he passed me I hit him with a piece of a pumpkin—which pleased the Indians very much, but hurt my feelings. About the time that these warriors came in, the green corn was beginning to be of use, so that we had either green corn or venison, and sometimes both, which was comparatively high living. When we could have plenty of green corn, or roasting corn, the hunters became lazy, and spent their time, as already mentioned, in singing and dancing, &c. They appeared to be fulfilling the Scriptures beyond those who profess to believe them, in that of taking no thought of to-morrow; and also in love, peace and friendship together, without dispute. In this manner we lived until October; then the geese, swans, ducks, cranes, &c., came from the North, and alighted on this little lake in an incredible number. Sunyendeand is a remarkable place for fish in the Spring, and fowl both in the Fall and Spring. As our hunters were now tired with indolence, and fond of their own kind of exercise, they all turned out to fowling, and in this could scarce miss of success; so that we had now plenty of hominy and the best of fowls; and sometimes, as a rarity, we had a little bread made of Indian corn meal, pounded in a hominy block, mixed with boiled beans, and baked into cakes under the ashes. This, with us, was called good living, though not equal to our fat roasted and boiled venison, when we went to the woods in the Fall; or bear's meat and beaver in the Winter; or sugar, bear's oil and dry venison in the Spring.

Some time in October, another adopted brother, older than Tontileaugo, came to pay us a visit at Sunyendeand, and asked me to take a hunt with him on Cuyahoga. I then went with Tecaughretanego to the mouth of the little lake, where we met with the company he intended going with, which was composed of Caughnewagas and Ottawas. Here I was introduced to a Caughnewaga sister, and others I had never before seen. My sister's name was Mary, which they pronounced *Maully*. I asked Tecaughretanego how it came that she had an English name; he said that he did not know that it was an English name; but it was the name the priest gave her when she was baptized, which he said was the name of the Mother of Jesus. He said there were a great many of the Caughnewagas and Wyandots that were a kind of half Roman Catholics; but as for himself, he said that the priest and him could not agree.

The Ottawas have a very useful kind of tents, which they carry with them, made of flags, plaited and stitched together in a very artful manner, so as to turn the rain and the wind well. Each mat is made fifteen feet long and about five feet broad. In order to erect this kind of tent, they cut a number of long straight poles, which they drive in the ground in the form of a circle, leaning inwards; then they spread the mats on these poles, beginning at the bottom and extending up, leaving only a hole in the top uncovered—and this hole answers the place of a chimney. They make fire of dry split wood in the middle, and spread down bark mats and skins for bedding, on which they sleep in a crooked posture, all round the fire, as the length of their beds will not admit of stretching themselves. In place of a door they lift up one end of a mat and creep in, and let the mat fall down behind them. These tents are warm and dry, and tolerably clear of smoke. Their lumber they keep under birch-bark canoes, which they carry out and turn up for a shelter, where they keep everything from the rain. Nothing is in the tents but themselves and their bedding.

About the first of December, 1755, we were preparing for leaving the river: we buried our canoes, and as usual hung up our skins, and every one had a pack to carry; the squaws also packed up their tents, which they carried in large rolls, that extended up above their heads; and though a great bulk, yet not heavy. We steered about a south-east course, and could not march over ten miles per day. At night we lodged in our flag tents, which, when erected, were nearly in the shape of a sugar-loaf, and about fifteen feet diameter at the ground. In this manner we proceeded about forty miles and wintered in these tents, on the waters of Beaver Creek, near a little lake or pond, which is about two miles long, and one broad, a remarkable place for beaver.

HABITS OF THE BEAVER—SMITH SNOWED UP AND LOST.

In conversation with Tecaughretanego, I happened to be talking of the beavers catching fish. He asked me why I thought that the beaver caught fish? I told him that I had read of the beaver making dams for the convenience of fishing. He laughed, and made game of me and my book. He said the man that wrote that book knew nothing about the beaver. The beaver never did eat flesh of any kind, but lived on the bark of trees, roots, and vegetable matter. In order to know certainly how this was, when we killed a beaver I carefully examined the intestines, but found no appearance of fish; I afterwards made an experiment on a beaver which we had, and found that it would neither eat fish nor flesh; therefore I acknowledged that the book that I had read was wrong.

I asked Tecaughretanego, what was the use of the beaver's stones, or glands, to them—as the she beaver has two pair, which are commonly called the oil stones, and the bark stones? He said that as the beavers are the dumbest of all animals and scarcely ever make any noise; and as they were working creatures, they made use of this smell in order to work in concert. If an old beaver was to come on the bank and rub his breech upon the ground and raise a perfume, the others will collect from different places and go to work; this is also of use to them in traveling, that they may thereby search out and find their company. Cunning hunters finding this out, have made use of it against the beavers, in order to catch them. What is the bait which you see them make use of, but a compound of the oil and bark stones. By this perfume, which is only a false signal, they decoy them to the trap.

Near this pond, beaver was the principal game. Before the water froze up, we caught a great many with wooden and steel traps; but after that, we hunted the beaver on the ice. Some places here the beavers build large houses to live in; and in other places they have subterraneous lodgings in the banks. Where they lodge in the ground, we have no chance of hunting on the ice; but where they have houses, we go with malls and handspikes, and break all the hollow ice, to prevent them from getting their heads above the water under it. Then we break a hole in the house, and they make their escape into the water; but as they cannot live long under water, they are obliged to go to some of those broken places to breathe, and the Indians commonly put in their hands, catch them by the hind leg, haul them on the ice, and tomahawk them. Sometimes they shoot them in the head, when they raise it above the water. I asked the Indians if they were not afraid to catch the beavers with their hands; they said no: they were not much of a biting creature; yet if they would catch them by the fore foot they would bite.

As it began to snow and blow most violently, I returned and proceeded after my company, and for some time could see their tracks; but the old snow being about three inches deep, and a crust upon it, the present driving snow soon filled up the tracks. As I had only a bow, arrows and tomahawk with me, and no way to strike fire, I appeared to be in a dismal situation—and as the air was dark with snow, I had little more prospect of steering my course than I would in the night. At length I came to a hollow tree, with a hole at one side that I could go in at. I went in, and found that it was a dry place, and the hollow about three feet diameter, and high enough for me to stand in. I found that there was also a considerable quantity of soft, dry, rotten wood around this hollow; I therefore concluded that I would lodge here, and that I would go to work, and stop up the door of my house. I stripped off my blanket, (which was all the clothes that I had, excepting breech-clout, leggins and moccasins,) and, with my tomahawk, fell to chopping at the top of a fallen tree that lay near, and carried wood and set it up on end against the door, until I had it three or four feet thick, all around, excepting a hole I had left to creep in at. I had a block prepared that I could haul after me, to stop this hole; and before I went in I put in a number of small sticks, that I might more effectually stop it on the inside. When I went in, I took my tomahawk and cut down all the dry, rotten wood I could get, and beat it small. With it I made a bed like a goose-nest or hog-bed, and with the small sticks stopped every hole, until my house was almost dark. I stripped off my moccasins, and danced in the centre of my bed for about half an hour, in order to warm myself. In this time my feet and whole body were agreeably warmed. The snow, in the meanwhile, had stopped all the holes, so that my house was as dark as a dungeon; though I knew that it could not be dark out of doors. I then coiled myself up in my blanket, lay down in my little round bed, and had a tolerable night's lodging.

When I awoke, all was dark—not the least glimmering of light was to be seen. Immediately I recollected that I was not to expect light in this new habitation, as there was neither door or window in it. As I could hear the storm raging, and did not suffer much cold as I was then situated, I concluded I would stay in my nest until I was certain it was day. When I had reason to conclude that it surely was day, I arose and put on my moccasins, which I had laid under my head to keep from freezing. I then endeavored to find the door, and had to do all by the sense of feeling, which took me some time. At length I found the block, but it being heavy, and a large quantity of snow having fallen on it, at the first attempt I did not move it. I then felt terrified —among all the hardships I had sustained, I never knew before what it was to be thus deprived of light. This, with the other circumstances attending it, appeared grievous. I went straightway to bed again, wrapped my blanket round me, and lay and mused awhile, and then prayed to Almighty God to direct and protect me, as he had done heretofore. I once again attempted to move away the block, which proved successful; it moved about nine inches—with this a considerable quantity of snow fell in from above, and I immediately received light; so that I found a very great snow had fallen, above what I had ever seen in one night. I then knew why I could not easily move the block, and I was so rejoiced at obtaining the light, that all my other difficulties seemed to vanish. I then turned into my cell and returned God thanks for having once more received the light of Heaven. At length I belted my blanket about me, got my tomahawk, bow and arrows, and went out of my den.

I was now in tolerable high spirits, though the snow had fallen above three feet deep, in addition to what was on the ground before; and the only imperfect guide I had, in order to steer my course to camp, was the trees, as the moss generally grows on the north-west side of them, if they are straight. I proceeded on, wading through the snow, and about twelve o'clock (as it appeared afterwards, from that time to night, for it was yet cloudy,) I came upon the creek that our camp was on, about half a mile below the camp; and when I came in sight of the camp, I found that there was great joy, by the shouts and yelling of the boys, &c.

When I arrived, they all came around me and received me gladly; but at this time no questions were asked, and I was taken into a tent, where they gave me plenty of fat beaver meat, and then asked me to smoke. When I had done, Tecaughretanego desired me to walk out to a fire they had made. I went out, and they all collected round me, both men, women and boys. Tecaughretanego asked me to give them a particular account of what had happened from the time they left me yesterday until now. I told them the whole of the story, and they never interrupted me; but when I made a stop, the intervals were filled with loud acclamations of joy. As I could not at this time talk Ottawa or Jibbewa well, (which is nearly the same,) I delivered my story in Caughnewaga. As my sister Molly's husband was a Jibbewa, and could understand Caughnewaga, he acted as interpreter, and delivered my story to the Jibbewas and Ottawas, which they received with pleasure. When all this was done, Tecaughretanego made a speech to me in the following manner:

"Brother:—You see we had prepared snow-shoes to go after you, and were almost ready to go when you appeared; yet, as you had not been accustomed to hardships in your country to the east, we never expected to see you alive. Now, we are glad to see you in various respects; we are glad to see you on your own account, and we are glad to see the prospect of your filling the place of a great man, in whose room you were adopted. We do not blame you for what has happened, we blame ourselves; because we did not think of this driving snow filling up the tracks, until after we came to camp.

"Brother:—Your conduct on this occasion hath pleased us much; you have given us an evidence of your fortitude, skill and resolution; and we hope you will always go on to do great actions, as it is only great actions that can make a great man."

The next morning some of the hunters went out on snow-shoes, killed several deer, and hauled some of them into camp upon the snow. They fixed their carrying-strings (which are broad in the middle and small at each end) in the fore feet and the nose of the deer, and laid the broad part of it on their head or about their shoulders, and pulled it along; and when it is moving, it will not sink in the snow much deeper than a snow-shoe; and when taken with the grain of the hair, slips along very easily. The snow-shoes are made like a hoop net, and wrought with buckskin thongs. Each shoe is about two feet and a half long, and about eighteen inches broad before, and small behind, with cross bars, in order to fix or tie them to the feet. After the snow had lain a few days, the Indians tomahawked the deer by pursuing them in this manner.

About two weeks after this there came a warm rain and took away the chief part of the snow, and broke up the ice; then we engaged in making wooden traps to catch beavers, as we had but few steel traps. These traps are made nearly in the same manner as the raccoon traps already described. One day as I was looking after my traps I got benighted, by beaver ponds intercepting my way to camp; and as I had neglected to take fire-works with me, and the weather was very cold, I could find no suitable lodging place; therefore, the only expedient I could think of to keep myself from freezing, was exercise. I danced and hallooed the whole night with all my night, and the next day came to camp. Though I suffered much more this time than the other night I lay out, yet the Indians were not so much concerned, as they thought I had fire-works with me; but when they knew how it was, they did not blame me. They said that old hunters were frequently involved in this place, as the beaver dams were one above another on every creek and run, so that it is hard to find a fording place. They applauded me for my fortitude, and said as they had now plenty of beaver skins, they would purchase me a gun at Detroit, as we were to go there the next Spring; and then if I should chance to be lost in dark weather, I could make fire, kill provision, and return to camp when the sun shined. By being bewildered on the waters of the Muskingum, I lost repute, and was reduced to the bow and arrow, and by lying out two nights here I regained my credit.

Singular Indian Customs—An Indian Drinking Frolic.

After some time the waters all froze again, and then, as formerly, we hunted beavers on the ice. Though beaver meat, without salt or bread, was the chief of our food this Winter, yet we had always plenty, and I was well contented with my diet, as it appeared delicious fare, after the way we had lived the Winter before. Some time in February we scaffolded up our furs and skins, and moved about ten miles in quest of a sugar camp, or a suitable place to make sugar, and encamped in a large bottom on the headwaters of Big Beaver Creek. We had some difficulty in moving, as we had a blind Caughnewaga boy, about fifteen years of age, to lead; and as this country is very brushy, we frequently had him to carry. We had also my Jibbewa brother-in-law's father with us, who was thought by the Indians to be a great conjurer—his name was Manetohcoa. This old man was so decrepid that we had to carry him this route upon a bier, and all our baggage to pack upon our backs.

Shortly after we came to this place, the squaws began to make sugar. We had no large kettles with us this year, and they made the frost, in some measure, supply the place of fire, in making sugar. Their large bark vessels, for holding the stock water, they made broad and shallow; and as the weather is very cold here, it frequently freezes at night in sugar time; and the ice they break and cast out of the vessels. I asked them if they were not throwing away the sugar? They said, no: it was water they were casting away, sugar did not freeze, and there was scarcely any in that ice. They said I might try the experiment, and boil some of it, and see what I would get. I never did try it; but I observed that after several times freezing, the water that remained in the vessel changed its color, and became brown and very sweet.

About the time we were done making sugar the snow went off the ground; and one night a squaw raised an alarm: she said she saw two men with guns in their hands, upon the bank on the other side of the creek, spying our tents—they were supposed to be Johnson's Mohawks. On this the squaws were ordered to slip quietly out some distance into the bushes; and all who had either guns or bows were to squat in the bushes near the tents; and if the enemy rushed up, we were to give them the first fire, and let the squaws have an opportunity of escaping. I got down beside Tecaughretanego, and he whispered to me not to be afraid, for he would speak to the Mohawks, and as they spoke the same tongue that we did, they would not hurt the Caughnewagas or me, but they would kill all the Jibbewas and Ottawas that they could, and take us along with them. This news pleased me well, and I heartily wished for the approach of the Mohawks.

Before we withdrew from the tents, they had carried Manetohcoa to the fire, and gave him his conjuring tools, which were dyed feathers, the bone of a shoulder-blade of a wild-cat, tobacco, &c.; and while we were in the bushes, Manetohcoa was in a tent at the fire, conjuring away to the utmost of his ability. At length he called aloud for us all to come in, which was quickly obeyed. When we came in, he told us that after he had gone through the whole of his ceremony, and expected to see a number of Mohawks on the flat bone when it was warmed at the fire, the pictures of two wolves only appeared. He said that though there were no Mohawks about, we must not be angry with the squaw for giving a false alarm; as she had occasion to go out and happened to see the wolves, though it was moonlight, yet she got afraid, and she conceited it was Indians with guns in their hands; so he said we might all go to sleep, for there was no danger—and accordingly we did.

The next morning we went to the place, and found wolf tracks, and where they had scratched with their feet like dogs; but there was no sign of moccasin tracks. If there is any such thing as a wizard, I think Manetohcoa was as likely to be one as any man, as he was a professed worshiper of the devil. But let him be a conjurer or not, I am persuaded that the Indians believed what he told them on this occasion as well as if it had come from an infallible oracle; or they would not, after such an alarm as this, go all to sleep in an unconcerned manner. This appeared to me the most like witchcraft of anything I beheld while I was with them.

Some time in March, 1757, we began to move back to the forks of Cuyahoga, which was about forty or fifty miles; and as we had no horses, we had all our baggage and several hundred weight of beaver skins, and some deer and bear skins—all to pack on our backs. The method we took to accomplish this, was by making short day's journeys. In the morning we would move on with as much as we were able to carry, about five miles, and encamp, and then run back for more. We commonly made three such trips in the day. When we came to the great pond, we staid there one day to rest ourselves, and to kill ducks and geese.

I remember that Tecaughretanego, when something displeased him, said, "God damn it!" I asked him if he knew what he then said? He said he did, and mentioned one of their degrading expressions, which he supposed to be the meaning, or something like the meaning, of what he had said. I told him that it did not bear the least resemblance to it; that what he had said was calling upon the Great Spirit to punish the object he was displeased with. He stood for some time amazed, and then said, if these be the meaning of these words, what sort of people are the whites? When the traders were among us, these words seem to be intermixed with all their discourse. He told me to reconsider what I had said, for he thought I must be mistaken in my definition; if I was not mistaken, he said the traders applied these words not only wickedly, but oftentimes very foolishly and contrary to sense or reason. He said he remembered once of a trader's accidentally breaking his gun-lock, and on that occasion calling out aloud, God damn it—surely, said he, the gun-lock was not an object worthy of punishment for Owananeeyo, or the Great Spirit; he also observed the traders often used this expression when they were in a good humor, and not displeased with anything. I acknowledged that the traders used this expression very often, in a most irrational, inconsistent and impious manner; yet I still asserted that I had given the true meaning of these words. He replied, if so, the traders are as bad as Oonasharoona, or the underground inhabitants, which is the name they give the devils, as they entertain a notion that their place of residence is under the earth.

We took up our birch-bark canoes, which we had buried, and found that they were not damaged by the Winter; but they not being sufficient to carry all that we now had, we made a large chestnut-bark canoe, as elm bark was not to be found at this place. We all embarked, and had a very agreeable passage down the Cuyahoga, and along the south side of Lake Erie, until we passed the mouth of the Sandusky; then the wind arose, and we put in at the mouth of the Miami of the Lake, at Cedar Point, where we remained several days, and killed a number of turkeys, geese, ducks and swans. The wind being fair, and the lake not extremely rough, we again embarked, hoisted up sails, and arrived safe at the Wyandot town, nearly opposite to Fort Detroit, on the north side of the river. Here we found a number of French traders, every one very willing to deal with us for our beaver.

We bought ourselves fine clothes, ammunition, paint, tobacco, &c., and, according to promise, they purchased me a new gun; yet we had parted with only about one-third of our beaver. At length a trader came to town with French brandy; we purchased a keg of it, and held a council about who was to get drunk, and who was to keep sober. I was invited to get drunk, but I refused the proposal—then they said that I must be one of those who were to take care of the drunken people. I did not like this; but of two evils I chose that which I thought was the least—and fell in with those who were to conceal the arms, and keep every dangerous weapon we could out of their way, and endeavor, if possible, to keep the drinking club from killing each other, which was a very hard task. Several times we hazarded our own lives, and got ourselves hurt, in preventing them from slaying each other. Before they had finished this keg, near one-third of the town was introduced to this drinking club; they could not pay their part, as they had already disposed of all their skins; but that made no odds—all were welcome to drink.

When they were done with this keg, they applied to the traders, and procured a kettle full of brandy at a time, which they divided out with a large wooden spoon—and so they went on, and never quit while they had a single beaver skin. When the trader had got all our beaver, he moved off to the Ottawa town, about a mile from the Wyandot town. When the brandy was gone, and the drinking club sober, they appeared much dejected. Some of them were crippled, others badly wounded, a number of their fine new shirts torn, and several blankets were burned. A number of squaws were also in this club, and neglected their corn planting. We could now hear the effects of the brandy in the Ottawa town. They were singing and yelling in the most hideous manner, both night and day; but their frolic ended worse than ours; five Ottawas were killed, and a great many wounded.

After this a number of young Indians were getting their ears cut, and they urged me to have mine cut likewise, but they did not attempt to compel me, though they endeavored to persuade me. The principal arguments they used were, its being a great ornament, and also the common fashion. The former I did not believe, and the latter I could not deny. The way they performed this operation was by cutting the fleshy part of the circle of the ear close to the gristle, quite through. When this was done, they wrapt rags round this fleshy part until it was entirely healed; they then hung lead to it, and stretched it to a wonderful length; when it was sufficiently stretched, they wrapped the fleshy part round with brass wire, which formed it into a semicircle, about four inches diameter.

Many of the young men were now exercising themselves in a game resembling foot ball; though they commonly struck the ball with a crooked stick made for that purpose; also a game something like this, wherein they used a wooden ball, about three inches diameter, and the instrument they moved it with was a strong staff, about five feet long, with a hoop-net on the end of it large enough to contain the ball. Before they begin the play, they lay off about half a mile distance in a clear plain, and the opposite parties all attend at the centre, where a disinterested person casts up the ball, then the opposite parties all contend for it. If any one gets it into his net, he runs with it the way he wishes to go, and they all pursue him. If one of the opposite party overtakes the person with the ball, he gives the staff a stroke, which causes the ball to fly out of the net; then they have a debate for it, and if the one that gets it can outrun all the opposite party, and can carry it quite out, or over the line at the end, the game is won; but this seldom happens. When any one is running away with the ball, and is likely to be overtaken, he commonly throws it, and, with this instrument, can cast it fifty or sixty yards. Sometimes, when the ball is at one end, matters will take a sudden turn, and the opposite party may quickly carry it out at the other end. Oftentimes they will work a long while back and forward, before they can get the ball over the line, or win the game.

About the first of November, a number of families were preparing to go on their Winter hunt, and all agreed to cross the lake together. We encamped at the mouth of the river the first night, and a council was held, whether we should cross through by the three islands, or coast it round the lake. These islands lie in a line across the lake, and are just in sight of each other. Some of the Wyandots or Ottawas frequently make their Winter hunt on these islands; though, excepting wild fowl and fish, there is scarcely any game here but raccoons, which are amazingly plenty, and exceedingly large and fat; as they feed upon the wild rice, which grows in abundance in wet places round these islands. It is said that each hunter, in one Winter, will catch one thousand raccoons. As the raccoons here lodge in rocks, the trappers make their wooden traps at the mouth of the holes; and as they go daily to look at their traps, in the Winter season they commonly find them filled with raccoons; but in the Spring, or when the frost is out of the ground, they say they can find their traps filled with large rattlesnakes; and therefore conclude that the raccoons are transformed. They also say that the reason why they are so remarkably plenty in the Winter is, every Fall the snakes turn into raccoons again.

Indian "Deer Drive" and "Ring Hunt"—Novel Fishing.

We concluded to coast it round the lake, and in two days we came to the mouth of the Miami of the Lake, and landed on Cedar Point, where we remained several days. Here we held a council, and concluded we would take a driving hunt in concert, and in partnership. The river in this place is about a mile broad, and as it and the lake forms a kind of neck, which terminates in a point, all the hunters (which were fifty-three) went up the river, and we scattered ourselves from the river to the lake. When we first began to move, we were not in sight of each other, but as we all raised the yell, we could move regularly together by the noise. At length we came in sight of each other and appeared to be marching in good order; before we came to the point, both the squaws and boys in the canoes were scattered up the river and along the lake to prevent the deer from making their escape by water. As we advanced near the point, the guns began to crack slowly; and after some time the firing was like a little engagement. The squaws and boys were busy tomahawking the deer in the water, and we shooting them down on the and; we killed in all about thirty deer, though a great many made their escape by water.

We had now great feasting and rejoicing, as we had plenty of hominy, venison and wild fowl. The geese at this time appeared to be preparing to make southward. As cold weather was now approaching, we began to feel the doleful effects of extravagantly and foolishly spending the large quantity of beaver we had taken in our last Winter's hunt. We were all nearly in the same circumstances—scarcely one had a shirt to his back; but each of us had an old blanket which we belted round us in the day, and slept in at night, with a deer or bear skin under us for our bed.

When we came to this place, we met with some Ottawa hunters, and agreed with them to take what they call a ring hunt, in partnership. We waited until we expected rain was near falling to extinguish the fire, and then we kindled a large circle in the prairie. At this time, or before the bucks began to run, a great number of deer lay concealed in the grass in the day, and moved about in the night; but as the fire burned in towards the centre of the circle, the deer fled before the fire; the Indians were scattered also at some distance before the fire, and shot them down every opportunity, which was very frequent, especially as the circle became small. When we came to divide the deer, there were about ten to each hunter, which were all killed in a few hours. The rain did not come on that night to put out the outside circle of the fire, and as the wind arose, it extended through the whole prairie, which was about fifty miles in length, and in some places nearly twenty in breadth. This put an end to our ring hunting this season, and was in other respects an injury to us in the hunting business; so that upon the whole we received more harm than benefit by our rapid hunting frolic. We then moved from the north end of the glades and encamped at the carrying place.

After some time, one of Tontileaugo's step-sons, (a lad of about eight years of age,) offended him, and he gave the boy a moderate whipping, which much displeased his Wyandot wife. She acknowledged that the boy was guilty of a fault, but thought that he ought to have been ducked, which is their usual mode of chastisement. She said she could not bear having her son whipped like a servant or slave— and she was so displeased that when Tontileaugo went out to hunt she got her two horses and all her effects, (as in this country the husband and wife have separate interests,) and moved back to the Wyandot camp that we had left.

When Tontileaugo returned he was much disturbed on hearing of his wife's elopement, and said that he would never go after her were it not that he was afraid that she would get bewildered, and that his children, that she had taken with her, might suffer. Tontileaugo went after his wife, and when they met they made up the quarrel, but he never returned, but left Tecaughretanego and his son, (a boy about ten years of age,) and myself, who remained here in our hut all Winter. Tecaughretanego had been a first-rate warrior, statesman and hunter, and though he was now near sixty years of age, was yet equal to the common run of hunters, but subject to rheumatism, which deprived him of the use of his legs.

Shortly after Tontileaugo left us, Tecaughretanego became lame, and could scarcely walk out of our hut for two months. I had considerable success in hunting and trapping. Though Tecaughretanego endured much pain and misery, yet he bore it all with wonderful patience, and would often endeavor to entertain me with cheerful conversation. Sometimes he would applaud me for my diligence, skill and activity—and at other times he would take great care in giving me instructions concerning the hunting and trapping business. He would also tell me that if I failed of success we would suffer very much, as we were about forty miles from any one living that we knew of; yet he would not intimate that he apprehended we were in any danger, but still supposed that I was fully adequate to the task.

When we came to the little lake at the mouth of Sandusky, we called at a Wyandot town that was then there, called Sunyendeand. Here we diverted ourselves several days, by catching rock fish in a small creek, the name of which is also Sunyendeand, which signifies rock fish. They fished in the night with lights, and struck the fish with gigs or spears. The rock fish there, when they begin first to run up the creek to spawn, are exceedingly fat, sufficiently so to fry of themselves. The first night we scarcely caught fish enough for present use, for all that was in the town.

The next morning I met with a prisoner at this place by the name of Thompson, who had been taken from Virginia. He told me, if the Indians would only omit disturbing the fish for one night, he could catch more fish than the whole town could make use of. I told Mr. Thompson that if he knew he could do this, that I would use my influence with the Indians, to let the fish alone for one night. I applied to the chiefs, who agreed to my proposal, and said they were anxious to see what the Big Knife (as they called the Virginian) could do. Mr. Thompson, with the assistance of some other prisoners, set to work, and made a hoop-net of elm bark; they then cut down a tree across the creek, and stuck in stakes at the lower side of it to prevent the fish from passing up, leaving only a gap at the one side of the creek; here he sat with his net, and when he felt the fish touch the net he drew it up, and frequently would haul out two or three rock fish that would weigh about five or six pounds each. He continued at this until he had hauled out a wagon load, and then left the gap open, in order to let them pass up, for they could not go far on account of the shallow water. Before day Mr. Thompson shut it up, to prevent them from passing down, in order to let the Indians have some diversion in killing them in daylight.

When the news of the fish came to town, the Indians all collected, and with surprise beheld the large heap of fish, and applauded the ingenuity of the Virginian. When they saw the number of them that were confined in the water above the tree, the young Indians ran back to the town, and in a short time returned with their spears, gigs, bows and arrows, &c., and were the chief part of that day engaged in killing rock fish, insomuch that we had more than we could use or preserve. As we had no salt, or any way to keep them, great numbers of turkey buzzards and eagles collected together and devoured them.

Some time in July, 1758, the Ottawas, Jibbewas, Potowatomies and Wyandots, rendezvoused at Detroit, and marched off to Fort Duquesne, to prepare for the encounter of General Forbes. The common report was, that they would serve him as they did General Braddock and obtain much plunder. From this time until Fall, we had frequent accounts of Forbes' army, by Indian runners, that were sent out to watch their motions. They espied them frequently from the mountains ever after they left Fort Loudon. Notwithstanding their vigilance, Colonel Grant, with his Highlanders, stole a march upon them, and in the night took possession of a hill about eighty rods from Fort Duquesne; this hill is, on that account, called Grant's Hill to this day. The French and Indians knew not that Grant and his men were there, until they beat the drum and played upon the bagpipes, just at daylight. They then flew to arms, and the Indians ran up under cover of the banks of the Allegheny and Monongahela, for some distance, and then sallied out from the banks of the rivers, and took possession of the hill above Grant; and as he was on the point of it, in sight of the fort, they immediately surrounded him; and as he had his Highlanders in ranks, and in very close order, and the Indians scattered and concealed behind trees, they defeated him with the loss only of a few warriors—most of the Highlanders were killed or taken prisoners.

When Tecaughretanego had heard the particulars of Grant's defeat, he said he could not well account for his contradictory and inconsistent conduct. He said, as the art of war consists in ambushing and surprising our enemies, and in preventing them from ambushing and surprising us, Grant, in the first place, acted like a wise and experienced officer, in artfully approaching in the night without being discovered; but when he came to the place, and the Indians were lying asleep outside of the fort, between him and the Allegheny river, in place of slipping up quietly and falling upon them with their broadswords, they beat the drums and played upon the bagpipes. He said he could account for this inconsistent conduct in no other way than by supposing that he had made too free with spirituous liquors during the night, and became intoxicated about daylight.

In April, 1759, Smith accompanied his Indian relatives to Montreal, and managed to secrete himself on board a French ship; was again taken prisoner and confined for four months; was finally exchanged, and reached home in 1760, to find his old sweet-heart married, and all supposing him dead. They were much surprised to see him so like an Indian in looks, gait and gesture.

Smith's Marriage—A Wilderness Hermit—Takes a British Fort.

In May, 1763, Smith married, and the same year the Indians again commenced to harass the whole Pennsylvania frontier. Very many of the inhabitants deserted their plantations, while those who remained raised and maintained bodies of riflemen. Smith was elected Captain of one of these troops of rangers, who were all dressed in Indian fashion. They did good service, scouring the whole line of frontier. He then accepted an ensigncy in the British regular service, which he soon after resigned and took service under General Armstrong. In '64, he went as Lieutenant on Bouquet's expedition against the western Indians.

The next year savage marauds and scalpings again took place, and as the traders were, contrary to law, furnishing the savages with goods, guns and ammunition, the back country was greatly excited. Smith, however, was not content with grumbling, but took a more summary course. Selecting ten of his old Indian fighters, he painted and disguised them, and waylaid a company of traders, firing on their packhorses from front to rear of their line, putting them to flight and burning up all their war-like goods. The traders complained at Fort Loudon, and securing a party of Highland soldiers, arrested a number of persons not at all concerned in the action. Smith at once raised three hundred riflemen, marched to the fort, and soon took enough of British troops in his possession to redeem all the prisoners. They also made continued war upon the traders, and kept guard and watch on the frontiers for several months.

In '66, Smith, captivated by the reports of the rich game country in the West, proceeded, with four active young fellows from Carlisle and a mulatto slave boy, and explored Kentucky and the region south of it (this was before Boone's time); also the region watered by the Cumberland and Tennessee rivers. Following the latter stream to the Ohio, his companions concluded to go to explore the Illinois country, but Smith determined to go east, through the vast wilderness, to Carolina. Taking only a little powder, he started off on his long and adventurous journey, accompanied only by the mulatto lad.

After about eight days of wilderness tramping, Smith received a painful cane stab in the foot; his leg commenced to swell, and finally became so intolerably painful that he had to perform a surgical operation in order to draw the huge splinter from his foot. He had nothing but a knife, a moccasin awl and a pair of bullet-moulds. But these, with the aid of the faithful darkey, proved efficient, but they were compelled to lie by here many, many weeks. He made the darkey hunt up Indian fomentations and poultices, using wood mosses instead of rags, and wrapping the whole around with elm-bark. A shelter was made with branches covered over with cane-tops, about a hundred yards distant from a regular buffalo trace, and with the aid of a Psalm Book and Watts upon Prayer, the two hermits got along very comfortably, Smith even composing poetry.

Some weeks after, Smith was able to travel slowly, and the two moved on, arriving in Carolina in October. He had, as he quaintly writes, "been now eleven months in the wilderness, and during this time I neither saw bread, money, women nor spirituous liquors, and three months of which I saw none of the human species except Jamie. When I came into the settlement, my clothes were almost worn out, and the boy had nothing on him that ever was spun—buckskin leggings, moccasins and breech-clout, a bear skin, dressed with the hair on, and a raccoon-skin cap. I was strictly examined by the inhabitants. I told them the truth, and where I came from, &c., but my story appeared so strange to them that they didn't believe me, asserting they had never heard of any one coming through the mountains from the mouth of the Tennessee, and if any undertook such a journey, surely no man would lend him his slave. On suspicion, they therefore took me into custody, and set a guard over me."

Meeting soon with an old acquaintance who vouched for him, poor

Smith was liberated, and, with an old beaver hat and blanket, buckskin leggins, moccasins, and a new shirt, which his pitying friend gave him, he marched on with Jamie, clad in his rough bear skin, and the twain presenting such a wild and uncouth spectacle, that Smith avers the dogs would come out and bark at them, and the settlers frequently stopped them on suspicion. He soon after obtained good clothes and a horse, and then, adds he, "no man ever asked me for a pass; therefore, I concluded that a horse thief, or even a robber, might pass without interruption provided he was only well dressed, whereas the shabby villain would be immediately detected."

In the Fall of 1767, Smith reached home, his wife and friends having again given him up as dead, since they had heard he was killed by Indians, and his horse brought into one of the Cherokee towns. In 1769, he and his "Indian boys" again commenced his war on the Indian-traders, for which some of his companions were arrested and lodged in Bedford jail—then, of course, a British post. Smith did not approve of the conduct of some of those who were arrested, but he could not bear to think of them chafing in irons, and so he boldly resolved to attempt a grand rescue. Collecting eighteen of his "black boys," he openly marched, with the avowed design of taking Fort Bedford, but employed a friend to go before as a spy. The next day they encamped near the crossings of the Juniata, about fourteen miles from the fort, and commenced erecting tents, as though intending to stay all night. None but Smith knew differently. At eleven at night, however, he roused his band and marched rapidly on towards the fort. Meeting his spy, he was told that the commandant had put thirty men on guard, and ridiculed the very idea of such a small rabble taking the fort.

Smith, finding the gate shut, moved his men quietly up under the Juniata's banks, where they lay concealed about a hundred yards from the fort gate. Soon as he found the gates open in the morning, the arms standing stacked, and the guards taking their morning dram, he, with his trusty followers, made a sudden rush inside the gate and took possession of the arms. They then raised a yell, hurriedly proceeded to the guard-house, found a blacksmith to remove the irons off the prisoners, and taking them all with them, rapidly left the place. "This, I believe," modestly adds Smith, "was the first British fort in America that was taken by what they called 'American rebels.'"

Some time after, while Smith was quietly riding from Bedford, *en route* to visit his lands located on the Yough, he was overtaken by some travelers on horseback who asked his name, and on his telling it, they pulled out their pistols and threatened to kill him if he didn't surrender himself as prisoner. But Smith was not that kind of a man. He stepped back, upped with his rifle, and upon one of the party snapping a pistol at him, let drive, dropping his enemy to the earth. The party, however, now made a rush on him, seized him, put him in Bedford guard-house, and held an inquest, bringing in Smith guilty of murder. As they were afraid to keep him at Bedford for fear of a rescue, he was sent privately to Carlisle, where he was heavily ironed and securely guarded.

Smith's arrest, it may well be supposed, created a terrible pother in the country round about. Hearing that a number of the old "black boys" were coming to tear down the jail, he told the sheriff he would not be rescued, but would stand his trial, and wrote a letter asking his old companions to keep off. They, hearing he was in irons, however, would come on. Smith asked the sheriff to take off his irons and he would make them a speech. This he did, begging them as the greatest favor his friends could do for him, to keep away and let him stand trial. That he was innocent and would surely be released. They retired but soon after met another force of three hundred rescuers, when the whole party returned to Carlisle and asserted that as he could never get a fair trial, they were resolved to rescue him. These also were persuaded to move off without attempting any violence.

Smith remained in prison four months, and when the Supreme Court sat, had his trial, the upshot of which was a verdict of "not guilty." Smith now quieted down and became a substantial citizen. In 1774, another Indian war commenced, in which Smith acted as Captain. At the outbreak of the Revolution, he was elected a member of the State Assembly, and afterwards headed his old Indian fighters and went on a scouting expedition against the British in Jersey. Preceding Washington, they waylaid the road at Rocky Hill, and with only thirty-six men attacked and defeated a force of two hundred. They afterwards made captive a lot of Hessians. Smith was soon seized with camp fever and lay at Burlington a long time. He then tried to get permission to raise a battalion of riflemen, to be dressed as Indians and to act as scouts, but Washington did not favor the idea, but offered him a majorship, which Smith, wishing to be with his own boys, declined.

In 1778, Smith secured a Colonel's commission, and was diligently and constantly employed protecting our frontier against British Indians. Soon after he commanded four hundred riflemen on a successful expedition against the French Creek Indians, and in 1788 he migrated West and settled in Bourbon county, Kentucky, representing his district in Assembly down to the present century.

CAPTAIN JACK, "THE WILD HUNTER OF THE JUNIATA."

About this period there flourished along the Pennsylvania border—at that time scarce extending much beyond the Susquehanna—a notable character by the name of Captain Jack, who was almost as much famed as his Indian namesake of Modoc notoriety has lately become. Although there is much of legend and mystery connected about the Juniata-valley Jack, this much is certain, that there was a bold hunter and "Indian-killer," known all along the Pennsylvania border, from the upper Susquehanna down to the Potomac, by that name. In Hazard's Register there is frequent mention of him. Colonel Armstrong, in his reports of his expedition against Captain Jacobs of the Delaware village of Kittanning, calls him—on account of his swarthy visage—"The Half-Indian." His monument can be now seen at Chambersburg, with the following inscription: "Colonel Patrick Jack, an officer of the Colonial and Revolutionary wars—died January 25th, 1821, aged ninety-one years."

Colonel George Croghan, who, while Braddock was preparing for his march, was engaged in beating up a number of Indians, scouts, etc., to serve as guides, distinctly states that Captain Jack was at the head of a body of bold hunter-rangers, skilled in woodcraft, expert in Indian fighting, clad, like their leader, in Indian attire, and offered them to Braddock, provided they were allowed to dress, march and fight as they pleased, and not to be subject to the strict regulations of a soldier's camp. "They are well armed," said Croghan, "and are equally regardless of heat or cold. They require no shelter for the night, *and ask no pay!*" This, of course, could not be permitted by such a strict and self-reliant martinet as Braddock, and the Rangers were suffered to depart. It is idle now to speculate what might have been the result of the British Expedition had these scouts, and a larger body of fighting Indians been allowed to accompany, or rather precede Braddock's army. Judging, however, from the late invaluable services of the Warm Spring Indians in tracking the Modocs to their lairs, beating up their fastnesses in the lava-beds, and bringing them to bay in such manner that nothing was left but surrender, it is certainly safe to assume that these Pennsylvania Rangers and Indians would have performed the same offices for Braddock, and rendered wholly impossible the disastrous defeat which we have taken such pains to describe.

Captain Jack's early history is shrouded in mystery, but it is the current tradition in middle Pennsylvania that he was a frontier settler, and that returning one evening from a long day's chase, he found his cabin a heap of smouldering ruins, and the blackened corpses of his murdered family scattered around. From that time he became a rancorous Indian hater and slayer. In '53 he held a sort of roving commission from Governor Hamilton—his home being in the Juniata valley—going under the names of "The Black Rifle," "The Black Hunter," and "The Wild Hunter of the Juniata." It is thought by some that "Jack's Mountain," in Pennsylvania, was called after him; but this, we think, is a mistake; it, as well as "Jack's Narrows," having taken their name from the fact—which caused a great deal of excitement at the time—of the atrocious murder, in 1744, of a noted Indian trader named Jack Armstrong, together with his two servants, Smith and Woodward, by a Delaware Chief called Musemeelin.

In Jones' "Juniata Valley," we find a lengthy account of Captain Jack. *He* makes him a hunter living on the Juniata, near a beautiful spring, having a mystery about him which no one ever succeeded in fathoming. He is described by Jones as a man of Herculean proportions, with an extremely swarthy complexion, and as a relentless Indian tracker and killer. The settlers about Aughwick (now Shirleysburg, Huntingdon county, Pa.,) as well as those in Path Valley and along the Juniata, "frequently found dead savages, some in a state of partial decay, and others with their flesh stripped by the bald eagles, on the spot where Jack's rifle had laid them low." "On one occasion," writes Jones, "Captain Jack had concealed himself in the woods by the side of the 'Aughwick Path,' where he lay in wait for a stray Indian. Presently a painted warrior, with a red feather waving from his head, and his body bedizened with gew-gaws recently purchased from a trader, came down the 'path.' A crack from Captain Jack's rifle, and the savage bounded into the air and fell dead without a groan. It appears that three others were in company—but had tarried at a spring—who, on hearing the discharge of a rifle, under the impression that their companion had shot a bear, gave a loud 'whoop.' Captain Jack immediately loaded, and when the Indians came up to the dead body, Jack again shot and killed a second one. The Indians then rushed into the thicket, and one of them getting a glimpse of Jack, shot at him, but missed. The 'Wild Hunter,' seeing that the chances were desperate, jumped out and engaged in a hand-to-hand encounter—the fourth savage being only armed with a tomahawk. He soon dispatched the third one by beating his brains out with a rifle; but the fourth one, an athletic fellow, grappled, and a long and bloody fight with knives followed, and only ceased when both were exhausted by loss of blood. The Indian managed to get away, and left the 'Black Hunter' the victor of the field. Weak and faint as Jack was, he scalped the three savages, and managed to work his way to the settlement, where his wounds—consisting of eight or ten stabs—were dressed."

"It is said," continues Jones, "that one night the family of an Irishman named Moore, residing in Aughwick, were suddenly awakened by the report of a gun. On opening the door, they found a dead Indian lying upon the very threshold. By the feeble light which shone through the door, they discovered the dim outline of the 'Wild Hunter,' who merely said: 'I have saved your lives,' and then plunged into the dark ravine and disappeared. With an eye like the eagle, an aim that was unerring, daring intrepidity, and a constitution that could brave the heat of Summer as well as the frosts of Winter, he roamed the valley like an uncaged tiger, the most formidable foe that ever crossed the redman's path. Of the final end of Captain Jack," concludes Jones, "we have nothing definite. One account says he went west, another that he died in 1772. It is said that his bones rest near the spring at the base of the mountain bearing his name, and this we are inclined to credit. The early settlers of the neighborhood believed that Captain Jack came down from the mountain every night at twelve o'clock to slake his thirst at his favorite spring; and half a century ago we might readily have produced the affidavits of twenty respectable men who had seen the 'Black Hunter' in the spirit, roaming over the land that was his in the flesh. The towering mountain, a hundred miles in length, bearing his name, will stand as an indestructible monument to his memory."

Chapter II.

THE CONSPIRACY OF PONTIAC.

> For he was of unblenching eye,
>   Honored in youth, revered in age;
> Of princely port and bearing high,
>   And brave and eloquent and sage.
> Ah, scorn not that a tawny skin
>   Wrapped his strong limbs and ample breast;
> A noble soul was pent within
>   As paler Saxon e'er possessed.
> Oft hath he gazed from yonder height,
>   When pausing 'mid the chase alone,
> On the fair realms beneath his sight,
>   And proudly called them all his own.—*J. H. Bryant.*

Upon the evacuation of Fort Duquesne, most of Forbes' army re-crossed the mountains, he himself being carried in a litter the whole way, and dying shortly after at Philadelphia. As the possession of the Forks of the Ohio was of immense importance to the whole country, it was determined to hold them, and for the present to erect a small stockade to be occupied by one hundred men, under Colonel Hugh Mercer—afterwards one of the most popular Generals of the Revolution and killed at the battle of Princeton. In September, 1759, was commenced the formidable fortification called Fort Pitt, which was completed the next year, having cost the British government sixty thousand pounds.

With Fort Duquesne's fall, all direct contest between the French and British ceased in the West. Canada was thenceforth the only scene of operations, though garrisons for awhile remained in the forts on French Creek. In '59 Ticonderoga, Crown Point, Niagara, and at length Quebec—assaulted by the famous Wolfe from the "Plains of Abraham"—yielded to the British, and in the Fall of '60, Montreal, Detroit, and all Canada were surrendered by Vaudreuil, the French Governor.

The long war was at length over; but it still remained to take possession of the frontier French posts, and it was while Major Rogers, captain of the far-famed American rangers, (half hunters, half woodsmen,) and a most gallant and skillful partisan officer, was marching to the front, that we first hear of the great and immortal Pontiac, the most noble and powerful Indian Chief that has ever appeared on the pages of American history. Rogers had left Montreal with two hundred of his rangers in fifteen whale-boats. Skirting along the northern shore of Ontario, they reached Fort Niagara on the 1st of October. Carrying their frail barks over the portage, they launched them once more on Lake Erie, and proceeded to the post at Presqu' Isle, (now Erie, Pa.,) and thence along its southern shore. Arriving at the mouth of the Chogage, the farthest point west that any body of troops under the British flag had ever penetrated, Rogers encamped in the neighboring forest. They had scarce landed before a number of chiefs appeared before their startled eyes, who stated they were an embassy from Pontiac, the great Lord of all that region, who would soon pay them a visit, and that the "pale-faces" must proceed no further.

Shortly after, Pontiac himself, majestic in appearance and attended by a number of his chiefs, made his appearance, and haughtily demanded of Rogers what his warriors were doing in that country, and how he *dared* enter it without his permission. The Major was too prudent to take offence at this arrogant style of address, but quietly answered that the French were defeated: that all Canada had surrendered, and that he had been ordered to take possession of Fort Detroit, and was now on his way thither. The proud chief only deigned to reply, "I shall stand in the path you are walking until morning," as much as to say, Proceed no farther without permission.

The next morning Pontiac reappeared, offered the pipe of peace, and said he was willing to live at peace with the English so long as they treated him with deference—not only this, but he dispatched messengers to the various Indian towns in front of Rogers, informing them that the Englishman had his authority to march through the country, and he employed a hundred of his warriors to drive the cattle which had been sent from Fort Pitt for the use of the troops. He kept near Rogers until his arrival at Detroit, and was the means of preventing a hostile Indian attack at the mouth of Detroit river. Hitherto Pontiac had been in word and deed the firm ally of the French, but he was shrewd, subtle and ambitious, and was too wise and crafty to press a failing cause. By making friends with the English, he hoped to advance his own ambitious projects and increase his influence over the north-western tribes. He confidently expected, likewise, that the newcomers would treat him and his authority with the same studied respect that the French had done. In all this he was doomed to a speedy and a mortifying disappointment. His tolerance, therefore, was soon succeeded by jealousy, which was easily, on opportunity, converted into rage and then revenge.

Pontiac at this time was principal Chief of the Ottawas, and was about fifty years of age. His powerful tribe had for some time been united with the Ojibwas and Pottawattamies, and he was their common head, exercising over them almost despotic authority and his power extending among all the surrounding nations. He was brave, shrewd, subtle and eloquent, and was a perfect master of all those arts by which the American savage is not only won, but retained. He had led his tribe, a few years before, at the bloody battle of Braddocks Fields. A short time previous he had saved the Detroit garrison from an attack from surrounding tribes. During the French war he had fought on the side of France, and had received especial marks of esteem from the Marquis de Montcalm.

When Rogers appeared with his whale-boats before Detroit, informing its French commandant that Canada had surrendered, and that he bore an order from Vaudreuil for the quiet evacuation of Detroit, he could not and would not believe it. The rangers landed on the opposite bank and pitched their tents upon a meadow. Two officers went across the stream to take possession. The authority from Vaudreuil was shown, and could not be disputed. In obedience thereto, the French garrison defiled upon the plain and grounded their arms. The *fleur de Lis* was lowered on the flag-staff, and the Cross of St. George took its place, while several hundred Indian warriors, late the active allies of France, looked on with wonder at the scene. They could not understand why so many men should humble themselves without a blow before those few impudent strangers. When it was all explained they were equally amazed at the forbearance of the conquerors in not killing their vanquished enemies on the spot. The forts of Miami, Onatanon and Machillimackinac soon after followed suit—still later the three remoter posts of St. Marie, Green Bay and St. Joseph.

First Mutterings of the Awful Storm—Pontiac's Subtlety.

Speedily, however, were heard the sullen mutterings of an awful storm. A deep-rooted hatred against the English soon grew up. They knew not like the French how to conciliate the Indians. They were stingy and niggardly with their gifts; they treated the Indian visitors at the forts with disdain and contempt, sometimes with personal rudeness and indignities; the French used to humor their ways and conform to their customs, marrying with them, dressing and living like them, and contributing liberally to all their amusements and native tastes. From the English they got little but harsh words or contemptuous blows. This hated nation, too, were steadily advancing, occupying all their best lands and the British fur-traders were cheating, rum-selling ruffians of the most degraded stamp, who debauched their women, encroached on their best trapping grounds and swindled them out of their furs with systematic villainy. Add to all this the fact that the French Canadians, who hoped that the hated British rule would be temporary, did all they possibly could to foment bad blood and to spread all manner of wicked reports and deceptions, and it is no marvel that the whole red race was ripe for revolt and conspiracy. In the language of a great Chippewa orator, the French had lived in the same lodge with them; they had sent them missionaries; had invited them to grand councils; had overwhelmed them with frequent and valuable presents, and had treated them as brothers. The English, however, had neglected all those acts of kindness and arts of courtesy and policy which had made the French so agreeable. The conduct of the French had never given rise to suspicion. That of the English had never given rest to it.

And now, too, a prophet—answering to Tecumseh's brother many years afterwards—arose conveniently among the Delawares to give as it were the sanction of the Great Spirit to all this discontent. He fairly hated the English and by all the arts known to the native dreamer and soothsayer, he went to and fro stirring up suspicion and discord. He dreamed dreams and saw visions, and all to the same purpose. The English had come to take away the beautiful country given them by the Great Spirit and they must be cut off or driven off.

Pontiac, actuated by revenge, ambition and patriotism, was really at the bottom of all this trouble. His sagacious, far-seeing mind, forecast the future and saw plainly that now, if ever, was the time to check the British advance. He sent out his ambassadors far and near. Bearing with them the war belt of wampum and the tomahawk stained in token of war, they roamed over all the country and called secret councils of all the tribes, advancing as far east as the Delaware and Shawnees of the Allegheny; the Cherokees and Catawbas of the south, and the Illinois and Muscatines of the west; and, first, a grand council of all the neighboring tribes, of which Pontiac was the supreme head and inspiration, was convened at the river Aux Ecorces. Here Pontiac exerted all those subtle arts for which he was so distinguished.

With a profound knowledge of the savage character, and especially aware of the great power of superstition on their minds, he related, among other things, a dream in which the Great Spirit had secretly disclosed to the Delaware prophet aforesaid, exactly what his red children must do. They were to abstain from the pale-faces' "fire-water;" to abandon all their manufactures; resume their bows and arrows, fire-arms and the skins of animals for clothing, "and why," the orator concluded, "Why, said the Great Spirit to the Delaware prophet, do you suffer these vile dogs in red clothing to enter your country and take the land I have given to you alone? Arise ! Drive them from it ! *Drive them!* When you are in distress *I* will help you !"

This speech was received with cries of vengeance. The scheme was fully debated and concluded. It was resolved that the work of extirpation should be commenced on the *same day* east and west ; north and south. That all should be kept secret as the grave and that in all cases, according to the universal Indian rule, resort should first be had to craft and artifice. Should *they* fail, then, *open war*.

With the subtle dissimulation of their race, the design was carefully concealed until all the tribes far and near should be ready to act in concert. Until that day arrived, the warriors still lounged about the forts, with calm, stony, imperturbable faces, begging as usual for tobacco and whiskey. Now and then some trader, coming in from Indian villages, would bring strange reports of mischief being on foot, or some swaggering half-breed would be heard boasting in his cups that he would now have abundance of hair-fringe for his hunting frock, but still there was no general alarm. Early in March, indeed, the plot was nearly discovered. Ensign Holmes, commanding at Fort Miami, was told by a friendly Indian, that the warriors of a neighboring friendly village had received a war belt and a peremptory command to destroy him and his garrison, which they were preparing to do. On being charged with this design, the wily savages did as they had often done before, and did do afterwards—they confessed the fault with much apparent humility, and blamed a far-distant tribe. Holmes wrote to Major Gladwyn, who was then the British commander of Detroit, who, in turn, informed General Amherst—but, also, that he thought the affair would soon blow over, and that, in the neighborhood of his own fort, the savages were perfectly tranquil, and yet, within cannon shot of this brave but deluded officer, dwelt and plotted the great Pontiac himself.

Well, the dread day agreed upon arrived at last, and the result was *nine British forts captured*, and in every case by artifice. Some of the garrisons were completely surprised and massacred on the spot; a few individuals in other cases escaped. Hundreds of Indian traders on their way to the different forts and tribes, were murdered and their goods and stores, either captured or destroyed. At the same time commenced a fierce, horrible and desolating war against the New York, Pennsylvania and Virginia borders. For weeks together, nothing was heard but news of whole families butchered and communities abandoned. Houses, stock, barns, *everything*, fell a prey to these human locusts, and the roads to the east were blocked with throngs of the poor, smitten and panic-stricken inhabitants. Other posts, too, would have fallen had not their commanders received timely intimations of the intended attack. The capture of so many by preconcerted strategy proves the scope and reach of the mind of Pontiac, the *brains* of the whole conspiracy. Generally the commanders were secured in the first instance by parties admitted within the forts, under the pretence of business or friendship. At Maumee, the officer was betrayed by a squaw, who, by piteous entreaties persuaded him to go out with her a couple of hundred yards to the succor, as she said, of a wounded and dying man. The Indians ambushed and shot him. We will here refer to the incidents attending the attack on some of the forts.

Machillimackinac Captured Through a Game of Ball.

And first Machillimackinac, standing on the south side of the strait between Lakes Huron and Michigan, opposite to where Mackinaw now stands. It was a very important post—a place of deposit and a point of departure between the upper and lower countries. An extensive square area, surrounded by high palisades, numerous houses, barracks and other buildings, formed a smaller square within, and in the vacant space could at that day be seen the red uniforms of British soldiers, the gray coats of Canadians, and the gaudy Indian blankets, mingled in picturesque confusion, while a multitude of half-breeds and squaws, with children of every hue, strolled restlessly about the place at the time. All the British troops had not yet arrived and the garrison was supplemented by Canadians, the only ordnance on the bastions being two small brass pieces.

The capture of this important post was given to the Sacs and Ojibwas, and the plan was thus:

The King's birthday having arrived, a game of baggattaway was proposed by the savages. This game is played with a bat and ball, the former being about four feet long, curved and terminating in a sort of a racket. Two posts are placed in the ground at a distance of half a mile from each other; each party has its post, and the game consists in throwing the ball, which is started at a point midway from the posts, and each party endeavoring to carry the ball to its own wicket. A well-contested game of this kind presents a scene of wonderful exertion and excitement. Hundreds of lithe and agile figures are leaping and bounding upon the plain. At times, the whole mass is crowded together, pushing, shoving, yelling and contending; and then they scatter again and leap over the ground like hounds in full cry, rushing and striking and tripping their adversaries.

At the proper moment it was easy for a selected party to throw the ball over the pickets of the fort, to be at once followed by a mad, shouting, tumultuous throng. Nothing could be more natural, or less likely to excite suspicion. This was, in fact, the very thing that was done, and to be still more sure of success, the Indians had persuaded many of the garrison and settlers to come without the pickets and lay wagers upon the keenly-contested game. Not fewer than four hundred were engaged on each side, and if possession of the fort could thus be gained, the rest was an easy matter.

There was there at this time an English trader, Alexander Henry by name. On his route thither he had been several times warned to turn back, and was at length compelled to assume the disguise of a Canadian *voyageur*. When his canoes reached the fort, he had been received coolly by the Indians. Soon after he heard that a large number of Ojibwas were about to call on him, which excited his suspicion and alarm. They came, about sixty in number, headed by Miniavavana— a chief of commanding stature, and a singularly fine face and manner. They walked in single file, each with a tomahawk in one hand and scalping knife in the other. Their bodies were naked from the waist up. They were decorated in true Indian fashion, their faces painted and their bodies worked up with white clay. The chief commenced the pow-wow by asking when he had left Montreal, and observed that the English must be brave men and not afraid of death, since they dared to come so fearlessly among their enemies.

After the pipes were smoked and while Henry was enduring all the tortures of suspense, the big chief made a more formal speech, in which he stated that the French King was their father, whom the English had made war on and were his enemies, and that his enemies were theirs, too; that the King of France was old and infirm and that, tired of making war, he had now fallen asleep and allowed the English to take Canada, but that his nap was almost done, and when he waked he would destroy the English utterly. He thus continued: "Englishman, although, indeed, you have conquered the French, you have not yet conquered us. We are not your slaves. These lakes, woods and mountains were left to *us* by our ancestors. We will part with them to none. Our young men have made war on your nation and many have been killed; it is our custom to retaliate until the spirits of the slain are satisfied, and this can be done only in two ways; first, by the blood of those who killed them; second, by covering the bodies of the dead by presents and thus allaying the resentment of the relatives. Englishman, *your* King has never sent us any presents, nor made treaty with us; wherefore, he and we are still at war. We consider, however, that you have ventured among us unarmed, to trade with us and shall regard you as a brother. You may sleep in quiet, and we present you this pipe."

A general smoke then ensued, and Henry made a formal reply. To this succeeded a request for whiskey. The trader reluctantly complied, and after distributing a few presents saw, with profound pleasure, the departure of his unwelcome guests. Soon after two hundred Ottawas came to the fort in a body, and summoned Henry and some other traders to their presence. Here they were told they must distribute their goods among the Indians, making a faithless promise to pay them in the Spring, and threatening death if they refused. Asking time to reflect on this gentle hint, the traders resolved to resist such a flagrant robbery, and accordingly, arming thirty of their men with muskets, they barricaded themselves in Henry's house and kept watch all night. No attack, however, occurred and soon after the garrison was reinforced by the timely arrival of troops.

Captain Etherington, the commandant of the fort, had received several warnings of the conspiracy among the Indians, but with that fatuity so common among British officers in America who despised their foes, not only disbelieved them, but threatened to send prisoner to Detroit the very next person who should keep the little settlement alarmed by such improbable and ridiculous tidings.

Henry, too, had received warning and afterwards blamed himself much for his total disregard of it. An Ojibwa Chief, Wawatam by name, had taken a great fancy to him and hinted several times that something unusual was on foot. One evening Henry's door was pushed open without ceremony and the dark figure of Wawatam glided silently in. He sat down with a dejected air and expressed surprise at finding his brother still in the fort; he was going next day to the Sault Ste Marie and begged Henry to go with him. He then asked if the English had heard no bad news, and said his own ears were filled with the songs of evil birds. Seeing that the unsuspecting trader was totally unsuspicious, he went away with a sad and mournful face, but returned next morning with his squaw and again pressed Henry to go with him. When the trader demanded the reason for his urgency, he asked if he did not know that many bad, strange Indians were encamped about the fort. To-morrow, he said, they would demand whiskey and would all get drunk and it would be dangerous to stay. Wawatam let fall other plain hints, which, had Henry understood Ojibwa better, could not fail to have moved him from his apathy. As it was, the chief and squaw took a mournful departure, but not before both had shed tears. There came no later warning.

The very next day happened the ball play alluded to. The incredulous Captain Etherington lounged outside the gate, having laid heavy wagers on the Ojibwas as against the Sacs. Several Indian chiefs and leading warriors, with eyes more snaky and glittering than usual, but apparently only intent upon watching the game, were grouped closely around. When the game was at its very highest and the surging crowd was swaying hither and yon, suddenly the ball soared high in the air and descending in a wide curve fell near the pickets of the fort. As if in pursuit of the fugitive ball, the players came rushing, in a maddened tumultuous throng, towards the chief gate which now stood invitingly open. One instant more and they had reached it. The dazed and stupefied English had no time to think or act. And now the shrill cries of the players all at once changed into the ferocious, blood-curdling war whoop. The warriors snatched from the outstretched hands of their squaws, their keen tomahawks which had been until now carefully concealed. Some of the Indians rushed fiercely on those without, while others bounded into the fort, and all was soon a frightful carnage. At the very first moment the throats of Etherington and his lieutenant were clutched by sinewy hands, and they were led into the woods. Within the fort all were butchered without mercy.

Henry was a witness to this horrid massacre, but not to the ball play, and has given a minute account of it and of his own subsequent adventures and narrow escapes. A canoe had just arrived from Detroit, and he was moving to the beach to hear the news when the murderous war whoop reached his startled ears. Going to his window he saw the infuriated mob of savages hacking and scalping all inside the fort. Seizing his fowling-piece, he waited, but of course in vain, for the drum to beat to arms. In this dreadful interval he saw several of his acquaintances fail and then scalped alive, while struggling between the knees of the fiends who held them. He then thought of his own safety, but knew not what to do or where to turn. He saw many of the French Canadians looking calmly on and thence thought one of their houses would offer the best security. Only a low fence separated his own house from M. Langlade—the noted partisan half-breed who led the Lake Indians at Braddock's defeat — over which he climbed and begged for concealment. Langlade turned again to the window, from which he and his family were gazing at the massacre, and with the expressive French shrug intimated he could do nothing. Henry's heart sank within him, but happily a Pawnee woman—one of the Sac captives and a slave of Langlade's—beckoned to him to follow her. She then showed him the door to the garret and bade him conceal himself. She then followed him to the garret, locked the door after him and took away the key.

Through an aperture, Henry's blood fairly curdled at witnessing the scalpings and mutilations of the dead and dying. From the hacked and slashed bodies of the slain, these insatiate demons were scooping up the blood in the hollow of their hands and quaffing it off amid shouts of rage and triumph. At last all being silent, there was a general cry of "all is finished." Just then were heard the footsteps of Indians entering Langlade's house and asking if any Englishmen were therein. Langlade said he could not say, but he thought not, but they might examine for themselves. The Pawnee woman had not only hidden him, but kept the secret.

THE TRADER HENRY'S NARROW ESCAPES FROM DEATH.

Henry now heard the wretches trying the garret door. Some delay was caused by the absence of the key. His feelings may be faintly imagined—not described. He looked anxiously about for a hiding-place, finally creeping in among a lot of birch-bark sugar vessels. An instant after, four savages, snuffing about like blood-hounds, entered with tomahawk in hand and all besmeared with gore. The throbbings of the poor fugitive's heart were almost loud enough to betray him. The Indians walked about in every direction, and one approached so closely that he almost touched the trembling, cowering white man, but the obscurity favored him, and they finally returned down stairs, loudly boasting to Langlade how many scalps they had taken.

Exhausted as he was by all he had gone through, Henry threw himself on a feather bed and went to sleep. At dusk, Madame Langlade entered and was surprised to see him, but told him she hoped he would escape. Next morning he was again on the rack. Indian voices were heard below, to the effect that Henry, the trader, had not yet been found, and that he must surely be somewhere concealed. He then had the unspeakable torture to hear the affrighted Madame Langlade argue in French with her husband—who must by this time have known of Henry's concealment—that he should be given up, as, should the savages discover that they had anything to do with it, they would avenge it on their children, and it was better he should die than they. The husband at first resisted, but finally suffered her to prevail, and told the savages that he had heard Henry was in the house, and that he would put him into their hands.

Judge of the poor man's horror at this revelation! Considering all further efforts at concealment vain, he rose from the bed and presented himself full in view to the savages now entering the garret, and who were all drunk and nearly naked. One huge chief named Wenniway, whom Henry well knew, had his entire body smeared with charcoal mixed with grease, with the exception only of one white spot, two inches in diameter, which encircled either eye. This fellow seized Henry by the coat with one hand, while with the other he flourished a large carving knife, threatening to run it in his bosom, and all the time glaring steadfastly into his eyes.

At length, after some seconds of dreadful suspense, he dropped his arm, saying, "I will not kill you!" adding that he had lost a brother by the English and that the trader should take his place.

This was a joyful reprieve to poor Henry, who was ordered down stairs and taken to the warrior's cabin, where he was again threatened with death, since not only there but everywhere else, the savages were infuriated and maddened with liquor. Wenniway, however, consented that the prisoner should stay at Langlade's house, and for the present all was safe.

Shortly after an Indian, who was largely in Henry's debt, called at the house and ordered him to follow him to the Ojibwa camp. Henry could do naught but obey, but seeing his dusky debtor moving briskly off towards the bushes, he refused to go further, asserting that he believed he meant to kill him. The savage said he was right, and seized the prisoner by the arm and raised his knife to strike. Henry flung the fellow from him, and ran for his life to the gate of the fort and called on Wenniway for protection. The chief ordered the savage to desist, but the latter, who was foaming at the mouth with rage, continued to strike furiously at him with his knife. Seeing Langlade's door open, the persecuted trader ran in and retreated to his snug garret, with the comfortable conviction, as he declares, that no Indian had power to harm him.

His confidence was somewhat shaken when he was suddenly aroused from sleep by a light shining in his eyes, and heard voices summoning him to descend. What was his surprise and joy to find in the room below, Captain Etherington, Lieut. Leslie, Bostwick a trader, with Father Jonois, a Jesuit priest. The savages were about to enjoy another grand debauch, and their chiefs, knowing the extreme danger to which the captives would be exposed during these mad orgies, had conveyed them all to the fort and put them in charge of the Canadians. Including officers, soldiers and traders, about twenty in all escaped the massacre.

When Henry entered the room he found his three companions in earnest debate as to seizing the fort again, which the Indians, drunken and with their usual recklessness, had actually left occupied by twenty Englishmen and about three hundred Canadians. They had even neglected to place a guard within the palisades. To close the gates and set the

Indians at defiance appeared to be no difficult matter. Through the dissuasions of the priest, who argued that the Canadians would probably prove treacherous, and that if a failure should result, every Englishman in the place would be butchered, the daring but feasible project was abandoned.

Next day Henry had to embark, in company with two traders and a soldier and guarded by seven Indians, in a canoe for the Isles du Castor. The heavy mists and the tempestuous weather compelled them to hug the shore, close beneath the wet, dripping forests. They had proceeded thus about twenty miles, when an Ottawa hailed them from the beach, asking the news and who were their prisoners. Some remarks followed while the canoe was approaching the shore, being in very shallow water. All at once a shrill yell was heard, and a hundred Ottawas, rising from among the trees and bushes, rushed into the water and seized upon the canoe and prisoners.

The astounded Ojibwas remonstrated in vain. The four whites were taken from them, and led to the shore. It turned out that the Ottawas were jealous and angry that the Ojibwas should have taken the fort and they have no share of the plunder. They professed much good will to the prisoners, assuring them that the Ojibwas were carrying them to the Isles du Castor merely to kill and eat them. The poor prisoners now found themselves on another canoe and going back to the fort so recently left. A flotilla of canoes, filled with Ottawas, accompanied them. They soon arrived, the Ojibwas looking on in silent amazement. The Ottawa warriors took no notice, but, all well armed, filed into the fort and took possession.

The English looked upon the new-comers as protectors, but were somewhat disappointed, for the next day the Ojibwa Chiefs invited the Ottawa leaders to a council, placed before them presents, and their great war-chief, Miniavavana, who had conducted the fort attack, addressed them with much feeling, saying that their conduct had much surprised him; that they had betrayed the common cause; opposed the will of the Great Spirit, which had decreed that every Englishman must die. Pontiac had taken Detroit (which was false,) and every other fort had been destroyed. All Indians but this band of Ottawas had taken up the hatchet, and the French king had awakened from his sleep. He concluded by exhorting them to join the rest.

The council now adjourned to the next day to give time to deliberate, when the rebuked Ottawas concurred with the Ojibwa views, and returned them some of the prisoners, retaining, however, the officers and a few of the soldiers. These they soon after carried to L'Arbre Croche and treated with kindness. The priest afterwards took a letter to Detroit from Etherington, telling Gladwyn of the capture of the fort and asking immediate aid. This, of course, as we shall soon show, Gladwyn could not do, he himself being in the most desperate straits.

The Ojibwas now carried the prisoners thus returned to them to one of their villages not far distant, and placed them in the council lodge as a prison, all who chose coming to jeer at and deride them. At the head sat the great war chief, Miniavavana, and, by his side, Henry's master, Wenniway. Shortly after, Henry observed an Indian stooping to enter at the low door, and to his great joy, recognized his friend and brother, Wawatam, who had, previous to the massacre, so earnestly begged him to go with him to the Sault. Wawatam said nothing, but as he passed the trader, pressed his hand, and then, proceeding to the head of the lodge, sat down with Wenniway and the war chief. After all had smoked awhile in silence, Wawatam went out, and soon returned with his squaw, bringing in her hand a valuable present, which she laid at the feet of the two chiefs. Wawatam then addressed them in an earnest and most feeling speech. Pointing to Henry, he expressed his surprise at seeing him a slave whom all knew was his brother, and if a relative to him, then also to them; and if so, then he could not, by their customs, be a slave. He then boldly charged Miniavavana with breach of faith, since, being fearful that Wawatam, on account of his love for Henry, would reveal the secret of the intended massacre, he had persuaded him to cross the lake, which Wawatam had agreed to do on the *express condition* that Miniavavana would protect Henry, his friend and brother. He now claimed the performance of this promise, and brought valuable presents to buy off any claim which any one could have upon his brother as a prisoner.

Wawatam had his will, and Henry soon found himself in the lodge of his rejoiced friend, where rich furs were spread for him to lie upon, food and drink brought for his refreshment, and everything done to promote his comfort that an ungrudging Indian hospitality could suggest. As he lay there in state in his lodge the next day, he heard a loud cry, and, looking through a crevice in the bark, saw the bodies of seven soldiers dragged out. He learned afterwards that a noted chief had just arrived from his wintering ground, and having come too late to take part in the fort massacre, he was anxious to manifest by this slaughter of victims how much he approved the proceedings. He had, therefore, calmly dispatched seven of the prisoners with his own knife.

After a great victory by the Indians, it often happens that bodies of their victims are consumed at a formal war feast, in order, as they superstitiously think, that thus their courage and hardihood may be increased. Such a feast now took place, many of the chiefs, however, partaking with repugnance. Up to this point all had been triumph and exultation, but now a revulsion of feeling began to set in. The bloody victors grew fearful of the consequences. Absurd and indefinite rumors of an approaching revenge on the part of the English were afloat in the camp and they thought best to shift position to some more defensible locality. Three hundred and fifty warriors, with their families and household effects, embarked in canoes for the Island of Machillimackinac, Wawatam and Henry being of the number. A storm arose and the flotilla was so much in imminent peril, that prayers to the Great Spirit went up and a dog was sacrificed to appease the angry Manitou of the waters. This island (now called Mackinaw), owing to its beautiful location, its natural bridges and caverns of rocks, its charming surroundings, and the excellent fish with which the waters teemed, had long been a favorite resort of the Indians, and the lodges were set up with joy. But on the very next day messengers arrived from Pontiac to the effect that he was now besieging Detroit, and urged them to come to his aid. Their fierceness, however, had now all died out. A senseless alarm prevailed among them. A vigilant watch was kept day and night. The fish having mysteriously disappeared, famine, too, began to be felt. No complaints were heard, but with that stoical resignation which so distinguishes the red race, they patiently endured the inevitable. They gradually had to disperse to localities where food was more abundant. Henry, painted and attired like an Indian, remained with his friend Wawatam all Summer and Winter, fishing and hunting the bear and moose for a subsistence.

Obstinate Defence of Presq' Isle Fort.

Let us now turn to the capture of Presq' Isle Fort, which stood near the site of the present town of Erie, on the lake of the same name. At one of its angles stood a massive, two-storied block-house, located on a projecting spit of land between the lake and a small brook, the bank of which, unfortunately, rose in a high, steep ridge, affording an excellent cover for assailants, while the lake bank offered similar facilities on another side.

At early dawn on the 15th of June, the little garrison, commanded by Ensign Christie, saw themselves surrounded by two hundred Huron savages. At the first alarm they abandoned the main fort and took to the block-house. The savages, availing themselves of every commanding position, crowded about the doomed fort and poured in a perfect hail of fire, searching out with their unerring missiles every vulnerable spot or crevice. They also shot fire arrows on the dry shingle roof, repeatedly setting it on fire, and hurled balls of burning pitch against the walls. Then they rolled logs to the top of the ridges and from behind these secure breastworks, they fired with still greater effect. Some even had the temerity to dart across the interval and attempt to shelter themselves in the ditch, but all of these were killed or wounded.

And now the tired defenders could see their implacable foes throwing up earth and stone behind their breastworks, a sure evidence of undermining. A still more imminent peril threatened in the total failure of water, which had been exhausted in putting out the frequent fires. To pproach the well on the parade ground would be instant death, and so a new well was dug in the block-house itself. Before it was completed, the roof was again on fire and all the water that remained was poured out. Again the flames burst forth, when a soldier averted the total destruction of the place by leaping upon the roof amid a hail of hurtling bullets and tearing off the blazing shingles.

Evening had now arrived. From earliest dawn, without one moment's intermission, the heroic little garrison had fought or toiled. All night long was seen the constant flashing of guns from the Indian entrenchments. Morning brought fresh perils. Fortunate was it that now the well was complete, for the indefatigable foe had pushed their subterranean approaches as far as the commandant's house, which was set on fire, stifling the defenders with the intense heat and smoke. The outer wall of the block-house itself scorched, blackened and at length burst into flame. Still this Spartan band refused to yield, but passing up water from the new well, they finally subdued the fierce flames.

The men were now utterly exhausted, yet still they toiled on within the wooden walls of their prison house, where the close air was sulphurous with the smoke of gunpowder. The fire continued until midnight of the second day, at which dread hour a bugle voice was heard crying out in French from the enemy's hold, that further resistance would be useless since all was now prepared for setting the block-house on fire from above and beneath at once. Christie asked if there were any among them who spoke English; upon which a soldier Briton who had been long prisoner with the savages, came out, in his Indian dress, from behind the breastwork. He promised, if they yielded now, their lives should be spared; if they longer fought, they must all be burned alive.

Christie, resolving to hold out as long as possible, asked them to wait till morning. Agreed to, and while some of the garrison watched, the rest sank down in their tracks and snatched a hasty sleep. Next morning Christie sent out two soldiers, as if to treat with the enemy, but, in reality, to learn truly whether they were able to set fire to the blockhouse. A preconcerted signal made by the two men, soon after reaching the breastwork, warned him that the insidious foe had made no idle boast. Two chiefs now met Christie between the breastwork and block-house, and to them this lake fort, defended with such intrepidity, was finally surrendered, on the express condition that the lives of the whole garrison should be spared, and they be allowed to retire to the nearest post.

The poor soldiers, pale, wild and haggard, like men who had passed through the fire and smoke of dreadful battle, now issued from the block-house, and were immediately seized and afterwards sent to Detroit, whence Christie soon after made a successful escape. The neighboring posts of Venango and Le Boeuf—the very ones which Washington visited while they belonged to France, several years before—fell an easy prey at the same time.

PONTIAC'S SIEGE OF DETROIT—AN OJIBWA MAID REVEALS THE PLOT.

And now what about Detroit, the most important and formidable post of all, and hence entrusted to the wily and powerful Pontiac himself! The British garrison, at this time consisting of a hundred and twenty soldiers, partly regulars and partly American rangers, with about forty fur-traders, was quartered in a well-built range of barracks within the fort, which contained within its enclosure about a hundred houses. Its form was nearly square, a wooden bastion at each corner, a block-house over each gateway, and the palisades surrounding and connecting all, about twenty-five feet high. Besides the barracks, the only public buildings were a council house and a rude little church.

The fur-traders, voyageurs and other Canadian occupants, could not be trusted in case of an Indian outbreak. The banks of the Detroit river, connecting Lakes Erie and St. Clair and running before the fort's gates, were sparsely settled for many miles, chiefly by Indian fishermen and Canadians engaged in the Indian trade. Two small armed schooners, the Beaver and Gladwyn, lay anchored in the stream, and several light pieces of artillery were mounted on the bastions. Within the limits of the settlement were three large Indian villages. A little below the fort were the Pottawattamies: directly across the river was a Wyandot village, and on the same side, five miles further up towards Lake St. Clair, Pontiac's band of Ottawas had an encampment. The fort was fortunate in having as commandant, Major Gladwyn, a British officer of pluck, merit and resolution, who had been one of Braddock's most trustworthy officers, and wounded at his memorable defeat.

On the afternoon of May 5th, a Canadian woman was on a visit to Pontiac's village to buy venison and maple sugar. She was startled at finding some of the warriors filing off the barrels of their guns, so as to reduce the length, stock and barrel, to about a yard. On her return she told what she had seen to some neighbors, when a blacksmith remarked that many of the savages had lately visited his shop and desired to borrow saws and files for a purpose which they would not disclose. The Canadians were suspicious. M. Gouin, an old and wealthy settler, went to Gladwyn and conjured him to be watchful. But little heed was given to the friendly advice.

In the Pottawattamie village lived a pretty Ojibwa girl who was on most intimate terms with Gladwyn. The very next day Catharine, as she was called, repaired to Gladwyn's quarters with a pair of elk-skin moccasins, wrought with porcupine quills in divers figures, which he had requested her to make. There was something unusual in her manner; her face was sad and downcast; she said little and soon left the room, but continued loitering around as if her errand were yet unaccomplished. At length Gladwyn's notice was attracted, and calling her in he pressed to know what was on her mind. She gave various excuses, but finally, on Gladwyn's urging her, she was induced to reluctantly reveal her dread secret.

To-morrow, she said, Pontiac, with a large crowd of chiefs, will come to the fort, each armed with a shortened gun hidden under his blanket. Pontiac would demand to hold a friendly council, and after his speech would be over he would offer a wampum belt, which would be the signal for an attack by the chiefs on the officers. These dispatched, they would then join their warriors in the streets, who, with curtailed rifles, likewise concealed, would push into the town under the pretence of trading. Every Englishman was to be butchered, but not the scalp of a Canadian would be touched.

Gladwyn, it may well be supposed, was astounded at this intelligence. He gathered all the information he could from the girl, and called his officers together. The garrison was weak, and the defences flimsy and in bad order. Every preparation was made to meet the possible if not probable emergency. Half the garrison were ordered under arms, and Gladwyn himself was so uneasy that he walked the ramparts that night and saw personally to every man's being at his post. As he thus anxiously paced the ramparts, he heard, at intervals, sounds of fearful portent—the dull, monotonous beat of the Indian drum and the wild chorus of quavering yells, as the warriors, around their distant camp fires, were celebrating in advance the triumphs of the dread to-morrow.

At early sun, a cloud of bark canoes could be seen sweeping swiftly down the Detroit river. The plains about the fort began to be dotted over with groups of squaws and warriors, some naked and others fantastically arrayed in barbarous finery. Grim warriors, closely wrapped in their gaudy blankets, could be seen stalking with erect forms, with

An Indian Maid Betraying Pontiac's Plot to Gladwyn.
SEE PAGE 123.

springy steps and restless, gleaming eyes towards the fort. Then with an air of assumed indifference they would lounge about or edge over towards the gate.

All this stirring panorama of savage life boded no good. It seemed to confirm the Indian girl's tale. None but Gladwyn and his officers knew the secret, and they were prepared. The chiefs, headed by the majestic figure of Pontiac, had now made a landing, and strode, with furtive looks and measured steps towards the great gate. All were at once admitted, Gladwyn choosing to convince his crafty foes that though their treachery was detected, it was also despised. The whole garrison had been early ordered under arms, and commands had been issued to the traders that, as a large concourse of savages was to be held in the town that morning, it would be well to close their stores and arm their men. A Canadian going to his home, had shortly before met Pontiac and his sixty chiefs, all marching in Indian file. As he stood aside to let them pass, he recognized among them an old and familiar acquaintance. The savage returned his salutation with a deep, sullen voice, opened for an instant the folds of his blanket, revealing the rifle beneath, and with a smile and gesture of a peculiar significance, strode on with his fellows.

And now the file of stern, proud and plumed chiefs are fairly within the palisades. All were wrapped to the throats with blankets. Their eyes gleamed around with the venom of the rattlesnake. As Pontiac's restless, roving glance caught the guard of soldiers and the rows of glistening arms ranged on either side of the gate, and as his quick ear caught the measured tap of the drum, he gave a sudden start, and a guttural exclamation of surprise and dismay came unbidden from his broad and swarthy breast. Even *his* vaunted stoicism was at fault as he beheld in these groups of soldierly and armed *engages* of the fur-traders, the probable ruin of his crafty plot. Stifling all signs of alarm, however, he and his haughty followers swept on to the council house. Entering, they saw Gladwyn and his officers seated in readiness to receive them, nor did their wary eyes fail to note that each had both sword and pistols in belt. All this, added to the fact of a larger number of troops than usual being visible, caused the conspirators to exchange meaning and uneasy glances.

"Why," coolly and calmly demanded Pontiac, "do I see so many of my father's young men standing with their guns in the street?" Gladwyn answered simply that it was for drill and exercise, with which answer Pontiac was fain to be content and straightway began his speech. Holding in his hand the fatal wampum belt, he professed the strongest attachment to the English and declared, with Indian figurativeness, that he had come to brighten the chain of friendship and smoke the pipe of peace. The officers watched him keenly, and when he raised the belt as if to give the preconcerted signal, at a motion from Gladwyn the clash of arms and peal of drum was heard from without.

Pontiac stood for a moment dazed and confounded! All his schemings dashed in an instant! The color mounted to his swarthy visage, and instead of giving the belt in the mode proposed, he handed it in the usual way and soon sat down alarmed and perplexed. The general version of this scene is, that Gladwyn rising from his seat, drew the chief's blanket aside, exposed the hidden gun and sternly rebuked him for his perfidy, but his own official letters do not confirm this, but state that he and his officers remained seated as before. It was manifestly his policy to prevent the fulfillment of the plot without bringing matters to an open rupture.

A silence which could be almost felt, ensued. At length Gladwyn arose, with calm eye and unruffled brow, and in a brief formal speech assured the assembled chiefs that he would extend friendship and protection so long as it was deserved, but that the first act of aggression on their part would be followed by a signal vengeance. The council then broke up, Pontiac stating that they would return in a few days with their squaws and children that they might all shake hands with their fathers, the English. The baffled and discomfited savages soon after took their departure, their hearts, if possible, burning with a still more venomous rancor at the ignominious failure of their deep-laid plot. This account differs materially from those given in the popular border books, but besides comporting better with the probabilities of the case, it agrees with Gladwyn's official report to Amherst, which distinctly states: "And Pontiac made a speech which I answered calmly, without intimating my suspicions of their intentions, and after receiving some trifling presents, they went away to their camp."

The foiled and chagrined Pontiac, baffled in the crafty scheme which he himself had conceived, retired to his hut to brood over his revenge. The snake was only scotched, not killed. He resolved to visit Gladwyn once more to convince him he had been deceived. The next day, bearing in his perfidious hand the sacred calumet of peace, he had the impudence to assert to the English that evil birds had sung lies in their ears; that they loved their English brothers, and to prove it, had come to smoke the pipe of peace. The same day he gathered the young men of all the tribes to a game of ball which took place with great noise and excitement. At nightfall the garrison was startled with loud discordant yells. The drums beat to arms and the troops were ordered to their posts. It proved, however, only the shouts of the victors, and all soon became silent as usual.

Hostilities Commenced.

The next day throngs of Indians commenced to gather about the fort and Pontiac, advancing singly from the multitude, approached the gate which he found barred against him. The baffled chief shouted to the sentinels and haughtily demanded why he was excluded. Gladwyn replied that he himself could enter if he wished, but his people must stay out. Thus openly rebuffed, the mask was now thrown off entirely. With a scowl of hate and an ejaculation of rage, Pontiac strode towards his followers who were lying in squads prone upon the ground, and at a signal all leaped up and ran like so many fiends towards the house of an Englishwoman who was at once made the first bloody victim. Another gang, with frightful yells, hurried to the river, leaped into their canoes, paddled swiftly to the Isle au Cochon and murdered an Englishman named Fisher, who lived there.

Hostilities Commenced—Officers Captured—Anecdotes of Pontiac.

Pontiac retired alone. He was terrible in his rage and none dare approach. Pushing a canoe from the shore, he drove it rapidly to the Ottawa town and imperiously ordered that it should be moved to the other shore. The enraged chief then, with tomahawk in hand, hideous in war paint and plumed for battle, leaped into the midst of his warriors, and brandishing his weapons, denounced vengeance on the cowardly English. The war dance over, a few hours found all the Ottawa community with huts pitched on the fort side of the river. A formidable band of ferocious Ojibwas from Saginaw river joined him. News came also to the fort of the murder of two English officers above Lake St. Clair.

The war had now commenced. Every Englishman in the fort was ordered under arms, and Gladwyn walked the ramparts all night. At the earliest streak of dawn the horrid war whoop was heard from all parts. The combined tribes environed the fort on every side but that on the river and a storm of leaden hail beat all day against the feeble barrier. With characteristic caution the savages scarcely ever revealed their forms. Within gunshot of the palisades was a cluster of outbuildings, behind which a swarm of the yelping reds found shelter, but at last, teased by their impudence, a cannon loaded with red-hot spikes was turned in their direction and the houses were soon in flames, upon which the disconcerted savages broke away in a body, and this was the first of a beleaguerment which endured for eight months and which was conducted with a skill, a system and a persistency that has no parallel in all Indian history. To give details of this long siege would fill a volume; we have only room for a mere mention of the more salient and interesting incidents which marked its course.

Gladwyn still believed that the whole outbreak was but a passing spasm of anger, and, being out of provisions, he concluded to open negotiations, under cover of which he could gather supplies. Accordingly La Butte, the interpreter, with two old Canadians, proceeded to the Indian camp and delivered their message. Pontiac was civil and courteous; listened patiently, but his heart was unmoved. The Canadians were deceived and La Butte hurried back with the report that peace might readily be had by a few timely gifts. On hurrying back, however, he found little progress had been made, Pontiac, with characteristic dissimulation, evading every direct proposal, but pretending that he wished to hold council with his English fathers and was especially desirous of seeing at his camp Major Campbell, the second in command, and a veteran officer who had gained their confidence by his justice and kindness. Gladwyn feared treachery, but the Major himself so pressed the mission that Campbell was at last permitted to depart to the Indian camp, accompanied by Lieutenant McDougal and several Canadians.

Meanwhile M. Gouin, in moving from lodge to lodge, soon saw and heard enough to convince him that the two officers were advancing into the lions' very jaws. He hastened to warn the advancing embassy. Too late! They would not be diverted but were soon approaching the little bridge that led over Parent's Creek, just beyond which lay Pontiac's camp. No sooner were the red uniforms noted than the swarming multitude raised a horrible outcry. The women and children seized clubs and stones and rushed forward as if intent upon making a gauntlet for the twain to run. Pontiac's stern voice, however, allayed the tumult. He shook hands and made a way for them to the central lodge, and pointing to some skins on the ground, bade them be seated. The lodge was at once thronged with chiefs, while a fierce, eager, jostling crowd of commoners glared at them, with tigerish looks, from the outside. Major Campbell answered Pontiac's curt speech, but was heard with an anxious silence. For a full hour the alarmed officers saw constantly before them the same dense throng of swarthy, inscrutable faces, bending on them a stony, unwavering glare. At length the anxious Major, desirous of testing his true position, arose to go to the fort. Pontiac made signs for him to resume his seat. "My father," he said in his deep, guttural tones, "will sleep to-night in the lodges of his red children."

The gray-haired veteran was a prisoner! Many were burning to sacrifice the two officers on the spot, but Pontiac was too politic for that extreme measure. They were conducted to the house of M.

Miloche and treated well. If two Indians had not happened at the time to be their prisoners at the fort, they would probably have had a short shrift. Next day Pontiac crossed to the Wyandot camp and succeeded in winning the whole tribe—which had hitherto been divided—to join in the war. They were the best fighters of all the tribes and soon after distinguished themselves.

Hostilities were now resumed, but with more system than before. At a meeting of officers, Gladwyn alone, it is said, favored holding out. Their condition was desperate. Provisions were scarce. The houses were of wood, thatched with straw, and could easily be inflamed, and a general onslaught—which could scarcely be resisted—was feared. This threat, however, was entirely contrary to Indian tactics. Their skill consists in winning without loss. A victory with them is considered dearly purchased by the death of a single warrior. Time passed on without any change or relief. For many weeks all slept in their clothes. Volunteer parties sallied out and cut down trees, or destroyed buildings until the dusky foe had no shelter. The two vessels in the river, sweeping the northern and southern curtains of the work with their fire, were of great aid in keeping off the swarming savages. Still, however, these wormed their way through the grass, or taking advantage of every shelter, would manage to crawl unobserved close to the palisades and let fly their arrows, tipped with burning tow. Water, however, was ever ready, and all such attempts proved abortive.

Pontiac neglected no art or wile that savage tactics could suggest. He even endeavored to draw from the French all they knew about the European methods of attacking a fortified place by regular approaches. He sent word, also, to Gladwyn, that if the place was given up, he might safely return with his whole force aboard his vessels, but that if he persisted, all would be burnt alive. Gladwyn answered, he cared nothing for empty threats; yet still he was overwhelmed with anxiety, for he now learned that over a hundred fierce Ojibwas from Grand river had joined Pontiac, and all, English and Canadian, slept, with arms ready, upon the ramparts. Every effort was made to gather and husband every kind of provisions, but, notwithstanding all, the post must have been abandoned had not a few Canadians provided it, in the most secret method, with cattle, hogs and other supplies. For a long time the Indians were kept ignorant of what was going forward in this line, and they themselves commenced to suffer from hunger.

Pontiac at first visited all the Canadian houses on both sides of the river and squeezed them bare of supplies. To deputations complaining of these proceedings, he made earnest and artful speeches, asserting that he and his men were fighting the British on French account; that he had not called on them for aid, but that his warriors must be fed. Pontiac then organized a regular commissariat and issued bills of credit drawn upon birch bark, signed with the figure of an otter, and, what is a greater marvel, they were punctually redeemed. Pontiac was the brains of all. He was ever on the alert, endeavoring to learn all he could, and exceedingly curious as to the best modes of making war and of manufacturing cloth, knives, guns, and other articles needed. General Gage himself stated, as a testimony to his keen and subtle genius, that he kept two secretaries, one to write and one to read messages, and managed to keep each of them ignorant of what was transacted by the other. Major Rogers, who was intimately acquainted with him, says: "He puts on an air of majesty and princely grandeur, and is greatly honored and revered by all his subjects. Although undeniably artful, treacherous and revengeful, yet, according to Indian ideas of honor and virtue, he was bold, fierce and ambitious." Two anecdotes will serve to show his character:

Some time after Rogers came up with his troops, he sent Pontiac a bottle of brandy, as a present, by the hands of a friendly Indian. Those about the chief, always suspicious that the English wished to dispatch such a powerful enemy and get him out of the way, argued that the brandy was drugged, and that he should not touch it. Pontiac listened quietly, poured out a cup of the liquor, and immediately quaffed it off, saying that the man whose life he had once saved had no power to kill him. At another time, during the siege, he quietly entered the house of M. Baby, who was the Canadian known to be most friendly to the English, and the one who had secretly supplied them with provisions, &c. Seating himself by the fire he, for some time, looked steadily at the embers. At length he said that he had heard the English had offered Baby a bushel of silver for the scalp of his friend, Pontiac. Baby indignantly scouted the story. Pontiac keenly studied his face, and said, "My brother has spoken the truth, and I will show that I believe him." He then remained all evening, and composedly wrapping himself in his blanket, he slept in full confidence till morning. At another time Baby complained that some Wyandots came night after night and stole his hogs and cattle. Pontiac stealthily arrived at the house about midnight, and pacing to and fro among his friend's barns, he at length discerned the dark forms of the plunderers stealing through the gloom. He appeared before them like an apparition. "Go back to your village, you Wyandot dogs! If you tread again on this man's lands, you die!" They slunk back abashed. Over the Wyandots Pontiac could claim no legitimate authority, yet his powerful spirit forced respect and obedience from all who approached him.

A Large Convoy Captured—A Thrilling Boat Scene.

While all this was going on, the British commandant at New York was ignorant of Gladwyn's danger. With the opening of Spring, however, a supply of provisions and ammunition had been sent up the lakes for the use of Detroit and other posts above. The boats of this convoy were now approaching, and Gladwyn's garrison awaited their coming with increasing anxiety. Gladwyn ordered one of his vessels to Niagara to hasten forward the convoy. The schooner set sail, but the very next day, as she lay becalmed at the entrance of Lake Erie, she was surrounded by a cloud of canoes, in the foremost of which was placed, as a protection from hostile shot, the veteran Major Campbell; but the brave old man at once called out never to mind him, but to fire away. Happily at that moment a fresh breeze sprang up, and the schooner escaped. On May 30th all Detroit was thrown into a wonderful stir by the announcement of a look-out that the long-expected convoy was in sight: at some distance below could be seen a line of boats, England's flag over them, and their oars flashing in the sun. With one accord the excited garrison and populace broke into three hearty cheers, while a cannon from one of the bastions sent out its roar of welcome. But suddenly every cheek was blanched with horror! Dark, naked figures were seen rising, with wild gesture, in the boats, while in lieu of the expected responsive salute could be faintly heard in the distance the triumphant whoop of the savage. Horrible thought! The convoy was in the hands of the enemy! Officers and men stood gazing with mournful silence, when a thrilling incident just then occurred which caused their hearts for a time to stand still.

In each of the approaching boats, of which there were eighteen, several of the captured soldiers were (guarded by many armed savages) compelled to act as rowers. In the first, as it happened somehow, were four soldiers but only three savages. As stated, one of the two vessels which lay along the water front of the fort had been sent to Niagara to hasten up this very convoy. The other lay anchored in the stream, and when the first of the advancing flotilla came opposite to it, the steersman conceived a daring plan of escape. He called to his comrade to seize the Indian who sat in front and throw him overboard. The man answered that he was not strong enough, and so, as if fatigued with rowing, the two changed places. As the bold soldier stepped forward, he suddenly seized the powerful savage by his scalp lock and with the other hand gripping his girdle, he gave him a lift and tossed him into the river. The boat rocked till the water surged over the gunwale. The indomitable savage, thus so unceremoniously treated, would not let go, but clinging fast to the soldier's clothes and drawing himself upwards, he stabbed the soldier again and again, and then dragged him over. Both went down the swift current, engaged in a death-grapple, and finally sank from sight, a few ripples and gurgles only serving to show the place of disappearance. The other two Indians leaped from the boat, while the two remaining soldiers shouted for aid and pulled for the vessel. The savages on shore opened a heavy fire, while the other boats darted forward in close pursuit. The poor soldiers strained every nerve to escape. One of them was soon wounded, and the light canoes rapidly gained on their boat. Escape seemed hopeless, when all at once flash! boom! and a ball from the anchored vessel came dancing along the water, marking its way by a line of foam and narrowly missing the foremost canoe. The pursuers paused in dismay; a second shot scatters the Indians on shore, and the prisoners reach the vessel in safety, and are soon surrounded with an eager, questioning throng.

The story they related was a sad one. Lieut. Cuyler had left Fort Niagara, May 13, with ninety-six men. They had made almost their whole journey without seeing a foe, when, on the 28th, the boats had landed not far from the mouth of Detroit river. A man and boy entered the woods to gather fire-wood, when a skulking savage leaped out and cleft his head with a single blow of his tomahawk. Cuyler immediately formed his band in a semicircle before the boats, when the enemy opened fire from their ambush, and after a hot blaze of musketry for a while, the whole painted, yelping body of them broke from the woods with horrible yells, and rushed with the greatest impetuosity upon the very centre of the line, which was at once broken and put to flight, the men becoming panic stricken, flinging down their guns and rushing to their boats. Five of these were gotten into the water and pushed off crowded with the terrified troops. Cuyler found himself utterly deserted, and was compelled to wade up to his neck and scramble into one of the boats. The yelling savages, crowding two more of the boats that were abandoned, gave immediate pursuit, capturing three of the five boats, their hapless crews making little or no resistance. The other two, in which was Cuyler, made their escape.

They rowed all night, landing in the morning on a small island. Between thirty and forty men were crowded in these two; the rest were all carried captive. Cuyler now turned back and made for Fort Sandusky, which finding destroyed, he rowed on to Presq' Isle, and thence back to Niagara. The victors in this well-planned stroke were the Wyandots or Hurons, who, for some days, had lain in ambush at the mouth of the Detroit. Seeing the confusion of the soldiers, they had forgotten their usual caution, and secured success by a prompt and vigorous rush. All the valuable stores fell prize to the savages, but the whiskey was nearly undoing them. It was carried to the respective camps, and for days they presented scenes of riot and revelry. The hot and maddening liquor was poured into birchen vessels, and the savages would crowd about, scoop it up in double-handfuls and quaff it off like so much water.

The effect may be imagined. While some sat apart totally overcome or wailing, whining and moaning in maudlin drunkenness, the major part were excited to beastly ferocity. Old quarrels were kindled afresh and jealousies among the different tribes awakened, and had not the poor squaws taken the precaution to hide all the weapons, there would have been a wholesale slaughter. As it was, some were killed, many were wounded, and others had their noses completely bitten off. The same evening two of the revelers came running directly towards the fort in all the vain-glory and pot-valor inspired by these deep potations, but being arrested by two leaden messengers, they leaped high into the air like a pair of wounded bucks and fell dead in their tracks.

Frightful Massacre of Prisoners—Capture of More Forts Announced.

Horrible, indeed, was the fate of all the poor prisoners! At night some Canadians came into the fort bringing appalling and sickening reports of the dreadful scenes enacted at the Indian camps. The soldiers, beginning to fear a like miserable fate, gathered about them, and, frozen with horror, listened to the shocking and frightful narratives. A deep gloom settled down upon the devoted garrison. Ten days after, naked corpses, gashed with knives, scorched with fire and mutilated out of all semblance to humanity, came floating down the pure waters of the Detroit, where fish came up to nibble and gnaw at the clotted blood that clung to their ghastly faces. We naturally hesitate to detail the awful tortures inflicted upon these unhappy prisoners. Sixty-four of the sixty-six were compelled to run the gauntlet, and were then subjected to all the numerous tortures that Indian ingenuity could devise. All, all their hellish skill was utterly exhausted in devising new modes of inflicting agony. The remaining two, who were too much exhausted to run the gauntlet, were inhumanly clubbed to death.

Not long after, the garrison saw issuing from the woods which extended beyond the pastures in the rear of the fort, a line of savages painted entirely black, each bearing a scalp fluttering from the end of a pole. This was to announce the fate of Fort Sandusky, which had been attacked by a band of Hurons. Among the few survivors was the commandant, Ensign Paully, who had been brought to Pontiac's camp, pelted by squaws and children with stones and sticks, and forced to sing and dance for the amusement of his tormentors. He was saved by a hideous old hag, who chose to adopt him in place of her deceased warrior. Having no other alternative but the stake, poor Paully for a while did the honors of the Ottawa family. Gladwyn soon received a letter from this impromptu Indian husband, giving a full account of Fort Sandusky's capture. Paully had been informed that seven Indians whom he knew, were waiting at the gate to speak with him. He ordered them to be admitted. Arrived at his quarters, two of the treacherous scoundrels seated themselves on either side, the rest being scattered about the room. The pipes were lighted and pow-wowing began, when a reddy, who stood in the door-way, made the signal, and suddenly the astounded Ensign was pounced upon and disarmed, while outside could be heard the confused noise of yells and shrieks, the firing of guns and the hurried tramp of feet. Soon after, led forth by his captors, Paully saw the parade ground strewn with the corpses of his butchered garrison. He was then put in a canoe, and as, amid thick darkness, the party pushed from the shore, their path was illumined by the sheets of flame bursting out on all sides from the doomed fort. On the heels of this news came the knowledge that two more strong bands of Ojibwas had joined Pontiac, swelling his force to near a thousand warriors.

The sleepless garrison, worn out by fatigue and privations, and harassed by constant petty attacks and alarms, were yet farther saddened by thickening tidings of disaster. Of all the posts scattered through the vast wilderness west of Niagara, their own and Fort Pitt alone held out. On June 15th a number of Pottawattamies approached the gate with four prisoners. The Indians wished an exchange, which was effected. They proved to be Ensign Schlosser and three privates from the post of St. Joseph, which stood at the head of Lake Michigan among the swamps and solitudes, and at an unmeasured distance from the abodes of civilization. On May 25th an officer learned that the fort was surrounded with savages, and that the parade was also crowded with them—all very insolent and disorderly.

While busying himself mustering together the Canadians, Ensign Schlosser heard a wild cry from the barracks. The sentinel at the gate was tomahawked and a free passage opened to the surging crowd without. In less than two minutes the fort was plundered, eleven men killed, and Schlosser with the only three survivors bound fast and carried to Detroit. Then came the awful news from Forts Machillimackinac and Miami and Presq' Isle—which we have already anticipated. Had American rangers garrisoned all these posts, some of them, it is probable, might have been saved, but foreign troops were not well qualified, either by discipline or experience, for coping with the wily and snaky redmen of the west. It required a long and a peculiar kind of training.

On June 19th a rumor reached Gladwyn from without that the vessel he had some time previously sent to Niagara had appeared off Turkey Island, and was awaiting a favorable breeze to work up the stream. She had gone to Niagara where she remained until Cuyler's return making known the miserable fate of his enterprise. Taking him and the survivors aboard, the vessel hastened back to Detroit, and was now almost within sight of the fort, but how to safely reach it—there was the problem remaining to be solved! The river channel was in some places narrow, and nearly a thousand Indians, led on by such a plotter as Pontiac, were on the alert to obstruct a passage. Nothing was heard more of the vessel for several days, when a great commotion was visible among the redskins outside, large parties of whom could be seen passing down the river. In the evening came the news that the vessel was attempting to ascend the stream and that all the savages had gone down to prevent her, upon which two cannon were fired as an announcement that the fort still stood.

Let us see how it fared on board the little ship so anxiously expected. She had entered the channel between the main shore and Fighting Island, having on board about sixty men, but only a few visible on deck. The rest were carefully kept concealed in the hope that thus an Indian attack might be induced. Just before reaching the narrowest part of the channel, the wind died away and the anchor was dropped. Right above, the redskins had erected on Turkey Island and behind a "blind" of bushes, a log breastwork. Ignorant of this but still wary and cautious, the crew kept strict watch for hours. At last night came down. The current plashed with a monotonous sound about the bows of the schooner, while on either hand the densely-wooded shores lay shrouded in deepest obscurity.

At length the keen-eyed sentinel in the shrouds thought he could discern various moving objects. The men were quietly ordered upon deck and all made ready for resisting an attack. A hammer blow on the mast was to be the signal to fire. A flotilla of birch canoes, filled with dark, crouching forms, kept gliding stealthily down and about the ship, when suddenly the dark side of the slumbering vessel burst into a blaze of musketry. From the ponderous jaws of the cannon also was belched forth a hail of hurtling grape which flew tearing among the frail canoes, destroying several, putting the rest to flight, killing fourteen Indians and wounding many more. Recovering from their surprise, the Indians commenced a fire from their concealed breastworks, upon which the schooner tripped her anchor and dropped down the river. Several days after she had better success, for although constantly fired on, she forced a channel and signalized her approach by sending a thick shower of grape among the huts of the Wyandot village, killing some and causing the rest to decamp yelpingly for the sheltering woods. Then furling her sails she lay peacefully at anchor beside her consort.

The schooner brought the long-needed supplies, as also the important news that the seven-year war was over and that peace had formally been declared between France and England. All Canada had been ceded to England, and the French about Detroit were subjects of King George. To many this news was exceedingly repugnant, and they went about the beleaguering hosts, asserting that the peace news was but a weak invention of Gladwyn; that the French King would never abandon his children, and that even then a great army was ascending the St. Lawrence, while another was coming over from the Illinois. Pontiac and his dusky bands clung tenaciously to this delusive hope, and he showed no let-up in his zeal and activity, but sent a message to Gladwyn strongly urging his surrender, adding that eight hundred Ojibwas were daily expected, and that all his influence could not prevent them from taking the scalp of every resisting Briton. The friendly invitation was rejected with scorn.

The Ottawa chief now made a determined effort to range the Canadians on his side and force them to take an active part. He called them to a grand council and harangued them with all the tact, fervor and eloquence of which he was the well-known master. He concluded thus: "You must be either wholly French or wholly English! If you are French, take up that war belt and lift the hatchet with us! but if English, then we declare war upon *you*. My brothers, I know this is a hard thing, but there is no choice. Look upon the belt and let us hear your answer?"

One of the Canadians made an answering speech, in which he held up the French King's proclamation, telling all his Canadian children to sit quiet and obey the English till he came, and pertinently asked Pontiac what he could reply to that. The Ottawa chief sat for a moment silent, mortified and perplexed, but made other speeches, the result of which was that he secured the enlistment of a lot of low, swaggering trappers, voyageurs, half-breeds and other nondescript vagabonds of the woods who were hanging about attired in Indian leggins and ornaments. The better class of Canadians, however, were shocked at this defection and protested against it. Pontiac, however, shook hands with the renegades, gave them a grand feast of dogs the next day, and the next night a mixed party of these whites and Indians entrenched themselves near the fort.

OLD MAJOR CAMPBELL BUTCHERED—INDIANS SEND DOWN FIRE RAFTS.

At daybreak they were detected; the gate was thrown open and Lieutenant Hay, with a picked party, rushed forth and dislodged them. It happened that a soldier who had been several years a Delaware prisoner, knelt down before one of the savages, who had been killed in the sortie, tore away the scalp and shook it exultingly towards the fugitives. This act excited wonderful rage among the Indians and proved the death warrant of poor Major Campbell. The same evening a white man was seen running briskly towards the fort, closely pursued by Indians. The panting fugitive was admitted by the wicket, and proved to be Paully, the commandant of Sandusky, who, as stated, had married an old squaw and was so profoundly disgusted with his bargain that he preferred to risk his death rather than longer endure her odious embraces.

Through him the horrified garrison heard of Major Campbell's fate. The Indian who had been that morning killed and scalped proved to be a nephew to Wasson, a great Ojibwa chief. On hearing of the death, the infuriated uncle blackened his face in sign of revenge, assembled party, and repairing to Meloche's house, where Campbell was confined, they seized, bound and shot him to death with arrows, and then mutilated his body in a most barbarous manner. His heart was eaten to make them courageous, a practice not uncommon among Indians after killing a foe of acknowledged bravery, and of which we shall give hereafter a most notable instance in the case of the gallant Major Sam McColloch, of West Virginia. Pontiac, according to some, was privy to the act, but according to others, he was greatly incensed at it and Wasson was obliged to fly to Saginaw to escape his fury. Lieutenant McDougal had previously made good his escape.

The two armed schooners now commenced to diversify the monotony of the long siege by tacking every now and then up and down the river and battering the Indian camps and villages. They soon became to the Indians objects of revengeful hate, and attention was turned to their destruction. One night in July a blazing raft, formed of two boats tied together by ropes and filled with pitch-pine and other combustibles, was sent down, but missed. Several nights after, the look-out saw a vivid, glowing spark on the water above, which grew brighter and brighter, and larger and larger, till it arose in a forked flame and then burst out into a conflagration. It was a fire raft and narrowly missed the vessels, passing down between them and the fort, brightly gilding their tracery of ropes and spars, lighting up the bastions and formal rows of palisades, disclosing the white Canadian cottages on either shore and revealing the dusky margin of the gloomy forest, behind and in front of them lines of dusky savages, who expectantly stood opposite to watch the effect of their artifice.

Lo and behold, now a flash is seen! a loud thunder breaks the stillness and a shower of grape drives the disappointed spectators under cover. Undeterred by these failures, the savages commence a third raft, much larger and different and more formidable in construction than the others, but on hearing that Gladwyn had moored boats connected by chains far in advance of the ships, they found their four days' work would be in vain and desisted.

It was now several months since the commencement of the siege. The Indians had displayed a higher degree of steadiness and persistence than had ever been displayed in their history, but some now commenced to flag in their zeal. A few Wyandots came to the fort and begged for peace, which was granted. Pottawattamies followed, who, upon delivering up the captives among them, were also allowed peace. The fort, however, was still closely besieged by the Ottawas and Ojibwas.

In the meantime, without the knowledge of the weary garrison, a strong reinforcement was on its way. Captain Dalzell had left Niagara with twenty-two barges, bearing two hundred and eighty men, with cannon, ammunition, &c. Passing Presq' Isle, they viewed with surprise its scorched and blackened block-house and the mines and breastworks made by the Indians: thence they went to Fort Sandusky—or rather its site—and marching inward, they burnt a Huron village, destroyed their crops, and successfully made their way up Detroit river, under cover of a heavy fog. As soon as the mists had rolled away, the garrison were summoned to behold the approaching convoy. A salute from the fort was at once answered from the boats, and all apprehension of its having fallen into the enemy's hands, was removed. The savages opened a hot fire, and managed to kill and wound fifteen of the troops, who belonged to the fifty-fifth and eightieth regiments, together with—last, but by no means least—twenty American rangers, headed by the gallant Major Rogers.

The ardent Dalzell wished to lose no time, and strongly insisted with Gladwyn that the hour was at length come when an overwhelming blow should be delivered to Pontiac. He asked permission to march out the following night and attack Pontiac's camp. Gladwyn, better acquainted with the strength and character of the foe he had opposed to him, was decidedly averse to the movement, but finally yielded a reluctant consent. Pontiac had lately moved his camp from the mouth of Parent's Creek, and was now posted several miles above, behind a great marsh, where his camp could be secure against the ship's cannon. Preparations were now actively made for an attack, but, by an inexcusable carelessness, the design was made known to a few Canadians.

A Fierce and Desperate Struggle at Bloody Run.

About two o'clock on the morning of July 31st, the devoted band, two hundred and fifty, all told, filed noiselessly out into the road and commenced their march, flanked on the water side by two large batteaux, each bearing a swivel on the bow. Lieutenant Brown had the advance, Captain Gray the centre, and Captain Grant the rear. The night was still, close and sultry, and the men marched in a light undress. The watch dogs barked as they passed the row of Canadian cottages, and the aroused inmates heard the heavy, measured tramp, tramp, tramp, and looked on the spectral band with alarm. Little did they think—these regulars never do—that Indian scouts watched every step of their progress, and that Pontiac, duly apprised of the projected attack, had broken up his camp, and was in rapid march against them, backed by all his warriors.

Scarce two miles from the fort, Parent's Creek—from that night called Bloody Run—descended a wild and broken defile and entered the Detroit amid a rank growth of grass and sedge. A few rods from its mouth the road crossed it by a narrow wooden bridge. Just beyond the bridge, the land rose in abrupt ridges parallel to the little stream, their tops garnished with rude entrenchments formerly made by Pontiac to protect his camp. Here were, too, piles of fire-wood, besides strong picket fences.

What choicer ground could be selected for a battlefield! So thought the astute and crafty Pontiac, and behind all these obstructions and entrenchments crouched his swarthy warriors, lying with gleaming eyes and panting bosoms but silent as snakes, as they heard the distant footfall of the foes they had so long waited for in vain. The fearless little command pushed rapidly through the dark towards the bridge, which was dimly visible in front, the ridges beyond seeming like a wall of blackness.

The advance was half way across the bridge and the main body just entering upon it, when a horrible din of blood-curdling yells and shrieks burst all at once out of the surrounding blackness, accompanied by the blaze and rattle of musketry. Half the advance melted away; the stunned and appalled survivors shrank back in affright, causing a sudden recoil of the whole body. Dalzell was the first to recover. Raising his bugle voice above the horrid clamor, he rallied his men, hurried to the front, and led them to the attack. Again the crouching redskins poured in a murderous, withering volley, and again the little command was checked: but their gallant leader shouted *forward!* and they dashed over the bridge and charged up the heights beyond.

Charged what! Not a redskin was there to oppose them! None could be found anywhere! Yet still their mysterious rifles flashed out constant destruction, and their screeching war whoops made the night hideous. The English forged forward amid the pitchy darkness, and soon became inextricably enmeshed amid a maze of outhouses and enclosures. The fire became hotter and hotter on the side of the Indians. To advance further would be a cruel and useless slaughter. There was nothing left but to retire and wait till daylight. Grant's company recrossed the bridge and took station on the road. A small party was left in advance to hold the foe in check, while the rest followed, and until the dead and wounded could be placed on board the boats. Before this difficult task was completed, heavy volleys were heard in the rear. It came from a large force of the savages stationed in Meloche's house and orchards. Grant pushed forward and drove them from the orchards and house at the point of the bayonet. From two Canadians found there, they learned that the savages had passed to the rear in great numbers, determined to occupy the houses and cut them off from the fort.

Instant withdrawal became their only salvation, and the men slowly and in order commenced their painful retreat. They did not meet with severe opposition until they had reached a cluster of outhouses connected by strong fences. Behind these was concealed a strong force of Indians, who suffered the advance to pass without a shot, but when the centre and rear came directly abreast of their ambuscade, they raised a horrid yell, and poured forth a regular *feu d'enfer*. The decimated soldiers were hardly saved here from a most disastrous panic. The river was on one side, and no escape but by the road. They broke ranks and crowded down upon each other like a flock of sheep, and had it not been for the presence and coolness of Dalzell, the confused retreat would have degenerated into a disgraceful rout. Like Braddock a few years before, he stormed, rebuked and beat back his men into ranks, and a random fire was at length returned.

It was still night, and nothing could be seen of the foe. The constant flashes of their guns only served to indicate their whereabouts; while a demoniac medley of yells and whoops and savage clamor drowned all voices. Into one house from which issued a fatal fire, Major Rogers and his Rangers burst their way, rushed in and expelled them. Captain Gray, while charging a large gang of redskins behind some fences, fell mortally wounded. No sooner, however, did the men resume their retreat, before the savages were at them again, hanging on their rear, picking off stragglers, and scalping the dead and wounded. The eye of the brave Dalzell caught sight of a wounded sergeant raising himself on his hands and gazing mutely after his retreating comrades. He rushed back to the rescue, but was himself shot dead, and none to turn back for him. The loss of the harassed command would have been much greater had not Major Rogers occupied a strong house commanding the road, made a most obstinate defence, and thus covered the retreat.

Meanwhile Captain Grant had made a stand in advance, and all as they came up, rallied around him, and made good the retreat with the exception of Rogers and his men, who, cooped up in the house spoken of, was besieged by full two hundred fierce and yelling savages. The batteaux which had gone down to the fort to discharge the wounded, at length returned to a point opposite this house and opened a fire from their swivels, thus enabling Rogers to reach the fort with no further loss. At about eight o'clock, after six hours of constant marching and fighting, the shattered detachment entered the fort once more, having lost full sixty of their number in killed and wounded. The loss to the enemy, led by Pontiac in person, was comparatively trifling. The rascals were greatly elated at their success, and sent runners far and near with the news, and fresh forces began to arrive daily.

A Bloody Repulse—Siege Abandoned—Death of Pontiac.

Well! Time passed on, nothing of note happening in the conduct of the siege until the memorable night of September 4th. The schooner Gladwyn had been sent to Niagara with dispatches. She was now returning, having on board Horst, master, Jacobs, mate, a crew of ten Provincials and six Iroquois, supposed to be friendly. On entering the Detroit, the Indians asked to be put ashore, which request was foolishly granted, they no doubt revealing to Pontiac the weakness of the crew. At nightfall the wind fell and the ship was compelled to anchor about nine miles below the fort. It grew exceedingly dark and those aboard kept up an incessant watch. Meantime three hundred and fifty savages had stealthily glided down the current in their birch canoes and were close upon the vessel before seen. Only time to fire one cannon ere the hungry horde were beneath the bows and clambering up her sides with their knives clenched tight between their teeth. A close fire of musketry seemed to have no effect, so, dropping their guns, the crew made at them with spears and hatchets and attacked the boarders with such tremendous energy that in a few minutes they had killed twice their own number.

Only for a moment, however, was the swarm of assailants checked. Horst, the master, was killed; several of the crew were disabled, when Jacobs, as he saw the assailants clambering over the bulwarks, called out lustily to blow up the ship. This desperate order saved the vessel. Some Wyandots heard the command and told the rest, when the panic-stricken crowd leaped overboard and were seen diving and swimming away in every direction to escape the expected explosion. The schooner reached harbor without further molestation with six of her crew unhurt. The enemy lost nearly thirty.

By the end of September, three of the tribes retired from the contest; but the Ottawas, led and inspired by the indomitable Pontiac, still continued petty hostilities. By November, however, a fatal blow was given to the hopes of the great chief in a letter sent by M. Neyon, commandant of Fort Chartres, the principal French post in the Illinois country. It assured Pontiac that France and England were now at peace and that hostilities which could lead to no good result, had better be abandoned. This message had great influence with the fickle Indians, and in rage and mortification Pontiac, with a number of his chiefs, left for the Maumee country in the hope of exciting the Indians there and renewing hostilities in the Spring. Shortly after, two friendly Wyandots gained secret admission to the fort and one of them unstringing his powder horn and taking off its false bottom, revealed a letter to Gladwyn from Major Wilkins—who was then expected from Fort Niagara—conveying the unwelcome tidings that his command had been overtaken by a storm; many of the boats had been wrecked; seventy men had been lost and all the stores and ammunition had been destroyed and the expedition had returned to Niagara.

Bad news enough! rendering the prospect of the coming Winter still more dreary. The besiegers had now, however, almost all scattered to their wintering grounds. It was impossible for them to remain longer in a body without actual starvation. The confederated tribes had failed to take Detroit, Fort Pitt and Niagara, the three most important fortresses in their country, and there was general disaffection among them. The siege proper may be said to terminate at this point, although for six months after, until relieved by General Bradstreet's army, the fort was environed by hostile bands and cut off from all provisions, communications, &c.

We can only simply refer to the decadence of Pontiac's power, and need not follow him in his broken fortunes. With soul unsubdued; with undying hatred to the English, and with one purpose so steadfast

Death of Pontiac.

and unfaltering as to almost reach the sublime, he continued to defy his foes and sought to confederate his friends. His exertions only grew the more daring as his fortunes became more desperate, but agencies were then at work all over the country, which at length convinced him that he had no longer a cause or a formidable following. He resolved, therefore, to accept the peace; to nurse his vengeance and to bide his time. He went the next year to Oswego; held a grand council with Sir William Johnson and the Iroquois sachems, and there made his last speech and sealed his submission to the English, renouncing forever the hopes which had so long nerved his ambitious soul. But the sacrifice almost broke his heart, and for the next two years he lived in such obscurity that history has no trace of him.

In 1769 he went with some attendant chiefs to visit his French friends at Fort St. Louis. The famous Pierre Chouteau of that post vividly remembered to the very last day of his life Pontiac's appearance at that memorable visit. He was arrayed in the full uniform of a French officer—a special mark of favor from the Marquis de Montcalm—and moved about with great dignity. Hearing that a large number of Indians were assembled at Cahokia, nearly opposite, he, in spite of all dissuasion to the contrary, crossed the river to visit them. His fame at once surrounded him with attentions, and he was induced to drink deeply. When the council was over he strode to the adjacent woods, where he was heard to sing his medicine songs. An English trader named Williamson was then in the village, and it is said bribed a Kaskaskia Indian to kill the great chief—the implacable foe to all Britons. As Pontiac entered the forest this assassin stole upon his track, and, watching his opportunity, buried a tomahawk in his brain.

This base and ignoble death caused great excitement among the western tribes, and most signally was it afterwards avenged, the Illinois tribes having been completely exterminated by the nations who almost worshipped Pontiac. The murdered chief lay where he fell until his old friend St. Ange sent to claim the body and buried it with warlike honors near his fort of St. Louis. In our account of Pontiac and the siege of Detroit, we have followed Parkman, whose monograph on Pontiac's Conspiracy is exceedingly full, exhaustive and reliable. He thus appropriately closes his notice of the great and imperial Ottawa chief: "Neither mound nor tablet mark the burial place of Pontiac. For a mausoleum, a city has risen above the great forest hero, and the race whom he hated with such burning rancor, trample with unceasing footsteps over his forgotten grave."

Guyasutha's Attack on Fort Pitt and Repulse.

Let us now go back and briefly narrate what occurred at Fort Pitt, one of the three frontier posts which escaped capture during Pontiac's war. It stood at the junction of the Allegheny and Monongahela, a little to one side of the ruins of the French Fort Duquesne, abandoned in 1758, and was a strong and formidable fortification, having five sides, the two towards the land of brick and the other three stockades. A broad moat, dry when the river was low, surrounded the fort.

Nothing occurred to alarm until May 27th, when prowling bands of Indians scoured the country around, scalping stragglers, shooting or driving off stock, and murdering Indian traders. Then came news of the wholesale butchery of traders in the Ohio country. Among the Hurons the traders were so numerous and formidable that the Indians gained possession of them by stratagem, telling them that the surrounding tribes had risen in arms and were killing all the whites they met, and that it would be impossible for them (the Hurons) to protect their friends, the traders, unless the traders would consent, for appearance sake, to be made prisoners. In that case they should be set at liberty soon as the danger was over. The deluded traders gave up their arms, submitted to be bound, and were inhumanly slaughtered to a man. At Fort Pitt every preparation was made for a vigorous defence. The garrison consisted of three hundred and thirty soldiers, traders and hunters, commanded by the gallant Captain Ecuyer, and for many days were kept in constant alarm. The surrounding woods were full of prowling savages, though as yet no general assault was attempted.

At length on June 22d a general fire was opened, which was replied to by a discharge of howitzers, the bursting shells appearing greatly to disconcert the assailants. Next morning a Delaware chief, Turtle's Heart by name, surrounded by other chiefs, boldly appeared before the fort and demanded its surrender, stating that six great nations had taken up the hatchet and had cut off all the frontier posts but that one. They must go back to the settlements or they would all be killed. Ecuyer replied, with a grim humor, which showed his confidence, that he could hold the fort against all the savages who should choose to combine against it; that they were very well off there and meant to stay; that he would tell them in confidence, but hoped they would not mention to other Indians, that a great army of six thousand was coming to Fort Pitt; another of three thousand had gone up the lakes, and a third had gone to the Virginia frontier, where, being joined by the Cherokees and Catawbas, (who were the most dreaded foes of the Ohio Indians,) they would come and destroy them. Therefore, they had better hide or they would get hurt. The chiefs were thus beaten at their own game, and taking fright at the three imaginary armies, disappeared and dispersed to attack weaker posts like Ligonier and Bedford. A few days later came in Ensign Price, followed by seven haggard, half-famished soldiers. They were the garrison of Le Bœuf on French Creek, attacked about same time as Presq' Isle and Venango. Price stated that the Indians had suddenly surrounded his block-house, showering bullets and fire-arrows against it, and had soon set it on fire. The yelling crowd then gathered in a half-circle about the gate, awaiting the moment when the inmates, stifled with flame and smoke, should rush out to their fate. But Price and his followers had hewn out a passage through the massive back wall of the block-house, and made good their escape to the surrounding woods, and thence to Fort Pitt. No man remained alive to tell how Fort Venango was taken, and it was not until long after that Sir William Johnson learned from a savage, who was present, that a large body of Senecas had gained entrance by a ruse, then closed the gates, fell upon the garrison, and butchered all but the commander, Lieutenant Gordon, whom they tortured to death over a slow fire for several successive nights.

Meanwhile every possible effort was made at Fort Pitt for the renewed attack which was daily expected. The rampart was repaired, a line of palisades was erected, the barracks were made bullet-proof to protect the women and children, of whom there were sheltered there more than a hundred. It was not, however, till the 26th of July, that there appeared a delegation, headed by Shingiss and Turtle's Heart, bearing a message from Pontiac to the effect that he was coming against the English at the forks of the Ohio with a great army, and that being a hungry and a headstrong people, they would eat up everything that came in their way. To this gentle hint, Ecuyer promptly replied that he despised the Ottawas; could and would hold his fort against all the Indians in the woods, and that if they came again about the fort, he would blow them to atoms with bombshells, and would fire bagfuls of bullets at them.

Ruse with a Stuffed Paddy—Bouquet Comes to the Rescue.

The savages at this retired in great disgust, and then organized a more serious attack. Crawling along and behind the steep banks of the rivers, they dug holes in them to conceal themselves and afford shelter from the garrison's fire. Snugly ensconced in these caverns, they kept up a severe and incessant hail on the fort, and often set it on fire with their arrows. It was dangerous to expose a head or any part of the body. They thus killed and wounded seven, including the brave and plucky Ecuyer himself. A soldier's letter from the fort, written at this time, and describing the above facts, says: "Some of our fellows, however, were more than a match for them. One day 'Brown Bill' procured some old clothes and straw, and stuffing a paddy he told us that night to lift it slowly above the stockade, and then let it fall quickly whenever it was fired at from the caves. He then took his station a few feet from it, and soon as his eye became accustomed to the darkness, bade us raise it up. We hoisted slowly, and a bullet at once passed through it, but instantly Bill, who could fire at a flash, put a ball through the Indian's head. We all laughed at the result, which made Bill tremendously angry. 'If you had held your jaw,' said he, 'the paddy might have served again, but now it's of no use, as the yellow-hides will smell a rat.' At last we got tired of being cooped up, but the following day chased the Indians from the banks of the river, where they most annoyed us. We built upon rollers a large flat-boat with high gunwales. The rowers were secured and port-holes bored all around; when finished and ready we rolled it into the Monongahela and anchored it so we could fire up the Allegheny. The Indians were astonished, afraid to attack either boat or fort, as they would be between two fires. We raked them from the boat along the river banks. They set up the most diabolical yells I ever heard, retired up stream, but never again ventured so close in daylight."

During all this time a terrible, scathing, ruthless border war was going on outside the forts along the whole line of frontier. Everywhere were experienced the same horrible cruelties—the sudden surprise, the massacre, the scalping, the burning. Many thousand people in Virginia were driven from their homes. The people of Pennsylvania suffered quite as much. They left all and crowded into the interior towns for safety, living as best they could in huts or tents, or on the charities of friends. Lancaster had become a frontier town. The colonial government was paralyzed by faction, and for a long time no adequate protection was furnished.

But this disgraceful state of things was about to end. Colonel Henry Bouquet, a Swiss, and one of the most able, resolute and energetic foreign officers that ever served in this country, was coming to the aid of Fort Pitt, and of the western frontier which that important post dominated. With every possible effort, he could only gather together about five hundred men, the shattered remains of two regiments of Highlanders, enfeebled by West Indian exposure and disease. Sixty of them were so weak that they had to be conveyed in baggage wagons. When Bouquet reached Carlisle he found the whole country in a pitiable panic. The roads were crowded with flying families, and the towns and villages were encumbered with a smitten and fugitive population. Instead of receiving supplies, therefore, as expected, he had to dispense them. Eighteen precious days were lost in collecting stores and providing transportation, and the little command commenced its long wilderness march of two hundred miles with the worst forebodings of the whole people. Just out of Carlisle they passed a forlorn and pitiable multitude of wretched refugees, who, unable to find shelter in the town, had encamped in the woods or adjacent fields, erecting huts of bark or branches and living on the charities of the town. Think of it! Crowds of poor men, women and children; bereft of home, friends and the means of supporting life; most of them haunted day and night with visions of the bloody knife and reeking scalps! It was enough, foreigners as they were, to move the hearts of the passing soldiers to pity, and to nerve their arms to deeds of vengeance. We will see how good a record they made.

The army pursued the route opened by Forbes on his expedition against Fort Duquesne, and first relieving Forts Bedford and Ligonier, both beleaguered by Indians, struck gallantly forth into the pathless wilderness. Bouquet had hoped at Ligonier to get some late tidings from Fort Pitt, but no word had been heard from there for a month. The woods were alive with savages, and every messenger between the two forts had been either killed or captured. Whether Fort Pitt stood or not, none knew—most probably not. The wagons were left behind, and everything needful packed on the horses, and, attended by the bleating of sheep and the lowing of cattle, the long, straggling train now wound its slow and toilsome way, like a huge serpent, through matted woods and across wild, dashing streams, dense walls of foliage on either side. Keen-eyed rangers scouted the woods on either flank. For nearly two days, in the sweltering heat of August, the troops fagged on. Before them now lay the dangerous defile of Turtle Creek, commanded for several miles by steep, craggy hills. Fearing an ambuscade, it was Bouquet's design to pass these by night, sweeping through so rapidly and stealthily that the savages could concert no attack. To do this a whole afternoon's rest was to be enjoyed at Bushy Run, which by noon of the 5th—after a wearisome march of seventeen miles—was declared to be only a half mile ahead. The jaded cattle and tired soldiers were pressing forward with renewed alacrity when their fond anticipations suffered a rude and cruel interruption.

Bouquet's Desperate Battle of Bushy Run.

A startling volley of firearms suddenly broke the forest stillness, causing every man's heart to leap to his throat and every man's hands to clutch his trusty musket. The drum beat to arms, the sharp command rang out loud and clear, but before ranks were closed up, the savages were upon them with a horrible din and clamor. Bouquet promptly ordered two companies to charge the ambuscade. As the files of gleaming bayonets steadily advanced, the savages broke and fled; but only for a moment. They soon gathered again, rushed in from all sides, and in great force occupied the heights, almost completely surrounding Bouquet's little army, and pouring in a most galling and fatal fire. A general charge along the whole line dislodged the swarming Indians from the heights, but the savages returned again and again to the attack, pouring in a murderous hail of fire in front and on both flanks, and even attacking the convoy in the rear.

The contest became hotter and hotter, the savages rushing to the attack with wonderful spirit and resolution, and the British holding their own with obstinacy and tenacity. It was life or death with them. Darkness alone ended the bloody battle. The brave little force was almost completely worn out. The day had been exceedingly sultry: they had fought for seven hours on empty stomachs; they were nearly tormented to death by thirst, and had coolly and with desperate courage withstood the galling hail from a fiery circle of whooping demons.

Right in the leafy wilderness where they had fought, on this hot, sultry August night, without one drop of water to cool their parched tongues and fevered bodies, the poor Highlanders sank down to rest. Over sixty of their number, including several officers, had been killed or wounded. A dropping fire, and occasional yells and whoops were kept up by the Indians; and in constant fear of a desperate night attack, the anxious hours were dragged through. At the very first streak of dawn a horrible din of yells and shrieks burst forth on all sides of them, and volley after volley of bullets came whistling among their thinned ranks. The combat raged fiercer and hotter than the day before. The Indians seemed more desperate and reckless. They would rush up to close quarters and fire from every bush and tree which could yield a cover. Although repulsed at every point, fresh Indians would take the places of the retreating, and the conflict raged more furiously as the day advanced. Yielding their ground when a charge was made, the crafty savages would vanish for a moment only to come out in a new spot.

The troops maddened by thirst, fainting from heat, and worn out by incessant charges which led to nothing, were almost completely exhausted. Their distress was so plainly visible, that the foe redoubled their horrid yells and fierce attacks, approaching so near as to deride and curse them in bad English. The whole camp was in utter confusion. The wounded and terror-stricken horses rushed frantically about, and the drivers concealed themselves or ran away, and all seemed lost. The defence became wavering and irresolute; all hope had gone, and death or torture menaced the jaded but still brave survivors. If anything was to be done, then was just the time, and no moment to spare.

Bouquet, happily, was equal to the occasion. In the very midst of despair he conceived and carried into immediate execution a masterly stratagem. He determined to get the Indians into one body, draw them into a trap, and then give them a furious bayonet charge, and so end the conflict. Two companies were ordered to fall back suddenly in the centre, while the troops on the flank should advance across the vacancy in the circle, as if to cover their retreat. Meanwhile another company of Light Infantry, with one of Grenadiers, were ordered to lie in ambush to support the first two companies on the feigned retreat. The stratagem took. These movements were mistaken for defeat and retreat. The yelling, screeching demons, believing that their time had come at last, leaped from cover on all sides and rushed headlong to the spot, pouring in a most galling fire. It seemed for a moment that nothing could withstand that impetuous advance and attack, but the two companies which had retreated, had, under cover of the dense woods and underbrush, made a rapid and secret detour, and now burst out on each flank of the yelling, onrushing crowd of savages, and discharged a heavy volley right into their very midst. The Indians, though taken completely by surprise, faced about with great intrepidity, and boldly returned the fire, and essayed to recover ground.

It was too late! With a wild, fierce yell of rage, the Highlanders were upon them with the cold steel. A well-conducted bayonet charge an Indian *has* never and *will* never stand. The shock was irresistible, and they fled in a tumultuous mob. Now the two other companies, who had been crouched in ambush, awaiting the moment to strike, put in an appearance. As the fugitive throng, pressed back by the advancing wall of bristling steel, passed directly across their front, they rose and poured in a destructive volley, which ended the whole matter. The four companies now uniting, soon changed flight to utter rout. No time was given them to reload; many were shot or driven down, while the rest were scattered in remediless confusion throughout the woods.

While all this took place in *one* part of the circle, the remaining savages on the other sides first watched, then wavered, then lost heart, and finally betook themselves to headlong flight. And thus was this gallant little force, and its brave and skillful commander, saved from a terrible disaster—snatched from the very jaws of death. Forty Indians, some of them their chief warriors, had been slain outright. Bouquet lost about fifty killed, and had about sixty wounded. The troops had so greatly suffered, and so many horses had been lost, that large amounts of stores had to be destroyed. The march was still difficult and tedious, though entirely unmolested, and it was not until four days after this bloody struggle that Bouquet arrived at Fort Pitt with his convoy, and thus raised the siege.

It was Guyasutha's band of besieging Indians which were so crushingly defeated at Bushy Run. They had gone out with confidence against the little force, judging shrewdly that if *it* could be defeated as was Braddock's much larger command but a few years previous, Fort Pitt must finally be theirs. Now all was altered. There was no rallying from that crushing overthrow, and the baffled Ohio savages retired sullenly to their homes beyond the Allegheny. Bouquet was most anxious to follow up his victory by marching at once into the heart of the enemy's country, and wringing from the hostile tribes a treaty, which would at once put an end to these scenes of rapine and slaughter, but his force was too small and the season too far advanced. He busied himself, therefore, during the Fall and Winter in restoring quiet along the frontier, and in gathering an adequate force for an early Spring campaign. It was not, however, till the next August that he was ready to move from Carlisle, his troops consisting of his old Highlanders—such as were left of them—a thousand Pennsylvanians, and a small but invaluable corps of Virginia rangers. With this imposing force the plan was for him to march against the Shawnees, Delawares and Mingoes of Ohio, while Colonel Bradstreet should advance into the lake country, reduce the Ottawas, Chippewas and Wyandots, and relieve Detroit. During the Spring and Summer, Indian marauds and massacres had been renewed with such devastating effect that Pennsylvania had at last been compelled, in compliance with the earnest demand of the whole frontier, to offer a high bounty for scalps—men, women and children.

On September 13th Bouquet arrived with his army at Fort Pitt. Various delegations from the Ohio tribes, who had all retired beyond the Muskingum, endeavored on various pretexts to delay the expedition until too late in the season, but Bouquet was perfectly convinced that the only possible peace was to be secured by a show of rigor and power. He could neither be wheedled or bullied into any fatal delay. And so on the 3d of October the army crossed the Allegheny, and defiling into the Indian trail, struck boldly out into the trackless wilderness. It was accompanied by long trains of pack horses and immense droves of cattle, and was preceded by three scouting parties of rangers, one of which kept the trail while the other two moved on the flanks. This whole expedition, together with the various incidents attending it, is replete with a romantic interest, but we have only room for results.

Boone marking out his own grave.—*See page 289.*

Bouquet in the Heart of the Indian Country.

The course lay along the Ohio to Big Beaver and thence to Yellow and Sandy Creeks directly to the Tuscarawas, a continuation of the Muskingum, which was reached on the tenth day. The march had been conducted in silence entirely through the vast primeval forest, and had been met with no obstructions whatever. They were now approaching the homes, hitherto sacred and secure, of the tribes which had been causing all the late mischief. News of their coming and of the imposing size of the army, as well as the skill and boldness of its commander, had long preceded them, and a great fear fell upon the contumacious tribes. Their hearts were now inclined to peace. Fleet runners went to and fro between the different towns. Grand councils were held; eloquent harangues were made; the young and ardent were overruled by the older and more prudent warriors, and the result was a large delegation of chiefs to sue for peace and endeavor to stay Bouquet's further progress.

A large bower was built near the camp for the conference. A grand parade was made that the chiefs might be duly impressed, and the negotiations commenced. The great chiefs Guyasutha, Turtle's Heart and Custaloga headed the deputation. Painted and plumed in all their savage pomp, they walked with majesty, not deigning to cast a glance at the grand military display around them. They seated themselves with stern, impassive looks, and an air of sullen dignity, while their black and sombre brows betrayed the hatred still rankling in their hearts. The pipe went round in solemn silence, and then from their pouches were drawn their strings of wampum, without which no conference can be conducted. The chiefs as usual laid the whole blame of the war on their young men, whom they said they could not control, and upon the nations who lived to the west of them. Bouquet, well understanding the Indian character and how best to treat them, now dismissed them, promising an answer the next day.

That day being very wet and rainy, however, he made no reply until the next, when the council being all duly assembled, Bouquet made a bold, haughty, uncompromising harangue, asserting that their excuses for the late marauds were weak and frivolous; reciting their numerous acts of perfidy; declaring that he would no longer be imposed upon; that he had brought with him the relations of the people they had massacred and made captive, and that he could scarce restrain them from taking revenge. He then gave them twelve days to deliver to him every person with white blood, in their hands—men, women and children—and to furnish said prisoners with horses, clothing and provisions to carry them back to Fort Pitt. These were the *only* terms on which he would make peace. The chiefs, finding Bouquet in dead earnest, were prompt to comply. His bold, resolute speech and mien made a profound impression on the haughty circle of swarthy listeners. Their stubborn pride was subdued, their arrogance abated, and the Delawares at once gave up eighteen prisoners then with them, and eighty-three small sticks denoting the number of other captives in their possession, whom they pledged themselves to bring in right away.

None of the Shawnee chiefs took part in this conference, but their deputy also promised, with sullen dejection, that his nation would comply with the terms. But Bouquet wisely determined to follow up his advantage and to march deeper into their country, shrewdly judging that the presence of his powerful force within easy striking distance of their towns, would be the best possible security for the prompt fulfillment of these promises; so, for the next three days, he marched down to the forks of the Muskingum, where he made a strong fortified camp, erecting redoubts, storehouses and other buildings for the reception of the expected captives, who were to be taken charge of by officers and matrons duly selected. The camp soon had the appearance of a little town, the order and regularity of which struck the onlooking and overawed Indians with astonishment. The constant sound of the axe, the lowing of cattle, the well-drilled army so rapidly located within the very heart of their own territory, moved them to such unusual activity, that on the 27th, messengers arrived from the Delaware king, Custaloga, that he was on his way with his prisoners, and a message of like effect from the Shawnees. About two weeks were spent at this camp, exchanging messages with relation to the prisoners, who were now being daily brought into camp. So strict was Bouquet in having all produced, that when Kings Beaver and Custaloga had brought in all but twelve, promising to bring them, too, in a few days, he refused to shake hands with or have a word to say to them until every single captive was in.

By the 9th of November there had been delivered of Virginians thirty-two males and fifty-eight females and children, and of Pennsylvanians forty-nine males and sixty-seven females and children, a total of two hundred and six. A hundred more were in the hands of the Shawnees, which, on account of those owning them having gone on a distant expedition, could not then be delivered, but they were solemnly promised early in the Spring at Fort Pitt. The Shawnees were ever a fierce, warlike and jealous tribe, and when the "pale-face" army entered their country, reports had reached them that their tribe was to be completely extirpated, upon which they had fully resolved to kill all their prisoners, and then to march out and give battle, and fight to the bitter end

Happily for them and the poor captives, they received a friendly message from Bouquet, sent as they were preparing to execute their horrible purpose, to the effect that peace would be made with them on the same terms as with the Delawares, if they would send in all of white blood with them.

Again, while actually on the way, they somehow heard that one of Bouquet's soldiers had been secretly killed near camp, and that some of their tribe were charged with the bloody deed. This decided them anew to make an heroic resistance, and collecting all their captives in a field, they were about to tomahawk them entire, when a runner fortunately arrived from Bouquet, who, on hearing of the report current among them, ridiculed it as absurd, and urged them to continue their journey

A final conference was now held, and peace granted, first to the Senecas and Delawares, and afterwards to the Shawnees, who had all along acted with such a sullen and disdainful haughtiness that Bouquet was fearful lest they should yet play him false. The biting blasts of Winter, however, commenced to prevail; the foliage had all fallen from the trees and every sign warned him that any longer delay would be dangerous. He was, therefore, obliged to rest satisfied with such prisoners as they saw fit to bring; exacting renewed promises that the rest should shortly be delivered at Fort Pitt, and compelling them to deliver to him six hostages for the faithful performance of all their pledges.

Touching Scenes on the Delivery of the Captives.

And now we enter upon the description of touching and pathetic scenes which have no parallel in history, and to which no pen could do justice. If the exhibitions of human tenderness and affection daily presented in that sylvan camp were not so well attested, they would seem actually incredible. They reflect as much honor on the Indians as on the whites—yes, far more! for these captives belonged to and were taken from a race they hated; whom they were taught to look upon as grasping, usurping and vindictive enemies. From the graphic account of Hutchins, the geographer, who accompanied the expedition, we quote as follows: "It was a most affecting spectacle to see fathers and mothers recognizing and clasping their once lost babes; husbands hanging around the necks of their newly-recovered wives; sisters and brothers unexpectedly meeting together after long separations, scarce able to speak the same language, or, for some time, to be sure they were children of the same parents. In all these interviews joy and rapture inexpressible were seen, while feelings of a very different nature were painted in the looks of others; flying from place to place in eager inquiries after relatives not found; trembling to receive an answer to their questions; distracted with doubts, hopes and fears on obtaining no account of those they sought for, or stiffened into living monuments of horror and woe on learning their unhappy fate.

"The Indians, too, as if wholly forgetting their usual savageness, bore a capital part in heightening this most affecting scene. They delivered up their beloved captives with the utmost reluctance; shed torrents of tears over them, recommending them to the care and protection of the commanding officer. Their regard to them continued all the time they remained in camp. They visited them from day to day; and brought them what corn, skins, horses and other matters they had bestowed on them, while in their families; accompanied with other presents and all the marks of most sincere and tender affection.

"Nay, they did not stop here, but, when the army marched, some of the Indians solicited and obtained leave to accompany their captives all the way to Fort Pitt, and employed themselves in hunting and bringing provisions for them on the road. A young Mingo carried this still further and gave an instance of love which would make a figure even in romance. A young woman from Virginia was among the captives, to whom he had formed so strong an attachment as to call her his wife. Against all remonstrances of the imminent danger to which he exposed himself by approaching the frontier, he persisted in following her, at the risk of being killed by the surviving relatives of many unfortunate persons who had been captured or scalped by those of his nation.

"These qualities in savages challenge our just esteem. Cruel and unmerciful as they are by habit and long example in war, yet whenever they come to give way to the native dictates of humanity, they exercise virtues which Christians need not blush to imitate. When they once determine to give life, they give everything with it. No woman thus saved is preserved for base motives, or need fear the violation of her honor. No child is otherwise treated by the persons adopting it than the children of their own body. Every captive whom their affection, their caprice, or whatever else, leads them to save, fares alike with themselves.

"Among the captives a woman was brought into the camp with a babe about three months old, at the breast. One of the Virginia volunteers soon knew her to be his wife, who had been taken by the Indians about six months before. She was immediately delivered to her overjoyed husband. He flew with her to his tent and clothed her and his child in proper apparel. But their joy, after the first transports, was soon damped by the reflection that another dear child of about two years old, captured with the mother and separated from her, was still missing, although many children had been brought in.

"A few days after a number of other prisoners were brought to the camp, among whom were several more children. The woman was sent for and one, supposed to be hers, was produced to her. At first sight she was uncertain, but viewing the child with great earnestness, she soon recollected its features and was so overcome with joy that literally forgetting her sucking child, she dropped it from her arms and catching up the new-found child in an ecstacy, pressed it to her breast and bursting into tears carried it off, unable to speak for joy. The father catching up the babe she had let fall, followed her in no less transport and affection.

"Among the children who had been carried off young and had long lived with the Indians, it is not to be expected that any marks of joy would appear on being restored to their parents or relatives. Having been accustomed to look upon the Indians as the only connections they had; having been tenderly treated by them and speaking their language, it is no wonder they parted from the savages with tears. But it must not be denied that there were even some grown persons who showed an unwillingness to return. The Shawnees were obliged to bind several of their prisoners and force them along to the camp; and some women who had been delivered up, afterwards found means to escape and run back to the Indian towns. Some, who could not make their escape, clung to their savage acquaintances at parting, and continued many days in bitter lamentations, even refusing sustenance."

All matters being now satisfactorily adjusted, the wilderness camp was broken up; the refreshed army commenced their backward march, and in ten days was back at Fort Pitt. Colonel Bouquet soon returned to Philadelphia, receiving, wherever he went, every possible mark of gratitude, but more especially from the overjoyed relatives of the many captives whom he had so happily restored to their families. The Assemblies of Pennsylvania and Virginia voted him addresses, while the home government promoted him to the rank of Brigadier General, placing him in command of the southern department. He did not long survive, however, to enjoy his honors, dying three years after at Pensacola.

We need only add, that the Shawnees faithfully redeemed their pledges. Ten chiefs, attended by about fifty warriors, came in with over a hundred captives to Fort Pitt the next May. In the grand council which ensued they said: "These captives have all been united to us by adoption, and although we deliver them up to you, we will always look upon them as our relations. We have taken as much care of them as if they were our own flesh and blood. They have become strange to your customs and manners, and we request you to use them kindly and tenderly."

Recovery of Captive Child on Bouquet's Expedition.
—See page 159.

THE DESPERATE BATTLE OF POINT PLEASANT.

Peace and quiet reigned for a time along the troubled and harassed western border. Now may be said to have commenced the explorations of the Great West by daring and adventurous hunters, and we approach a new and a very interesting era in American history. The glowing reports brought back by Smith, Finley, Boone, Stewart and their companions, as well as many Indian traders, excited a wide-spread longing among the young men of the old settlements, to migrate to the West. It was pictured to their fancies as a new Eldorado—a magnificent region, abounding in vast forests, clear streams teeming with fish and in every species of fragrant flowers. It was a boundless land; with soft and genial clime; with soil of wondrous freshness, and the luxuriant woods stocked with game in every variety, from the beaver to the buffalo. The savages who either inhabited or roamed over this "hunter's paradise," seeing the land sold from under their feet by the Iroquois of New York, and witnessing with a fierce anger and jealousy this new tide of hardy and daring pioneers, naturally began to grow restless and hostile. A deep and bitter feeling of hate and rancor was evidently growing in their proud and haughty bosoms. But still remembering British power and past punishment, they managed to keep the peace until 1774, when a canoe filled with friendly redmen was attacked below Wheeling by Michael Cresap, and another attack was made by the same party upon an Indian camp at the mouth of Captina Creek, twenty miles below.

These were clearly the exciting causes of what is known in history as "Dunmore's war of 1774." It is true, however, that the magazine was fully charged before, only needing the match to explode it. These bloody deeds were immediately followed by a horrid and entirely unprovoked massacre of Indians at the mouth of Yellow Creek, in which were killed some of the relatives of Logan, the famous Mingo Chief. This cowardly and treacherous butchery was perpetrated by thirty-two men led by Daniel Greathouse, and reflects the deepest dishonor upon all concerned. The pretext to the attack was, that as the Captina massacre shortly before would undoubtedly provoke an Indian war, it was better to take the initiative. Opposite the mouth of Yellow Creek was the house of a man named Baker. Greathouse's party being gathered there, saw the encampment of an Indian hunting party across the Ohio, and an ambush being laid, Greathouse crossed the river under the mask of friendship to ascertain the number. The presence of women and children clearly proved to him that it was no war party.

While there a squaw urged him to retire at once as the Indians were drinking heavily, and, being excited by the murders of their people below Wheeling, might do him mischief. Greathouse reported to his band that the savages were too strong for an open assault, but urged Baker to give all the Indians who came over as much rum as they could drink. A canoe with six warriors, two squaws and a little girl soon crossed, and the men becoming hopelessly drunk, were set upon by a few of Greathouse's men—the rest protesting against the atrocious and perfidious murder—and all were cruelly butchered but the girl. The Indians in camp, hearing the firing on the other side, sent a canoe paddled by two men, to ascertain the cause. These, too, were shot down like dogs, as soon as they made the beach. A larger canoe was then manned by a number of savages and sent across. They were received by a fatal volley from an ambush on shore, and the survivors compelled to return. Shots were then exchanged across the Ohio, but without further damage. These two massacres embraced the whole of Logan's family.

A prodigious excitement prevailed along the Virginia frontier after these wanton and unholy deeds, and the scattered settlers, knowing full well that the savages would retaliate, lost no time in erecting forts and stations for their protection. Many of these were for the next twenty years famous as the scenes of many a desperate struggle. Expresses were also dispatched to Governor Dunmore, at Williamsburg, to send out immediate aid. Measures were at once adopted by the House of Burgesses for organizing and equipping an adequate force. Boone and Stoner were ordered to bring in the surveyors, out in various directions, which task was promptly and successfully executed; but the unfortunate traders then busy in the Indian country, peddling their wares from town to town, could not be so easily warned or rescued. Some of these fell the first victims to the redman's vengeance. One near the town of White Eyes, the great Peace Chief of the Delawares, was literally hacked to pieces, and the fragments of his body hung up on the bushes. The kindly chief, however—of whom we shall hear much hereafter—gathered them together and buried them; they were disinterred and again scattered by the infuriated perpetrators, but the kindness of the chief was as persistent as their hatred, and again he collected the *disjecta membra* and hid them in a secret place.

It being thought best to assume the offensive, a force of four hundred was hastily gathered at Fort Henry, (now Wheeling, West Va.,) and, led by Colonel Angus McDonald and piloted by Jonathan Zane, a hurried expedition was made against Wappatomica, on the Muskingum, situated near what is now Coshockton, Ohio. The march was a success. The savages having been frustrated in an expected surprise of the invaders, deserted their town, sued for peace, and delivered up five chiefs as hostages. It being found, however, that the Indians meant war, and were only desirous of gaining time until their forces should be gathered, the Virginians proceeded to destroy their towns and crops, and retreated, carrying three chiefs to Fort Henry. But this only incensed the savages. The storm that had been aroused was too violent and wide-spread to be easily allayed. Nothing but blood could wipe out their wrongs. While the other Indians were hesitating on their course, and the great Cornstalk was exerting himself to placate his angry followers, Logan, who, by the wanton murder of his relatives, had been converted into a bitter foe of the whites, suddenly swooped down like a whirlwind upon the Monongahela settlements and carried away nineteen scalps.

But Logan, although a much-wronged man, was also a kind man. At this very attack, a man named Robinson was making off for the woods when he heard behind him a voice crying out in very good English, "Stop! I won't hurt you!" "Yes, you will," replied Robinson. "No, I won't, but if you don't stop, by —— I'll shoot you!" Robinson still forged ahead, but while looking over his shoulder to watch the expected tomahawk, he stumbled over a log, fell, and was immediately clutched by his pursuer, who told him he must quietly go captive, and assured him he should not be hurt. It was Logan! He continued his kindness, for when Robinson was afterwards compelled to run the gauntlet, the Mingo chief so instructed him that he escaped without injury. He was afterwards tied to a stake to be burned, but the chief ran and spoke strongly for some time in behalf of the captive. Three times was the intended victim tied to the stake, but at length Logan's masterly eloquence prevailed, and he was released, taken to Logan's own lodge, and some time after returned home. Robinson afterwards used to say that Logan's countenance, when speaking, was the most striking and impressive that he ever beheld. Logan made as strenuous efforts afterwards, as we shall see, to procure the release of the famous Simon Kenton.

Predatory bands of Indians now pushed forward in various directions, and the border suffered greatly from marauds and attacks, from June until September. In the meantime two formidable bodies of troops were slowly gathering to beat back these desolating savage gangs and restore quiet to the frontier. The one from South and West Virginia was to be led by General Andrew Lewis: the other from North and

East Virginia to be under command of Governor Dunmore himself, and which, descending the Ohio from Fort Pitt, was to meet Lewis' army at the mouth of the Kanawha. Lewis, with eleven hundred men, reached the point agreed upon on the 6th of October, but, Dunmore not having arrived, he sent scouts—both Simon Girty and Simon Kenton were acting as scouts in this campaign, a fact, as will be hereafter shown, to which Kenton owed his life—and soon received dispatches to the effect that the plan of campaign was altered; that he (Dunmore) would proceed directly against the Shawnee towns on the Scioto, and Lewis was ordered to join him before those towns.

This could not be done, however, without a desperate struggle—one of the most severe and well-fought battles that has ever occurred between the red and white races. The next morning, October 10th, '74, General Lewis was preparing to move as directed, when a scout reported that he and a companion had been out hunting, and had discovered a large body of Indians just rising from their encampment, which covered about four acres, and that while his partner had been shot, he had made good his escape. As this meant that the Indians were strong enough to cross the Ohio to take the offensive, all was, of course, immediate surprise and confusion, but General Lewis, calm as was the morning itself, lighted his pipe with the greatest coolness and ordered out the regiment under Colonel Chas. Lewis, his brother, and that of Colonel Fleming, to reconnoitre the ground.

General Andrew Lewis—The Battle Rages—The Savages Retreat.

Before battle is joined, however, let us say something of the commander of this gallant army, which contained the very flower of Virginia, and embraced many names afterwards highly distinguished. General Andrew Lewis had served as Captain of the Virginia Rangers at the disastrous battle of Braddocks Fields, and had five brothers in his company. He afterwards served as Major in Washington's regiment, Forbes' army, and was with Major Grant in that officer's foolish bravado before Fort Duquesne, having the misfortune to be wounded and taken prisoner. McClung asserts—with what authority we are ignorant—that while he and Grant were on parole at the French fort, a quarrel broke out between them, much to the amusement of the French. Grant, in his dispatches captured by the Indians, had made Lewis the scapegoat for his own defeat, whereas, in truth, the only execution that was done was effected by the Virginia troops. On leaving the fort, Lewis went in search of Grant, and, drawing his sword, directed his former commander to defend himself on the spot. Grant contemptuously refused to comply, upon which Lewis cursed him for a liar and a coward, and, in the presence of two French officers, actually spat in his face.

General Lewis' person considerably exceeded six feet in height, as did, indeed, that of most every man under him. He had a splendid *physique*, and was of a very imposing appearance. His countenance was stern and manly, expressive of that daring and energy which ever distinguished him. His manners were cold, plain and unbending, and his conversation short, pithy and to the point. At the general treaty with the tribes in '63, General Lewis was the "observed of all observers," and his majestic military appearance not only attracted attention but inspired awe. The Governor of New York then declared that he "looked like the genius of the forest, and that the earth seemed to tremble beneath his footsteps." The General had a brother and three sons—two of them privates—in his division.

Colonel Charles Lewis now instantly advanced, and was soon engaged with the enemy, composed of Shawnees, Mingoes, Delawares and Tawas, about a thousand strong, led by the celebrated Shawnee chief, Cornstalk, and assisted by his son, Elenipsico, by Logan, Red Eagle and other prominent chiefs. Colonel Fleming, who advanced along the Ohio, also found the enemy close by, and a very hot and fierce struggle at once ensued. Colonel Charles Lewis, being in full uniform, and a conspicuous mark for the enemy, was soon mortally wounded, as was also, soon after, Colonel Fleming. The troops were much discouraged, and being pressed by the savages with unusual vigor, were compelled to beat a retreat. At this critical moment, General Lewis ordered up Field's regiment, which, meeting the retiring troops, rallied them again, and not only restored the fortunes of the day, but compelled the Indians, in *their* turn, to retreat to a very strong position—one that was not easily assailable.

The contest now became more desperate than ever and was still stubbornly maintained by both parties—who were about equal in numbers—with consummate skill, valor and energy. The savages, sure of success when they previously beheld the troops give way, fought with a vigor and steadiness never surpassed in all the annals of savage warfare. Neither party would retreat; neither could advance. The noise of the terrible conflict was tremendous. The cheers of the whites and the yells of the infuriated savages, together with the incessant discharge of firearms, kept up an appalling din. The love for scalps on the part of the redskins caused them to make many daring dashes and imprudent exposures, and three of them were successively shot down over one body, in an attempt to secure the trophy they so much coveted.

The action was fought on the narrow point of land between the Ohio and Kanawha. As the repeated efforts of the whites to carry the enemy's position grew more desperate, the Indian line began to waver, and at several points, to give way. The deep voice of Cornstalk could now be distinctly heard above all the din of battle as he urged his dusky crew to the conflict and shouted: "Be strong! Be strong!" He even buried his keen tomahawk in the brain of one of his faltering warriors and indignantly shaming the rest, made good again the line of battle.

Colonel Field fell about this time, and, at length, General Lewis, alarmed at the extent of his losses and the obstinacy of his swarthy foe, made an effort to turn the enemy's flank by way of Crooked Creek, with three of his best companies. This timely manoeuvre was partially successful. The enemy's fire began to slacken, and at last they began to retire slowly and in such order that they laid ambushes for all the whites who pressed on them too fast. So the contest lasted till dark, when Cornstalk effected a secure retreat. The Virginian loss was severe, embracing three Provincial officers and some sixty men killed and ninety-six wounded. The enemy's loss was also heavy, but its extent could never be exactly ascertained, as during the very hottest of the action they were seen busily engaged throwing the dead into the Ohio and carrying off their wounded. Thirty-three dusky bodies were found on the field the next day. During the night they crossed the Ohio and made off for the Scioto towns.

This battle was the very last that took place under British dominion. It was one of the longest and most obstinately-contested struggles that ever occurred on the western frontier, lasting from sunrise to sunset. The line of battle was at times a mile long, and at points the contestants came to close quarters with tomahawks and clubbed muskets. The Indian army comprised the pick of the Ohio tribes. Cornstalk's towering form could frequently be seen gliding from point to point, rebuking the fearful and reassuring the wavering. It is asserted that on the evening preceding the battle, this distinguished chief, fearing the issue of the approaching struggle, openly proposed in council to go in person to the camp of General Lewis and negotiate an honorable peace. His voice, however, was overruled. "Then," said he, "since you are resolved to fight you *shall* fight. It is likely we will have hard work to-morrow, but if any warrior shall attempt to run away, I will kill him with my own hand."

SUBSEQUENT ATROCIOUS MURDER OF CORNSTALK AND HIS SON.

We may as well here follow the brave Cornstalk until he met his sad fate in the year '77. It is not a little singular that all the prominent chiefs who commanded in this battle were murdered, and two of them close by the battlefield. Not very long after this action, Captain Arbuckle commanded the fort erected at Point Pleasant, and the next year, when the revolutionary struggle had commenced, and British agents were exerting themselves to excite the Indians to take sides against the patriots, Cornstalk and Red Hawk—not showing the unquenchable hatred which always animated the Shawnees against the Americans—visited Arbuckle and declared that the Shawnees were determined on war, and he supposed that he and his would be reluctantly compelled to drift with the stream. Arbuckle on hearing this, resolved to detain the two chiefs, hoping thereby to keep their tribe neutral.

One day Elenipsico, Cornstalk's son, crossed the Ohio on a visit to his father. He is said to have been a very noble and promising young chief. The very next morning two hunters from the fort were ambushed in the woods and one of them, Gillmore by name, was killed. The soldiers of the company to which Gillmore belonged crossed the Kanawha and brought back his mutilated remains. The canoe had scarce touched the shore when Captain Hall's men cried out "Let us kill the Indians in the fort." Captain Hall placed himself at their head, and they all marched up the bank, maddened with rage and carrying their loaded firelocks in their hands. Colonel Stewart and Captain Arbuckle exerted themselves in vain to prevent the bloody, treacherous deed, but exasperated to fury by the spectacle of Gillmore's scalped head, they rushed into the fort, threatening instant death to all who dared oppose them.

The interpreter's wife, who had been a captive among the Indians and felt an affection for the visitors, ran forward and told them that Hall's soldiers were coming to take their lives because they believed that the Indians who killed Gillmore had come with Cornstalk's son the preceding day. This the young chief solemnly denied, averring that he knew nothing whatever of them. His father, perceiving that Elenipsico was in great agitation, encouraged him, and urged him to cast aside all fear. "If, my son," said he, "the Great Spirit has seen fit that we should die together, it is His will, and you ought to die like a man." As the soldiers approached the door, Cornstalk rose, and with great dignity advanced to meet them, receiving eight or nine balls in his body and sank to instant death without a groan. His son remained still and passive and was next shot dead in the seat he occupied. Red Hawk made an attempt to escape by the chimney but was dragged out and dispatched. The remaining Shawnee was shamefully mangled and the horrid tragedy was over.

THE MURDER OF THE GREAT CHIEF BALD EAGLE.

We might have mentioned one other cause, somewhat similar to the one just related, as contributing to the Indian rancor against the "Long Knives," as they called the Virginians. The wanton murder, some little time before, of Bald Eagle, an aged Delaware sachem, was peculiarly irritating to that warlike nation. He spoke the English language with great fluency, and being remarkably fond of tobacco, sweetmeats, and rum, all of which were generally offered to him in profusion in the settlements, he was a frequent visitor at the fort erected at the mouth of the Kanawha, and familiarly acquainted even with the children. He usually ascended the river alone, in a bark canoe, and, from the frequency and harmlessness of his visits, his appearance never excited the least alarm. A white man, who had suffered much from the Indians, encountered the old chief one evening alone upon the river, returning peaceably from one of his usual visits. A conference ensued, which terminated in a quarrel, and the old man was killed upon the spot. The murderer, having scalped his victim, fixed the dead body in the usual sitting posture in the stern of the boat, replaced the pipe in his mouth, and, launching the canoe again upon the river, permitted it to float down with its burden undisturbed. Many settlers beheld it descending in this manner, but, from the upright posture of the old man, they supposed that he was only returning, as usual, from a visit to the whites. The truth, however, was quickly discovered, and inflamed his tribe with the most ungovernable rage. Vengeance was vowed for the outrage, and amply exacted.

After the battle of Point Pleasant, General Lewis crossed the Ohio and marched rapidly towards the Scioto to meet Governor Dunmore, according to orders. At the Pickaway Plains, and within easy striking distance of old Chillicothe and the chief Indian towns, he was met by a message from Dunmore, who was encamped not far distant, ordering him to stop, as he, Dunmore, was about to negotiate a peace with the Indians. Indignant at the manner in which he had been treated, and finding his rear threatened by a large force of savages, Lewis kept on, disregarding likewise a second dispatch, until he had approached within a few miles of old Chillicothe. The Governor now became uneasy, and, accompanied by White Eyes, the celebrated Delaware chief, he peremptorily ordered Lewis to halt.

It is asserted that at this untimely arrest of their march, and when they were in position and in condition to inflict condign punishment and to conquer a lasting peace, it was with difficulty that the Virginian commander could restrain his men from killing Dunmore, who was deemed a traitor to his country. Lewis was now ordered to return forthwith to Point Pleasant and disband, while Dunmore returned to Camp Charlotte and concluded a treaty. The chief orator on the Indian side was Cornstalk, who openly charged the whites with being the sole cause of the war, enumerating the many provocations received by them, and dwelling at length and with force upon the murder of Logan's family. His clear, bugle voice could be distinctly heard over the whole camp of twelve acres. He had ever been the friend of the whites, and after his late defeat by General Lewis, he led his broken and scattered bands to their towns, and immediately convened a council to determine upon what was next to be done. The stern old chief arose, and glancing around with eagle eye upon the assembly of chiefs and oldest warriors, he put the question: "What shall we do now? The 'Long Knives' are coming upon us by two routes. Shall we turn out and fight them?" No response being made, he continued: "Shall we kill all our squaws and children, and then fight until we are all killed ourselves?" Still the congregated warriors were silent, and, after a moment's hesitation, Cornstalk struck his tomahawk into the war post, and with compressed lips and flashing eye, gazed around the assembled throng and said, with great emphasis: "Since you are not inclined to fight, I will go and make peace;" and thus it was he met Dunmore before the arrival of General Lewis. This ended the campaign, and a temporary and hollow peace was patched up. Next year came the Revolution.

SKETCH OF LOGAN, THE FAMED MINGO CHIEF.

<blockquote>Mislike me not for my complexion
The shadowed livery of the burnished sun.—*Shakspeare.*</blockquote>

There was one chief, however, whose face was not seen and whose voice was not heard at the camp of Lord Dunmore, and that was Logan, the far-famed Mingo (which means Iroquois) Chief. He, however, is said to have sent the following speech, which has been published over the whole world, and has ever since its publication formed a staple model of oration for aspiring youth: "I appeal to any white man to say, if ever he entered Logan's cabin hungry, and he gave him not meat; if ever he came cold and naked, and he clothed him not. During the course of the last long and bloody war, Logan remained idle in his cabin, an advocate for peace. Such was my love for the whites that my countrymen pointed as they passed, and said, 'Logan is the friend of white men.' I had even thought to have lived with you, but for the injuries of one man, Colonel Cresap, who last Spring, in cold blood and unprovoked, murdered all the relations of Logan, not even sparing my women and children. There runs not a drop of my blood in the veins of any living creature. This called on me for revenge. I have sought it; I have killed many; I have fully glutted my vengeance. For my country I rejoice at the beams of peace. But do not harbor a thought that mine is the joy of fear. Logan never felt fear! He will not turn on his heel to save his life. Who is there to mourn for Logan? Not one."

Jefferson published this speech in 1784, employing the following complimentary language concerning it: "I may challenge the whole orations of Demosthenes and Cicero to pronounce a single passage superior to the speech of Logan, a Mingo Chief, to Lord Dunmore." The speech immediately became immensely popular; was copied into various tongues, and was published into books of oratory for the instruction of youth. In 1797, Luther Martin, a very able Maryland lawyer, and a son-in-law of Michael Cresap, addressed a long letter to a public declaimer—who had been regularly reciting this alleged speech of Logan— in which he asserted, in effect, that the whole letter was an entire fiction; that neither it nor anything like it had been spoken, written or delivered by Logan; that its sole author was Jefferson himself; that the charge contained in the speech was a vile calumny, and that in support of these assertions he was ready to enter the lists with Jefferson.

Jefferson, finding his veracity and integrity thus openly and boldly impeached, addressed letters to various persons with the purpose of establishing the genuineness of the alleged speech of Logan. He asserted, however, that he first heard of the speech in the circle of Lord Dunmore, and the officers who had been at Camp Charlotte with him; that it had already then been long current and published; that for over twenty years, it had passed uncontradicted, and that if it were not true, he, as well as multitudes of others, were innocently deceived, and that as for doing an injury to Captain Cresap, he was entirely guiltless, having no knowledge of him nor any desire to do him any injustice.

We need not go into the details of this long controversy, which excited a great deal of noise and feeling at the time, and which have been quoted at length by many historians. The information which Jefferson elicited from those in a position to be more fully acquainted with the matter, was exceedingly full and precise, and we think most clearly established the following facts: that *a* speech called Logan's was undoubtedly delivered to Lord Dunmore in '74, at Camp Charlotte, near old Chillicothe; that Mr. Jefferson was honest in the whole matter, and fully believed that Logan had written or delivered the speech which he published as his; that *Captain* Cresap, and not *Colonel* Cresap, as he is styled in the speech, was concerned in the wanton killing of Indians about that time, but that said Cresap was in no manner concerned, as the speech makes Logan say, in the massacre at Yellow Creek, where Logan's relatives were slaughtered.

Colonel Ebenezer Zane, the founder of Wheeling and a gentleman of indisputable veracity, stated that he knew positively, and could abundantly prove, that Cresap was engaged in the attack on two parties of Indians below Wheeling, just before the massacre at the mouth of Yellow Creek, but that at that last massacre Cresap was not present, neither had he, Zane, any doubt but that these three attacks were the cause of Dunmore's war which immediately followed. James Chambers, who lived near Baker's house, opposite Yellow Creek, and was perfectly cognizant of all the facts of the massacre, deposed that Captain Cresap was *not* there that day; that Cresap's party had confessed in his presence that they had attacked Indians just previous, friends and relatives of Logan, and that the woman killed at Baker's was Logan's sister. Judge James testified that in '74 he lived near Fort Henry, and knew that there was a war club with a note attached, left at the house of a settler, whose family were cut off by Logan's party, of which the following is a copy: "Captain Cresap—What did you kill my people on Yellow Creek for? The white people killed my kin at Conestoga a great while ago, and I thought nothing of that. But you killed my kin again on Yellow Creek, and took my cousin prisoner. Then I thought I must kill, too, and I have been three times to war since, but the Indians are not angry—only myself. Captain John Logan. July 21st, 1774."

Confirmatory of the above, we have the testimony of Mr. Robinson, the person whom we have already mentioned as having been captured by Logan in person and afterwards saved by him from the torture, who testifies that Logan always treated him with exceeding kindness and conversed frequently with him, always charging Captain Cresap with the murder of his family; that on July 21st (the very date of the paper given above) Logan brought him, Robinson, a piece of paper and told him he must write a letter for him, which he meant to carry and leave in some house where he should kill somebody: that he made ink with gunpowder, and that he, Robinson, then wrote the letter by his direction, addressing Captain Cresap in it, and that the purport of it was to ask why he had killed his people, &c., and signed it with Logan's name, which letter Logan took and set out again for war, and that he understood that among the Indians killed at Yellow Creek was a sister of Logan, *enceinte*, whom the whites mutilated and stuck on a pole: that he, Robinson, was released in November, but while he remained, his Indian relatives by adoption were exceedingly indulgent to him, never allowing him to do any work.

We next have a very important and highly interesting letter from General Gibson, who deposed that he was with Dunmore at Camp Charlotte: that at the request of the Indians that Dunmore should send some one to their town who could understand their language, he, Gibson, was so dispatched: that on his arrival at the town, Logan came to where deponent was sitting with Cornstalk and other chiefs and asked him to walk out with him: that they then went together into a copse of woods, where they sat down, when Logan, after shedding abundance of tears, delivered to him the speech nearly as related by Jefferson. Gibson further deposed that he then told Logan that it was *not* Colonel Cresap who had murdered his relatives, and that although his son, Captain Michael Cresap, was with the party who killed a Shawnee chief and other Indians, yet he was not present when his relatives were killed opposite the mouth of Yellow Creek.

To our mind the evidence presented is entirely conclusive, and if the speech generally accredited to Logan is a fabrication at all, it is the fabrication of Gibson and not of Jefferson. We will only add a few facts relating to the life and death of a chief who has been embalmed in history with so much romantic interest attached to his memory. He was the second son of Shikellimus, a celebrated chief of the Cayuga nation, who lived at Shamokin, or Conestoga, Pa., and who was a zealous and faithful friend of Christianity and the English. His son was called Logan after the benevolent James Logan, of Pennsylvania, with whom Shikellimus was long on intimate terms. Exactly when Logan emigrated west is not known, nor indeed is much of his life while in Pennsylvania. It is certain, however, that he always had the reputation of being a just, noble and friendly Indian.

Judge Brown, of Mifflin county, asserts that he was the first settler in the Kisacoquillas valley, Pa., and that when a young man he and three others had wandered out one day in search of springs. The party started after a bear and became separated. Brown was looking about for the bear's tracks when all at once he came upon what is now called the Big Spring, and, setting his rifle against a bush, he ran down to get a drink from its pure, sparkling waters. Upon putting his head down, he saw reflected in the water, on the opposite side, the shadow of a tall Indian: he sprang to his rifle, when the savage gave a yell, whether for peace or war the young hunter could not exactly make out, but upon Brown seizing his rifle and facing the stranger, the savage knocked up the pan of his gun, threw out the priming, and extended his open palm in token of amity. After putting down the guns they both shook hands again. This was Logan, "the best specimen of humanity," writes Brown, "I ever met with, either white or red. He could speak a little English, and told me there was another white hunter a little way down the stream, and guided me to his camp." This proved to be Samuel Maclay, also searching for lands to settle on. The two young men thus made known to each other through Logan, were intimate friends ever after.

A few days after they went to Logan's Spring, about six miles distant, where was their Indian friend's camp, and Maclay and Logan soon became engaged in shooting at a mark for a dollar a shot. Logan lost four or five times and confessed himself beaten. When the two whites were about to leave, Logan went into his hut and brought out as many deer skins as he had lost dollars, but Maclay refused to take them, alleging that they had been his guests and did not come to rob him; that the shooting was only a trial of skill and the bet merely nominal. Upon this Logan drew himself up with great dignity and said, "Me bet to make you shoot your best—me gentleman, and me take your dollar if me beat." Maclay, seeing that he would affront his sensitive friend, was obliged to take the skins, and so nice was Logan's sense of honor that he could not be prevailed on to take even a horn of powder in return. Logan soon went to the Allegheny, and Brown never saw him again.

Heckewelder, the Moravian missionary, was among the very earliest residents in the West, and asserts that Logan was introduced to him by an Indian as the friend of the white people, and that he thought him an Indian of superior talents. He exclaimed against the whites for imposing liquor on the Indians, but confessed his own fondness for it. Heckewelder was then living at the Moravian town on the Beaver, and Logan was living at the mouth of that stream. The next year, when the Moravians were passing down the Beaver, on their way to the Muskingum, Heckewelder called at Logan's settlement, and was received with every possible civility. Indian reports of Logan, after the murder of his relatives in '74, state that during Dunmore's war, he took all the revenge he could, and was loth to lay down the hatchet. His expressions denoted a deep melancholy. Life, he said, had become a torment to him. He knew no more what pleasure was; thought it would have been better had he never been born. Report further states that he became delirious, declared he would kill himself, went to Detroit, drank very freely, and did not seem to care what became of him. In this condition he left Detroit, and on his way between that place and Miami was murdered. Heckewelder continues that when he was on his way to Detroit in '81, he was shown the spot where his death occurred. Zeisberger, a far-famed and entirely credible missionary among the Delawares, stated that he knew Logan from a boy; that he was a man of talents, judgment and quick apprehension, and doubted not in the least that Logan sent to Dunmore the speech that has become of such worldwide celebrity.

When Simon Kenton was being carried prisoner to Sandusky, and had been treated very harshly—a savage having shortly before cut through his shoulder with an axe—he arrived at Logan's tent, and says that the Mingo chief walked gravely up to where he stood and said: "Well, young man, these young men seem very mad at you." "Yes, sir, they certainly are," naturally replied poor Kenton. "Well, don't be disheartened. I am a great chief. You are to go to Sandusky; they speak of burning you there, but I will send two runners to-morrow to speak good for you." This he did, and until their return Kenton was kindly treated, being permitted to spend much of his time with Logan, who conversed freely and in the most friendly manner. In the evening Logan was closeted with the two runners, but did not visit Kenton till next morning, when he walked up to him, gave him a piece of bread, told him that he must be carried to Sandusky, and without another word turned upon his heel and left him. Kenton says that Logan's form was striking and manly, his countenance calm and noble, and he spoke English fluently and correctly.

This was in '78. A Captain John Dunkin, according to a contribution in the *American Pioneer*, was also taken prisoner the same year, and saw a good deal of Logan, who spoke both English and French, and told Dunkin that he, Logan, had two souls—one good, one bad; when the good soul was uppermost, he was kind and humane, but when the bad soul ruled he was savage and cruel. Dunkin said that he was killed by his own brother-in-law on returning from a council in Detroit. It is much to be regretted that a chief who was so uniformly friendly to the whites, and who, during his whole life, exhibited so many noble and interesting traits of character, should have been so wronged and abused by reckless, wanton borderers, as to turn all his sweetness into gall, and to render bitter and wretched the whole balance of his life. Had his family been spared, his life would probably have been widely different. Let us drop a tear over human passion, and let the name of Logan live among those of the good and noble.

THE MASSACRE OF THE CONESTOGA INDIANS.

Logan, in the letter attached to a war club, left at a borderer's house, used these significant words: "The white people killed my kin at Conestoga a great while ago, and I thought nothing of *that*, but you killed my kin again at Yellow Creek," &c. This allusion was to the massacre in 1763, over ten years previous, of a small settlement of friendly and inoffensive Iroquois at Conestoga, near Lancaster. The perpetrators of this cruel and cowardly slaughter were a company of fanatical backwoodsmen of the Scotch-Irish stock, called the Paxton Boys, who lived at Paxton, Derry and Donegal, old settlements near Harrisburg. These rude and hardy borderers, consisting of scouts, rangers, hunters, farmers and traders, had suffered enormously for years by Indian forays and scalpings and were goaded almost to desperation at their loss of relatives, property and stock. They looked upon the redmen as so many dogs, and, many of them being religious zealots, found abundant warrant in Scripture for treating the Indians like the Canaanites of old, to "smite them and utterly destroy them: to make no covenant with them nor show mercy unto them."

These hot-headed and tempestuous fanatics were about as much exasperated at the Quakers and the Provincial Legislature as they were against the savages themselves. They complained, and with much show of justice, that while they on the harassed and smitten border, were scourged and peeled, the Legislature and the Quakers sat at their ease, perfectly indifferent, wasting the precious days in factious wrangling and more careful of the copper-colored pagans than they were of them. It is difficult for us in these times, and only reading of the devastating outrages of savages as a matter of remote interest, to understand the intense bitterness and implacable, unquenchable hatred that many of the frontiermen had against the redmen, whom they deemed the authors of all their woes and the barriers to their success as land-getters. The misery of the matter was that with many this hate was blind and indiscriminate. They placed *all* Indians in the same category, only fit to be tracked and hunted like wild beasts and utterly swept off the face of the earth.

This little band of lounging, broom-selling Conestogas were unfortunate enough to incur the suspicion of the Paxton Boys and were charged, if not with secretly indulging in the border murders and robberies, at least with stealthily abetting them and sneakingly conveying information to the actual depredators. The Paxton Boys had formed themselves into a body of rangers for the protection of the frontier, under the auspices of their pastor, the Rev. Colonel Elder, who went about with cocked hat and rifle slung on shoulder—and under the leadership of Captain Lazarus Stewart and Matthew Smith, daring and reckless partisan Captains of the day. Smith heard through some wandering scouts that an Indian, who was known to have committed some late atrocities, had been traced to the Conestoga settlement. This was enough to fire his excitable heart, and hastily collecting a few of his " boys," of like mind with himself, they reached the peaceable Indian hamlet. Here Smith dismounted, and crawling forward, rifle in hand, to reconnoitre, saw, or fancied he saw, a number of armed warriors in the cabins.

The party being too weak for an attack, returned to Paxton. Runners were sent out, and the very next day a body of fifty-seven mounted men, bloodily resolute on extirpating the Conestogas, set out, arriving at their destination by daybreak. Separating into small squads, they stealthily surrounded the humble cabins. An Indian, alarmed at the strange sounds without, issued from one of the huts and came in their direction. "He is the very one that killed my mother!" asserted one with an oath, and drawing sight he was ruthlessly shot down. This was signal enough with men only too anxious to commence the slaughter. With an appalling shout they now rushed forward out of the night; burst into the peaceful cabins; shot, stabbed, tomahawked and scalped all they could find therein to the number of fourteen men, women and children, and then, seizing on whatever booty offered, they set fire to the hamlet. The rest of the hapless community were scattered about the neighborhood.

On the return of these night-prowlers from their unholy mission, they were met by Thomas Wright, who testified afterwards that, struck by their disordered appearance, and seeing a bloody tomahawk at each saddle bow, he asked where they had been and what doing, and on being told, they, seeing the horror depicted on his countenance, demanded of him if he believed in the Bible, and if the Scriptures did not command that the heathen should be destroyed. The devil could always quote Scripture for his purpose, and strangely believing or affecting to believe that they had been doing good service, these bloody miscreants quietly dispersed to their homes.

A prodigious excitement was caused by these lawless and execrable proceedings. The community was divided in opinion, but the great majority being of those who had personally suffered from savage barbarities, either upheld or excused the massacre. The affrighted and horror-stricken remnant of the Conestogas knew not what to do or where to turn to escape the fury of their rancorous foes, but at length were advised to appeal to the sheriff of the county for protection, and were conducted amid growing excitement to Lancaster and lodged in the stone county jail, so strong that it was thought to afford ample protection.

The news of this flagrant outrage spread like wild-fire. The Governor issued a proclamation denouncing the inhuman act and offering a reward for the perpetrators. But the blood of the Paxton Boys was now inflamed. Hearing that an Indian, charged with shedding the blood of one of their number, was among these jail refugees, a party of over fifty assembled secretly, and boldly marched off towards Lancaster. It is said that the design of the leader, Lazarus Stewart, was only to demand this one man and to put him singly to death in case he were found guilty of murder. But unfortunately human passion once thoroughly aroused cannot be so easily allayed. It gets beyond control and resembles the tiger's fierceness upon the taste of blood. The fighting parson, Elder, used all his influence to divert them from their unlawful design. He overtook them on horseback, plead, remonstrated and threatened, but all to no purpose. He then, as a last resort, reined up his horse in front so as to block up the narrow path and *commanded* them to disperse. Upon this, Matthew Smith, pointing his rifle at his pastor's heart, ordered him to make room or he would fire. A passage was thus made and the determined band soon clattered into the streets of Lancaster; turned their panting horses into a tavern yard; hurried to the jail in a body; burst open the door and rushed in with horrid yells and armed to the teeth with rifle, knife and tomahawk.

The poor Indians to the number of near twenty were huddled together in the jail yard. They heard with dismay the furious clamor and saw with horror the inbursting mob of cruel and yelling persecutors. It was said, on the testimony, that several of them snatched up billets of wood in self-defence. Whether this may have changed the purpose of the invaders will never be known, but certain it is that they were now ferociously assaulted, trampled over, slashed with knives and tomahawks, and shot with rifles, and so close, too, that heads were blown to pieces and brains scattered about over the walls and ground. While this was going on, the magistrates and chief citizens were in church attending the Christmas service. The door was suddenly thrown open and the horror-stricken assemblage could hear the broken exclamations of "Murder!—the jail!—the Paxton Boys!—the Indians!"

It was enough to curdle the blood of all there. Before any, however, could reach the jail, the bloody deed had been finished, and the murderers were seen galloping in a body out of the town. Franklin, in his account of the massacre, asserts that when the wretched victims discovered the horrible purpose of the rioters, "they divided into their little families, the children clinging to their parents; they fell on their knees, protested their innocence, declared love to the English, asserting that, in their whole lives, they had never done them injury, and in this posture they all received the hatchet." This picture may be somewhat overdrawn, but certain it is that all who witnessed the shocking spectacle united in declaring that the poor wretches met their fate with that unflinching stoicism which characterizes their race. A company of Highland soldiers on their way from Fort Pitt to Philadelphia, were encamped at the time in or near the town. It is said that they refused to interfere, but this is not very probable, since the whole dread tragedy, so carefully had it been concocted and so silently and swiftly executed, only occupied about a quarter of an hour.

The people now crowded into the jail yard to gaze stupidly upon the ghastly, pitiable spectacle. That it was a revolting sight the following extract of a letter addressed to Heckewelder, the missionary, by a respectable and intelligent citizen of the place, fully attests. We quote: "From fifteen to twenty Indians were placed there for protection. The first notice I had of this affair was while at my father's store, near the court house. I saw a number of people running down street towards the gaol, which enticed me and other lads to follow. At about sixty yards from the jail we met from twenty-five to thirty men, well mounted on horses, and armed with rifles, tomahawks and scalping-knives, fully equipped for murder. I ran into the prison yard, and there, Oh, what a horrid sight presented itself to my view! Near the back door of the prison lay an old Indian and his squaw, particularly well known and esteemed by the people of the town on account of their placid and friendly conduct. His name was Will Sock. Across him and his squaw lay two children of about the age of three years, whose heads were split with the tomahawk and their scalps all taken off. Towards the middle of the jail yard lay a stout Indian shot in the breast. His legs were chopped with the tomahawk, his hands cut off, and finally a rifle-ball discharged in his mouth, so that his head was blown to atoms, and the brains were splashed against and were yet hanging to the wall for three or four feet around. This man's hands and feet had also been chopped off with a tomahawk. In this manner lay the whole of them— men, women and children, spread about the prison yard—shot, scalped, hacked, cut to pieces."

But this was not to be the end. A dreadful ferment was created all along the border by this atrocious massacre. The people of the frontier knew that many of the men engaged in the deed were not brutal ruffians, but were among the best and most substantial residents, who had long and effectively been employed, too, as rangers in protecting the whole border. They knew, also, how much that border had suffered from savage atrocities, and while they heartily condemned the crime, they inclined to excuse the perpetrators of it. But in Philadelphia it was widely different. They there looked upon the massacre in some such light as we would now regard it. They—Quakers especially—assailed not only the murderers, but the whole Presbyterian sect with a perfect tempest of reproach and abuse. In obedience to public clamor, large rewards were offered for the arrest of the criminals, but these shrank not from the trial, but boldly proclaimed the necessity of their act, and defended it by argument and Scripture. So great was the excitement along the frontier that to arrest the ringleaders of the murderous band would have been almost impossible, or, at least, would have required the assistance of a large military force.

The excitement, instead of decreasing by time, daily augmented, but not altogether from this one cause. The backwoods people had always suspected the Moravian or Christianized Indians of complicity in the attacks of the heathen Indians, and several attempts had been made to assault and drive them out of their country. So dangerous became their position that at last, though some time before the proceedings just narrated, the Quaker assembly was compelled to disarm and then remove these converted Indians to Philadelphia for safety. Much against their will, they had, in the midst of Winter, to prepare for migration. Their total number was one hundred and forty. It was in November when the forlorn procession—the aged, the young, the sick and the blind borne in wagons, while the rest went on foot—commenced its weary journey. At every village and hamlet they were rudely greeted with curses and threats. In passing through Germantown they were insulted by an infuriate mob, but, meek and gentle, the jaded pilgrims answered not, but steadily kept moving on, arriving at the Philadelphia barracks in safety.

Here the soldiers quartered there, obstinately refused them admission, and the shrinking, cowering fugitives were compelled to stand in the street for five hours, constantly exposed to a hooting, yelling and cursing rabble, who threatened to kill them outright. The soldiers still persisting in their contumacy, the deplorable procession again took up its dreary march, followed by an angry and tumultuous mob of many thousands and proceeded some six miles further to Province Island, and were there lodged in some waste buildings. Here they held their regular religious meetings and remained peaceably until the massacre of the Conestogas, already related, put an entirely different complexion on matters. Those engaged in that successful piece of butchery, were soon heard to boast that they would finish this Indian business at Philadelphia. The idea, strange as it may seem, soon grew rapidly into favor. The disgraceful conduct of the Quakers—they alleged—in maintaining, at public expense, a lot of savages all through the Winter, who in Spring would be found scalping and butchering upon the border, was constantly rung upon with all the changes.

Meetings were now held, inflammatory harangues delivered, false and absurd reports were industriously circulated, and soon these reckless and hot-headed borderers, finding their sentiments were re-echoed from a noisy and lawless party in Philadelphia itself, began to clamor to be led on to that city. Once before they had sent thither a wagon load of the scalped and mutilated bodies of their neighbors to impress the Quakers with a realizing sense of how they on the frontier were treated by their special pets, the Indians. Now they resolved to go themselves, armed cap-a-pie, and to demand protection. This was, indeed, no empty threat, for a force estimated at from five to fifteen hundred men mustered in January, under their most popular leaders, and actually took up the march to Philadelphia.

The ostensible object of this audacious excursion was the destruction of the Moravian Indians; what political designs against the Quakers lay back of this have never been divulged. Their numbers gathered strength at every mile, and the prodigious excitement which the thick-crowding reports of this singularly daring expedition engendered in Philadelphia may be faintly imagined. Terror and confusion were universal, and the city was working like a hive of bees. Even the non-resisting Quakers were aroused to a sense of what was due from their manhood in this alarming exigency. The magistrates were pressingly urged to take immediate measures for repelling force by force. Eight pieces of heavy ordnance were drawn up to the barracks, where the alarmed Indians were now confined. The citizens, and even many of the young Quakers, took up arms and stationed themselves at these barracks, which they put in as good a condition of defence as possible.

On the night of February the 5th, the mob of borderers were announced as approaching. Every preparation was made to receive them. The whole city was in an uproar. The bells were rung, the streets were illuminated, and the citizens, being suddenly awakened from sleep, were ordered to the town hall to receive their arms and ammunition. Two companies of volunteers repaired to the barracks, and four more cannon were mounted. These prompt and decided preparations caused the approaching mob to pause and ponder. Some gentlemen were deputed to visit them and ask their cause of complaint. With great presumption and arrogance, they asserted there were several murderers among the Moravians, and insolently demanded that these should be delivered up to them. To pacify them, one of the ringleaders was induced to enter the barracks and asked to point out the offenders. Each shrinking Indian was examined, but not one was found against whom any crime could be truthfully charged. The rioters, on hearing this, then asserted that the Quakers must have removed and secreted the criminal Indians. *This* was proved false, and the turbulent invaders were forced to relinquish their design and to take up the homeward march.

The Indians now became objects of great curiosity, and were visited by thousands of all ranks and conditions. Their Sunday services were attended by crowds of respectful listeners, and the soldiers themselves were won to kindness by their meekness and sincerity. Yet still their condition was a very hard one. Accustomed to the free, roaming life of the woods, confinement bore disastrously upon them. The high-seasoned food disagreed with them, and as the Summer advanced, fevers and small-pox broke out among them, causing great loss and almost despair. No less than fifty-six of them died during this long captivity, while the remainder were not released until March, 1765, after the Indian war was well over. They now settled at a new place which they built up near Wyalusing Creek, and called Friedenshutten (Tents of Peace). They were now at peace, and at length, after all their severe trials and troubles, were, for a season, contented, happy and prosperous.

CHAPTER III.

THE LIFE AND CUSTOMS OF THE WESTERN PIONEERS.

> Not with the bold array
> Of armies dread, came they
> Proud conquest on.
> Through a long warfare rude,
> With patient hardihood,
> By toil and strife and blood,
> The soil was won.—*L. Y. Cist.*

We now arrive at a period in Western Border History which, if it have not for the reader so much of a general interest, has yet a more special fascination since it abounds in a series of remarkable personal adventures and captivities; in fierce and obstinate individual conflicts, and in incidents of varied and thrilling interest. By the close of Dunmore's war, and at the outbreak of the Revolution, the tide of emigration had fairly set in for the West. It was relentless as fate—as irresistible as old ocean's onrolling waves. The restless, adventurous pioneer still pushed on and on; penetrating deeper and deeper into the wilderness; ready to bid a stern defiance to all who opposed, and holding on to the soil he had so valorously won, with a grim and unflinching tenacity. Often rudely checked, they were never disheartened; sought out and harassed by a foe that neither pitied or slumbered, they still fought on and on. Ever environed by perils; subjected to every variety of exposure and privation; frequently decimated by savage marauds and forays, and having those most dear to their hearts killed, scalped or carried into captivity, yet they never turned back upon foe, but met him or hunted him with resolute heart, unquailing eye, and with a cool, reckless courage that was almost sublime.

Thus the borderers grew stronger, bolder and more stubborn as the years rolled on. The ringing sounds of their keen axes could be ever heard in new clearings, and within the deepest core of the wilderness; strange forests were notched or girdled in each successive year, serving to mark additional claims; the jealous denizens of the woods would come suddenly upon roving surveying parties with pole and chain, and goaded to madness at the sight, would attack them with vindictive bitterness. An undying and implacable hatred grew up between the two races, as fierce and bitter as that which formerly existed between Moor and Spaniard, and engendered, too, by much the same cause. One sight of each other was the signal for a grapple and a deadly struggle. With kindled eye and expanded nostril, they swiftly rushed to the conflict, inspired by

> That stern joy which warriors feel
> In meeting foemen worthy of their steel.

Now it was that such daring and indomitable characters as Boone, Kenton, Harrod, Brady, Logan, Sevier, the Poes, the Zanes, the McCollochs and the Wetzells, first came to the fore-front—the most prominent types of their class; to whom fear was utterly unknown; who all had a certain free dash of the wilderness in their ways and wanderings; whose very buckskin garments had the odor of the forest mould or herbage about them, and who soon learned to surpass even their swarthy foes themselves in woodcraft, in trailing, in artful strategy and in hand-to-hand combat.

For several years, parts of the Monongahela valley, the region about Fort Pitt and the West Virginia valleys had been sparsely settled, and the Zanes had formed a flourishing colony at Fort Henry, (now Wheeling.) Most of the emigrants came by way of Redstone, (now Brownsville,) on the Monongahela, and since, by Dunmore's treaty at Camp Charlotte a peace or rather a temporary truce was patched up, the settlers came out in swarms, extending as far west as Kentucky. It was the true, genuine spirit of the Anglo-Saxon which spurned all restraint and subdued all things to its will, that impelled them, and they clustered about the various outposts of civilization, prepared to "do or die"—to wrest a generous living from the teeming soil, or leave their bones within its bosom. Those who located along the Ohio differed from those who selected lands in the interior. They were more ambitious of pushing themselves forward and many of them, anticipating the time when the Indian territory across the Ohio would be thrown open to settlement, crossed to explore the country and to pick out for themselves the choice spots.

Around these they would generally mark trees or otherwise define boundaries by which they could be afterwards identified. There were, also, at every frontier post, persons who were attracted thither by their love of hunting and by a genuine attachment for the wild, unshackled scenes of a ranger's life. Existence in the house or in forts was inexpressibly irksome to them. They only felt perfectly free and joyous when roaming the unbounded forests, couched on their beds of leaves or skins at night, and utterly heedless of all restraint or trammel.

This constant practice in the "mimicry of war" soon begot a nerve and skill which enabled them to cope successfully with the wily savage. They were perfectly at home in the woods by day or by night, and could steer their way to any part of the compass with as much unerring certainty as the redskins themselves. It was, notwithstanding the excessive hazard in time of war, a free and happy life, and it is no marvel that so many of the frontier men and youth became completely enamored of this Gypsey abandon of the forest, passing most of their time in vagabondizing hither and yon, "wandering at their own sweet will." When gathered about their fire at night, the stars glimmering dimly through the roof above them, they could right heartily join in the "Song of the Pioneer:"

> The hunt, the shot, the glorious chase;
> The captured elk or deer;
> The camp, the big, bright fire, and then
> The rich and wholesome cheer;
> The sweet, sound sleep at dead of night
> By the camp fire blazing high,
> Unbroken by the wolf's long howl
> Or the panther springing by.

As one of their own number truthfully writes: "Various as may have been their objects in emigrating, no sooner had they come together than there existed in each settlement a perfect unison of feeling. Similitude of situation and commonality of danger, operating as a magic charm, stifled in their birth all those little bickerings which are so apt to disturb the quiet of 'society.' Ambition of preferment and the pride of place, too often but hindrances to social intercourse, were unknown among them. Equality of condition rendered them strangers alike to the baneful distinctions created by wealth as to other adventitious circumstances. A sense of mutual dependence for their common security locked them in amity; and, conducting their several purposes in harmonious concert, together they toiled and together suffered.

"In their intercourse with others they were kind, beneficent and disinterested; extending to all the most generous hospitality which their circumstances could afford. That selfishness which prompts to liberality for the sake of remuneration, and proffers the civilities of life with an eye to individual interest, was unknown to them. They were kind for kindness' sake, and sought no other recompense than the never-failing concomitant of good deeds—the reward of an approving conscience. Such were the early pioneers of the West, and we might even now profit from the contemplation of their humble virtues, hospitable homes, and spirits patient, noble, proud and free—their self-respect grafted on innocent thoughts; their days of health and nights of sleep—their toils by danger dignified, yet guiltless—their hopes of cheerful old age and a quiet grave, with cross and garland over its green turf. and their grandchildren's love for an epitaph.

The great object with most who moved West was, of course, to better their condition, and this more especially after the Revolution. Land was the great *desideratum*, and it could be obtained literally "for the taking up." The methods in which this was done are best described by Rev. Joseph Doddridge, D. D., whose father moved into West Virginia in 1773, just before the outbreak of Dunmore's, or, as it is sometimes called, Cresap's war. Brought up in a rude wilderness cabin, the Doctor spent his whole life amid the dangers and vicissitudes which made up the backwoodsman's life, and has written very graphically of the sports, customs, struggles, privations and vicissitudes which went to make up the pioneer's average life. His earliest recollections were of the humble log cabin, the protecting fort, the encircling woods, the excitements of the chase, and the perils of the redskin scalp-hunters. His infant slumbers were disturbed by the yell of the Indian, and the scene of his boyish sports was a dense and sombre forest, in which danger lay ambushed in so many shapes that even the lads of the border grew cunning in eluding or self-possessed in meeting it. We shall hereafter quote freely and liberally from his famous "Notes," now long out of print.

THE TITLE TO LANDS—THE HARDSHIPS OF SETTLERS.

"Our early land laws allowed four hundred acres and no more to a settlement right. Many of our first settlers seemed to regard this as enough for one family, and believed that any attempt to get more would be sinful, although they might have evaded the law, which allowed of but one settlement right to any one individual, by taking out the title papers in the names of others, to be afterwards transferred to them as if by purchase. Some few, indeed, pursued this practice, but it was generally held in detestation.

The division lines between those whose lands adjoined were generally made in an amicable manner before any survey was made by the parties concerned. In doing this they were guided mainly by the tops of ridges and water courses. Hence, the greater number of farms in the western parts of Pennsylvania and Virginia bore a striking resemblance to an amphitheatre. The buildings occupied a low situation, and the tops of the surrounding hills were the boundaries of the tract to which the family mansion belonged. Our forefathers were fond of farms of this description, because, as they said, 'Everything comes to the house down hill.' In the hilly parts of the State of Ohio, the land having been laid out by straight parallel lines, the farms present a different aspect. There the buildings frequently occupy the tops of the hills.

Our people had become so accustomed to the mode of 'getting land for taking it up,' that for a long time it was believed that the west side of the Ohio would ultimately be disposed of in the same way. Hence, almost the whole region between the Ohio and Muskingum was parceled out in 'tomahawk improvements,' but those so claiming were not satisfied with a single four hundred acre tract. Many owned a great number of tracts of the best land, and thus, in imagination, were as 'wealthy as a South Sea dream.' Some of these land jobbers did not content themselves with marking trees at the usual height with the initials of their names, but climbed up the large beeches and cut the letters in their retentive bark, from twenty to forty feet from the ground. To enable them to identify these trees at a future period, they made marks on the trees around as references. At an early period of our settlements there was an inferior kind of land title, denominated a 'tomahawk right.' This was made by deadening a few trees near a spring, and marking on one or more of them the initials of the name of the person by whom the improvement was made. Rights acquired in this way were frequently bought and sold.

The settlement of a new country in the immediate neighborhood of an old one is not attended with much difficulty, because supplies can be readily obtained from the latter; but the settlement of a country more remote is quite a different thing, because at the outset, food, raiment and the implements of husbandry are only obtained in small supplies and with great difficulty. The task of making new establishments in a remote wilderness, in time of profound peace, is sufficiently difficult, but when, in addition to all the unavoidable hardships attending on this business, those resulting from an extensive and furious warfare with savages are superadded, toil, privations and sufferings are then carried to the full extent of the capacity of men to endure them.

Such was the wretched condition of our forefathers in making their settlements. To all these other difficulties and privations, the Indian war was a weighty addition. This destructive warfare they were compelled to sustain almost single-handed, because the Revolutionary contest gave full employment for the military strength and resources on the east side of the mountains.

AMUSING EXPERIENCES OF YOUNG DODDRIDGE—COFFEE AND GAME.

"Some of the early settlers took the precaution to come over the mountains in the Spring, leaving their families behind, to raise crops of corn, and then return and bring them out in the Fall. This was the better way. Others, especially those whose families were small, brought them with them in the Spring. My father took the latter course. His family was but small, and he brought them all with him. The Indian meal which he transported over the mountains was expended six weeks too soon, so that for that length of time we had to live without bread. The lean venison and the breast of wild turkeys, we were taught to call *bread*. The flesh of the bear was denominated *meat*. This artifice did not succeed very well; after living in this way for some time, we became sickly; the stomach seemed to be always empty and tormented with a sense of hunger. I remember how narrowly the children watched the growth of the potato tops, pumpkin and squash vines, hoping from day to day to get something to answer in the place of bread. How delicious was the taste of the young potatoes when we got them! What a jubilee when we were permitted to pull the young corn for roasting-ears! Still more so, when it had acquired sufficient hardness to be made into johnny-cakes, by the aid of a tin grater. We then became healthy, vigorous, and contented with our situation, poor as it was.

The furniture of the table, for several years after the settlement of the country, consisted of a few pewter dishes, plates and spoons, but mostly of wooden bowls, trenchers and noggins. If these last were scarce, gourds and hard-shelled squashes made up the deficiency. The iron pots, knives and forks, were brought from the east side of the mountains, along with salt and iron, on pack-horses. These articles of furniture corresponded very well with the articles of diet. 'Hog and hominy' was a dish of proverbial celebrity. Johnny-cake or 'pone' was at the outset of the settlements the only form of bread in use for breakfast and dinner; at supper, milk and mush was the standard dish. When milk was scarce, hominy supplied its place, and mush was frequently eaten with sweetened water, molasses, bear's oil, or the gravy of fried meat.

In our display of furniture, delf, china and silver were unknown. The introduction of delf-ware was considered by many of the backwoods people as a wasteful innovation. It was too easily broken, and the plates dulled their scalping and clasp knives. Tea and coffee, in the phrase of the day, 'did not stick to the ribs.' The idea then prevalent was that they were only designed for people of quality, who did not labor, or for the rich. A genuine backwoodsman would have thought himself disgraced by showing a fondness for such 'slops.'

I well recollect the first time I ever saw a teacup and saucer, and tasted coffee. My mother died when I was about six or seven years of age. My father then sent me to Maryland, with a brother of my grandfather, Mr. Alexander Wells, to go to school. At Colonel Brown's, in the mountains, at Stony Creek glades, I for the first time saw tame geese, and by bantering a pet gander, I got a severe biting by his bill, and a beating by his wings. I wondered very much that birds so large and strong, should be so much tamer than the wild turkey; at this place, however, all was right, excepting the large birds which they called geese. The cabin and furniture were such as I had been accustomed to see in the backwoods, as my country was then called.

At Bedford, everything was changed. The tavern at which my uncle put up, was a stone house, and to make the changes still more complete, it was plastered on the inside, both as to the walls and ceiling. On going into the dining-room, I was struck with astonishment at the appearance of the house. I had no idea that there was any house in the world that was not built of logs; but here I looked round and could see no logs, and above I could see no joists; whether such a thing had been made by the hands of man, or had grown so of itself, I could not conjecture. I had not the courage to inquire anything about it. When supper came on, my confusion was 'worse confounded.' A little cup stood in a bigger one, with some brownish-looking stuff in it, which was neither milk, hominy, nor broth; what to do with these little cups, and the little spoons belonging to them, I could not tell; but I was afraid to ask anything concerning the use of them.

I, therefore, watched attentively to see what the big folks would do with their little cups and spoons. I imitated them and found the taste of the coffee nauseous beyond anything I had ever tasted in my life. I continued to drink as the rest of the company did, but with tears streaming from my eyes; but when it was to end, I was at a loss to know, as the little cups were filled immediately after being emptied. This circumstance distressed me very much, as I durst not say I had enough. Looking attentively at the grown persons, I saw one man turn his cup bottom upwards and put his little spoon across it. I observed that after this his cup was not filled again. I followed his example, and to my great satisfaction, the result as to my cup was the same.

A neighbor of my father, some years after the settlement of the country, had collected a small drove of cattle for the Baltimore market. Amongst the hands employed to drive them, was one who had never seen any condition of society but that of the woodsmen. At one of their lodging-places in the mountain, the landlord and his hired man, in the course of the night, stole two of the bells belonging to the drove, and hid them in a piece of woods.

The drove had not gone far in the morning before the bells were missed, and a detachment went back to recover them. The men were found reaping the field of the landlord. They were accused of the theft, but they denied the charge. The torture of 'sweating,' according to the custom of that time, that is, of suspension by the arms pinioned behind the backs, brought a confession. The bells were procured and hung round the necks of the thieves. In this condition they were driven on foot before the detachment until they overtook the drove, which by this time had gone nine miles. A halt was called, and a jury selected to try the culprits. They were condemned to receive a certain number of lashes on the bare back, from the hand of each drover. The man above alluded to was the owner of one of the bells; when it came to his turn to use the hickory, 'now,' says he to the thief, 'you infernal scoundrel, I'll work your jacket nineteen to the dozen—only think what a rascally figure I should make in the streets of Baltimore without a bell on my horse!'

The man was in earnest; in a country where horses and cattle are pastured in the range, bells are necessary to enable the owners to find them; to the traveler who encamps in the wilderness, they are indispensable, and the individual described had probably never been placed in a situation in which they were not requisite

Hunting and Hunters of the Border—Life in the Woods.

"Hunting was an important part of the employment of the early settlers. For some years after their emigration, the forest supplied them with the greater part of their subsistence; some families were without bread for months at a time, and it often happened that the first meal of the day could not be prepared until the hunter returned with the spoils of the chase. Fur and peltry were the circulating mediums of the country; the hunter had nothing else to give in exchange for rifles, salt, lead and iron. Hunting, therefore, was the employment, rather than the sport, of the pioneers; yet it was pursued with the alacrity and sense of enjoyment which attend an exciting and favorite amusement. Dangerous and fatiguing as are its vicissitudes, those who become accustomed to the chase generally retain through life their fondness for the rifle.

The class of hunters with whom I was acquainted, were those whose hunting ranges were on the western side of the river, and at the distance of eight or nine miles from it. Fall and Winter was the time for deer, and Winter and Spring for fur-skinned animals, which could be hunted in any month with an R in it. As soon as the leaves were pretty well down and the weather became rainy, accompanied with slight snows, these men, often acting the part of husbandmen, began to feel that they were also hunters, and grew restless and uneasy at home. Everything about them became disagreeable. The house was too warm; the feather bed too soft, and even the good wife was not thought, for the time being, an agreeable companion. The mind of the hunter was wholly occupied with the camp and the chase.

I have often seen them get up early in the morning, at this season, walk hastily out and look anxiously to the woods and snuff the autumnal winds with the highest rapture; then return into the house and cast a quick and attentive look at the rifle, which was always suspended to a joist by a couple of buck-horns or wooden forks. The hunting dog, understanding the intentions of his master, would wag his tail, and by every blandishment in his power, express his readiness to accompany him to the woods. A hunt usually occupied several days, and often extended to weeks; the hunter living in a camp, hidden in some secluded place, to which he retired every night, and where he kept his store of ammunition and other plunder. There were individuals who re mained for months together in the woods, and spent the greater part of their lives in these camps, which are thus described:

A hunting-camp, or what was called a half-faced cabin, was of the following form: the back part of it was sometimes a large log; at the distance of eight or ten feet from this, two stakes were set in the ground a few inches apart; and at the distance of eight or ten feet from these, two more, to receive the ends of poles for the sides of the camp. The whole slope of the roof was from the front to the back. The covering was made of slabs, skins or blankets, or, if in the Spring of the year, the bark of the hickory or ash tree. The front was left entirely open. The fire was built directly before this opening. The cracks between the poles were filled with moss. Dry leaves served for a bed. It is thus that a couple of men, in a few hours, will construct for themselves a temporary, but tolerably comfortable defence against the inclemencies of the weather.

The site for the camp was selected with all the sagacity of the woodsmen, so as to have it sheltered by the surrounding hills from every wind, but more especially from those of the north and south. These shelters were so artfully concealed, as to be seldom discovered except by accident. An uncle of mine, of the name of Samuel Teter, occupied the same camp for several years in succession. It was situated on one of the southern branches of Cross Creek. Although I lived many years not more than fifteen miles from the place, it was not till within a few years ago, that I discovered its situation. It was shown me by a gentleman living in the neighborhood. Viewing the hills round about it, I soon discovered the sagacity of the hunter in the site of his camp. Not a wind could touch him; and unless by the report of his gun or the sound of his axe, it would have been mere accident if an Indian had discovered his concealment.

Hunting was not a mere ramble in pursuit of game, in which there was nothing of skill and calculation; on the contrary, the hunter, before he set out in the morning, was informed by the state of weather in what situation he might reasonably expect to meet with his game; whether on the bottoms, or on the sides or tops of the hills. In stormy weather, the deer always seek the most sheltered places, and the leeward sides of hills. In rainy weather, when there is not much wind, they keep in the open woods, on the highest ground. In every situation, it was requisite for the hunter to ascertain the course of the wind, so as to get to leeward of the game. This he effected by putting his finger in his mouth and holding it there until it became warm, then holding it above his head; the side which first became cold, showed which way the wind blew.

As it was requisite, too, for the hunter to know the cardinal points, he had only to observe the trees to ascertain them. The bark of an aged tree is thicker and much rougher on the north than on the south side. The same thing may be said of the moss. The whole business of the hunter consists in a series of stratagems. From morning till night he was on the alert to gain the wind of his game, and approach it without being discovered. If he succeeded in killing a deer, he skinned it, and hung it up out of the reach of the wolves, and immediately resumed the chase till the close of the evening, when he bent his course towards his camp; when he arrived there he kindled up his fire, and, together with his fellow-hunter, cooked his supper. The supper finished, the adventures of the day furnished the tales for the evening. The spike buck, the two and three-pronged buck, the doe and barren doe, figure through their anecdotes.

After hunting awhile on the same ground, the hunters became acquainted with nearly all the gangs of deer within their range, so as to know each flock when they saw them. Often some old buck, by means of his superior sagacity and watchfulness, saved his little gang from the hunter's skill, by giving timely notice of his approach. The cunning of the hunter and of the old buck were staked against each other, and it frequently happened that at the conclusion of the hunting season, the old fellow was left the free, uninjured tenant of his forest; but if his rival succeeded in bringing him down, the victory was followed by no small amount of boasting. Many of the hunters rested from their labors on the Sabbath day; some from a motive of piety; others said that whenever they hunted on Sunday they were sure to have bad luck for the remainder of the week."

Weddings in the Olden Time—Strange Frolics and Customs.

"For a long time after the first settlement of a country, the inhabitants in general married young. There was no distinction of rank, and very little of fortune. On these accounts the first impression of love resulted in marriage, and a family establishment cost but a little labor and nothing else. A wedding engaged the attention of a whole neighborhood, and the frolic was anticipated by old and young with eager expectation. This is not to be wondered at when it is told that a wedding was almost the only gathering which was not accompanied with the labor of reaping, log-rolling, building a cabin, or planning some scout or campaign."

Among other graphic sketches, the reverend historian gives the following deeply interesting account of a wedding in the olden times:

"In the morning of the wedding-day, the groom and his attendants assembled at the house of his father, for the purpose of reaching the mansion of his bride by noon, which was the usual time for celebrating the nuptials; which for certain must take place before dinner. Let the reader imagine an assemblage of people, without a store, tailor or mantua-maker within a hundred miles, and an assemblage of horses, without a blacksmith or saddler within an equal distance. The gentlemen, dressed in shoepacks, moccasins, leather breeches, leggins, and linsey hunting shirts, all home made; the ladies, in linsey petticoats, and linsey or linen short gowns, coarse shoes and stockings, handkerchiefs, and buckskin gloves, if any. If there were any buckles, rings, buttons or ruffles, they were relics of old times—family pieces from parents or grandparents.

The horses were caparisoned with old saddles, old bridles or halters, and pack-saddles, with a bag or blanket thrown over them; a rope or string as often constituted the girth as a piece of leather. The march in double file was often interrupted by the narrowness and obstructions of our horse-paths, as they were called, for we had no roads; and these difficulties were often increased, sometimes by the good, and sometimes by the ill will of neighbors, by felling trees and tying grape-vines across the way. Sometimes an ambuscade was formed by the way-side, and an unexpected discharge of several guns took place, so as to cover the wedding company with smoke. Let the reader imagine the scene which followed; the sudden spring of the horses, the shrieks of the girls, and the chivalric bustle of their partners to save them from falling. Sometimes, in spite of all that could be done to prevent it, some were thrown to the ground. If a wrist, an elbow, or an ankle, happened to be sprained, it was tied up with a handkerchief, and little more said or thought about it."

THE RUN FOR THE BOTTLE—THE JIGS, REELS AND MERRY-MAKINGS.

Another ceremony commonly took place before the party reached the home of the bride. It was after the practice of making whiskey began, which was at an early period. When the party were about a mile from the place of their destination, two young men would single out to run for the bottle; the worse the path—the more logs, brush and deep hollows the better, as these obstacles afforded an opportunity for the greater display of intrepidity and horsemanship. The English fox chase, in point of danger to riders and horses, is nothing to this race for the bottle.

The start was announced by an Indian yell; logs, brush, muddy hollows, hill and glen were speedily passed by the rival steeds. The bottle was always filled for the occasion, so that there was no use for judges, for the first who reached the door was presented with the prize. On returning in triumph he announced his victory over his rivals by a shrill whoop. At the head of the troop he gave the bottle, first to the groom and his attendants, and then to each pair in succession to the rear of the line, and then putting the bottle in the convenient and capacious bosom of his hunting shirt, he took his station in line.

The ceremony of the marriage preceded the dinner, which was a substantial backwoods feast of beef, pork, fowls, and sometimes venison and bear meat roasted and boiled, with plenty of potatoes, cabbage, and other vegetables. During the dinner the greatest hilarity always prevailed, although the table might be a large slab of timber hewed out with a broad axe, supported by four sticks set in auger holes; and the furniture, some old pewter dishes and plates, eked out with wooden bowls and trenchers. A few pewter spoons, much battered about the edges, were seen at some tables; the rest were made of horn. If knives were scarce, the deficiency was made up by the scalping knives which every man carried in sheaths suspended to the belt of the hunting shirt.

"After dinner the dancing commenced, and generally lasted till the next morning. The figures of the dances were three and four-handed reels and jigs. The commencement was always a square four, which was followed by what was called 'jigging it off:' that is, two of the four would single out for a jig, and be followed by the remaining couple. The jigs were often accompanied with what was called 'cutting out;' that is, when either of the parties became tired of the dance, on intimation, the place was supplied by some one of the company, without any interruption to the dance. In this way it was often continued till the musician was heartily tired of his situation. Towards the latter part of the night, if any of the company, through weariness, attempted to conceal themselves for the purpose of sleeping, they were hunted up, paraded on the floor, and the fiddler ordered to play 'Hang out till tomorrow morning.'

About nine or ten o'clock a deputation of the young ladies stole off the bride and put her to bed. In doing this it frequently happened that they had to ascend a ladder instead of stairs, leading from the dining and ball room to a loft, the floor of which was made of clap-boards lying loose. This ascent, one might think, would put the bride and her attendants to the blush; but as the foot of the ladder was commonly behind the door, purposely opened for the occasion, and its rounds at the inner ends were well hung with hunting shirts, dresses, and other articles of clothing—the candles being on the opposite side of the house, the exit of the bride was noticed but by few. This done, a deputation of young men, in like manner, stole off the groom and placed him snugly by the side of his bride, while the dance still continued; and if seats happened to be scarce, every young man was obliged to offer his lap as a seat for one of his girls. Late at night refreshment in the shape of 'black Betty'—the bottle—was sent up the ladder, with sometimes substantial accompaniments of bread, beef, pork and cabbage. The young couple were compelled to eat and drink of whatever was offered them. The feasting and dancing often lasted several days, at the end of which the whole company were so exhausted with loss of sleep, that many days' rest was requisite to fit them to return to their ordinary labors. Sometimes it happened that neighbors or relations not asked to the wedding, took offence, and revenged themselves by cutting off the manes, foretops and tails of horses belonging to the wedding company."

How the Couple were Settled—Feasting and House-Warming.

The same writer thus describes the usual manner of settling the young couple in the world:—"A spot was selected on a piece of land of one of the parents. Shortly after the marriage, a day was appointed for building the cabin. The choppers, carpenters, &c., arranged all the day before. The clap-boards for the roof were split with a large frow, four feet long, and as wide as the timber would allow. They were used without planing or shaving. The puncheons for the floor were made by splitting trees eighteen inches in diameter, and hewing the faces of them with a broad-axe. They were half the length of the floor they were intended to make.

The second day was allotted for the raising. In the morning all the neighbors assembled and selected four corner men, whose business it was to notch and place the logs. The rest of the company supplied them with material. By the time the cabin was a few rounds high, the sleepers and floor began to be laid. The door was made by sawing or cutting the logs in one side, so as to make an opening about three feet wide, which was secured by upright pieces of timber, through which holes were bored into the ends of the logs for the purpose of pinning them fast. A similar opening, but wider, was made in one end for a chimney. This was built of logs, and was large enough to admit of a back and jambs of stone. At the square, two end logs projected a foot or more to receive the bunting poles against which the ends of the first row of clap-boards for the roof were supported.

The roof was formed by making the end logs shorter, until a single log formed the comb: on these parallel logs the clap-boards were placed, the ranges of them lapping some distance over those next below them, and kept in their places by logs placed at a proper distance upon them. The roof, and sometimes the floor, were finished on the same day of the raising.

A third day was commonly spent by a few carpenters in leveling off the floor and making a clap-board door and a table, which latter was made of a split slab and supported by four round limbs set in auger holes. Some three-legged stools were made in the same manner. Some pins stuck in the logs at the back of the house supported some clap-boards, which served for shelves. A single fork, placed with its lower end in a hole in the floor and its upper end fastened to a joist, served for a bedstead by placing a pole in the fork, with one end through a crack between the logs at the end of the wall. This front pole was crossed by a shorter one within the fork, with its outer end through another crack. From the front pole, through a crack between the logs of the end of the house, the boards were put on which formed the bottom of the bed. Sometimes other poles were pinned to the forks a little distance above these for the purpose of supporting the front and foot of the bed, while the walls were the support of its back and head.

A few pegs around the walls for a display of the coats of the women and hunting shirts of the men, and two small forks or buck's horns protruding from a joist for the rifle and shot-pouch, completed the carpenter work. In the meantime the masons were also at work. With the heart-pieces of the clap-board timber, they made billets for chinking up the cracks between the logs of the cabin and the chimney. A large bed of mud mortar was made for daubing over these cracks so filled, and a few stones formed the back and jambs of the chimney.

The cabin being thus finished, the ceremony of house-warming took place before the young couple were allowed to move into it. This 'warming' was a dance lasting a whole night, indulged in by the bride and groom, relatives and neighbors. On the day following, the young couple took possession of their new mansion. At house-raisings, log-rollings and harvest parties, every one was expected to do his duty faithfully. A person who shirked his duty on these occasions, was called a 'Laurence,' or some other still more opprobrious epithet, and if it ever came his turn to require a like aid, the idler soon felt his punishment in the general refusal to attend his call. Every man, too, of full age and size, was expected to do his full share of military or scouting duty. If he did not, he was 'hated out as a coward.' Even the want of any article of war equipments, such as ammunition, a sharp flint, a priming wire, a scalping knife or tomahawk, was thought highly disgraceful."

Border Customs and Battles—Tattling—Thieves, &c.

"A man who, without good cause, failed to go out on a scout or campaign when it came to his turn, met with an expression of contempt in the countenances of all his neighbors, and epithets of dishonor were fastened upon him without mercy. Debts, which make such an uproar in civilized life, were then but little known. After the depreciation of the continental currency, they had no money of any kind, but paid for everything by peltry, produce or labor. A good cow and calf were often the price of a bushel of alum salt. Any petty theft was punished with all the infamy that could be heaped upon the offender.

A man on a campaign stole from his comrade a cake out of the ashes. He was immediately named 'the bread rounds!' This epithet of reproach was bandied about thus: when he came in sight of a group of men, one of them would call out 'Who comes there?' Another would answer 'The bread rounds.' If any meant to be more serious, he would call out 'Who stole a cake out of the ashes?' Another would answer out the thief's name in full; to this a third would give confirmation by exclaiming 'That's true and no lie!' This kind of tongue-lashing he was doomed to bear for the rest of the campaign, as well as for years after.

If a theft was detected on the frontier, it was deemed a detestable crime and the maxim was 'a thief must be whipped!' If the theft was serious, a jury of the neighborhood, after hearing the testimony, would condemn the culprit to Moses' Law—that is, to forty stripes, save one. If the theft was trifling, the offender was doomed to carry on his back the U. S. flag of thirteen stripes, which stripes were well and heartily laid on. This was followed by sentence of exile. He had to decamp in so many days, under penalty of having his stripes doubled. If a woman was given to tattling and slander, she was allowed to say what she pleased without being believed, her tongue being said to be no scandal.

With all their rudeness these people were given to hospitality and freely divided their rough fare with a neighbor or a stranger, and would have been offended at the offer of pay. In their forts and settlements, they lived, worked, fought, feasted and suffered together in cordial harmony. They were warm and constant in their friendships. On the other hand, they were revengeful in their resentments, and the point of honor sometimes led to personal combats. If one called another a liar, he was considered as having given a challenge which the one who received it must accept or be deemed a coward. If the injured party was unable to fight the aggressor, he might get a friend to do it for him. The same thing took place on a charge of cowardice or any other dishonorable action—a battle must follow. Thus circumstanced, our people in early times were very cautious of speaking evil of their neighbors.

Sometimes pitched battles occurred, in which time, place and seconds were appointed beforehand. I remember seeing one of these in my father's fort. One of the young men knew well that he should get the worst of the battle, and no doubt repented the engagement, but there was no getting over it. The point of honor demanded the risk of a battle. He took his whipping; the contestants then shook hands, and that was an end of it. The mode of battle in those days was dangerous in the extreme; although no weapons were used, fists, teeth and feet were used at will, but, above all, the detestable practice of gouging, by which eyes were sometimes put out, rendered this mode of fighting frightful indeed. The ministry of the Gospel contributed immensely to the happy change which has been effected in our western society. At an early period in our settlement, three Presbyterian clergymen commenced their labors. They were pious, patient, laborious men, who collected their people into regular congregations, and did all for them that circumstances would allow. It was no disparagement to them that their first churches were in the shady groves, and their first pulpits a kind of tent, constructed of a few rough slabs and covered with clapboards."

The Household Customs—Hunters in Indian Dress.

"The women did the offices of the household, milked the cows, cooked the mess, prepared the flax, spun, wove, and made the garments of linen or linsey. The men hunted and brought in the meat; they planted, ploughed and gathered the corn. Grinding it into meal at the handmill or pounding it into hominy in the mortar, was occasionally the work of either or the joint labor of both. The men alone exposed themselves to danger, fought the Indians, cleared the land, reared the hut or built the fort in which the women were placed for safety. Much use was made of the skins of deer for dress, while the bear and buffalo skins were consigned to the floor for beds and covering. Wooden vessels, either *turned* or *coopered*, were in common use as furniture. A tin cup was as rare a luxury as an iron fork.

Every hunter carried his knife; it was no less the implement of a warrior; not unfrequently the rest of the family were left with but one or two for the use of all. When the bed was, by chance or refinement, elevated above the floor, it was often laid on slabs placed across poles and supported on forks; or, when the floor was of puncheons, the bedstead was hewed pieces, pinned on upright posts or let into them by auger holes. The food was of the most wholesome kind. The richest milk, the finest butter and best meat that ever delighted man's palate, were eaten with a relish which health and labor only could command. Hats were made of native fur, and the buffalo wool employed to make cloth, as was also the bark of the wild nettle. There was some paper money in the country. If there was any gold and silver, it was suppressed. The price of a beaver hat was, in the depreciated currency of the day, worth five hundred dollars.

The hunting shirt was universally worn by the men. This was a kind of loose frock, reaching half way down the thighs, with large sleeves, open before, and so wide as to lap over a foot or more when belted. The cape was large and sometimes handsomely fringed with a raveled piece of cloth of a different color from that of the hunting shirt itself. The bosom of this shirt served as a wallet to hold a chunk of bread, cakes, jerk, tow for wiping the barrel of the rifle, or any other necessary for the hunter or warrior. The belt, which was always tied behind, answered several purposes besides that of holding the dress together. In cold weather, the mittens, and sometimes the bullet-bag, occupied the front part of it. To the right side was suspended the tomahawk, and to the left the scalping knife in its leathern sheath.

The hunting shirt was generally made of linsey; sometimes of coarse linen, and a few of dressed deer skins. These last were very cold and uncomfortable in wet weather. The skirt and jacket were of the common fashion. A pair of drawers or breeches and leggins were the dress of the thighs and legs; a pair of moccasins answered for the feet much better than shoes, and were made of dressed deer skin. They were mostly made out of a single piece, with a gathering seam along the top of the foot, and another from the bottom of the heel, without gathers, as high as the ankle joint, or higher. Flaps were left on each side to reach some distance up the leg, and were adapted to the ankles and lower part of the leg by thongs of deer skin, so that no dust, snow or gravel could find its way within.

The moccasins in general use cost but a few hours of labor to fashion, and were done by a moccasin awl made from the back spring of an old clasp knife. This awl, with its buck-horn handle, was an appendage of every bullet-pouch strap, together with a roll of buckskin thongs for mending moccasins, which was the labor of almost every evening. They were sewed and patched together with deer-skin thongs, or whangs, as they were commonly called. In cold weather, these moccasins were well stuffed with deer's hair or dry leaves, so as to keep the feet comfortably warm; but in wet weather it was usually said that wearing them was only 'a decent way of going barefooted,' and such, indeed, was the fact, owing to the spongy texture of the leather of which they were made.

Owing to the defective covering of the feet more than to anything else, the greater number of hunters and warriors were afflicted with rheumatism in the limbs. Of this disease they were all apprehensive in cold or wet weather, and therefore always slept with their feet to the fire, to prevent or cure it as well as they could. This kept them from being confirmed cripples for life.

In the latter years of the Indian war, our young men became more enamored of the Indian dress. The drawers were laid aside, and the leggins made longer, so as to reach the upper part of the thigh. The Indian breech-cloth was adopted. This was a piece of linen cloth, nearly a yard long and eight or nine inches broad, hanging before and behind over the belt, sometimes ornamented with coarse embroidery. To the same belt which secured the breech-cloth, strings, supporting the long leggins, were attached. When this belt, as was often the case, passed over the hunting shirt, the upper part of the thighs and part of the hips were naked. The young warrior, instead of being abashed by this nudity, was proud of his Indian dress. In some few instances I have seen them go into places of public worship in this dress. Their appearance, however, did not much add to the devotion of the young ladies. The linsey coats and bed gowns, which were the universal dress of our women in early times, would make a strange figure at this day. They knew nothing of the ruffles, leghorns, curls, combs, rings, and other jewels with which the ladies now decorate themselves. Such things were not then to be had. Instead of the toilet, they had to handle the distaff or shuttle—the sickle or weeding hoe—contented if they could obtain their linsey clothing and cover their heads with a sun-bonnet made of six or seven hundred linen."

THE SPORTS AND PASTIMES OF THE PIONEERS.

"The sports of the pioneers were such as might be expected among a people who, owing to circumstances as well as education, set a higher value on physical than mental endowments and on skill in hunting and bravery in war, than any polite accomplishment or the fine arts. Many of the sports were imitative of the exercises and stratagems of hunting and war. Boys were taught the use of the bow and arrow at an early age, and acquired considerable adroitness in their use, so as to kill a bird or a squirrel. One important pastime of boys was that of imitating the noise of every bird and beast of the woods. This faculty was not merely a pastime, but a very necessity of education, on account of its practical utility. Imitating the gobbling and other sounds of the wild turkey, often brought those watchful and keen-eyed tenants of the forest within reach of the rifle. The bleating of the fawn brought its dam to her death in the same way. The hunter often collected a company of mopish owls to the trees about his camp and amused himself with their hoarse screaming. His howl would raise and obtain responses from a pack of wolves so as to inform him of their whereabouts, as well as to guard him against their depredations.

This imitative faculty was sometimes requisite as a measure of precaution in war. The Indians, when scattered about in a neighborhood, often collected together by imitating turkeys by day and wolves by night. In similar situations our people did the same. I have often witnessed the consternation of a whole neighborhood in consequence of the screeching of owls. An early and correct use of this imitative faculty was considered as an indication that its possessor would become in due time a good hunter and a valiant warrior.

Throwing the tomahawk was another boyish sport in which many acquired considerable skill. The tomahawk, with its handle of a certain length, will make a given number of turns within a certain distance; say, in five steps it will strike with the edge, the handle downwards—at the distance of seven and a half it will strike with the edge, the handle upwards, and so on. A little experience enabled the boy to measure the distance with his eyes when walking through the woods, and to strike a tree with his tomahawk in any way he chose. A well-grown boy at the age of twelve or thirteen, was furnished with a small rifle and shot pouch. He then became a foot soldier and had his porthole assigned him. Hunting squirrels, turkeys and raccoons, soon made him expert in the use of his gun.

Shooting at a mark was a common diversion among the men when their stock of ammunition would allow it; this, however, was far from being always the case. The present mode of shooting off-hand was not then in practice. This mode was not considered as any trial of a gun; nor, indeed, as much of a test of the skill of a marksman. Their shooting was from a rest, and as great a distance as the length and weight of the barrel of the gun would throw a ball on a horizontal level. Such was their regard to accuracy in those sportive trials of their rifles, and in their own skill in the use of them, that they often put moss or some other soft substance on the log or stump from which they shot, for fear of having the bullet thrown from the mark by the spring of the barrel. When the rifle was held to the side of a tree for a rest, it was pressed against it as tightly as possible, for the same reason. Rifles of former times were different from those of modern date; few of them carried more than forty-five bullets to the pound. Bullets of a less size were not thought sufficiently heavy for hunting or war.

The athletic sports of running, jumping and wrestling, were the pastimes of boys in common with men. Dramatic narrations, chiefly concerning Jack and the Giant, furnished our young people with another source of amusement during their leisure hours. The different incidents of the narration were easily committed to memory, and have been handed down from generation to generation. The singing of the first settlers was rude enough. 'Robin Hood' furnished a number of our songs; the balance were mostly tragical; these were denominated 'love songs about murder.' As to cards, dice, backgammon and other games of chance, we knew nothing about them. They are among the blessed gifts of civilization! Dancing was the principal amusement of our young people of both sexes. Their dances, to be sure, were of the simplest forms; three-handed and four-handed reels and jigs. Country (contra) dances, cotillions and minuets, were unknown. I remember to have seen, once or twice, a dance which was called 'The Irish Trot.'"

THE CAPTIVITY OF JOHN McCULLOUGH.

Written by Himself After Eight Years a Captive.

We have quoted liberally from Dr. Doddridge, because he himself lived on the border; was an actor in the stirring scenes which occurred during the Indian wars, and, being well acquainted with the early pioneers and their ways and customs, has graphically pictured them, writing only of what he himself saw or knew. Such a chronicle, therefore, is obviously worth a score of those written at this late day and from a modern stand point.

For a somewhat similar reason we publish a few simple narratives of captivities, because, like that of Smith's, already related, they furnish the most faithful transcript of Indian daily life and habits. They treat of a singular and deeply interesting period and condition in our history —the like of which has never occurred since and can never occur again. Before, therefore, we proceed to the settlement of Kentucky, or sketch the lives of the remarkable worthies who traveled or fought over that "dark and bloody ground," we select two narratives of captivities which happened contemporaneously with that of Captain Smith. And first, we give an abridgment of what John McCullough saw and suffered during an eight years' residence among redskins. We quote:

I was born in Newcastle county, in the State of Delaware. When I was five years old my father moved his family from thence to the back parts of then Cumberland (now Franklin) county, to a place well known by the name of Conococheague settlement, about a year before what has been generally termed Braddock's war. Shortly after the commencement of the war, he moved his family into York county, where he remained until the Spring of 1756, when we ventured home; we had not been long at home until we were alarmed again; we then fled down to Antietam settlement, where we remained until the beginning of harvest, then ventured home to secure our crops; we stopped about three miles from home, where we got a small cabin to live in until my father went home and secured the grain.

On the 26th of July, 1756, my parents and oldest sister went home to pull flax, accompanied by one John Allen, a neighbor, who had business at Fort Loudon, and promised to come that way in the evening to accompany them back. Allen had proceeded but about two miles toward Loudon when he heard the Indians had killed a man that morning, about a mile and a half from where my parents were at work; he then, instead of going back to accompany them home, agreeably to his promise, took a circuitous route of about six or seven miles, for fear of Indians. When he came home, my brother and I were playing on the great road, a short distance from the house; he told us to go immediately to the house or the Indians would catch us, adding, at the same time, that he supposed they had killed our father and mother by that time.

We were small; I was about eight years old, my brother was but five; we went to the house, the people were all in a bustle, making ready to go to a fort about a mile off. I recollect of hearing them say, that somebody should go and give my parents notice; none would venture to go; my brother and I concluded that we would go ourselves; accordingly we laid off our trowsers and went off in our shirts, unnoticed by any person, leaving a little sister about two years old sleeping in bed; when we got in sight of the house we began to halloo and sing, rejoicing that we had got home; when we came within about fifty or sixty yards of the house, all of a sudden the Indians came rushing out of a thicket upon us; they were six in number, to wit, five Indians and one Frenchman; they divided into two parties; three rushed across the path before, and three behind us. This part of the scene appears to me yet more like a dream than anything real: my brother screamed aloud the instant we saw them; for my part, it appeared to me that the one party were Indians and the other white people; they stopped before us; I was making my way betwixt two of them, when one of the hind party pulled me back by my shirt; they instantly ran up a little hill to where they had left their baggage; there they tied a pair of moccasins on my feet; my brother at that instant broke off from them, running towards the house, screaming as he went; they brought him back, and started off as fast as I was able to run along with them, one of them carrying my brother on his back.

We ran alongside of the field where my parents were at work; they were only intercepted from our view by a small ridge in the field, that lay parallel to the course we were running; when we had got about seventy or eighty perches from the field, we sat down in a thicket of bushes, where we heard our father calling us; two of the Indians ran off towards the house, but happily missed him, as he had returned back to the field, supposing that we had gone back again. The other four started off with us as fast as I was able to travel along with them, jumping across every road we came to, one catching by each arm and slinging me over the road to prevent our tracks from being discovered.

We traveled all that day, observing still when we came to an eminence, one of them would climb up a tree, and point out the course they should take, in order, I suppose, to avoid being discovered. It came on rain towards evening; we traveled on till a good while after night; at last we took up our lodging under a large tree; they spread down a blanket for us to lie on, and laid another over us; an Indian laid down on each side of us on the edge of our cover, the rest laid down at our head and feet. At break of day we started again; about sunrise we heard a number of axes at a short distance from us; we also discovered where logs had been dragged on the ground the day before; they immediately took the alarm and made off as quick as possible. Towards evening we stopped on the side of a mountain; two of the Indians and the Frenchman went down into the valley, leaving one to take care of us; they were not long gone till we heard them shooting; in a short time they came back, carrying a parcel of hogs on their backs, and a fowl they had killed; also a parcel of green apples in their bosoms; they gave us some of the apples, which was the first nourishment we got from the time we were taken.

We then went down the mountain into an obscure place, where they kindled a fire and singed the hair off the hogs and roasted them; the fowl they roasted for us. We had not been long there till we heard the war halloo up the run from where we had our fire, and the two Indians came to us, whom I mentioned had ran towards the house when they heard my father calling us; they had a scalp with them, and by the color of the hair I concluded that it had been my father's, but I was mistaken; it was the scalp of the man they killed the morning before they took us; this scalp they made two of, and dried them at the fire. After roasting the meat and drying the scalps, we took to the mountain again; when we had got about half way up, we stopped and sat down on an old log—after a few minutes' rest they rose up, one after another, and went to the sides of rocks and old logs and began to scrape away the leaves, where they drew out blankets, bells, a small kettle, and several other articles which they had hidden when they were coming down.

We got over the mountain that evening; about sunset we crossed a large road in sight of a waste house; we went about a quarter of a mile further and encamped by the side of a large run; one of then went about two or three hundred yards from the camp and shot a deer and brought it to the camp on his back. I had been meditating my escape from the time we crossed the road. Shortly after dark we laid down; I was placed next to the fire, my brother next, and an Indian laid down on the edge of the blanket behind us. I awoke some time in the night, and roused my brother, whispering to him to rise, and we would go off; he told me that he could not go; I told him that I would go myself, but he replied that he did not care. I got up as softly as I could, but had not got more than three or four yards from the fire till the Indian who lay at our backs raised his head and said, "*Where you go?*" I told him I was going for a call of nature; he said, "*make haste, come sleep.*" I went and laid down again.

Next morning four of the Indians and the Frenchman went off on a scout, leaving one to take care of us. About the middle of the day they came running the way we came the evening before—they hallooed as soon as they came in sight; by the time they got to the camp, the one who took care of us took me on his back and ran as fast as he could for about a quarter of a mile, then threw me down, broke a twig and switched me along until we got on the mountain again; about an hour after, we began to gather whortleberries, as they were very plenty on the mountains; lucky, indeed, for us, for I verily believe we would have starved, had it not been for the berries, for we could not eat the meat without bread or salt. We got off the mountain that evening, and encamped in a thicket; it rained that night and the next morning; they had made a shade of some of their spare blankets; we were long in starting the next morning. Whilst we were sitting about the fire we heard the report of two guns at a little distance directly the way we came the evening before; they started up in an instant, and picked up their blankets and other things. The one who carried me before took me on his back and ran as fast as he could for about half a mile, then threw me down and whipped me along as he had done the day before.

McCullough's Idea of the Devil—How He was Made Hardy.

It must be observed that they always carried my brother time about; for my part it was the only two rides I got from the day I was taken till we got to Fort Duquesne (now Pittsburgh.) I must pass over many occurrences that happened on our way to Pittsburgh, excepting one or two. The morning before we came to *Kee-ak-kshee-man-nit-toos*, which signifies Cut Spirit, an old town at the junction of *La-el-han-neck*, or Middle Creek, and *Can-na-maugh*, or Otter Creek. The morning before we got there, they pulled all the hair out of our heads, except a small spot on the crown, which they left. We got to the town about the middle of the day, where we got some squashes to eat; the next morning we set out for Fort Duquesne—the morning after that we came to several Indian camps—they gave us some bread, which was the first we tasted from the time we were taken. About a mile or two before we came to the fort, we met an old Indian, whose dress made him appear very terrifying to us; he had a brown coat on him, no shirt, his breast bare, a breech-clout, a pair of leggins and moccasins, his face and breast painted rudely with vermilion and verdigris, a large bunch of artificial hair, dyed of a crimson color, fixed on the top or crown of his head, a large triangular piece of silver hanging below his nose, that covered almost the whole of his upper lip; his ears (which had been cut according to their peculiar custom) were stretched out with fine brass wire, made in the form (but much larger) of what is commonly fixed in suspenders, so that, perhaps, he appeared something like what you might apprehend to be a likeness of the devil.

As he approached toward us, the rest said something to him—he took hold of me by the arm, and lashed me about from side to side; at last he threw me from him as far as he was able, then took hold of my brother and served him the same way. Shortly after that they stopped and painted us, tying or fixing a large bunch of hawk's feathers on the top of each of our heads, then raised the war halloo, viz.: one halloo for each scalp, and one for each prisoner, still repeating at certain intervals; we met several Indians who came running out to meet us—we were taken to the middle of their encampment into one of their chief's huts; after they had given a narrative of their adventures, the old chief drew out a small bag from behind his bed and took out a large belt of wampum and fixed it around my neck. We then started down to the fort; a great number of Indians of both sexes were paraded on each side of the path to see us as we went along; some of them were shoving in little fellows to strike us, and others advising me to strike them, but we seemed to be both afraid of each other; we were taken into a French house, where a number of Indians were sitting on the floor; one of the chiefs took my brother by the hand and handed him to a Frenchman who was standing at a room door, which was the last sight I had of him.

After that he took me by the hand, and made a speech for about half an hour, then handed me to an Indian, who was sitting on the hearth smoking his pipe; he took me between his legs, (he could talk very good English,) and asked me several questions, telling me that I was his brother, that the people had killed a brother of his about a year before, and that these good men (meaning the warriors who took us) had gone and brought me to release his deceased brother; he also told me that he had been raised amongst the white people, and that he had been taught to read when he was young, but that he had almost forgot it. I believe he was telling the truth, for he knew all the letters and figures. He then took me by the hand and led me to the *Al-lee-ge-ning*, or Allegheny river, which signifies an impression made by the foot of a human being; for, said they, the land is so rich about it that a person cannot travel through the lands adjoining it without leaving the mark of their feet. We got in a canoe and went across the river, where a great number of Indians were encamped. He led me through their encampment; toward evening we came back. Shortly after our return two young fellows took me by the hand and led me to the river; we got into a canoe and paddled about thirty or forty yards from the shore, when they laid down their paddles and laid hold of me by the wrists, and plunged me over head and ears under the water, holding me down till I was almost smothered, then drew me up to get breath. This they repeated several times.

I had no other thought but that they were going to drown me. I was at every interval pleading with them not to drown me; at last one of them said, "*me no killim, me washim*." I pleaded with them to let me in shallow water, and I would wash myself; accordingly they did—I then began to rub myself; they signified to me to dive; I dipped my face into the water and raised it up as quick as I could: one of them stepped out of the canoe and laid hold of me on the back of my neck, and held me down to the bottom, till I was almost smothered, before he let me go. I then waded out; they put a new ruffled shirt on me, telling me that I was then an Indian, and that they would send me away to the rest of their friends. Accordingly I was sent off the next day with a female friend, to an uncle of my adopted brother's, who lived at a town called *She-nang-go*, on Beaver Creek. Nothing remarkable happened during our journey, excepting several falls that I got off a young horse I was set on to ride.

On the third or fourth night we arrived in *She-nang-go*, about an hour after dark: after the female friend whom I was sent with had informed the family who I was, they set up a lamentable cry for some time: when their lamentation was over, they came to me one after another and shook me by the hand, in token that they considered me to stand in the same relationship to them as the one in whose stead I was placed. The next morning I was presented to my uncle, with whom I lived about a year. He was blind of one eye—a very good-natured man. In the beginning of Winter he used to raise me up by daylight every morning, and make me sit down in the creek up to my chin in the cold water, in order to make me hardy, as he said, whilst he would sit on the bank smoking his pipe, until he thought I had been long enough in the water, and he would then bid me dive. After I came out of the water he would order me not to go near the fire until I would be dry. I was kept at that till the water was frozen over; he would then break the ice for me and send me in as before. Some time in the Winter, perhaps not long before Christmas, I took very sick; I lay all Winter at the fire side, and an old squaw attended me (what bt

14

dle attendance I got); she used to go out in the snow and hunt up herbs by the old tops; the roots of which she would boil and make a kind of drink for me. She would never suffer me to taste cold water, or any kind of flesh, or anything that was sweet or salt. The only nourishment that I was suffered to take was honey, or dumplings, made of coarse Indian meal boiled in water. As I said before, I lay all Winter at the fire side; I had nothing but a small blanket to cover me, part of which I drew under me for my bed; my legs drew up so that I was obliged to crawl when I had occasion to go out of doors. I remained in that situation till corn-planting time, when I began to get better. They anointed my knees and hams with bear's oil, and made me keep my knees stretched out as tight as I could bear them, by which means I got the use of my joints in about a month's time.

AN INDIAN BOY SHOT AND KILLED—McCULLOUGH SUSPECTED.

Shortly after I got able to run about, a dreadful accident happened by my hands, in the following manner: The most of the Indians of the town were either at their corn fields or out a fishing—my uncle had been unwell for some time—he was below the town at the creek side, where he had an Indian doctor sweating him and conjuring out his disorder. He had a large pistol, which he had hung up by the guard at the head of his bed. There were two brothers, relations of ours, the oldest was perhaps about my own age, the other about two years younger. The oldest boy took down the pistol and cocked it, threatening, for diversion, to shoot his brother: the little fellow ran off from us. I assisted him to let down the cock of the pistol, which he held in his left hand with the muzzle towards his body, and his right hand against the cock; I would then (after cautioning him to turn the muzzle past his body) draw the trigger, and he would let down the cock slowly. I advised him several times to lay by the pistol, which he would do; but as soon as his brother would come back to us, he would get it again. At last his brother got afraid and would not come near us any more.

He then threatened to shoot me; I fled out of the house from him. The town lay in a semi-circular form, round a bend of the creek; there happened to be a woman at the upper end of the town (as we lived at the lower end) that had observed me when I fled out of the house from him—he immediately called me back to assist him to let down the cock; I refused to go, unless he would turn the butt of the pistol to me, which he did; I went in, in haste (and forgot to caution him to hold the muzzle to one side) and drew the trigger; the consequence was, the pistol went off and shot him in the stomach. The pistol flew out of our hands; he laid his hands across his breast and ran out of the house, screaming aloud as he ran; I ran out of the house and looked after him; he went towards their own door, (about forty or fifty yards off,) but quit screaming before he fell. It was late in the evening; his mother and grandmother were coming from their corn field at that instant; his grandmother just cast her eye towards him, as she came past him, and came to me where I was standing; before they got near me, I told her that *Watook*, (for that was his name,) had shot himself; she turned away from me without saying anything. In a short time all the Indians in the town collected about me, examining me, and getting me to show them what way he took to shoot himself; I told them that he took the pistol in his left hand and held the muzzle to his stomach, whilst he pushed the trigger from him with his thumb: I held to the one story. At last the woman (whom I mentioned had seen me when I fled out of the house from him) came and told them that she was standing out of doors looking at me across the bend of the creek, at the time she heard the report of the pistol, and that I was standing a considerable distance from the house at the time—at which they all dispersed. There was something very singular in this affair, as the same woman and her husband, about a year after the above accident, were the means of saving my life when I was apparently drowned, as I shall have occasion to mention hereafter.

It happened to be the first funeral that I had seen amongst them, and not being acquainted with their customs, I was put to a terrible fright; shortly after dark they began to fire their guns, which they always do when any one dies. As all the family had gone to the wake, I was left by myself in the house; when the firing began I concluded that they were about to take my life; I therefore crept under a bed that was set upon forks drove into the ground, a considerable height off the floor, where I lay as close to the wall as I could get, till about break of day, when I was roused by the report of their guns again. I did not go near the corpse—however, I heard them say, that he bled none, as the wadding and the blaze of the powder had followed the ball into his body. There were several young squaws who had seen us running about with the pistol; they frequently charged me with being the cause of the boy's death, which I always denied, but *Queek-queek-co-moochque* a little white girl, (a prisoner,) who lived with the family that the deceased belonged to, was like to be the worst evidence against me— she told that she saw me have the pistol in my hands several times—but the woman's evidence overruled the whole of them; however, their minds were not entirely divested of the thought that I had taken his life, as they often cast it up to me afterwards, that I had shot *Watook;* especially when I would happen to get into a quarrel with any of the little fellows, they would tell me that I had killed one of them already, and that I wanted to kill another; however, I declared the thing was merely accidental.

When I reflect on the above accident, and the circumstances attending it, my mind flows with gratitude to that Almighty Being whose wise providence directs the affairs of the world; I do not say that a lie is justifiable in the sight of God, yet I am led to believe that the woman was guided by Providence in telling a manifest falsehood, which, perhaps, was the means of prolonging my days; as I am led to believe, had the true circumstances of the case been known to them, I never should have seen the light of another day; nor should I have expected that my body would have been laid under the ground, but that I would rather have been thrown into the creek, to be devoured by fish, or left above ground to be devoured by vermin, as I knew to be the case with two men, which I shall mention before I close this narrative.

Some time in the Summer following, we went to a treaty with the French at Presq' Isle. On our way there, we went by an Indian town at or near where Meadville now stands; just as we got to the town, we observed a number of batteaux coming down French Creek; the French came to the shore where we were; one of them offered to purchase me from the Indians; he offered for me an old spade, wanting the handle, (which, perhaps, was the lowest value that ever was set upon me). They laughed scornfully at him for his folly; however, they decamped immediately, for fear the French might come and steal me away by night. When we got to Presq' Isle, I was given up to my Indian mother, whom I had never seen before. After the treaty was over, my old uncle returned to Shenango, and left me with my old mother and two brothers something older than myself; we had a step-father also, who hunted for us. We moved from Presq' Isle near to Fort *Le Bœuf*, where my mother had raised a small patch of corn; we lived there till the Fall, occasionally going to the fort to draw rations, as the French constantly supplied the Indians with provisions whilst they lay about the fort. The French always observed to fire off a swivel, as a salute, when the Indians came to the fort with prisoners or scalps.

Towards Fall my old brother (I call him old because he was the oldest of the family—he was not more than twenty-two or three) came to us; I had not seen him from the time I was given to him at Fort Duquesne (or Pittsburgh) till then; he came to take us to Shenango to live amongst the rest of our friends. We had but one horse to carry our provisions; our apparel we carried on our backs like the terrapin, so that we had to travel on foot. We were a long time on the way, as they frequently stopped three or four days at a place to hunt. We arrived at Shenango in the beginning of Winter. Not long after our arrival, I took a severe turn of the pleurisy, and lay very ill for about twenty days; my old mother and an old aunt paid great attention to me; observing, with regard to my drink and diet, as my former attendant had done before.

Captive Nearly Drowned—A Squaw Whipped for Abusing Him.

The next Summer I had like to lose my life; all the Indians of the town, excepting one man and a woman, were out at their corn fields, leaving the young ones to take care of their houses. About ten o'clock of the day, four of the little fellows and I went into the creek to bathe ourselves; the creek is perhaps about sixty or seventy yards wide; there is a ridge of rocks that reaches across the stream, where I had often observed the Indians wading across, the water being deep at each side; I ventured to wade over, and made out very well until I got about a rod off the shore on the opposite side; when the water began to get too deep for me, I turned about, proud of my performance. When I had got about half way back, I missed my course, and all at once stepped over the edge of the rocks and went down over head and ears; I made a few springs as high as I could above the water; at last I swallowed so much water, not having yet learned to swim, I was obliged to give over. When the little fellows who came to bathe along with me, saw that I had given myself up, they raised the scream. The woman whom I mentioned before, came running to the bank to see what was the matter; they told her that *Isting-go-weh-hing* (for that was the name they gave me) was drowned. She immediately ran to the house and awaked her husband, who came as quick as possible (as they told me afterwards) to my relief; as I kept afloat all the time, he waded up to his chin before he could get a hold of me by the leg, he then trailed me through the water until he got to the rocks that I had stepped over, he then laid me on his shoulder and brought me out to the bank, where he threw me down, supposing that I was dead.

It happened that my head was down hill; the water gushed out of my mouth and nose; they had previously sent off one of the little boys to inform my friends of the accident. After some time I began to show some signs of life. He then took me by the middle, clasping his hands across my belly, and shook me, the water still running plentifully out of my mouth and nose. By the time my friends arrived, I began to breathe more freely. They carried me up the bank to a *weik-waum*, or house, and laid me down on a deer skin, where I lay till about the middle of the afternoon; at last I awoke out of sleep and was surprised to see a great number of Indians of both sexes standing around me. I raised my head, my old brother advanced toward me, and said, "*au moygh-t-ha-heeh a-moigh*," that is, "rise, go and bathe yourself." I then recollected what I had been doing. He told me that if he would see me in the creek again he would drown me outright; however, the very next day I was paddling in the water again.

Some time whilst we resided at *She-nang-go*, (perhaps in the latter end of November,) about thirty warriors returned through *She-nang-go* from a tour; they were of the Mingo nation: they had a number of scalps with them and a prisoner, a man of about twenty-five years of age; one of the party had got wounded in the body; the prisoner had a large bundle of blankets tied up and slung on his back, with a *hap-pees*, for the wounded Indian to sit on. I make no doubt but that he had carried him the whole way from where he received the wound, which, I presume, could not be less that two hundred miles. They tarried about two hours in town, then started off again. The prisoner had to take the wounded Indian on his back again and march off; I understood they had to go a considerable distance beyond Presq' Isle, which, I presume, could not be less than three hundred and fifty or four hundred miles that the poor, unfortunate prisoner had to carry the wounded Indian on his back, before they would get to their destination. However, he had one advantage over what other prisoners had to undergo, that was, he was exempt from a severe beating at every town they went through before they got to their destination, which every grown person has to suffer, as I shall relate hereafter. I understood by them that it was a general custom among all their nations, that if any one happened to get wounded, that the rest would do their utmost to take a prisoner or prisoners to carry him.

We lived about two years and a half in Shenango; we then moved to where they were settling a new town, called *Kseek-he-ooing*, that is, a place of salt; a place now well known by the name of Salt Licks, on the west branch of Beaver, where we lived about one year: we moved there about the time that General Forbes took Fort Duquesne from the French. My brother had been about three years married; they had a young son, whom they thought a great deal of; my sister-in-law was very cross to me when my brother was absent; he had heard of it, and asked me, when we were by ourselves, if his wife did not strike me sometimes, when he was absent. I told him she did. He bid me to let him know if ever she would strike me again; not long after, my brother being absent, she went to the corn field to work, and left her son in my care;

as soon as she left us, I began to divert myself with a foot ball; the little fellow was running after me crying aloud, and his mother heard him. While I was engaged in my diversions, she came behind me unnoticed, and knocked me down with the handle of a billhook. I took the first opportunity to inform my brother how she had treated me; he advised her not to treat me so any more, telling her what the consequence would be if she did. She was highly affronted at him, and went off and left us About three days after she came back, attended by a female cousin of hers, to carry off her movables; whilst she was gathering up her goods, my brother stepped out and began to try the strength of some small branches that had been recently chopped off a green tree; at seeing that, she fled out of the house and ran as fast as she was able. He pursued her, and whipped her severely; she ran back to the house for protection and squatted down behind his mother, who had occasionally come to see us; it put the thoughts of leaving us out of her head; neither did she ever strike me afterwards.

A Novel Punishment—He Escapes from his Own Father.

Some time while we resided at *Kseek-he-ooing*, or Salt Licks, *Mos-sooh-whese*, or Ben Dickson, invented a kind of punishment to inflict on boys who would do mischief, such as quarreling, plundering watermelon or cucumber patches, &c., in the following manner: There is a kind of fish that abounds in the western waters, called a gar, that has a very long bill and long, sharp teeth; he took the bill of one of those fish and wrapped a thin rag round it, projecting the teeth through the rag. He took any one who would do any kind of mischief, and after wetting their thighs and legs, he would score them from the hip down to the heel, three or four times on each thigh and leg, and sometimes, if they were found guilty a second or third time, he would score them from the top of the shoulder down to the wrists, and from the top of the shoulder, on the back, to the contrary hip, crossways. It happened once that a nephew of his, a very mischievous boy, threw the entrails of a turtle in my face, then ran off as quick as he could from me round the house; I picked up a stone and pursued him, and threw it after him; it happened to light on the top of his head and knocked him down, and cut his head badly, or, it is probable, he would have concealed it, as he well knew what the consequence would be; for his back, arms, thighs and legs were almost constantly raw by the frequent punishments he got for his mischief.

However, *Mos-sooh-whese* happened to be out a fishing at the time; he was informed when he came home of what had taken place; I was apprehensive of what would be my doom, and was advised by my friends to hide myself; accordingly I got into a small addition to the house, where a number of bales of deer skin and fur were piled up; I had not been long there until I heard him inquiring for me; they told him that I had gone down to the creek, and was not returned yet: he therefore ordered one of my brothers, (who had been with him a fishing the day before,) to stand up until he would score him; as my brother was partly man grown, he refused; a struggle ensued—my brother, however, was obliged to give up. The reason he gave for punishing others who were not present at the time the mischief was done was, that if they should be present at the time that any one was promoting mischief, he should do his best endeavor to prevent it, or inform against those who had done it—as the informer was always exempted from the punishment aforesaid. I then heard him say, that if I was to stay away a year he would score me; he then went to the creek on the hunt of me; after he was gone they told me that I might as well come out as conceal myself; accordingly I did. In a short time he came back, grinning and showing his teeth as if he had got a prize; he ordered me to stand up at the side of a post; I obeyed his orders; he then took and wet my thighs and legs, to prevent the skin from tearing; he took the gar's bill, and gave me four scores, or scrapes, with it, from the point of the hip down to the heel—the mark of which I will carry to my grave.

My oldest brother was from home at the time the above punishment was inflicted on us; he came home that same night; I scarcely ever saw him more out of humor than when he found the way we had been treated. He said, (whether he was in earnest or not, I cannot tell,) that if he had been at home he would have applied his *tim-ma-keek-can* to *Mos-sooh-whese's* head rather than suffer such an ignominious punishment, as he conceived it, to be inflicted on any of his family. However, he told *Mos-sooh-whese* never to do the like again without his consent. I was very near being innocently punished about a year afterwards, notwithstanding I had more than a dozen of witnesses to prove that I was not, in the course of that day, where the mischief was done: which was only the plundering of a watermelon patch.

Whilst we were living at *Kseek-he-ooing*, one Andrew Wilkins, a trader, came to the town, and was taken ill while there—he sent me to the other end of the town with some beads to purchase a fowl for him to work off a physic with; when I came back, he was sitting alone in the house: as he could talk the Indian tongue tolerably well, he began to question me about where I was taken from; I told him from Conococheague—he asked my name; I told him. As soon as he returned to Shippensburg, (which was his place of residence,) he informed my father that he had seen me, which was the first account they received of me from the time I was taken. The next Spring we moved to a town about fifteen miles off, called *Ma-hon-ing*, which signifies a lick. Some time in the Summer following, my father came to Mahoning, and found me out. I was shy in speaking to him, even by an interpreter, as I had at that time forgot my mother tongue. My Indian brother not being at home, my father returned to Pittsburgh and left me.

My brother was gone to *Tus-ca-la-ways*, about forty or fifty miles off, to see and hear a prophet that had just made his appearance amongst them; he was of the Delaware nation; I never saw nor heard him. It was said, by those who went to see him, that he had certain hieroglyphics marked on a piece of parchment, denoting the probation that human beings were subjected to whilst they were living on earth, and also denoting something of a future state. They informed me that he was almost constantly crying whilst he was exhorting them. I saw a copy of his hieroglyphics, as numbers of them had got them copied and undertook to preach, or instruct others.

The first (or principal doctrine) they taught them was to purify themselves from sin, which, they taught, they could do by the use of emetics, and abstinence from carnal knowledge of the different sexes; to quit the use of firearms, and to live entirely in the original state that they were in before the white people found out their country; nay; they taught that that fire was not pure that was made by steel and flint, but that they should make it by rubbing two sticks together, which I have frequently assisted to do, in the following manner: Take a piece of red cedar, have it well seasoned, get a rod of bor-tree, well seasoned, gouge out a small bit with the point of a knife, cut off the cedar about an eighth of an inch from the edge, set the end of the bor-tree in it, having first stuck a knife in the side of the cedar, to keep the dust that will rub out by the friction; then take it between the hands and rub it, pressing hard on the cedar and rubbing as quick as possible; in about half a minute the fire will kindle. It was said that their prophet taught them, or made them believe, that he had his instructions immediately from *Keesh-she-la-mil-lang-up*, or a being that *thought* us into being, and that by following his instructions, they would, in a few years, be able to drive the white people out of their country.

I knew a company of them who had secluded themselves for the purpose of purifying from sin, as they thought they could do; I believe they made no use of firearms. They had been out more than two years before I left them; whether they conformed rigidly to the rules laid down to them by their prophet, I am not able to say with any degree of certainty—but one thing I know, that several women resorted to their encampment; it was said, that they made use of no other weapons than their bows and arrows: they also taught, in shaking hands, to give the left hand in token of friendship, as it denoted that they gave the heart along with the hand—but I believe that to have been an ancient custom among them, and I am rather of opinion, that the practice is a caution against enemies—that is, if any violence should be offered, they would have the right hand ready to seize their *tim-ma-keek-can*, or tomahawk, or their *paughk-sheek-can*, or knife, to defend themselves, if necessary.*

The Fall following, my father went out to Fort Venango, or French Creek, along with Wilkins. Wilkins sent a special messenger to Mahoning, for my brother to take me to Venango, telling him that my father would purchase me from him; accordingly he took me off without letting me know his intention, or, it is probable, I would not have gone with him. When we got to Venango, we encamped about a mile from the garrison; my brother went to the garrison to bargain with my father for me, but told me nothing of it. The next morning my father and two others came to our camp, and told me that my brother wanted to see me at the fort; I went along with them; when we got there he told me that I must go home with my father, to see my mother and the rest of my friends; I wept bitterly—all to no purpose; my father was ready to start; they laid hold of me and set me on a horse—I threw myself off; they set me on again, and tied my legs under the horse's belly, and started away for Pittsburgh.

We encamped about ten or fifteen miles from Venango; before we lay down, my father took his garters and tied my arms behind my back; however, I had them loose before my father lay down; I took care to keep it concealed from them by keeping my arms back as if they were tied. About midnight, I arose from between my father and John Simeons, who was to accompany us to Pittsburgh; I stepped out from the fire and sat down as if I had a real necessity for doing so; my father and Simeons arose and mended up the fire; whilst they were laying the chunks together, I ran off as fast as I could; I had got near a hundred yards from the camp, when I heard them hunting a large dog, which they had along with them, after me; I thought the dog would certainly overtake me; I therefore climbed up a tall tree, as fast as I could; the dog stopped at the root of the tree, but as they continued to hunt him on, he ran off again—they came past the tree; after they

---

*The observant reader will note that these were the peculiar doctrines of Pontiac and his Delaware prophet, and the incident so attested by a captive boy, proves that Pontiac had his emissaries out through all the tribes, trying to excite a general war. The murder of the traders, mentioned later was part of the same plan.

passed by me, I climbed further up, until I got to some limbs, where I could rest myself; the dog came back to the tree again—after a short time they came back and stood a considerable time at the root of the tree—then returned to the fire; I could see them distinctly from where I was.

I remained on the tree about an hour; I then went down and steered through the woods till I found the road; I went about two or three miles along it, and the wolves were making a hideous noise all around me; I went off the road a short distance and climbed up a dogwood sapling, and fixed myself on the branches of it, where I remained till break of day; I then got on the road again; I ran along as fast as I was able, for about five miles, where I came to an Indian camp; they told me that I had better not keep the road, alleging that I would certainly be pursued; I took their advice and went off the road immediately, and steered through the woods till I got to where my friends were encamped; they advised me to take along the road that we came, when we came there; telling me that they were going to return home that day; I made no delay, but went on about ten miles, and there waited till they came up with me. Not long after I left them, my father came to the camp; they denied that they had seen me—supposing that I had gone on to Mahoning by myself, telling him that if I had, that they would take me to Pittsburgh that Fall.

Soon after we got home to Mahoning, instead of taking me to Pittsburgh, agreeable to their promise, they set out on their Fall hunt, taking me along with them; we staid out till some time in the Winter before we returned. We lived about a mile out of Mahoning; there were some traders at *Kseek-he-ooing*, or Salt Licks, early in the Spring. A nephew of my adopted brother's had stolen a horse from one Tom Green, a trader; he pursued the thief to Mahoning; he was gone out a trapping when Green came after him. Green waited three days on the Indian's return with the horse. The third night, about midnight, there came an alarm, which was notified by hallooing *Qua-ah !* still repeating four halloos at a time, at certain intervals. When we heard the alarm, my oldest brother went off to the town, to see what was the matter. In about two hours he returned; Green asked him what was the matter—he told him that it was some foolish young fellows that had done it, for diversion. Green did not seem to be satisfied with the answer. However, about sunrise *Mus-sooh-whese,* (an Indian, my adopted brother's nephew, known by the name of Ben Dickson, among the white people,) came to our house; he had a pistol and a large scalping knife, concealed under his blanket, belted round his body. He informed *Ket-too-ha-lend* (for that was my adopted brother's name) that he came to kill Tom Green; but *Ket-too-ha-lend* endeavored to persuade him off it. They walked out together, and Green followed them, endeavoring, as I suppose, to discover the cause of the alarm the night before; in a short time they returned to the house, and immediately went out again. Green asked me to bring him his horse, as we heard the bell a short distance off; he then went after the Indians again, and I went for the horse.

As I was returning, I observed them coming out of a house about two hundred yards from ours; *Ket-too-ha-lend* was foremost, Green in the middle; I took but slight notice of them, until I heard the report of a pistol; I cast my eyes towards them and observed the smoke, and saw Green standing on the side of the path, with his hands across his breast; I thought it had been him that shot; he stood a few moments, then fell on his face across the path; I instantly got off the horse, and held him by the bridle. *Ket-too-ha-lend* sunk his pipe tomahawk into his skull, *Mos-sooh-whese* stabbing him under the arm-pit with his scalping knife; he had shot him between the shoulders with his pistol. The squaws gathered about him, stripped him naked, trailed him down the bank, and plunged him into the creek; there was a "fresh" in the creek at the time, which carried him off. *Mos-sooh-whese* then came to me, (where I was holding the horse, as I had not moved from the spot where I was when Green was shot,) with the bloody knife in his hand; he told me that he was coming to kill me next; he reached out his hand and took hold of the bridle, telling me that that was his horse; I was glad to parley with him on the terms, and delivered the horse to him. All the Indians in the town immediately collected together, and started off to the Salt Licks, where the rest of the traders were, and murdered the whole of them, and divided their goods amongst them, and likewise their horses. My adopted brother took two horse loads of beaver skin, and set off with them to *Tus-ca-la-ways*, where a number of traders resided, and sold the fur to them.

There happened to be an old Indian, who was known amongst the traders by the name of Daniel; he cautioned the traders not to purchase the fur from him, assuring them that he had murdered some traders —to convince them, he showed them that the skins were marked with so many different marks, which convinced him in his opinion; however, either through fear or some other motive, they exchanged goods for the fur; the same evening, old Daniel offered his services to them, assuring them that he would endeavor to conduct them safe into Pittsburgh, adding that, if they would not take his advice, he was sure they would be all murdered by daylight the next morning; they took his advice, and, as they lived about a mile out of town, they had an opportunity of going away without being discovered; they started shortly after dark, as was conjectured by the Indians, leaving all their merchandise behind them; how many there were of them I do not recollect of hearing; however, as I heard, they went on safe until they got to *Ksack-hoong*, an old Indian town at the confluence of the Beaver and Ohio, where they came to an Indian camp unawares; probably the Indians had discovered them before they reached the camp, as they were ready for them; as soon as they made their appearance the Indians fired on them —the whole of them fell, excepting old Daniel and one Calhoun, who made his escape into Pittsburgh; old Daniel had a bullet shot into his saddle, close behind him, the mark of which I frequently saw, after he made his escape back to his friends.

Mahoning lay on the frontier, as they had evacuated all their towns to the north of it when the war commenced. Shortly after the commencement of the war, they plundered a tanyard near to Pittsburgh, and carried away several horse-loads of leather; they also committed several depredations along the Juniata; it happened to be at a time when the small-pox was in the settlement where they were murdering, and the consequence was, a number of them got infected, and some died before they got home, others shortly after; those who took it after their return, were immediately moved out of the town, and put under the care of one who had had the disease before. In one of their excursions, they took some prisoners—among them was one of the name of Beatty, whom they beat unmercifully when they took him to Mahoning; they set him to make bridles for them, (that is, to fill old bits,) of the leather they took from Pittsburgh; he appeared very cross; he would often run at the little fellows with his knife or awl, when they came to look at him where he was at work; however, they soon took him off to *Cay-a-haw-ga*, a town not far distant from Lake Erie.

We remained in Mahoning till shortly after the memorable battle at Bushy Run; we then moved to *Cay-a-haw-ga;* the day before we got there they began to be alarmed at Beatty's behavior; they held a council and agreed to kill him, lest he should take some of their lives. They led him about fifty or sixty perches out of the town, some walking before and some behind him; they then shot him with arrows. I went out the evening after we got there, along with some little fellows, to see him; he was a very disagreeable sight to behold; they had shot a great number of arrows into his body—then went off and left him exposed to the vermin!

The same year that Beatty was taken, *Ket-too-ha-lend* was the *Moy-a-sooh-whese*, or foreman, of a party consisting of nine Indians; they came to a house where there were two men and a woman who had killed a hog, and had a large pot of water on the fire, making ready to scald it—*Ket-too-ha-lend* rushed into the house—the rest stopped at the outside; he seized the woman and shoved her out of the door, and told the rest to take care of her; one of the men broke out of the house and made off, whilst the other catched hold of *Ket-too-ha-lend* by the arm, and endeavored to put him into the pot of boiling water, shoving him back to the corner of the house, where two guns were standing— he said he frequently called on the rest to come in to assist him, but none of them would venture in. The man was constantly looking about, either for assistance or from fear of the rest of the Indians; he therefore, after he was almost exhausted, watched his opportunity, and suddenly putting his hand up behind the man's back, and catching hold of his queue, jerked his head back, by which means he got his other arm disengaged, and drew his *tim-ma-keek-can*, or tomahawk, and knocked him on the head. But, to his great mortification, when he came out, he found the woman whom he had shoved out of the door lying dead and scalped.

We stayed but a short time in *Cay-a-haw-ga*, then moved across the country to the forks of *Moosh-king-oong*, (Muskingum,) which signifies clear eyes, as the river abounds with a certain kind of fish that have very clear eyes; from thence we took up the west branch to its source, and from thence I know not where. Nothing remarkable happened during our peregrinations, excepting that we suffered by hunger, it being in the Winter; we sometimes had to make use of the stems of turkey quills for food, by running them under hot embers till they would swell and get crisp. We have subsisted on gum bark, and sometimes on white plantain; but the greater part of our time on a certain kind of root that has something of the resemblance of a potato.

In the Spring we returned to the west branch of *Moosh-king-oong*, and settled in a new town, which he called *Kta-ho-ling*, which signifies a place where roots have been dug up for food. We remained there during the Summer. Sometimes in the Summer, whilst we were living at *Kta-ho-ling*, a great number of Indians collected at the forks of *Mooshking-oong*; perhaps there were three hundred or upwards; their intention was to come to the settlements and make a general massacre of the whole people, without any regard to age or sex; they were out about ten days, when the most of them returned; having held a council, they concluded that it was not safe for them to leave their towns destitute of defence. However, several small parties went on to different parts of the settlements; it happened that three of them, whom I was well acquainted with, came to the neighborhood of where I was taken from— they were young fellows, perhaps none of them more than twenty years of age—they came to a school house, where they murdered and scalped the master and all the scholars, excepting one, and a full cousin of mine. I saw the Indians when they returned home with the scalps; some of the old Indians were very much displeased at them for killing so many children, especially *Neep-paugh-whese*, or Night Walker, an old chief or Half King—he ascribed it to cowardice, which was the greatest affront he could offer them.*

In the Fall they were alarmed by a report that the white people were marching out against them, which, in a short time, proved to be true; Colonel Bouquet, with an army, was then actually marching out against them. As the Delaware nation was always on the frontier, (which was the nation I was amongst,) they had the first notice of it, and immediately gave the alarm to the other nations adjoining them. A council was called: the result was, that they were scarce of ammunition, and were not able to fight him; that they were then destitute of clothing; and that, upon the whole, it was best to come to terms of peace with the white people. Accordingly they sent off special messengers to meet the army on their march, in order to let them know that they were disposed to come to terms of peace with them. The messengers met the army at Tuscalaways. They crept up to the camp after dark, and informed the guard that they were sent by their nation to sue for peace. The commander of the army sent for them to come into camp; they went and delivered their mission. The Colonel took care to take hostages for their fidelity; the remainder were suffered to return; but he told them he would march his army on to *Moosh-king-oong*, where he expected to meet their chiefs and warriors, to come to terms of peace with him, assuring them, at the same time, that he would not treat with them but upon condition that they would deliver up all the prisoners they had in their possession. The messengers returned, and gave a narrative of their mission. The *Sha-a-noo-wack*, or Shawanese, were not satisfied with the terms; however, as the Delawares had left hostages with the commander of the army, the Shawanese acquiesced to come to terms of peace jointly with the other tribes. Accordingly the army marched on to *Moosh-king-oong*. The day they arrived there, an express was sent off to one of their nearest towns, to inform them that they were ready to treat with them.

---

* This refers to a horrid massacre in Pennsylvania, of a whole school, in August, '64. The remains of the murdered and mutilated scholars were all interred together, in a large and rudely constructed box, just as they were found. The name of the teacher was Brown. Seventy-nine years after an exhumation took place, and the bones were again committed to earth, and a mound raised to perpetuate the memory of this sad spot. The school house was truly a solitary one, and some of its remains exist to the present day.

We then lived about ten miles from *Moosh-king-oong;* accordingly they took all the prisoners to the camp, myself among the rest, and delivered us up to the army. We were immediately put under a guard— a few days after, we were sent under a strong guard to Pittsburgh. On our way two of the prisoners made their escape, to wit, one Rhoda Boyd and Elizabeth Studibaker, and went back to the Indians. I never heard whether they were ever brought back or not. There were about two hundred of us—we were kept a few days in Pittsburgh. There was one John Martin, from the Big Cove, came to Pittsburgh after his family, who had been taken by the Indians the Fall before I was taken: he got leave from the Colonel to bring me down along with his family. I got home about the middle of December, 1764, being absent (as I heard my parents say) eight years, four months and sixteen days. Previous to my return, my father had sold his plantation, where I was taken from, and bought another about four miles from the former, where I have resided ever since.

When I reflect on the various scenes of life I came through during my captivity, methinks I see the hand of Providence, remarkably conspicuous, throughout the whole. First, What but the hand of Providence directed them to take us alive, when our scalps might have answered the same purpose? or that they should, when apparently in danger, risk their lives by the incumbrance of us, by carrying us on their backs? Secondly, That they should not have drowned me outright, when they washed me in the Allegheny river? Thirdly, That they took any care of me, when I was apparently on the point of death, by two severe fits of sickness? Fourthly, That they should have taken any notice of me when I was, to all appearances, drowned at Shenango? Nay, I have often thought that the hand of Providence guided me in making my escape from my father, as, in all probability, I would have been at the school where the master and scholars were murdered, as I had two cousins among the number, one of whom was scalped, and who, I believe, is yet alive; or even when *Mus-sooh-whese* came to me, after he had murdered Green, with the bloody knife in his hand. I say, methinks I see the hand of Providence remarkably displayed throughout the whole.

How often are we exposed to dangers, which we have neither had knowledge of nor power to prevent? I could have related many dangers that I was exposed to during my captivity, which I have thought proper to omit in the foregoing narrative; as I am conscious that there are numbers, who never have had the trial of what they were able to undergo, would be ready to charge me with falsehood, as I have often observed what other narrators have met with.

THE CAPTIVITY AND ESCAPE OF THE BARD FAMILY.

Collected from his Papers by his Son, Archibald Bard.

My father, Richard Bard, lived in York county, now Adams, and owned the mill now called Marshall's mill, in what is called Carroll's tract, where, on the morning of the 13th of April, 1758, his house was invested by a party of nineteen Indians. They were discovered by a little girl called Hannah M'Bride, who was at the door, and on seeing them, screamed, and ran into the house. At this time there were in the house, my father, mother, and Lieutenant Thomas Potter, (brother of General Potter,) who had come the evening before, (being a full cousin,) together with a child of about six months old, and a bound boy. The Indians rushed into the house and one of them, with a large cutlass in his hand, made a blow at Potter, but he so managed it as to wrest the sword from the Indian and return the blow, which would have put an end to his existence had not the point struck the ceiling, which turned the sword so as to cut the Indian's hand.

In the meantime, Mr. Bard (my father) laid hold of a horseman's pistol that hung on a nail, and snapped it at the breast of one of the Indians, but there being tow in the pan it did not go off; at this the Indians, seeing the pistol, ran out of the house. By this time one of the Indians at the door had shot at Potter, but the ball took him only in the little finger. The door was now shut and secured as well as possible; but finding the Indians to be very numerous, and having no powder or ball, and as the savages might easily burn down the house by reason of the thatched roof and the quantity of mill wood piled at the back of the building, added to the declarations of the Indians that they would not be put to death, determined them to surrender; on which a party of the Indians went to a field and made prisoners Samuel Hunter and Daniel M'Manimy. A lad by the name of William White, coming to the mill, was also made a prisoner. Having secured the prisoners, they took all the valuable effects out of the house and set fire to the mill. They then proceeded toward the mountain, and my mother, inquiring of the Indians who had care of her, was informed that they were of the Delaware nation.

At the distance of about seventy rods from the house, contrary to all their promises, they put to death Thomas Potter, and having proceeded on the mountain about three or four miles, one of the Indians sunk the spear of his tomahawk into the breast of the small child, and after repeated blows, scalped it. After crossing the mountain, they passed the house of Mr. Halbert T——, and seeing him out, shot at him, but without effect. Thence, passing late in the evening M'Cord's old fort, they encamped about half a mile in the gap. The second day, having passed into the Path valley, they discovered a party of white men in pursuit of them; on which they ordered the prisoners to hasten, for should the whites come up with them, they should be all tomahawked. Having been thus hurried, they reached the top of the Tuskarora mountain, and all had set down to rest, when an Indian, without any previous warning, sunk a tomahawk into the forehead of Samuel Hunter, who was seated by my father, and by repeated blows put an end to his existence. He was then scalped, and the Indians, proceeding on their journey, encamped that evening some miles on the north of Sideling Hill.

The next day they marched over the Allegheny mountain, through what is now called Blair's gap. On the fifth day, whilst crossing Stony Creek, the wind blew a hat of my father's from the head of the Indian in whose custody he was. The Indian went down the stream some distance before he recovered it. In the meantime my father had passed the creek, but when the Indian returned he severely beat my father with the gun, and almost disabled him from traveling any further. And now, reflecting that he could not possibly travel much further, and that, if this was the case, he would immediately be put to death, he determined to attempt his escape that night. Two days before this, the half of my father's head was painted red. This denoted that a council had been held, and that an equal number were for putting him to death and for keeping him alive, and that another council was to have taken place to determine the question. Being encamped, my parents, who before this had not liberty to speak to one another, were permitted to assist each other in plucking a turkey, and being thus engaged, the design of escaping was communicated to my mother. After some of the Indians had laid down, and one of them was amusing the others with dressing himself with a gown of my mother's, my father was called to go for water. He took a quart, and emptying it of the water it contained, stept about six rods down to the spring. My mother perceiving this, succeeded so well in confining the attention of the Indians to the gown, that my father had got about one hundred yards, when the Indians from one fire cried to those of another—"*your man is gone.*"

They ran after him and one having brought back the quart, said: "*here is the quart, but no man.*" They spent two days in looking after him, while the prisoners were confined in the camp; but after an unsuccessful search, they proceeded down the stream to the Allegheny river, thence to Fort Duquesne, now Fort Pitt. After remaining there one night and a day, they went about twenty miles down the Ohio, to an Indian town, on entering which a squaw took a cap off my mother's head, and, with many others, severely beat her. Now, almost exhausted with fatigue, she requested leave to remain at this place, and was told she might, if she preferred being scalped to proceeding. They then took her to a town called Cususkey. On arriving at this place, Daniel M'Manimy was detained outside the town, but my mother, the two boys and girls, were taken into the town, at the same time having their hair pulled, faces scratched, and beaten in an unmerciful manner.

Horrible Death by Torture of Daniel M'Manimy.

Here I shall extract from my father's papers the manner and circumstances of M'Manimy's death. This account appears to have been obtained from my mother, shortly after her return, who received it from those who had been eye witnesses of the tragical scene. The Indians formed themselves into a circle round the prisoner, and commenced by beating him; some with sticks, and some with tomahawks. He was then tied to a post near a large fire, and after being tortured some time with burning coals, they scalped him, and put the scalp on a pole to bleed before his face. A gun barrel was then heated red hot, and passed over his body, and with a red-hot bayonet they pierced his body, with many repetitions. In this manner they continued torturing him, singing and shouting, until he expired. Shortly after this, my mother set out from this place, leaving the two boys and girl, whom she never saw again until they were liberated. She was now distressed beyond measure; going she knew not where, without a comforter, without a companion, and expecting to share the fate of M'Manimy in the next town she would reach. In this distressed situation she met a number of Indians, among whom was a captive woman. To her my mother made known her fears, on which she was informed that her life was not in danger, for that belt of wampum, said she about your neck, is a certain sign that you are intended for an adopted relation.

They soon after arrived at a town, and being taken into the council house, two squaws entered in—one stepped up and struck my mother on the side of the head. Perceiving that the other was about to follow this example, she turned her head and received a second blow. The warriors were highly displeased at such acts in a council house, being contrary to usage. Here a chief took my mother by the hand, and delivered her to two Indian men, to be in the place of a deceased sister. She was put in charge of a squaw in order to be cleanly clothed. She had remained here, with her adopted friends, near a month, when her party began to think of removing to the head waters of the Susquehanna, a journey of about two hundred miles. This was very painful to my mother, having already traveled about two hundred miles over mountains and swamps, until her feet and legs were extremely swollen and sore. Fortunately, on the day of their setting out, a horse was given to her by her adopted brother; but before they had traveled far, one of the horses in the company died, when she was obliged to surrender hers to supply its place. After proceeding on her journey some miles, they were met by a number of Indians, one of whom told her not to be discouraged, as a peace was about to take place shortly, when she would have leave to return home. To this information she was the more disposed to give credit, as it came from one who was a chief counselor in the Delaware nation, with whom she was a prisoner. Having arrived near the end of her journey, to her great surprise, she saw a captive dead by the road side, having been tomahawked and scalped. She was informed that he had endeavored to escape, but was overtaken at this place.

On arriving at the place of destination, having, in all, traveled near five hundred miles, the fatigue which she had undergone, with cold and hunger, brought on a severe fit of sickness, which lasted near two months. In this doleful situation, having no person to comfort or sympathize with her—a blanket was her only covering, and her bed was the cold earth, in a miserable cabin; boiled corn was her only food—she was reduced to so weak a state as to consider herself as approaching the verge of dissolution. But, recovering from her sickness, she met with a woman with whom she had been formerly acquainted. This woman had been in captivity some years, and had an Indian husband by whom she had one child. My mother reproved her for this, but received for answer, that before she had consented, they had tied her to a stake in order to burn her. She added, that as soon as their captive women could speak the Indian tongue, they were obliged to marry some one of them or be put to death. This information induced her to determine never to learn the Indian language, and she adhered to this determination all the time she remained with them, from the day of her captivity to that of her releasement, a space of two years and five months. She was treated during this time, by her adopted relations, with much kindness; even more than she had reason to expect.

I shall now return to the narration of facts respecting my father, after he had made his escape from the Indians, as before stated. The Indians, as soon as he was missed, gave chase. Finding himself closely pursued, he hid in a hollow log until they had gone by and out of hearing, when, turning in a different direction, he resumed his flight. Two days, it has been said, were spent by the Indians in search of him; in the meantime, with much fatigue and suffering, he came to a mountain four miles across, and at the top covered with snow. By this time he was almost exhausted, having traveled nearly constantly for two days and nights, and being without food, except a few buds plucked from the trees as he went along; his shoes were worn out; and the country he traveled through being extremely rough and in many places covered with briers of a poisonous nature, his feet were very much lacerated and swollen. To add to his difficulties, the mountain was overgrown with laurel, and the snow lodged upon its leaves so bent it down that he was unable in many places to get along in his weak condition, except by creeping upon his hands and knees under the branches.

Three days had now elapsed since his escape; and although he feared that the Indians were still in pursuit of him, and that by traveling along the mountain they would find his tracks in the snow and by that means be led to his place of concealment, yet he found himself so lame that he could proceed no farther. His hands also, by crawling upon them in the snow, became almost as much swollen as his feet. He was therefore compelled to lie by, without much prospect indeed of ever proceeding any farther on his journey. Besides the danger of being overtaken by his savage pursuers, he was, in fact, in a starving condition, not having tasted food since his escape, except the buds already mentioned, plucked, as he journeyed on, from the bean-wood, or red-bud tree, as it is called. On the fifth day, however, as he was creeping on his hands and knees (not being able yet to walk) in search of buds or herbs to appease his hunger, he was fortunate enough to see a rattlesnake, which he killed and ate raw. After lying by three or four days, he allayed the swelling of his feet by puncturing the festered parts with a thorn; he then tore up his breeches, and with the pieces bound up his feet as well as he could. Thus prepared, he again set out upon his journey, limping along with great pain; but he had no other alternative, except to remain where he was and die. He had gone but a few miles when, from a hill he had just ascended, he was startled by the welcome sound of a drum; he called as loud as he could, but there was no one to answer; it was but a delusion of the imagination. Sad and disappointed, he journeyed on again, and on the eighth day crossed the Juniata by wading it, which, on account of his lameness, he accomplished with great difficulty.

It was now night and very cold, and his clothes being wet he was so benumbed that he was afraid to lie down lest he should perish; and he, therefore, lame and wearied as he was, determined to pursue his journey, although it was very dark. Providential circumstance! for in the course of the night, as he wandered on, he scarcely knew whither, he was attracted by the sight of a fire apparently abandoned the day before, probably by a party of the settlers who were out in pursuit of the savages. Remaining here till morning, he discovered a path leading in the direction of the settlements, which he followed with as much speed as he was able. This was the ninth day since his escape, during which time a few buds and four snakes were all he had to subsist on. In the afternoon of this day he was alarmed by suddenly meeting at a turn of his path three Indians; but they proved friendly, and instead of killing him, as he expected when he first saw them, they conducted him in a few hours to Fort Littleton, (in Bedford county,) a place well known to him, where he remained a few days, until sufficiently recruited in strength to proceed home.

Some time after my father's return home, he went to Fort Pitt, which was then in the hands of the English, and a number of Indians being on the opposite side of the river, about to form a treaty, he one evening went over to make inquiry concerning my mother. My father observed among them several who were present when he was taken prisoner; to these he discovered himself. But they professed not to know him, on which he inquired of them if they did not recollect having been at the taking of nine persons, referring them to the time and place. They then acknowledged it, and inquired of him how he got home, &c., after which he made inquiry concerning my mother, but they said they knew nothing of her, but promised to give him some information by the time of his return the next day. He then returned to the fort. Shortly after this, a young man, who had been taken by the Indians when a child, followed him, and advised him not to return, for that when he had left them he had heard them say that they never had a stronger desire for anything than to have sunk the tomahawk into his head, and that they had agreed to kill him on his return next day. After this man had requested my father not to mention anything of his having been with him, or of the subject of their conversation, he returned to camp.

I may here state that from the time that my father was taken by the Indians until my mother was released, he did little else than wander from place to place, in quest of information respecting her, and after he was informed where she was, his whole mind was bent upon contriving plans for her redemption. Desiring, with this view, to go again to Pittsburgh, he fell in with a brigade of wagons, commanded by Mr.

Irvine; with them he proceeded as far as Bedford, but finding this a tedious way of traveling, he spoke to the commanding officer of the place to get Captain White Eyes, who commanded a party of Indians, to promise to accompany him to Pittsburgh. This was accordingly done, and the Indians having agreed to take him safe to Pitt, my father set out with them, having a horse and a new rifle. They had proceeded but about two miles, when an Indian turned off the road and took up a scalp which that morning had been taken off one of the wagoners. This alarmed my father not a little; but having proceeded about ten miles further, the Indians again turned off the road, and brought several horses and a keg of whiskey which had been concealed. Shortly after this, the Indians began to drink so as to become intoxicated. White Eyes then signified to my father that as he had ran off from them, he would then shoot him, and raised his gun to take aim; but my father, stepping behind a tree, ran round it while the Indian followed. This for a time gave great amusement to the bystanders, until a young Indian stepped up, twisted the gun out of the hands of White Eyes, and hid it under a log.

The Indians became considerably intoxicated, and scattered, leaving White Eyes with my father. White Eyes then made at him with a large stick, aiming at his head, but my father threw up his arm, and received so severe a blow as to blacken it for weeks. At this time an Indian of another nation, who had been sent as an express to Bedford, came by. Captain White Eyes applied to him for his gun to shoot my father, but the Indian refused, as they were about making peace, and the killing of my father would bring on another war: (being of different nations they were obliged to speak in English.) By this time my father, finding himself in a desperate situation, resolved, at all events, to attempt an escape; he said to Captain White Eyes, "our horses are going away," and went towards them, expecting every minute to receive a ball in his back, but coming up to his horse, he got on him and took to the road; he had gone but a short distance when he saw the Indian who had taken the gun out of White Eyes' hand sleeping at a spring, and I have often heard him say had it been any of the other Indians he would have shot him. Fearing pursuit, he rode as fast as his horse could go, and, having traveled all night, he got to Pittsburgh the next morning shortly after sunrise, and he was not there more than three hours until the Indians were in after him: but from a fear of injury being done my mother, should he kill them, he suppressed his anger, and passed the matter by

Here he had an opportunity of writing her a letter, requesting her to inform her adopted friends, that if they would bring her in, he would pay them forty pounds. But having waited for an answer until he became impatient, he bargained with an Indian to go and steal her away. But the night before he was to start, he declined going, saying that he would be killed if he went. In this situation he resolved, at all hazards, to go himself and bring her; for which purpose he set out and went to a place on the Susquehanna; I think it was called Shamokin, not far from what is called the Big Cherry Trees. From here he set out on an Indian path, along which he traveled until evening, when he was met by a party of Indians who were bringing in my mother; the Indians passed him by, and raised the war halloo—my mother felt distressed at their situation, and my father, perceiving the Indians not to be in a good humor, began to promise them their pay, as he had promised them by letter, when they would come to Shamokin, but the Indians told him that if he got them among the whites he would then refuse to pay them, and that they would then have no redress; finding they were thus apprehensive, he told them to keep him as a hostage out in the woods and send his wife into town, and he would send an order for the money to be paid them, and that if it was not done they might do with him as they pleased. This had the desired effect. They got quite good humored and brought them in, on doing which the money was paid agreeably to promise.

Before my father and mother left Shamokin, he requested an Indian who had been an adopted brother of my mother, if ever he came down amongst the white people to call and see him. Accordingly, some time afterwards the Indian paid him a visit, he living then about ten miles from Chambersburg. The Indian having continued for some time with him, went to a tavern, known by the name of McCormack's, and there became somewhat intoxicated, when a certain Newgen, (since executed in Carlisle for stealing horses,) having a large knife in his hand, struck it into the Indian's neck, edge foremost, designing thereby to thrust it between the bone and throat, and by drawing it forwards to cut his throat, but he partly missed his aim, and only cut the forepart of the windpipe. On this Newgen had to escape from justice; otherwise the law would have been put in force against him. And it has been remarked, that ever after he continued to progress in vice until his death. A physician was brought to attend the Indian; the wound was sewed up, and he continued at my father's house until he had recovered, when he returned to his own people, who put him to death, on the pretext of his having, as they said, joined the white people.

In August, 1764, (according to the best accounts of the time,) my father and his family, from fear of the Indians, having moved to my grandfather **Thomas Poe's**, about three miles from his own place, he took a black girl with him to his own place to make some hay—and being there at his work, a dog which he had with him began to bark and run towards and from a thicket of bushes. Observing these circumstances he became alarmed, and, taking up his gun, told the girl to run to the house, as he believed there were Indians near. So they made toward the house, and had not been there more than an hour, when from the loft of the house they saw a party, commanded by Captain Potter, late General Potter, in pursuit of a party of Indians who had that morning murdered a school master of the name of Brown, with ten small children, and scalped and left for dead one by the name of Archibald McCullough, who recovered and was living not long since. It was remarkable that, with but few exceptions, the scholars were much averse to going to school that morning. And the account given by McCullough is, that when the master and scholars met at the school, two of the scholars informed him that on their way they had seen Indians, but the information was not attended to by the master, who ordered them to their books; soon afterwards two old Indians and a boy rushed up to the door. The master, seeing them, prayed them only to take his life and spare the children; but, unfeelingly, the two old Indians stood at the door whilst the boy entered the house and, with a piece of wood made in the form of an Indian maul, killed the master and scholars, after which the whole of them were scalped.

ORIGIN OF THE INDIAN TERM "LONG-KNIVES."

Some years after the old French war, several settlers at the mouth of Decker's Creek, on the Monongahela, were cut off by a party of Delawares. Of these was Thomas Decker himself. But two or three of the settlers escaped, and one of these, making his way to Redstone, (Brownsville, Pa.,) gave information of the massacre. Captain Paull, of that post, sent a runner to Fort Pitt with full news of the Indian foray, and notifying Colonel Gibson of the probable line of retreat of the savages. Gibson proceeded down the river with the hope of intercepting them, and happened accidentally upon a small party of Iroquois or Mingoes, encamped on Cross Creek, and under command of a prominent chief by the name of Little Eagle. Discovering the whites about the same moment that they saw him, he gave a frightful yell and discharged his piece at the white leader. The ball passed through the Colonel's coat but did no other injury. With the quickness of the crouching panther, Gibson sprang upon his swarthy foe, and with one dexterous and powerful sweep of his sword, severed the head of Little Eagle from his shoulders.

Two others were shot dead by the whites, but the rest escaped and reported to their tribes that a white officer had cut off the head of their chief with a *long knife*. This is said to have been the origin of the epithet "long-knives," applied throughout the Indian wars to the Virginians, and afterwards used generally to denote all the "pale faces" on the Western Border. Gibson, himself a Virginian, then acquired among the Ohio Indians the sobriquet of "Long-Knife Warrior," and was known by it all his life afterwards.

JOHN HARRIS, THE FOUNDER OF HARRISBURG, PA.

"John Harris' Ferry," over the Susquehanna, was a frontier locality so well known before the Revolution to the whole country that its fame far excelled posts of much greater pretension and was even widely known abroad. It was quite common for letters from England, Ireland and Scotland to be addressed, "Care of John Harris, Harris' Ferry, North America."

The first John Harris was a Yorkshireman, who married in Philadelphia an Englishwoman of great energy and force of character, Esther Say by name, and who settled on the Susquehanna about 1724. Here was born, in 1726, the son, John Harris, the founder of Harrisburg, and said to have been the first white child born in Pennsylvania, west of the Conewago Hills.

A number of Indian villages were then scattered along the Susquehanna and Juniata rivers, and Harris, Sr., soon became an extensive trader, having connected with his cabin a large range of sheds, which were sometimes literally filled with skins and furs, stored there by the various Indian traders from the west and which were transported to Philadelphia on pack-horses. In the words of the memorable Parson Elder, he was as " honest a man as ever broke bread."

On one occasion a wandering band of Indians came to his house and demanded rum, as the modern whiskey was not then made in Pennsylvania. Seeing they were already intoxicated and fearing mischief, Harris refused. At this they became furious, seized and tied him to a mulberry tree to burn him. He was released by other friendly Indians coming across the river to his relief. In remembrance of this, he directed his body to be buried beneath that tree. He died in 1748, and his remains still repose at the roots of this famous mulberry, the stump of which is said to be still standing.

Of Esther, Harris' wife, several characteristic anecdotes are told. Here is one: The mansion was surrounded by a stockade as security against Indians. A British officer was one night staying at the house, when, by accident, the gate of the stockade was left unfastened. The officer, dressed in full regimentals, was seated with Harris and wife at the table. An Indian stealthily entered the gate, thrust his rifle through one of the port holes and fired away—it is supposed at the officer. The night being damp, the gun only *flashed*. Instantly Mrs. Harris blew out the candle to prevent a second aim and thus saved a human life.

John Harris, Jr., became a large farmer and trader; was a man of great energy and enterprise, and had an extensive western acquaintance. It was during his life that the *ferry* became so well known. He owned the ground on which Harrisburg now stands. When the Revolution broke out, he thought a Declaration of Independence premature, fearing that the colonies could not cope with the mother country, but after it was once declared, he took his wife and son aside and read it aloud, saying, "The act is now done and we must take sides. The war cannot be carried on without money. Now, we have £3000 in the house and, if you are agreed, I will take it to Philadelphia and put it in the treasury to carry on the war. If we succeed in obtaining an independence, we may lose our money—as the government may not be able to pay it back—but we will get our land." It was done and Harris died a rich man.

DR. BENJAMIN FRANKLIN AS A COMMANDER.

It is not generally known that during the Indian ravages consequent upon Braddock's defeat, the learned and amiable philosopher and statesman, Dr. Franklin, did service as a military officer and was sent to Northwestern Pennsylvania to establish a line of forts. He says he undertook this military business, although he did not conceive himself well qualified for it. " I had but little difficulty," he writes, "in raising men, having soon five hundred and sixty under my command. My son, who had seen service, was my aid-de-camp and of great value to me. The Indians had burned Gnadenhutten, a village settled by the Moravians, and massacred the inhabitants. It was January, 1756, when we set out upon this business of building forts. We had not marched many miles before it began to rain and continued all day. There were no habitations on the road till we arrived, at night, at a German's house, where, and in his barn, we were all huddled together as wet as water could make us. It was well we were not attacked, for our arms were of the most ordinary sort and our men could not keep the locks dry. The Indians are dexterous in contrivances for that purpose, for they met that day eleven farmers and killed ten of them; the one that escaped told us that the guns would not go off, the priming being wet.

"At Gnadenhutten we hutted ourselves and commenced burying the dead. Next morning our fort (Fort Allen) was planned and was finished in a week. However contemptible, it was a sufficient defence against Indians without cannon. We met no Indians, but found the places where they lay to watch us. There was an art in their contrivances worth mentioning. It being Winter, fire was necessary for them, but a common fire would have betrayed by its light and smoke; they had, therefore, dug holes about three feet in diameter and somewhat deeper. We found where they had, with their hatchets cut off the charcoal from the sides of burnt logs lying in the woods. With these coals they had made small fires in the bottoms of the holes, and we observed among the weeds and grass the prints of their bodies, made by their lying all round, with their legs hanging down in the holes to keep their feet dry and warm, which, with them, is an essential point. This kind of fire could not reveal them by its light, flame, sparks or even smoke.

"We had for our chaplain a zealous Presbyterian minister, Mr. Beatty, who complained to me that the men would not attend his prayers and exhortations. I had observed that they were punctual at their rum rations, half a gill morning and evening, upon which I said: It is, perhaps, below the dignity of your profession to act as steward of the rum, but if you were to distribute it only just after prayers, you would have them all about you. He liked the thought, undertook the task, and never were prayers more generally or punctually attended."

CONRADE WEISER AND THE ONONDAGA CHIEF.

For near thirty years Conrade Weiser was a very prominent man in Pennsylvania. During that period his name occurs in the Colonial Records oftener than that of any other. He came to this country early in life and lived most of his time after 1714 among the Six Nations of New York. He was so greatly esteemed by them as to be adopted into their tribes, and thus he became perfectly familiar with their language. Desiring to visit Pennsylvania, the Indians brought him down the Susquehanna to Harris' Ferry, (now Harrisburg,) and thence he found his way to Philadelphia, where he met Wm. Penn. He soon became confidential messenger and interpreter for the colony among the savages, and was an active agent in many of the most important treaties. In '37 he was sent by the Colony of Virginia to visit the grand Six-Nation's council at Onondaga. He started in the dead of Winter, accompanied by a German and three friendly Indians, five hundred miles through a pathless wilderness, and was nearly frozen and starved to death.

In '44 he was in like manner dispatched to Shamokin. On all these journeys he noted down interesting observations, and it is from his published letters in the State Records that we glean most valuable information about early Indian doings and sentiment. He afterwards established an Indian agency and trading house at Reading, Pa., but was kept so constantly on the go that he had but little time to attend to private affairs. In '55, during the border war, he was appointed Colonel of a regiment of Rangers and did good service. The Indians always entertained a high respect for his character, and for years after his death were in the habit of making visits of affectionate remembrance to his grave. The Rev. Henry A. Muhlenberg was his grandson.

Dr. Franklin relates that Conrade Weiser told him the following: In going through the Six-Nation country to carry a message from Pennsylvania, he called at the cabin of Cannassatego, an influential old Onondaga Chief, who embraced him, spread furs for him, placed before him beans and venison and some rum and water. When he was well refreshed, Cannassatego asked him many questions, and when the discourse began to flag, the old chief said: "Conrade, you have lived long among the white people and know something of their customs; I have been sometimes at Albany and have observed that once in seven days they shut up their shops and assemble in a great house. Tell me what they do there?" "They meet there," replied Weiser, "to hear and learn good things."

"I do not doubt that they tell you so, Conrade, they have told me the same; but I *do* doubt the truth of what they say, and I will give you my reasons. I went lately to Albany to sell my skins and buy rum, powder, blankets, &c. You know I used generally to deal with Hans Hanson, but I was a little minded this time to try some one else. However, I called first upon Hans and asked how much for beaver. He said he could not give more than four shillings a pound, but, says he, I cannot talk on business now; this is the day we meet to learn good things. So I thought to myself if I cannot do any business I might as well go to meeting too, and I went with Hans. There stood up a man in black and began to talk to the people very angrily. I didn't understand what he said, but perceiving he looked much at Hans and me, I fancied he was angry at seeing me there; so I went out, sat down near the big house, struck a fire and lit my pipe. I thought, too, the man had said something about beaver, so when they came out I said, 'Well, Hans, I hope you have agreed to give more than four shillings per pound for beaver pelts?' 'No,' said he, 'I cannot give so much—not more than three and six.' I then spoke to several more, but they all sang the same song—*three and six, three and six, three and six.* This made it clear to me that my suspicion was right, and that whatever they said they met for, the real business was to learn how to cheat the Indians in the price of beaver.

"Consider but a little, Conrade, and you must think with me. If they met so often to learn good things, they would have learned some before this, but they are still ignorant. You know our practice. If a white man travels our way and enters our cabin, we all treat him as I now treat you—dry him if he's wet, warm him if he's cold, give him meat and drink and spread soft furs for him to sleep on, and we ask nothing in return. But if I go into a white man's house in Albany and ask for meat and drink they say, 'Get out, you Injun dog.' So you see they have not yet learned those little good things which our mothers have taught us. Depend upon it, Weiser, these meetings are held to help cheat the Indians in beaver skins."

We may as well present here another characteristic speech of Cannassatego, also given by Franklin. At the very large and important council held at Lancaster in 1744, at which two hundred and fifty chiefs and warriors were present, this Onondaga Chief was the great orator. When the main business was all satisfactorily finished, an invitation was extended to the chiefs by the Commissioner of Virginia to send some of their youth there to be educated. To this Cannassatego replied:

"Brother, we must let you know that we love our children too well to send them so great a way. We thank you for the invitation, but our customs being different from yours, you must excuse us. We have had some experience in this. Several of our young people were formerly brought up at northern colleges. They were instructed in all your sciences, but when they came back to us, they were bad runners; ignorant of every means of living in the woods; unable to bear either cold or hunger; knew neither how to build a cabin or take a deer or kill an enemy; spoke our language badly; were, therefore, neither fit for hunters, warriors or counselors—they were totally good for nothing. To show, however, that we are grateful for your offer, if the gentlemen from Virginia will send us a dozen of their sons, we will teach them all we know and make *men* of them."

BORDER FORTS, STATIONS AND BLOCK-HOUSES.

Constant reference is made throughout all border chronicles to forts and to settlers fleeing to them for refuge. These were not only places of defence but places of residence of families belonging to a neighborhood. As Indian warfare consisted in an indiscriminate slaughter of all ages and both sexes, it was as requisite to provide for the safety of women and children as well as for the men. A fort, according to Doddridge, consisted of cabins, block-houses and stockades. A range of cabins, separated by divisions of logs, commonly formed one side, at least, of the fort. The walls on the outside were ten or twelve feet high, the slope of the roof being turned wholly inward. Very few of the cabins had puncheon floors, but nearly all earthen.

The block-houses were built at the angles of the fort, projecting about two feet beyond the outer walls of the cabins and stockades. Their upper stories were about eighteen inches every way larger in dimension than the under ones, so as to allow the occupants to fire straight down and prevent the enemy from making a lodgment under their walls. In some forts, instead of block-houses, the angles were furnished with bastions. A large folding gate, made of thick slabs and situated nearest the spring, served to close or open the fort. The stockade, bastion, cabins and block-house walls were furnished with port holes at proper heights and distances. The whole of the outside was made completely bullet-proof.

It may be truly said that "necessity is the mother of invention," for the whole of this work was made without the aid of a single nail or spike of iron; and for this reason: such things were not to be had. In some places, less exposed, a single block-house, with a cabin or two, constituted the whole fort.

Such refuges may appear very trifling compared with formidable military garrisons, but they answered the purpose admirably, since Indians had no artillery and seldom attacked, and scarcely ever took one of them. The families belonging to these forts were so attached to their own cabins on their farms, that they seldom moved into their forts in the Spring until compelled by some alarm; that is, when it was announced by some murder that the savages were hovering about the settlement.

Doddridge in the above is scarcely explicit enough. De Hass supplements the information and draws a closer distinction between the various places of defence in times of Indian hostilities. A *fort* was generally a stockade enclosure, embracing cabins, &c., for the accommodation of several families, with, generally, block-houses on two or on all four of its corners. A *station* was a parallelogram of cabins, united by palisades, so as to present a continued wall on the outer side, the cabin doors opening into a common square on the inner side. A *block-house* was a square, double-storied structure, the upper story projecting over the lower about two feet, which space was left so that the inmates could shoot from above upon an enemy attempting to fire or climb its walls. But one door opened into these rude buildings, and that was always very strong, so as to defy entrance by any ordinary means of assault. They were generally considered the safest for a small number. The men generally remained above, and many are the tales of border war wherein a few determined spirits successfully withstood the combined and persistent attacks of hundreds of Indians.

A SINGULAR WILL CASE ON THE BORDER.

As illustrative of the peculiar results arising from carrying children into captivity, we may mention the famous Grey Property Case, which was in controversy for about fifty years before the various Pennsylvania courts, and which was noted for many amusing scenes and the marked originality of many of the principal personages therewith connected.

Robert Hagg, Samuel Bingham, James and John Grey, were the first four settlers in Tuscarora valley, Pa., arriving there in 1749, and building Bingham's Fort. In '56, the year after Braddock's defeat, John Grey went with pack-horses to Carlisle to procure salt. As Grey was returning a bear crossed his path, which so frightened his horse that he was thrown and severely injured. This delay brought him back to Fort Bingham just after it was burned and every person either killed or made prisoner, including his wife and only daughter, three years old. The unhappy husband and father then joined Colonel Armstrong's expedition against Kittanning, in the hope of hearing of the fate of his family, but returned in such bad health that he died soon after, leaving by will his wife one-half and his daughter the other half of his fine farm, if they ever returned from captivity. If his daughter did *not* return or was not alive, he willed the second half to his sister, on condition of her releasing a claim she held against him.

In the meantime, Mrs. Grey and child, and other captives taken at Fort Bingham, were carried to Kittanning and afterwards to the French Fort Duquesne, and thence to Canada. About a year after, Mrs. Grey concealed herself among some deer skins in the wagon of a white trader and was brought off, leaving her little daughter in captivity. She returned home, proved her husband's will, and took possession of her half of the property. She afterwards married a Mr. Williams, but had no issue. In '64, some seven years after her escape, a number of the captive children, recovered by Colonel Bouquet, were taken to Philadelphia to be recognized. Mrs. Grey attended, but no child appeared that she recognized as her dear little Jenny. There was one there, however, unclaimed, of about the same age. Some one, conversant with the terms of Grey's will, whispered to the mother to claim this child for the purpose of holding the other half of the property. She did so—took back the child and brought her up as her own.

Time wore away, and the girl grew up gross and ugly in her person, awkward in her manners, and, as subsequent events proved, loose in her morals. Notwithstanding all these drawbacks, however, she contrived to captivate a Mr. Gillespie, who married her. The property then went over, by purchase or gift, to Rev. McKee, and then to his nephew. After a lapse of many years, the children of James Grey, heirs of John Grey's sister, got hold of information leading them to doubt the identity of the returned captive, and a law suit was brought about in 1789. It would literally puzzle a "Philadelphia lawyer" to describe the multiform and complicated phases which the case assumed during a legal contest of more than fifty years. There were many families interested, as also many prominent lawyers.

Mrs. Grey (or Mrs. Williams) said that when they were crossing Sideling Hill, she had examined the child Jane and found a mark by which she was able to recognize her. A Mr. Innis, one of the captives with her, testified that he one day chided Mrs. Williams for keeping a child not her own. "You know why I keep this girl," she answered. Mrs. Innis had herself lost three children, and told Mrs. W. that the child was not hers, but was a German girl, and could not talk English when she came to Montreal. Mrs. W., one witness testified, said, "No, that is not my daughter, but Woods knows where my daughter is, and has promised to get her." The *real* daughter was never recovered. Woods testified that he had been told by Indians that the real Jenny Grey was a fine, big girl, and lived near Sir William Johnson's, in the Mohawk valley, which information he had given to Mrs. Grey, the mother; that George Croghan, the famous Indian agent, had told him since and asserted that *he* procured the child, Jenny Grey, from the Indians, and had put her into a good family to be brought up. Finally the Indian, Hutson, came to Woods' house and asserted that little Jenny was now a fine woman, had a large house and children, and lived near Sir William Johnson's seat, in New York State.

Old Mrs. McKee, who spoke with a rich Irish brogue, was the principal living witness, and frequently convulsed the court by entering largely—much too largely—into the early history of the valley. She described the spurious girl as "a big, black, ugly Dutch lump, and not to be compared to the beautiful Jennie Grey." Her historical revelations so interested one of the jurymen, himself an old settler, that he sent for he old lady to come to the hotel and enter more at large into "the days of Auld Lang Syne." The old man was a little deaf, and Mrs. McKee's voice so loud and shrill that one of the opposing counsel overheard the old lady, and next day ludicrously exposed the poor juryman amidst the roars of the court and bar. The case, of course, had to be then tried before another jury, but was finally decided, in 1833, against the identity of the adopted child, and the property vested accordingly.

SIR WILLIAM JOHNSON, BARONET.

"A Fine Old Irish Gentleman, all of the Olden Time."

The battle of Lexington, which inaugurated the American Revolution, took place April 19th, 1775, but still the late peace effected with the Ohio tribes by Lord Dunmore continued during most of that year. Occasionally there were ominous symptoms that the savages were being tampered with by English agents, and the frontiers were kept very anxious for fear there should be a general alliance between the British and the confederated western tribes. The action and policy, therefore, of Colonel Guy Johnson, son-in-law of and successor to Sir William Johnson, General Superintendent of Indian Affairs, was narrowly watched, and gave much reason for alarm. Colonel Guy, Colonel Claus, Sir John Johnson and Joseph Brant, the celebrated Mohawk Chief, were all loyal to the core, and were using their strongest efforts to array the powerful Six Nations actively on the same side. Sir William Johnson, Baronet, had died in July, 1774, and it is high time we should give a sketch of a distinguished man, who had for so many years exercised such an almost omnipotent sway over American-Indian tribes. He was truly a most remarkable character, whose whole life was a romance, and crowded with interesting personal adventure.

Coming to America from Ireland while a young man, under the auspices of his uncle, Admiral Sir Peter Warren, he threw himself boldly into the wilderness, and, with but little assistance, became the architect of his own fame and fortune. From the humble position as agent of the landed property of his uncle, he was, successively, a farmer, dealer in peltries, a merchant, government contractor, a successful general, a Baronet of the British realm, and, for over a score of years, the Chief Superintendent of Indian Affairs on this continent, possessing more influence among the Indian tribes from the Hudson to the Mississippi, than any one man either before or since.

In 1775 such were his abilities and his commanding power over the redmen of the forest, that to him was entrusted, with the rank of Major General, the task of capturing Crown Point. At the same time he was appointed Superintendent of Indian Affairs. He fought soon after a decisive action with Baron Dieskau and defeated him badly, which victory was the only one during the whole year's campaign, and was so greatly esteemed by King George that he created Johnson a Baronet, while the Parliament presented him with five thousand pounds. In '58 he, by his intimate acquaintance with the temper of the Indians and by his wonderful influence over them, effected a peace with fifteen different tribes. In '59 he defeated the French army under D' Aubrey, and captured Fort Niagara. In '60 he assisted at the capture of Montreal, since which time he acted as Indian Superintendent.

It was among the Six Nations, however, that he ruled supreme, having a far larger authority over them than any of their own sachems. He was well calculated to conciliate and retain the affections of these warlike tribes. In person he was an uncommonly tall, well-made man, having a fine countenance and an imposing address. He was likewise shrewd, sagacious and possessed a most intimate knowledge of Indian tastes, customs and languages, and therefore knew best how to please the redmen. He purchased from the Indians a large and fertile tract of land upon the Mohawk river, where, having cleared the ground, he built two spacious and stately places of residence, known afterwards over all the country by the names of Johnson Castle and Johnson Hall. The first was on the Mohawk river and slightly fortified. The last was built on a gentle eminence, environed by most fertile and delightful plains, with an ample and well-cultivated domain, and that again encircled by European settlers who had first gone there as architects or workmen, but who had been induced, by Sir William's liberality or the singular beauty of the district, to remain. His trade with the Six Nations was very much to their as well as his own advantage, he supplying them on more equitable terms than any trader, and not indulging them in strong liquors which others were accustomed to do. The Castle contained the stores in which all goods meant for the Indian traffic were laid up and the peltries received in exchange. The Hall was his Summer residence, around which his chief improvements were laid.

"Here," wrote Mrs. Grant, a Scotch lady who visited Sir William, and published her travels, "this singular man lived like a little sovereign; kept a most bountiful table for strangers and officers, and, by confiding entirely in the Indians, and treating them with unvarying truth and justice, without ever yielding to solicitation what he had once refused, he taught them to repose entire confidence in him. He, in his turn, became attached to them; wore, in Winter, almost entirely their dress and ornaments, and contracted a kind of alliance with them; for, becoming a widower in the prime of life, he had connected himself with an Indian maiden, (daughter of a sachem,) who possessed an uncommonly agreeable person and good understanding; and whether ever formally married to him or not, according to our usage, contrived to live with him in great union and affection all his life.

"So perfect was his dependence on these people that when they returned from their Summer excursions and exchanged their pelts for firearms, &c., they used to pass a few days at the Castle, when his family and most of his domestics were down at the Hall. There they were all liberally entertained by their friend, and five hundred of them have been known, for nights together, after drinking pretty freely, to lie around him on the floor, while he was the only white person in a house containing great quantities of everything that was to them valuable or desirable."

The Peculiar Education of Sir William's Two Daughters.

"While Sir William thus united in his mode of life the calm urbanity of a liberal and extensive trader with the splendid hospitality, the numerous attendance and the plain, though dignified, manners of an ancient baron, the female part of his family were educated in a manner so entirely dissimilar from that of all other young people of their sex and station, that as a matter of curiosity it is worthy a recital. These two young ladies, his daughters, inherited, in a great measure, the personal advantages and strength of understanding for which their father was so distinguished. Their mother dying when they were very young, bequeathed the care of them to a friend, the widow of an officer who had fallen in battle. I am not sure whether this widow was devout and shunned the world for fear of its pollutions, or whether romantic, and so despised its selfish, bustling spirit; but so it was, that she seemed utterly to forget it, and to devote herself to her fair pupils. To these she taught needle-work of the most elegant and ingenious kinds; also reading and writing, and thus quietly passed their childhood, their mistress not taking the smallest concern in family management, nor, indeed, the least interest in any worldly thing but themselves. Far less did she inquire about the fashions or diversions which prevailed in a world that she had renounced, and from which she wished to see her pupils forever estranged.

"Never was anything so uniform as their dress, their occupations, and the general tenor of their lives. In the morning they rose early, read their prayer book, I believe, but certainly their Bible; fed their birds; tended their flowers, and breakfasted. Then they were employed for some hours, with unwearied perseverance, at fine needle-work on the ornamental parts of dress which were the fashion of the day, without knowing to what use these were to be put, since they never wore them. They had not, at the age of sixteen, ever seen a lady excepting each other and their governess. They then read as long as they chose, either the voluminous romances of the last century, of which their friend had an ample collection, or Rollins' Ancient History, the only books they had ever seen. After dinner they regularly, in Summer, took a long walk, or, in Winter, an excursion in the sledge with their friend. They then returned and resumed their wonted occupations, with the sole variation of a stroll in the garden in Summer and a game of chess or shuttle-cock in Winter.

"Their dress was to the full as simple and uniform as everything else; they wore wrappers of the finest chintz and green silk petticoats, and this the whole year round without variation. Their hair, which was long and beautiful, was tied behind with a simple ribbon; a large calash shaded each from the sun, and in Winter they had long scarlet mantles that covered them from head to foot. Their father did not live with them, but visited them every day in their apartments. This innocent and uniform life they led till the death of their monitress, which happened when the eldest was not quite seventeen. On some future occasion I shall satisfy the curiosity which this short but faithful account of these amiable recluses has possibly excited."

Mrs. Grant, so far as we can learn, never *did* satisfy curiosity about these "amiable recluses," and we beg to supplement her story by jotting down a few facts from Sir William's life. She never mentions a son John, who was the eldest of his three children, and who afterwards inherited his father's title and estate and became one of the most bitter and destructive tories during our Revolution. The mother was a plain but sensible German girl, of no social standing and but little education, Catharine Weisenberg by name, and was married to Sir William about the year 1740. When she died is not known, but it is thought it was about 1745. The two "recluses," mentioned by Mrs. Grant, were named Mary and Nancy. In 1763, the former and younger was married to Guy Johnson, her cousin, and for some time the private secretary of his uncle. Shortly after, Nancy married Colonel Claus.

Two spacious stone houses, each surrounded by an extensive domain, were built for these sons-in-law of Sir William in 1766. Both after became famous tories during the Revolution, and by means of their long acquaintance and large influence over the Six Nations were enabled to do great mischief. They afterwards (as did Sir John Johnson) removed to Canada and were gifted by the crown with large possessions, to compensate them for their immense landed property which was confiscated at the outbreak of the Revolution.

Sir William Marries Molly Brant, an Indian Maiden.

It was somewhere about 1748 that Sir William took up with Molly Brant, sister to the far-famed war chief, Joseph Brant, (Thayendanegea of the Revolution,) and the Indian maiden, who possessed an "uncommonly agreeable person and good understanding," as mentioned by Mrs. Grant. With her as his Indian wife, united according to the custom of the tribes, Sir William lived in great harmony and affection till his death, always treating her with respect and consideration, of which, according to all accounts, she was well worthy. Sir William had by her no less than eight children, to each of whom, as well as to the mother, he bequeathed, by will, generous sums of money and large tracts of land. Most of them migrated to Canada at the time of our Revolution, and their descendants are among the most respectable persons of that province.

Sir William's love for Miss Molly, as she was generally called, had a rather wild and romantic commencement. The story runs that she was born in Ohio, and that her mother had moved back to the Mohawk valley, with her and her brother Joseph. It was at a regimental militia muster that the Baronet first saw her, at which time she was a wild, laughing, beautiful girl of about sixteen. She, on this occasion, made one of a multitude of spectators, mainly Indians. One of the field officers passing by her on his prancing steed, by way of banter, she laughingly asked permission to mount behind him. Not for one moment supposing she could perform the exploit, he said she might. At the word she leaped upon the crupper with the agility of a gazelle. The horse sprang off at full speed, and, clinging to the officer, her gay-colored blanket flying and her raven tresses streaming to the wind, she flew about the parade ground swift as an arrow, to the infinite merriment of the onlooking throng. The Colonel, (for he had not at that time been titled, and was little over thirty years old,) who was a witness of the entertaining spectacle, so admired the spirit of the young squaw, and became so enamored of her person, that he at once took her to his house and made her its keeper.

Sir William Johnson died July 11th, 1774. It has been asserted, and largely believed, that his end was greatly hastened, if not caused, by the worries and perplexities occasioned by the approaching Revolution. There can be no doubt but that this royal beneficiary had many serious troubles of mind regarding the conflicts and growing discontents between the colonists and the mother country, but it is a grave error to conclude for certain that had he lived another year, he would have espoused the cause of the crown. Many remarks he made, and parts of his letters written during these preliminary troubles, show that he condemned England for some of her acts toward this country, and that he sympathized with Americans in many of their grievances. That he perished by his own hand in consequence of the clouds that were then darkening the political sky, or immediately after having received dispatches from England instructing him, in the event of hostilities, to use his influence with the Indians on behalf of the crown—and both these assertions have diligently been circulated—has not one tittle of evidence to support them. His demise occurred from entirely natural causes. For many years he was subject to alarming attacks of illness of a dysenteric character, which often prostrated him on his bed for weeks together. Even so far back as 1767 he had been induced by his faithful Mohawks to visit a medicinal spring whose healing waters had long had great repute among the tribes. Accompanied by Indian guides, and borne on a rude Indian litter, he proceeded through the wilderness to Saratoga Lake, and thence to what is now known as Cliff Rock Spring. Close to this healing fountain, in a rough bower of bark and boughs, reclined the first white man that is known to have visited the now world-famous Saratoga Springs. He was soon called away, however, on business, but short as his sojourn was there, such was the benefit derived, that he was enabled to travel part of the way back on foot.

The closing scenes of the English Baronet's days were in harmony with all his previous life and have much in them of the touching and picturesque. We have already given a full account of the wanton murders committed in the Spring of '74 and under the lead of Captain Cresap and Daniel Greathouse, upon Indians living on the Ohio below Fort Pitt, and more especially on the relatives of Logan, the famous Mingo Chief. The news of these outrages was received by the Six Nations with alarm. They were very deeply moved and greatly exasperated. Logan, the principal sufferer, was the son of Shikellimus, a distinguished Cayuga Sachem, and therefore one of their own flesh and blood. They at once desired Sir William to hold a congress with them upon this serious news. This was granted and by the 7th of July about six hundred Iroquois had assembled at the Hall. Sir William had for some weeks been indefatigable in his efforts to restrain the Six Nations from taking any part in the war, which, in consequence of these outrages, had already broken out upon the border, and by the time the congress was assembled was so physically exhausted as to bring on a sharp attack of his old complaint—dysentery. On the 8th and 9th the congress—involving almost constant exertion on the Baronet's part—was in full progress. On the 11th he made a lengthy speech of full two hours' duration, delivered with all the fire and fervor of an Indian orator, to which, although seated under a burning July sun, the Indians listened with grave attention.

The great cause was gained, but it was at the expense of the life of its advocate. Scarcely had his strange and swarthy audience dispersed ere he had to be supported to his library. An express was immediately sent for his son, who was distant nine miles. Mounting a fleet English blood horse, John rode to the Hall with such uncommon speed that his gallant horse fell dead when within a mile of the house, having run upwards of eight miles in a quarter of an hour. Sir John borrowed another horse and pushed on to the Hall. He found his honored father in the arms of a faithful body slave. He spoke to him but received no answer, and in a few minutes more the Baronet was no more.

Upon the announcement of this sudden and shocking death to the large assemblage of Indians, who had so long loved and trusted him for his justice and integrity, they appeared stupefied and fell into the greatest confusion and distress, declaring that they were now left without a protector, and would at once send "speech belts" to all the Indian tribes. Colonel Guy Johnson, however, solemnly promised them that he would take charge of their affairs and carry out Sir William's wishes until His Majesty's pleasure was known. They then became calm, and on the 13th attended the august funeral in a body, behaving with the greatest decorum and exhibiting the most lively marks of real sorrow. The next day they performed the ceremony of condolence, Conoghquieson, a distinguished Oneida Chief, beginning the touching ceremony, and delivering an affecting speech, in which he earnestly exhorted Colonel Johnson to follow the footsteps of their great brother Wawaghiyagey, who *never deceived them.*

Colonel Guy Johnson, in accordance with a request forwarded by the Baronet to the Crown a few weeks before his death, was continued as General Indian Superintendent. He was assisted by Colonel Claus, his brother-in-law, who had been for a number of years the Baronet's deputy in Canada, and was well qualified to give advice.

A Late Visit to Johnson Hall and Castle.

During the present Summer (1875) we proceeded, via the Hudson river, to the beautiful Mohawk valley, for the express purpose of visiting the scene of Sir William's long labors, and the baronial residences which are so inseparably connected with his name and memory. We were most richly repaid for our trouble. Leaving Albany by rail, we passed through the old Dutch town of Schenectady, and stopped first at Amsterdam.

Here taking a horse and buggy, we first visited Guy Park, where stands the hall built, in 1766, by Sir William Johnson, for his nephew and son-in-law, Colonel Guy Johnson. It is situate near the Mohawk, in the midst of a grove of venerable elms, and can easily be seen from the cars on the N. Y. Central Road. It is a solid, substantial, double stone house, somewhat modernized, it is true, but still showing what it was in times long past—one of the finest structures in the colony. The grounds around, which were selected for Sir William by the Indians by reason of their fertility, still maintain their old reputation. The widow lady who now owns Guy Park says her large farm is as rich and productive as any in the Mohawk valley. A short distance further west once stood the hall built, at same time and in same style, for Colonel Daniel Claus, another son-in-law of Sir William's. It was burnt down during the Revolution. A body of six hundred and forty acres was the gift with each house.

About a mile west of Guy Park, the Mohawk river and the N. Y. Central Road running directly in front, stands Fort Johnson, or Johnson Castle, as it was frequently called in olden times. The property is located at the base of a hill called Mount Johnson, and was bought by Sir William in 1742. The next year he erected a solid, massive stone mansion, which looks, even now, as if it would stand for another hundred years. It is occupied at present by a family by the name of Aiken, who have put very few repairs upon it. The walls are very thick and strong; the timbers, especially in the attic, very sound and staunch, and the small, square panes of glass are set in heavy sash. Altogether, the house is an excellent specimen of the old-style mansion, and would be considered an elegant structure even at the present day. A venerable grove of locusts in front serves to somewhat obscure the view of it from the railroad.

Here Sir William lived constantly until the construction of Johnson Hall, in 1763, and even then he occupied it during the Winters. Johnson Hall is situate a few miles back off the Mohawk, on the edge of the flourishing town now known as Johnstown. It is easiest reached by rail from Fonda, but we preferred a ride via Tribes Hill, over the breezy, verdant uplands, and were accompanied much of the way by the hum of the mowing machine. We never remember to have passed over a more charming country, or to have had a more delightful ride. On reaching Johnstown we soon found the hall. Everybody knew it. It stands upon a gentle elevation, and is now the property of Mr. Wells, who very freely allowed us admission, and took great pains to show everything of interest. Although both house and grounds have been greatly altered and modernized, we can even now judge well what they must have been originally.

The hall is a two-storied double mansion, built of wood, in the most substantial, conscientious manner, with raised panels on the outside in imitation of stone. It was, without doubt, in its day the most spacious and elegant edifice in the colony outside of New York City. The hall is fully fifteen feet wide, and the ceilings over twelve feet high, surrounded with massive wooden cornices of carved work. The sides of the rooms are elegantly wainscoted with pine panels and heavy carved work. A broad staircase of easy ascent leads from the lower to the upper hall, ornamented with massive mahogany balustrades, which still, at every foot, bear the marks of the tomahawk's hacking, said by tradition to have been notched there by Chief Brant himself when he fled the valley with Sir John Johnson in 1776, "to protect the house from the torch of Indians who would understand and respect these signs." W. L. Stone, however, the biographer of Sir William, thinks it far more probable that the hacking was done by some vandal soldier in the service who, not being allowed by his superior officer to burn the building, vented his malice in the above manner.

Of the garden and nursery, situated to the south of the hall, and which in the olden times were the delight of the Baronet, and the pride of the surrounding country, no vestige remains. Some of the poplars, however, which he planted, still stand green and vigorous. The hall was formerly flanked by two stone block-houses, with sundry loop holes for musketry cut directly under the eaves. But one of these—now converted into a servants' dwelling—yet stands, the other having been burned down many years ago. Of the stone wall which surrounded the whole place as a protection against attack, but little now remains.

Mr. Wells informed us that a subterranean passage led from the main building to the block-house on the left, and thence another communicated with the block-house on the right flank. These passages, however, as well as the port holes in the remaining block-house, have been filled up. Although the building never experienced a siege, yet it was twice fortified, once, as stated, by a strong stone rampart in 1763, by Sir William, and again in 1776, by Sir John Johnson, previous to his flight into Canada.

When Sir William died he was—part by purchase and part by gift of the crown—the largest landed possessor in America, next to the Penns. His magnificent estate, however, was confiscated during the Revolution and his halls passed out of the family into the hands of strangers. Mr.

252 OUR WESTERN BORDER.

Wells informed us that occasionally some of the descendants of the Johnson and Brant families pay Johnson Hall a visit and are deeply interested in all the localities associated with his name.

Boone's combat with two savages.—*See page* 263.

CHAPTER IV.

DANIEL BOONE, PIONEER OF KENTUCKY.

> Here once Boone trod—the hardy Pioneer,
> The only white man in the wilderness.
> Oh, how he loved, alone, to hunt the deer;
> Alone at eve his simple meal to dress.
> No mark upon the tree, nor print nor track
> To lead him forward or to guide him back;
> He roved the forest—king, by main and might—
> Looked up to the sky, and shaped his course aright.
> In hunting shirt and moccasin arrayed;
> With bear-skin cap and pouch and trenchant blade;
> How carelessly he leaned upon his gun!
> Sceptre of the wild that hath so often won.—*F. W. Thomas.*

American History presents no character of such fascination and popularity as that of Daniel Boone, the pioneer hunter of Kentucky; and this, not simply because he was a daring and adventurous woodsman, or because the free life of the wilderness has ever its special charms and romance, but because of the singular modesty, simplicity and guilelessness of the man's character. Like all truly brave men, Boone had a vast amount of quiet, unostentatious force. No man was freer from a boastful, vaunting spirit. It is likewise gross error to consider him as nothing but a daring hunter, whose life was passed in constant conflict with wild beasts or with still more savage Indians. Although an unlettered man, Boone must occupy a higher plane in our history than that; he was a pioneer, a leader and a masterful director, as well as a hunter, and was as closely connected with civilization and its beneficial achievements as he was with the woody solitude and the perils of varied adventure. He is chiefly admired because he is the completest and most admirable specimen of the class to which he belonged.

George Boone, his grandfather, came to this country from England, bringing with him nine sons and ten daughters, the very kind of family men needed to populate the boundless wastes of America. Daniel Boone was the son of Squire Boone; was born in Berks county, Pa., in 1734, but the family soon moved to the South Yadkin, N. C. Daniel was then about nineteen, a fine, active, stalwart man, exceedingly fond of roving in the surrounding forests, and particularly skilled with the rifle. But little is known of his early manhood, as he has modestly forborne to say anything of himself, saving so far as he is connected with Kentucky. We know for certain, however, that he took great delight in long and solitary wilderness excursions, and was early enamored of the untrammeled freedom of the boundless forests.

Of his romantic courtship and marriage, we will treat elsewhere, when we come to sketch the life of his most excellent wife, Rebecca. For some time he lived happily with her on the banks of the Yadkin, occasionally disturbing the toiling monotony of his farmer's life by long hunting rambles. For instance, Ramsay's Tennessee gives a fac-simile of a rude inscription drawn by Boone on a tree in that State, announcing his killing of a bear in 1760, at the age of twenty-six. In '64 he had even stood within the eastern border of Kentucky and bathed in the waters of the Cumberland. It was while viewing the vast herds of buffalo from a spur of the Cumberland mountains, that he exclaimed: "I am richer than the one mentioned in Scripture who owned the cattle of a thousand hills, for I own the wild beasts of more than a thousand valleys."

Kentucky as it Was in the Olden Time.

In '67 Findley, the first white man who ever explored Kentucky, returned from his solitary vagabondizing and gave such glowing accounts of that magnificent country—its hills and valleys; its park-like forests; its dense canebrakes and—above all to affect a zealous hunter—its exhaustless variety of game, from the beaver to the buffalo, that Boone's ardor was kindled and he determined to visit the new Eldorado and Paradise for hunters, in person. That Kentucky at that early day presented irresistible attractions for the adventurer, can readily be judged from the accounts of all who traversed it. Captain Imlay, who, in early times, visited it in the Spring, and was enraptured with the panorama of bewildering beauty which everywhere met his eye, wrote: "Everything here assumes a dignity and splendor I have never seen in any other part of the world. Here an eternal verdure reigns and the brilliant sun piercing through the azure heavens, produces in this prolific soil an early maturity truly astonishing. Flowers full and perfect as if they had been cultivated by the hand of a florist, with all their captivating odors and with all the variegated charms which color and nature can here produce, decorate the smiling groves. Soft zephyrs gently breathe on sweets and the inhaled air gives a voluptuous glow of health and vigor that seems to ravish the intoxicated senses. The sweet song sters of the forest appear to feel the influence of the genial clime, and in more soft and modulated tones warble their tender notes in unison with love and nature. Everything here gives delight, and we feel a glow of gratitude for what an all-bountiful Creator has bestowed upon us."

Filson, another visitor of the long ago, wrote: "The soil is of a loose, deep, black mould without sand—in the best lands about two feet deep and exceedingly luxuriant in all its productions. The country is well timbered, producing large trees of many kinds, and to be exceeded by no country in variety"—among others, sugars, coffee, pawpaw and honey locusts. Of the fine cane, so famous for its buffalo paths; its plenteousness of bear and other wild game, and its ranges for cattle, he says: "This plant grows from three to twelve feet high; is of a hard substance, with joints at eight or ten inches distance along the stalk, from which proceed leaves like those of the willow. There are many canebrakes so thick and tall that it is difficult to pass through them. Where no cane grows there is an abundance of wild rye, clover and buffalo grass, covering vast tracts of country, and affording excellent food for cattle. Here are seen the finest crown-imperial in the world; the cardinal flower so much extolled for its scarlet color; and all the year, excepting the Winter months, the plains and valleys are adorned with a variety of flowers of the most admirable beauty. Here is also found the tulip-bearing laurel tree, or magnolia, which is very fragrant and continues to blossom and seed for several months together. By casting an eye over the map and viewing round the heads of Licking from the Ohio, and round the heads of the Kentucky and Dick's rivers, and down Green river to the Ohio again, one may view within that compass of above a hundred miles square, the most extraordinary country on which the sun has ever shone."

This is a glowing but not an overdrawn picture of Kan-tuck-ee as she was of old, robed in all her primeval beauty. Others have said that the herbage was of such lushness and exuberance that you could track a man through it at a run on a fleet horse. Indeed, we opine, that few of our day can realize the surpassing richness and luxuriance of favored portions of the virgin western wilderness. For instance Spencer, in his Narrative of Captivity, says:

"Our western Winters were much milder, our Springs earlier and our Autumns longer than now. On the last of February, some of the trees were putting forth foliage; in March the red bud, the hawthorn and the dog wood, in full bloom, checkered the hills, and in May the ground was covered with the May apple, bloodroot, ginseng, violets and a great variety of herbs and flowers. Flocks of paroquets were seen, decked in their rich plumage of green and gold. Birds of every species and hue were flitting from tree to tree, and the beautiful red bird and the plaintive dove could be seen, and the rumbling drum of the partridge or the loud gobble of the wild turkey, heard from all sides. Here might be seen the clumsy bear, doggedly running off; there the timid deer watchfully resting, cautiously feeding, or, aroused from his matted thicket, gracefully bounding off. It seemed an earthly paradise, and but for the apprehension of the wily copperhead, silently coiled beneath the leaves; the horrid rattlesnake, who, however, more chivalrous, apprised one of his danger, and the still more fearful and insidious savage, who, crawling upon the ground or noiselessly approaching behind trees and thickets, sped the deadly shaft or fatal bullet, you might have fancied you were in the confines of Eden or the borders of Elysium."

The author of Miami County Traditions says: "The country all around the settlement presented the most lovely appearance; the earth was like an ash-heap for mellowness and nothing could exceed the luxuriance of primitive vegetation; indeed, our cattle often died from excess of feeding, and it was somewhat difficult to rear them on that account. The white weed, or bee harvest, as it is called, so profusely spread now over our bottoms and woodlands, was not then seen among us; the sweet annis, nettles, wild rye and pea vine, now so scarce, then everywhere abounded. They were almost the entire herbage of our bottoms; the last two gave subsistence to our cattle, and the first, with other nutritious roots, were eaten by our swine with the greatest avidity. In the Spring and Summer months, a drove of hogs could be scented at a considerable distance from the flavor of the annis root."

Is it any wonder, then, that the early hunters became enamored of these western Edens, so prodigal of sweetness as to throw an atmosphere of fragrance even about a drove of vulgar unsavory swine! But our readers must forgive this tempting side ramble. *Revenons a nos moutons.*

To one of Boone's tastes, the scenes so enthusiastically described by Findley presented charms not to be longer resisted, so joining, in 1769, Findley and four others of like mind and tastes with himself, he left his family on the Yadkin and pushed boldly for the West. We cannot, of course, in a work as this, essay to give the details of a life like Boone's, so absolutely crowded with personal adventure, and so must content ourselves with a most meagre outline of his future happenings.

On the 7th of June they reached Red river, and from a neighboring eminence were enabled to survey the vast plain of Kentucky. Here they built a cabin, in order to afford them a shelter from the rain—which had fallen in immense quantities on their march—and remained in a great measure stationary until December, killing a great quantity of game immediately around them. Immense herds of buffalo ranged through the forest in every direction, feeding on the leaves of the cane or the rich and spontaneous fields of clover. On the 22d of December, Boone and John Stuart, one of his companions, left their encampment, and following one of the numerous paths which the buffalo had made through the cane, they plunged boldly into the interior of the forest. They had as yet seen no Indians, and the country had been reported as totally uninhabited. This was true in a strict sense, for although the southern and north-western tribes were in the habit of hunting here as upon neutral ground, yet not a single wigwam had been erected, nor did the land bear the slightest mark of having ever been cultivated. The different tribes would fall in with each other, and from the fierce conflicts which generally followed these casual rencontres, the country had been known among them by the name of "*the dark and bloody ground!*"

BOONE CAPTURED FOR THE FIRST TIME AND ESCAPES.

The two adventurers soon learned the additional danger to which they were exposed. While roving carelessly from canebrake to canebrake, and admiring the rank growth of vegetation, and the variety of timber which marked the fertility of the soil, they were suddenly alarmed by the appearance of a party of Indians, who, springing from their place of concealment, rushed upon them with a rapidity that rendered escape impossible. They were almost instantly seized, disarmed and made prisoners. Their feelings may be readily imagined. They were in the hands of an enemy who knew no alternative between adoption and torture, and the numbers and fleetness of their captors rendered escape by open means impossible, while their jealous vigilance seemed equally fatal to any secret attempt. Boone, however, was possessed of a temper admirably adapted to the circumstances in which he was placed. Of a cold and saturnine, rather than an ardent disposition, he was never either so much elevated by good fortune or depressed by bad, as to lose for a moment the full possession of all his faculties. He saw that immediate escape was impossible, but he encouraged his companion, and constrained himself to follow the Indians in all their excursions with so calm and contented an air, that their vigilance insensibly began to relax.

On the seventh evening of their captivity, they encamped in a thick

17

canebrake, and, having built a large fire, lay down to rest. The party whose duty it was to watch, were weary and negligent, and about midnight Boone, who had not closed an eye, ascertained from the deep breathing all around him that the whole party, including Stuart, were in a deep sleep. Gently and gradually extricating himself from the Indians who lay around him, he walked cautiously to the spot where Stuart lay, and having succeeded in awakening him without alarming the rest, he briefly informed him of his determination, and exhorted him to arise, make no noise, and follow him. Stuart, although ignorant of the design, and suddenly aroused from sleep, fortunately obeyed with equal silence and celerity, and within a few minutes they were beyond hearing. Rapidly traversing the forest, by the light of the stars and the barks of the trees, they ascertained the direction in which the camp lay, but upon reaching it on the next day, to their great grief, they found it plundered and deserted, with nothing remaining to show the fate of their companions; and, even to the day of his death, Boone knew not whether they had been killed or taken, or had voluntarily abandoned their cabin and returned. Here in a few days they were accidentally joined by Boone's brother and another man, who had followed them from Carolina, and fortunately stumbled upon their camp. This accidental meeting in the bosom of a vast wilderness, gave great relief to the two brothers, although their joy was soon overcast.

Boone and Stuart, in a second excursion, were again pursued by savages, and Stuart was shot and scalped, while Boone fortunately escaped. As usual, he has not mentioned particulars, but barely stated the event. Within a few days they sustained another calamity, if possible still more distressing. Their only remaining companion was benighted in a hunting excursion, and, while encamped in the woods alone, was attacked and devoured by the wolves.

The two brothers were thus left in the wilderness alone, separated by several hundred miles from home, surrounded by hostile Indians, and destitute of everything but their rifles. After having had such melancholy experience of the dangers to which they were exposed, we would naturally suppose that their fortitude would have given way, and that they would instantly have returned to the settlements. But the most remarkable feature in Boone's character was a calm and cold equanimity, which rarely rose to enthusiasm, and never sunk to despondency. His courage undervalued the danger to which he was exposed, and his presence of mind, which never forsook him, enabled him, on all occasions, to take the best means of avoiding it. The wilderness, with all its dangers and privations, had a charm for him which is scarcely conceivable by one brought up in a city, and he determined to remain alone, whilst his brother returned to Carolina for an additional supply of ammunition, as their original supply was nearly exhausted.

"I was," he says, "left by myself, without bread, salt or sugar, without the company of my fellow-creatures, or even a horse and dog."

His situation, we should now suppose, was in the highest degree gloomy and dispirited. The dangers which attended his brother on his return were nearly equal to his own; and each had left a wife and children, which Boone acknowledged cost him many an anxious thought. But the wild and solitary grandeur of the country around him, where not a tree had been cut, nor a house erected, was to him an inexhaustible source of admiration and delight; and he says himself, that some of the most rapturous moments of his life were spent in those lonely rambles. The climate was superb. The forests were magnificent with their exuberance of rustling foliage, and in sunny openings lay verdant savannas covered with the lushest of grasses and perfectly enameled with flowers. Upon these and along several streams and extensive canebrakes, immense herds of the unwieldy buffalo could be seen rolling along. The majestic trees were festooned with vines, from which, in early Autumn, hung grapes as luscious as those of Eshcol. In fact, it was a "land of Canaan, flowing with milk and honey." The utmost caution was necessary to avoid the savages, and scarcely less to escape the ravenous hunger of the wolves that prowled nightly around him in immense numbers. He was compelled frequently to shift his lodging, and by undoubted signs, saw that the Indians had repeatedly visited his hut during his absence. He sometimes lay in canebrakes, without fire, and heard the yell of the Indians around him. Fortunately, however, he never encountered them, although he took long rambles all over Northern Kentucky.

On the 27th of July, 1770, his brother returned with a supply of ammunition on two well-laden horses; and with a hardihood which appears almost incredible, they ranged through the country in every direction, and without injury, until March, 1771. They then returned to North Carolina, where Daniel rejoined his family, after an absence of three years, during nearly the whole of which time he had never tasted bread or salt, nor seen the face of a single white man, with the exception of his brother, and the friends who had been killed. He here determined to sell his farm and remove with his family to the wilderness of Kentucky—an astonishing instance of hardihood, and we should even say indifference to his family, if it were not that his character has uniformly been represented as mild and humane as it was bold and fearless.

Boone Moves his Family to Kentucky—Loses a Son.

Accordingly, on the 25th of September, 1771, having disposed of all the property which he could not take with him, he took leave of his friends and commenced his journey to the west. A number of milch cows and horses, laden with a few necessary household utensils, formed the whole of his baggage. His wife and children were mounted on horseback and accompanied him, every one regarding them as devoted to destruction. In Powell's valley, they were joined by five more families and forty men well armed. Encouraged by this accession of strength, they advanced with additional confidence, but had soon a severe warning of the further dangers which awaited them. When near Cumberland Mountain, their rear was suddenly attacked with great fury by a scouting party of Indians, and thrown into considerable confusion. The party, however, soon rallied, and being accustomed to Indian warfare, returned the fire with such spirit and effect, that the Indians were repulsed with slaughter. Their own loss, however, had been severe. Six men were killed upon the spot, and one wounded. Among the killed was Boone's eldest son—to the unspeakable affliction of his family. The disorder and grief occasioned by this rough reception, seems to have affected the emigrants deeply, as they instantly retraced their steps to the settlements on Clinch river, forty miles from the scene of action. Here they remained until June, 1774, probably at the request of the women, who must have been greatly alarmed at the prospect of plunging more deeply into a country upon the skirts of which they had witnessed so keen and bloody a conflict.

At this time Boone, at the request of Governor Dunmore, of Virginia, conducted a number of surveyors to the falls of Ohio, a distance of eight hundred miles. Of the incidents of this journey, we have no record whatever. After his return he was engaged under Dunmore, until 1775, in several affairs with the Indians, and at the solicitation of some gentlemen of North Carolina, he attended at a treaty with the Cherokees, for the purpose of purchasing the lands south of Kentucky river.

It was under the auspices of Colonel Henderson that Boone's next visit to Kentucky was made. Leaving his family on Clinch river, he set out, at the head of a few men, to mark out a road for the pack-horses or wagons of Henderson's party. This laborious and dangerous duty he executed with his usual patient fortitude, until he came within fifteen miles of the spot where Boonsborough afterwards was built. Here, on the 22d of March, his small party was attacked by the Indians, and suf-

Capture of the Boone and Calloway Girls.

SEE PAGE 26.

fered a loss of four men killed and wounded. The Indians, although repulsed with loss in this affair, renewed the attack with equal fury on the next day, and killed and wounded five more of his party. On the 1st of April, the survivors began to build a small fort on the Kentucky river, afterwards called Boonsborough, and, on the 4th, they were again attacked by the Indians, and lost another man. Notwithstanding the harassing attacks to which they were constantly exposed, (for the Indians seemed enraged to madness at the prospect of them building houses on their hunting grounds,) the work was prosecuted with indefatigable diligence, and on the 14th was completed.

Boone instantly returned to Clinch river for his family, determined to bring them with him at every risk. This was done as soon as the journey could be performed, and Mrs. Boone and her daughters were the first white women who stood upon the banks of the Kentucky river, as Boone himself had been the first white man who ever built a cabin upon the borders of the State. The first house, however, which ever stood in the *interior* of Kentucky, was erected at Harrodsburg, in the year 1774, by James Harrod, who conducted to this place a party of hunters from the banks of the Monongahela. This place was, therefore, a few months older than Boonsborough. Both soon became distinguished, as the only places in which hunters and surveyors could find security from the fury of the Indians.

Within a few weeks after the arrival of Mrs. Boone and her daughters, the infant colony was reinforced by three more families, at the head of which were Mrs. McGary, Mrs. Hogan and Mrs. Denton. Boonsborough, however, was the central object of Indian hostilities, and scarcely had his family become domesticated in their new possession when they were suddenly attacked by a party of Indians, and lost one of their garrison. This was in December, 1775.

CAPTURE OF BOONE'S DAUGHTER AND THE CALLOWAY GIRLS.

In the following July, however, a much more alarming event occurred. Boone's daughter, Jemima, in company with Betty and Fanny Calloway, crossed the Kentucky river in a canoe, and while amusing themselves along the leafy bank by splashing the water about with their paddles, they were seen by five lurking savages. One of them, stealthily gliding into the stream, seized the tying rope and succeeded in noiselessly dragging the canoe into a little leafy nook out of sight of the fort. The loud shrieks of the now terrified girls quickly alarmed the family. The small garrison was dispersed in their usual occupations; but Boone hastily collected a small party of eight men, and pursued the enemy

So much time, however, had been lost, that the Indians had got several miles the start of them. The pursuit was urged through the night with great keenness, by woodsmen capable of following a trail at all times, and on the following day they came up with them. The attack was so sudden and furious, that the Indians were driven from the ground before they had time to tomahawk their prisoners, and the girls were recovered without having sustained any other injury than excessive fright and fatigue. Nothing but a barren outline of this interesting occurrence has been given. We know nothing of the conduct of the Indians to their captives, or of the situation of the young ladies during the short engagement, and cannot venture to fill up the outline from imagination. The Indians lost two men, while Boone's party was uninjured.

From this time until the 15th of April, 1777, the garrison was incessantly harassed by flying parties of Indians. While ploughing their corn, they were waylaid and shot; while hunting, they were chased and fired upon; and sometimes a solitary Indian would creep up near the fort, in the night, and fire upon the first of the garrison who appeared in the morning. They were in a constant state of anxiety and alarm, and the most ordinary duties could only be performed at the risk of their lives. On the 15th the enemy appeared in large numbers, hoping to crush the infant settlement at a single blow. Boonsborough, Logan's Fort and Harrodsburg were attacked at one and the same time. But, destitute as they were of artillery, scaling ladders, and all the proper means of reducing fortified places, they could only distress the men, alarm the women and destroy the corn and cattle. Boonsborough sustained some loss, as did the other stations, but the enemy, being more exposed, suffered so severely as to cause them to retire with precipitation.

No rest, however, was given to the unhappy garrison. On the 4th of July following they were again attacked by two hundred warriors, but the enemy were repulsed with loss. The Indians retreated, but a few days afterwards fell upon Logan's station with great fury, having sent detachments to alarm the other stations, so as to prevent the appearance of reinforcements at Logan's. In this last attempt they displayed great obstinacy, and as the garrison consisted only of fifteen men, they were reduced to extremity. Not a moment could be allowed for sleep. Burning arrows were shot upon the roofs of the houses, and the Indians often pressed boldly up to the gates, and attempted to hew them down with their tomahawks. Fortunately, at this critical time, Colonel Bowman arrived from Virginia with one hundred men well armed, and the savages precipitately withdrew, leaving the garrison almost exhausted with fatigue and reduced to twelve men.

Boone's Fight with Two Savages—He is taken Captive.

A brief period of repose now followed, in which the settlers endeavored to repair the damages done to their farms. But a period of heavy trial to Boone and his family was approaching. In January, 1778, accompanied by thirty men, Boone went to the Blue Licks to make salt for the different stations, and used to go out to hunt for them regularly. One day, according to Flint, his biographer, he had wandered some distance from the river, and suddenly encountered two savages. He could not retreat, and so slipped behind a tree, and then exposed himself to attract their aim. The first shot, and Boone dropped at the flash as if killed. To make the second throw away his shot, he again exposed part of his person. The eager savage instantly fired, and Boone evaded the shot as before. The two Indians were now, with nervous hands, attempting to reload. Boone now drew a fatal bead on the foremost, and he fell, pierced to the heart. The two antagonists now advanced—Boone flourishing his knife and the savage his tomahawk—to the dead body of the fallen Indian. Boone placed his foot on the body, and received the tomahawk on his rifle. In the attitude of striking, the unwary savage had exposed his body, in which the remorseless knife was plunged to the hilt.

On the 7th of February following, while out hunting, he fell in with one hundred and two Indian warriors, on their march to attack Boonsborough. He instantly fled, but being nearly fifty years old, was unable to contend with the fleet young men who pursued him, and was a second time taken prisoner. As usual, he was treated with kindness until his final fate was determined, and was led back to the Licks, where his men were still encamped. Here his whole party, to the number of twenty-seven, surrendered themselves, upon promise of life and good treatment, both of which conditions were faithfully observed.

Had the Indians prosecuted their enterprise, they might, perhaps, by showing their prisoners and threatening to put them to the torture, have operated so far upon the sympathies of the garrison as to have obtained considerable results. But nothing of the kind was attempted. They had already been unexpectedly successful, and it is their custom after either good or bad fortune, immediately to return home and enjoy the triumph. Boone and his party were conducted to the old town of Chillicothe, where they remained till the following March. No journal was written during this period, by either Boone or his party. We are only informed that his mild and patient equanimity wrought powerfully upon the Indians; that he was adopted into a family, and uniformly treated with the utmost affection. One fact is given us which shows his acute observation and knowledge of mankind. At the various shooting matches to which he was invited, he took care not to beat them *too* often. He knew that no feeling is more painful than that of inferiority, and that the most effectual way of keeping them in a good humor with *him*, was to keep them in a good humor with themselves. He, therefore, only shot well enough to make it an honor to beat him, and found himself an universal favorite.

On the 10th of March, 1778, Boone was conducted to Detroit, when Governor Hamilton himself offered £100 for his ransom; but so strong was the affection of the Indians for their prisoner, that it was positively refused. Several English gentlemen, touched with sympathy for his misfortunes, made pressing offers of money and other articles, but Boone steadily refused to receive benefits which he could never return. The offer was honorable to them, and the refusal was dictated by rather too refined a spirit of independence. Boone's anxiety on account of his wife and children was incessant, and the more intolerable, as he dared not excite the suspicion of the Indians by any indication of a wish to rejoin them.

Upon his return from Detroit, he observed that one hundred and fifty warriors of various tribes had assembled, painted and equipped for an expedition against Boonsborough. His anxiety at this sight became ungovernable, and he determined, at every risk, to effect his escape. During the whole of this agitating period, however, he permitted no symptoms of anxiety to escape him. He hunted and shot with them, as usual, until the morning of the 16th of June, when, taking an early start, he left Chillicothe and directed his route to Boonsborough. The distance exceeded one hundred and sixty miles, but he performed it in four days, during which he ate only one meal. He appeared before the garrison like one rising from the dead. His wife, supposing him killed, had transported herself, children and property to her father's house, in North Carolina; his men, suspecting no danger, were dispersed to their ordinary avocations, and the works had been permitted to go to waste. Not a moment was to be lost. The garrison worked day and night upon the fortifications. New gates, new flanks and double bastions, were soon completed. The cattle and horses were brought into the fort, ammunition prepared, and everything made ready for the approach of the enemy within ten days after his arrival. At this time, one of his companions in captivity arrived from Chillicothe, and announced that his escape had determined the Indians to delay the invasion for three weeks.

During this interval, it was ascertained that numerous spies were traversing the woods and hovering around the station, doubtless for the purpose of observing and reporting the condition of the garrison. Their report could not have been favorable. The alarm had spread very generally, and all were upon the alert. The attack had been delayed so long that Boone began to suspect that they had been discouraged by the report of the spies; and he determined to invade them. Selecting nineteen men from his garrison, he put himself at their head, and marched with equal silence and celerity against the town on Paint Creek, on the Scioto. He arrived, without discovery, within four miles of the town, and there encountered a party of thirty warriors on their march to unite with the grand army in the expedition against Boonsborough. Instantly attacking them with great spirit, he compelled them to give way with some loss, and without any injury to himself. He then halted, and sent two spies in advance to ascertain the condition of the village. In a few hours they returned with the intelligence that the town was evacuated. He instantly concluded that the grand army was on its march against Boonsborough, whose situation, as well as his own, was exceedingly critical. Retracing his steps, he marched day and night, hoping still to elude the enemy and reach Boonsborough before them. He soon fell in with their trail, and making a circuit to avoid them, he passed their army on the sixth day of his march, and on the seventh reached Boonsborough.

SEVERE SIEGE OF BOONSBOROUGH—INDIAN STRATAGEMS FOILED.

On the eighth the enemy appeared in great force. There were nearly five hundred Indian warriors, armed and painted in their usual manner, and what was still more formidable, they were conducted by a Canadian officer, well skilled in the usages of modern warfare. As soon as they were arrayed in front of the fort, the British colors were displayed, and an officer with a flag was sent to demand the surrender of the fort, with a promise of quarter and good treatment in case of compliance, and threatening "the hatchet," in case of a storm. Boone requested two days for consideration, which, in defiance of all experience and common sense, was granted. This interval, as usual, was employed in preparation for an obstinate resistance. The cattle were brought into the fort, the horses secured, and all things made ready against the commencement of hostilities.

Boone then assembled the garrison and represented to them the condition in which they stood. They had not to deal with Indians alone, but with British officers, skilled in the art of attacking fortified places, sufficiently numerous to *direct*, but too few to *restrain* their savage allies. If they surrendered, their lives might and probably would be saved; but they would suffer much inconvenience, and *must* lose all their property. If they resisted, and were overcome, the life of every man, woman and child would be sacrificed. The hour was now come in which they were to determine what was to be done. If they were inclined to surrender, he would announce it to the officer; if they were resolved to maintain the fort, he would share their fate, whether in life or death. He had scarcely finished, when every man arose and in a firm tone announced his determination to defend the fort to the last.

Boone then appeared at the gate of the fortress, and communicated to Captain Duquesne the resolution of his men. Disappointment and chagrin were strongly painted upon the face of the Canadian at this answer; but endeavoring to disguise his feelings, he declared that Governor Hamilton had ordered him not to injure the men if it could be avoided, and that if nine of the principal inhabitants of the fort would come out into the plain and treat with them, they would instantly depart without further hostility. The insidious nature of this proposal was evident, for they could converse very well from where they then stood, and going out would only place the officers of the fort at the mercy of the savages—not to mention the absurdity of supposing that this army of warriors would "*treat*," but upon such terms as pleased them, and no terms were likely to do so, short of a total abandonment of the country. Notwithstanding these objections, the word "treat," sounded so pleasantly in the ears of the besieged, that they agreed at once to the proposal and Boone himself, attended by eight of his men, went out and mingled with the savages, who crowded around them in great numbers, and with countenances of deep anxiety.

The treaty then commenced and was soon concluded. What the terms were, we are not informed, nor is it a matter of the least importance, as the whole was a stupid and shallow artifice. This was soon made manifest. Duquesne, after many very pretty periods about "*bienfaisance and humanite*," which should accompany the warfare of civilized beings, at length informed Boone, that it was a singular custom with the Indians, upon the conclusion of a treaty with the whites, for two warriors to take hold of the hand of each white man. Boone thought this rather a singular custom, but there was no time to dispute about etiquette, particularly as he could not be more in their power than he already was; so he signified his willingness to conform to the Indian mode of cementing friendship. Instantly, two warriors approached each white man, with the word "brother" upon their lips, but a very different expression in their eyes, and grappling him with violence, attempted to bear him off. "Go!" shouted Blackfish to his savages. The whites probably expected such a consummation, and all at the same moment sprung from their enemies. The struggle was violent, but of short duration. Boone and his fellows tossed the savages from them, and in the midst of rifle balls from the fort and of bullets, tomahawks and arrows from the foe, the heroic little band escaped into the fortress and securely barred the gate, all being uninjured save Boone's brother, Squire.

The attack instantly commenced by a heavy fire against the picketing, and was returned with fatal accuracy by the garrison. The Indians quickly sheltered themselves, and the action became more cautious and deliberate. Finding but little effect from the fire of his men, Duquesne next resorted to a more formidable mode of attack. The fort stood on the south bank of the river, within sixty yards of the water. Commencing under the bank, where their operations were concealed from the garrison, they attempted to push a mine into the fort. Their object, however, was fortunately discovered by the quantity of fresh earth which they were compelled to throw into the river, and by which the water became muddy for some distance below. Boone, who had regained his usual sagacity, instantly cut a trench within the fort in such a manner as to intersect the line of their approach, and thus frustrated their design. The enemy exhausted all the ordinary artifices of Indian warfare, but were steadily repulsed in every effort. Finding their numbers daily thinned by the deliberate but fatal fire of the garrison, and seeing no prospect of final success, they broke up on the ninth day of the siege and returned home. The loss of the garrison was two killed and four wounded. On the part of the savages, thirty-seven were killed and many wounded, who, as usual, were carried off. This was the last siege sustained by Boonsborough. The country had increased so rapidly in numbers, and so many other stations lay between Boonsborough and the Ohio, that the savages could not reach it without leaving enemies in the rear.

In the Autumn of this year Boone returned to North Carolina for his wife and family, who, as already observed, had supposed him dead, and returned to her father. There is a hint in Mr. Marshall's history, that the family affairs, which detained him in North Carolina, were of an unpleasant character, but no explanation is given. In the Summer of 1780 he returned to Kentucky with his family, and settled at Boonsborough. Here he continued busily engaged upon his farm until the 6th of October, when, accompanied by his brother, he went to the Lower Blue Licks, for the purpose of providing himself with salt. This spot seemed fatal to Boone. Here he had once been taken prisoner by the Indians and here he was destined, within two years, to lose his youngest son, and to witness the slaughter of many of his dearest friends. His present visit was not free from calamity. Upon their return, they were encountered by a party of Indians, and his brother, who had accompanied him faithfully through many years of toil and danger, was killed and scalped before his eyes. Unable either to prevent or avenge his death, Boone was compelled to fly, and by his superior knowledge of the country, contrived to elude his pursuers. They followed his trail, however, by the scent of a dog, that pressed him closely, and prevented his concealing himself. This was one of the most critical moments of his life, but his usual coolness and fortitude enabled him to meet it. He halted until the dog, baying loudly upon his trail, came within gunshot, when he deliberately turned and shot him dead. The thickness of the wood and the approach of darkness then enabled him to effect his escape.

During the following year Boonsborough enjoyed uninterrupted tranquility. The country had become comparatively thickly settled, and was studded with fortresses in every direction. Fresh emigrants with their families were constantly arriving; and many young unmarried women, (who had heretofore been extremely scarce,) had ventured to risk themselves in Kentucky. They could not have selected a spot where their merit was more properly appreciated, and were disposed of very rapidly to the young hunters, most of whom had hitherto, from necessity, remained bachelors. Thriving settlements had been pushed beyond the Kentucky river, and a number of houses had been built where Lexington now stands.

The year 1781 passed away in perfect tranquility, and, judging from appearances, nothing was more distant than the terrible struggle that awaited them. But during the whole of this year the Indians were meditating a desperate effort to crush the settlements at a single blow. They had become seriously alarmed at the tide of emigration, which rolled over the country and threatened to convert their favorite hunting ground into one vast cluster of villages. The game had already been much dispersed; the settlers, originally weak and scattered over the south side of the Kentucky river, had now become numerous, and were rapidly extending to the Ohio. One vigorous and united effort might still crush their enemies, and regain for themselves the undisputed possession of the western forests. A few renegade white men were mingled with them, and inflamed their wild passions by dwelling upon the injuries which they had sustained at the hands of the whites, and of the necessity for instant and vigorous exertion, or of an eternal surrender of every hope either of redress or vengeance. Among these the most remarkable was *Simon Girty*. Runners were dispatched to most of the northwestern tribes, and all were exhorted to lay aside private jealousy and unite in a common cause against these white intruders. In the meantime, the settlers were busily employed in opening farms, marrying and giving in marriage, totally ignorant of the storm which was gathering upon the lakes.

Defeat of Captain Estill—A Well-fought Action.

In the Spring of 1782, after a long interval of repose, they were harassed by small parties, who preceded the main body, as the pattering and irregular drops of rain are the precursors of the approaching storm. In the month of May, a party of twenty-five Wyandots secretly approached Estill's station, and committed shocking outrages in its vicinity. Entering a cabin which stood apart from the rest, they seized a woman and her two daughters, who, having been violated with circumstances of savage barbarity, were tomahawked and scalped. Their bodies, yet warm and bleeding, were found upon the floor of the cabin. The neighborhood was instantly alarmed. Captain Estill speedily collected a body of twenty-five men, and pursued their trail with great rapidity. He came up with them on Hinkston fork of Licking, immediately after they had crossed it, and a most severe and desperate conflict ensued. The Indians at first appeared daunted and began to fly, but their chief, who was badly wounded by the first fire, was heard in a loud voice, ordering them to stand and return the fire, which was instantly obeyed.

The creek ran between the two parties, and prevented a charge on either side, without the certainty of great loss. The parties, therefore, consisting of precisely the same number, formed an irregular line, within fifty yards of each other, and sheltering themselves behind trees or logs, they fired with deliberation, as an object presented itself. The only manœuvre which the nature of the ground permitted, was to extend their lines in such a manner as to uncover the flank of the enemy, and even this was extremely dangerous, as every motion exposed them to a close and deadly fire. The action, therefore, was chiefly stationary, neither party advancing or retreating, and every individual acting for himself. It had already lasted more than an hour, without advantage on either side or any prospect of its termination. Captain Estill had lost one-third of his men, and had inflicted about an equal loss upon his enemies, who still boldly maintained their ground and returned his fire with equal spirit. To have persevered in the Indian mode of fighting, would have exposed his party to certain death, one by one, unless all the Indians should be killed first, who, however, had at least an equal chance with himself. Even victory, bought at such a price, would have afforded but a melancholy triumph; yet it was impossible to retreat or advance without exposing his men to the greatest danger.

After coolly revolving these reflections in his mind, and observing that the enemy exhibited no symptoms of discouragement, Captain Estill determined to detach a party of six men, under Lieutenant Miller, with orders to cross the creek above, and take the Indians in flank, while he maintained his ground, ready to co-operate as circumstances might require. But he had to deal with an enemy equally bold and sagacious. The Indian chief was quickly aware of the division of the force opposed to him, from the slackening of the fire in front, and, readily conjecturing his object, he determined to frustrate it by crossing the creek with his whole force, and overwhelming Estill, now weakened by the absence of Miller. The manœuvre was bold and masterly, and was executed with determined courage. Throwing themselves into the water, they fell upon Estill with the tomahawk, and drove him before them with slaughter. Miller's party retreated with precipitation, and even lie under the reproach of deserting their friends and absconding, instead of occupying the designated ground. Others contradict this statement, and affirm that Miller punctually executed his orders, crossed the creek, and, falling in with the enemy, was compelled to retire with loss.

Estill's party, finding themselves furiously charged, and receiving no assistance from Miller, who was probably at that time on the other side of the creek, in execution of his orders, would naturally consider themselves deserted, and when a clamor of that kind is once raised against a man, (particularly in a defeat,) the voice of reason can no longer be heard. Some scapegoat is always necessary. The broken remains of the detachment returned to the station, and filled the country with consternation and alarm, greatly disproportioned to the extent of the loss. The brave Estill, with eight of his men, had fallen, and four were wounded—more than half of their original number.

This, notwithstanding the smallness of the numbers, is a very remarkable action, and perhaps more honorable to the Indians than any one on record. The numbers, the arms, the courage and the position of the parties were equal. Both were composed of good marksmen and skillful woodsmen. There was no surprise, no panic, nor any particular accident, according to the most probable account, which decided the action. A delicate manœuvre, on the part of Estill, gave an advantage, which was promptly seized by the Indian chief, and a bold and masterly movement decided the fate of the day.

The news of Estill's disaster was quickly succeeded by another, scarcely less startling to the alarmed settlers. Captain Holder, at the head of seventeen men, pursued a party of Indians who had taken two boys from the neighborhood of Hoy's station. He overtook them after a rapid pursuit, and in the severe action which ensued, was repulsed with the loss of more than half his party. The tide of success seemed completely turned in favor of the Indians. They traversed the woods in every direction, sometimes singly and sometimes in small parties, and kept the settlers in constant alarm.

GIRTY'S DESPERATE ATTACK ON BRYANT STATION.

At length, early in August, the great effort was made. The allied Indian army, composed of detachments from nearly all the northwestern tribes, and amounting to nearly six hundred men, under the lead of Simon Girty, the notorious renegade, commenced their march from Chillicothe, under command of their respective chiefs, aided and influenced by Girty, M'Kee, and other renegade white men. With a secrecy and celerity peculiar to themselves, they advanced through the woods without giving the slightest indication of their approach, and on the night of the 14th of August, they appeared before Bryant's station, as suddenly as if they had risen from the earth, and surrounding it on all sides, calmly awaited the approach of daylight, holding themselves in readiness to rush in upon the inhabitants the moment the gates were opened in the morning. The supreme influence of fortune in war, was never more strikingly displayed. The garrison had determined to march on the following morning, to the assistance of Hoy's station, from which a messenger had arrived the evening before, with the intelligence of Holder's defeat. Had the Indians arrived only a few hours later they would have found the fort occupied only by old men, women and children, who could not have resisted their attack for a moment. As it was, they found the garrison assembled and under arms, most of them busily engaged throughout the whole night, in preparing for an early march the following morning. The Indians could distinctly hear the bustle of preparation, and see lights glancing from block-houses and cabins during the night, which must have led them to suspect that their approach had been discovered. All continued tranquil during the night, and Girty silently concerted the plan of attack.

The fort, consisting of about forty cabins placed in parallel lines, stood upon a gentle rise on the southern bank of the Elkhorn, a few paces to the right of the road from Maysville to Lexington. The garrison was supplied with water from a spring at some distance from the fort, on its northwestern side—a great error in most of the stations, which, in a close and long-continued siege, must have suffered dreadfully for the want of water. The great body of Indians placed themselves in ambush within half rifle shot of the spring, while one hundred select men were placed near the spot where the road runs after passing the creek, with orders to open a brisk fire and show themselves to the garrison on that side, for the purpose of drawing them out, while the main body held themselves in readiness to rush upon the opposite gate of the fort, hew it down with their tomahawks, and force their way into the midst of the cabins.

At dawn of day, the garrison paraded under arms, and were preparing to open their gates and march off, as already mentioned, when they were alarmed by a furious discharge of rifles, accompanied with yells and screams, which struck terror to the hearts of the women and children, and startled even the men. All ran hastily to the picketing, and beheld a small party of Indians exposed to open view, firing, yelling and making the most furious gestures. The appearance was so singular, and so different from their usual manner of fighting, that some of the more wary and experienced of the garrison instantly pronounced it a decoy party, and restrained their young men from sallying out and attacking them, as some of them were strongly disposed to do. The opposite side of the fort was instantly manned, and several breaches in the picketing rapidly repaired.

The Heroism of the Kentucky Women.

Their greatest distress arose from the prospect of suffering for water. The more experienced of the garrison felt satisfied that a powerful party was in ambuscade near the spring, but at the same time they supposed that the Indians would not unmask themselves until the firing upon the opposite side of the fort was returned with such warmth as to induce the belief that the feint had succeeded. Acting upon this impression, and yielding to the urgent necessity of the case, they summoned all the women, without exception, and explaining to them the circumstances in which they were placed, and the improbability that any injury would be offered to them until the firing had been returned from the opposite side of the fort, they urged them to go in a body to the spring, and each to bring up a bucketful of water. Some of the ladies, as was natural, had no relish for the undertaking, and asked why the men could not bring water as well as themselves! observing that *they* were not bullet-proof, and that the Indians made no distinction between male and female scalps.

To this it was answered that women were in the habit of bringing water every morning to the fort, and that if the Indians saw them engaged as usual, it would induce them to believe that their ambuscade was undiscovered, and that they would not unmask themselves for the sake of firing at a few women, when they hoped, by remaining concealed a few moments longer, to obtain complete possession of the fort; that if *men* should go down to the spring, the Indians would immediately suspect that something was wrong, would despair of succeeding by ambuscade, and would instantly rush upon them, follow them into the fort, or shoot them down at the spring. The decision was soon over. A few of the boldest declared their readiness to brave the danger, and the younger and more timid rallying in the rear of these veterans, they all marched down in a body to the spring, within point blank shot of more than five hundred Indian warriors!

Some of the girls could not help betraying symptoms of terror, but the married women, in general, moved with a steadiness and composure which completely deceived the Indians. Not a shot was fired. The party were permitted to fill their buckets, one after another, without interruption, and although their steps became quicker and quicker on their return, and when near the gate of the fort, degenerated into rather an unmilitary celerity, attended with some little crowding in passing the gate, yet not more than one-fifth of the water was spilled, and the eyes of the youngest had not dilated to more than double their ordinary size.

Being now amply supplied with water, they sent out thirteen young men to attack the decoy party, with orders to fire with great rapidity, and make as much noise as possible, but not to pursue the enemy too far, while the rest of the garrison took post on the opposite side of the fort, cocked their guns, and stood in readiness to receive the ambuscade as soon as it was unmasked. The firing of the light parties on the Lexington road was soon heard, and quickly became sharp and serious, gradually becoming more distant from the fort. Instantly Girty sprang up, at the head of his five hundred warriors, and rushed rapidly upon the western gate, ready to force his way over the undefended palisades. Into this immense mass of dusky bodies the garrison poured several rapid volleys of rifle balls with destructive effect. Their consternation may be imagined. With wild cries they dispersed on the right and left, and in two minutes not an Indian was to be seen. At the same time, the party who had sallied out on the Lexington road, came running into the fort at the opposite gate, in high spirits, and laughing heartily at the success of the manœuvre.

A regular attack, in the usual manner, then commenced, without much effect on either side, until two o'clock in the afternoon, when a new scene presented itself. Upon the first appearance of the Indians in the morning, two of the garrison, Tomlinson and Bell, had been mounted on fleet horses and sent to Lexington, announcing the arrival of the Indians and demanding reinforcements. Upon their arrival, a little after sunrise, they found the town occupied only by women and children and a few old men, the rest having marched, at the intelligence of Holder's defeat, to the general rendezvous at Hoy's station. The two couriers instantly followed at a gallop, and overtaking them on the road, informed them of the danger to which Lexington was exposed during their absence.

The whole party, amounting to sixteen horsemen, and more than double that number on foot, with some additional volunteers from Boone's station, instantly countermarched, and repaired with all possible expedition to Bryant's station. They were entirely ignorant of the overwhelming numbers opposed to them, or they would have proceeded with more caution. Tomlinson had only informed them that the station was surrounded, being himself ignorant of the numbers of the enemy. By great exertions, horse and foot appeared before Bryant's at two in the afternoon, and pressed forward with precipitate gallantry to throw themselves into the fort. The Indians, however, had been aware of the departure of the two couriers, who had, in fact, broken through their line in order to give the alarm, and expecting the arrival of reinforcements, had taken measures to meet them.

Running a Bloody Gauntlet—Girty Chaffed by Reynolds.

To the left of the long and narrow lane, where the Maysville and Lexington road now runs, there were more than one hundred acres of green standing corn. The usual road from Lexington to Bryant's ran parallel to the fence of this field, and only a few feet distant from it. On the opposite side of the road was a thick wood. Here more than three hundred Indians lay in ambush, within pistol shot of the road, awaiting the approach of the party. The horsemen came in view at a time when the firing had ceased and everything was quiet. Seeing no enemy, and hearing no noise, they entered the lane at a gallop, and were instantly saluted with a shower of rifle balls from each side, at the distance of ten paces. At the first shot, the whole party set spurs to their horses, and rode at full speed through a rolling fire from either side, which continued for several hundred yards, but owing partly to the furious rate at which they rode; partly to the clouds of dust raised by the horses' feet, they all entered the fort unhurt. The men on foot were less fortunate. They were advancing through the cornfield, and might have reached the fort in safety but for their eagerness to succor their friends. Without reflecting that, from the weight and extent of the fire, the enemy must have been ten times their number, they ran up with inconsiderate courage to the spot where the firing was heard, and there found themselves cut off from the fort, and within pistol shot of more than three hundred savages.

Fortunately, the Indian guns had just been discharged, and they had not yet leisure to reload. At the sight of this brave body of footmen, however, they raised a hideous yell, and rushed upon them, tomahawk in hand. Nothing but the high corn and their loaded rifles could have saved them from destruction. The Indians were cautious in rushing upon a loaded rifle with only a tomahawk, and when they halted to load their pieces, the Kentuckians ran with great rapidity, turning and dodging through the corn in every direction. Some entered the wood and escaped through the thickets of cane, some were shot down in the cornfield, others maintained a running fight, halting occasionally behind trees, and keeping the enemy at bay with their rifles, for, of all men, the Indians are generally the most cautious in exposing themselves to danger. A stout, active young fellow, was so hard pressed by Girty and several savages, that he was compelled to discharge his rifle, (however unwillingly, having no time to reload it,) and Girty fell. It happened, however, that a piece of thick sole-leather was in his shot-pouch at the time, which received the ball, and preserved his life, although the force of the blow felled him to the ground. The savages halted upon his fall, and the young man escaped.

Although the skirmish and race lasted for more than an hour, during which the cornfield presented a scene of turmoil and bustle which can scarcely be conceived, yet very few lives were lost. Only six of the white men were killed and wounded, and probably still fewer of the enemy, as the whites never fired until absolutely necessary, but reserved their loads as a check upon the enemy. Had the Indians pursued them to Lexington, they might have possessed themselves of it without resistance, as there was no force there to oppose them; but after following the fugitives for a few hundred yards, they returned to the hopeless siege of the fort.

It was now near sunset, and the fire on both sides had slackened. The Indians had become discouraged. Their loss in the morning had been heavy, and the country was evidently arming, and would soon be upon them. They had made no impression upon the fort, and without artillery could hope to make none. The chiefs spoke of raising the siege and decamping, but Girty determined, since his arms had been unavailing, to try the efficacy of negotiation. Near one of the bastions there was a large stump, to which he crept on his hands and knees, and from which he hailed the garrison. "He highly commended their courage, but assured them that further resistance would be madness, as he had six hundred warriors with him, and was in hourly expectation of reinforcements, with artillery, which would instantly blow their cabins into the air; that if the fort was taken by storm, as it certainly would be, when their cannon arrived, it would be impossible for him to save their lives; but if they surrendered at once, he gave them his honor that not a hair of their heads should be injured.

"He told them his name, inquired whether they knew him, and assured them that they might safely trust to his honor." The garrison listened in silence to this speech, and many of them looked very blank at the mention of the artillery, as the Indians had, on one occasion, brought cannon with them, and destroyed two stations. But a young man by the name of Reynolds, highly distinguished for courage, energy and a frolicsome gaiety of temper, perceiving the effect of Girty's speech, took upon himself to reply to it. To Girty's inquiry of "whether the garrison knew him?" Reynolds replied, "that he was very well known— that he himself had a worthless dog to which he had given the name of 'Simon Girty,' in consequence of his striking resemblance to the man of that name. That if he had either artillery or reinforcements, he might bring them up and be ———. That if either himself or any of the naked rascals with him found their way into the fort, they would disdain to use their guns against them, but would drive them out again with switches, of which they had collected a great number for that purpose alone; and, finally, he declared that *they* also expected reinforcements —that the whole country was marching to their assistance, and that if Girty and his gang of murderers remained twenty-four hours longer before the fort, their scalps would be found drying in the sun upon the roofs of their cabins."

Girty took great offence at the tone and language of the young Kentuckian, and retired with an expression of sorrow for the inevitable destruction which awaited them on the following morning. He quickly rejoined the chiefs, and instant preparations were made for raising the siege. The night passed away in uninterrupted tranquility, and at daylight in the morning the Indian camp was found deserted. Fires were still burning brightly, and several pieces of meat were left upon their roasting sticks, from which it was inferred that they had retreated a short time before daylight.

Early in the day reinforcements began to drop in, and, by noon, one hundred and sixty-seven men were assembled at Bryant's station. Colonel Daniel Boone, accompanied by his youngest son, headed a strong party from Boonsborough; Trigg brought up the force from the neighborhood of Harrodsburg, and Todd commanded the militia around Lexington. Nearly a third of the whole number assembled was composed of commissioned officers, who hurried from a distance to the scene of hostilities, and, for the time, took their station in the ranks. Of those under the rank of Colonel, the most conspicuous were, Majors Harland, McBride, McGary, and Levi Todd, and Captains Bulger and Gordon. Of the six last-named officers, all fell in the subsequent battle except Todd and McGary. Todd and Trigg, as senior Colonels, took the command, although their authority seems to have been in a great measure nominal. That, however, was of less consequence, as a sense of common danger is often more binding than the strictest discipline. A tumultuous consultation, in which every one seemed to have a voice, terminated in a unanimous resolution to pursue the enemy without delay.

It was well known that General Logan had collected a strong force in Lincoln, and would join them at farthest in twenty-four hours. It was distinctly understood that the enemy was at least double, and, according to Girty's account, more than treble their own numbers. It was seen that their trail was broad and obvious, and that even some indications of a tardiness and willingness to be pursued had been observed by their scouts, who had been sent out to reconnoitre, and from which it might reasonably be inferred that they would halt on the way—at least, march so leisurely as to permit them to wait for the aid of Logan. Yet so keen was the ardor of officer and soldier, that all these obvious reasons were overlooked, and in the afternoon of the 18th of August, the line of march was taken up, and the pursuit urged with that precipitate courage which has so often been fatal to Kentuckians. Most of the officers and many of the privates were mounted.

THE DISASTROUS BATTLE OF "THE BLUE LICKS."

The Indians had followed the buffalo trace, and, as if to render their trail still more evident, they had chopped many of the trees on each side of the road with their hatchets. These strong indications of tardiness, made some impression upon the cool and calculating mind of Boone, but it was too late to advise retreat. They encamped that night in the woods, and on the following day reached the fatal boundary of their pursuit. At the Lower Blue Licks, for the first time since the pursuit commenced, they came within view of an enemy. As the miscellaneous crowd of horse and foot reached the southern bank of Licking, they saw a number of Indians ascending the rocky ridge on the other side. They halted upon the appearance of the Kentuckians, gazed at them for a few moments in silence, and then calmly and leisurely disappeared over the top of the hill.

A halt immediately ensued. A dozen or twenty officers met in front of the ranks, and entered into consultation. The wild and lonely aspect of the country around them, their distance from any point of support, with the certainty of their being in the presence of a superior enemy, seems to have inspired a seriousness bordering upon awe. All eyes were now turned upon Boone, and Colonel Todd asked his opinion as to what should be done. The veteran woodsman, with his usual unmoved gravity, replied, "that their situation was critical and delicate—that the force opposed to them was undoubtedly numerous and ready for battle, as might readily be seen from the leisurely retreat of the few Indians who had appeared upon the crest of the hill; that he was well acquainted with the ground in the neighborhood of the Lick, and was apprehensive that an ambuscade was formed at the distance of a mile in advance where two ravines, one upon each side of the ridge, ran in such a manner that a concealed enemy migh assail them at once both in front and flank, before they were apprised of the danger.

"It would be proper, therefore, to do one of two things: either to await the arrival of Logan, who was now undoubtedly on his march to join them; or, if it was determined to attack without delay, that one-half of their number should march up the river, which there bends in an elliptical form, cross at the rapids, and fall upon the rear of the enemy, while the other division attacked in front. At any rate, he strongly urged the necessity of reconnoitering the ground carefully before the main body crossed the river." Such was the counsel of Boone. And although no measure could have been much more disastrous than that which was adopted, yet it may be doubted if anything short of an immediate retreat upon Logan, could have saved this gallant body of men from the fate which they encountered. If they divided their force, the enemy, as in Estill's case, might have overwhelmed them in detail—if they remained where they were, without advancing, the enemy would certainly have attacked them, probably in the night, and with a certainty of success. They had committed a great error at first in not waiting for Logan, and nothing short of a retreat, which would have been considered disgraceful, could now repair it.

Boone was heard in silence and with deep attention. Some wished to adopt the first plan—others preferred the second, and the discussion threatened to be drawn out to some length, when the boiling ardor of McGary, who could never endure the presence of an enemy without instant battle, stimulated him to an act which had nearly proved destructive to his country. He suddenly interrupted the consultation with a loud whoop, resembling the war cry of the Indians, spurred his horse into the stream, waved his hat over his head and shouted, " Let all who are not cowards follow me ! " The words and the action together, produced an electric effect. The mounted men dashed tumultuously into the river, each striving to be foremost. The footmen were mingled with them in one rolling and irregular mass. No order was given and none observed. They struggled through a deep ford as well as they could, McGary still leading the van, closely followed by Majors Harland and McBride.

With the same rapidity they ascended the ridge, which, by the trampling of buffalo for ages, had been stripped bare of all vegetation, with the exception of a few dwarfish cedars, and which was rendered still more desolate in appearance by the multitude of rocks, blackened by the sun, which were spread over its surface. Upon reaching the top of the ridge, they followed the buffalo traces with the same precipitate ardor—Todd and Trigg in the rear; McGary, Harland, McBride and Boone in front. No scouts were sent in advance—none explored either flank—officers and soldiers seemed alike demented by the contagious example of a single man, and all struggled forward, horse and foot, as if to outstrip each other in the advance.

Suddenly, the van halted. They had reached the spot mentioned by Boone, where two ravines headed on each side of the ridge. Here a body of Indians presented themselves, and attacked the van. McGary's party instantly returned the fire, but under great disadvantage. They were upon a bare and open ridge—the Indians in a bushy ravine. The centre and rear, ignorant of the ground, hurried up to the assistance of the van, but were soon stopped by a terrible fire from the ravine that flanked them. They found themselves enclosed as if in the wings of a net, destitute of a proper shelter, while the enemy were, in a great measure, covered from their fire. Still, however, they maintained their ground.

Boone's Son Killed—Thrilling Incidents—Reynolds' Capture.

The action now became fierce and bloody. The parties gradually closed, the Indians emerged from the ravine, and the fire became mutually destructive. The officers suffered dreadfully. Todd and Trigg, in the rear—Harland, McBride, and young Boone, in front, were already killed. The Indians gradually extended their line, to turn the right of the Kentuckians, and cut off their retreat.

This was quickly perceived by the weight of the fire from that quarter, and the rear instantly fell back in disorder, and attempted to rush through their only opening to the river. The motion quickly communicated itself to the van, and a hurried retreat became general. The Indians instantly sprang forward in pursuit, and falling upon them with their tomahawks, made a cruel slaughter. From the battle ground to the river, the spectacle was terrible. The horsemen generally escaped, but the foot, particularly the van, which had advanced farthest within the wings of the net, were almost totally destroyed. Colonel Boone, after witnessing the death of his son Israel, and many of his dearest friends, found himself almost entirely surrounded at the very commencement of the retreat. Several hundred Indians were between him and the ford, to which the great mass of the fugitives were bending their flight, and to which the attention of the savages was principally directed. Being intimately acquainted with the ground, he, together with a few friends, dashed into the ravine which the Indians had occupied, but which most of them had now left to join the pursuit.

After sustaining one or two heavy fires, and baffling one or two small parties, who pursued him for a short distance, he crossed the river below the ford, by swimming, and entered the wood at a point where there was no pursuit, returning by a circuitous route to Bryant's station. In the meantime, the great mass of the victors and vanquished crowded the bank of the ford. The slaughter was great in the river. The ford was crowded with horsemen and foot and Indians, all mingled together. Some were compelled to seek a passage above by swimming—some, who could not swim, were overtaken and killed at the edge of the water. A man by the name of Netherland, who had formerly been strongly suspected of cowardice, here displayed a coolness and presence of mind equally noble and unexpected. Being finely mounted, he had outstripped the great mass of fugitives, and crossed the river in safety. A dozen or twenty horsemen accompanied him, and having placed the river between him and the enemy, showed a disposition to continue their flight, without regard to the safety of their friends who were on foot and still struggling with the current. Netherland instantly checked his horse, and in a loud voice called upon his companions to halt—fire upon the Indians, and save those who were still in the stream. The party instantly obeyed—and, facing about, poured a fatal discharge of rifles upon the foremost of the pursuers. The enemy instantly fell back from the opposite bank, and gave time for the harassed and miserable footmen to cross in safety. The check, however, was but momentary. Indians were seen crossing in great numbers above and below, and the flight again became general. Most of the foot left the great buffalo track, and, plunging into the thickets, escaped by a circuitous route to Bryant's.

But little loss was sustained after crossing the river, although the pursuit was urged keenly for twenty miles. From the battle ground to the ford the loss was very heavy; and at that stage of the retreat there occurred a rare and striking instance of magnanimity, which it would be criminal to omit. The reader cannot have forgotten young Reynolds, who replied with such rough and ready humor to the pompous summons of Girty, at the siege of Bryant's. This young man, after bearing his share in the action with distinguished gallantry, was galloping with several other horsemen in order to reach the ford. The great body of the fugitives had preceded them, and their situation was in the highest degree critical and dangerous.

About half way between the battle ground and the river, the party overtook Captain Patterson, on foot, exhausted by the rapidity of the flight, and, in consequence of former wounds received from the Indians, so infirm as to be unable to keep up with the main body of the men on foot. The Indians were close behind him, and his fate seemed inevitable. Reynolds, upon coming up with the brave officer, instantly sprang from his horse, aided Patterson to mount upon the saddle, and continued his own flight on foot. Being remarkably active and vigorous, he contrived to elude his pursuers, and, turning off from the main road, plunged into the river near the spot where Boone had crossed, and swam in safety to the opposite side. Unfortunately he wore a pair of buckskin breeches, which had become so heavy and full of water as to prevent his exerting himself with his usual activity, and while sitting down for the purpose of pulling them off, he was overtaken by a party of Indians and made prisoner.

A prisoner is rarely put to death by the Indians, unless wounded or infirm, until their return to their own country; and then his fate is decided in solemn council. Young Reynolds, therefore, was treated kindly, and compelled to accompany his captors in the pursuit. A small party of Kentuckians soon attracted their attention, and he was left in charge of three Indians, who, eager in pursuit, in turn committed him to the charge of one of their number, while they followed their companions. Reynolds and his guard jogged along very leisurely—the former totally unarmed, the latter with a tomahawk and rifle in his hands. At length the Indian stopped to tie his moccasin, when Reynolds instantly sprung upon him, knocked him down with his fist, and quickly disappeared in the thicket which surrounded them. For this act of generosity, Captain Patterson afterwards made him a present of two hundred acres of first-rate land.

Late in the evening of the same day, most of the survivors arrived at Bryant's station. The awful tidings spread rapidly throughout the country, and the whole land was covered with mourning. Sixty of the very flower of Kentucky had been killed in the battle and flight, and seven had been taken prisoners, of whom some were afterwards put to death by the Indians, as was said, to make their loss even. This account, however, appears very improbable. It is almost incredible that the Indians should have suffered an equal loss. Their superiority of numbers, their advantage of position, (being in a great measure sheltered, while the Kentuckians, particularly the horsemen, were much exposed,) the extreme brevity of the battle, and the acknowledged boldness of the pursuit, all tend to contradict the report that the Indian loss exceeded ours. We have no doubt that some of the prisoners were murdered after arriving at their towns, but cannot believe that the reason assigned for so ordinary a piece of barbarity was the true one. Still the execution done by the Kentuckians, while the battle lasted, seems to have been considerable, although far inferior to the loss which they themselves sustained.

Hugh McGary's Fiery Character and his Defence.

Todd and Trigg were a severe loss to their families, and to the country generally. They were men of rank in life, superior to the ordinary class of settlers, and generally esteemed for courage, probity and intelligence. The death of Major Harland was deeply and universally regretted. A keen courage, united to a temper the most amiable, and an integrity the most incorruptible, had rendered him extremely popular in the country. Together with his friend McBride, he accompanied McGary in the van, and both fell in the commencement of the action. McGary, notwithstanding the extreme exposure of his station, as leader of the van, and consequently most deeply involved in the ranks of the enemy, escaped without the slightest injury. This gentleman will ever be remembered as associated with the disaster of which he was the immediate, although not the original, cause. He has always been represented as a man of fiery and daring courage, strongly tinctured with ferocity, and unsoftened by any of the humane and gentle qualities which awaken affection. In the hour of battle, his presence was invaluable, but in civil life, the ferocity of his temper rendered him an unpleasant companion.

Several years after the battle of the Blue Licks, a gentleman of Kentucky, since dead, fell in company with McGary at one of the circuit courts, and the conversation soon turned upon the battle. McGary frankly acknowledged that he was the immediate cause of the loss of blood on that day, and, with great heat and energy, assigned his reasons for urging on the battle. He said that in the hurried council which was held at Bryant's, on the 18th, he had strenuously urged Todd and Trigg to halt for twenty-four hours, assuring them that, with the aid of Logan, they would be able to follow them even to Chillicothe if necessary, and that their numbers *then* were too weak to encounter them alone. He offered, he said, to pledge his head that the Indians would not return with such precipitation as was supposed, but would afford ample time to collect more force, and give them battle with a prospect of success.

He added, that Colonel Todd scouted his arguments, and declared that "if a single day was lost the Indians would never be overtaken— but would cross the Ohio and disperse; that now was the time to strike them, while they were in a body—that to talk of their numbers was nonsense—the more the merrier!—that for his part he was determined to pursue without a moment's delay, and did not doubt that there were brave men enough on the ground to enable him to attack them with effect." McGary declared, "that he felt somewhat nettled at the manner in which his advice had been received; that he thought Todd and Trigg jealous of Logan, who, as senior Colonel, would be entitled to the command upon his arrival; and that, in their eagerness to have the honor of the victory to themselves, they were rashly throwing themselves into a condition which would endanger the safety of the country.

"However, sir," (continued he, with an air of unamiable triumph,) "when I saw the gentlemen so keen for a fight, I gave way, and joined in the pursuit as willingly as any; but when we came in sight of the enemy, and the gentlemen began to talk of 'numbers,' 'position,' 'Logan,' and 'waiting,' I burst into a passion, d——d them for a set of cowards, who could not be wise until they were scared into it, and swore that since they had come so far for a fight, they *should fight*, or I would disgrace them forever! That when I spoke of waiting for Logan on the day before, they had scouted the idea, and hinted about 'courage'—that now it would be shown who had courage, or who were d——d cowards, who could talk big when the enemy were at a distance, but turned pale when danger was near. I then dashed into the river, and called upon all who were not cowards to follow!" The gentleman upon whose authority it is given added, that even then, McGary spoke with bitterness of the deceased Colonels, and swore that they had received just what they deserved, and that he for one was glad of it.

On the very day on which this rash and unfortunate battle was fought Colonel Logan arrived at Bryant's station, at the head of no less than four hundred and fifty men. He here learned that the little army had marched on the preceding day, without waiting for so strong and necessary a reinforcement. Fearful of some such disaster as had actually occurred, he urged his march with the utmost diligence, still hoping to overtake them before they could cross the Ohio; but within a few miles of the fort, he encountered the foremost of the fugitives, whose jaded horses, and harassed looks, announced but too plainly the event of the battle. As usual with men after a defeat, they magnified the number of the enemy and the slaughter of their comrades. None knew the actual extent of their loss. They could only be certain of their own escape, and could give no account of their companions. Fresh stragglers constantly came up, with the same mournful intelligence; so that Logan, after some hesitation, determined to return to Bryant's until all the survivors should come up. In the course of the evening, both horse and foot were reassembled at Bryant's, and the loss was distinctly ascertained.

Although sufficiently severe, it was less than Logan had at first apprehended; and having obtained all the information which could be collected, as to the strength and probable destination of the enemy, he determined to continue his march to the battle ground, with the hope that success would embolden the enemy, and induce them to remain until his arrival. On the second day he reached the field. The enemy were gone, but the bodies of the Kentuckians still lay unburied, on the spot where they had fallen. Immense flocks of buzzards were soaring over the battle ground, and the bodies of the dead had become so swollen and disfigured, that it was impossible to recognize the features of their most particular friends. Many corpses were floating near the shore of the northern bank, already putrid from the action of the sun, and partially eaten by fishes. The whole were carefully collected, by order of Colonel Logan, and interred as decently as the nature of the soil would permit. Being satisfied that the Indians were by this time far beyond his reach, he then retraced his steps to Bryant's station and dismissed his men.

As soon as intelligence of the battle of the Blue Licks reached Colonel George Rogers Clark, who then resided at the falls of Ohio, he determined to set on foot an expedition against the Indian towns, for the purpose, both of avenging the loss of the battle, and rousing the spirit of the country, which had begun to sink into the deepest dejection. He proposed that one thousand men should be raised from all parts of Kentucky, and should rendezvous at Cincinnati, under the command of their respective officers, where he engaged to meet them at the head of a part of the Illinois regiment, then under his command, together with one brass field piece, which was regarded by the Indians with superstitious terror. The offer was embraced with great alacrity; and instant measures were taken for the collection of a sufficient number of volunteers.

The whole force of the interior was assembled, under the command of Colonel Logan, and descending the Licking in boats prepared for the purpose, arrived safely at the designated point of union, where they were joined by Clark, with the volunteers and regular detachment from below. No provision was made for the subsistence of the troops, and the sudden concentration of one thousand men and horses upon a single point, rendered it extremely difficult to procure the necessary supplies. The woods abounded in game—but the rapidity and secrecy of their march, which was absolutely essential to the success of the expedition, did not allow them to disperse in search of it. They suffered greatly, therefore, from hunger as well as fatigue; but all being accustomed to privations of every kind, they prosecuted their march with unabated rapidity, and appeared within a mile of one of their largest villages, without encountering a single Indian. Here, unfortunately, a straggler fell in with them, and instantly fled to the village, uttering the alarm whoop repeatedly in the shrillest and most startling tones. The troops pressed forward with great dispatch, and, entering their town, found it totally deserted. The houses had evidently been abandoned only a few minutes before their arrival. Fires were burning, meat was upon the roasting sticks, and corn was still boiling in their kettles. The provisions were a most acceptable treat to the Kentuckians, who were well nigh famished, but the escape of their enemies excited deep and universal chagrin.

After refreshing themselves, they engaged in the serious business of destroying the property of the tribes with unrelenting severity. Their villages were burnt, their corn cut up, and their entire country laid waste. During the whole of this severe but necessary occupation, scarcely an Indian was to be seen. The alarm had spread universally, and every village was found deserted. Occasionally, a solitary Indian would crawl up within gunshot and deliver his fire; and once a small party, mounted upon superb horses, rode up with great audacity, within musket shot, and took a leisurely survey of the whole army, but upon seeing a detachment preparing to attack them, they galloped off with a rapidity that baffled pursuit.

Boone's Last Days—Driven to Missouri—Touching Scenes.

Boone accompanied this expedition, but, as usual, has omitted everything which relates to himself. Here the brief memoir of Boone closes. It does not appear that he was afterwards engaged in any public expedition or solitary adventure. He continued a highly respectable farmer-citizen of Kentucky for several years, until the country became too thickly settled for *his* taste. As refinement of manners advanced, and the general standard of intelligence became elevated by the constant arrival of families of rank and influence, the rough old woodsman found himself entirely out of his element. The all-engaging subject of politics, which soon began to agitate the country with great violence, was to him as a sealed book or an unknown language, and for several years he wandered among the living groups which thronged the court yard or the churches, like a venerable relic of other days. He was among them, but not of them! He pined in secret for the wild and lonely forests of the west—for the immense prairie, trodden only by the buffalo or the elk, and became eager to exchange the listless languor and security of a village for the healthful exercise of the chase or the more thrilling excitement of savage warfare.

In 1792, he dictated his brief and rather dry memoirs to some young gentleman who could write, and who garnished it with a few flourishes of rhetoric, which passed off upon the old woodsman as a precious morsel of eloquence. He was never more gratified than when he could sit and hear it read to him, by some one who was willing, at so small an expense, to gratify the harmless vanity of the kind-hearted old pioneer. He would listen with great earnestness, and occasionally rub his hands, smile and ejaculate, "all true!—every word true!—not a lie in it!" He never spoke of himself unless particularly questioned; but this written account of his life was the Delilah of his imagination. The idea of "seeing his name in print," completely overcame the cold philosophy of his general manner, and he seemed to think it a masterpiece of composition.

A disastrous reverse increased his discontent. He had, after the Revolution, collected much of his means to purchase land warrants, but while on his way to Richmond, was robbed of the whole and left destitute. Ignorant, too, of the niceties of the law, he found that even those lands he had located and thought his own, were defective in title, and so it came to pass that the old pioneer, although the first to explore the magnificent domain of Kentucky, could at length claim of her soil only the six feet that belonged to every child of Adam. Sore, wounded and dissatisfied, but never, that we can hear, embittered, Boone forever left Kentucky; turned his back upon civilization and its legal chicanery; settled for awhile with his faithful wife on the Kanawha in Virginia, and finally joined his son Daniel in what is now Missouri, but what was then part of the Spanish territory. The Spanish authorities at St. Louis gave him a grant of land, and at length he found peace again and lived by his traps and rifle, sending the spoils of the hunt to St. Louis.

He had left Kentucky in debt, but living in a time when it was not considered exactly honorable to break up "full handed," or to compound with creditors at fifty cents on the dollar, he worked manfully along until he had raised some money, and then once more appeared in Boonsborough a stranger in a strange land. The honest old man sought out his creditors, took each one's word for the amount of his indebtedness to him, and, after satisfying every claim, dollar for dollar, he shouldered his trusty rifle and started again for his western home.

But marked changes were going on even in that remote wilderness. His western paradise was soon disturbed by intruders. The territory had changed hands from Spain to France and then to the United States. He now used to make long trapping and hunting excursions up the Missouri river and its tributaries. At one time he took pack-horses and went to the Osage, taking with him a negro lad. Soon after preparing his camp, he lay a long time sick. One pleasant day, when able to walk out, he took the boy to a slight eminence and marked out his own grave, enjoining the lad, in case of his (Boone's) death, to wash his body and wrap it in a clean blanket. He was then to dig a grave exactly as he had marked it, drag his body and put it therein and then plant posts at the head and foot, and mark the trees so the place could be found by his friends. Special messages were then given about his horses, rifle, &c. All these directions were given, as the boy declared, with entire calmness and serenity.

He did not die then, however, but soon after became landless again. His title was declared invalid and, at seventy-six, the venerable pioneer was a second time left without one acre in all that boundless domain. But this did not sour him. His sweetness of disposition still continued.

and with an enduring and touching faith, he sent, in 1812, a memorial to the Kentucky Senate, asking their influence in form of a petition to Congress to confirm his Spanish title to ten thousand acres. This was done, much to Boone's satisfaction, most promptly and heartily, but Congress hesitated, and at length, in 1814, gave him title to less than a thousand.

While his claim was pending, the most terrible disaster of his life befell the old man in the loss of his dear and most faithful wife, Rebecca. He wept over her coffin as one who "would not be comforted." With her he buried all his earthly affections. He left his own humble cabin and took up his residence with his son, Major Nathan Boone. He now returned to his forest rambles and hunting sports, and when about eighty-two years old, he made a hunting excursion as far as Fort Osage on the Kansas, one hundred miles from his dwelling. On all these distant adventures, he took with him a companion bound by written agreement, that wherever he died, he was to convey and bury his body beside that of his wife overlooking the Missouri.

In 1819 a distinguished artist visited Boone at his dwelling near the Missouri, for the purpose of taking his portrait, and found him in a "small, rude cabin, indisposed and reclining on his bed. A slice from the loin of a buck, twisted about the ramrod of his rifle, within reach of him as he lay, was roasting before the fire. Several other cabins, arranged in the form of a parallelogram, were occupied by the descendants of the pioneer. Here he lived in the midst of his posterity. His withered energies and locks of snow, indicated that the sources of existence were nearly exhausted."

Boone died of fever on the 26th of September, 1820, in the eighty-seventh year of his age, and at the residence of his son-in-law in Flanders, Calloway county, Mo., and was buried by the side of his wife. It is said that when too old to hunt, he would seat himself, with his trusty old rifle in hands and with eyes turned towards the forest, and thus gaze wistfully for hours, living over again in memory, doubtless, the active and stirring scenes of his youth and manhood beneath similar sombre shades. When intelligence of his death reached the Missouri Legislature, an adjournment and the usual badge of mourning for thirty days was voted.

In 1845 a committee, appointed by the Kentucky Legislature, visited Missouri and had the bodies of the old pioneer and his wife, Rebecca, removed to Frankfort, and on the 13th of September, 1845, the ashes of the revered and illustrious dead were recommitted to Kentucky dust amid the most solemn and imposing ceremonies. It was a great day in Kentucky, and one long to be held in sacred remembrance. An immense concourse of citizens had assembled from all parts of the State. The funeral procession was more than a mile in length. The hearse, profusely decorated with flowers and evergreens, was drawn by four white horses and accompanied, as pall bearers, by such distinguished pioneers as Colonel R. M. Johnson, General James Taylor, General R. McAfee, Colonel John Johnston, of Ohio, and Colonel Wm. Boone, of Shelby. The affecting funeral ceremonies were performed in a beautiful hollow near the grave, the oration having been delivered by the Hon. J. J. Crittenden.

It is a common error to suppose that Boone was a very ignorant, illiterate man. He could both read and write, and his spelling was no worse than that of his cotemporary, General George Rogers Clark, and other prominent men of his day and generation. Governor Morehead, in his commemorative address, says of Boone:

"His life is a forcible example of the powerful influence a single absorbing passion exerted over the destiny of an individual. Possessing no other acquirements than a very common education, he was enabled, nevertheless, to maintain through a long and useful career, a conspicuous rank among the most distinguished of his cotemporaries. He united in an eminent degree the qualities of shrewdness, caution, courage and uncommon muscular strength. He was seldom taken by surprise; he never shrank from danger, nor cowered beneath the pressure of exposure and fatigue. His manners were simple and unobtrusive—exempt from the rudeness characteristic of the backwoodsman. In his person there was nothing remarkably striking. He was five feet ten inches in height and of robust and powerful proportions. His countenance was mild and contemplative. His ordinary habits were those of a hunter. He died as he lived, in a cabin, and perhaps his trusty rifle was the most valuable of all his chattels."

Two Characteristic Anecdotes of Daniel Boone.

Boone, according to James Hall, was once resting in the woods with a small number of his followers, when a large party of Indians came suddenly upon them and halted—neither party having discovered the other until they came in contact. The whites were eating, and the savages, with the ready tact for which they are famous, sat down with perfect composure, and also commenced eating. It was obvious they wished to lull the suspicions of the white men, and seize a favorable opportunity for rushing upon them. Boone affected a careless inattention, but, in an undertone, quietly admonished his men to keep their hands upon their rifles. He then strutted towards the reddies unarmed and leisurely picking the meat from a bone. The Indian leader, who was somewhat similarly employed, arose to meet him.

Boone saluted him, and then requested to look at the knife with which the Indian was cutting his meat. The chief handed it to him without hesitation, and our pioneer, who, with his other traits, possessed considerable expertness at sleight of hand, deliberately opened his mouth and affected to swallow the long knife, which, at the same instant, he threw adroitly into his sleeve. The Indians were astonished. Boone gasped, rubbed his throat, stroked his body, and then, with apparent satisfaction, pronounced the horrid mouthful to be *very good*.

Having enjoyed the surprise of the spectators for a few moments, he made another contortion, and drawing forth the knife, as they supposed, from his body, coolly returned it to the chief. The latter took the point cautiously between his thumb and finger, as if fearful of being contaminated by touching the weapon, and threw it from him into the bushes. The pioneer sauntered back to his party, and the Indians, instantly dispatching their meal, marched off, desiring no further intercourse with a man who could swallow a scalping knife.

From Collins' Kentucky we derive the following: One morning in 1777, several men in the fields near Boonsborough were attacked by Indians, and ran towards the fort. One was overtaken and tomahawked within seventy yards of the fort, and while being scalped, Simon Kenton shot the warrior dead. Daniel Boone, with thirteen men, hastened to help his friends, but they were intercepted by a large body of Indians, who got between them and the fort. At the first fire from the Indians, seven whites were wounded, among them Boone. An Indian sprang upon him with uplifted tomahawk; but Kenton, quick as a flash, sprang toward the Indian, discharged his gun into his breast, snatched up the body of his noble leader, and bore it safely into the fort. When the gate was closed securely against the Indians, Boone sent for Kenton: "Well, Simon," said the grateful old pioneer, "you have behaved yourself like a man to-day—indeed, you are a fine fellow." Boone was a remarkably silent man, and this was great praise from him.

KENTUCKY SPORTS—BOONE BARKING SQUIRRELS BY RIFLE.

We have individuals in Kentucky, wrote Audubon, the famous naturalist, that, even there, are considered wonderful adepts in the management of the rifle. Having resided some years in Kentucky, and having more than once been witness of rifle sport, I shall present the results of my observation, leaving the reader to judge how far rifle shooting is understood in that State:

Several individuals who conceive themselves adepts in the management of the rifle, are often seen to meet for the purpose of displaying their skill; and, betting a trifling sum, put up a target, in the centre of which, a common-sized nail is hammered for about two-thirds its length. The marksmen make choice of what they consider a proper distance, and which may be forty paces. Each man cleans the interior of his tube, which is called *wiping* it, places a ball in the palm of his hand, pouring as much powder from his horn as will cover it. This quantity is supposed to be sufficient for any distance short of a hundred yards. A shot which comes very close to the nail is considered that of an indifferent marksman; the bending of the nail is of course somewhat better; but nothing less than hitting it right on the head is satisfactory. One out of the three shots generally hits the nail; and should the shooters amount to half-a-dozen, two nails are frequently needed before each can have a shot. Those who drive the nail have a further trial among themselves, and the two best shots out of these generally settles the affair, when all the sportsmen adjourn to some house, and spend an hour or two in friendly intercourse, appointing, before they part, a day for another trial. This is technically termed, "*driving the nail.*"

Barking of squirrels is delightful sport, and, in my opinion, requires a greater degree of accuracy than any other. I first witnessed this manner of procuring squirrels while near the town of Frankfort. The performer was the celebrated Daniel Boone. We walked out together and followed the rocky margins of the Kentucky river until we reached a piece of flat land, thickly covered with black walnuts, oaks, and hickories. As the general *mast* was a good one that year, squirrels were seen gamboling on every tree around us. My companion, a stout, hale, athletic man, dressed in a homespun hunting shirt, bare legged and moccasined, carried a long and heavy rifle, which, as he was loading, he said had proved efficient in all of his former undertakings, and which he hoped would not fail on this occasion, as he felt proud to show me his skill. The gun was wiped, the powder measured, the ball patched with six-hundred-thread linen, and a charge sent home with a hickory rod. We moved not a step from the place, for the squirrels were so thick that it was unnecessary to go after them.

Boone pointed to one of these animals, which had observed us, and was crouched on a bough about fifty paces distant, and bade me mark well where the ball should hit. He raised his piece gradually until the *bead* or sight of the barrel was brought to a line with the spot he intended to hit. The whip-like report resounded through the woods and along the hills in repeated echoes. Judge of my surprise, when I perceived that the ball had hit the piece of bark immediately underneath the squirrel and shivered it into splinters; the concussion produced by which had killed the animal, and sent it whirling through the air as if it had been blown up by the explosion of a powder magazine. Boone kept up his firing, and before many hours had elapsed, we had procured as many squirrels as we wished. Since that first interview with the veteran Boone, I have seen many other individuals perform the same feat.

The *snuffing of a candle* with a ball, I first had an opportunity of seeing near the banks of the Green river, not far from a large pigeon roost, to which I had previously made a visit. I had heard many reports of guns during the early part of a dark night, and knowing them to be those of rifles, I went forward towards the spot to ascertain the cause. On reaching the place I was welcomed by a dozen tall, stout men, who told me they were exercising for the purpose of enabling them to shoot after night, at the reflected light from the eyes of a deer or wolf by torchlight. A fire was blazing near, the smoke of which rose curling among the thick foliage of the trees. At a distance which rendered it scarcely distinguishable, stood a burning candle, but which, in reality, was only fifty yards from the spot on which we all stood. One man was within a few yards of it to watch the effect of the shots, as well as to light the candle should it chance to go out, or to replace it should the shot cut it across. Each marksman shot in his turn. Some never hit either the snuff or the candle, and were congratulated with a loud laugh; while others actually snuffed the candle without putting it out, and were recompensed for their dexterity with numerous hurrahs. One of them, who was particularly expert, was very fortunate, and snuffed the candle three times out of seven, while the other shots either put out the candle or cut it immediately under the light.

Of the feats performed by the Kentuckians with the rifle, I might say more than might be expedient on the present occasion. By the way of recreation, they often cut off a piece of the bark of a tree, make a target of it, using a little powder wetted with water or saliva, for the bullseye, and shoot into the mark all the balls they have about them, picking them out of the wood again.

GENERAL SIMON KENTON, alias BUTLER.

He has a Battle and Thinks He has Committed Murder.

Tread lightly ! This is hallowed ground. Tread reverently here !
Beneath this sod, in silence, sleeps the brave old Pioneer;
Who never quailed in darkest hour; whose heart ne'er felt a fear,
Tread lightly, then ! and now bestow the tribute of a tear.
For ever in the fiercest and the thickest of the fight,
The dusk and swarthy foemen felt the terror of his might.—*Wm. Hubbard.*

The most daring and adventurous of Boone's companions was the far-famed Simon Kenton, who was born in Fauquier county, Virginia, on the 15th of May, 1755, the ever-memorable year of Braddock's defeat. Of his early years nothing is known. His parents were poor, and until the age of sixteen, his days seem to have passed away in the obscure and laborious drudgery of a farm. He was never taught to read or write, and to this is the poverty and desolation of his old age, in a great measure, to be attributed. At the age of sixteen, by an unfortunate adventure, he was launched into life, with no other fortune than a stout heart and a robust set of limbs.

It seems that, young as he was, his heart had become entangled in the snares of a young coquette in the neighborhood, who was grievously perplexed by the necessity of choosing *one* husband out of *many* lovers. Young Kenton and a robust farmer by the name of Leitchman—William Veach, according to Collins and McDonald—seem to have been the most favored suitors, and the young lady, not being able to decide upon their respective merits, they took the matter into their own hands, and, in consequence of foul play on the part of Leitchman's friends, young Kenton was beaten with great severity. He submitted to his fate for the time, in silence, but internally vowed that, as soon as he had obtained his full growth, he would take ample vengeance upon his rival for the disgrace he had sustained at his hands. He waited patiently until the following Spring, when, finding himself six feet high and full of health and action, he determined to delay the hour of retribution no longer.

He accordingly walked over to Leitchman's house one morning, and finding him busily engaged in carrying shingles from the woods, he stopped him, told him his object, and desired him to adjourn to a spot more convenient for the purpose. Leitchman, confident in his superior age and strength, was not backward to indulge him in so amiable a pastime, and having reached a solitary spot in the woods, they both stripped and prepared for the encounter. The battle was fought with all the fury which mutual hate, jealousy, and herculean power on both sides, could supply, and after a severe round, in which considerable damage was done and received, Kenton was brought to the ground Leitchman (as usual in Virginia) sprang upon him without the least scruple, and added the most bitter taunts to the kicks with which he saluted him, from his head to his heels, reminding him of his former defeat, and rubbing salt into the raw wounds of jealousy by triumphant allusions to his own superiority both in love and war. During these active operations on the part of Leitchman, Kenton lay perfectly still, eying attentively a small bush which grew near him. It instantly occurred to him that if he could wind Leitchman's hair, (which was remarkably long,) around this bush, he would be able to return those kicks which were now bestowed upon him in such profusion. The difficulty was to get his antagonist near enough. This he at length effected in the good old Virginia style, viz.: by biting him *en arriere*, and compelling him, by short springs, to approach the bush, much as a bullock is goaded on to approach the fatal ring, where all his struggles are useless. When near enough, Kenton suddenly exerted himself violently, and succeeded in wrapping the long hair of his rival around the sapling. He then sprung to his feet, and inflicted a terrible revenge for all his past injuries. In a few seconds Leitchman was gasping, apparently in the agonies of death. Kenton instantly fled, without even returning for an additional supply of clothing, and directed his steps westward. This was in April, 1771.

During the first day of his journey, he traveled in much agitation He supposed that Leitchman was dead, and that the hue and cry would instantly be raised after himself as the murderer. The constant apprehension of a gallows lent wings to his flight, and he scarcely allowed himself a moment for refreshment, until he had reached the neighborhood of the Warm Springs, where the settlements were thin and the immediate danger of pursuit was over. Here, he fortunately fell in with an exile from the State of New Jersey, of the name of Johnson, who was traveling westward on foot, and driving a single pack-horse, laden with a few necessaries, before him. They soon became acquainted, related their adventures to each other, and agreed to travel together. They plunged boldly into the wilderness of the Allegheny mountains, and subsisting upon wild game and a small quantity of flour, which Johnson had brought with him, they made no halt until they arrived at a small settlement on Cheat river, one of the prongs of the Monongahela.

Here the two friends separated, and Kenton (who had assumed the name of Butler) attached himself to a small company headed by John Mahon and Jacob Greathouse, who had united for the purpose of exploring the country. They quickly built a large canoe, and descended the river as far as the Province's settlement. There Kenton became acquainted with two young adventurers, Yager and Strader, the former of whom had been taken by the Indians when a child, and had spent many years in their village. He informed Kenton that there was a country below, which the Indians called Kan-tuck-ee, which was a perfect Elysium: that the ground was not only the richest, and the vegetation the most luxuriant in the world, but that the immense herds of buffalo and elk, which ranged at large through its forests, would appear incredible to one who had never witnessed such a spectacle. He added, that it was entirely uninhabited, and was open to all who chose to hunt there; that he himself had often accompanied the Indians in their grand hunting parties through the country, and was confident that he could conduct him to the same ground, if he was willing to venture.

Kenton closed with the proposal, and announced his readiness to accompany him immediately. A canoe was speedily procured, and the three young men committed themselves to the waters of the Ohio, in search of the enchanted hunting ground, which Yager had visited in his youth, while a captive among the Indians. Yager had no idea of its exact distance from Province's settlement. He recollected only that he had crossed the Ohio in order to reach it, and declared that, by sailing down the river for a few days, they would come to the spot where the Indians were accustomed to cross, and assured Kenton that there would be no difficulty in recognizing it; that its appearance was different from all the rest of the world, &c.

Fired by Yager's glowing description of its beauty, and eager to reach this new Eldorado of the west, the young men rowed hard for several days, confidently expecting that every bend of the river would usher them into the land of promise. No such country, however, appeared; and at length Kenton and Strader became rather skeptical as to its existence at all. They rallied Yager freely upon the subject, who still declared positively that they would soon witness the confirmation of all that he had said. After descending, however, as low as the spot where Manchester now stands, and seeing nothing which resembled Yager's country, they held a council, in which it was determined to return and survey the country more carefully—Yager still insisting that they must have passed it in the night. They accordingly retraced their steps, and successively explored the land about Salt Lick, Little and Big Sandy, and Guyandotte. At length, being totally wearied out in searching for what had no existence, they turned their attention entirely to hunting and trapping, and spent nearly two years upon the Great Kanawha, in this agreeable and profitable occupation. They obtained clothing in exchange for their furs, from the traders of Fort Pitt, and the forest supplied them abundantly with wild game for food.

In March, 1773, while reposing in their tent after the labors of the day, they were suddenly attacked by a party of Indians. Strader was killed at the first fire, and Kenton and Yager with difficulty effected their escape, being compelled to abandon their guns, blankets and provisions, and commit themselves to the wilderness, without the means of sheltering themselves from the cold, procuring a morsel of food, or even kindling a fire. They were far removed from any white settlement, and had no other prospect than that of perishing by famine, or falling a sacrifice to the fury of such Indians as might chance to meet them. Reflecting, however, that it was never too late for men to make an effort against being utterly lost, they determined to strike through the woods for the Ohio river, and take such fortune as it should please heaven to bestow.

Directing their route by the barks of trees, they pressed forward in a straight direction for the Ohio, and during the first two days allayed the piercing pangs of hunger by chewing such roots as they could find on their way. On the third day their strength began to fail, and the keen appetite which at first had constantly tortured them, was succeeded by a nausea, accompanied with dizziness and sinking of the heart, bordering on despair. On the fourth day they often threw themselves upon the ground, determined to await the approach of death—and as often were stimulated by the instinctive love of life, to arise and resume their journey. On the fifth, they were completely exhausted, and were able only to crawl, at intervals. In this manner, they traveled about a mile during the day, and succeeded, by sunset, in reaching the banks of the Ohio. Here, to their inexpressible joy, they encountered a party of traders, from whom they obtained a comfortable supply of provisions.

The traders were so much startled at the idea of being exposed to perils, such as those which Kenton and Yager had just escaped, that they lost no time in removing from such a dangerous vicinity, and instantly returned to the mouth of the Little Kanawha, where they met with Dr. Briscoe at the head of another exploring party. From him Kenton obtained a rifle and some ammunition, with which he again plunged alone into the forest and hunted with success until the Summer of '73 was far advanced. Returning, then, to the Little Kanawha, he found a party of fourteen men, under the direction of Dr. Wood and Hancock Lee, who were descending the Ohio with the view of joining

Captain Bullitt, who was supposed to be at the mouth of Scioto, with a large party. Kenton instantly joined them, and descended the river in canoes as far as the Three Islands, landing frequently and examining the country on each side of the river. At the Three Islands they were alarmed by the approach of a large party of Indians, by whom they were compelled to abandon their canoes and strike diagonally through the wilderness for Greenbriar county, Virginia. They suffered much during this journey from fatigue and famine, and were compelled at one time (notwithstanding the danger of their situation,) to halt for fourteen days and wait upon Dr. Wood, who had unfortunately been bitten by a copperhead snake, and rendered incapable of moving for that length of time. Upon reaching the settlements the party separated.

Kenton, not wishing to venture to Virginia, (having heard nothing of Leitchman's recovery,) built a canoe on the banks of the Monongahela, and returned to the mouth of the Great Kanawha, hunted with success until the spring of '74, when the war, called sometimes Dunmore's and sometimes Cresap's war, broke out between the Indian tribes and the colonies, occasioned, in a great measure, by the murder of the family of the celebrated Indian chief, Logan. Kenton was not in the great battle near the mouth of the Kanawha, but, with the notorious renegade, Simon Girty, acted as a spy throughout the whole of the campaign, in the course of which he traversed the country around Fort Pitt and a large part of the present State of Ohio.

When Dunmore's forces were disbanded, Kenton, in company with two others, determined on making a second effort to discover the rich lands bordering on the Ohio, of which Yager had spoken. Having built a canoe and provided themselves abundantly with ammunition, they descended the river as far as the mouth of Big Bone Creek, upon which the celebrated Lick of that name is situated. They there disembarked, and explored the country for several days; but not finding the land equal to their expectations, they reascended the river as far as the mouth of Cabin Creek, a few miles above Maysville.

HERDS OF ELK AND BUFFALO—HENDRICKS BURNT—KENTON'S FIGHT.

From this point they set out with a determination to examine the country carefully until they could find land answering in some degree to Yager's description. In a short time they reached the neighborhood of Mayslick, and, for the first time, were struck with the uncommon beauty of the country and fertility of the soil. Here they fell in with the great buffalo trace, which, in a few hours, brought them to the Lower Blue Lick. The flats upon each side of the river were crowded with immense herds of buffalo that had come down from the interior for the sake of the salt, and a number of elk were seen upon the bare ridges which surrounded the springs. Their great object was now achieved. They had discovered a country far more rich than any which they had yet beheld, and where the game seemed as abundant as the grass of the plain.

After remaining a few days at the Lick, and killing an immense number of deer and buffalo, they crossed the Licking and passed through the present counties of Scott, Fayette, Woodford, Clarke, Montgomery and Bath, when, falling in with another buffalo trace, it conducted them to the Upper Blue Lick, where they again beheld elk and buffalo in immense numbers. Highly gratified at the success of their expedition, they quickly returned to their canoe, and ascended the river as far as Green Bottom, where they had left their skins, some ammunition and a few hoes, which they had procured at Kanawha, with the view of cultivating the rich ground which they expected to find.

Returning as quickly as possible, they built a cabin on the spot where the town of Washington, Ky., now stands, and having cleared an acre of ground in the centre of a large canebrake, they planted it with Indian corn. Strolling about the country in various directions, they one day fell in with two white men, near the Lower Blue Lick, who had los¹ their guns, blankets and ammunition, and were much distressed for provisions and the means of extricating themselves from the wilderness. They informed them that their names were Fitzpatrick and Hendricks; that, in descending the Ohio, their canoe had been overset by a sudden squall; that they were compelled to swim ashore, without being able to save anything from the wreck; that they had wandered thus far through the woods, in the effort to penetrate through the country to the settlements above, but must infallibly perish unless they could be furnished with guns and ammunition. Kenton informed them of the small settlement which he had opened at Washington, and invited them to join him and share such fortune as Providence might bestow. Hendricks consented to remain, but Fitzpatrick, being heartily sick of the woods, insisted upon returning to the Monongahela. Kenton and his two friends accompanied Fitzpatrick to "the point," as it was then called, being the spot where Maysville now stands, and having given him a gun, &c., assisted him in crossing the river, and took leave of him on the other side.

In the meantime, Hendricks had been left at the Blue Licks, without a gun, but with a good supply of provisions, until the party could return from the river. As soon as Fitzpatrick had gone, Kenton and his two friends hastened to return to the Lick, not doubting for a moment that they would find Hendricks in camp as they had left him. Upon arriving at the point where the tent stood, however, they were alarmed at finding it deserted, with evident marks of violence around it. Several bullet holes were to be seen in the poles of which it was constructed, and various articles belonging to Hendricks were tossed about in too negligent a manner to warrant the belief that it had been done by him. At a little distance from the camp, in a low ravine, they observed a thick smoke, as if from a fire just beginning to burn. They did not doubt for a moment that Hendricks had fallen into the hands of the Indians, and believing that a party of them were then assembled around the fire which was about to be kindled, they betook themselves to their heels, and fled faster and farther than true chivalry perhaps would justify.

They remained at a distance until the evening of the next day, when they ventured cautiously to return to camp. The fire was still burning, although faintly, and after carefully reconnoitering the adjacent ground, they ventured at length to approach the spot, and there beheld the skull and bones of their unfortunate friend. He had evidently been roasted to death by a party of Indians, and must have been alive at the time when Kenton and his companion approached on the preceding day. It was a subject of deep regret to the party that they had not reconnoitered the spot more closely, as it was probable that their friend might have been rescued. The number of Indians might have been small, and a brisk and unexpected attack might have dispersed them. Regret, however, was now unavailing, and they sadly retraced their steps to their camp at Washington, pondering upon the uncertainty of their own condition, and upon the danger to which they were hourly exposed from the numerous bands of hostile Indians who were prowling around them in every direction.

They remained at Washington, entirely undisturbed, until the month of September, when again visiting the Lick, they saw a white man, who informed them that the interior of the country was already occupied by the whites, and that there was a thriving settlement at Boonsborough. Highly gratified at this intelligence, and anxious once more to enjoy the society of men, they broke up their encampment at Washington, and visited the different stations which had been formed in the country. Kenton sustained two sieges in Boonsborough, and served as a spy, with equal diligence and success, until the summer of '78, when Boone, returning from captivity, as has already been mentioned, concerted an expedition against the small Indian towns on Paint Creek.

Kenton acted as a spy on this expedition, and after crossing the Ohio, being some distance in advance of the rest, he was suddenly startled by hearing a loud laugh from an adjoining thicket, which he was just about to enter. Instantly halting, he took his station behind a tree, and waited anxiously for a repetition of the noise. In a few minutes two Indians approached the spot where he lay, both mounted upon a small pony, and chatting and laughing in high good humor. Having permitted them to approach within good rifle distance, he raised his gun, and aiming at the breast of the foremost, pulled the trigger. Both Indians fell —one shot dead, the other severely wounded. Their frightened pony galloped back into the cane, giving the alarm to the rest of the party, who were some distance in the rear. Kenton instantly ran up to scalp the dead man and to tomahawk his wounded companion, according to the usual rule of western warfare; but, when about to put an end to the struggles of the wounded Indian, who did not seem disposed to submit very quietly to the operation, his attention was arrested by a rustling in the cane on his right, and turning rapidly in that direction, he beheld two Indians within twenty steps of him, very deliberately taking aim at his person.

A quick spring to one side, on his part, was instantly followed by the flash and report of their rifles—the balls whistled close to his ears, causing him involuntarily to duck his head, but doing him no injury. Not liking so hot a neighborhood, and ignorant of the number which might be behind, he lost no time in regaining the shelter of the woods, leaving the dead Indian unscalped and the wounded man to the care of his friends. Scarcely had he treed, when a dozen Indians appeared on the edge of the canebrake, and seemed disposed to press on him with more vigor than was consistent with the safety of his present position. His fears, however, were instantly relieved by the appearance of Boone and his party, who came running up as rapidly as a due regard for the shelter of their persons would permit, and opening a brisk fire upon the Indians, quickly compelled them to regain the shelter of the canebrake, with the loss of several wounded, who, as usual, were carried off. The dead Indian, in the hurry of the retreat, was abandoned, and Kenton at last had the gratification of taking his scalp.

Boone, as has already been mentioned, instantly retraced his steps to Boonsborough; but Kenton and his friend Montgomery determined to proceed alone to the Indian town, and at least to obtain some recompense for the trouble of their journey. Approaching the village with the cautious stealthy pace of the cat or panther, they took their station upon the edge of a cornfield, supposing that the Indians would enter it, as usual, to gather roasting ears. They remained here patiently all day, but did not see a single Indian, and heard only the voices of some children who were playing near them. Being disappointed in the hope of getting a shot, they entered the Indian town in the night, and stealing four good horses, made a rapid night's march for the Ohio, which they crossed in safety, and on the second day afterwards reached Logan's fort with their booty.

Scarcely had he returned, when Colonel Bowman ordered him to take his friend Montgomery, and another young man named Clark, and go on a secret expedition to an Indian town on the Little Miami, against which the Colonel meditated an expedition, and of the exact condition of which he wished to have certain information. They instantly set out, in obedience to their orders, and reached the neighborhood of the town without being discovered. They examined it attentively, and walked around the houses during the night with perfect impunity.

Kenton Passes Through Some Remarkable Adventures.

Thus far all had gone well—and had they been contented to return after the due execution of their orders, they would have avoided the heavy calamity which awaited them. But, unfortunately during their nightly promenade, they stumbled upon a pound in which were a number of Indian horses. The temptation was not to be resisted. They each mounted a horse, but not satisfied with that, they could not find it in their hearts to leave a single animal behind them, and as some of the horses seemed indisposed to change masters, the affair was attended with so much fracas, that at last they were discovered. The cry ran through the village at once, that the Long Knives were stealing their horses right before the doors of their wigwams, and old and young, squaws, boys and warriors, all sallied out with loud screams to save their property from these greedy spoilers. Kenton and his friends quickly discovered that they had overshot the mark, and that they must ride for their lives; but even in this extremity, they could not bring themselves to give up a single horse which they had haltered; while two of them rode in front and led the horses, the other brought up the rear, and plying his whip from right to left, did not permit a single animal to lag behind.

In this manner they dashed through the woods at a furious rate, with the hue and cry after them, until their course was suddenly stopped by an impenetrable swamp. Here, from necessity, they paused for a few moments and listened attentively. Hearing no sounds of pursuit, they resumed their course, and skirting the swamp for some distance, in the vain hope of crossing it, they bent their course in a straight direction towards the Ohio. They rode during the whole night without resting a moment—and halting for a few minutes at daylight, they continued their journey throughout the day, and the whole of the following night, and by this uncommon expedition, on the morning of the second day they reached the northern bank of the Ohio. Crossing the river would now ensure their safety, but this was likely to prove a difficult undertaking, and the close pursuit which they had reason to expect, rendered it necessary to lose as little time as possible. The wind was high and the river rough and boisterous. It was determined that Kenton should cross with the horses, while Clark and Montgomery should construct a raft in order to transport their guns, baggage and ammunition to the opposite shore.

The necessary preparations were soon made, and Kenton, after forcing his horses into the river, plunged in himself and swam by their side. In a very few minutes the high waves completely overwhelmed him and forced him considerably below the horses, which stemmed the current much more vigorously than himself. The horses being thus left to themselves, turned about and swam again to the shore, where Kenton was compelled to follow them. Again he forced them into the water, and again they returned to the same spot, until Kenton became so exhausted by repeated efforts as to be unable to swim. A council was then held and the question proposed: "What was to be done?" That the Indians would pursue them, was certain—that the horses would not, and could not be made to cross the river in its present state, was equally certain. Should they abandon their horses and cross on the raft, or remain with their horses and take such fortune as heaven should send? The latter alternative was unanimously adopted.

Should they now move up or down the river, or remain where they were? The latter course was adopted. It was supposed that the wind would fall at sunset, and the river become sufficiently calm to admit of their passage, and as it was supposed that the Indians might be upon them before night, it was determined to conceal the horses in a neighboring ravine, while they should take their stations in the adjoining woods. A more miserable plan could not have been adopted. The day passed away in tranquility, but at night the wind blew harder than ever, and the waters became so rough that even their raft would have been scarcely able to cross. Not an instant more should have been lost in moving from so dangerous a post; but, as if totally infatuated, they remained where they were until morning—thus wasting twenty-four hours of most precious time in total idleness. In the morning the wind abated, and the river became calm—but it was now too late. Their horses, recollecting the difficulty of the passage on the preceding day, had become as obstinate and heedless as their masters, and positively and repeatedly refused to take the water.

Finding every effort to compel them entirely unavailing, their masters at length determined to do what ought to have been done at first. Each resolved to mount a horse and make the best of his way down the river to Louisville. Had even this resolution, however tardily adopted, been executed with decision, the party would probably have been saved, but, after they were mounted, instead of leaving the ground instantly, they went back upon their own tra, in the vain effort to regain possession of the rest of their horses, which had broken from them in the last effort to drive them into the water. They thus wearied out their good genius, and literally fell victims to their love for horse-flesh.

They had scarcely ridden one hundred yards, (Kenton in the centre, the others upon the flanks, with an interval of two hundred yards between them,) when Kenton heard a loud halloo, apparently coming from the spot which they had just left. Instead of getting out of the way as fast as possible, and trusting to the speed of his horse and the thickness of the wood for safety, he put the last cap-stone to his imprudence, and, dismounting, walked leisurely back to meet his pursuers, as if to give them as little trouble as possible. He quickly beheld three Indians and one white man, all well mounted. Wishing to give the alarm to his companions, he raised his rifle to his shoulders, took a steady aim at the breast of the foremost Indian, and drew the trigger. His gun had become wet on the raft, and flashed. The enemy were instantly alarmed, and dashed at him.

Now, at last, when flight could be of no service, Kenton betook himself to his heels, and was pursued by four horsemen at full speed. He instantly directed his steps to the thickest part of the woods, where there was much fallen timber and rankness of underwood, and had succeeded, as he thought, in baffling his pursuers, when, just as he was leaving the fallen timber and entering the open woods, an Indian on horseback galloped round the corner of the woods, and approached him so rapidly as to render flight useless. The horseman rode up, holding out his hand and calling out, "brother! brother!" in a tone of great affection. Kenton observed that if his gun would have made fire he would have "brothered" him to his heart's content, but, being totally unarmed, he called out that he would surrender if he would give him quarter and good treatment. Promises were cheap with the Indians, and he showered them out by the dozen, continuing all the while to advance with extended hands and a writhing grin upon his countenance, which was intended for a smile of courtesy. Seizing Kenton's hand, he grasped it with violence.

Kenton, not liking the manner of his captor, raised his gun to knock him down, when an Indian, who had followed him closely through the brushwood, instantly sprang upon his back and pinioned his arms to his side. The one who had just approached him then seized him by the hair and shook him until his teeth rattled, while the rest of the party coming up, they all fell upon Kenton with their tongues and ramrods, until he thought they would scold or beat him to death. They were the owners of the horses which he had carried off, and now took ample revenge for the loss of their property. At every stroke of their ramrods over his head, (and they were neither few nor far between,) they would repeat, in a tone of strong indignation, "Steal Indian hoss!! hey!!"

Their attention, however, was soon directed to Montgomery, who, having heard the noise attending Kenton's capture, very gallantly hastened up to his assistance; while Clark very prudently consulted his own safety by betaking himself to his heels, leaving his unfortunate companions to shift for themselves. Montgomery halted within gunshot, and appeared busy with the pan of his gun, as if preparing to fire. Two Indians instantly sprang off in pursuit of him, while the rest attended to Kenton. In a few minutes Kenton heard the crack of two rifles in quick succession, followed by a halloo, which announced the fate of his friend. The Indians quickly returned, waving the bloody scalp of Montgomery, and with countenances and gestures which menaced him with a similar fate. They then proceeded to secure their prisoner. They first compelled him to lie upon his back and stretch out his arms to their full length. They then passed a stout stick at right angles across his breast, to each extremity of which his wrists were fastened by thongs made of buffalo's hide. Stakes were then driven into the earth near his feet, to which they were fastened in a similar manner. A halter was then tied around his neck and fastened to a sapling which grew near, and finally a strong rope was passed under his body, lashed strongly to the pole which lay transversely upon his breast, and finally wrapped around his arms at the elbows, in such a manner as to pinion them to the pole with a painful violence, and render him literally incapable of moving hand, foot or head, in the slightest manner.

Simon Kenton takes a Mazeppa ride.
SEE PAGE 305.

Kenton Tries a Mazeppa Ride—Escape and Recapture.

> They tied his hands, Mazeppa like
> And set him on his steed,
> Wild as the mustang of the plains,
> And, mocking, bade him speed.
> Then sped the courser like the wind,
> Of curb and bit all freed,
> O'er flood and field; o'er hill and dale,
> Wherever chance might lead.

During the whole of this severe operation, neither their tongues nor hands were by any means idle. They cuffed him from time to time, with great heartiness, until his ears rang again, and abused him for "a teef!—a hoss steal!—a rascal!" and, finally, for a "d—d white man!" All the western Indians had picked up a good many English words—particularly our oaths, which, from the frequency with which they were used by our hunters and traders, they probably looked upon as the very root and foundation of the English language. Kenton remained in this painful attitude throughout the night, looking forward to certain death, and most probable torture, as soon as he reached their towns. Their rage against him seemed to increase rather than abate, from indulgence, and in the morning it displayed itself in a form at once ludicrous and cruel.

Among the horses which Kenton had taken, and which their original owners had now recovered, was a fine but wild young colt, totally unbroken, and with all his honors of mane and tail undocked. Upon him Kenton was mounted, without saddle or bridle, with his hands tied behind him, and his feet fastened under the horse's belly. The country was rough and bushy, and Kenton had no means of protecting his face from the brambles, through which it was expected that the colt would dash. As soon as the rider was firmly fastened upon his back, the colt was turned loose with a sudden lash, and dashed off like a dart through the briars and underbrush, but after executing many curvets and caprioles, to the great distress of his rider but to the infinite amusement of the Indians, he appeared to take compassion upon his rider, and falling into a line with the other horses, avoided the brambles entirely, and went on very well. In this manner he rode through the day. At night he was taken from the horse and confined as before.

On the third day they came within a few miles of Chillicothe. Here the party halted and dispatched a messenger to inform the village of their arrival, in order to give them time to prepare for his reception. In a short time Blackfish, one of their chiefs, arrived, and regarding Kenton with a stern countenance, thundered out, in very good English,

"You have been stealing horses?" "Yes, sir." "Did Captain Boone tell you to steal our horses?" "No, sir; I did it of my own accord." This frank confession was too irritating to be borne. Blackfish made no reply, but brandished a hickory switch, which he held in his hand, and applied it so briskly to Kenton's naked back and shoulders, as to bring the blood freely, and occasion acute pain.

Thus alternately beaten and scolded, he marched on to the village. At the distance of a mile from Chillicothe, he saw every inhabitant of the town, men, women and children, running out to feast their eyes with a view of the prisoner. Every individual, down to the smallest child, appeared in a paroxysm of rage. They whooped, they yelled, they hooted, they clapped their hands, and poured upon him a flood of abuse to which all that he had yet received was gentleness and civility. With loud cries they demanded that their prisoner should be tied to the stake. The hint was instantly complied with. A stake was quickly fastened in the ground. The remnants of Kenton's shirt and breeches were torn from his person, (the squaws officiating with great dexterity in both operations,) and his hands being tied together and raised above his head, were fastened to the top of the stake. The whole party then danced around him until midnight, yelling and screaming in their usual frantic manner, striking him with switches, and slapping him with the palms of their hands. He expected every moment to undergo the torture of fire, but *that* was reserved for another time. They wished to prolong the pleasure of tormenting him as much as possible, and after having caused him to anticipate the bitterness of death until a late hour of the night, they released him from his stake and conveyed him to the village.

Early in the morning he beheld the scalp of Montgomery stretched upon a hoop, and drying in the air before the door of one of their principal houses. He was quickly led out and ordered to run the gauntlet. A row of boys, women and men extended to the distance of a quarter of a mile. At the starting place stood two grim-looking warriors, with butcher knives in their hands—at the extremity of the line was an Indian beating a drum, and a few paces beyond the drum was the door of the council house. Clubs, switches, hoe handles and tomahawks were brandished along the whole line, causing the sweat involuntarily to stream from his pores, at the idea of the discipline which his naked skin was to receive during the race. The moment for starting arrived—the great drum at the door of the council house was struck— and Kenton sprung forward in the race. He avoided the row of his enemies, and turning to the east, drew the whole party in pursuit of him. He doubled several times with great activity, and at length, ob-

Escape and Recapture.

serving an opening, he darted through it, and pressed forward to the council house with a rapidity which left his pursuers far behind. One or two of the Indians succeeded in throwing themselves between him and the goal—and from these alone he received a few blows, but was much less injured than he could at first have supposed possible.

As soon as the race was over, a council was held in order to determine whether he should be burnt to death on the spot, or carried round to the other villages and exhibited to every tribe. The arbiters of his fate sat in a circle on the floor of the council house, while the unhappy prisoner, naked and bound, was committed to the care of a guard in the open air. The deliberation commenced. Each warrior sat in silence, while a large war club was passed round the circle. Those who were opposed to burning the prisoner on the spot were to pass the club in silence to the next warrior; those in favor of burning, were to strike the earth violently with the club before passing it. A teller was appointed to count the votes. This dignitary quickly reported that the opposition had prevailed; that his execution was suspended for the present, and that it was determined to take him to an Indian town on Mad river called Wappatomica. His fate was quickly announced to him by a renegade white man, who acted as interpreter. Kenton felt rejoiced at the issue, but naturally became anxious to know what was in reserve for him at Wappatomica. He accordingly asked the white man what the Indians intended to do with him upon reaching the appointed place: "BURN YOU, G——d d——n you!!!" was the ferocious reply. He asked no further question, and the scowling interpreter walked away.

Instantly preparations were made for his departure, and to his great joy, as well as astonishment, his clothes were restored to him, and he was permitted to remain unbound. Thanks to the ferocious intimation of the interpreter, he was aware of the fate in reserve for him, and secretly determined that he would never reach Wappatomica alive if it was possible to avoid it. Their route lay through an unpruned forest, abounding in thickets and undergrowth. Unbound, as he was, it would not be impossible to escape from the hands of his conductors; and if he could once enter the thickets, he thought that he might be enabled to baffle his pursuers. At the worst, he could only be retaken— and the fire would burn no hotter after an attempt to escape than before. During the whole of their march, he remained abstracted and silent—often meditating an effort for liberty, and as often shrinking from the peril of the attempt.

At length he was aroused from his reverie by the Indians firing off their guns and raising the shrill scalp halloo. The signal was soon answered, and the deep roll of a drum was heard far in front, announcing to the unhappy prisoner that they were approaching an Indian town where the gauntlet, certainly, and perhaps the stake, awaited him. The idea of a repetition of the dreadful scenes which he had already encountered, completely banished the indecision which had hitherto withheld him, and with a sudden and startling cry he sprang into the bushes and fled with the speed of a wild deer. The pursuit was instant and keen, some on foot, some on horseback. But he was flying for his life—the stake and the hot iron, and the burning splinters were before his eyes—and he soon distanced the swiftest hunter that pursued him. But fate was against him at every turn. Thinking only of the enemy behind, he forgot that there might also be enemies in front, and before he was aware of what he had done, he found that he had plunged into the centre of a fresh party of horsemen, who had sallied from the town at the firing of the guns, and happened unfortunately to stumble upon the poor prisoner, now making a last effort for freedom. His heart sunk at once from the ardor of hope to the very pit of despair, and he was again haltered and driven before them to town like an ox to the slaughter house.

Upon reaching the village, (Pickaway,) he was fastened to a stake near the door of the council house, and the warriors again assembled in debate. In a short time they issued from the council house and, surrounding him, they danced, yelled, &c., for several hours, giving him once more a foretaste of the bitterness of death. On the following morning their journey was continued, but the Indians had now become watchful, and gave him no opportunity of even attempting an escape. On the second day he arrived at Wappatomica. Here he was again compelled to run the gauntlet, in which he was severely hurt; and immediately after this ceremony he was taken to the council house, and all the warriors once more assembled to determine his fate.

He sat silent and dejected upon the floor of the cabin, awaiting the moment which was to deliver him to the stake, when the door of the council house opened, and Simon Girty, James Girty, John Ward and an Indian, came in with a woman (Mrs. Mary Kennedy) as a prisoner, together with seven children and seven scalps. Kenton was instantly removed from the council house, and the deliberations of the assembly were protracted to a very late hour, in consequence of the arrival of the last-named party with a fresh drove of prisoners.

Simon Girty Intercedes and Saves his Friend.

At length he was again summoned to attend the council house, being informed that his fate was decided. Regarding the mandate as a mere prelude to the stake and fire, which he knew were intended for him, he obeyed it with a calm despair which had now succeeded the burning anxiety of the last few days. Upon entering the council house he was greeted with a savage scowl, which, if he had still cherished a spark of hope, would have completely extinguished it. Simon Girty threw a blanket upon the floor, and harshly ordered him to take a seat upon it. The order was not immediately complied with, and Girty impatiently seized his arm, jerked him roughly upon the blanket, and pulled him down upon it. In the same rough and menacing tone, Girty then interrogated him as to the condition of Kentucky. "How many men are there in Kentucky?" "It is impossible for me to answer that question," replied Kenton, "but I can tell you the number of officers and their respective ranks—you can then judge for yourself." "Do you know William Stewart?" "Perfectly well—he is an old and intimate acquaintance." "What is your own name?" "Simon Butler!" replied Kenton.

Never did the annunciation of a name produce a more powerful effect. Girty and Kenton (then bearing the name of Butler) had served as spies together in Dunmore's expedition. The former had not then abandoned the society of the whites for that of the savages, and had become warmly attached to Kenton during the short period of their services together. As soon as he heard the name he became strongly agitated, and, springing from his seat, he threw his arms around Kenton's neck, and embraced him with much emotion. Then turning to the assembled warriors, who remained astonished spectators of this extraordinary scene, he addressed them in a short speech, which the deep earnestness of his tone and the energy of his gesture rendered eloquent. He informed them that the prisoner, whom they had just condemned to the stake, was his ancient comrade and bosom friend; that they had traveled the same war path, slept under the same blanket, and dwelt in the same wigwam. He entreated them to have compassion upon his feelings—to spare him the agony of witnessing the torture of an old friend by the hands of his adopted brothers—and not to refuse so trifling a favor as the life of a white man, to the earnest intercession of one who had proved by the most faithful service, that he was sincerely and zealously devoted to the cause of the Indians.

The speech was listened to in unbroken silence. As soon as he had finished, several chiefs expressed their approbation by a deep guttural interjection, while others were equally as forward in making known their objections to the proposal. They urged that his fate had already been determined in a large and solemn council, and that they would be acting like squaws to change their minds every hour. They insisted upon the flagrant misdemeanor of Kenton; that he had not only stolen their horses, but had flashed his gun at one of their young men—that it was in vain to suppose that so bad a man could ever become an Indian at heart, like their brother Girty—that the Kentuckians were all alike—very bad people—and ought to be killed as fast as they were taken—and, finally, they observed that many of their people had come from a distance solely to assist at the torture of the prisoner—and pathetically painted the disappointment and chagrin with which they would hear that all their trouble had been for nothing.

Girty listened with obvious impatience to the young warriors, who had so ably urged against a reprieve—and starting to his feet, as soon as the others had concluded, he urged his former request with great earnestness. He briefly, but strongly, recapitulated his own services, and the many and weighty instances of attachment which he had given. He asked if *he* could be suspected of partiality to the whites? When had he ever before interceded for any of that hated race? Had he not brought seven scalps home with him from the last expedition? and had he not submitted seven white prisoners that very evening to their discretion? Had he expressed a wish that a single one of the captives should be saved. *This* was his first and should be his last request: for if they refused to *him* what was never refused to the intercession of one of their natural chiefs, he would look upon himself as disgraced in their eyes, and considered as unworthy of confidence. Which of their own natural warriors had been more zealous than himself? From what expedition had he ever shrunk? What white man had ever seen his back? Whose tomahawk had been bloodier than his? He would say no more. He asked it as a first and last favor; as an evidence that they approved of his zeal and fidelity, that the life of his bosom friend might be spared. Fresh speakers arose upon each side, and the debate was carried on for an hour and a half with great heat and energy.

During the whole of this time Kenton's feelings may readily be imagined. He could not understand a syllable of what was said. He saw that Girty spoke with deep earnestness, and that the eyes of the assembly were often turned upon himself with various expressions. He felt satisfied that his friend was pleading for his life, and that he was violently opposed by a large part of the council. At length, the war club was produced and the final vote taken. Kenton watched its progress with thrilling emotion, which yielded to the most rapturous delight, as he perceived that those who struck the floor of the council house were decidedly inferior in number to those who passed it in silence. Having thus succeeded in his benevolent purpose, Girty lost no time in attending to the comfort of his friend. He led him to his own wigwam, and from his own store gave him a pair of moccasins and leggins, a breech-cloth, a hat, a coat, a handkerchief for his neck and another for his head.

The whole of this remarkable scene is in the highest degree honorable to Girty, and is in striking contrast to most of his conduct after his union with the Indians. No man can be completely hardened, and no character is at all times the same. Girty had been deeply offended with the whites; and knowing that his desertion to the Indians had been universally and severely reprobated, and that he himself was regarded with detestation by his former countrymen, he seems to have raged against them from these causes, with a fury which resembled rather the paroxysm of a maniac than the deliberate cruelty of a naturally ferocious temper. Fierce censure never reclaims, but rather drives to still greater extremities; and this is the reason that renegades are so much fiercer than natural foes, and that when females fall, they fall irretrievably.

For the space of three weeks Kenton lived in perfect tranquility. Girty's kindness was uniform and indefatigable. He introduced Kenton to his own family, and accompanied him to the wigwams of the principal chiefs, who seemed all at once to have turned from the extremity of rage to the utmost kindness and cordiality. Fortune, however, seemed to have selected him for her football, and to have snatched him from the frying pan only to throw him into the fire. About twenty days after his most providential deliverance from the stake, he was walking in company with Girty and an Indian named Redpole, when another Indian came from the village towards them, uttering repeatedly a whoop of a peculiar intonation. Girty instantly told Kenton that it was the "distress halloo," and that they must all go instantly to the council house. Kenton's heart involuntarily fluttered at the intelligence, for he dreaded all whoops, and hated all council houses—firmly believing that neither boded him any good. Nothing, however, could be done to avoid whatever fate awaited, and he sadly accompanied Girty and Redpole back to the village.

Upon approaching the Indian who had hallooed, Girty and Redpole shook hands with him. Kenton likewise offered his hand, but the Indian refused to take it—at the same time scowling upon him ominously. This took place within a few paces of the door of the council house. Upon entering, they saw that the house was unusually full. Many chiefs and warriors from the distant towns were present; and their countenances were grave, severe and forbidding. Girty, Redpole and Kenton walked around, offering their hands successively to each warrior. The hands of the first two were cordially received—but when poor Kenton anxiously offered *his* hand to the first warrior, it was rejected with the same scowling eye as before. He passed on to the second, but was still rejected—he persevered, however, until his hand had been refused by the first six—when, sinking into despondence, he turned off and stood apart from the rest.

The debate quickly commenced. Kenton looked eagerly towards Girty, as his last and only hope. His friend looked anxious and distressed. The chiefs from a distance arose one after another, and spoke in a firm and indignant tone, often looking at Kenton with an eye of death. Girty did not desert him—but his eloquence appeared wasted upon the distant chiefs. After a warm debate, he turned to Kenton and said, "Well, my friend! *you must die!*" One of the stranger chiefs instantly seized him by the collar, and the others surrounding him, he was strongly pinioned, committed to a guard, and instantly marched off. His guards were on horseback, while the prisoner was driven before them on foot with a long rope around his neck, the other end of which was held by one of the guard. In this manner they had marched about two and a half miles, when Girty passed them on horseback, informing Kenton that he had friends at the next village, with whose aid he hoped to be able to do something for him. Girty passed on to the town, but finding that nothing could be done, he would not see his friend again, but returned to Wappatomica by a different route.

A Savage Axe Blow—Kenton Meets Chief Logan.

They passed through the village without halting, and at a distance of two and a half miles beyond it, Kenton had again an opportunity of witnessing the fierce hate with which these children of nature regarded an enemy. At the distance of a few paces from the road, a squaw was busily engaged in chopping wood, while her lord and master was sitting on a log smoking his pipe and directing her labors, with the indolent indifference common to the natives, when not under the influence of some exciting passion. The sight of Kenton, however, seemed to rouse him to fury. He hastily sprang up, with a sudden yell, snatched the axe from the squaw, and rushing upon the prisoner so rapidly as to give him no opportunity of escape, dealt him a blow with the axe which cut through his shoulder, breaking the bone and almost severing the arm from the body. He would instantly have repeated the blow, had not Kenton's conductors interfered and protected him, severely reprimanding the Indian for attempting to rob them of the amusement of torturing the prisoner.

They soon reached a large village upon the head waters of the Scioto, where Kenton, for the first time, beheld the celebrated Mingo Chief, Logan, so honorably mentioned in Jefferson's Notes on Virginia. Logan walked gravely up to the place where Kenton stood, and the following short conversation ensued: "Well, young man, these young men seem very mad at you?" "Yes, sir, they certainly are." "Well, don't be disheartened; I am a great chief; you are to go to Sandusky—they speak of burning you there—but I will send two runners to-morrow to speak good for you." Logan's form was striking and manly—his countenance calm and noble, and he spoke the English language with fluency and correctness. Kenton's spirits instantly rose at the address of the benevolent chief, and he once more looked upon himself as providentially rescued from the stake.

On the following morning two runners were dispatched to Sandusky, as the chief had promised, and until their return Kenton was kindly treated, being permitted to spend much of his time with Logan, who conversed with him freely and in the most friendly manner. In the evening the two runners returned, and were closeted with Logan. Kenton felt the most burning anxiety to know what was the result of their mission, but Logan did not visit him again until the next morning. He then walked up to him, accompanied by Kenton's guards, and, giving him a piece of bread, told him that he was instantly to be carried to Sandusky; and without uttering another word, turned upon his heel and left him.

Again Kenton's spirits sunk. From Logan's manner, he supposed that his intercession had been unavailing, and that Sandusky was destined to be the scene of his final suffering. This appears to have been the truth. But fortune, who, to use Lord Lovat's expression, had been playing at cat and mouse with him for the last month, had selected Sandusky for the display of her strange and capricious power. He was driven into the town, as usual, and was to have been burnt on the following morning, when an Indian Agent, named Drewyer, interposed, and once more rescued him from the stake. He was anxious to obtain intelligence for the British commandant at Detroit, and so earnestly insisted upon Kenton's being delivered up to him, that the Indians at length consented, upon the express condition that after the required information had been obtained, he should again be placed at their discretion. To this Drewyer consented, and without further difficulty, Kenton was transferred to his hands. Drewyer lost no time in removing him to Detroit.

On the road he informed Kenton of the condition upon which he had obtained possession of his person, assuring him, however, that no consideration should induce him to abandon a prisoner to the mercy of such wretches. Having dwelt at some length upon the generosity of his own disposition, and having sufficiently magnified the service which he had just rendered him, he began, at length, to cross-question Kenton as to the force and condition of Kentucky, and particularly as to the number of men at Fort McIntosh. Kenton very candidly declared his inability to answer either question, observing that he was merely a private, and by no means acquainted with matters of an enlarged and general import; that his great business had heretofore been to endeavor to take care of himself—which he had found a work of no small difficulty. Drewyer replied that he believed him, and from that time Kenton was troubled with no more questions.

His condition at Detroit was not unpleasant. He was compelled to report himself every morning to an English officer, and was restricted to certain boundaries through the day; but in other respects he scarcely felt that he was a prisoner. His battered body and broken arm were quickly repaired, and his emaciated limbs were again clothed with a proper proportion of flesh. He remained in this state of easy restraint from October, 1777, until June, 1778, when he meditated an escape. There was no difficulty in leaving Detroit—but he would be compelled to traverse a wilderness of more than two hundred miles, abounding with hostile Indians, and affording no means of sustenance beyond the wild game, which could not be killed without a gun. In addition to this, he would certainly be pursued, and, if retaken by the Indians, he might expect a repetition of all that he had undergone before, without the prospect of a second interposition on the part of the English. These considerations deterred him for some time from the attempt, but at length his patience became uncontrollable, and he determined to escape or perish in the attempt.

He took his measures with equal secrecy and foresight. He cautiously sounded two young Kentuckians then at Detroit, who had been taken with Boone at the Blue Licks and had been purchased by the British. He found them as impatient as himself of captivity and resolute to accompany him. Charging them not to breathe a syllable of their design to any other prisoners, he busied himself for several days in making the necessary preparations. It was absolutely necessary that they should be provided with arms, both for the sake of repelling attacks and for procuring the means of subsistence; and at the same time it was very difficult to obtain them without the knowledge of the British commandant. By patiently waiting their opportunity, however, all these preliminary difficulties were overcome. Kenton formed a close friendship with two Indian hunters, deluged them with rum, and bought their guns for a mere trifle. After carefully hiding them in the woods, he returned to Detroit, and managed to procure another rifle, with powder and balls, from a Mr. and Mrs. Edger, citizens of the town. They then appointed a night for the attempt, and agreed upon a place of rendezvous.

All things turned out prosperously. They met at the time and place appointed without discovery, and, taking a circuitous route, avoided pursuit, and traveling only during the night, they at length arrived safely at Louisville, after a march of thirty days.

Thus terminated one of the most remarkable series of adventures in the whole range of western history. Kenton was eight times exposed to the gauntlet—three times tied to the stake—and as often thought himself on the eve of a terrible death. All the sentences passed upon him, whether of mercy or condemnation, seemed to have been only pronounced in one council in order to be reversed in another. Every friend that Providence raised up in his favor was immediately followed by some enemy, who unexpectedly interposed, and turned his short glimpse of sunshine into deeper darkness than ever. For three weeks he was see-sawing between life and death, and during the whole time *he* was perfectly passive. No wisdom, or foresight, or exertion, could have saved him. Fortune fought his battle from first to last, and seemed determined to permit nothing else to interfere. Scarcely had he reached Kentucky when he was embarked in a new enterprise.

BUTLER CHANGES HIS NAME TO KENTON—HIS LAST YEARS.

This was in July, '79, and, in a few days, the restless borderer sought out new hazards and adventures, and, down to '82, was constantly engaged, by turn, as scout, guide, hunter and officer. Having acquired some valuable tracts of land, he concluded to make a settlement on Salt river. Hearing now, for the first time, from his old Virginia home, and that not only his father, but the rival whom he supposed he had killed, were still living, a great load was lifted from his heart. He now dropped the name of Butler and assumed his own proper name of Kenton, and concluded to pay Virginia a visit.

His meeting with his venerable father was something like that between the old Patriarch Jacob and his son Joseph, whom he had given up for lost. Joseph, however, only *sent* for his father's family, but Simon *went* for his, for after visiting all his old friends, his former rival included, he gave such glowing accounts of Kentucky that the whole family concluded to return with him. While, however, engaged in constructing a Kan-tuck boat at Redstone, on the Monongahela, his father sickened and died. The rest made their way down the Ohio to Limestone, (now Maysville,) which was the great point for entering Kentucky.

At his old camp near Maysville, Kenton soon commenced a flourishing colony, but being located so near the hostile Indian country, just across the Ohio, he had ever a constant, unintermittent warfare with the savages. Their scalping and horse-stealing incursions were frequent, and twice Kenton guided large retaliating parties into the very heart of their country. He had learned from his old commander, General Clarke, the efficacy of "carrying the war into Africa," and no blow was delivered by the Indians but what there was a prompt and most effective rejoinder. In '93, after many small but sanguinary hand-to-hand struggles, Kenton ambushed at the river-crossing the last swarthy invaders from the Ohio country, succeeding in killing six.

And so, after a bitter and most obstinate struggle of over twenty years, Kentucky was forever lost to the redman. In their best blood, the dogged pioneers had written their title to the soil, and now held it with an iron and an unyielding grip. Kenton, with a valiant band of Kentuckians, served as Major in "Mad Anthony Wayne's" '94 campaign, but was not present at its crowning triumph—the Battle of the Fallen Timbers. There the power and spirit of the Northwestern Confederacy were forever broken, and the borders at length enjoyed peace.

But, as with Boone, so now with Kenton; vexatious troubles fell upon him on account of land titles. They who had borne the "heat and burthen of the day" were vexed and harassed by "eleventh-hour men" coming in to enjoy the fruits secured to them by the toil, blood and perils of those who had preceded them. Kenton now, when his skill and services as a bold and watchful Indian fighter were no longer needed, was cast aside like an old shoe. He had braved the stake, the gauntlet and the tomahawk in vain. His very body, even, was taken for debt, and he was actually imprisoned for twelve months upon the very spot upon which he had built the first cabin, planted the first corn, and about which he had fought the savages in a hundred fierce encounters. The first pioneer was stripped by crafty, greedy speculators of nearly all the broad, fat acres he had so bloodily earned. Beggared by losses and law suits, he moved over to the Ohio wilderness—some say in '97 and some say in 1802. A few years after he was elected Brigadier General of the Ohio militia, and, in 1810, he united himself with the Methodist Episcopal Church, and ever after lived a consistent Christian life.

In 1813 the staunch old patriot joined the Kentucky troops under Governor Shelby, and was present at the Battle of the Thames. But this was his last battle, except the hard "battle of life," which he sternly fought to the very last. He returned to his obscure cabin in the woods, and remained at and near Urbana till 1820, when he moved to Mad River, in sight of the old Shawnee town of Wappatomica, where he had once been tied to the Indian stake. Even here he was pursued by judgments and executions from Kentucky, and, to prevent being driven from his own cabin by whites, as he formerly was by reds, he was compelled to have some land entered in the name of his wife and children.

Kenton still had some large tracts of mountain lands in Kentucky, but they had become forfeit to the State for taxes. He first tried boring on some of them to make salt, but this failing, his only alternative was to appeal to the Kentucky Legislature to release the forfeiture. So, in 1824, when about seventy years old, he mounted his sorry old horse, and, in his tattered garments, commenced his weary pilgrimage. The second night he stopped at the house of James Galloway, of Xenia, Ohio, an old friend and pioneer. Looking at his shabby appearance and his wretched saddle and bridle, Galloway gave vent to his honest indignation.

"Kenton," he said, "you have served your country faithfully, even to old age. What expedition against the British and savages was ever raised in the west, but what you were among the most prominent in it? Even down to the last war, you were with Harrison at the taking of Proctor's army in Canada; an old gray-headed warrior, you *could* not stay at home while your country needed your services, and look how they have neglected you! How can you stand such treatment?" But the patriot Kenton could and would hear no word against his country. Rising from his seat, he cast a fiery look at his old friend, clinched his fist and with an angry stamp of his foot, he exclaimed with warmth: "Don't say that again, Galloway! If you do, I will leave your house forever and never again call you my friend."

Kenton at last reached Frankfort, now become a thrifty and flourishing city. Here he was utterly unknown. All his old friends had departed. His dilapidated appearance and the sorry condition of his horse and its wretched equipments only provoked mirth. The grizzled old pioneer, was like Rip Van Winkle appearing after his long sleep. He wandered up and down the streets, "the observed of all observers." The very boys followed him. At length the scarred old warrior was recognized by General Fletcher, an old companion-in-arms. He grasped him by the hand, led him to a tailor's shop, bought him a suit of clothes and hat, and after he was dressed took him to the State Capitol.

Here he was placed in the Speaker's chair and introduced to a crowded assembly of judges, citizens and legislators, as the second pioneer of Kentucky. The simple-minded veteran used to say afterwards that " it was the very proudest day of his life," and ten years subsequently, his friend Hinde asserted, he was wearing the self-same hat and clothes. His lands were at once released and shortly after, by the warm exertion of some of his friends, a pension from Congress of two hundred and fifty dollars was obtained, securing his old age from absolute want.

Without any further marked notice, Kenton lived in his humble cabin until 1836, when, at the venerable old age of eighty-one, he breathed his last, surrounded by his family and neighbors and supported by the consolations of the Gospel. He died in sight of the very spot where the savages, nearly sixty years previous, proposed to torture him to death.

General Kenton was of fair complexion, six feet one inch in height. He stood and walked very erect, and, in the prime of life, weighed about a hundred and ninety pounds. He never was inclined to be corpulent, although of sufficient fullness to form a graceful person. He had a soft, tremulous voice, very pleasing to the hearer; auburn hair and laughing gray eyes, which appeared to fascinate the beholder. He was a pleasant, good-humored and obliging companion. When excited or provoked to anger, which was seldom the case, the fiery glance of his eye would almost curdle the blood of those with whom he came in contact. His wrath, when aroused, was a tornado. In his dealing he was perfectly honest. His confidence in man and his credulity were such, that the same man might cheat him twenty times—and, if he professed friendship, might still continue to cheat him. Kentucky owes it to justice and gratitude, to gather up General Kenton's remains and place them alongside of those of Boone, in the sacred soil he was among the first and the boldest to defend.

> Ah, can this be the spot where sleeps
> The bravest of the brave?
> Is this rude slab the only mark
> Of Simon Kenton's grave?
> These fallen palings, are they all
> His ingrate country gave,
> To one who periled life so oft
> Her homes and hearths to save?

THE WETZEL FAMILY—FATHER AND FIVE SONS.

LEWIS, THE RIGHT ARM OF THE WHEELING BORDER.

> He needs no guide in the forest,
>   More than the hunter bees;
> His guides are the cool, green mosses
>   To the northward of the trees.
> Nor fears he the foe whose footsteps
>   Go light as the Summer air.
> His tomahawk hangs in his shirt belt,
>   And the scalp-knife glitters there.
> The stealthy Wyandots tremble,
>   And speak his name with fear;
> For his aim is sharp and deadly,
>   And his rifle's ring is clear.—*Florus B. Plympton.*

In the year 1772, there came with the four Zane brothers, who settled at the mouth of Wheeling Creek, in the West Virginian Panhandle, a rough but brave and honest old German by the name of John Wetzel—not Whetzell or Whitzell, as the old Border books have it. He was the father of five sons—Martin, George, John, Jacob and Lewis, and two daughters—Susan and Christina.

At that time there were only three other adventurers in that whole wilderness region—the two Tomlinsons, located on the Flats of Grave Creek, and a mysterious man by the name of Tygert, at the mouth of Middle Island Creek. Who this latter was, or what became of him, no one has ever learned. Andrew Zane, shortly after his own arrival, went a short distance down the Ohio on a hunting excursion, and was surprised to find this lone hunter's cabin where he supposed the foot of white man had never yet trodden.

The whole of this Wetzel family were hunters and Indian fighters, but the most daring and reckless of all, and the one who has left the greatest name on the western border, was Lewis Wetzel. Of him more anon. We now propose first to treat of the father and brothers. The elder Wetzel spent much of his time in locating lands, hunting and fishing. In the very hottest time of the Indian troubles, he was so rash as to build his cabin at some distance from the fort. His neighbors frequently admonished him against exposing himself thus to the enemy; but disregarding their advice, and laughing at their fears, he continued to widen the range of his excursions, until at last he fell a victim to the active vigilance of the tawny foe. He was killed near Captina, in 1787, on his return from Middle Island Creek, under the following circumstances: Himself and companion were in a canoe, paddling slowly near the shore, when they were hailed by a party of Indians, and ordered to land. This they of course refused, when immediately they were fired upon, and Wetzel was shot through the body. Feeling himself mortally wounded, he directed his companion to lie down in the canoe, while he, (Wetzel,) so long as strength remained, would paddle the frail vessel beyond reach of the savages. In this way he saved the life of his friend, while his own was ebbing fast. He died soon after reaching the shore, at Baker's station, and his humble grave can still be seen near the site of that primitive fortress. A rough stone marks the spot, bearing, in rude but perfectly distinct characters, "J. W., 1787."

Martin Wetzel made Captive—Kills Three Savages.

Martin, who was the oldest of the family, was once surprised and taken prisoner by the Indians, and remained with them a long time. By his cheerful disposition and apparent satisfaction with their mode of life, he disarmed their suspicion, acquired their confidence, and was adopted into one of their families.

He was free, hunted around the town, returned, danced and frolicked with the young Indians, and appeared perfectly satisfied with his change of life. But all the time his heart was brooding on an escape, which he wished to render memorable by some tragic act of revenge upon his confiding enemies. In the Fall of the year, Martin and three Indians set off to make a Fall hunt. They pitched their camp near the head of Sandusky river. When the hunt commenced, he was very careful to return first in the evening to the camp, prepare wood for the night, and do all other little offices of camp duty to render them comfortable. By this means he lulled any lurking suspicion which they might entertain towards him. While hunting one evening, some distance from the camp, he came across one of his Indian camp-mates. Martin watched for a favorable moment, and as the Indian's attention was called in a different direction, he shot him down, scalped him, and threw his body into a deep hole, which had been made by a large tree torn up by the roots, and covered his body with logs and brush, over which he strewed leaves to conceal the body. He then hurried to the camp to prepare, as usual, wood for the night.

When night came, one of the Indians was missing, and Martin expressed great concern on account of the absence of their comrade. The other Indians did not appear to be the least concerned at the absence of their companion; they both alleged that he might have taken a large circle, looking for new hunting ground, or that he might have pursued some wounded game till it was too late to return to camp. In this mood the subject was dismissed for the night; they ate their supper and lay down to sleep. Martin's mind was so full of the thoughts of home, and of taking signal vengeance on his enemies, that he could not sleep; he had gone too far to retreat, and whatever was done must be done quickly. Being now determined to effect his escape at all hazards, the question he had to decide was whether he should make attack on the two sleeping Indians, or watch for a favorable opportunity of dispatching them one at a time. The latter plan appeared to him to be less subject to risk or failure. The next morning he prepared to put his determination into execution.

When the two Indians set out on their hunt, he determined to follow one of them (like a true hunting dog on a slow trail) till a fair opportunity should present itself of dispatching him without alarming his fellow. He cautiously pursued him till near evening, when he openly walked to him, and commenced a conversation about their day's hunt. The Indian being completely off his guard, suspecting no danger, Martin watched for a favorable moment, when the Indian's attention was drawn to a different direction, and with one sweep of his vengeful tomahawk laid him lifeless on the ground, scalped him, tumbled his body into a sink-hole and covered it with brush and logs. He then made his way to the camp, with a firm determination of closing the bloody tragedy by killing the third Indian. He went out and composedly waited at the camp for the return of the Indian. About sunset he saw him coming, with a load of game that he had killed swung on his back. Martin went forward under the pretense of aiding to disencumber him of his load. When the Indian stooped down to be detached of his load Martin, with one fell swoop of his tomahawk, laid him in death's eternal sleep. Being now in no danger of pursuit, he leisurely packed up what plunder he could conveniently carry with him, and made his way to the white settlements, where he safely arrived with the three Indian scalps, after an absence of nearly a year.

JOHN WETZEL ON A HORSE-STEALING EXPEDITION.

In the year 1791 or '92, the Indians having made frequent incursions into the settlements along the river Ohio, between Wheeling and the Mingo Bottom, sometimes killing or capturing whole families; at other times stealing all the horses belonging to a station or fort, a company consisting of seven men, rendezvoused at a place called the Beech Bottom, on the Ohio river, a few miles below where Wellsburg, W. Va., has been erected. This company were John Wetzel, William M'Cullough, John Hough, Thomas Biggs, Joseph Hedges, Kinzie Dickerson, and a Mr. Linn. Their avowed object was to go to the Indian town to steal horses. This was then considered a legal, honorable business, as the border was then at open war with the Indians. It would only be retaliating upon them in their own way. These seven men were all trained to Indian warfare and a life in the woods from their youth. Perhaps the western frontier, at no time, could furnish seven men whose souls were better fitted, and whose nerves and sinews were better strung to perform any enterprise which required resolution and firmness.

They crossed the Ohio, and proceeded with cautious steps and vigilant glances on their way through the cheerless, dark and almost impenetrable forest in the Indian country, till they came to an Indian town, near where the head waters of the Sandusky and Muskingum rivers interlock. Here they made a fine haul, and set off homeward with about fifteen horses. They traveled rapidly, only making a short halt, to let their horses graze and breathe a short time to recruit their strength and activity. In the evening of the second day of their rapid retreat, they arrived at Wells Creek, not far from where the town of Cambridge, Ohio, has been since erected. Here Mr. Linn was taken violently sick, and they must stop their march, or leave him alone to perish in the dark and lonely woods. Our frontiermen, notwithstanding their rough and unpolished manners, had too much of my Uncle Toby's "sympathy for suffering humanity," to forsake a comrade in distress. They halted, and placed sentinels on their back trail, who remained there till late in the night, without seeing any signs of being pursued. The sentinels then returned to the camp, Mr. Linn still lying in excruciating pain. All the simple remedies in their power were administered to the sick man, without producing any effect.

Being late in the night, they all lay down to rest, except one who was placed as guard. Their camp was on a small branch. Just before daybreak the guard took a small bucket, and dipped some water out of the stream; on carrying it to the fire he discovered the water to be muddy. The muddy water waked his suspicion that the enemy might be approaching them and be walking down in the stream, as their footsteps would be noiseless in the water. He waked his companions, and communicated his suspicion. They arose, examined the branch a little distance, and listened attentively for some time, but neither saw nor heard anything, and then concluded it must have been raccoons, or some other animals paddling in the stream. After this conclusion the company all lay down to rest, except the sentinel, who was stationed just outside of the light. Happily for them the fire had burned down, and only a few coals afforded a dim light to point out where they lay.

The enemy had come silently down the creek, as the sentinel suspected, to within ten or twelve feet of the place where they lay, and fired several guns over the bank. Mr. Linn, the sick man, was lying with his side towards the bank, and received nearly all the balls which were at first fired.

The Indians then, with tremendous yells, mounted the bank with loaded rifles, war clubs and tomahawks, rushed upon our men, who fled barefooted, and without arms. Mr. Linn, Thomas Biggs and Joseph Hedges were killed in and near the camp. William M'Cullough had run but a short distance when he was fired at by the enemy. At the instant the firing was given, he jumped into a quagmire and fell; the Indians supposing that they had killed him, ran past in pursuit of others. He soon extricated himself out of the mire, and so made his escape. He fell in with John Hough, and came into Wheeling. John Wetzel and Kinzie Dickerson met in their retreat, and returned together. Those who made their escape were without arms, without clothing or provisions. Their sufferings were great; but this they bore with stoical indifference, as it was the fortune of war. Whether the Indians who defeated our heroes followed in pursuit from their towns, or were a party of warriors, who accidentally happened to fall in with them, has never been ascertained. From the place they had stolen the horses, they had traveled two nights and almost two entire days, without halting, except just a few minutes at a time, to let the horses graze. From the circumstance of their rapid retreat with the horses, it was supposed that no pursuit could possibly have overtaken them, but that fate had decreed that this party of Indians should meet and defeat them. As soon as the stragglers arrived at Wheeling, Captain John M'Cullough collected a party of men, and went to Wells Creek and buried the unfortunate men who fell in and near the camp. The Indians had mangled the dead bodies at a most barbarous rate. Thus was closed this horse-stealing tragedy. Those who survived this tragedy continued to hunt and to fight as long as the war lasted. John Wetzel and Dickerson died in the country near Wheeling. John Hough died near Columbia, Ohio. The brave Captain William M'Cullough fell in 1812, in the campaign with General Hull.

John Wetzel Captures an Obstinate Savage.

John Wetzel and Veach Dickerson associated to go on an Indian scout. They crossed the Ohio at the Mingo Bottom, three miles below where the town of Steubenville has since been constructed. They set off with the avowed intention of bringing an Indian prisoner. They painted and dressed in complete Indian style, and could talk some in their language. What induced them to undertake this hazardous enterprise is now unknown; perhaps the novelty and danger of the undertaking prompted them to action. No reward was given for either prisoners or scalps; nor were they employed or paid by government. Every man fought on his own hook, furnished his own arms and ammunition, and carried his own baggage. This was, to all intents, a democratic war, as every one fought as often and as long as he pleased; either by himself, or with such company as he could confide in. As the white men on the frontier took but few prisoners, Wetzel and Dickerson concluded to change the practice, and bring in an Indian to make a pet.

Whatever whim may have induced them, they set off with the avowed intention of bringing in a prisoner, or losing their own scalps in the attempt. They pushed through the Indian country with silent tread and a keen lookout, till they went near the head of the Sandusky river, where they came near a small Indian village. They concealed themselves close to a path which appeared to be considerably traveled. In the course of the first day of their ambush, they saw several small companies of Indians pass them. As it was not their wish to raise an alarm among the enemy, they permitted them to pass undisturbed. In the evening of the next day they saw two Indians coming sauntering along the road in quite a merry mood. They immediately stepped into the road, and with a confident air, as if they were meeting friends, went forward until they came within reach of the enemy. Wetzel now drew his tomahawk, and with one sweep knocked an Indian down; at the same instant Dickerson grasped the other in his arms, and threw him on the ground. By this time Wetzel had killed the other, and turned his hand to aid in fastening the prisoner. This completed, they scalped the dead Indian, and set off with the prisoner for home.

They traveled all night on the war path leading towards Wheeling. In the morning they struck off from the path, and making diverse courses, and keeping on the hardest ground, where their feet would make the least impression, they pushed along till they had crossed the Muskingum some distance, when their prisoner began to show a restive, stubborn disposition; he finally threw himself on the ground and refused to rise. He held down his head, and told them they might tomahawk him as soon as they pleased, for he was determined to go no farther. They used every argument they could think of to induce him to proceed, but without any effect. He said he would prefer dying in his native woods than to preserve his life a little longer, and at last be tortured by fire, and his body mangled for sport, when they took him to their towns. They assured him his life would be spared, and that he would be well used and treated with plenty. But all their efforts would not induce him to rise to his feet. The idea that he would be put to death for sport, or in revenge, in presence of a large number of spectators, who would enjoy with rapture the scenes of his torture and death, had taken such a strong hold of his mind, that he determined to disappoint the possibility of their being gratified at his expense. As it was not their wish to kill him from coaxing they concluded to try if a hickory, well applied, would not bend his stubborn soul. This, too, failed to have any effect. He appeared to be as callous and indifferent to the lash as if he had been a cooper's horse. What invincible resolution and fortitude was evinced by this son of the forest! Finding all their efforts to urge him forward ineffectual, they determined to put him to death. They then tomahawked and scalped him, and left his body a prey to the wild beasts of the forest and to the birds of the air. The scalp-hunters then returned home with their two scalps; but vexed and disappointed that they could not bring with them the prisoner.

JACOB WETZEL AND SIMON KENTON ATTACK AN INDIAN CAMP.

Of Jacob Wetzel's history, writes McDonald, I can give but a meagre account, although I have heard of many of his exploits in the old Indian war. But my recollection of them is so indistinct and confused, that I will not attempt to relate but one of the numerous fights in which he was engaged. In that battle he had a comrade who was his equal in intrepidity, and his superior in that cautious prudence which constitutes the efficient warrior. That headstrong fury with which many of our old frontiermen rushed into danger, was the cause of many distressing disasters. They frequently, by their headlong course, performed such successful actions, that if any military exploits deserve the character of sublime, they were eminently such.

The following relation I had from General Kenton. He and Wetzel made arrangements to make a Fall hunt together, and for that purpose they went into the hilly country near the mouth of the Kentucky river. When they arrived where they intended to make their hunt, they discovered some signs of Indians having preoccupied the ground. It would have been out of character in a Kenton and a Wetzel to retreat without first ascertaining the description and number of the enemy. They determined to find the Indian camp, which they believed was at no great distance from them, as they had heard reports of guns late in the evening and early the next morning in the same direction. This convinced them that the camp was at no great distance from the firing. Our heroes moved cautiously about, making as little sign as possible, that they might not be discovered by the enemy. Towards evening of the second day after they arrived on the ground, they discovered the Indian camp.

They kept themselves concealed, determined, as soon as night approached, to reconnoitre the situation and number of the enemy; and then govern their future operations as prudence might dictate. They found five Indians in the camp. Having confidence in themselves and in their usual good fortune, they concluded to attack them boldly. Contrary to military rules, they agreed to defer the attack till light. In military affairs it is a general rule to avoid night fights, except where small numbers intend to assault a larger force. The night is then chosen, as in the darkness the numbers of the assailants being uncertain, may produce panics and confusion, which may give the victory to far inferior numbers. Our heroes chose daylight and an open field for the fight. There was a large fallen tree lying near the camp; this would serve as a rampart for defence and would also serve to conceal them from observation till the battle commenced. They took their station behind the log, and there lay till broad daylight, when they were able to draw a clear bead.

Jacob Wetzel had a double-barreled rifle. Their guns were cocked—they took aim, and gave the preconcerted signal—fired, and two Indians fell. As quick as thought, Wetzel fired his second load, and down fell the third Indian. Their number was now equal, so they bounded over the log, screaming and yelling at the highest pitch of their voices, to strike terror into their remaining enemies, and were among them before they recovered from the sudden surprise. The two remaining Indians, without arms, took to their heels, and ran in different directions. Kenton pursued one, whom he soon overhauled, tomahawked and scalped, and then returned with the bloody trophy to the camp. Shortly after Wetzel returned with the scalp of the fifth Indian. This was a wholesale slaughter, that but few except such men as Kenton and Wetzel would have attempted.

LEWIS WETZEL, THE BOONE OF WEST VIRGINIA.

> Stout-hearted Lewis Wetzel
> Rode down the river shore,
> The wilderness behind him
> And the wilderness before.—*Plympton.*

But of all the Wetzel family Lewis was the most famous. Without him the history of Northwestern Virginia would be like the "play of Hamlet with Hamlet left out." His presence was a tower of strength to the settlers, and for many years he was esteemed the right arm of their defence. With most of the famed hunters of the west, Indian fighting was only an episode—frequently a compulsory one—of their stormy lives, but with Wetzel it was a *life business*. He plunged recklessly into the fearful strife, and was never contented unless roaming the wilderness solitudes, trailing the savages to their very homes and rushing to combat, regardless of time, place or numbers. Bold, wary and tireless, he stood without an equal in the perilous profession to which he had sworn to devote himself.

No man on the western frontier was more dreaded by the enemy, and none did more to beat him back into the heart of the forest, and reclaim the expanseless domain which we now enjoy. By many he is regarded as little better than a semi-savage—a man whose disposition was that of an enraged tiger—whose only propensity was for blood, but this De Hass (excellent authority) asserts was not true. He was never known to inflict unwonted cruelty upon women and children, as has been charged upon him; and he never was found to torture or mutilate his victim, as many of the traditions would indicate. He was revengeful, because he had suffered deep injury at the hands of that race, and woe to the Indian warrior who crossed his path. He was literally a man without fear. He was brave as a lion, cunning as a fox; "daring where daring was the wiser part—prudent when discretion was valor's better self." He seemed to possess, in a remarkable degree, that intuitive knowledge which can alone constitute a good and efficient hunter, added to which, he was sagacious, prompt to act, and always aiming to render his actions efficient. Such was Lewis Wetzel, the celebrated Indian hunter of Western Virginia.

At the time of his father's death, Lewis was about twenty-three years of age, and, in common with his brothers, or those who were old enough, swore sleepless vengeance against the whole Indian race. Terribly did he and they carry that resolution into effect. From that time forward, they were devoted to the woods; and an Indian, whether in peace or war, at night or by day, was a doomed man in the presence of either. The name of Wetzel sent a thrill of horror through the heart of the stoutest savage, before whom a more terrible image could not be conjured up than one of these relentless "Long Knives."

The first event worthy of record, in the life of our hero, occurred when he was about fourteen years of age. The Indians had not been very troublesome in the immediate vicinity of his father's, and no great apprehensions were felt, as it was during a season of comparative quietude. On the occasion referred to, Lewis had just stepped from his father's door, and was looking at his brother Jacob playing, when, suddenly turning toward the corn crib, he saw a gun pointing around the corner. Quick as thought he jumped back, but not in time to escape the ball; it took effect upon the breast bone, carrying away a small portion, and cutting a fearful wound athwart the chest. In an instant, two athletic warriors sprang from behind the crib, and quietly making prisoners of the lads, bore them off without being discovered. On the second day they reached the Ohio, and crossing near the mouth of McMahan's Creek, gained the Big Lick, about twenty miles from the river.

During the whole of this painful march, Lewis suffered severely from his wound, but bore up with true courage, knowing that if he complained, the tomahawk would be his doom. That night, on lying down, the Indians, contrary to their custom, failed to tie their prisoners. Lewis now resolved to escape, and in the course of an hour or so, satisfying himself that the Indians were asleep, touched Jacob, and both arose without disturbing their captors. Lewis, leading the way, pushed into the woods. Finding, however, that he could not travel without moccasins, he returned to the camp and soon came back with two pair, which, having fitted on, Lewis said: "Now I must go back for father's gun." Securing this, the two boys started for home. Finding the path, they traveled on briskly for some time; but hearing a noise, listened and ascertained the Indians were in pursuit. The lads stepped aside as the pursuers came up, and then again moved on. Soon they heard the Indians return, and by the same plan effectually eluded them. Before daylight they were again followed by two on horseback, but, resorting to a similar expedient, readily escaped detection. On the following day, about eleven o'clock, the boys reached the Ohio, at a point opposite Zane's Island. Lashing together two logs, they crossed over, and were once more with their friends.

Lewis Wetzel Slays Three Savages by Loading as He Runs.
SEE PAGE 329.

LEWIS WETZEL KILLS THREE SAVAGES IN A RUNNING FIGHT.

Shortly after Crawford's defeat, a man named Thomas Mills, in escaping from that unfortunate expedition, reached the Indian Spring, about nine miles from Wheeling, on the present National Road, where he was compelled to leave his horse and proceed to Wheeling on foot. Thence he went to Van Metre's Fort, and, after a day or two of rest, induced Lewis Wetzel to go with him to the spring for his horse. Lewis cautioned him against the danger, but Mills was determined, and the two started. Approaching the spring, they discovered the horse tied to a tree, and Wetzel at once comprehended their danger. Mills walked up to unfasten the animal, when instantly a discharge of rifles followed, and the unfortunate man fell, mortally wounded.

Wetzel now turned, and, knowing his only escape was in flight, plunged through the enemy, and bounded off at the very extent of his speed. Four fleet Indians followed in rapid pursuit, whooping in proud exultation of soon overhauling their intended victim. After a chase of half a mile, one of the most active savages approached so close that Wetzel was afraid he might throw his tomahawk, and instantly wheeling, shot the fellow dead in his tracks.

In early youth Lewis had acquired the habit of loading his gun while at a full run, and now he felt the great advantage of it. Keeping in advance of his pursuers during another half mile, a second Indian came up, and, turning to fire, the savage caught the end of his gun, and, for a time, the contest was doubtful. At one moment the Indian, by his great strength and dexterity, brought Wetzel to his knee, and had nearly wrenched the rifle from the hands of his antagonist, when Lewis, by a renewed effort, drew the weapon from the grasp of the savage, and, thrusting the muzzle against the side of his neck, pulled the trigger, killing him instantly. The two other Indians, by this time, had nearly overtaken him; but leaping forward, he kept ahead, until his unerring rifle was a third time loaded.

Anxious to have done with that kind of sport, he slackened his pace, and even stopped once or twice to give his pursuers an opportunity to face him. Every time, however, he looked round, the Indians treed, unwilling any longer to encounter his destructive weapon. After running a mile or two farther in this manner, he reached an open piece of ground, and, wheeling suddenly, the foremost Indian jumped behind a tree, but which, not screening his body, Wetzel fired, and dangerously wounded him. The remaining Indian made an immediate retreat, yelling as he went, "*No catch dat man, him gun alway loaded.*"

In the Summer of 1786, the Indians having become troublesome in the neighborhood of Wheeling, particularly in the Short Creek settlement, and a party having killed a man near Mingo Bottom, it was determined to send an expedition after the retreating enemy, of sufficient force to chastise them most effectually. A subscription or pony purse was made up, and one hundred dollars were offered to the man who should bring in the first Indian scalp. Major McMahan, living at Beach Bottom, headed the expedition, and Lewis Wetzel was one of his men They crossed the river on the 5th of August, and proceeded, by a rapid march, to the Muskingum. The expedition numbered about twenty men; and an advance of five were detailed to reconnoitre. This party reported to the commander that they had discovered the camp of the enemy, but that it was far too numerous to think of making an attack. A consultation was thereupon held, and an immediate retreat determined on.

During the conference Lew. Wetzel sat upon a log, with his gun carelessly resting across his knees. The moment it was resolved to retreat, most of the party started in disordered haste; but the commander, observing Wetzel still sitting on the log, turned to inquire if he was not going along. "No," was his sullen reply; "I came out to hunt Indians, and now that they are found, I am not going home, like a fool, with my fingers in my mouth. I am determined to take an Indian scalp or lose my own." All arguments were unavailing, and there they were compelled to leave him: a lone man, in a desolate wilderness, surrounded by an enemy—vigilant, cruel, bloodthirsty, and of horrid barbarity— with no friend but his rifle, and no guide but the sure index which an All-Wise Providence has deep set in the heavens above. Once by himself, and looking around to feel satisfied that they were all gone, he gathered his blanket about him, adjusted his tomahawk and scalping knife, shouldered his rifle, and moved off in an opposite direction, hoping that a small party of Indians might be met with. Keeping away from the larger streams, he strolled on cautiously, peering into every dell and suspicious cover, and keenly sensitive to the least sound of a dubious character.

Nothing, however, crossed his path that day. The night being dark and chilly, it was necessary to have a fire; but to show a light, in the midst of his enemy, would be to invite to certain destruction. To avoid this, he constructed a small coal pit out of bark, dried leaves, etc., and covering these with loose earth, leaving an occasional air hole, he seated himself, encircling the pit with his legs, and then completed the whole by covering his head with the blanket. In this manner he would produce a temperature equal, as he expressed it, to that of a "stove room." This was certainly an original and ingenious mode of getting up a fire, without, at the same time, endangering himself by a light.

During most of the following day he roamed through the forest without noticing any "signs" of Indians. At length smoke was discovered, and going in the direction of it, he found a camp, but tenantless. It contained two blankets and a small kettle, which Wetzel at once knew belonged to two Indians, who were, doubtless, out hunting. Concealing himself in the matted undergrowth, he patiently awaited the return of the occupants. About sunset, one of the Indians came in and made up the fire, and went to cooking his supper. Shortly after, the other came in. They ate their supper, and began to sing, and amuse themselves by telling comic stories, at which they would burst into roars of laughter. Singing and telling amusing stories, was the common practice of the white and redmen, when lying in their hunting camps.

About nine or ten o'clock, one of the Indians wrapped his blanket around him, shouldered his rifle, took a chunk of fire in his hand and left the camp, doubtless with the intention of going to watch a deerlick. The fire and smoke would serve to keep off the gnats and mosquitoes. It is a remarkable fact, that deer are not alarmed at seeing fire, from the circumstance of meeting it so frequently in the Fall and Winter seasons, when the leaves and grass are dry, and the woods on fire. The absence of the Indian was a cause of vexation and disappointment to our hero, whose trap was so happily set that he considered his game secure. He still indulged the hope that the Indian would return to camp before day, but in this he was disappointed. There are birds in the woods which commence chirping just before break of day, and, like the cock, give notice to the woodsman that light will soon appear. Lewis heard the wooded songsters begin to chatter, and determined to delay no longer the work of death for the return of the other Indian.

He walked to the camp with a noiseless step, and found his victim buried in profound sleep, lying upon one side. He drew his scalping knife, and with the utmost force, impelled by revenge, sent the blade through his heart. He said the Indian gave a short quiver, a convulsive motion, and then laid still in the sleep of death. Lewis scalped him, and set out for home. He arrived at the Mingo Bottom only one day after his unsuccessful companions. He claimed and received the reward.

He Shoots a Red Gobbler and Attacks a Camp of Four.

A most fatal decoy, on the frontier, was the turkey call. On several occasions, men from the fort at Wheeling had gone across the hill in quest of a turkey, whose plaintive cries had elicited their attention, and, on more than one occasion, the men never returned. Wetzel suspected the cause, and determined to satisfy himself. On the east side of the Creek Hill, and at a point elevated at least sixty feet above the water, there is a capacious cavern, (we have seen this cavern within the year,) the entrance to which, at that time, was almost obscured by a heavy growth of vines and foliage. Into this the alluring savage would crawl, and could there have an extensive view of the hill front on the opposite side. From that cavern issued the decoy of death to more than one incautious soldier and settler. Wetzel knew of the existence and exact locality of the cave, and accordingly started out before day, and, by a circuitous route, reached the spot from the rear. Posting himself so as to command a view of the opening, he waited patiently for the expected cry. Directly the twisted tuft of an Indian warrior slowly rose in the mouth of the cave, and, looking cautiously about, sent forth the long, shrill, peculiar "cry," sounding like chug-a-lug, chug-a-lug, chug-a-lug, chug, and immediately sank back out of view. Lewis screened himself in his position, cocked his gun, and anxiously waited for a reappearance of the head. In a few minutes up rose the tuft; Lewis drew a fine aim at the polished head, and the next instant the brains of the savage were scattered about the cave. *That* turkey troubled the inhabitants no longer, and tradition does not say whether the place was ever after similarly occupied.

A singular custom with this daring borderer was to take a Fall hunt into the Indian country. Equipping himself, he set out and penetrated to the Muskingum, and fell upon a camp of four Indians. Hesitating a moment, whether to attack a party so much his superior in numerical strength, he determined to make the attempt. At the hour of midnight, when naught was heard but the long, dismal howl of the wolf,

> "Cruel as death, and hungry as the grave,
> Burning for blood, bony, gaunt and grim,"

he moved cautiously from his covert, and, gliding through the darkness, stealthily approached the camp, supporting his rifle in one hand and a tomahawk in the other. A dim flicker from the camp fire faintly revealed the forms of the sleepers, wrapped in that profound slumber, which, to part of them, was to know no waking. There they lay, with their dark faces turned up to the night-sky, in the deep solitude of their own wilderness, little dreaming that their most relentless enemy was hovering over them.

Quietly resting his gun against a tree, he unsheathed his knife, and, with an intrepidity that could never be surpassed, stepped boldly forward like the minister of death, and, quick as thought, cleft the skull of one of his sleeping victims. In an instant, a second one was similarly served; and, as a third attempted to rise, confused by the horrid yells with which Wetzel accompanied his blows, he too shared the fate of his companions, and sank dead at the feet of his ruthless slayer. The fourth darted into the darkness of the woods and escaped, although Wetzel pursued him some distance. Returning to camp, he scalped his victims, and then left for home. When asked, on his return, what luck? "Not much," he replied. "I treed four Indians, but one got away." This unexampled achievement stamped him as one of the most daring, and, at the same time, successful hunters of his day. The distance to and from the scene of this adventure could not have been less than one hundred and seventy miles.

During one of his scouts in the immediate neighborhood of Wheeling, our hero took shelter, on a stormy evening, in a deserted cabin on the bottom, not far from what was then the residence of Mr. Hamilton Woods. Gathering a few broken boards, he prepared a place, in the loft, to sleep. Scarcely had he got himself adjusted for a nap when six Indians entered, and, striking a fire, commenced preparing their homely meal. Wetzel watched their movements closely, with drawn knife, determined, the moment he was discovered, to leap into their midst, and, in the confusion, endeavor to escape. Fortunately, they did not see him; and, soon after supper, the whole six fell asleep. Wetzel now crawled noiselessly down, and hid himself behind a log, at a convenient distance from the door of the cabin. At early dawn, a tall savage stepped from the door, and stretching up both hands in a long, hearty yawn, seemed to draw in new life from the pure, invigorating atmosphere. In an instant Wetzel had his finger upon the trigger, and the next moment the Indian fell heavily to the ground, his life's blood gushing upon the young grass, brilliant with the morning dew-drops. The report of the rifle had not ceased echoing through the valley, ere the daring borderer was far away, secure from all pursuit.

Some time after General Harmar had erected a fort at the mouth of the Muskingum river, where Marietta now stands, about 1789, he employed some white men to go, with a flag, among the nearest Indian tribes, to prevail with them to come to the fort, and there to conclude a treaty of peace. A large number of Indians came, on the general invitation, and encamped on the Muskingum river, a few miles above its mouth. General Harmar issued a proclamation, giving notice that a cessation of arms was mutually agreed upon, between the white and redmen, till an effort for a treaty of peace should be concluded.

As treaties of peace with Indians had been so frequently violated, but little faith was placed in the stability of such engagements by the frontiermen; notwithstanding that they were as frequently the aggressors as were the Indians. Half the backwoodsmen of that day had been born in a fort, and grew to manhood, as it were, in a siege. The Indian war had continued so long, and was so bloody, that they believed war with them was to continue as long as both survived to fight. With these impressions, as they considered the Indians faithless, it was difficult to inspire confidence in the stability of treaties. While General Harmar was diligently engaged with the Indians, endeavoring to make peace, Lewis Wetzel concluded to go to Fort Harmar, and, as the Indians would be passing and repassing between their camp and the fort, he would have a fair opportunity of killing one.

He associated with himself in this enterprise, a man named Veach Dickerson, who was only a small grade below him in restless daring. As soon as the enterprise was resolved on, they were impatient to put it in execution. The more danger, the more excited and impatient they were to execute their plan. They set off without delay, and arrived at the desired point, and sat themselves down in ambush, near the path leading from the fort to the Indian camp. Shortly after they had concealed themselves by the wayside, they saw an Indian approaching on horseback, running his horse at full speed. They called to him, but, owing to the clatter of the horse's feet, he did not hear or heed their call, but kept on at a sweeping gallop. When the Indian had nearly passed, they concluded to give him a shot as he rode. They fired; but, as the Indian did not fall, they thought they had missed him.

As the alarm would soon be spread that an Indian had been shot at, and as large numbers of them were near at hand, they commenced an immediate retreat to their home. As their neighbors knew the object of their expedition, as soon as they returned they were asked, what luck? Wetzel answered that they had bad luck—they had seen but one Indian, and he on horseback—that they had fired at him as he rode, but he did not fall, but went off scratching his back, as if he had been stung by a yellowjacket. The truth was, they had shot him through the hips and lower part of the belly. He rode to the fort, and that night expired of his wounds. It proved to be a large, fine-looking savage, of considerable celebrity, and known by the name of George Washington.

It was soon rumored to General Harmar that Lewis Wetzel was the murderer. General Harmar sent a Captain Kingsbury, with a company of men, to the Mingo Bottom, with orders to take Wetzel, alive or dead—a useless and impotent order. A company of men could as easily have drawn Beelzebub out of the bottomless pit, as take Lewis Wetzel, by force, from the Mingo Bottom settlement. On the day that Captain Kingsbury arrived, there was a shooting match in the neighborhood, and Lewis was there. As soon as the object of Captain Kingsbury was ascertained, it was resolved to ambush the Captain's barge, and kill him and his company.

Happily Major McMahan was present to prevent this catastrophe, who prevailed on Wetzel and his friends to suspend the attack till he would pay Captain Kingsbury a visit; perhaps he would induce him to return without making an attempt to take Wetzel. With a great deal of reluctance, they agreed to suspend the attack till Major McMahan should return. The resentment and fury of Wetzel and his friends were boiling and blowing like the steam from a scape pipe of a steamboat. "A pretty affair this," said they, "to hang a man for killing an Indian, when they are killing some of our men almost every day." Major McMahan informed Captain Kingsbury of the force and fury of the people, and assured him that, if he persisted in the attempt to seize Wetzel, he would have all the settlers in the country upon him; that nothing could save him and his fellows from massacre but a speedy return. The Captain took his advice, and forthwith returned to Fort Harmar. Wetzel considered the affair now as finally adjusted.

As Lewis was never long stationary, but ranged, at will, along the river from Fort Pitt to the Falls of the Ohio, and was a welcome guest and perfectly at home wherever he went, shortly after the attempt to seize him by Captain Kingsbury, he got into a canoe, with the intention of proceeding down the Ohio to Kentucky. He had a friend, by the name of Hamilton Carr, who had lately settled on the island near Fort Harmar. Here he stopped, with the view of lodging for the night. By some means, which never were explained, General Harmar was advised of his being on the island. A guard was sent, who crossed to the island, surrounded Mr. Carr's house, went in, and, as Wetzel lay asleep, he was seized by numbers, his hands and feet securely bound, and he was hurried off into a boat, and from thence placed in a guard-room, where he was loaded with irons.

Handcuffed by General Harmar and Makes his Escape.

The ignominy of wearing iron handcuffs and hobbles, and being chained down, to a man of his independent and resolute spirit, was more painful than death. Shortly after he was confined, he sent for General Harmar, and requested a visit. The General went. Wetzel admitted, without hesitation, "that he had shot the Indian." As he did not wish to be hung like a dog, he requested the General to give him up to the Indians, there being a large number of them present. "He might place them all in a circle, with their scalping knives and tomahawks, and give him a tomahawk and place him in the midst of the circle, and then let him and the Indians fight it out the best way they could." The General told him, "that he was an officer appointed by the law, by which he must be governed. As the law did not authorize him to make such a compromise, he could not grant his request." After a few days' longer confinement, he again sent for the General to come and see him; and he did so. Wetzel said "he had never been confined, and could not live much longer if he was not permitted some room to walk about in."

The General ordered the officer on guard to knock off his iron fetters, but to leave on his handcuffs, and permit him to walk about on the point at the mouth of the Muskingum; but to be sure and keep a close watch upon him. As soon as they were outside the fort gate, Lewis began to caper and dance about like a wild colt broke loose from the stall. He would start and run a few yards, as if he was about making an escape, then turn round and join the guards. The next start he would run farther, and then stop. In this way he amused the guard for some time, at every start running a little farther. At length he called forth all his strength, resolution and activity, and determined on freedom or an early grave. He gave a sudden spring forward, and bounded off at the top of his speed for the shelter of his beloved woods. His movement was so quick, and so unexpected, that the guards were taken by surprise, and he got nearly a hundred yards before they recovered from their astonishment. They fired, but all missed; they followed in pursuit, but he soon left them out of sight.

As he was well acquainted with the country, he made for a dense thicket, about two or three miles from the fort. In the midst of this thicket, he found a tree which had fallen across a log, where the brush was very close. Under this tree he squeezed his body. The brush was so thick that he could not be discovered unless his pursuers examined very closely. As soon as his escape was announced, General Harmar started the soldiers and Indians in pursuit. After he had lain about two hours in his place of concealment, two Indians came into the thicket, and stood on the same log under which he lay concealed; his heart beat so violently he was afraid they would hear it thumping. He could hear them hallooing in every direction as they hunted through the brush. At length, as the evening wore away the day, he found himself alone in the friendly thicket. But what should he do? His hands were fastened with iron cuffs and bolts, and he knew of no friend, on the same side of the Ohio, to whom he could apply for assistance.

He had a friend who had recently put up a cabin on the Virginia side of the Ohio, who, he had no doubt, would lend him every assistance in his power. But to cross the river was the difficulty. He could not make a raft with his hands bound, and though an excellent swimmer, it would be risking too much to trust himself to the stream in that disabled condition. With the most gloomy foreboding of the future, he left the thicket as soon as the shades of night began to gather, and directed his way to the Ohio, by a circuitous route, which brought him to a lonely spot, three or four miles below the fort. He made to this place, as he expected guards would be set at every point where he could find a canoe. On the opposite shore he saw an acquaintance, Isaac Wiseman by name, fishing in a canoe. Not daring to call to him, as he could not know whether his enemies were not within sound of his voice, he waved his hat for some time to attract the notice of his friend, having previously induced him to direct his eye that course by a gentle splashing in the water.

This brought Wiseman to his assistance, who readily aided his escape. Once on the Virginia shore he had nothing to fear, as he had well-wishers all through the country, who would have shed blood, if necessary, for his defence. It was not, however, until years had elapsed, and General Harmar returned to Philadelphia, that it became safe for Wiseman to avow the act, such was the weakness of civil authority and the absolute supremacy of military rule on the frontier. A file and hammer soon released him from the heavy handcuffs. After the night's rest had recruited his energies, he set out for fresh adventures, his friend having supplied him with a rifle, ammunition and blanket. He took a canoe and went down the river for Kentucky, where he should feel safe from the grasp of Harmar and his myrmidons.

Subsequently to Wetzel's escape, General Harmar removed his headquarters to Fort Washington, Cincinnati. One of his first official acts there, was to issue a proclamation, offering considerable rewards for the apprehension and delivery of Lewis at the garrison there. No man, however, was found base or daring enough to attempt this service.

On his way down Wetzel landed at Point Pleasant, and, following his usual humor, when he had no work among Indians on the carpet, ranged the town, for a few days, with as much unconcern as if he were on his own farm. Lieutenant Kingsbury, attached to Harmar's own command, happened to be at the mouth of the Kanawha at the time, and scouting about, while ignorant of Wetzel's presence, met him—unexpectedly to both parties. Lewis, being generally on the *qui vive*, saw Kingsbury first, and halted with great firmness in the path, leaving to the Lieutenant to decide his own course of procedure, feeling himself prepared and ready, whatever that might be. Kingsbury, a brave man himself, had too much good feeling toward such a gallant spirit as Wetzel to attempt his injury, if it were even safe to do so. He contented himself with saying, "*Get out of my sight, you Indian killer!*" And Lewis, who was implacable to the savage only, retired slowly and watchfully, as a lion draws off measuring his steps in the presence of the hunters, being as willing to avoid unnecessary danger as to seek it when duty called him to act.

He regained his canoe and put off for Limestone, Ky., at which place, and at Washington, the county town, he established his headquarters for some time. Here he engaged on hunting parties, or went out with the scouts after Indians. When not actually engaged in such service, he filled up his leisure hours at shooting matches, foot racing or wrestling with other hunters. Major Fowler, of Washington, who knew him well during this period, described him as a general favorite, no less from his personal qualities than for his services.

While engaged in these occupations at Maysville, Lieutenant Lawler, of the regular army, who was going down the Ohio to Fort Washington, in what was called a Kentucky boat, full of soldiers, landed at Maysville, and found Wetzel sitting in one of the taverns. Returning to the boat, he ordered out a file of soldiers, seized Wetzel and dragged him on board the boat, and, without a moment's delay, pushed off, and that same night delivered him to General Harmar, at Cincinnati, by whom the prisoner was again put in irons, preparatory to his trial and consequent condemnation, for what Lewis disdained to deny or conceal, the killing of the Indian at Marietta. But Harmar, like St. Clair, although acquainted with the routine of military service, was destitute of that practical good sense, always indispensable in frontier settlements, in which such severe measures were more likely to rouse the settlers to flame than to intimidate them; and soon found the country around him in arms.

The story of Wetzel's captivity—captured and liable to punishment for shooting an Indian merely—spread through the settlement like wildfire, kindling the passions of the frontiermen to a high pitch of fury.

Petitions for his release came in to General Harmar, from all quarters and all classes of society. To these, at first, he paid little attention. At length the settlements along the Ohio, and some even of the back counties, began to embody in military array to release the prisoner *vi et armis*. Representations were made to Judge Symmes, which induced him to issue a writ of *habeas corpus* in the case. John Clawson, and other hunters of Columbia, who had gone down to attend his trial, went security for Wetzel's good behavior; and, being discharged, he was escorted with great triumph to Columbia, and treated at that place to his supper, etc.

HIS HAIR REACHED TO HIS CALVES—THRILLING ADVENTURE.

Judge Foster, who gave these last particulars, described him at this period, (August 26th, 1789,) as about twenty-six years of age, about five feet ten inches high. He was full breasted, very broad across the shoulders; his arms were large; skin, darker than the other brothers; his face, heavily pitted with the small-pox; his hair, of which he was very careful, reached, when combed out, to the calves of the legs; his eyes remarkably black and "piercing as the dagger's point," and, when excited, sparkling with such vindictive glances as to indicate plainly it was hardly safe to provoke him to wrath. He was taciturn in mixed company, although the fiddle of the party among his social friends and acquaintances. His morals and habits, compared with those of his general associates and the tone of society in the West of that day, were quite exemplary. He certainly had a rare scalp—one for which the savages would at any time have given a dozen of their best warriors.

Shortly after his return from Kentucky, a relative, from Dunkard Creek, invited Lewis home with him. The invitation was accepted, and the two leisurely wended their way along, hunting and sporting as they traveled. On reaching the home of the young man, what should they see but, instead of the hospitable roof, a pile of smoking ruins! Wetzel immediately examined the trail, and found that the marauders were three Indians and one white man, and that they had taken one prisoner. That captive proved to be the betrothed of the young man, whom nothing could restrain from pushing on in immediate pursuit.

Placing himself under the direction of Wetzel, the two strode on, hoping to overhaul the enemy before they had crossed the Ohio. It was found, after proceeding a short distance, that the savages had taken great care to obliterate their trail; but the keen discernment of Wetzel once on the track, and there need not be much difficulty. He knew they would make for the river by the most expeditious route, and therefore, disregarding their trail, he pushed on, so as to head them at the crossing place. After an hour's hard travel, they struck a path which the deer had made, and which their sagacity had taught them to carry over knolls, in order to avoid the great curves of ravines. Wetzel followed the path because he knew it was almost in a direct line to the point at which he was aiming. Night coming on, the tireless and determined hunters partook of a hurried meal, then again pushed forward, guided by the lamps hung in the heavens above them, until, toward midnight, a heavy cloud shut out their light and obscured the path.

Early on the following morning they resumed the chase, and, descending from the elevated ridge, along which they had been passing for an hour or two, found themselves in a deep and quiet valley, which looked as though human steps had never before pressed its virgin soil. Traveling a short distance, they discovered fresh footsteps in the soft sand, and, upon close examination, the eye of Wetzel's companion detected the impress of a small shoe, with nail-heads around the heel, which he at once recognized as belonging to his affianced. Hour after hour the pursuit was kept up; now tracing the trail across the hills, over alluvium, and often detecting it where the wily captors had taken to the beds of streams. Late in the afternoon they found themselves approaching the Ohio, and, shortly after dark, discovered, as they struck the river, the camp of the enemy on the opposite side, and just below the mouth of Captina. Swimming the river, the two reconnoitered the position of the camp, and discovered the locality of the captive. Wetzel proposed waiting until daylight before making the attack, but the almost frantic lover was for immediate action. Wetzel, however, would listen to no suggestion, and thus they waited the break of day.

At early dawn the savages were up and preparing to leave, when Wetzel directed his companion to take good aim at the white renegade, while he would make sure work of one of the Indians. They fired at the same moment, and with fatal effect. Instantly the young man rushed forward to release the captive; and Wetzel, reloading, pursued the two Indians who had taken to the woods to ascertain the strength of the attacking party. Wetzel pursued a short distance, and then fired his rifle at random, to draw the Indians from their retreat. The trick succeeded, and they made after him with uplifted tomahawks, yelling at the height of their voices. The adroit hunter soon had his rifle loaded, and wheeling suddenly, discharged its contents through the body of his nearest pursuer. The other Indian now rushed impetuously forward, thinking to dispatch his enemy in a moment. Wetzel, however, kept dodging from tree to tree, and, being more fleet than the Indian, managed to keep ahead until his unerring gun was again loaded, when, turning, he fired, and the last of the party lay dead before him.

Soon after this, our hero determined to visit the extreme South, and for that purpose engaged on a flat boat about leaving for New Orleans. Many months elapsed before his friends heard anything of his whereabouts, and then it was to learn that he was in close confinement at New Orleans, under some weighty charge. What the exact nature of this charge was, has never been fully ascertained; but it is very certain he was imprisoned and treated like a felon for nearly two years. The charge is supposed to have been of some trivial character, and has been justly regarded as a great outrage. It was alleged, at the time of his arrest, to have been for uttering counterfeit coin; but this being disproved, it was then charged that he had been guilty of an *amour* with the wife of a Spaniard.

Of the nature of these charges, however, but little is known. He was finally released by the intervention of our government, and reached home by way of Philadelphia, to which city he had been sent from New Orleans. He remained but two days on Wheeling Creek after his return, and De Hass learned from several citizens who saw him then that his personal appearance was much changed. From the settlement he went to Wheeling, where he remained a few days, and then left again for the South, vowing vengeance against the person whom he believed to have been accessory to his imprisonment, and in degrading his person with the vile rust of a felon's chain. During his visit to Wheeling, he remained with George Cookis, a relative. Mrs. Cookis plagued him about getting married, and jocularly asked whether he ever intended to take a wife. "No," he replied, "there is no woman in this world for me, but I expect there is one in heaven."

After an absence of many months, he again returned to the neighborhood of Wheeling; but whether he avenged his real or imaginary wrongs upon the person of the Spaniard alluded to, is not known. His propensity to roam the woods was still as great as ever; and an incident occurred which showed that he had lost none of his cunning while undergoing incarceration at New Orleans. Returning homeward, from a hunt north of the Ohio, somewhat fatigued and a little careless of his movements, he suddenly espied an Indian, in the very act of raising his gun to fire. Both immediately sprang to trees, and there they stood for an hour, each afraid of the other.

What was to be done? To remain there the whole day, for it was then early in the morning, was out of the question. Now it was that the sagacity of Wetzel displayed itself over the child-like simplicity of the savage. Cautiously adjusting his bear-skin cap to the end of his ramrod—with the slightest, most dubious and hesitating motion, as though afraid to venture a glance—the cap protruded. An instant, a crack, and off was torn the fatal cap, by the sure ball of the vigilant savage. Leaping from his retreat, our hero rapidly advanced upon the astonished Indian, and ere the tomahawk could be brought to its work of death, the tawny foe sprang convulsively into the air, and, straightening as he descended, fell upon his face quite dead.

Wetzel was universally regarded as one of the most efficient scouts and most practiced woodsmen of the day. He was frequently engaged by parties who desired to hunt up and locate lands, but were afraid of the Indians. Under the protection of Lewis Wetzel, however, they felt safe, and thus he was often engaged for months at a time. Of those who became largely interested in western lands was John Madison, brother of James, afterward President Madison. He employed Lewis Wetzel to go with him through the Kanawha region. During their expedition they came upon a deserted hunter's camp, in which were concealed some goods. Each of them helped himself to a blanket, and that day, in crossing Little Kanawha, they were fired upon by a concealed party of Indians, and Madison was killed.

General Clark, the companion of Lewis in the celebrated tour across the Rocky Mountains, had heard much of Lewis Wetzel in Kentucky, and determined to secure his services in the perilous enterprise. A messenger was accordingly sent for him, but he was reluctant to go. However, he finally consented, and accompanied the party during the first three months' travel, but then declined going any farther, and returned home. Shortly after this he left again, on a flat boat, and never returned. He visited a relative named Philip Sikes, living about twenty miles in the interior from Natchez, and there made his home until the Summer of 1808, when he died. The late venerable David McIntyre, of Belmont county, Ohio, one of the most reliable and respectable men in the State, said that he met Lewis Wetzel at Natchez, in April 1808, and remained with him three days. That Lewis told him he would visit his friends during the then approaching Summer. But, alas, that visit was never made! His journey was to "that undiscovered country, from whose bourne no traveler returns."

The number of scalps taken by the Wetzels in the course of the long Indian war, exceeds belief. There is no doubt they were very little short of one hundred. War was the business of their lives. They would prowl through the Indian country singly, suffer all the fatigues of hasty marches in bad weather, or starvation lying in close concealment, watching for a favorable opportunity to inflict death on the devoted victims who would be so unfortunate as to come within their vindictive grasp.

As to Martin and John Wetzel, wrote McDonald, I have but a faint recollection of their personal appearance. Jacob Wetzel was a large man, of full habit, but not corpulent. He was about six feet high, and weighed about two hundred pounds. He was a cheerful, pleasant companion, and in every respect as much of a gentleman in his manners as most of the frontiermen. They were all dark skinned and wore their hair, which was very long and thick, curled, and no part of it was suffered to be cut off. Lewis Wetzel had a full breast, and was very broad across the shoulders; his arms were large; his limbs were not heavy; his skin was darker than his brothers; his face considerably pitted by the small-pox; his hair, of which he was very careful, reached, when combed out, to the calves of his legs; his eyes were remarkably black, and when excited, (which was easily done,) they would sparkle with such a vindictive glance as almost to curdle the blood to look at him. In his appearance and gait there was something different from other men. Where he professed friendship, he was as true as the needle to the pole; his enmity was always dangerous. In mixed company he was a man of few words; but with his particular friends he was a social, and even a cheerful companion. Notwithstanding their numberless exploits in war, they were no braggadocios. When they had killed their enemies, they thought no more about it than a butcher would after killing a bullock. .It was their trade.

Happily all the old frontiermen were not such dare-devils as were the Wetzels. If they had been, the country could never have been settled. The men who went forward with families, and erected blockhouses and forts, and remained stationary to defend them, and to cultivate the earth, were the most efficient settlers. The Wetzels, and others of the same grit, served as a kind of out-guards, who were continually ranging from station to station in search of adventure; so that it was almost impossible for large bodies of the enemy to approach the settlements without being discovered by those vigilant, restless rangers, who would give the alarm to the forts. In this way all were useful; even the timid (for there were some such) would fight in defence of their fort.

Chapter V.

THE ZANE FAMILY, WHO SETTLE WHEELING.

>   Our forest life was rough and rude,
>   And dangers closed us round;
>   But here, amid the green old trees,
>   *Freedom* was sought and found.
>   Oft through our cabins, wintry blasts
>   Would rush with shriek and moan;
>   We cared not. Though they were but frail,
>   We felt they were our own.
>   Oh, free and manly lives we led,
>   Mid verdure or mid snow;
>   In the days when we were Pioneers,
>   Full fifty years ago.—*W. D. Gallagher.*

On a bright sunny morning of June, 1779, a bold and stalwart youth, clad in hunting shirt and buckskins, stood upon the high bluff just above the confluence of Wheeling Creek with the Ohio. He was, save the companionship of his faithful dog, utterly alone. The morning mist that covered the Ohio and the bottoms and valleys adjacent, was lazily lifting under the beams of a fervid sun. Not a breath of air disturbed the glittering dewdrops which sparkled upon the fresh green frondage, and as the ravished eye of the intrepid pioneer took in, feature by feature, the glorious panorama of hill and valley, wood and water, plain and island, now unrolled before him, his heart bounded with delight, and his "prophetic ken" forecast the future. That matchless scene of beauty was to him "a joy forever."

This solitary adventurer was Ebenezer Zane, scarce yet twenty-three years old. He was one of that "wild-turkey breed" of heroes, with heart full of that game spirit of old, which compelled him to abandon home and society, and strike out alone through the wilderness. He was so much delighted with what he now saw, and so impressed with the manifest advantages of the location, that he concluded to found a settlement there. Building himself a rude cabin, and remaining one season on the Ohio, hunting and exploring, he returned to Berkely county,

East Virginia, for his family. Acquainting his friends with the magnificent country he had traversed, he induced a few farmers, of like spirit with himself, to accompany him to the wilderness in 1772.

Deeming it unsafe as well as unwise to carry his family direct to their new abode, he left them at Redstone, on the Monongahela, while he, accompanied by his brothers, Silas, Andrew and Jonathan, (of whom more anon,) and by Bonnet, Wetzel, Messer and one or two others, crossed to the Ohio by way of Catfish Camp, (now Washington, Pa.) When within a few hundred yards of the forks of Wheeling Creek, some six or seven miles back from the Ohio, an incident occurred, says De Hass, the historian of Western Virginia, trivial in its character but important in its results.

Wetzel was riding in advance, when suddenly the girth of his saddle broke, compelling him to dismount. Meantime, Silas Zane passed on and coming to the forks of the creek, and greatly admiring the locality commenced tomahawking his right. "Tomahawk rights" were made by deadening a few trees and marking the bark of one or more with the initials of the person who claimed the locality. These "rights" were generally respected by the primitive settlers, and were frequently bought and sold. The land thus secured by Silas Zane, one thousand acres, is now one of the most valuable and highly improved farms in all Virginia.

The little band soon stood on the commanding bluff above Wheeling Creek and as they gazed at the magnificent outstretch below them, at once admitted that the "half had not been told them." With sturdy arms they soon opened a clearing and let the blessed sunshine into the heart of the sombre forest. Completing his cabin, Ebenezer Zane removed his family and soon the Wheeling settlement began to grow and flourish. Zane's clearing embraced about ten acres, all now a part of the city of Wheeling.

His wife was Elizabeth McColloch, sister to the two daring borderers whom we shall speedily mention. She bore him no less than thirteen children, the descendants of whom are now scattered all over the "Great West." She was a matron of remarkable force of character as well as kindness of heart, and her zeal, devotion and generosity were celebrated the whole length of the border. She was especially famous for her skill in the healing art, and many were the sick and wounded whom she tended with her own hands and restored to health when all had despaired.

To give one instance only, she and Rebecca Williams dressed the wounds of a scout by name of Thomas Mills, who had been brought into the fort shot by Indians in no less than fourteen places, while engaged spearing fish by moonlight. None thought it possible he could

survive, but by simple applications and warm fomentations his indefatigable nurses not only saved his life, but preserved an arm and leg
which were broken and which all said must come off.

The fort built by the Wheeling settlers for protection was first called
Fort Fincastle and afterwards Fort Henry, and for many years was a
famous one on the border, having withstood two memorable sieges—
one in 1777 and one in 1782. In the first Colonel Ebenezer Zane's
home, situate just outside the stockade, was burnt down, but in the last,
the new one had been fortified and withstood a desperate attack, giving
rise to one of the most noted scenes in western history and known as
"Betty Zane's Powder Exploit."

Colonel Zane's intercourse with the Indians during times of peace,
was marked with kindness, justness and honorable dealing. After the
country became settled, he received from time to time various marks of
distinction from Colonial, State and National governments. He was
a true gentleman—brave, upright and generous, quick and impetuous in
his temper and blunt of speech, but true of heart and of great enterprise. His personal appearance was marked. Although not very tall,
he was uncommonly active and athletic, and in feats of strength and
prowess was a match for almost any man in his settlement. His complexion was very dark, his brows were beetling and bushy; his nose
very prominent and his eyes black and piercing. He was a devoted
hunter and spent much of his time in the woods; but few men could
out-shoot and fewer still out-run him. In '96, the government, recognizing Colonel Zane's energy and capacity, employed him to open the
National Road from Wheeling to Maysville, Ky. This duty, assisted by
his brother Jonathan, a son-in-law and a noted Indian guide, he performed satisfactorily, and as a reward, Congress granted him the privilege of locating military warrants upon three sections of land—the first
to be at the crossing of the Muskingum (now Zanesville); the second
at the crossing of the Hock-Hocking, (now Lancaster), and the third
on the east side of the Scioto, opposite Chillicothe. These fine possessions, as well as other large bodies of land he had acquired, became
very valuable, and at his death in 1811, at the age of sixty-four, the
Colonel was very wealthy.

ZANE'S FOUR BROTHERS AND SISTER BETTY—SHOOTING ADVENTURES

Colonel Zane's sister Elizabeth was a lady of beauty and accomplish-
ments, having been educated at a Quaker school in Philadelphia. At a
very early age she became famous for the powder exploit, hereafter to
be mentioned. Of his brothers, Silas and Andrew, although prominent

settlers and noted hunters, but little has been preserved of note. The latter was killed by Indians while crossing the Scioto. Isaac was a more singular and conspicuous character. When only nine years of age he was taken captive by the Indians, carried to their town and there remained four years without seeing a white man. Like many another white lad in similar circumstances, he became so enamored of the free and untrammeled life of the wilderness, that he preferred it to all others. Isaac soon became a thorough Indian, not only in dress and habits but also in complexion. Arrived at manhood, he married the sister of a distinguished Wyandot Chief, by whom he raised a family of eight children. He acquired, with his tawny spouse, large landed possessions, and became a very important character in the Indian Confederacy; but, notwithstanding all this, he ever remained true to the whites, and was often the means of communicating important intelligence of Indian attacks, preparing the backwoods settlements for bloody visitations. For instance, in 1777, General Hard of Fort Pitt, sent word to Wheeling that Isaac Zane had secretly conveyed information to him that a large army of savages were about to strike a terrible blow upon the border, and asking him to put the whole line on guard. By this timely notice every post on the border was prepared for the attack, and when it finally fell on Wheeling they were all ready there and escaped with comparatively little damage. In consideration of Isaac Zane's valuable services, the government granted him a patent for ten thousand acres of land on Mad river, where he lived and died. The centre of this tract is now Zanesfield, Logan county, Ohio.

Jonathan, another brother, was perhaps the most experienced hunter and woodsman of his day—a man of great energy, resolution and restless activity. He knew the woods as a farmer does his fields, and used to make long excursions in search of game and frequently in search of Indians. He rendered invaluable services to the Virginia border in the capacity of spy and ranger. He had the confidence of all the backwoods settlements, and was noted for his strong, earnest will and his indomitable courage. He frequently acted as guide to noted expeditions, more especially to that of Crawford, in 1782. In the one under Brodhead, in '79, he was severely wounded. It was he who strongly admonished Crawford against proceeding, as all the signs gave evidence that the Indians were retiring before him in order to gain time, and that in the end they would overwhelm the whites. He died in Wheeling, leaving large landed possessions and several children, the founders of well known western families.

Jonathan prided himself especially on his skill as a marksman. Once, while returning home through some high weeds from hunting some horses, he saw five savages jump into the Ohio, and swim for Zane's Island, right opposite Wheeling. Drawing a careful bead on one tufted head, he fired and the Indian sank to rise no more. Loading and firing as fast as possible, he aimed at one head after another, until three more sank from sight. The fifth and last one, alarmed at the terrible fate of his companions, and hoping to escape the deadly aim of Zane's unerring rifle, took refuge behind a "sawyer," or up-sticking log, near the island. It was some time before Zane could catch sight of any part of the Indian exposed, but at last he saw, or thought he saw, a portion of his abdomen protruding from under the log. Drawing a fine sight, off went the piece, and the savage, after clinging tenaciously for awhile to his log, was observed floating down stream.

We have stated that Colonel Eb. Zane was also a dead shot. About the year 1781, some of the whites in the fort observed a savage on the island going through certain insulting gestures. He thought he was beyond all reach of danger. Colonel Zane's attention having been drawn to the indelicate performances, said he guessed he would spoil his sport. So charging his rifle with an additional ball, he waited patiently for the fellow to reappear. In a moment the savage's naked body was seen emerging from behind a large sycamore, and commencing anew his performances. The Colonel drew on him a most careful aim, and the next instant the red harlequin was seen going through a painful gyration not down "in the bill."

MAJOR SAMUEL McCOLLOCH AND HIS FAMOUS LEAP.

The story of McColloch's ride for life is as familiar as that of Putnam's, and his subsequent leap as that of the mailed Marcus Curtius and his noble steed, but few know anything of his history. There were two Major McCollochs, John and Samuel, both famed on the Virginia border for their daring exploits, and to the former has often been attributed the mad leap adown Wheeling hill. But De Hass has incontestibly proved that it was Sam., the elder brother, who did the gallant deed. The family was one of the earliest and most noted that settled on Short Creek, West Virginia. There were three brothers, all noted for bravery, and two sisters, in every way worthy of them. Elizabeth, as stated, was the honored wife of Colonel Ebenezer Zane; her whole life was a model of love, virtue and gentle kindness.

As an Indian hunter, Major Sam. had few superiors. He tracked his wily foe with wonderful sagacity, and would unwind his most secret trail with the unerring and instinctive tenacity of a bloodhound. He could not be frightened or shaken off. It was mainly to his energetic operations and daring exploits that the frontier was so often saved from savage depredation; and, by cutting off the Indian retreat, by attacking their hunting camps, and by annoying them in every possible way, the Major soon became to them an object of fear and intense hatred. He was a marked man, and sleepless vengeance was vowed against him.

At the close of the memorable siege of Fort Henry, in 1777, the Major had brought forty mounted men from Short Creek. The gates were joyfully thrown open to receive them, for never was reinforcement more timely, since the heroic little garrison had been very hardly pressed. A rush was made by the wary foe to prevent an entrance. All, however, succeeded in squeezing in but the gallant Major himself, who, anxious for the safety of his men, held back until completely hemmed in by desperate foes bent upon cutting him off. Finding himself in the most imminent peril of capture, there was nothing left but flight. He was admirably mounted on a noble steed of great stride and power, and giving him the spur, off they dashed, pursued by a yelling mob of exultant savages, on the road leading to the summit of the high hill back of the fort, and thence to Van Metre's Fort, on Short Creek.

Knowing the deadly rancor which the savages entertained for him, and seeing their desperate endeavors to entrap him, the Major goaded on his horse, who rushed up the hill at heart-burst speed, and at length reached the top. Galloping ahead of his pursuers, the Major was congratulating himself on his lucky escape, when, just as he gained a point in the path, lo and behold! there encountered him a considerable body of Indians, just returning from a plundering expedition among the settlements.

In an instant his full danger was comprehended. With foes in the path behind and in front, and both parties spreading about him on the third side, escape seemed utterly out of the question. What was to be done? He saw his pursuers in a yelling curve about him, stealthily gliding around among the trees, as if to completely hem him in. To fall into their hands was agonizing to think of. But one only avenue of escape remained, and that was by the precipice to one side. Death among the rocks and brambles seemed to him, in his extremity, preferable to the knife and fagot of the pitiless savage, and so he made quick resolve to try a plunge over the precipice. Without a moment's hesitation, then, for the savages were crowding in upon him, he firmly adjusted himself in his seat, grasped securely the bridle with his left hand, and supporting his rifle in the right, pushed his unfaltering horse over the abyss.

A plunge, a crash, crackling timber and tumbling rocks were all that the dazed and astounded savages could see or hear. They looked bewildered, one upon the other. The hill where their rash and reckless foe had gone over was near three hundred feet high, and in some places the slope was almost precipitous; while, therefore, they could not but admire his audacity and rejoice that their most inveterate enemy was finished at last, they regretted that he had been so unexpectedly spared their tortures. They crowded to the edge of the cliff, but what was their amazement and disgust to see the fiery steed, with the invulnerable Major sitting erect upon his back, dashing across the creek which ran at the base of the hill, and then careering across the peninsula at a free and rapid stride. They were safe at last, and the baffled savages had nothing else to do but return dejected and discomfited to camp.

After a life of such deeds of "daring emprise," it is sad to chronicle the Major's sad and untimely fate. In the Fall of '82, Major McColloch and his brother John started out on horseback for Van Metre's Fort, to track up some "Indian sign." They scouted closely and cautiously, proceeding almost as far as Fort Henry and not discovering any traces of Indians, had gone nearly back to "Girty's Point" on the river, when all at once a deadly discharge of rifles took place from a matted covert close by the path, by which the Major was vitally hit, falling dead from his horse. John escaped himself, but his horse was killed.

Major Sam. McColloch's Famous Leap Down Wheeling Hill.
SEE PAGE 350.

Quick as thought, however, he leaped from the writhing animal and sprang to the back of his dead brother's horse, and made off to give the alarm. As yet no enemy had been seen; but turning in his saddle, after a quick dash of fifty yards or so, the path was filled with whooping savages, and one fellow was seen in the very act of scalping the unfortunate Major. This was too much for the infuriated brother. In an instant his rifle was at his shoulder and flash! crack! the mutilating savage was rolling on the leaves in the agonies of death. With the exception of a slight bullet scratch on the hip, John escaped to the fort unhurt and aroused the settlement.

The next day a party went out fron Van Metre's and gathered up the mutilated remains of the poor Major. The savages had actually disemboweled him, but the viscera all remained except the heart. Some years subsequently an Indian, who had been one of the attacking party on this occasion, confessed to some whites that the heart of Major McColloch had been divided and *eaten* by the party; "so that," he concluded, "we be bold like Major McColloch." On another occasion the Indian, in speaking of the incident, said: "The whites (meaning John McColloch) had killed a great captain, but they (the Indians) had killed a greater one."

John McColloch afterwards became almost as distinguished as his lamented brother. He did glorious service in the Revolution; was a most devoted patriot and filled many posts of trust and honor. Samuel at the time of his "untimely taking off" had only been married six months.

BENJAMIN LOGAN AND HIS HEROIC DEEDS.

Among the earliest and most respectable of the emigrants to Kentucky, was General Benjamin Logan. His father was an Irishman, who had left his own country early in the eighteenth century and settled in Pennsylvania, from which he subsequently removed to Augusta county, Virginia. Here he shortly afterward died. Young Logan, as the eldest son, was entitled, by the laws of Virginia, to the whole of the landed property, (his father having died intestate). He refused, however, to avail himself of this circumstance, and, as the farm upon which the family resided was too small to admit of a division, he caused it to be sold, and the money to be distributed among his brothers and sisters, reserving a portion for his mother. At the age of twenty-one he removed from Augusta county to the banks of the Holston, where, shortly afterward, he purchased a farm and married.

In 1774 he accompanied Dunmore in his expedition, probably as a private. In 1775 he removed to Kentucky, and soon became particularly distinguished. His person was striking and manly, his hair and complexion very dark, his eye keen and penetrating, his countenance grave, thoughtful, and expressive of a firmness, probity and intelligence which were eminently displayed throughout his life. His education was very imperfect, and confined simply to the arts of reading and writing. Having remained in Kentucky, in a very exposed situation, until the Spring of 1776, he returned for his family, and brought them out to a small settlement, called Logan's Fort, not far from Harrodsburg. The Indians during this Summer were so numerous and daring in their excursions, that Logan was compelled to remove his wife and family for safety to Harrodsburg, while he himself remained at his cabins and cultivated a crop of corn.

In the Spring of 1777 his wife returned to Logan's Fort, and several settlers having joined him, he determined to maintain himself there at all risk. His courage was soon put to the test. On the morning of the 20th of May, a few days after his wife had rejoined him, the women were milking the cows at the gate of the little fort, and some of the garrison attending them, when a party of Indians appeared and fired upon them. One man was shot dead and two more wounded, one of them mortally. The whole party, including one of the wounded men, instantly ran into the fort and closed the gate. The enemy quickly showed themselves upon the edge of a canebrake, within close rifle shot of the gate, and seemed numerous and determined. Having a moment's leisure to look around, they beheld a spectacle which awakened the most lively interest and compassion.

A man named Harrison had been severely wounded, and still lay near the spot where he had fallen, within full view both of the garrison and the enemy. The poor fellow was, at intervals, endeavoring to crawl in the direction of the fort, and had succeeded in reaching a cluster of bushes, which, however, were too thin to shelter his person from the enemy. His wife and family were in the fort, and in deep distress at his situation. The enemy undoubtedly forbore to fire upon him, from the supposition that some of the garrison would attempt to save him, in which case they held themselves in readiness to fire upon them from the canebrake. The case was a very trying one. It seemed impossible to save him without sacrificing the lives of several of the garrison, and their numbers already were far too few for an effectual defence, having originally amounted only to fifteen men, three of whom had already been put *hors de combat*.

Yet the spectacle was so moving, and the lamentation of his family so distressing, that it seemed equally impossible not to make an effort to relieve him. Logan endeavored to persuade some of his men to accompany him in a sally, but so evident and appalling was the danger, that all at first refused; one herculean fellow observing that he was "a weakly man," and another declaring that he was sorry for Harrison, "but that the skin was closer than the shirt." At length John Martin collected his courage, and declared his willingness to accompany Logan, saying, that "he could only die once, and that he was as ready now as he ever would be." The two men opened the gate and started upon their forlorn expedition, Logan leading the way.

They had not advanced five steps, when Harrison, perceiving them, made a vigorous effort to rise, upon which Martin, supposing him able to help himself, immediately sprung back within the gate. Harrison's strength almost instantly failed, and he fell at full length upon the grass. Logan paused a moment after the desertion of Martin, then suddenly sprung forward to the spot where Harrison lay, rushing through a tremendous shower of rifle balls which was poured upon him from every spot around the fort capable of covering an Indian. Seizing the wounded man in his arms, he ran with him to the fort, through the same heavy fire, and entered it unhurt, although the gate and picketing near him were riddled with balls, and his hat and clothes pierced in several places.

A Perilous Journey after Powder—Bowman's Singular Behavior.

The fort was now vigorously assailed in the Indian manner, and as vigorously defended by the garrison. The women were all employed in moulding bullets, while the men were constantly at their posts. The weakness of the garrison was not their only grievance. A distressing scarcity of ammunition prevailed, and no supply could be procured nearer than Holston. But how was it to be obtained? The fort was closely blockaded, the Indians were swarming in the woods, and chances were sadly against the probability of the safe passage of any courier through so many dangers! Under these circumstances, Logan determined to take the dangerous office upon himself. After encouraging the men as well as he could, with the prospect of a safe and speedy return, he took advantage of a dark night, and crawled through the Indian encampment without discovery.

Shunning the ordinary route through Cumberland Gap, he arrived at Holston by by-paths which no white man had yet trodden; through canebrakes and thickets; over tremendous cliffs and precipices, where the deer could scarcely obtain footing, and where no vestige of any of the human family could be seen. Having obtained a supply of powder and lead, he returned through the same almost inaccessible paths to the fort, which he found still besieged and now reduced to extremity. The safe return of their leader inspired them with fresh courage, and in a few days the appearance of Colonel Bowman's party compelled the Indians to retire.

During the whole of this and the next year, the Indians were exceedingly troublesome. The Shawnees particularly distinguished themselves by the frequency and inveterate nature of their incursions; and as their capital, Chillicothe, was within striking distance, an expedition was set on foot against it in 1779, in which Logan served as second in command. Captain James Harrod and John Bulger accompanied the expedition; the former of whom, shortly afterward, perished in a lonely ramble; and the latter was killed at the Blue Licks. Colonel Bowman commanded in chief. The detachment amounted to one hundred and sixty men; consisted entirely of volunteers, accustomed to Indian warfare, and was well officered, but not so fortunate in its commander.

They left Harrodsburg in July, and took their preliminary measures so well that they arrived within a mile of Chillicothe without giving the slightest alarm to the enemy. Here the detachment halted at an early hour in the night, and, as usual, sent out spies to examine the condition of the village. Before midnight they returned, and reported that the enemy remained unapprised of their being in the neighborhood, and were in the most unmilitary security. It was determined that Logan, with one-half of the men, should turn to the left and march half way around the town, while Bowman, at the head of the remainder, should make a corresponding march to the right; that both parties should proceed in silence, until they had met at the opposite extremity of the village, when, having thus completely encircled it, the attack was to commence.

Logan, who was bravery himself, performed his part of the combined operation with perfect order and in profound silence, and having reached the designated spot, awaited with impatience the arrival of his commander. Hour after hour stole away, but Bowman did not appear. At length daylight appeared. Logan, still expecting the arrival of his Colonel, ordered the men to conceal themselves in the high grass and await the expected signal to attack. No orders, however, arrived. In the meantime, the men, in shifting about through the grass, alarmed an Indian dog, the only sentinel on duty. He instantly began to bay loudly, and advanced in the direction of the man who had attracted his attention. Presently a solitary Indian left his cabin and walked cautiously toward the party, halting frequently, rising upon tiptoes, and gazing around him.

Logan's party lay close, with the hope of taking him without giving the alarm; but at that instant a gun was fired in an opposite quarter of the town, as was afterwards ascertained, by one of Bowman's party, and the Indian, giving one shrill whoop, ran swiftly back to the council house. Concealment was now impossible. Logan's party instantly sprang up from the grass and rushed upon the village, not doubting for a moment that they would be gallantly supported. As they advanced they perceived Indians, of all ages and of both sexes, running to the great cabin, near the centre of the town, where they collected in full force, and appeared determined upon an obstinate defence. Logan instantly took possession of the houses which had been deserted, and, rapidly advancing from cabin to cabin, at length established his detachment within close rifle shot of the Indian redoubt.

He now listened impatiently for the firing which should have been heard from the opposite extremity of the town, where he supposed Bowman's party to be, but to his astonishment, everything remained quiet in that quarter. In the meantime, his own position had become critical. The Indians had recovered from their panic and kept up a close and heavy fire upon the cabins which covered his men. He had pushed his detachment so close to the redoubt, that they could neither advance nor retreat without great exposure. The enemy outnumbered him, and gave indications of a disposition to turn both flanks of his position and thus endanger his retreat.

Under these circumstances, ignorant of the condition of his commander, and cut off from communication with him, he formed the bold and judicious resolution, to make a movable breastwork of the planks which formed the floor of the cabins, and under cover of it, to rush upon the stronghold of the enemy and carry it by main force. Had this gallant determination been carried into effect, and had the movement been promptly seconded, as it ought to have been by Bowman, the conflict would have been bloody, and the victory decisive. Most probably not an Indian would have escaped, and the consternation which such signal vengeance would have spread throughout the Indian tribes, might have repressed their incursions for a considerable time. But before the necessary steps could be taken, a messenger arrived from Bowman, with orders "to retreat!"

Astonished at such an order, at a time when honor and safety required an offensive movement on their part, Logan hastily asked if Bowman had been overpowered by the enemy? No! Had he ever beheld an enemy? No! What, then, was the cause of this extraordinary abandonment of a design so prosperously begun? He did not know: the Colonel had ordered a retreat! Logan, however reluctantly, was compelled to obey. A retreat is always a dispiriting movement, and, with militia, is almost certain to terminate in a complete rout. As soon as the men were informed of the order, a most irregular and tumultuous scene commenced. Not being buoyed up by the mutual confidence which is the offspring of discipline, and which sustains regular soldiers under all circumstances, they no longer acted in concert.

Each man selected the time, manner and route of his retreat for himself. Here a solitary Kentuckian would start up from behind a stump, and scud away through the grass, dodging and turning to avoid the balls which whistled around him. There a dozen men would run from a cabin, and scatter in every direction, each anxious to save himself, and none having leisure to attend to their neighbors. The Indians, astonished at seeing men rout themselves in this manner, sallied out of their redoubt and pursued the stragglers, as sportsmen would cut up a scattered flock of wild geese. They soon united themselves to Bowman's party, who from some unaccountable panic of their commander, or fault in themselves, had stood stock still near the spot where Logan had left them the night before.

All was confusion. Some cursed their Colonel; some reproached other officers; one shouted one thing, one bellowed another; but all seemed to agree that they ought to make the best of their way home, without the loss of a moment's time. By great exertions on the part of Logan, well seconded by Harrod, Bulger, and the late Major G. M. Bedinger, of the Blue Licks, some degree of order was restored, and a tolerably respectable retreat commenced. The Indians, however, soon surrounded them on all sides, and kept up a hot fire, which began to grow fatal. Colonel Bowman appeared quite bewildered, and sat upon his horse like a pillar of stone, neither giving an order, nor taking any measures to repel the enemy. The sound of rifle shots had, however, completely restored the men to their senses, and they readily formed in a large hollow square, took trees, and returned the fire with equal vivacity. The enemy were quickly repelled, and the troops recommenced their march.

But scarcely had they advanced half a mile, when the Indians reappeared, and again opened a fire upon the front, rear and both flanks. Again a square was formed, and the enemy repelled; but scarcely had the harassed troops recommenced their march, when the same galling fire was opened upon them from every tree, bush and stone capable of concealing an Indian. Matters now began to look serious. The enemy were evidently endeavoring to detain them, until fresh Indians could come up in sufficient force to compel them to lay down their arms. The men began to be unsteady, and the panic was rapidly spreading from the Colonel to the privates. At this crisis, Logan, Harrod, Bedinger, etc., selected the boldest and best mounted men, and dashing into the bushes on horseback, scoured the woods in every direction, forcing the Indians from their coverts, and cutting down as many as they could overtake.

This decisive step completely dispersed the enemy, and the weary and dispirited troops continued their retreat unmolested. They lost nine killed and a few others wounded. But the loss of reputation on the part of the Colonel was incalculable, for, as usual, *he* was the scapegoat upon whose head the disgrace of the miscarriage was laid. No good reason has ever been assigned for the extraordinary failure of his own detachment; and the subsequent panic which he displayed when harassed in the woods, affords room for suspicion that either the darkness of the night, or the cry of an owl (for he did not see the face of an enemy) had robbed the Colonel of his usual presence of mind.

Logan returned to Kentucky with a reputation increased rather than diminished, by the failure of the expedition. His conduct was placed in glaring contrast to that of his unfortunate commander, and the praise of the one was in exact correspondence to the censure of the other. No other affair of consequence occurred until the rash and disastrous battle of the Blue Licks, in which, as we have seen, Logan was unable to share. He seems to have remained quietly engaged in agricultural pursuits until the Summer of 1788, when he conducted an expedition against the Mack-a-chack towns on Mad river, which, as usual, terminated in burning their villages, and cutting up their cornfields; serving to irritate, but not to subdue the enemy. A single incident attending this expedition, deserves to be commemorated. We give the first version from McClung:

THE MURDER OF MOLUNTHA BY THE FIERCE HUGH McGARY.

Upon approaching a large village of the Shawnees, from which, as usual, most of the inhabitants had fled, an old chief, named Moluntha, came out to meet them, fantastically dressed in an old cocked hat, set jauntily upon one side of his head, and a fine shawl thrown over his shoulders. He carried an enormous pipe in one hand, and a tobacco pouch in the other, and strutted out with the air of an old French beau to smoke the pipe of peace with his enemies, whom he found himself unable to meet in the field.

Nothing could be more striking than the fearless confidence with which he walked through the foremost ranks of the Kentuckians, evidently highly pleased with his own appearance, and enjoying the admiration which he doubted not that his cocked hat and splendid shawl inspired. Many of the Kentuckians were highly amused at the mixture of dandyism and gallantry which the poor old man exhibited, and shook hands with him very cordially. Unfortunately, however, he at length approached Major McGary, whose temper, never particularly sweet, was as much inflamed by the sight of an Indian, as that of a wild bull by the waving of a red flag. It happened, unfortunately, too, that Moluntha had been one of the chiefs who commanded at the Blue Licks, a disaster which McGary had not yet forgotten.

Instead of giving his hand as the others had done, McGary scowled upon the old man, and asked him if "he recollected the Blue Licks?" Moluntha smiled, and merely repeated the word "Blue Licks!" when McGary instantly drew his tomahawk and cleft him to the brain. The old man received the blow without flinching for a second, and fell dead at the feet of his destroyer. Great excitement instantly prevailed in the army. Some called it a ruthless murder, and others swore that he had done right; that an Indian was not to be regarded as a human being, but ought to be shot down as a wolf whenever and wherever he appeared. McGary himself raved like a madman at the reproach of his countrymen, and declared, with many bitter oaths, that he would not only kill every Indian whom he met, whether in peace or war, at church or market, but that he would equally as readily tomahawk the man who blamed him for the act.

Nothing else, worthy of being mentioned, occurred during the expedition, and Logan, upon his return, devoted himself exclusively to the civil affairs of the country, which about this time began to assume an important aspect.

Another Account of Moluntha's Murder—A Spirited Lad.

General Lytle, then a lad of only sixteen, was present at Logan's destruction of the Mack-a-chack towns on Mad river, and gives a graphic account of the whole affair. Logan, he says, burned eight towns, destroyed many fields of corn, took seventy or eighty prisoners, and killed twenty warriors, among them Moluntha, the head chief of the nation. This last act caused deep shame, regret and humiliation to the commander-in-chief and his troops.

"I was extremely solicitous, says Lytle, to try myself in battle. The commander of the centre line waved his sword over his head as a signal for the troops to advance. Colonel Daniel Boone and Major Simon Kenton commanded the advance, and Colonel Trotter the rear. As we approached within half a mile of the town on the left, we saw the savages retreating in all directions, making for the swamps, thickets and high prairie grass. General Logan waved his sword, and in a voice of thunder exclaimed, '*Charge!* from right to left!' The horses appeared as impatient for the onset as their riders. I heard of but one savage, with the exception of the chief, cry for quarter. They fought with desperation so long as they could raise gun, knife or tomahawk. We dispatched all the warriors we overtook, and sent the women and children prisoners to the rear.

"We pushed ahead, still hoping to overtake a larger body, when we might have something like a general engagement. I was mounted on a very fleet grey horse. Fifty of my companions followed me. I had not advanced more than a mile before I discovered some of the enemy running along the edge of a thicket of hazel and plum bushes. I made signs to the men in my rear to come on. I obliqued across the plain to get ahead of them, and when I had arrived within easy shot I dismounted and raised my gun. The warrior I was about to shoot held up his hand in token of surrender, and I heard him order the other Indians to stop.

"By this time the men behind had arrived, and were in the act of firing. I called them not to fire, as the Indians had surrendered. The warrior who had surrendered to me, came walking towards me, calling his women and children to follow. I advanced to meet him, with my right hand extended, but before I could reach him, our men of the right wing had surrounded him. I rushed in among the horses. While he was giving me his hand, several of our men wished to tomahawk him. I informed them they would have to tomahawk me first. We led him back to the place where his flag had been. Among the prisoners we then took were the chief, his three wives—one of them a young and handsome woman—another of them, the famous Grenadier Squaw, and two or three fine young lads. The rest were children.

"One of these lads was a remarkably interesting youth, about my own age and size. He clung closely to me, and appeared to notice nearly everything that was going on.

"When we arrived at the town, a crowd of our men pressed around to see the chief. I stepped aside to fasten my horse, and my prisoner lad clung close to my side. A young man by the name of Cumer had been to one of the springs to drink. He discovered the young savage by my side, and came running towards me. The young Indian supposed he was advancing to kill him. As I turned around, in the twinkling of an eye, he let fly an arrow at Cumer, for he was armed with a bow. It passed through Cumer's dress and grazed his side. The jerk I gave his arm undoubtedly saved Cumer. I took away his arrows and sternly reprimanded him. I then led him back to the crowd which surrounded the prisoners.

"At the same moment Colonel Hugh McGary, the same man who had caused the disaster at the battle of the Blue Licks some years before, coming up, General Logan's eye caught that of McGary's. 'Colonel McGary,' said he, 'you must not molest these prisoners!' 'I will see to that,' said McGary, in reply. I forced my way through the crowd to the chief, with my young charge by the hand. McGary ordered the crowd to open and let him in. He came up to the chief, and his first salutation was, 'Were you at the defeat of the Blue Licks?' The Indian, not knowing the meaning of the words, or not understanding the purport of the question, answered, 'Yes.' McGary instantly seized an axe from the hands of the Grenadier Squaw, and raised it to make a blow at the chief. I threw up my arm to ward off the blow. The handle of the axe struck me across the left wrist, and came near breaking it. The axe sunk into the head of the chief to the eyes, and he fell dead at my feet. Provoked beyond measure at this wanton barbarity, I drew my knife for the purpose of avenging the cruelty by dispatching McGary. My arm was arrested by one of our men, which prevented me from inflicting the thrust. McGary escaped from the crowd.

"While out with Captain Stucker after a drove of hogs we saw running about, I saw an Indian coming along with a deer on his back. The fellow happened to raise his eyes the same moment, and look across the prairie to the upper town and saw it all in flames. In the act of turning my head to tell Captain Stucker of the savage, I discovered Hugh Ross, at a distance of sixty or seventy yards, approaching us. I made a motion with my hand to Ross to squat down; then taking a tree between me and the Indian, I stepped somewhat nearer to get a fairer shot—when, at the instant I raised my gun past the tree, the Indian being about a hundred yards distant, Ross's ball whistled by me so close that I felt the wind of it, and struck the savage in the calf of one of his legs. The Indian that moment dropped his deer and sprang into the high grass of the prairie, when, before I could draw sight on him, he was lost to view.

"I was provoked at Ross for shooting when I was near enough to have killed him, and now the consequence would be that some of our men would lose their lives, as an Indian will only give up with life itself. Captain Irwin rode up at this moment with his troop of horse, and asked me where the Indian was. I pointed as nearly as I could to the spot, cautioning the Captain if he missed him the first charge to pass on out of his reach before he wheeled to recharge, or the Indian would kill some of his men in the act of wheeling. Whether the Captain heard me, I cannot say; at any rate, the warning was not attended to, for after passing the Indian a few steps, Captain Irwin ordered his men to wheel and recharge across the woods, and in the act of executing the movement, the Indian raised up and shot the Captain dead on the spot, still keeping below the level of the grass to deprive us of any opportunity of putting a bullet through him. The troop charged again; but the Indian was so active that he had darted into the grass some rods from where he had fired at Irwin, and they again missed him.

"By this time several footmen had came up. Captain Stucker and myself had each of us taken a tree that stood out on the edge of the prairie among the grass, when a Mr. Stofford came up and put his head first past one side and then past the other of the tree I was behind. I told him not to expose himself that way or he would get shot in a twinkling. I had hardly spoken the last word, when the Indian again raised up out of the grass. His gun, Stucker's and my own, with four or five behind us, all cracked at the same instant. Stofford fell at my side, while we rushed on the wounded Indian with our tomahawks. Before we had got him dispatched he had made ready the powder in his gun and a ball in his mouth, preparing for a third fire, with bullet holes in his breast that might all have been covered with a man's open hand. We found with him Captain Beaseley's rifle—the Captain having been killed at the Lower Blue Licks a few days before the army passed through that place on their way to the towns.

"Next morning General Logan ordered an attack on a town seven or eight miles northwest of where we then were. This town was also burnt, together with an English block-house, of huge size and thickness. Mr. Isaac Zane was at that time living at the village, he being married to a squaw, and having there at the time his wife and several children. The name of the Indian chief killed by McGary was Moluntha, the Great Sachem of the Shawnees. The Grenadier Squaw, his wife, was sister to Cornstalk, who (basely murdered) died at Point Pleasant."

Jonathan Alder, an account of whose captivity we give further on, was living with the Indians at the time. He says the approach of Logan's army was communicated by a Frenchman, but that as the whites arrived sooner than expected, the surprise was complete. Most of the Indians were absent hunting at the time. A runner came early one morning to the village where Alder lived, and said that Mack-a-chack had been destroyed. Alder, with the people of the village, principally squaws and children, retreated two days, and suffered greatly for want of food. Not one among them could hunt, and they had to live for eight days on paw-paws, muscles and craw fish. All that Winter they lived on raccoons, with no salt, and without bread, hominy or corn. So hard were they pushed that for a time they had to subsist on a sort of wild potato, as the raccoons had been suckled down so poor that dogs would hardly eat them, but *they* threw them on the fire, singed the hair off, and ate skin and all."

At Colonel Grant's defeat in Indiana, a desperate action, this same Lytle, then but seventeen years of age, had both his arms shattered, his face powder-burnt, his hair singed to the roots, and no less than *nineteen bullets* passed through his body and clothing. In this condition, a retreat being ordered, he succeeded in bringing off the field several of his friends, generously aiding the wounded and exhausted by placing them on horses, while he himself ran forward in advance of the last remnant of the retreating party to stop the only boat on the Ohio at that time which could take them across the river and save them. On reaching the water he found the boat just putting for the Kentucky shore and the ferrymen very reluctant to obey his order, one of them declaring "that it was better a few should perish than that all should be sacrificed." Taking aim with his rifle, Lytle now swore he would shoot the first man who pulled an oar until all his friends were aboard. In this way all were secured, but the boat being crowded almost to dipping Lytle disdained to get aboard, but running up the bank to where some horses stood panting under the willows, he leaped to the back of the strongest he could find, boldly plunged into the stream and holding on to the mane by his teeth, succeeded in reaching the middle of the river, where he was taken aboard bleeding and almost fainting from his wounds. By this time the balls of the enemy were rattling like hail about the boat, but they escaped after all.

MOLUNTHA'S SON LAWBA AND HIS ROMANTIC DEATH.

The brave and spirited lad, son of Moluntha, who was saved by Lytle, had afterwards a prominent and honorable career. He was taken with other prisoners to Kentucky, but General Logan was so pleased with his spirit and brightness, that he made him a member of his own household, and he there grew up to manhood, being afterwards known as Captain Logan. His Indian name was Spemica Lawba, or The High Horn. He afterwards rose to the rank of Civil Chief, on account of his many estimable qualities. His personal appearance was commanding, he being six feet in height and weighing near two hundred pounds. He, from that time, continued the unwavering friend of the Americans, and fought on their side with great bravery. He lost his life in 1812 under melancholy and romantic circumstances, which indicated that he was a man of the keenest sense of honor.

In November, 1812, General Harrison directed Logan to take a small party and reconnoitre the country towards Maumee Rapids. Being met by a far superior body of the enemy, they were compelled to retreat. Logan, Bright Horn and Captain Johnny, effected their escape to the left wing of the army, under command of General Winchester. A certain general of Kentucky troops, without the slightest grounds, accused Logan of infidelity to the cause and of giving intelligence to the enemy. Indignant and outraged at the base charge, Logan determined to give proof of his loyalty in a way that could not be mistaken, and said he would start out on a scout the very next morning, and either return with trophies or leave his bones bleaching in the woods.

Accordingly, at the earliest dawn, he was off, in company with Captain Johnny and Bright Horn. At their first nooning they were suddenly surprised by a party of seven savages, among whom were young Elliott, a half breed, and the famous Pottawattamie Chief, Winnemac. Logan made no resistance, but, with great presence of mind, extended his hand to Winnemac, and proceeded to inform him that he and his companions had been disgusted with the American service, and were on their way to the British. Winnemac was suspicious, and proceeded to disarm and surround the three, and then started off for the British camp. Winnemac afterwards became more confident and was induced to restore to the prisoners their arms again. While doggedly trudging along, Logan managed to communicate to his two friends a plan of attack. The guns being loaded, they only had to put some extra bullets in their mouths to be ready for a prompt reload. Captain Johnny was noticed in this sly manœuvre and adroitly averted suspicion by remarking, " me chaw heap tobac."

Evening camp was made on Turkeyfoot, and while most of the captors were roaming around after supper in search of blackhaws, Logan gave the signal, and all fired at those remaining. Two dropped at once, but the third required a second shot, and in the meantime the remainder of the party hurried back, returned the fire, and all " treed." There being four of the enemy and only three of Logan's party, all the movements of the enemy could not be watched. The unwatched foe thus was enabled to pass around until Logan's person was uncovered by his tree, and then shot him through the body. By this time Logan's party had wounded two of the four, causing them to fall back.

Captain Johnny now mounted Logan on one horse and Bright Horn, also wounded, on another, and started them for Winchester's Camp, which they reached about midnight. Captain Johnny, with Winnemac's scalp, got in on foot next morning. It was subsequently learned that the two wounded of the enemy died, making five out of the seven slain by Captain Logan's party. When Logan's wound and the occasion of it became noised about the camp, it produced a deep and mournful sensation. Logan's popularity was great, being very largely esteemed for his fidelity and the nobility of his nature. He lived but two or three days, ever in extreme bodily agony, and was buried at Fort Winchester with the honors of war.

Previous to his death, he related the particulars of the fight to a friend, declaring that he prized his honor more than his life, and now that he had vindicated that, he died satisfied. Shortly after, while writhing with pain, he was observed to smile, and, upon being asked the cause, replied that when he recalled the manner in which Captain Johnny took off the scalp of Winnemac, while at the same time he was obliged to keep moving around with one eye watching the movements of the roving fourth Indian, he could not refrain from laughing—an incident showing " the ruling passion strong in death."

Logan left a dying request to Colonel Johnston, that his two sons should be educated in Kentucky, under care of Major Hardin. When peace was restored, Johnston made application to the chiefs of Lawba's tribe to fulfill his dying wish, but they were embarrassed and unwilling to comply, and in this the mother of the two boys agreed. On no account would they send them to Kentucky, but would consent that they might be schooled at Piqua, Ohio, which was done, the boys boarding in a religious family. The mother, however, was a bad woman, and thwarted all plans for her sons' improvement, frequently taking them off for weeks, giving them bad advice and buying whiskey several times to make them drunk. She finally persuaded them off altogether. Both mother and children afterwards emigrated west, and there became the wildest of their race.

Two Adventures of Captain Johnny—A Desperate Indian Duel.

There was a certain Indian called John Cush, who lived much among the whites about Chillicothe. He was a large, muscular man, pleasant and good humored. Every Fall he would take to the woods on a grand hunt. In the Fall of 1779, he happened on Captain Johnny's camp while a white rum trader was there. Cush and Johnny, being pretty wild with liquor, fell into a quarrel but were separated. Both, however, being terribly enraged, arranged for a duel next morning with knives and tomahawks. They stuck a post on the south side of a log; made on the log a notch, and agreed that when the shadow of the post struck the notch the duel should commence. When the shadow drew near the spot, they deliberately and in gloomy silence took their station on the log.

At length, the shadow having touched the notch, the two desperadoes, thirsting for each other's blood, simultaneously sprang to their feet with each a tomahawk in the right hand and a scalping knife in the left hand, and flew at each other with the fury of catamounts, swinging their tomahawks around their heads and yelling in the most terrific manner. Language fails to describe the horrid scene. After several passes and many wounds, Johnny's tomahawk fell on Cush's head and left him lifeless on the ground.

About the year 1800, while Johnny was at his hunting camp, he and his wife had a quarrel and mutually agreed to separate. After they had divided their property, the wife insisted on keeping the one child, a little boy of two or three years. The wife laid hold of the child and the wrathful husband attempted to wrest it from her. At length, Johnny's passion being roused to fury, he raised his ponderous fist, knocked his wife down, seized the boy, and, carrying him to a neighboring log, deliberately cut him into two parts, and then throwing one-half to his wife, bade her take it but never again to show her face or he would treat her in the same manner. Thus ended this cruel and brutal scene of savage tragedy.

CAPTAIN WILLIAM HARDIN, PIONEER OF KENTUCKY.

One of the earliest settlers in Kentucky was Captain William Hardin, a noted hunter and Indian fighter—a man of dauntless courage and resolution—cool, calm and self-possessed in the midst of most appalling dangers, and perfectly skilled in all the wiles and arts of border warfare. Soon after Captain Hardin had erected a station in what is now the county of Breckinridge, intelligence was received that the Indians were building a town on Saline Creek, in the present State of Illinois Hardin, not well pleased that the savages should establish themselves in such close vicinity to his little settlement, determined to dislodge them. He soon had collected around him a force of eighty select men; the hardiest and boldest of those noted hunters whose lives were passed in a continual round of perilous adventure.

When this force reached the vicinity of the lick, they discovered Indian signs, and approaching the town cautiously, they found it in the possession of three warriors who had been left to guard the camp. Hardin ordered his men to fire on them, which they did, killing two. The third attempted to make his escape, but was shot down as he ran. He succeeded, however, in regaining his feet and ran fifty yards, leaped up a perpendicular bank, six feet high, and fell dead.

In the meantime, Hardin, correctly supposing that the main body of the Indians were out on a hunting expedition, and would shortly return, made immediate preparation for battle. He accordingly selected a place where a few acres of timbered land were surrounded on all sides by the prairie. Here he posted his men with orders to conceal themselves behind the trees, and reserve their fire until the Indians should approach within twenty-five yards. Soon after the little band had taken their position, they discovered the Indians rapidly approaching on their trail and numbering apparently between eighty and a hundred men. When the savages had arrived within one hundred yards of the position of the Kentuckians, one of the men, in his impatience to begin the battle, forgot the order of the Captain, and fired his gun. Immediately the Indians charged, and the fight commenced in earnest.

At the first fire Captain Hardin was shot through the thighs. Without, however, resigning his command, or yielding to the pain of his wound, he sat down on a large log, and, during the whole action, continued to encourage his men and give forth his orders, with as much coolness, promptitude and self-possession, as if engaged in the most ordinary avocation. This more than Spartan firmness and resolution was not, however, anything very remarkable in the early history of Kentucky. Every battlefield furnished many examples of similar heroism. The iron men of those times seem, indeed, to have been born insensible to fear and impregnable to pain. The coolness, courage and unyielding determination of Hardin, in this trying situation, no doubt contributed greatly to the success of the day; and after a severe contest, in which some thirty of the savages fell, they were finally repulsed. The loss of the whites, in killed and wounded, was very considerable. During the action the parties were frequently engaged hand to hand.

CAPTAIN BLAND BALLARD AND HIS ADVENTURES

This distinguished pioneer went to Kentucky in 1777; was, like his compeers, long engaged in the defence of the country of his adoption, and, after serving in Bowman's campaign in '79, accompanied General Clark's expedition against the Pickaway towns in '81, on which occasion he was severely wounded. In '86 he served as a spy for Clark, and in '91 as guide, and was with General Wayne at the decisive battle of Fallen Timbers in '94.

During his three years' service as spy with Clark he had many exciting rencontres with Indians. One occurred near Louisville. He was scouting down the river and heard, early one morning, a noise on the Indiana shore. He sought concealment, and, when the fog cleared, discovered a canoe with three savages approaching. When within range he fired and killed one. The others jumped overboard and tried to get their canoe into deep water, but before they succeeded he shot a second, and finally the third. Upon reporting to General Clark the game he had bagged, a party was sent down and buried the three bodies. For this service Clark gave him a *linen* shirt, of which the tough pioneer was very proud, his previous shirts being only of buckskin.

A few years later the savages attacked the little fort on Tick Creek, where his father resided. Ballard, Sr., had moved outside the fort to be near a sugar camp. When a younger brother had gone out to chop some wood for the fire, he was shot by prowling Indians, who then assailed the cabin. The inmates barred the door and prepared for defence. His father was the only man in the house, and the only men in the fort were one old man and Bland Ballard, the latter of whom, as soon as he heard firing, proceeded as near as was safe to his father's cabin and commenced using his unerring rifle with the best effect. The savages had burst into the cabin and killed old Ballard, but not before *he* had first killed two of *them*. They also murdered young Ballard's full sister, a half sister, his step-mother, and tomahawked his younger sister, who, however, afterwards recovered. The step-mother was pursued out of the back door by an eager savage, and just as his tomahawk descended, a bullet from young Ballard's rifle laid him low. The savage and the step-mother expired together. The Indians numbered fifteen, but before they got fairly off with their booty, had lost six or seven.

At one time Ballard was taken captive by five Indians, a little above Louisville, and taken to their camp, where he was treated well, but they neglected to tie him. The next day, while they were engaged in horse-racing, his guards left him to enjoy the sport. Near him stood a fine black horse, recently stolen from Beargrass. Springing to his back, Ballard made off, when the character of the race changed, it being now one for life and death. He was pursued for over twenty miles to the river, but succeeded in making good his escape, the gallant horse who had saved him dying, however, shortly after, from his extraordinary exertions.

At another time the Indians stole his horse at night. He distinctly heard them while they took the beast from the door to which he was tied. Ballard's energy and sagacity, however, were such that, by taking a short cut, "across country," he was enabled to get in advance of the exultant thieves before they reached the Ohio. Putting himself in ambush by the trail they would most likely pass, a party of three soon hove in sight. Drawing a careful bead on the Indian mounted on his own horse, he dropped him, and Ballard not only succeeded in catching the frightened animal in its flight, but in escaping without any injury.

In after life Major Ballard repeatedly represented the people of Shelby county in the Legislature; commanded a company under Harrison in 1812–13, and was wounded and taken prisoner at the battle of the Raisin. In 1847 Ballard was living yet, a fine specimen of the old-style Kentucky Pioneer.

EXCITING ADVENTURE OF "BIG JOE LOGSTON."

The subject of our sketch had somewhat notable parents. Old Joe Logston was a very large, athletic man, with uncommon muscular strength. His wife was not remarkable in height, but, like the Dutchman's horse, was built right up from the ground and had the strength of three ordinary women. The son was no discredit to them, but soon outstripped his father in strength, size and activity. It was often said to growing, stout-looking youth, "You'll soon be as great as Big Joe Logston." The family lived at first in one of the most rugged and inhospitable regions of the Allegheny Mountains, from which Joe sometimes descended in order to exchange his pelts for lead, powder and other articles. While in society he entered with great zest into all the various athletic sports of the day. No Kentuckian could ever with greater propriety than he, have said, "I can out-run, out-leap, out-jump, throw down, drag out and whip any man in the country." As to the use of the rifle he was reputed one of the quickest and surest centre-shots to be found. With all this, as is usual with men of true grit, Joe was good natured and never sought a quarrel. For many years he waged a stubborn and unintermittent war with the bears, panthers, wolves and rattlesnakes with which his wild haunts abounded, but he persistently maintained his ground until, like Daniel Boone before him, he learned to tire of encroachments on hunting grounds he began to deem his own. One man pitched his cabin six miles east of him, another a few miles west, and finally one, with a numerous family, had the impudence to locate within two miles of him, which was too much, so, in great disgust, he gathered up his traps and migrated to Barren river, Ky., where he was in no danger of hearing the crack of any man's rifle but his own. No one, it may easily be believed, was better qualified to live on a perilous and exposed frontier than Joe. His part of the country was subject to frequent visitations from the Cherokees, and they bore him about as much love as he did them. There was not a particle of fear in Joe's composition. Among a race of men unusually daring and reckless, Joe was considered uncommonly so. Hitherto he had only encountered and overcome wild beasts, but now he had a different foe to deal with, and as "it stirs the more to rouse a lion than to start a hare," Joe was kept somewhat excited. The savages soon made a sudden hostile attack, and all that escaped slaughter were driven into one of the rude stockades of the border. Joe did not relish this. He soon became restless at his confinement and would insist on some of his more unrecking companions going outside to hunt up the abandoned cattle. Finding none to join him, he, mounted on his good nag, sallied out alone.

He ransacked the woods all day, but finding no cattle, which, indeed, had been driven off by the wily savages, he was returning along the path to the fort and came under a fruitful grapevine, whose rich and tempting clusters hung within reach. Laying his rifle across the pommel of his saddle, he plucked his hat full of the fragrant fruit and then rode carelessly along, eating his grapes, until the cracks of two rifles, one from either side of his woodland path, gave him a rude awakening from his repast. One of the balls passed directly through the paps of his breast, which, for a male, were remarkably prominent. The other ball struck his poor beast just behind the saddle and he sank in his tracks.

Joe was greatly surprised but not discomfited. He might now have taken to his heels, and so fleet was he that none could have caught him. But our Kentuckian was not of that kind. The wound in his breast and his rude fall aroused his ire, so that when one athletic Indian leaped towards him, Joe drew a rapid bead on him, which his quick and wary antagonist seeing, sprang behind two pretty large saplings, some small distance apart, but neither of them large enough to cover his body. He now commenced dancing from one to the other in order to disturb the white man's aim until his companion could shoot him down. Joe followed the motions of the big savage with his gun, but kept one wary eye peering about for the other redskin, whom at last he discovered loading a gun behind a tree not quite large enough to cover him. When in the act of pushing down his bullet, he exposed one of his hips. This was Joe's opportunity, so, wheeling suddenly about, he let fly and brought the fellow quickly to earth.

The big savage then, with a horrid yell, rushed upon him with his uplifted tomahawk. Here were two stout warriors met, each determined to do or die. The reddy had rather the advantage in size and activity, but Joe in weight and muscular strength. The savage made a halt at the distance of fifteen feet, and cast his hatchet. Joe quickly, however, had his eye on it and dodged, and the keen weapon whizzed past harmless and beyond the reach of either. Quick as thought Kantuck clubbed his rifle and sprang forward in his turn, but his opponent leaped into some brush and dodged behind the saplings to avoid the blows. At length Joe, thinking his chance had come at last, made a side blow with such force that, missing the dodging Indian, it struck a tree, was broken close to the barrel, and, what was worse, flew out of his stunned hands quite beyond reach.

Here was a pretty fix for a modest man to be in! The infuriated savage now gave another exulting and blood-curdling yell, and sprang at him like a wild beast. Neither of them had any weapon, and the Indian, seeing Logston bleeding freely, thought he could easily throw and master his burly antagonist. He argued without his host. The two grappled at once, and a most desperate struggle ensued. Joe could throw the slippery savage down but could not hold him there, for, being naked from the waist up, and with his hide oiled, he would still elude his foe's grasp, and spring to his feet again. After throwing the reddy thus several times, and finding the desperate exertion was fast pumping all his wind out of him, Joe was rapidly forced to the conclusion that he must at once change his tactics or lose his scalp. He now threw the Indian once again, but this time without attempting to hold him; he jumped back from him, and as his panting foe was staggering to his pins, somewhat weak and "groggy," let fly a terrible fist blow, about as persuasive as the playful kick of a mule, which caused the other to fall back, and as he would rise again, Logston would give him blow after blow, the Indian rising slower and sadder each time. Old Kantuck now had it his own way, and at last succeeded in delivering a terrible blow in the burr of the ear, which felled the big savage, and left him without either breath or motion.

Joe now jumped upon him, and, thinking he could dispatch him by choking, grasped his neck with his left hand, while keeping his right ready for emergencies. But the big Indian was no such a man, and Logston found his right arm in motion, and, on casting his eye down, discovered him making an effort to unsheath a knife that was hanging at his belt. The blade was short and so sunk in its sheath that it was necessary to force it up gradually by pressing against the point. This, indeed, was what the game savage was doing, and with good success. His watchful antagonist, however, kept a wary eye upon it, but he allowed the savage to work away until the handle was out, when Joe suddenly grasped it, jerked it out of the sheath and sunk it up to the handle into the Indian's breast, who gave a death groan and expired.

The other Indian was now to be thought of. It was not certain yet how far he had been crippled. It was found he had been severely wounded, but that, with the well-known desperation and thirst for revenge which characterizes the American savage, he had crawled some distance towards them, had propped his broken back against a log, and was trying to raise his gun to shoot, but in attempting to do this he would fall forward, and had to push against his gun to raise himself again. Logston, seeing that he was safe from him, made as soon as possible for the fort, which he reached about nightfall, and a pitiable plight he was in—blood and dirt from the crown of his head to the sole of his moccasin; no horse, no hat and no gun. They would scarce believe his bloody story, but next morning a company was made up to go to the battle ground. When they approached there was no appearance of dead Indians, and nothing of all Joe had talked of but the dead horse.

A trail, however, was soon found, and an appearance as if something had been dragged along it. On pursuing it they found the big Indian, dead as Julius Cæsar, lying behind a log and covered up with leaves. Still following the trail some hundred yards further, they found the broken-backed Indian, lying on his back, with his own knife sticking up to the hilt in his body, just below the breast bone, evidently showing that he had killed himself. After a long search they at last found the knife by which the big savage had been killed, forced down into the ground, apparently by the weight of a heel. This had been done by the crippled Indian, and the great efforts he must have made in his crippled and desperate condition to effect his purpose, furnishes one more instance of what Indians are capable under the greatest extremities. Some years after peace had been declared with the Indians, that frontier, like many others, became infested with a gang of outlaws, and it was in a contest between them and a band of "regulators" that Big Joe Logston lost his life.

JACK WELLS' DREAM AND WHAT CAME OF IT.

About the year 1777 a singular circumstance took place in Bedford county, Pa. A rather wealthy man named Jack Wells had gone with his family to the nearest fort for protection. In the Fall he took six or seven men, and an Irish girl to cook, and returned to his clearing to secure his potato crop. The night before starting back, Wells dreamed he had been attacked and gored by a bull. So strong an impression did this dream make, that he was sure some great danger impended, and so told his people. He slept again, and dreamed he was about to shoot a deer, and that when cocking his gun the main-spring broke. He again awoke, went to his gun to examine if all were right, and in cocking it, the main-spring broke. He was now alarmed, and they made haste to depart. To prevent delay, the girl was put on the only horse and started off first.

Before they had gone far, Wells' dog ran back as if scenting danger. Wells called him again and again, but he invariably kept running back to the house. Not wishing to abandon him, Wells started back, when five Indians sprang up from behind a fallen tree and came forward with extended hands. The men fled at once, and so would Wells, but he thought it useless. As the savages approached, however, he fancied the looks of one very powerful fellow boded no good, and he determined to risk flight. As the Indian approached, Wells flung at him his broken rifle and dashed off for the woods. Instead of firing, the savages joined in pursuit, seeming desirous of taking him prisoner. When, however, they found the fugitive was gaining on them, at a signal, they all stopped still in their tracks and fired at him together. Every bullet struck him, but without dropping him or retarding his flight.

Soon after he passed the place where his companions were concealed, and begged them, for God's sake, to fire and save him and themselves. They were afraid, and kept quiet. Wells continued his flight at heartburst speed, and soon overtook the girl on the horse. She, brave woman, quickly understood his danger, instantly dismounted, and urged him to take her place while she should hide herself. He mounted, but without whip, and could not get the old Bucephalus out of a trot. This delay soon brought the Indians within sight, and soon as they were near enough they fired, one of the balls striking him in the hip and lodging in his groin. But this saved his life, for the noise frightened the old horse into a gallop, and he escaped, but suffered severely for some time afterwards.

The Indians were afterwards pursued in their turn, and being surprised at their morning meal, four of them were killed and one escaped. A prisoner with this tribe afterwards related, however, that this fifth savage came home with leaves stuffed in bullet holes in his chest. A scout by the name of John Lane was out shortly after, under Captain Phillips, but became separated from the rest. On returning to the fort, he found them still absent and led another party in search of them. Within only a mile or two of the fort they found Captain Phillips and the whole of his men, fifteen in number, killed and scalped. When found they were all tied to saplings, and their bodies completely riddled. Another party, under Captain Dorsey, were cut off near the same time. The small predatory excursions of the Indians were sometimes quite as destructive as their regular encounters.

MAJOR ROBERT BENHAM AND HIS STRANGE ADVENTURE.

In the Autumn of 1779, a number of keel boats were ascending the Ohio, under the command of Major Rodgers, and had advanced as far as the mouth of Licking without accident. Here, however, they observed a few Indians standing upon the southern extremity of a sand bar, while a canoe, rowed by three others, was in the act of putting off from the Kentucky shore, as if for the purpose of taking them aboard. Rodgers instantly ordered the boats to be made fast on the Kentucky shore, while the crew, to the number of seventy men, well armed, cautiously advanced in such a manner as to encircle the spot where the enemy had been seen to land. Only five or six Indians had been seen, and no one dreamed of encountering more than fifteen or twenty enemies.

When Rodgers, however, had, as he supposed, completely surrounded the enemy, and was preparing to rush upon them from several quarters at once, he was thunderstruck at beholding several hundred savages suddenly spring up in front, rear and upon both flanks! They instantly poured in a close discharge of rifles, and then, throwing down their guns, fell upon the survivors with the tomahawk. The panic was complete and the slaughter prodigious. Major Rodgers, together with forty-five of his men, were almost instantly destroyed. The survivors made an effort to regain their boats, but the five men who had been left in charge of them had immediately put off from shore in the hindmost boat, and the enemy had already gained possession of the others. Disappointed in the attempt, they turned furiously upon the enemy, and, aided by the approach of darkness, forced their way through their lines, and, with the loss of several severely wounded, at length effected their escape to Harrodsburg.

Among the wounded was Captain Robert Benham. Shortly after breaking through the enemy's line, he was shot through both hips, and, the bones being shattered, he instantly fell to the ground. Fortunately a large tree had lately fallen near the spot where he lay, and, with great pain, he dragged himself into the top, and lay concealed among the branches. The Indians, eager in pursuit of the others, passed him without notice, and by midnight all was quiet. On the following day, the Indians returned to the battle ground, in order to strip the dead and take care of the boats. Benham, although in danger of famishing, permitted them to pass without making known his condition, very correctly supposing that his crippled legs would only induce them to tomahawk him upon the spot, in order to avoid the trouble of carrying him to their town.

He lay close, therefore, until the evening of the second day, when, perceiving a raccoon descending a tree near him, he shot it, hoping to devise some means of reaching it, when he could kindle a fire and make a meal. Scarcely had his gun cracked, however, when he heard a human cry, apparently not more than fifty yards off. Supposing it to be an Indian, he hastily reloaded his gun, and remained silent, expecting the approach of an enemy. Presently the same voice was heard again, but much nearer. Still Benham made no reply, but cocked his gun, and sat ready to fire as soon as an object appeared. A third halloo was quickly heard, followed by an exclamation of impatience and distress, which convinced Benham that the unknown must be a Kentuckian. As soon, therefore, as he heard the expression, "Whoever you are, for God's sake, answer me !" he replied with readiness, and the parties were soon together.

Benham, as we have already observed, was shot through both legs. The man who now appeared had escaped from the same battle, *with both arms broken!* Thus each was enabled to supply what the other wanted. Benham, having the perfect use of his arms, could load his gun and kill game with great readiness, while his friend, having the use of his legs, could kick the game to the spot where Benham sat, who was thus enabled to cook it. When no wood was near them, his companion would rake up brush with his feet, and gradually roll it within reach of Benham's hands, who constantly fed his companion and dressed *his* wounds as well as his own—tearing up both of their shirts for that purpose. They found some difficulty in procuring water at first; but Benham, at length, took his own hat, and placing the rim between the teeth of his companion, directed him to wade into the Licking up to his neck and dip the hat into the water by sinking his own head. The man who could walk was thus enabled to bring water, by means of his teeth, which Benham could afterward dispose of as was necessary.

In a few days they had killed all the squirrels and birds within reach, and the man with the broken arms was sent out to drive game within gunshot of the spot to which Benham was confined. Fortunately, wild turkeys were abundant in those woods, and his companion would walk around and drive them toward Benham, who seldom failed to kill two or three of each flock. In this manner they supported themselves for several weeks, until their wounds had healed so as to enable them to travel. They then shifted their quarters, and put up a small shed at the mouth of the Licking, where they encamped until late in November, anxiously expecting the arrival of some boat which should convey them to the Falls of Ohio.

On the 27th of November they observed a flat boat moving leisurely down the river. Benham instantly hoisted his hat upon a stick and hallooed loudly for help. The crew, however, supposing them to be Indians—at least suspecting them of an attempt to decoy them ashore—paid no attention to their signals of distress, but instantly put over to the opposite side of the river, and, manning every oar, endeavored to pass them as rapidly as possible. Benham beheld them pass him with a sensation bordering on despair; for the place was much frequented by Indians, and the approach of Winter threatened them with destruction unless speedily relieved. At length, after the boat had passed him nearly half a mile, he saw a canoe put off from its stern, and cautiously approach the Kentucky shore, evidently reconnoitering them with great suspicion.

He called loudly upon them for assistance, mentioned his name, and made known his condition. After a long parley, and many evidences of reluctance on the part of the crew, the canoe at length touched the shore, and Benham and his friend were taken on board. Their appearance excited much suspicion. They were almost entirely naked, and their faces were garnished with six weeks' growth of beard. The one was barely able to hobble on crutches, and the other could manage to feed himself with one of his hands. They were instantly taken to Louisville, where their clothes (which had been carried off in the boat which deserted them) were restored to them, and after a few weeks' confinement, both were perfectly restored.

Benham afterward served in the northwest throughout the whole of the Indian war, accompanied the expeditions of Harmar and Wilkinson, shared in the disaster of St. Clair, and afterward in the triumph of Wayne. Upon the return of peace, he bought the land upon which Rodgers had been defeated, and ended his days in tranquillity, amid the scenes which had witnessed his sufferings.

McCONNEL'S CAPTURE AND SIGNAL REVENGE.

Early in the Spring of 1780, according to Rev. McClung, Mr. Alexander McConnel, of Lexington, Ky., went into the woods on foot, to hunt deer. He soon killed a large buck, and returned home for a horse, in order to bring it in. During his absence, a party of five Indians, on one of their usual skulking expeditions, accidentally stumbled on the body of the deer, and perceiving that it had been recently killed, they naturally supposed that the hunter would speedily return to secure the flesh. Three of them, therefore, took their stations within close rifle shot of the deer, while the other two followed the trail of the hunter, and waylaid the path by which he was expected to return. McConnel, expecting no danger, rode carelessly along the path which the two scouts were watching, until he had come within view of the deer, when he was fired upon by the whole party, and his horse killed. While laboring to extricate himself from the dying animal, he was seized by his enemies, instantly overpowered and borne off as a prisoner.

His captors, however, seemed to be a merry, good-natured set of fellows, and permitted him to accompany them unbound; and, what was rather extraordinary, allowed him to retain his gun and hunting accoutrements. He accompanied them with great apparent cheerfulness through the day, and displayed his dexterity in shooting deer for the use of the company, until they began to regard him with great partiality. Having traveled with them in this manner for several days, they at length reached the banks of the Ohio river. Heretofore, the Indians had taken the precaution to bind him at night, although not very securely; but on that evening he remonstrated with them on the subject, and complained so strongly of the pain which the cords gave him, that they merely wrapped the buffalo tug loosely around his wrists, and having tied it in an easy knot, and attached the extremities of the rope to their own bodies, in order to prevent his moving without awakening them, they very composedly went to sleep, leaving the prisoner to follow their example or not, as he pleased.

McConnel determined to effect his escape that night, if possible, as on the following night they would cross the river, which would render it much more difficult. He, therefore, lay quietly until near midnight, anxiously ruminating upon the best means of effecting his object. Accidentally casting his eyes in the direction of his feet, they fell upon the glittering blade of a knife, which had escaped its sheath, and was now lying near the feet of one of the Indians. To reach it with his hands without disturbing the two Indians to whom he was fastened, was impossible, and it was very hazardous to attempt to draw it up with his feet. This, however, he attempted. With much difficulty he grasped the blade between his toes, and, after repeated and long-continued efforts, succeeded at length in bringing it within reach of his hands.

To cut his cords was then but the work of a moment, and gradually and silently extricating his person from the arms of the Indians, he walked to the fire and sat down. He saw that his work was but half done; that if he should attempt to return home, without destroying his enemies, he would assuredly be pursued and probably overtaken, when his fate would be certain. On the other hand, it seemed almost impossible for a single man to succeed in a conflict with five Indians, even although unarmed and asleep. He could not hope to deal a blow with his knife so silently and fatally, as to destroy each one of his enemies in turn, without awakening the rest. Their slumbers were proverbially light and restless; and if he failed with a single one, he must instantly be overpowered by the survivors. The knife, therefore, was out of the question.

After anxious reflection for a few minutes, he formed his plan. The guns of the Indians were stacked near the fire; their knives and tomahawks were in sheaths by their sides. The latter he dared not touch for fear of awakening their owners; but the former he carefully removed, with the exception of two, and hid them in the woods, where he knew the Indians would not readily find them. He then returned to the spot where the Indians were still sleeping, perfectly ignorant of the fate preparing for them, and taking a gun in each hand, he rested the muzzles upon a log within six feet of his victims, and having taken deliberate aim at the head of one and the heart of another, he pulled both triggers at the same moment.

Both shots were fatal. At the report of their guns the others sprang to their feet, and stared wildly around them. McConnel, who had run instantly to the spot where the other rifles were hid, hastily seized one of them and fired at two of his enemies, who happened to stand in a line with each other. The nearest fell dead, being shot through the centre of the body; the second fell also, bellowing loudly, but quickly recovering, limped off into the woods as fast as possible. The fifth, and only one who remained unhurt, darted off like a deer, with a yell which announced equal terror and astonishment. McConnel, not wishing to fight any more such battles, selected his own rifle from the stack, and made the best of his way to Lexington, where he arrived safely within two days.

Shortly afterward, Mrs. Dunlap, of Fayette, who had been several months a prisoner amongst the Indians on Mad river, made her escape, and returned to Lexington. She reported that the survivor returned to his tribe with a lamentable tale. He related that they had taken a fine young hunter near Lexington, and had brought him safely as far as the Ohio; that while encamped upon the bank of the river, a large party of white men had fallen upon them in the night, and killed all his companions, together with the poor, defenceless prisoner, who lay bound hand and foot, unable either to escape or resist!

AN ADVENTURE OF THE THREE BROTHERS McAFEE.

Early in May, 1781, McAfee's station, in the neighborhood of Harrodsburg, was alarmed. On the morning of the 9th, Samuel McAfee, accompanied by another man, left the fort in order to visit a small plantation in the neighborhood, and at the distance of three hundred yards from the gate, they were fired upon by a party of Indians in ambush. The man who accompanied him instantly fell, and McAfee attempted to regain the fort. While running rapidly for that purpose, he found himself suddenly intercepted by an Indian, who, springing out of the canebrake, planted himself directly in his path. There was no time for compliments. Each glared upon the other for an instant in silence, and both raising their guns at the same moment, pulled the triggers together. The Indian's rifle snapped, while McAfee's ball passed directly through his brain. Having no time to reload his gun, he sprang over the body of his antagonist, and continued his flight to the fort.

When within one hundred yards of the gate he was met by his two brothers, Robert and James, who, at the report of the guns, had hurried out to the assistance of their brother. Samuel hastily informed them of their danger, and exhorted them instantly to return. James readily complied, but Robert, deaf to all remonstrances, declared that he must have a view of the dead Indian. He ran on for that purpose, and having regaled himself with that spectacle, was hastily returning by the same path, when he saw five or six Indians between him and the fort, evidently bent upon taking him alive. All his activity and presence of mind were now put in requisition. He ran rapidly from tree to tree, endeavoring to turn their flank and reach one of the gates, and after a variety of turns and doublings in the thick wood, he found himself pressed by only one Indian. McAfee, hastily throwing himself behind a fence, turned upon his pursuer, and compelled him to take shelter behind a tree.

Both stood still for a moment, McAfee having his gun cocked, and the sight fixed upon the tree, at the spot where he supposed the Indian would thrust out his head in order to have a view of his antagonist. After waiting a few seconds he was gratified. The Indian slowly and cautiously exposed a part of his head, and began to elevate his rifle. As soon as a sufficient mark presented itself McAfee fired, and the Indian fell. While turning, in order to continue his flight, he was fired on by a party of six, which compelled him again to tree. But scarcely had he done so, when, from the opposite quarter, he received the fire of three more enemies, which made the bark fly around him and knocked up the dust about his feet. Thinking his post rather too hot for safety, he neglected all shelter and ran directly for the fort, which, in defiance of all opposition, he reached in safety, to the inexpressible joy of his brothers, who had despaired of his return.

The Indians now opened a heavy fire upon the fort, in their usual manner; but finding every effort useless, they hastily decamped, without any loss beyond the two who had fallen by the hands of the brothers, and without having inflicted any upon the garrison. Within half an hour, Major McGary brought up a party from Harrodsburg at full gallop, and, uniting with the garrison, pursued the enemy with all possible activity. They soon overtook them, and a sharp action ensued. The Indians were routed in a few minutes, with the loss of six warriors left dead upon the ground, and many others wounded, who, as usual, were borne off. The pursuit was continued for several miles, but from the thickness of the woods and the extreme activity and address of the enemy, was not very effectual. McGary lost one man dead upon the spot and another mortally wounded.

BRYANT'S AND HOGAN'S PARTIES ATTACKED BY SAVAGES.

About the same time Bryant's station was much harassed by small parties of the enemy. This, as we have already remarked, was a frontier post, and generally received the brunt of Indian hostility. It had been settled in 1779 by four brothers from North Carolina, one of whom, William, had married a sister of Colonel Daniel Boone. The Indians were constantly lurking in the neighborhood, waylaying the paths, stealing their horses and butchering their cattle. It at length became necessary to hunt in parties of twenty or thirty men, so as to be able to meet and repel those attacks, which were every day becoming more bold and frequent.

One afternoon, about the 20th of May, William Bryant, accompanied by twenty men, left the fort on a hunting expedition down the Elkhorn Creek. They moved with caution, until they had passed all the points where ambuscades had generally been formed, when, seeing no enemy, they became more bold, and determined, in order to sweep a large extent of country, to divide their company into two parties. One of them, conducted by Bryant in person, was to descend the Elkhorn on its southern bank, flanking out largely, and occupying as much ground as possible. The other, under the orders of James Hogan, a young farmer in good circumstances, was to move down in a parallel line upon the north bank. The two parties were to meet at night, and encamp together at the mouth of Cane Run.

Each punctually performed the first part of their plans. Hogan, however, had traveled but a few hundred yards, when he heard a loud voice behind him exclaim, in very good English, "Stop, boys!" Hastily looking back, they saw several Indians, on foot, pursuing them as rapidly as possible. Without halting to count numbers, the party put spurs to their horses and dashed through the woods at full speed, the Indians keeping close behind them, and at times gaining upon them. There was a led horse in company, which had been brought with them for the purpose of packing game. This was instantly abandoned, and fell into the hands of the Indians. Several of them lost their hats in the eagerness of flight; but quickly getting into the open woods, they left their pursuers so far behind that they had leisure to breathe and inquire of each other whether it was worth while to kill their horses before they had ascertained the number of the enemy.

They quickly determined to cross the creek, and await the approach of the Indians. If they found them superior to their own and Bryant's party united, they would immediately return to the fort; as, by continuing their march to the mouth of Cane Run, they would bring a superior enemy upon their friends, and endanger the lives of the whole party. They accordingly crossed the creek, dismounted and awaited the approach of the enemy. By this time it had become dark. The Indians were distinctly heard approaching the creek upon the opposite side, and, after a short halt, a solitary warrior descended the bank, and began to wade through the stream.

Hogan waited until he had emerged from the gloom of the trees which grew upon the bank, and as soon as he had reached the middle of the stream, where the light was more distinct, he took deliberate aim and fired. A great splashing in the water was heard, but presently all became quiet. The pursuit was discontinued, and the party, remounting their horses, returned home. Anxious, however, to apprise Bryant's party of their danger, they left the fort before daylight on the ensuing morning, and rode rapidly down the creek, in the direction of the mouth of Cane. When within a few hundred yards of the spot where they supposed the encampment to be, they heard the report of many guns in quck succession. Supposing that Bryant had fallen in with a herd of buffalo, they quickened their march, in order to take part in the sport.

The morning was foggy, and the smoke of the guns lay so heavily upon the ground that they could see nothing until they had approached within twenty yards of the creek, when they suddenly found themselves within pistol shot of a party of Indians, very composedly seated upon their packs and preparing their pipes. Both parties were much startled, but quickly recovering, they sheltered themselves, as usual, and the action opened with great vivacity. The Indians maintained their ground for half an hour with some firmness, but being hard pressed in front and turned in flank, they at length gave way, and, being closely pursued, were ultimately routed with considerable loss, which, however, could not be distinctly ascertained. Of Hogan's party, one man was killed on the spot, and three others wounded, none mortally.

It happened that Bryant's company had encamped at the mouth of Cane, as had been agreed upon, and were unable to account for Hogan's absence. About daylight they had heard a bell at a distance, which they immediately recognized as the one belonging to the led horse which had accompanied Hogan's party, and which, as we have seen, had been abandoned to the enemy the evening before. Supposing their friends to be bewildered in the fog and unable to find their camp,

Bryant, accompanied by Grant, one of his men, mounted a horse and rode to the spot where the bell was still ringing. They quickly fell into an ambuscade, and were fired upon. Bryant was mortally, and Grant severely, wounded, the first being shot through the hip and both knees, the latter through the back.

Being both able to keep the saddle, however, they set spurs to their horses, and arrived at the station shortly after breakfast. The Indians, in the meantime, had fallen upon the encampment and instantly dispersed it; and, while preparing to regale themselves after their victory, were suddenly attacked, as we have seen, by Hogan. The timidity of Hogan's party, at the first appearance of the Indians, was the cause of the death of Bryant. The same men who fled so hastily in the evening were able the next morning, by a little firmness, to vanquish the same party of Indians. Had they stood at first, an equal success would probably have attended them, and the life of their leader would have been preserved.

A SCHOOLMASTER ATTACKED BY A WILD CAT.

We have now to notice an adventure of a different kind, and which, from its singularity, is entitled to a place in our pages. In 1783 Lexington was only a cluster of cabins, one of which was used as a school house. One morning in May, McKinney, the teacher, was sitting alone at his desk, busily engaged in writing, when, hearing a slight noise at the door, he turned his head and beheld—what do you suppose, reader? A tall Indian in his war paint, brandishing his tomahawk or handling his knife? No! an enormous cat, with her forefeet upon the step of the door, her tail curled over her back, her bristles erect, and her eyes glancing rapidly through the room as if in search of game.

McKinney's position at first completely concealed him, but a slight and involuntary motion of his chair, at sight of this shaggy inhabitant of the forest, attracted puss's attention, and their eyes met. McKinney, having heard much of the power of "the human face divine" in quelling the audacity of wild animals, attempted to disconcert the intruder by a frown. But puss was not to be bullied. Her eyes flashed fire, her tail waved angrily, and she began to gnash her teeth, evidently bent upon serious hostility. Seeing his danger, McKinney hastily arose and attempted to snatch a cylindrical rule from a table which stood within reach, but the cat was too quick for him.

Darting upon him with the proverbial activity of her tribe, she fastened upon his side with her teeth, and began to rend and tear with her claws like a fury. McKinney's clothes were, in an instant, torn from his side and his flesh dreadfully mangled by the enraged animal, whose strength and ferocity filled him with astonishment. He in vain attempted to disengage her from his side. Her long, sharp teeth were fastened between his ribs, and his efforts served but to enrage her the more. Seeing his blood flow very copiously from the numerous wounds in his side, he became seriously alarmed, and not knowing what else to do, he threw himself upon the edge of the table, and pressed her against the sharp corner with the whole weight of his body.

The cat now began to utter the most wild and discordant cries, and McKinney at the same time lifting up his voice in concert, the two together sent forth notes so doleful as to alarm the whole town. Women, who are always the first in hearing or spreading news, were now the first to come to McKinney's assistance. But so strange and unearthly was the harmony within the school house, that they hesitated long before they ventured to enter. At length the boldest of them rushed in, and seeing McKinney bending over the corner of the table, and writhing his body as if in great pain, she at first supposed that he was laboring under a severe fit of the colic; but quickly perceiving the cat, which was now in the agonies of death, she screamed out, "Why, good heaven! Mr. McKinney, what is the matter?"

"I have caught a cat, madam!" replied he, gravely turning around, while the sweat streamed from his face, under the mingled operation of fright and fatigue, and agony. Most of the neighbors had now arrived, and attempted to disengage the dead cat from her antagonist; but so firmly were her tusks locked between his ribs, that this was a work of no small difficulty. Scarcely had it been effected, when McKinney became very sick, and was compelled to go to bed. In a few days, however, he had totally recovered, and so late as 1820 was alive, and a resident of Bourbon county, Ky., where he was often heard to affirm, that he, at any time, had rather fight two Indians than one wild cat.

DAVID MORGAN'S DESPERATE COMBAT WITH TWO SAVAGES.

About the same time a conflict more unequal, and equally remarkable, took place in another part of the country. David Morgan, a relation of the celebrated General Daniel Morgan, had settled upon the Monongahela during the earlier period of the Revolutionary war, and at this time had ventured to occupy a cabin at the distance of several miles from any settlement. One morning, having sent his younger children out to a field at a considerable distance from the house, he became uneasy about them, and repaired to the spot where they were working, armed, as usual, with a good rifle. While sitting upon the fence, and giving some directions as to their work, he observed two Indians upon the other side of the field, gazing earnestly upon the party. He instantly called to the children to make their escape, while he should attempt to cover their retreat.

The odds were greatly against him, as, in addition to other circumstances, he was nearly seventy years of age, and, of course, unable to contend with his enemies in running. The house was more than a mile distant, but the children, having two hundred yards the start, and being effectually covered by their father, were soon so far in front that the Indians turned their attention entirely to the old man. He ran, for several hundred yards, with an activity which astonished himself, but perceiving that he would be overtaken long before he could reach his home, he fairly turned at bay, and prepared for a strenuous resistance. The woods through which they were running were very thin, and consisted almost entirely of small trees, behind which it was difficult to obtain proper shelter.

When Morgan adopted the above-mentioned resolution, he had just passed a large walnut, which stood like a patriarch among the saplings which surrounded it, and it became necessary to run back about ten steps in order to regain it. The Indians became startled at the sudden advance of the fugitive, and were compelled to halt among a cluster of saplings, where they anxiously strove to shelter themselves. This, however, was impossible; and Morgan, who was an excellent marksman, saw enough of the person of one of them to justify him in risking a shot. His enemy instantly fell, mortally wounded. The other Indian, taking advantage of Morgan's empty gun, sprang from his shelter and advanced rapidly upon him. The old man, having no time to reload his gun, was compelled to fly a second time. The Indian gained rapidly upon him, and, when within twenty steps, fired, but with so unsteady an aim that Morgan was totally unhurt, the ball having passed over his shoulder.

He now again stood at bay, clubbing his rifle for a blow; while the Indian, dropping his empty gun, brandished his tomahawk and prepared to throw it at his enemy. Morgan struck with the butt of his gun and the Indian whirled his tomahawk at one and the same moment. Both blows took effect, and both were at once wounded and disarmed. The breech of the rifle was broken against the Indian's skull, and the edge of the tomahawk was shattered against the barrel of the rifle, having first cut off two of the fingers of Morgan's left hand. The Indian then attempting to draw his knife, Morgan grappled him and bore him to the ground. A furious struggle ensued, in which the old man's strength failed, and the Indian succeeded in turning him.

Planting his knee on the breast of his enemy, and yelling loudly, as is usual with them upon any turn of fortune, he again felt for his knife, in order to terminate the struggle at once; but having lately stolen a woman's apron and tied it around his waist, his knife was so much confined that he had great difficulty in finding the handle. Morgan, in the meantime, being a regular pugilist, according to the custom of Virginia, and perfectly at home in a ground struggle, took advantage of the awkwardness of the Indian, and got one of the fingers of his right hand between his teeth. The Indian tugged and roared in vain, struggling to extricate it. Morgan held him fast, and began to assist him in hunting for the knife. Each seized it at the same moment, the Indian by the blade and Morgan by the handle, but with a very slight hold.

The Indian, having the firmest hold, began to draw the knife further out of its sheath, when Morgan, suddenly giving his finger a furious bite, twitched the knife dexterously through his hand, cutting it severely. Both now sprang to their feet, Morgan brandishing his adversary's knife, and still holding his finger between his teeth. In vain the poor Indian struggled to get away, rearing, plunging and bolting, like an unbroken colt. The teeth of the white man were like a vise, and he at length succeeded in giving him a stab in the side. The Indian received it without falling, the knife having struck his ribs; but a second blow, aimed at the stomach, proved more effectual, and the savage fell. Morgan thrust the knife, handle and all, into the cavity of the body, directed it upward, and starting to his feet, made the best of his way home.

The neighborhood was quickly alarmed; and, hurrying to the spot where the struggle had taken place, they found the first Indian lying where he had fallen, but the second had disappeared. A broad trail of blood, however, conducted to a fallen tree-top, within one hundred yards of the spot, into which the poor fellow had dragged himself, and where he now lay, bleeding but still alive. He had plucked the knife from his wound, and was endeavoring to dress it with the stolen apron —which had cost him his life—when his enemies approached. The love of life was still strong within him, however. He greeted them with what was intended for an insinuating smile, held out his hand and exclaimed, in broken English, "How de do, broder? how de do? Glad to see you!" But, poor fellow! the love was all on his side. Their brotherhood extended only to tomahawking, scalping and skinning him, all of which operations were performed within a few minutes after the meeting. To such an extent had mutual injury inflamed both parties.

EVENTS FROM DUNMORE'S WAR TO MORAVIAN MASSACRE.

In presenting biographical sketches of the leading early pioneers of the West, we were obliged to depart somewhat from the chronological sequence of events. We had proceeded as far as the treaty made by Lord Dunmore with the Ohio Indians in 1774. On April 19th of the next year (1775) was fought the opening battle of the American Revolution. This august event created a mighty change everywhere. During most of the year, however, there was peace on the western border, save occasional acts of hostility on the part of the Shawnees and other hostile tribes, instigated no doubt by British agents. The frontiers were in a great state of anxiety and apprehension regarding a close alliance between England and the confederated western tribes.

Sir William Johnson, the British Superintendent of Indian Affairs, had, as we have shown, a most potent influence among the redmen of the whole country. He, more than any other, could hold them in check or incite them to an open rupture. To cope with these tribes alone would be comparatively an easy matter, but to deal with them when constantly goaded on and assisted by British wealth and power, and more especially when the whole fighting strength of the country was drawn eastward to contend with the large and well-drilled armies of Britain, was quite a different matter.

Sir William was now dead, it is true, but it was not long before his successors—his son, sons-in-law and the powerful Mohawk Chief, Brant, arrayed themselves openly against the colonies. Their bad influence with the Six Nations was greatly dreaded by Washington and the Continental leaders, and an early effort was made to have the New York nations remain neutral. This was no easy task, for the tory leaders were already busy among them, and at last the Johnsons, gathering a force of five hundred tories and savages, moved westward to Oswego and held a council, the result of which was that four out of the six nations composing the Iroquois, allied themselves openly or secretly with the British. Through emissaries dispatched thence to the western tribes, they, too, were soon divided in council, and—already angered by the constant invasion of their hunting grounds by the pioneers, and by the constant robbery of the lands under their feet through artful and despoiling treaties—their straggling scalping parties so filled the woods that no family was safe outside a fort. Had a Pontiac then been alive to merge and weld them into one hostile and cosentient mass; to inspire and lead them on to action, it would have gone hard, indeed, with the whole western frontier.

To counteract the malevolent operations of the British and the Mohawk Valley tories, Congress, in July, formed three Indian Departments—a northern one for the Six Nations and those tribes north and east of them; a middle one for the western tribes, and a southern one for the Cherokees, Catawbas, and all tribes south of Kentucky. The commissioners of these several departments were to keep close watch and ward over their respective tribes, as well as upon the King's superintendents and agents among them. They were to endeavor to hold the natives quiet and neutral in the Revolutionary contest. Councils were also suggested, and "talks" prepared to send to the different tribes to explain the nature of the struggle between England and America.

The first conference was held at Albany in August, at which, however, the Six Nations were not fully represented, and some even of those who were present immediately afterwards went over to the British. The second conference was held in October at Fort Pitt, and was well attended by delegates from the western tribes, who were much divided in opinion among themselves.

THE DELAWARE CHIEFS, CAPTAINS PIPE AND WHITE EYES.

The commissioners having first informed the assembled chiefs of the nature of the dispute between the mother country and America, illustrated it in the following manner: "Suppose a father had a little son whom he loved and indulged while young, but, growing up to be a youth, began to think of having some help from him; and, making up a small pack, he bid him carry it for him. The boy cheerfully takes this pack up, following his father with it. The father, finding the boy willing and obedient, continues in this way, and as the boy grows stronger, so the father makes the pack bigger and heavier; yet, as long as the boy is able to carry the pack, he does so without grumbling. At length, however, the boy having arrived at manhood, and while the father is making up a pack for him, in comes a person of an evil disposition, and learning who was to be the carrier of the pack, advises the father to make it heavier, for surely the son is able to carry a larger pack. The father, listening rather to the bad adviser than consulting his own judgment and his feelings of tenderness, follows the bad advice of the hard-hearted adviser, and makes up a very heavy load for his son to carry.

"The son, now grown up, and examining the weight of the load he is to carry, addresses the parent in these words: 'Dear father, this pack is too heavy for me to carry; do, pray, lighten it! I am willing to do what I can, but am unable to carry *this* load.' The father's heart having become hardened, and the bad adviser urging him to whip him if he disobey and refuse to carry the pack, now arrogantly demands his son to take up his pack and move off, or he will whip him, and already takes up the stick to beat him. 'So,' says the son, 'am I to be served thus for not doing what I am unable to do? Well, if entreaties are all nothing with you, father, and the matter is to be decided by blows, whether I am able or not to carry this pack, so heavy, then I have no other chance left me but that of resisting your unreasonable demand by strength, and thus, by striking each other, learn who is the strongest.'"

The chiefs were furthermore warned not to mix in this family quarrel on penalty of being considered parties to it, but to "sit still" until the contest should be over, and not take up the hatchet for either side; but if they should move in this quarrel, and the Americans should prove victorious, then they would surely be terribly punished.

At this time a delegation of the Senecas, the most numerous as well as the most warlike of the Six Nations, were at Pittsburgh, to learn what part the western Indians, and more especially the Delawares, would take during the contest. Hearing Captain White Eyes, a mighty Chief of the Delawares, declaring openly in favor of the Americans and their cause, they were very much chagrined and incensed. They sharply and haughtily reminded him that the Delawares had been conquered by the Six Nations; were nothing but women, and wore petticoats. This was indeed true. The Delawares had long been subject to the Iroquois, and had been so chased about and driven from pillar to post by their conquerors, that, for the sake of peace and independence, they had crossed the mountains and settled in the Ohio country. For many years back they had been thriving and growing more powerful and independent, and now it was high time to assert themselves and hurl back the Iroquois' insults with defiance.

White Eyes therefore arose, and with an air of disdain, replied: "I well know that the Six Nations esteem the Delawares as a conquered people and their inferiors. You say that you once conquered us; that you cut off our legs; put petticoats upon us; gave us a hoe and a corn-pounder, saying: 'Now, women, your business henceforward shall be to plant and hoe corn and pound the same for us, men and warriors!' Look at my legs! If, as you say, they were cut off, they have grown again to their proper size; the petticoat I have thrown away and have put on again my own dress; the corn-hoe and pounder I have exchanged for these firearms, and I declare here and now, that *I am a man*, and," waving his hand in the direction of the Allegheny river, he continued proudly, "all the country on the other side of that river is *mine!*"

No address so bold or daring had ever before been delivered by a Delaware chief to the Six Nations, and it was afterwards made the occasion for a division of the nation. There were many Delawares who were greatly alarmed at the haughty and arrogant language of their chief to the Six Nations, to whom they had been so long subject, and of whose power and resentment they stood in mortal dread. So the Monseys, under the lead of their chief, Newalike, withdrew from the Turtle Tribe and united themselves to the Wolf Tribe of Delawares, under Captain Pipe. They then retired to a new settlement near Lake Erie, and took good care to let the Six Nations know that they did not at all approve of what Captain White Eyes had said.

This Captain Pipe was a very artful, designing man, and a chief of considerable ability and influence. He had for some time plotted for a division of his nation. His ambitious spirit would brook no rival, and while White Eyes leaned to the Americans, Pipe's intriguing heart belonged wholly to the British and to the Indian Confederacy which affiliated with them. The affairs of the Indians at this juncture were so mixed up with those of the Moravian or Christian Delawares, settled at that time on the Muskingum, that it is very hard to separate them. We shall, however, treat of the Muskingum settlements further on. Netawatwees, the head chief of the Delawares, had always been the warm friend of the Moravians; had invited them to settle near him; had extended to them every aid and courtesy, and was at one time, like King Agrippa of old, almost " persuaded to be a Christian " himself.

The efforts of this wise and venerable chief were now devoted to preserving peace. In this noble aim, he was ably seconded by Killbuck and Big Cat. But his best endeavors were ever frustrated by the restless Captain Pipe, who was warlike and vengeful, ever brooding over old resentments. This redskin Mephistopheles now kept aloof from the council of the nation, and busily spread the report that White Eyes had made secret engagements with the Americans with a view to the enslavement of his own people. White Eyes minded him not, but even headed a deputation to the Wyandots in the interest of peace; but they refused his peace belts, and a British officer, who was there, even snatched them from his hands, cut them to pieces and then insultingly told the chief to " begone if he set any value on his head."

Shortly after an embassy of twenty warriors arrived among the still steadfast Delawares, and demanded their assistance, stating that all the western tribes had confederated as one man for the war, and that the Turtle Tribe of Delawares alone stood out for an inglorious, ignominious peace. Meanwhile every variety of artful report was industriously circulated, in order to pervert the minds of the young and ardent Delawares, and to compel them, as it were, to take the war path. Unfortunately, just previous to this crisis, Netawatwees died at Pittsburgh, declaring, as his last will, that the Gospel should be preached to the Indians without any let or hindrance. This resolve was not only endorsed but steadfastly carried out by White Eyes, and on the Moravians positively declaring that they would forsake the country if the Delawares should go to war, all their chiefs, in solemn conclave assembled, resolved to keep the peace and maintain a strict neutrality at any and at every hazard.

Early in 1778 the hostile savages began again to commit depredations against the border, stealing horses, burning houses, plundering, murdering and destroying. On returning from these bloody and merciless marauds, they would frequently pass with their prisoners and scalps through the peaceable Indian settlements, in order to exasperate the frontiermen, and make them believe *them* the guilty aggressors.

SIMON GIRTY, ELLIOTT AND MCKEE DESERT FROM FORT PITT.

Truly a troubled and tempestuous time had these friendly Indians, and to cap the climax of their miseries, there now arrived at the Delaware town Goschochking, (now Coshocton, Ohio,) a squad of twelve base deserters from Fort Pitt, led on by those notorious tories, Simon Girty, Matthew Elliott and Alexander McKee—the last, Sir William Johnson's old deputy among the Indians. "It was enough," dolefully writes Heckewelder, "to break the hearts of the missionaries." This tory defection, just at this alarming juncture, caused quite as much terror and anxiety among the Delawares as it did among the whites themselves. The mouths of these malevolent renegades were filled with all manner of evil and lying. They impudently asserted that Washington had been killed; that his armies were cut to pieces by the British; that Congress had been dispersed; that the whole East was in possession of the enemy, and that the force at Fort Pitt had nothing left for it to do but to possess the Indian lands, killing men, women and children.

The effect of these false and malicious stories, just at a time when Captain Pipe had been so long working to win over the Delaware tribe to take open sides with the British and to make a combined maraud against the border, was prodigious. Captains White Eyes, Killbuck and Big Cat, however, stood firm, and did all they could to allay the excitement. A grand council of the nation was called to discuss Pipe's earnest advice that arms should be immediately taken up against the Americans. White Eyes, the noble old chief, made a most spirited and vehement address to all the hot-blooded young warriors; denounced Girty and his *confreres* as liars, and begged just for ten days, and then, if no news came to disprove what had been told them by these deserters, he would not only favor immediate hostilities, but he would himself lead them on: "Not like the bear hunter," he sarcastically concluded, "who sets the dog on the animal to be beaten about with his paws, while he keeps at a safe distance. No, he would lead them on in person; place himself in the front, and be the first to fall."

The ten days were at length decreed. It was a most anxious and critical time. As day after day passed without further news from Fort Pitt, those Indians who desired peace wavered, and, finally, were so despondent and hopeless that they no longer made opposition to Pipe and his war tribe; but the fiery young zealots of *both* tribes commenced sounding the war drum, shaving their heads, laying on the scalp plume, and otherwise preparing to set off on a bloody raid against the white settlements.

But God did not so will it. Just in the very nick of time, the young Moravian, John Heckewelder, had arrived from the East at Fort Pitt, and, hearing of the late defection, set off without one instant's delay to the Moravian towns. Here he found everything in the direst confusion. The last day of the ten was at hand, and the whole fighting strength of the Delawares, together with a large force of Wyandots from Sandusky, were to start off early next morning on the war path.

Not one moment to be lost! Spent and jaded as he was, Heckewelder soon mounted a fresh horse, and rode thirty miles farther to Goschochking, the chief Delaware town, which he found in great commotion, all the braves being decked out for war. His reception was discouraging. Even Captain White Eyes and the other chiefs who had always befriended the Moravians, drew back in the coldest and most haughty manner when the hand was extended. At length the great chief, White Eyes, boldly stepped forward and said that if what Girty and his party asserted were so, the Delawares no longer had a friend among the Americans, and wanted to know the exact truth. He then asked· "Is Washington killed? Are the American armies cut to pieces? Is there no longer a Congress? and are the few thousands who escaped the British armies, embodying themselves at Fort Pitt to take the Indian's country, slaughtering even our women and children?"

Heckewelder then stood up, his honest face and truthful manner carrying conviction with every word, and denounced all Girty's stories as utter fabrications. He asserted, on the contrary, that Burgoyne's whole army had just surrendered, and that he (Heckewelder) was the bearer of the most friendly messages from General Hand and Colonel Gibson, of Fort Pitt, advising them to continue neutral.

In proof of his statement, Heckewelder put a newspaper in White Eye's hands, containing the account of the battle of Saratoga and the surrender of Burgoyne, which the glad old chief, now completely reassured, held up before his people, saying: "See, my friends and relatives! this document containeth great events—not the song of a bird, but the truth!" Then, stepping up to Heckewelder, he joyfully said: "You are welcome with us, brother."

Thus, for the time, did all Pipe's machinations and ambitious schemes come to naught. His mortified spies slunk back to their own Wolf tribe, while Captain White Eyes, knowing that Girty, Elliott and McKee had gone on to the Shawnee towns on the Scioto with the same fabrications, immediately dispatched fleet runners thither with the following message: "Grandchildren! Ye Shawneese! Some days ago a flock of birds, that had come on from the East, lit at Goschochking, imposing a song of theirs upon us, which song had nigh proved our ruin. Should these birds, which, on leaving us, took their flight towards Scioto, endeavor to impose a song on you likewise, do not listen to them, for they lie."

DEATH OF CAPTAIN WHITE EYES—A HORRID MASSACRE.

This, as stated, took place in the Spring of '78, and ever after, this precious trio of tories—Girty, Elliott and McKee—were a full match, in every species of hostile attack and savage depredation, with that other trio of the Mohawk Valley—Johnson, Butler and Brant.

Shortly after the desertion, Captain White Eyes returned to Fort Pitt to be nearer Colonel George Morgan, the Indian agent, and with his aid to prevent his nation from being dragged into war. He was also, seeing the flourishing condition of the Moravian settlements on the Muskingum, exceedingly anxious to have his tribe embrace Christianity, but God did not so will it, for while accompanying General McIntosh to the Tuscarawas, where Fort Laurens was to be built for the protection of the peaceable Indians, he was seized with the small-pox and died, greatly lamented by both reds and whites. He was a wise, sensible and peaceable chief, always friendly to Christianity and the cause of the colonies. Pipe, however, heard of this removal of his rival with ill-concealed joy, and promptly remarked, in a council of chiefs, that "the Great Spirit had put him out of the way that the nation might be saved." White Eyes' death was, according to Indian custom, at once made known to all the nations around, and even the distant Cherokees sent to Goschochking a deputation of fourteen chiefs to condole with the mourning Delawares. White Eyes' successor being very young in years, three other chiefs, Killbuck, Big Cat and Tetepachksi, officiated till he should become of age; and when, afterwards, Pipe and the war party became supreme, retired with him to Smoky Island, across the river from Fort Pitt, for protection. It will be seen shortly, how foully this young chief was dealt with.

The most remarkable event that happened in 1779, was the wonderful expedition of George Rogers Clark—called the Hannibal of the West—against the British force in the northwest, and his capture of the posts of Kaskaskia and Vincennes. But those events were of such a singular character and were attended with so many romantic features and deeds of daring, that we shall give them a special and separate mention.

A HORRID MASSACRE.

During three years, '79, '80 and '81, Indian cruelties and devastations in the West continued with more or less constancy and severity. The borders were greatly drained of their fighting strength to supply the eastern armies, then waging a war to the death with all the power of Great Britain. The West was necessarily left to maintain itself as best it could against the whole confederacy of western tribes, backed by English hate and wealth; inspired from British forts and more especially from Detroit, and officered by British or tory leaders.

In the Spring of '82, however, occurred a dread and lamentable event, which not only rests as an indelible stain upon the fair fame of the western border, but which added for a long time a rancorous bitterness to all the subsequent savage warfare. We allude, of course, to the dastardly and execrable massacre of the Moravian Indians on the Muskingum. For some time the whole frontier had been in a very excited and discontented state, and that Spring savage barbarities had commenced earlier than usual. On account of the constant harassment by Indians, the failure of Clark's and Gibson's expeditions, and the almost total annihilation of Colonel Archibald Lochry's command of over one hundred of the very bravest and foremost riflemen of Westmoreland county, there existed universal gloom and dismay. Add to this the long and angry controversy which had prevailed about the boundary between Virginia and Pennsylvania, ending in disputed authority, vexatious suits, insecure titles, excuses for neglect of military duty, and a want of authority by the county lieutenants over the militia for twenty miles on either side of the line in dispute, and the terribly demoralized state of the West can be fully imagined.

So restless and disheartened had the settlers become, that very many talked of flying back east of the mountains, while a new scheme of emigration to the Ohio, championed by an adventurer of the name of Jackson, had—wild and dangerous as it was—created quite an excitement, and had won very many adherents. As there were a large number of bitter tories then in the West, it was shrewdly suspected at Fort Pitt that so hazardous and foolhardy a project would never have been entertained except with the promise of a British protectorate from Detroit. They must either have been cut to pieces by the Indians, or have had an understanding with the British, who instigated all the border marauds of that day. May 25th was appointed for the rendezvous.

But this was not all, nor the worst. As Doddridge in his Notes says: "It would seem that the long continuance of the Indian war had debased a considerable portion of our population to the savage state. Having lost so many relatives by the Indians, and witnessed their horrid murders and other depredations upon so extensive a scale, they became subjects of that indiscriminating thrist for revenge, which is such a prominent feature in the savage character."

We cannot well present an intelligible statement of what occurred on the border in 1782, without giving an account—as brief as is consistent with clearness—of the Moravian Missions west of the Alleghenies. The earlier history of the Moravians *east* of the mountains and their dealings with the natives, are replete with interest and a mournful pathos, and would fill a volume, but with that branch of the subject we have nothing to do.

Chapter VI.

GOD'S MIGHTY WORK IN THE WILDERNESS.

> Where late the war whoop's hideous sound
> Alone disturbed the silence round ;
> Where late the godless wigwam stood,
> Deep in the unbounded range of wood ;
> Where lately, armed for deadly strife,
> With tomahawk and scalping knife,
>   The Natives strove;
> Now dove-eyed Peace triumphant reigns,
> And o'er the cultivated plains,
> In converse sweet, dusk maids and swains,
>   Contented rove.

Never, to our thinking, in all the history of Christ's Church, was there a missionary enterprise with so touching a story; that was so clearly blessed of God in its spiritual results, or that, for some inscrutable Providence, was permitted to be so harrowed and storm-tossed as the Moravian Mission among the western Indians.

The Delawares were a noble, intelligent and virtuous tribe, as compared with redmen generally, and peculiarly susceptible to Gospel teachings. Among them the missionaries worked east of the Alleghenies for years, converting thousands; forming them into separate industrious communities; teaching all the arts of peaceful civilization, and assisting them to live pure, devoted and consistent Christian lives.

The western explorations of Frederick Post, a very devout man of God, satisfied his Church that a most promising field of missionary enterprise invited beyond the Alleghenies. The first decided attempt was made on the upper Allegheny, and many were converted; among others, Allemewi, a blind old Delaware chief. Wars and troubles, however, soon arose, and it was concluded to accept the invitation of Pankake and Glickhican, and move further west, where the Delawares were more numerous and all favorably inclined.

Accordingly, in April, 1770, a fleet of sixteen canoes, filled with missionaries and their little band of disciples, the firstlings of the Faith, descended the Allegheny from Lawunakhannek, to Pittsburgh; thence down the Ohio to the Big Beaver; thence up said river twenty miles, where a debarkation was effected and a settlement made. The Indians soon flocked in from far and near, and were "astonished at their doctrine." Chiefs and warriors, great and small, wise and simple, were in like manner attracted; but when Glickhican, one of the best, greatest and most influential Delaware war chiefs, as also the wife of Allemewi, became converts, the excitement increased and widened.

A beautiful and prosperous village arose, which was called Friedenstadt, or Village of Peace. The land was rich, and the woods filled with every variety of game, as were the streams with fish. Churches, schools, mills and workshops were erected; the lands were surrounded with good fences, and cultivated with the latest improved implements; horses, cattle, hogs, &c., were multiplied, and, in a word, the "wilderness blossomed as the rose," and all was peace and happiness.

But soon the low, depraved, vagabondish "Indian trader," with his cheap daubs, gewgaws and abominable whiskey, made his appearance; perverting and demoralizing the faithful, sowing jealousies, and creating great trouble generally. In the meantime, persistent invitations had been extended to the Moravians by the Great Council of Delawares in Ohio, to come further west and settle near them on the Muskingum. This invitation was soon after more urgently repeated by the great and good Delaware chief, Netawatwees, backed by the Wyandot chiefs, who promised all the land they needed and constant protection.

In '75 this invitation was accepted, and, a large number of disciples from east of the mountains having migrated, Friedenstadt was abandoned the next year for the new village of Schoenbrun, (Beautiful Spring,) on the Tuscarawas branch of the Muskingum, some going by land, and twenty-two large canoes going by water down the Beaver and Ohio, and then up the Muskingum nearly two hundred miles.

It would take many pages even to briefly relate the varied and deeply interesting history of the Christian villages located in those years on this river. Schoenbrun was followed by Gnadenhutten; then by Lichtenau, and when, in '79, that village had to be abandoned, because lying directly on the great war path between the British Indians and the American borders, was followed by Salem.

These three all grew fat and flourished. Indians crowded in from all sides. Even one tribe of Miami Shawnees moved near to be under their benign influence. The reports of the love, harmony and abundance which existed among these three communities of converts spread far and near, and exercised a most happy influence. Their fields of waving corn could be counted by the hundred acres; the hills were dotted with fine horses and cattle; while droves of hogs roamed and fattened in the woods. Chapels, schools, houses and workshops were built, and the voice of prayer and praise was alternated with the busy hum of industry. On still nights the inhabitants of each village could hear the sounds of the church bell from the neighboring village; rude cabins made way for comfortable two-story houses of hewn logs; traveling bands of Indians were always treated hospitably and fed with abundance and variety; war, and all that led to or made for it, was forever forsworn, and every tribe in Ohio saw, heard, understood and wondered.

Alas! this was too good a state of things to last! The contrast was too marked. Prosperity begets envy, and those bereft of everything soon learn to hate those who are blessed with everything. The conjurers and "medicines" of the various tribes saw "an unknown God" set up for worship; felt their own power and influence waning, and denounced the new religion as making squaws of their chiefs and warriors. They execrated the "praying Indians" for their neutrality; made border-scalpers return by their towns so as to draw on them the vengeance of the whites; accused them of constantly conveying news to Forts Pitt and McIntosh, so that all Indian raids aborted.

In all this they were aided and even surpassed by those three artful and desperate tories and renegades, Girty, Elliott and McKee, who were constantly, like Saul of Tarsus, "breathing out threatenings and slaughter against the disciples of the Lord." They all saw that the Delaware nation persisted in maintaining strict neutrality in the war between the British and Americans, and made repeated efforts first to sow dissensions; then break up the Moravian towns; then waylay and kill the missionaries, and, all these failing, to make the British at Detroit, and Pomoacon, the Huron Half King, remove the "praying Indians" back out of the way.

The missionary Senseman had been attacked near Schoenbrun; Edwards and Young were shot at while planting potatoes near Gnadenhutten; Heckewelder had been thrice waylaid and assaulted; while Zeisberger had been ambushed by a hired gang of eight Mingoes. Just as Simon Girty, their leader, leaped into the path before him, shouting, "This is the man; now do your work as promised," some Delaware hunters providentially appeared and effected a rescue. If any was more persistent in his hatred to the Moravians than Girty, it was Elliott, who was infinitely more artful and sneaking. Pipe, whose prophetess wife had been finally converted to the new doctrines, was quite as bad and hateful as either. If Girty and Elliott were the crafty, designing plotters, Pipe and the Huron Half King, Pomoacon, were the pliant tools. We have already related how Pipe at length succeeded in dividing the Lenni-

Lenape in two, taking with him the Wolf tribe, which was for war, and leaving the Turtle tribe, which was for peace, on the Muskingum.

Alas! for the worried and harrowed Moravian towns, their great and good protector, Netawatwees, had died at Fort Pitt in '76, desiring, as his last will and testament, that his nation should embrace the Gospel. His successor, the *greater* Captain White Eyes, although, like King Agrippa, "almost persuaded to be a Christian," had contented himself with remaining their staunch and unwavering friend, and had died the very next year. Soon after, the young chief who was lineally to succeed them, was compelled, by Pipe and tribal dissensions, to move with his guardians, Killbuck and Big Cat, to Smoky Island, under the protecting guns of Fort Pitt.

What more was left for the peeling and scattering of these persecuted heathen converts? The ignoble trio of tories and deserters from Fort Pitt having been baffled in all their bad schemes, now applied for aid to the Six Nations of New York, who claimed all the Ohio soil and a protectorate over the western tribes. These steady friends of the British would not openly interfere, but were found ready enough to relegate the cowardly business to others, so they sent to the Chippewas and Ottawas the following pleasant message: "We herewith make you a present of the Christian Indians on the Muskingum to make broth of." These two nations were too proud to engage in such contemptible work, alleging that "their 'Grandfather' had done them no injury." The same summons was then sent to the Wyandots, who were nearly connected with the Six Nations, but even they at first refused, since the Delawares were their "cousins," and they had formerly contracted to be protectors of the Christian Indians.

POMOACON DESTROYS TOWNS AND CARRIES MORAVIANS CAPTIVE.

The machinations of Girty, Pipe and the rest soon persuaded the Half King to lead a hostile expedition against the Moravian towns. Accordingly, with a cohort of three hundred chosen warriors, Pomoacon "came down like a wolf on the fold." British guns were in their hands; the British flag waved over them, and Elliott, a British captain, was at their head. It was either removal or death.

Great and unspeakable was the consternation among these three peaceful communities at the sudden appearance of so many fierce and hostile warriors. The gist of the Half King's commands was that the believing Indians "were sitting just half way between two powerful, angry gods, who stood with their mouths wide open and looking ferociously at each other; that if they didn't move back out of the road they would be ground to powder by the teeth of either one or the other, or perhaps by both. He urged them not to stand stupidly gazing at their horses, flocks and standing crops, but to rise, take their teachers, and he would lead them to a fat and rich place, near his own town, where game, fish and corn were plenty."

No use to argue! A whole week was spent in that way, the unruly rabble becoming each day more violent and aggressive, wantonly shooting down cattle, pillaging houses, and riding over fenced grounds. The interception of some messengers who had secretly been dispatched to Fort Pitt, and the escape thither of a squaw who had ridden off Pipe's famous riding horse, brought matters to a crisis, and the missionaries and their chief assistants were arrested and menaced with death. This so alarmed the more timid of the congregations that they finally consented to leave their beautiful villages behind, and go whither their cruel and merciless persecutors directed.

The last parting was a most touching one. The chapel was thrown open and crowded with people, many of the heathen savages having also flocked in. After hymn singing by the united congregations, all joining their sad wails together, Zeisberger, their most beloved minister, calmly arose and preached a touching and most powerful sermon from Isaiah liv: 8—" In a little wrath I hid my face from thee for a moment, but with everlasting kindness will I have mercy on thee, saith the Lord, thy Redeemer."

The scene then presented was certainly one of very extraordinary interest. The venerable missionary was most profoundly grieved and touched, and discoursed with unwonted force and feeling; Joachim, the native chapel interpreter, spoke with equal freedom and unction, and as his clear, ringing tones resounded through the crowded assemblage, weeping and wailings arose on all sides. It was like an inspiration—as if the tongue had been "touched with a live coal from off the altar." Even the on-looking heathen were moved to tears.

But why dwell longer on these sad and harrowing scenes? These persecuted Christians, "hunted like a partridge upon the mountain," placed their beloved pastors in their midst, and took up their melancholy pilgrimage for the distant Sandusky; all their comfortable homes abandoned; over three hundred acres of standing corn left in the ear; most of their cattle shot or driven to the woods; their bountiful stores of meat, honey, tools, &c., left behind, and nothing to look forward to but a dreary Winter of cold and privations.

They were just a month on their way, and suffered untold hardships. But these were as nothing to what followed. The promised Paradise turned out a bleak, wintry desert. The wretched victims were cast

26

adrift in the barren woods, while the Half King and his exultant followers continued on to their own town. Some miserable hovels were knocked up. Many of their cattle now died of absolute starvation, and amid want, pinching cold, and sick and starving children, passed the terrible Winter of '81. Added to all this, their missionaries were now dragged to Detroit and confronted with Pipe, their chief tormentor and accuser.

On being ordered by the British commandant, De Peyster, to make good his constant charges against the Muskingum Moravians, that truculent worthy, much to the surprise of all, called on his chiefs to "get on their legs and speak." Alas! these were utterly dumb! A second command, and Pipe arose in a most embarrassed manner, and recalled all he had ever said against the Moravians; taking the blame on himself and tribe, and concluded with the request that the missionaries should be treated well, and sent back to their suffering congregations. Being thus triumphantly acquitted, this was done, De Peyster making all the amends in his power by sending with them food, clothes and his best wishes.

The year 1782 opened very miserably for the poor wanderers. They had, it is true, built a new chapel and continued their devotions, but suffered so terribly from cold and want of provisions, that many sickened and died. They were straitened to that degree as to be obliged to live on the carcasses of their starved cattle, and many sucking babes perished miserably. Each grown person was reduced to one pint of corn per day. The famine now increased; corn advanced to half a dollar per quart, and very little to be had at that; their children distressed them by their constant wails for food, and, to save them and theirs from sheer starvation, they concluded to return to their forsaken towns on the Muskingum, and gather the corn from the large crops they had left standing in the ear. They accordingly set out—men, women and children, with horses to bring back the food—in three divisions, and numbering one hundred and fifty souls.

Girty and the Half King all this time continued increasingly hostile. Their object was to drive the "praying Indians" out of the country altogether. To this end new charges were trumped up against the missionaries, the Half King threatening that if they were not removed he "would know what to do." A special order from Detroit was sent to Girty to conduct them again to Detroit, and should they refuse to come, Pomoacon was bidden to aid him.

The grief and consternation of the poor Indians when they found they must lose their pastors and teachers, was indescribable. They lost both sleep and appetite, and hurried off messengers to hasten back the expedition which had left for the Muskingum in quest of corn. Alas!

most of these were fated never to come back, or to look again on the faces of their beloved teachers.

On March 14th, just as the missionaries were preparing to set off, they heard the "alarm yell" sound, and, on going out, found a "runner" returning from the Muskingum with the sad news that while the one hundred and fifty Indians were busy gathering their maize, a party of Virginians had come upon them and made them all prisoners, killing some and taking the remainder to Pittsburgh.

With this heavy news the missionaries started. How would their hearts have bled had they known the whole dread story, in all its horrid and sickening details! They surely must have concluded that the Half King's rhetorical figure was not overdrawn, and that between the two angry gods standing opposed to each other with mouths open, the one on the Sandusky and the other on the Ohio, they and their flocks were being ground to powder.

HORRIBLE MASSACRE OF MORAVIANS AT GNADENHUTTEN.

In order to render the account of the Gnadenhutten massacre more *actual* to our readers, we borrow a chapter from our Historical Work of "Simon Girty, the Renegade." The narration therein given is faithful to history, having been carefully gathered from every reliable source, while the dialogue style makes the whole drama, as it were, more present and realistic. In order to a fuller understanding of the scene presented, we may premise that two companies of border scouts, out on an Indian trail in search of a party of captives, meet and encamp by appointment —only two months after the massacre—near the burnt and deserted village of Gnadenhutten. Captain Sam. Brady, the noted scout and one of the prominent characters of the romance, desirous of witnessing the deserted ruins, and the scene of a butchery, the details of which were then in every mouth on the frontier, is piloted at night to the ruins by Rev. Edward Christy. This young divine, having lost his betrothed by Indians, had accompanied Williamson's slaughtering expedition, and was a protesting and horrified witness of the dreadful drama. We now quote:

* * * "Let me see," replied Christy, reflectively, "it was the 4th of March that our company of about a hundred, gathered from

the Ohio shore and the various settlements along Short, Buffalo, Raccoon, Ten Mile, and other creeks, assembled at Mingo Bottom. Most of us were good and true men, who were much exasperated at Indian incursions and atrocities and determined to retaliate. Since all the signs favored the Moravians as either the perpetrators or the instigators of these thefts and scalpings, and as we did not know their characters so well as they were known at Fort Pitt, we were honest in our ends; but still there were many Indian haters among us; people who looked upon them as of no more account than mad curs, to be shot on sight; others, who had a religious or rather fanatical hate of all redmen, and very many rough, lawless desperadoes, who coveted their lands, horses and pelts, and who, by their boldness and violence, were allowed to have far too much influence among us. There was the mischief! It was an odd and incongruous mixture of good and bad.

"Well, in about two days we came in sight of this town. We found out afterwards that about one hundred and fifty men, women and children, all told, had come down from Sandusky to gather their corn, and that the day before our coming, a party of Wyandots passing through here confessed to a border murder, and advised them all to be off or they would be attacked. A conference was then held here by the leaders of the three villages, and the conclusion was, that as they had always been peaceable and friendly to the whites, feeding and relieving their captives and sending the settlements early intelligence of expected raids, they certainly had nothing to fear; but it was also resolved, that as they had gathered their corn and were all ready to go back, they would start from home on the 6th, the very day we arrived.

"Our videttes having informed us that most of the reddys were across the river, the band was divided into two equal parts; one to cross over about a mile below Gnadenhutten and secure those who were gathering corn, and the other, with which I was, to attack this village itself. The first party found young Shabosch about a mile from here out catching horses. He was shot and scalped by a Captain Builderbeck.* Finding no canoes for crossing, and the river being high and running ice, young Dave Slaughter swam over and brought back an old sugar trough, which would only carry two at a time.

---

*This Captain Builderbeck was a large, fine looking, and very daring borderer, who was some years after captured by Indians. On giving his name, a look of intelligence immediately circulated among his captors. He was recognized as the man who fired the first shot at the Moravian massacre, and as the slayer of the much-esteemed Shabosch, and was at once killed and scalped under circumstances of great cruelty. It may here also be stated that, although Colonel David Williamson escaped immediate retribution for his share in the massacre, and was even afterwards made sheriff of Washington county, Pa., yet towards the end of his life he became wretchedly poor, and died in the Washington, Pa., jail.

"This was slow work, and a good many stripped, and, putting guns and clothes on board, swam over. Fearing the noise of their shot would alarm the Indians, they sent word for us to advance on the town, which we did with a rush, finding it, much to our surprise, completely deserted—all but one man, who was just pushing off in a canoe, and who was instantly killed.

"The other party hurried along with all speed; hailed the corn gatherers as friends and brothers; told them they had heard of their sufferings and bad treatment among the Hurons, and offered to take them to Fort Pitt and protect and support them.

"This was joyful news to the Indians, for they had been so starved and maltreated that any change was for the better. So they gathered about, shook hands and exchanged congratulations with each other. They were then advised to leave off work and cross to Gnadenhutten.

"Meanwhile, as we afterwards learned, a native teacher, by name of Martin, from Salem, on the west side of the river, five miles below, was out with his son and saw the tracks of our shodden horses, for we had a good many mounted men with us; and being surprised thereat, ascended a hill to reconnoitre. Seeing whites and reds all together, talking and chatting in the most friendly manner, he sent his son across, while he rode rapidly off to Salem, and told them there what he had seen, giving it as his opinion that God had ordained that they should not perish on the Sandusky barrens, and that these whites were sent to succor them. Two brethren were then dispatched to this village, and finding all favorable, returned with some of our band to Salem, who, on repeating the same promises that were made by the whites here, all came trooping up the west bank.

"Unfortunately, our party who went to Salem set fire to the church and houses there, which at once excited disapproval and suspicion. It was explained, however, that as they were going to abandon the place, it had been done to prevent its occupation by the enemy."

"They must have been a very credulous folk," here put in Brady, "to be so easily deceived."

"Well, I've heard that our boys talked religion to them, praised their church, called them good Christians, and made so many fine promises that their suspicions seem to have been completely lulled. On arriving opposite this place, however, their eyes were opened very quick; but it was now too late. They discovered blood on the sandy beach, and more of it in the canoe by which they crossed."

"But when they found themselves betrayed, why didn't they fly to arms?" wonderingly asked Brady.

"Ah, that was the most curious part of the whole performance," said

Christy. "Both lots of Indians had freely and unhesitatingly yielded up guns, axes and knives, on solemn promise being made that when arrived at Pittsburgh all should be promptly returned to the right owners; besides, by their religion, they were non-combatants.

"Up to this point, I cannot say but what I, and many who afterwards joined me in a solemn protest against the subsequent atrocities, acquiesced. But now all disguise was thrown off, and we immediately saw that, guilty or not guilty, these poor creatures, of all ages and both sexes, were doomed to a horrid death. I almost shudder at the thought of what followed.

The Indians Told to Prepare for Death—Touching Scenes.

"Brady, do you see that blotch of deep shadow yonder, marking a oak in the river bank?"

"Just in front of those two spectral-looking chimney-stacks? Yes; what of it?"

"'Twas the road to the ferry; and right on that bluff above, the two lots of dismayed Indians met and exchanged sad greetings and suspicions. They had much reason. For, *presto, presto*, and the scene was now abruptly changed. The looks of their captors lowered; their faces became clouded and sullen; their words grew fierce and insolent. They roughly separated the women and children, and confined them in one cabin, and then drove the shocked and unresisting males into another, impudently charging them with being warriors and enemies instead of peaceful Christians; with having the stolen goods of murdered borderers in their possession, and triumphantly pointing to pewter dishes and spoons, and to branded horses as proof of the alleged robberies.

"'Twas in vain that the branding irons made by native blacksmiths were shown, and that the astonished Indians accounted—as I heard their teachers do in each case—for every article in their possession—what had been made by themselves and what had been bought from traders or carried from the East. It was the old fable of the Wolf and the Lamb. They were doomed to destruction, and as the terrible truth gradually took possession of them, a feeling of horror was depicted on their tearful countenances.

"A council was now held by the miscreant band, and a violent and bloodthirsty feeling soon developed itself. Angry words arose, followed by menacing gestures. Suggestions of pity and moderation were rudely scoffed at, and it soon became manifest that the hundred were to be ruled and domineered by a few fierce, violent, fanatical spirits—turbulent, tempestuous borderers, with mouths filled with whiskey, tobacco and big oaths, and who hated and hunted Indians like snakes."

"But where was the craven Williamson all this time?" queried Brady, indignantly; "and why didn't he at once rebuke and beat down this dastardly treachery?"

"Well, Williamson did what he could in a mild, arguing sort of way. I'll give him *that* credit. But his band was militia, all of equal authority, collected from various places, many of them unknown to him; and, although a brave and humane man himself, he hadn't that kind of quiet moral force that such a lawless band required. All he and the officers generally dared to do was to refer the matter to the men and take a vote *

"Well, by —, there's just where he made a fatal mistake," hotly put in Brady. "I've served through the Revolution, and know well how a few bold, blustering bullies can make a whole regiment do wrong against their will. No use for an officer to temporize and argue with that strain of men. He must take the bull by the horns, and dare do his whole duty. If Dave Williamson had stepped sternly out; boldly denounced and forbidden such villainy, and called on his command to *obey* orders, and not *discuss* them, the few cut-throat savages would have at once slunk away, and the rest asserted themselves."

"I believe you, Captain," answered the young divinity student, quietly; "but would have believed you just as readily if you hadn't challenged your Maker to back you up. 'Thou shalt not take the name of the Lord thy God in vain.'"

"I ask your pardon, sir," answered Brady, confusedly, feeling the rebuke was deserved. "I forgot your cloth, and we borderers fall into a rough way of speaking; but I get so riled up at the memory of the Moravian butchery that I want to talk as strong as I feel."

Mr. Christy bowed gravely, and continued: "Well, whether the Colonel could or could *not* control his men, it is certain he *didn't;* but pusillanimously shifted the responsibility on his band by a vote 'whether the Moravian Indians should be taken prisoners to Pittsburgh or put to death,' and requested that all those who were in favor of saving their lives should step out of the line and form a second rank.

---

*In justice to the memory of Colonel Williamson, I have to say that, although at that time very young, I was personally acquainted with him, and say with confidence he was a brave man, but not cruel. He would meet an enemy in battle and fight like a soldier, but not murder a prisoner.—*Dod drüige's Notes.*

From the best evidence before us, Colonel Williamson deserves not the censure belonging to this campaign. He is acknowledged on all hands to have been a brave and meritorious officer, and had he possessed proper command, none can doubt but what the result would have been very different.— *De Hass' History of Western Virginia.*

"Would you believe it, Brady, only eighteen out of all that party dared to put themselves on the side of right and justice—just a *paltry eighteen*. The rest were overawed or demonized, I don't know which. I was shocked! confounded! speechless with amazement! had talked with a number of the teachers and leading Indians, and was perfectly convinced they were good and sincere Christians, ever on the side of peace, and having nothing whatever to do with border raids and savageries.

"I supposed that, having the same proofs, many others were likewise so convinced, but when I saw this sparse little group of protesters, I thought 'twas high time to do *my duty* if the Colonel wouldn't do *his*. So I held a brief consultation with our party, and then harangued the whole assemblage, protesting, in the most solemn manner, against such a horrible piece of hypocrisy and outrage. I went over all the circumstances of the case; showed how we had disarmed and then enticed over these inoffensive Christians; what they had already suffered from Girty and the Ohio tribes, and finished by calling God to witness that we would be innocent of their blood."

"The base, infernal butchers," said Brady. "I hope you put it to them hot and strong."

"I did, indeed, Captain; stronger than they would bear, for, while the better part of them slunk away beyond the sound of my voice, and others winced and uneasily affected to scoff and jeer at my reproofs, the bolder scoundrels gathered about me with scowling faces and menacing gestures; called me a young milksop, a chicken-hearted boy, a black-coated pedagogue, old McMillan's baby darling, and what not.

"I tell you, Brady, I seemed to be looking into the fierce, savage faces of a pack of famished, blood-thirsty wolves; their yellow eyes shot fire; their teeth gnashed like fangs; they glared at me horribly, nervously rubbing their hands together as if they wanted to tear me to pieces. I couldn't believe these were my gay, roystering companions of the day previous. Like tigers, the smell of blood seemed to have completely crazed them, and whetted their appetites for more."

"It's marvelous," here interrupted Brady. "It does seem as if the long Indian wars had actually debased a large number of our frontier people to the savage state. Having lost so many friends and relatives by the reddys, and heard of so many horrid murders and scalpings, they are possessed with an insatiate thirst for blood, and look upon *all* Indians as wild varmints to be killed and scalped on sight. They are *worse* than the savages themselves. Well, what next?"*

---

*The sentiment here expressed by Brady is the same as written by Dr. Joseph Doddridge, an historian of that period, in his Notes on Indian Wars.

"Oh, our steadfast little band of malcontents barely escaped violence, and retired to the edge of the woods, protesting in God's name against the diabolical atrocity resolved upon. Meanwhile the assassins —for I can call them by no milder name—debated as to the mode of death. Some even advised burning the Moravians alive, as they were cooped up in the two cabins. At last it was decided to kill and scalp them wholesale, and then burn their towns and carry off all their horses, skins, &c.

"You may faintly imagine, but I can't hope to describe, the scene that ensued when this terrible news was told the victims. The males soon quieted down into a sort of sullen, stoical indifference, but the tears and wails and shrieks among the women and children were truly heart-rending. They might have moved hearts of stone—*not* of adamant.

"A petition now came up from the poor betrayed innocents that they might have some time to prepare for death. They called God to witness their guiltlessness, but were ready to suffer for His sake, only asking that they might sing and pray together, and make their peace with Him.

"This was grudgingly granted. It was now night. The heavens were overcast. The wind arose, and soughed mournfully through the forest where our little party sat sad and indignant; but above all the noise and bluster of the winds, floated the strong, sweet sounds of public worship.

"I could scarce believe my own ears, and several of us wended our way to the cabins, passing the huge fires around which were assembled the main portion of the expedition. Approaching a window, I stepped upon a log, looked in, and beheld one of the most touching scenes man ever saw. The hymns were just over, and now strong, brawny, swarthy-hued men were passing around shaking each other's hands and kissing each other's cheeks. Some faces were bedewed with tears, and some convulsed with agony, but most had on them the joyful, exultant expression of the victory almost won—a prefiguration, as it were, of the coming glory. Now they tenderly asked each other's pardon for offences given or griefs occasioned; now they kneeled and offered, with uplifted faces—which seemed to brighten with a radiance almost celestial—fervent prayers to God, their Saviour, and then, as one or another would touchingly allude to their wives and children—so near to them and yet so far from them—the whole assemblage would burst out into tears and convulsive sobbings.

"Oh, Brady, 'twas just awful! I never expect to witness on earth another such moving sight. I never hope to see God's grace and power so manifested, or His name so magnified. No heathen curses or boastings; no revilings of their cruel, merciless murderers, or calling down upon them of Almighty vengeance. All was love and joy, and resignation to God's will. Some even had the amazing grace to imitate our Saviour, and cry out, 'Father, forgive them; they know not what they do.'

"The scene among the poor women and children was somewhat similar, only infinitely more harrowing and agonizing. Ruthlessly torn from those who should have been their stay and support in these last trying hours, how could their sobs and wails and pitiful cries be pent up! And how, hearing and seeing all this, and not old enough to have the martyr's faith and joy in death, could tender, innocent children, who laugh or weep like a capricious April day, be expected to bear up against such an overwhelming woe!

"Excited by a louder and more distressful wail—more like a shriek—than usual, I summoned up courage to take one glance within. Merciful Father! One was enough! An exemplary believer, Christina by name, from Bethlehem, Pa., had just finished an exhortation for all to stand firm to the death; that there was no hope left but in a merciful Saviour; and that if those present could not see their husbands or fathers in *this* world, they soon would in another and better.

"The poor creatures did not seem to realize their awful fate till then, and such a heart-rending wail arose from the whole assemblage as would have moved the dead. I saw fond mothers, with tears streaming down their tawny faces, convulsively embrace their dear little children, and children—some of them scarcely knowing what it all meant—clinging to their parents amid harrowing cries and sobbings; but, most touching sight of all! a number of little ones of both sexes had quietly fallen asleep, and were lying around, with tearful, passionate, agonized mothers' faces hanging over them.

"Horror-stricken, I almost fell from my position at the window, and rushed off to find Williamson. I implored him to come back with me and gaze upon that dolorous scene. He declined, kindly, but firmly; said he deeply regretted the way matters stood, but was powerless to do anything. 'Twas as much as his life was worth. He had done all he could, but each man had as much authority as himself, and all were stubbornly bent on vengeance.

"I then asked permission to enter the two cabins and mingle with the victims, and help prepare them for the dreadful fate awaiting them. This raised a storm of indignant reproach among the men who, attracted by the discussion, had gathered about. Some of them had imbibed freely from a keg of sacramental wine they had discovered, and were rude and turbulent.

"I rejoined our little party, and sadly awaited the morning. The 8th of March dawned gloomily. The air was raw and chilly, and gusts of wind and soft snow would at times sweep through the air. Two houses were chosen for the execution, one for the men and the other for the women and children. To these the wanton murderers appropriately gave the name of 'slaughter-houses!' You see those two naked chimneys? 'Tis all that's left of them; but come, Brady! let's go nearer, that I may explain what happened next."

Driven into Two Slaughter-houses and Inhumanly Butchered.

The twain silently arose from an old canoe which had served as a seat, and almost shudderingly advanced to where the "slaughter-houses" had stood. The moon was now obscured behind a heavy, rapidly-drifting cloud. A brisk breeze brought mournful sounds from the encircling forests. They now stood upon the very edge of the cellar where lay the scorched and half-consumed remains of twenty women and thirty-four children.

Nothing there but a heap of charred and blackened ruins! A rank, fetid, charnel-house odor filled the air and offended the nostrils. A blue smoke was even yet rising from one corner of the crushed and fallen timbers. The scene was weird and uncanny. The gloom and desolation became oppressive. Neither spake. At last Brady whispered:

"For God's sake, Christy, let's get out of this! It's simply horrible! I'm not easily moved, but what you've told me this night; this sacrificial stench of burnt flesh, and that pile of still smouldering ruins, shock me deeply. I seem to see the whole awful scene before me, and feel it down to the very marrow of my bones."

"And so I," replied Christy, in low, earnest tones, while tightly clutching Brady's arm. "It's given me the horrors for two months. I saw but a small part of the damnable atrocities, and yet enough to curdle my blood, and at night, especially, the hellish saturnalia rise up before me in ghostly procession. I cannot shut them out. They grip and shake me like a hideous nightmare, and yet they do my soul good. 'Though He slay me, yet will I trust in Him.' But come! you must see the other one;" and Christy dragged his companion hurriedly forward to the cellar, where lay buried amid the charred and smoking *debris*, the remains of forty-two slaughtered male converts.

This cellar presented about the same dismal and forlorn aspect as did the other. As the two stood gloomily looking down upon the desolate ruins, all at once Brady, in his turn, tightly grasped his companion's arm and hoarsely whispered:

"My God, Christy, what's that! Don't you hear something down there? Listen!"

"No, I don't," after a pause. "You ain't trying to frighten me, Brady? I'm not of that—"

"Hist! hist! there 'tis again! By Heaven, I tell you there *is* a strange sound down there—a sort of grating, grinding, crunching noise. It stopped for a moment, but I heard it just now again. Must be some varmint"—and Brady hunted around by the obscure light, and found a heavy stick of charred wood, which he, with a shout, hurled down into the cellar.

An instant noise and rush were heard from various parts of the ruins, accompanied by short, angry yelps and snarls, and immediately after could be seen leaping up from under the arched timbers and darting off, several gaunt and shaggy forms, which soon disappeared in the adjacent woods.

"Must be Indian dogs left here, and looking for their poor, lost masters," nervously whispered Christy.

"Dogs be hanged," quickly answered Brady; "they're ravenous wolves gone down beneath that pile of burnt stuff to gnaw the bones of the dead. Thought I couldn't be mistaken in those crunching, mumbling sounds. Now come away, I tell you! I'll stop here no longer. It's a horrible charnel-house—would as soon breathe the stifling odor of the Catacombs," and Brady led the way from the place with quick, impatient strides.

They soon left the deserted village behind them; entered the dense, sombre woods; sped along till the camp fires were in full view, and then sat down on a mossy log to rest. Here Brady felt again at home, but nothing was said for some little time. At length, while taking off his skin cap, thridding his thick chestnut curls with his fingers, and wiping the thick beads from his brow, Brady smilingly remarked:

"Glad to get out of *that* graveyard, anyhow! It's strange, Christy, how the night will affect a strong man. Now I'm no chicken, and am deemed a pretty tough, weather-beaten old hunter. Scarcely know what nerves are in the daytime, and yet many a night in the woods, on a 'painter' or Indian hunt, I've started up and found my head filled with the sickliest kind of fancies—thought Indians were on all sides of me. Every dancing, rustling leaf above my head would take strange, fantastic shapes in the flickering firelight, and make me as nervous as a girl with the megrims, or as a cat in a strange garret. I'd pish and pshaw, and shut my eyes tight, but not the slightest use. I never could get to sleep again without jumping up, giving the fire a turn, taking a pipe of tobacco, and then, maybe, going over several times my 'Now I lay me's,' &c."

"It *is* odd," laughed Christy. "I have the same experience. Night makes mountains out of mole hills, and it's a capital time for nursing up all one's pet troubles. Great pity that our feelings, and even our faith, should depend on the state of our liver, and on whether we've eaten pork and cabbage, or corn pone and venison for supper. I'll tell you one thing, though, Brady. I don't believe certain ones I could name of Williamson's gang would dare go within a stone's throw of that village by night, and as for gazing down at either one of those cellars, 'twould be worse on them than a regular scalping; but shall I go on, or wait another time?"

"Oh, yes, go on! go on! Make a finish of it at once!" said Brady. "I'm daily learning how little better many Christian whites are than wild beasts, and how much worse oftentimes than heathen."

"'But for the grace of God there goes John Bunyan!' said once the 'inspired tinker,' on seeing a drunken, worthless wretch reeling down the street of Bedford, and I suspect," added Christy, "we all have that same tendency of going back to our original wildness which fruit trees are said to possess. But to resume:

"On the morning of the 8th the doomed Christians again commenced their devotions, but were interrupted by one of the executioners bluntly asking if they were not yet ready for death. The reply came in the affirmative; they had commended their souls to God and were now prepared for the sacrifice.

"The cabin in which the males were confined belonged to a cooper, and one of the party—you'd be shocked, Brady, if I called him by name—taking up a cooper's mallet, said: 'How exactly this will answer for the business,' and commencing with Abraham, who I learned was a most devoted and exemplary disciple, he felled, as a butcher would so many beeves, no less than *fourteen Christians!* He now handed the bloody mallet to another miscreant, with the remark: 'My arm fails me! Go on in the same way! I think *I've* done pretty well!' and so the horrid, hellish work went on till over forty were thus dropped, scalped and hacked to pieces.

"In the other house, Judith, an aged and remarkably pious and gentle widow, was the first victim. Christina, before mentioned, fell on her knees and begged for life. In vain! In vain! The tigers had again tasted blood. In both houses men, women and children were bound by ropes in couples, and were thus 'led like lambs to the slaughter.' Most all of them, I heard—for I only saw that part of the butchery which I was compelled to witness—marched cheerfully, and some smilingly, to meet their death.

"And in this atrocious and inhuman manner," solemnly continued Christy, "died, in all, over ninety Christian Indians, and may God have had mercy on their souls, and given them, in Heaven, that joy and peace which His enemies prevented them from knowing on earth."

"Amen!" added Brady, in his deep, bass tones, "and may His curse and punishment equally follow—"

"Stop! stop! my hasty friend. 'Vengeance is mine: I will repay, sayeth the Lord.' We can safely rest this matter with Him. 'The mills of the Gods grind slow, but they grind exceeding fine.' Five of the slain were extremely aged and accomplished native teachers—two of them originally converts to Brainard, in New Jersey, and one, the famous fighting chief, Glickhiccan.

"But the children! Ah, the tender, innocent children! whose loving voices of praise had so often ascended from the home, the school and the chapel; my heart faileth me to describe the shocking and harrowing scene of their horrid death. Their agonizing cries pierce my ears; their pitiful, beseeching young faces wring my heart even to this day."

One Little Boy Saved—Slaughter Renewed at Smoky Island.

"My God! what sickening savagery!" gasped Brady. "It fairly stuns and appalls me! And were none of those precious innocents allowed to live?"

"I'll tell you, my friend, for your query leads me to the part *I* took in the tragedy. After exhausting every effort to stay the carnage, I had, with very many others, kept aloof from the slaughter pens, but all at once heard a piercing shriek, and saw a bright, active young lad of about eight years running for dear life in my direction, and pursued by one of the murderers with a gory, uplifted tomahawk. I immediately sprang towards him. The little fellow saw me; ran as hard as his tiny legs would carry him, and wound his arms tight about my limbs, crying—'Good pale face! save 'ittle Injun boy. Don't let him kill Benny! oh, don't!'

"I would have saved that life with my own! Raising my rifle and drawing a bead on him, I sternly warned off the pursuing cut-throat. Fortunately those who saw the affair were as much moved as I was, and backed me up at once. And so the bloody miscreant was forced to retire sullenly without his prey."

"And what became of the lad?" eagerly asked Brady.

"He's at my father's house on Buffalo Creek, and—oh, strange inconsistency of man!—the very caitiffs who were so pitiless at the carnage, overwhelmed the little fellow with their attentions on the route home. He became a great favorite with all. Happily for him he has a child's memory, and is now as merry and frolicsome as any of my little brothers with whom he plays. I intend raising him and making a missionary of him, as the only reparation I can give for *my* share in this disgraceful expedition." *

"Oh, *you're* not to blame," said his companion, "and I thank you in the name of our common humanity for what you were able to do; but what became of those at the upper village?"

"Why, soon as the slaughter was over, a party of the most insatiable of the freebooters scurried off on horseback to Schoenbrun; but, thank God, the game had fled. The village was found completely deserted, so setting fire to it, they returned and finished their devastation here, by first burning the two 'slaughter-houses,' and then the chapel, school house and all the other buildings.

"Hastily gathering up their ill-gotten and blood-stained plunder, they started for home, driving before them about fifty stolen horses. Some time after they marched to Smoky Island, opposite Fort Pitt; attacked a settlement of peaceful and friendly Delawares there, under Killbuck, Big Cat, and the young chief who was to succeed White Eyes; killed and scalped him with many others; drove off the other chiefs and a sergeant's guard from the fort; crossed to Pittsburgh, boasting of their inhuman atrocities, and ended by having a public vendue of all the blankets, guns, horses and other booty, so vilely and meanly stolen; and so my story's ended."

"And a sad and shameful one it is," said Brady, as he rose slowly to his feet. "I fairly shudder at it—can scarce credit it—seems like some horrid nightmare! Come! I feel sore about this. Let's to camp! There's no use in a hell if not meant for just such fellows."

We may add here some few additional facts derived from Moravian writers, and of which, of course, Mr. Christy was then ignorant. Two Indian lads, respectively aged fourteen and fifteen, made a miraculous escape from the 'slaughter-houses.' One (Thomas by name) was knocked down and scalped with the rest, but after a while, coming to his senses, he saw Abel, a friend, also scalped, covered with blood and trying to get on his feet. Fearing a return of the murderers, Thomas lay down and feigned death. True enough, the murderers did return, and seeing

---

* One little boy of eight years old (named Benjamin) was happily saved by a humane white man of the party, who privately took him off to his home, where he raised him to a man, whence he afterwards returned to the Indian country.—*Heckewelder, Mor. Missions.*

Abel still living, chopped his head off. Thomas now crept over all dead, mutilated bodies, stole out at the door, and concealed himself until dark and escaped.

The other lad referred to as escaping was in the house with the women and children, and raising a loose plank which served as a trap into the cellar, he and a companion slipped into the basement, and lay there during the whole time of the butchery, the blood of the slaughtered women and children running down upon them in streams through the crevices of the rough plank floor. At dark they both attempted to escape by a small hole which served for a window. The smaller one succeeded, but his companion stuck fast and was burnt with the house.

These two lads, the only human beings, besides the child mentioned, who escaped the slaughter, took to the woods at different times, and with that unerring sagacity which seems to be an instinct with Indians of all ages, made a straight course home. The next day they met on the trail, and also fell in with the spared fugitives from Schoenbrun. These latter had providentially been warned in time for all to escape.

A runner named Stephen had been sent down from Sandusky by the missionaries Zeisberger and Heckewelder to the three Moravian towns, summoning the corn-gathering parties to return. As he was much spent on arriving at Schoenbrun, two fresh messengers were sent on to Gnadenhutten and Salem. On approaching the former, they saw tracks of shodden horses; then came on the scalped and mangled body of young Shabosch, and then saw in the distance the whites and Indians all crowded together. Hastening back with the news, the Indians at Schoenbrun at once took to the woods near by, and were there concealed when the monsters visited and burned their beautiful village.

Many attempts—some of them of late years—have been made by historical writers to exculpate Williamson in regard to this terrible butchery. *It cannot be done!* The damned blood spot will *not* out at the bidding of any feeble apologist. The commander of the expedition must be held, not only as *particeps criminis*, but as its very "head and front." Dr. Doddridge asserts that, as a militia officer, Williamson could advise but not command, and that "his only fault was that of too easy compliance with popular prejudice." It is a gross abuse of words to call that a *fault* which should be deemed a flagrant *crime*.

If the Colonel had but dared to head the eighteen protestants, and had boldly and firmly opposed the dastardly ruffians, not a man, woman or child would have bled. He did *not* so dare, but shirked his plain duty, bandying honied words and flimsy arguments when he should have thundered out commands or presented rifles. As with Macbeth, "All great Neptune's ocean cannot wash this blood clean from his hand."

The whole massacre leaves a stain of deepest dye on the page of American history. It was simply atrocious and execrable—a blistering disgrace to all concerned; utterly without excuse and incapable of defence. It damns the memory of each participator "to the last syllable of recorded time." All down the ages the "massacre of the Innocents" will be its only parallel. We must go to the Thugs of India or the slaughterers of African Dahomey for its superior.

SKETCH OF SIMON GIRTY, THE "WHITE SAVAGE."

> The outlawed white man, by Ohio's flood,
> Whose vengeance shamed the Indian's thirst for blood;
> Whose hellish arts surpassed the redman's far;
> Whose hate enkindled many a border war,
> Of which each aged grandame hath a tale
> At which man's bosom burns, and childhood's cheek grows pale.

From the Spring of 1778—when Girty, in company with Matthew Elliott, Alexander McKee, and other well-known tories, fled from Fort Pitt to the British Indians—down to General Wayne's battle of the Fallen Timbers, in '94, where the power of the western tribes was utterly and forever broken, no name on the whole frontier was so widely known or so universally dreaded as that of Simon Girty—the "White Savage," as he was styled by the missionary Heckewelder. Scarce a scalping party, maraud or massacre occurred during those troublous times, that was not blamed on the Girtys—for there were three brothers of the family, all operating and influential with the western Indians. The hated name was a terror in every pioneer's cabin, and the mere mention of it would cause woman's cheek to blanch, and children's hair to stand with fear.

For a score of years Simon Girty was the Raw-head-and-bloody-bones of the border. That he was not so cruel and debased as represented; that many of the frontier stories and traditions of him were absolute fictions, and that frequently enormities which were perpetrated by his two brothers, George and James, were falsely charged on Simon, is now, in the light of subsequent facts not then known, sure and certain. There is so much stuff and mystery concerning him in the old border books, that it is difficult to come at the exact truth, but, after a painstaking research, we think the following sketch, in which "naught is extenuated and naught set down in malice," comes nearer the truth than anything that has yet been published.

Simon Girty, Sr., was an Indian trader, regularly licensed by the Colony of Pennsylvania, and plying his perilous and vagabondish vocation among the western savages. He was a vulgar, violent old curmudgeon of an Irishman, and said to have been so besotted with liquor as to have turned his wife's love to hate, and to have been killed by her paramour. He left four boys: Thomas, Simon, George and James. Some time during Braddock's war, in 1755, the last three were made captive by the Indians; but Thomas, who was the best and most respectable of the brood, always remained quietly at home, on a little run emptying into the Allegheny, near Fort Pitt, and called to this day "Girty's Run."

Simon was adopted by the Indians under the name of Katepacomen, and became, in dress, language and habits, a thorough Indian, and was ever after much enamored of their free, wilderness life, with all its unshackled liberties and absence of restraints. George was adopted by the Delawares; became a fierce and ferocious savage, and is said, after a long career of outrageous cruelties, to have been cut off in a drunken broil. James was adopted into the Shawnee tribe; soon grew depraved, and became a cruel and blood-thirsty raider on the Kentucky border, sparing not even women and children from the horrid torture.

It was an old and true border saying, that you could never make a white man out of an Indian, but could very easily make an Indian out of a white man. There is something in the unsettled, free-and-easy life of the wild woods which possesses very strong and almost irresistible fascinations, and we have already shown that many of the white captives restored by the savages to Bouquet—even women and children—refused to leave their Indian relatives. When compelled, however, to return to their old homes, they parted amid the most touching tears and sobbings, many afterwards escaping back to those who had so tenderly adopted and cared for them. Of this number was young Simon, but being forcibly returned to the settlements, he took up his home near Fort Pitt.

We hear no more of him until Dunmore's bloody war of 1774, brought about by the wanton murder of Logan's relatives at the mouth of Yellow Creek. In this campaign, in company with Simon Kenton, he served as hunter and scout, and subsequently acted as Indian agent. He also then became well acquainted with Colonel Crawford, and was a guest of his at the cabin on the Yough. Like the famous Frenchman, Joncaire, Girty never felt so much at home as in the woods and among the wigwams or council fires of Indians, where he could harangue the assembled warriors of different tribes. At the outbreak of the Revolution he was a commissioned officer of militia at Pittsburgh, espousing the Patriot cause with zeal and serving it with fidelity until his desertion to the Indians from Fort Pitt, in March, 1778, with the notorious Matthew Elliott, Alexander McKee, and a squad of twelve soldiers. This tory defection, just at that unfavorable juncture, caused the greatest alarm along the entire frontier. We have already related at length the commotion it occasioned among the Delawares, then divided into peace and war factions.

Why did Girty, an officer in the American service, desert to the British? Most of the histories of the day say it was because he failed to get promoted to the regular army, or was mortified because one younger than he, and whom he thought not so deserving as himself, was advanced before him. From all the most reliable sources, we gather the true reason was, that Girty found himself looked upon at Fort Pitt with suspicion because he was known to be a tory at heart, and under the influence of the mischievous and notorious Dr. Connelly, of Virginia, who had not only laid claim to all Southwestern Pennsylvania as a part of Virginia, but had enforced said claims by a series of violent and outrageous proceedings, rending the whole section into warring factions, and even seizing and occupying Fort Pitt itself.

Be this as it may—and it is not at this late day of prime importance —Girty now headed his course for Detroit, and was captured by the Wyandots, but claimed by the Senecas as their prisoner, because he had once been adopted into their tribe. This claim, Leather Lips, a prominent and truculent old Huron chief, stoutly resisted, and the Mingoes were obliged to yield their point. On Girty's affirming that he had been badly treated at Fort Pitt because he was true to the King, and that being forced to leave the fort, he was now on his way to Detroit to join the British, he was released, and was soon after welcomed by the cruel Governor Hamilton, the "British Hair Buyer."

Girty was now just in his element. Talking several Indian languages, and employed by Hamilton in the Indian department, he was sent back to Sandusky to assist the savages in their harassing marauds against our border, and soon arose to a very bad eminence among them. He had never lost his relish for the free, untamed life of the forest. He was a true Indian in all his habits, longings and ambitions, and, like all apostates on whom the door of return is forever closed, soon became noted for his hate and desperate activity. He outdid the redskins themselves in the fierceness and cruelty of his wrath. When not ruthlessly worrying and harassing the frontier by his sudden forays and scalpings and torturings, he was ever busy, with diabolical hate and activity, in planning the destruction of the Moravians. He was their inveterate foe, and finally made Pomoacon, the Half King of the Hurons, the instrument of their forced abandonment of their three peaceful and flourishing towns on the Muskingum, and their removal, just on the eve of the Winter of 1781, to the inhospitable wilds and barrens about Sandusky.*

---

*To show Girty's violence when in liquor, as also his hatred to the Moravians, we quote from their missionary, Heckewelder, who, after the destruction of their towns on the Muskingum, had been forcibly removed to the Sandusky. Girty, on departing south on a scalping raid, had ordered a Frenchman to drive the Moravian teachers "the same as if we were cattle, and never to make a halt

Girty, however, was not *all*, or always bad. Many of the atrocities committed by his brothers, George and James, were falsely blamed on him. He was a savage by taste and education, and conformed to Indian usages, but it is known that he was his own worst enemy. Unfortunately inheriting a love for rum, it became his master. At such times he was cruel, vindictive and relentless. When sober he was a far better and kinder man.

Of Girty's personal courage, even to fool-hardiness, there is little question. He once had a quarrel with a Shawnee chief, caused, it is said, by some trade misunderstanding. While bandying words with each other, the Indian, by innuendo, questioned his opponent's courage. Girty instantly pointed to a half keg of powder, which happened to be at the camp, and snatching a fire-brand, called upon the chief to stand by him. The latter, at this strange hari-kari test of courage, hastily evacuated the premises.

In the sketch of Simon Kenton, a notable instance of Girty's goodness and kindness of heart is given at length. Through his importunities also many prisoners were saved from death and torture. He was reported honest, and was careful to fulfill all his engagements. It was said of him that he once sold his horse rather than incur the odium of violating his promise. He was brave and determined, and it was his dearest wish that he might die in battle. Jonathan Alder, who was for many years a captive among the Indians, and had occasion to know the renegade well, said that Girty was a warm friend to many prisoners, and that he had known him to purchase, at his own expense, several boys who were prisoners, and take them to the British to be educated. Lyon, in his narrative of captivity, when a half-grown boy, says Girty was very kind to him, taking him on his knee and promising to have him well cared for. Mrs. Thomas Cunningham, of West Virginia—after

---

even for the purpose of the women giving suckle to their children." This Lavallie would not do; but treated the missionaries with great kindness, and kept them several weeks at Lower Sandusky, while a boat should be sent from Detroit for them. We now quote from Heckewelder, page 332:—
"We had become uneasy lest Girty should find us still here on his return from war. He did return and behaved like a madman on hearing that we were here, and that our conductor had disobeyed his orders. He flew at the Frenchman most furiously, striking at him, and threatening to split his head. He swore the most horrid oaths respecting us, and continued in that way until after midnight. His oaths were all to the purport that he would never leave the house until he had split our heads in two with his tomahawk, and made our brains stick to the walls of the room. He had somewhere procured liquor, and would, at every drink, renew his oaths, which he repeated until he fell asleep. Never before did any of us hear the like oaths, or know anybody to rave like him. He appeared like an host of evil spirits. He would sometimes come up to the bolted door between us and him, threatening to chop it to pieces, to get at us. No Indian we had ever seen drunk would have been a match for him. How we should escape the clutches of this white beast in human form no one could see; nor how relieved from the hands of this wicked white savage, whose equal, we were led to believe, was (perhaps) not to be found among mankind."

seeing her oldest boy tomahawked and scalped, and the brains of her little daughter dashed out against a tree, all in her very presence, was carried into captivity. She suffered untold agony during her long march to the Indian town, her only nourishment for ten days being the head of a wild turkey and a few paw-paws; but, after a long absence, she was returned to her husband through the intercession of Simon Girty, who, happening to pass her way, ransomed and sent her home.

And finally, as Colonel Thomas Marshall was floating down the Ohio in an ark, he was hailed by a man who said he was James Girty, and that he had been stationed there by his brother Simon to warn all boats of the danger from decoys. The Indians, James said, had become jealous of Simon, who deeply regretted the injury which he had inflicted upon his countrymen, and who wished to be restored to their society. Every effort would be made, by white men and children, to entice boats ashore; but they must keep the middle of the river, and steel their hearts against every attempt. This warning, by whatever motive, was of service to many families. Thus much of Simon Girty, and some things to his credit, showing that he was not always the inhuman monster which old histories and traditions have painted him.

Girty Marries the Beautiful Kate Malott.

We must consider Girty, then, as having a dual character, and as the old Greek, sure of justice, appealed "from King Philip drunk to King Philip sober," a like appeal, in Girty's case, would probably have had the same effect. There was, besides, for many years, a streak of romance running through the renegade's life not yet known to the public or to history. It was communicated to us by Lyman C. Draper, a collector and historian of perfect reliability.

In March, 1779, a family of French descent, by the name of Malott, left Maryland for Kentucky. At Fort Redstone, on the Monongahela, where it was general for all emigrants to take arks or boats for Kentucky, they were joined by some other families, and embarked in two boats, one of them, a stock boat, in front, under charge of Peter Malott, the head of the family. Mrs. Malott and her five children were in the rear boat, commanded by Captain Reynolds, an officer of the Revolution. Mrs. Reynolds and seven children, Mrs. Hardin and two children, and others, were also in this boat.

This Reynolds boat was attacked and captured by some twenty-five Indians of mixed tribes at the head of Long Reach, some forty miles below Wheeling. Captain Reynolds had been shot dead in the first onset, and another man and a child of Mrs. Hardin were also killed. The

Indians secured much booty and no less than nineteen prisoners, whom they took, some to the Delaware and some to the Wyandot towns. The Malott stock boat was not captured. Mrs. Reynolds, being subsequently taken to Detroit, succeeded, by her energy and the influence of Colonel De Peyster—the Governor after Hamilton's capture by General Clarke—in collecting her scattered family and returning East. Catharine Malott, the oldest daughter of the family, was in her fifteenth year at the time of the capture, and was carried to one of the Shawnee towns on Mad river. Simon Girty seems to have come across her on one of his circuits among the various Indian towns, and fell violently in love with her. This was about three years after her capture, and while her mother was known by Girty to be in Detroit for the purpose of collecting her family from captivity. Indeed, it is probable that Girty had been employed by Mrs. Malott to trace up, if possible, her lost children. However this may be, he found Catharine now grown and very pretty, and adopted into an Indian family. They refused to give the girl up, but on Girty's promising to bring her back after she had seen her mother in Detroit, he succeeded in getting Catharine away. Once in Detroit, he married her, with, it is probable, the mother's approval. One of the captives said she was "a right pretty girl; reported to be the prettiest in Detroit." They had several children, and she survived her husband many years, and died at a very advanced age. Peter Malott, the father, returned to Maryland, and Draper thinks married again, never having succeeded in getting his captured family together.

For some few years after this marriage Girty was comparatively quiet, attending to the cares of his growing family, and largely occupied in trading with the savages. He lived at various localities among them, chiefly at Girty's Point, on the Maumee river, five miles above Napoleon. Quite a number of places in Ohio, however, bear his name. The ill-fated expeditions of General Harmar, in 1790, and of General St. Clair, in 1791, found him busy with his old associates, Elliott and McKee, in the council and in the field, and wielding much influence among the savage tribes. At their grand council, held after St. Clair's disastrous and overwhelming defeat, Girty was the only white man permitted to be present, and his voice and influence were for continuing the war.

At St. Clair's defeat he was present, and took an active part, receiving a severe sabre cut on the head. He is said to have found and recognized the body of General Richard Butler, second in command.

At another grand Indian conference, held in 1793, Girty still thundered for war, and was especially active in organizing and marshaling the forces against Wayne in 1793-4. He was present at the decisive battle of the Fallen Timbers, fought the same year, which forever crushed the power of the confederate Indian tribes, and ended in the treaty of Greenville, which at last brought peace. Girty now sold his trading establishment on the St. Mary river, located at a place called Girty's town—now St. Marys—and went back to Detroit, where his growing family lived.

He seemed to be perpetually haunted by the fear of falling into American hands; and when Detroit was finally yielded by the British, in 1796, and the boats, laden with our troops, came in sight, it is said he could not wait for the return of the ferryboat, but plunged his horse into the Detroit river and made for the Canada shore, pouring out a volley of curses, as he rode up the opposite bank, upon the American officers and troops.

He now settled quietly down on a farm near Malden, Canada, on the Detroit river, about fifteen miles below the city, and we hear no more of him until the war of 1812. During the invasion of Canada he followed the course of the British retreat, but returned to his family at Malden, and died in 1815, aged near seventy years, and totally blind. William Walker saw him at Malden in 1813, and describes him as being broad across the chest, with strong, round, compact limbs, and apparently endowed by nature with great powers of endurance.

Mr. D. M. Workman, of Ohio, says: "In 1813 I went to Malden and put up at a hotel kept by a Frenchman. I noticed in the bar-room a gray-headed and blind old man. The landlady, who was his daughter, a woman of about thirty years of age, inquired of me, 'Do you know who that is?' pointing to the old man. On my replying 'No;' she replied, 'It is Simon Girty.' He had then been blind about four years. In 1815 I returned to Malden, and ascertained that Girty had died a short time previous. Girty was a man of extraordinary strength, power of endurance, courage and sagacity. He was in height about five feet ten inches, and strongly made."

Girty took to hard drinking some time after his marriage, and for several years he and his wife lived apart. Draper visited Canada and saw one of Girty's daughters and some of the grandchildren, as also other descendants of the Malott family, which likewise settled in Western Canada, and he writes us of them and of Girty, as follows: "They were fine, worthy people, and some of the females quite attractive and intelligent. Our border histories have given only the worst side of Girty's character. He had redeeming traits. He was uneducated—only a little above the average Indian, I infer. He did what he could, unless infuriated by liquor, when, as Heckewelder states, he was boisterous, and probably dangerous. He certainly befriended Simon Kenton, and tried to save Crawford, but could not. In the latter case he had to dissemble somewhat with the Indians, and a part of the time appear in their presence as if not wishing to befriend him, when he knew he could not save him, and did not dare to shoot him, as he himself was threatened with a similar fate."

As to the stories told of Girty's heartless behavior at the prolonged tortures of his old friend Crawford, we are, like Draper, very skeptical. In our account of Crawford's sufferings, we have given what we could gather. Of Girty's courage and even recklessness there is ample testimony.

CAPTAIN SAM. BRADY, THE DARING PARTISAN LEADER.

> He knew each pathway through the wood,
> Each dell unwarmed by sunshine's gleam;
> Where the brown pheasant led her brood,
> Or wild deer came to drink the stream.

Who in the West has not heard of Samuel Brady, the Captain of the Spies, and of his wonderful exploits and hairbreadth escapes? A soldier from the first drum-tap of the Revolution, he commenced his service at Boston. He was in all the principal engagements of the war until the battle of Monmouth, when he was promoted to a captaincy and ordered to Fort Pitt to join General Broadhead, with whom he became a great favorite, and was almost constantly employed in partisan scouting. In '78 his brother, and in '79 his father, were cruelly killed by Indians. This made Captain Brady an Indian killer, and he *never changed his business*. The redman never had a more implacable foe, or a more relentless tracker. Being as well skilled in woodcraft as any Indian of them all, he would trail them to their very lairs with all the fierceness and tenacity of the sleuth hound. We could fill pages with the mere mention of his lone vigils, his solitary wanderings, and his terrible revenges. His hate was undying; it knew no interval—his revenge no surfeit. Day and night, Summer and Winter were all the same, if it gave him chance to feed fat his ancient grudge.

He commenced his scouting service about 1780, when he was only twenty-four years old, having been born in Shippensburg in 1756. A bolder or braver man never drew sword or pulled trigger. During the whole of the fierce, protracted and sanguinary war which ravaged the western border from 1785 to 1794, he was a dread terror to the savages and a tower of strength to the white settlers. His ubiquitous presence, backed by the band of devoted followers, who ever stepped in his footprints, was felt as a security everywhere. His the step that faltered not; his the eye that quailed not, and his the heart that knew never the meaning of fear. Many a mother has quieted the fears and lulled to sleep her infant family by the assurance that the rapid Allegheny, or the broad Ohio, the dividing lines between the whites and Indians, was safe because he there kept watch and ward.

But to begin at the beginning. When the company of volunteer riflemen, of which Brady was a member, lay in the "Leaguer of Boston," frequent skirmishes took place. On one occasion, Lowden was ordered

CAPT. SAM. BRADY, THE DARING PARTISAN LEADER.

—*See page 426.*

to select some able-bodied men, and wade to an island, when the tide was out, and drive out some cattle belonging to the British. He considered Brady too young for this service, and left him out of his selection; but, to the Captain's astonishment, Brady was the second man on the island, and behaved most gallantly. On another occasion, he was sitting on a fence with his Captain, viewing the British works, when a cannon ball struck the fence under them. Brady was first up, caught the Captain in his arms and raised him, saying, with great composure, "We are not hurt, Captain." Many like instances of his coolness and courage happened while the army lay at Boston.

At the battle of Princeton he was under Colonel Hand, of Lancaster, and had advanced too far; they were nearly surrounded—Brady cut a horse out of a team, got his Colonel on, jumped on behind him, and both made their escape. At the massacre at Paoli, Brady had been on guard, and had laid down with his blanket buckled round him. The British were nearly on them before the sentinel fired. Brady had to run; he tried to get clear of his blanket coat, but could not. As he jumped a post and rail fence, a British soldier struck at him with his bayonet and pinned the blanket to the rail, but so near the edge that it tore out. He dashed on—a horseman overtook him and ordered him to stop. Brady wheeled, shot him down and ran on. He got into a small swamp in a field. He knew of no person but one being in it beside himself; but in the morning there were fifty-five, one of whom was a Lieutenant. They compared commissions; Brady's was the oldest; he took the command and marched them to headquarters.

Captain Brady Makes a Scout to Upper Sandusky.

In 1780 the Indians became very troublesome to the settlements about Pittsburgh, and Washington, knowing well that the most effectual way to deal with them was to strike them in their very homes, ordered Colonel Broadhead, of Fort Pitt, to dispatch a suitable person to their towns to ascertain their strength and resources. Broadhead sent for Brady, showed him Washington's letter, and a draft or map of the country he must traverse; very defective, as Brady afterwards discovered. Selecting a few soldiers, and four Chickasaw Indians as guides, Brady crossed the Allegheny and was at once in the enemy's country. Brady was versed in all the wiles of Indian "strategie," and, dressed in the full war dress of an Indian warrior, and well acquainted with their language, he led his band in safety near to the Sandusky towns without seeing a hostile Indian. But his Chickasaws now deserted. This was alarming, for it was probable they had gone over to the enemy.

However, he determined to proceed. With a full knowledge of the horrible death that awaited him if taken prisoner, he passed on, until he stood beside the town on the bank of the river.

His first care was to provide a secure place of concealment for his men. When this was effected, having selected one man as the companion of his future adventures, he waded the river to an island partially covered with driftwood, opposite the town, where he concealed himself and comrade for the night. The next morning a dense fog spread over the hill and dale, town and river; all was hid from Brady's eyes, save the logs and brush around him. About eleven o'clock it cleared off, and afforded him a view of an immense number of Indians engaged in the amusement of the race ground. They had just returned from Virginia or Kentucky, with some very fine horses. One gray horse in particular attracted his notice. He won every race until near the evening, when, as if envious of his speed, two riders were placed on him and thus he was beaten. The starting post was only a few rods above where Brady lay, and he had a pretty fair chance of enjoying the amusement, without the risk of losing anything by betting on the race.

He made such observations through the day as was in his power, waded out from the island at night, collected his men, went to an Indian camp he had seen as he came out; the squaws were still there, took them prisoners, and continued his march homeward. The map furnished by General Broadhead was found defective, the distance represented being much less than it really was. The provisions and ammunition of the men were exhausted by the time they reached the Big Beaver, on their return. Brady shot an otter, but could not eat it. The last load was in his rifle. They arrived at an old encampment, and found plenty of strawberries, with which they appeased their hunger.

Having discovered a deer track, Brady followed it, telling the men he would perhaps get a shot at it. He had gone but a few rods when he saw the deer standing broadside to him. He raised his rifle and attempted to fire; but it flashed in the pan, and he had not a priming of powder. He sat down, picked the touch-hole, and then started on. After going a short distance the path made a bend, and he saw before him a large Indian on horseback, with a white child before and its mother behind him on the horse, and a number of warriors marching in the rear. His first impulse was to shoot the Indian on horseback; but, as he raised his rifle, he observed the child's head to roll with the motion of the horse. It was fast asleep, and tied to the Indian. He stepped behind the root of a tree, and waited until he could shoot without danger to the child or its mother.

When he considered the chance certain, he fired, and the Indian, child and mother, all fell from the horse. Brady called to his men, with a voice that made the forest ring, to surround the Indians, and give them a general fire. He sprang to the fallen Indian's powder horn, but could not pull it off. Being dressed like an Indian, the woman thought he was one, and said, "Why did you shoot your brother!" He caught up the child, saying, "Jenny Stoop, I am Captain Brady; follow me, and I will secure you and your child." He caught her hand in his, carrying the child under the other arm, and dashed into the brush. Many guns were fired at him but no ball touched, and the Indians, dreading an ambuscade, were glad to make off. The next day he arrived at Fort M'Intosh, with the woman and her child. His men had got there before him. They had heard his war whoop, and knew they were Indians he had encountered, but having no ammunition, had taken to their heels and run off.

A Conflict at "Brady's Bend"—His Adventure with Phouts.

The incursions of the Indians had become so frequent, and their outrages so alarming, that it was thought advisable to retaliate upon them the injuries of war, and to carry into the country occupied by them the same system with which they had visited the settlements. For this purpose an adequate force was provided, under the immediate command of Broadhead, the command of the advance guard of which was confided to Captain Brady.

The troops proceeded up the Allegheny river, and had arrived near the mouth of Redbank Creek, now known by the name of Brady's Bend, without encountering an enemy. Brady and his rangers were some distance in front of the main body, as their duty required, when they suddenly discovered a war party of Indians approaching them. Relying on the strength of the main body, and its ability to force the Indians to retreat, and anticipating, as Napoleon did in the battle with the Mamelukes, that, when driven back, they would return by the same route they had advanced on, Brady permitted them to proceed without hindrance, and hastened to seize a narrow pass, higher up the river, where the rocks, nearly perpendicular, approached the river, and a few determined men might successfully combat superior numbers.

In a short time the Indians encountered the main body under Broadhead, and were driven back. In full and swift retreat they pressed on to gain the pass between the rocks and the river, but it was occupied by Brady and his rangers, who failed not to pour into their flying columns a most destructive fire. Many were killed on the bank, and many more in the stream. Cornplanter, afterwards the distinguished Chief of the Senecas, but then a young man, saved himself by swimming. The celebrated war chief of this tribe, Bald Eagle, was of the number slain on this occasion.

After the savages had crossed the river, Brady was standing on the bank wiping his rifle, when an Indian, exasperated at the unexpected defeat and disgraceful retreat of his party, and supposing himself now safe from the well-known and abhorred enemy of his race, commenced abusing him in broken English, calling Brady and his men cowards, squaws, and the like, and putting himself in such attitudes as he probably thought would be most expressive of his utter contempt of them. When Brady had cleaned his rifle and loaded it, he sat down by an ash sapling, and, taking sight about three feet above the Indian, fired. As the rifle cracked, the Indian was seen to shrink a little and then limp off. When the main army arrived, a canoe was manned, and Brady and a few men crossed to where the Indian had been seen. They found blood on the ground, and had followed it but a short distance when the Indian jumped up, struck his breast and said, "I am a man." It was Brady's wish to take him prisoner, without doing him further harm. The Indian continuing to repeat, "I am a man"—"Yes," said an Irishman, who was along, "By St. Patrick, you're a purty boy," and, before Brady could arrest the blow, sunk his tomahawk into the Indian's brain.

The army moved onward, and after destroying all the Indians' corn, and ravaging the Kenjua flats, returned to Pittsburgh.

Shortly after Brady's return from Sandusky, he proposed to Phouts— a Dutchman of uncommon strength and activity and well acquainted with the woods—to go scouting up the Allegheny. Phouts jumped at this, and, raising himself on tip-toe, and bringing his heels hard down on the ground, by way of emphasis, said: "By dunder und lightnin', Captain, I would rader go mit you as to any of de finest weddins in dis guntry!"

Next morning they stealthily left the fort, traveled all day, and discovered smoke, denoting Indians. Brady desired Phouts to stay still while he would reconnoitre, but the irrepressible Dutchman refused, saying, "No, by dunder, I will see him, too." So they crept up and discovered only an old Indian by the fire. Phouts was for shooting him at once, but Brady prevented, as he judged that those absent from the camp were quite numerous. Next morning he fell upon a large trail of Indians, about a day or more old, so Brady determined to go back and take the old savage prisoner, and carry him back to Pittsburgh. The Indian was lying on his back, his faithful dog by his side. Brady now silently crept forward, tomahawk in hand, until within a few feet of the Indian, when, uttering a fierce yell, he made a spring like a panther and clutched the Indian hard and fast by the throat. The old fellow struggled violently at first, but seeing he was held with firm and tenacious grip, he gracefully submitted to the inevitable. The dog behaved very civilly, uttering merely a few low growls. Phouts now came up and the prisoner was tied. When the Indian found he was treated kindly and was to be carried to Pittsburgh, he showed them a canoe, and all embarked and encamped all night at the mouth of the little run.

Next morning Brady started to get some "jerk" they had hung up, leaving Phouts in charge of the prisoner. The Indian complained to the Dutchman that the cords hurt his wrists very much, and he, being a tender and kind-hearted fellow, took off the cords entirely, at which the redskin appeared very grateful. While, however, Phouts was busy with something else, the wary savage sprang to the tree against which Phouts' gun stood leaning, and leveled at the Dutchman's breast. The trigger was pulled, but fortunately the bullet whistled harmlessly past, taking off part of Phouts' bullet pouch. One stroke of Phouts' tomahawk settled the old Indian forever, nearly severing the head from the body.

Brady, hearing the report of the rifle and the yell of Phouts, hastily ran back, where he found the Dutchman astride of the Indian's body, calmly examining the rent in his own pouch. "In the name of Heaven," said Brady, "what have you done?" "Yust look, Gabtain," answered the fearless Phouts, "vat dis d—d red rascal vas apout;" holding up to view the hole in his belt. The Indian's scalp was then taken off, they got into their canoe and returned safely to Pittsburgh.

Saves Himself by a Shrewd Device—A Wholesale Kill.

Beaver Valley and the region about Fort McIntosh was one of Brady's famous scouting grounds. In one of his trapping and hunting excursions thereabouts, he was surprised and taken prisoner by a party of Indians who had closely watched his movements. To have shot or tomahawked him would have been but a small gratification to that of satiating their revenge by burning him at a slow fire, in the presence of all the Indians of their village. He was therefore taken alive to their encampment, on the west bank of the Beaver river, about a mile and a half from its mouth. After the usual exultations and rejoicings at the capture of a noted enemy, and causing him to run the gauntlet, a fire was prepared, near which Brady was placed after being stripped, and with his arms unbound. Previous to tying him to the stake, a large circle was formed around of Indian men, women and children, dancing and yelling, and uttering all manner of threats and abuses that their small knowledge of the English language could afford.

The prisoner looked on these preparations for death and on his savage foe with a firm countenance and a steady eye, meeting all their threats with Indian fortitude. In the midst of their dancing and rejoicing, a squaw of one of their chiefs came near him, with a child in her arms. Quick as thought, and with intuitive prescience, he snatched it from her and threw it toward the fire. Horror stricken at the sudden outrage, the Indians simultaneously rushed to rescue the infant from the flames. In the midst of this confusion, Brady darted from the circle, overturning all that came in his way, and rushed into the adjacent thicket, with the Indians yelling at his heels. He ascended the steep side of a hill amidst a shower of bullets, and darting down the opposite declivity, secreted himself in the deep ravines and laurel thickets that abound for several miles to the west. His knowledge of the country, and wonderful activity, enabled him to elude his enemies, and reach the settlements in safety. Another version of this event furnished us, makes it the squaw herself that the Captain pushed on the fire.

From one of Brady's spies, who, in 1851, had not answered to the roll-call of death—one who served with him three years, during the most trying and eventful period of his life—De Hass has gathered the following incident: On one of their scouting expeditions into the Indian country, the spies, consisting at that time of sixteen men, encamped for the night at a place called "Big Shell Camp." Toward morning, one of the guard heard the report of a gun, and immediately communicating the fact to his commander, a change of position was ordered. Leading his men to an elevated point, the Indian camp was discovered almost beneath them. Cautiously advancing in the direction of the camp, six Indians were discovered standing around the fire, while several others lay upon the ground, apparently asleep. Brady ordered his men to wrap themselves in their blankets and lie down, while he kept watch. Two hours thus passed without anything material occurring.

As day began to appear, Brady roused his men and posted them side by side, himself at the end of the line. When all were in readiness, the commander was to touch, with his elbow, the man who stood next to him, and the communication was to pass successively to the farthest end. The orders then were, the moment the last man was touched, he should shoot, which was to be the signal for a general discharge. With the first faint ray of light rose six Indians, and stood around the fire. With breathless expectation the whites waited for the remainder to rise, but failing, and apprehending a discovery, the Captain moved his elbow, and the next instant the wild woods rang with the shrill report of the rifles of the spies. Five of the six Indians fell dead, but the sixth, screened behind a tree, escaped. The camp being large, it was deemed unsafe to attack it further, and a retreat was immediately ordered.

Soon after the above occurrence, in returning from a similar expedition, and when about two miles from the mouth of Yellow Creek, at a place admirably adapted for an ambuscade, a solitary Indian stepped forward and fired upon the advancing company. Instantly, on firing, he retreated toward a deep ravine, into which the savage hoped to lead his pursuers. But Brady detected the trick, and, in a voice of thunder, ordered his men to tree. No sooner had this been done, than the concealed foe rushed forth in great numbers, and opened upon the whites a perfect storm of leaden hail. The brave spies returned the fire with spirit and effect; but as they were likely to be overpowered by superior numbers, a retreat was ordered to the top of the hill, and thence continued until out of danger. The whites lost one man in this engagement, and two wounded. The Indian loss is supposed to have been about twenty, in killed and wounded.

Curing a "Sick Gun"—A Brace at a Single Shot

Captain Brady possessed all the elements of a brave and successful scout. Like Marion, "he consulted with his men respectfully, heard them patiently, weighed their suggestions, and silently made his own conclusions. They knew his determination only by his actions." Brady had but few superiors as a woodsman: he would strike out into the heart of the wilderness, and, with no guide but the sun by day and the stars by night, or, in their absence, then by such natural marks as the bark and tops of trees, he would move on steadily in a direct line toward his point of destination. He always avoided beaten paths and the borders of streams, and never was known to leave his track behind him. In this manner he eluded pursuit and defied detection. He was often vainly hunted by his own men, and was more likely to find them than they him.

When Brady was once out on a forest excursion with some friendly Indians killing game for the Fort Pitt garrison, his tomahawk slipped and severely wounded his knee, obliging him to camp out for some time with the Indians. One of these, who had taken the name of Wilson, Brady saw one evening coming home in a great hurry and kicking his squaw. Without saying a word he then began to unbreech his gun. The squaw went away, and returned soon after with some roots, which, after washing clean, she put into a kettle to boil. While boiling, Wilson corked up the muzzle of his gun and stuck the breech into the kettle, and continued it there until the plug flew out of the muzzle. He then took it out and put it into the stock. Brady, knowing the Indians were very "superstitious," did not speak to him until he saw him wiping his gun. He then called to him, and asked what was the matter. Wilson came to the Captain and said that his gun had been very sick, that she could not shoot; he had been just giving her a vomit, and she was now well. Whether the vomit helped the gun or only strengthened Wilson's nerves, the Captain could not tell, but he averred that Wilson killed ten deer the next day.

Near Beaver, Pa., (formerly Fort McIntosh,) exist three localities, respectively called Brady's Run, Brady's Path and Brady's Hill. The following incident, furnished us, ended on the last. The Captain started from Pittsburgh with a few picked men on a scout towards the Sandusky villages. On their return they were hotly pursued, and all killed but the leader. He succeeded in getting back as far as the hill now called after him, not wounded, but nearly dead with fatigue. He knew well he was being relentlessly tracked, and that if he did not resort to some shrewd Indian trick, he would be lost. After cudgeling his brains awhile he hit upon the following:

Selecting a large tree lately blown down, and having a very thick, leafy end, he walked back very carefully in his tracks for a few hundred yards, then turned about and again trod in his old steps as far as the tree. This was to insure the Indians following him thither. He then walked along the trunk and snugly ensconced himself among the dense frondage at its end. Here he sat with rifle, specially loaded, all ready for duty. He counted upon his pursuers tracking him that far, and then, seeing no further trace of him, and it being at the end of a long day's tramp, that they would squat on the tree in a line for consultation. Nor was he disappointed. After he had been thus secreted for some time, and was gaining a fine rest, three Indians, with eyes bent earthwards like nosing hounds, came up in hot pursuit. Coming to the tree, they closely examined for the trail beyond, but not finding any, they were nonplused, and sat down to confab together.

The waiting scout now raised his long, black, unerring tube, drew a careful bead for his line shot, when flash! crack! and down tumbled one of his quarry dead and the other two wounded. With a silent chuckle at the success of his wile, Brady leaped to the encounter with clubbed rifle, and, after a brief struggle, succeeded in killing both savages. Quietly securing the whole three scalps, he made his way back to the fort. They had to hunt in gangs who would take Brady.

THE LONE HUNTER'S REVENGE—A DREAD HOLOCAUST.

At another time, about the close of the Revolution, Brady started with two tried companions—Thomas Bevington and Benjamin Biggs—from Fort McIntosh to Fort Pitt. They debated for some time which side of the Ohio they would take, but finally selected the northern, or Logstown shore, along which ran the beaten Indian trail. Moving rapidly forward they came to where Sewickley now stands, but where at that time was only the solitary cabin of a hunter named Albert Gray—one of that roving, dare-devil, wild-turkey breed, that must be always a little in advance of outposts.

Upon approaching this cabin, Brady suddenly came upon "Indian sign," and bidding his men crouch down, went ahead to reconnoitre. In a short time he heard a noise to one side, and beheld Gray himself coming along on horseback, with a deer laid across behind. Brady being dressed and painted, as usual, like an Indian, had to wait till the hunter was abreast, when he suddenly sprang forth and jerked Gray from his horse, saying hurriedly, as the other offered fierce resistance, "Don't strike; I am Captain Brady! for God's sake keep quiet!" The twain now stealthily advanced, and to their horror saw the ruins of Gray's little cabin smoking in the distance. It was as Brady feared. The savages had been at their hellish work. Gray's feelings may be imagined. Unrecking of the danger, he madly rushed forward, rifle in hand, more cautiously followed by the ranger. The ruins were carefully examined, but finding no bodies, it was concluded that the whole family were made captive. Not an instant to be lost! The retreating trail was broad and fresh, denoting a large party of Indians. The two lurking scouts were now rejoined, and an eager, anxious conference followed. One advised to go to Fort Pitt and the other to Fort McIntosh, about equidistant, for aid, but Brady said, "Come! Follow me!"

The pursuit was commenced at two P. M. Brady was a thorough woodsman, and knew the "lay" of that country, with its ravines, points and short cuts, better than the redskins themselves. Sure, by the tread of the trail, that the marauders were making for Big Beaver ford, he so shaped his course as to intercept, or, failing in that, to overtake them at this point. Right as a trivet; for on approaching the river he found their plain trail, making, as Brady supposed, for a wild, secluded glen through which a stream, now known as Brady's Run, brawled its devious way.

A close inspection and study of the traces indicated a party of at least a dozen. The odds were very large, but the anguish and impatience of the bereaved husband and father were so great that a sudden night attack was resolved upon. Secreting themselves, therefore, they patiently bided their time until dusk, when, crossing the Beaver, they entered the savage and sequestered ravine on the other side, and soon descried—right beside a famous spring—the camp fire of the cruel kidnappers. The unrecking Indians were at their evening meal, the captives—among whom was a strange woman and two children beside Gray's—sitting apart by themselves. The sight of his wife and children made Gray's heart thump, and he was like a bloodhound held in leash. But Brady sternly rebuked his impatience, and firmly restrained him. Their only chance for success was to wait until the reds were asleep. If evil had been intended to the captives, it would have been inflicted before that. They must trust only to knife and tomahawk, and must all crawl to the side of the sleeping savages, each man selecting his victim.

And now the fire has nearly died out, and the Indian camp is at rest. No watch dog there to betray the four scouts, who, making no more noise than their own shadows, draw themselves, like so many serpents, slowly but surely forward. A branch suddenly snaps beneath the knee of Biggs! Not much of a noise, but loud and distinct enough to cause one of the swarthy sons of the forest to spring to a sitting position, and—with head bent in direction of the alarm, and with ear intensely attent to the slightest sound—to listen, listen, listen. The four avengers lay prone on the grass, their hands on their knife handles and their hearts beating like muffled drums. The strain was truly dreadful, but perfect silence is maintained—no sound but the faint chirp of a wood cricket—so delicate that scarce could anything live between it and silence.

The dusky statue, his suspicions at length lulled, gives the dying embers a stir, and, with a sleepy yawn, sinks again to slumber. He has thus lighted his own and his companions' way to death, for when all was again quiet, a low cluck from Brady gives the signal of advance. Noiselessly as rattlers, each of the four drags himself alongside of a sleeping savage, a tomahawk in each right hand and a knife between the teeth. The four gleaming instruments of vengeance are now suspended above the unconscious sleepers, and at another low cluck from Brady, a hail of murderous blows descends.

What a contrast now! the whole camp is a scene of the direst confusion and alarm. The remaining savages leap to their feet in a vain endeavor to escape the pursuing blades. Every one is sooner or later dispatched. The captives at first fled in alarm, but finding preservers at hand, soon returned and were restored to their friends. The spring by the side of which the Indians camped was afterwards, in memory of this swift retribution and dreadful tragedy, called the "Bloody Spring."

Tracked by a Dog—An Indian Camp Attacked.

Once on returning from a scout, Brady was keeping a sharp lookout in expectation of being trailed, and taking every precaution to avoid pursuit, such as keeping on the driest ridges and walking on logs whenever they suited his course, he found he was followed by Indians. His practiced eye would occasionally discover in the distance, an Indian hopping to or from a tree, or other screen, and advancing on his trail. After being satisfied of the fact, he stated it to his men and told them no Indian could thus pursue him, after the precautions he had taken, without having a dog on his track. "I will stop," said Brady, "and shoot the dog and then we can get along better." He selected the root of a tall chestnut tree which had fallen westward, for his place of ambush. He walked from the west end of the tree or log to the east, and sat down in the pit made by the raising of the roots. He had not been long there when a small slut mounted the log at the west end and with her nose to the trunk approached him. Close behind her followed a plumed warrior. Brady had his choice. He preferred shooting the slut, which he did; she rolled off the log stone dead, and the warrior, with a loud whoop, sprang into the woods and disappeared. He was followed no further.

On another occasion the Indians had made a destructive raid upon the Sewickley settlement and the Fort Pitt soldiers were out to chastise them. Brady took five men and his *pet* Indian and also went out, but in an entirely different direction. He crossed the Allegheny and proceeded straight up that stream, rightly conjecturing that the invaders must have descended it in canoes. He, therefore, carefully examined the mouths of all the little streams on his way, and when opposite to the Mahoning, his sagacity was rewarded, for there lay the canoes drawn up to the bank. He instantly retreated down the river, and at night made a raft and crossed to the other side. He then proceeded up to the creek, and found that the Indians had in the meantime crossed it, as the canoes were now on the other side.

The country at the mouth of the Mahoning being rough and the stream high, the current was very rapid, and it was not until after several ineffectual attempts, that the Brady party crossed, two or three miles from the mouth. Then they made a fire, dried their clothes, inspected their arms, and moved towards the Indian camp, which was on the second bank of the river. Brady placed his men at some distance on the lower bank. The Indians had captured a stallion, which they had fettered and turned to pasture on the lower bank. One of them, probably the owner, came down to him frequently, and troubled our party greatly. The horse, too, seemed desirous to keep with them, and it required considerable circumspection to avoid all intercourse with either. Brady became so provoked that he strongly desired to kill the Indian, but his calmer judgment prevented this, as likely to hazard a more important achievement.

Brady being desirous to ascertain the numbers of the Indians and the position of the guns, crept up so close that the *pet* Indian would accompany him no further. While he was thus watching, an Indian rose and came so close to him that he could have touched him with his foot. However, he discovered nothing, and returned to his blanket and was soon asleep.

Brady returned to his men and posted them, and in silence they awaited the light. When it appeared, the Indians arose and stood around their fires. When the signal was given, seven rifles cracked and five Indians fell dead. Brady gave his well-known war cry, and the party charged and secured all the guns. The remaining Indians instantly fled. One was pursued by the trace of his blood, but soon he seemed to have succeeded in staunching this. The *pet* Indian then gave the cry of a young wolf, which was answered by the wounded man, and the pursuit was renewed. A second time the wolf cry was given and answered, and the pursuit continued into a " wind-fall."

Here the savage must have seen his pursuers, for he answered no more; but Brady, three weeks afterwards, found his body. Taking the horse and the plunder, the party returned to Pittsburgh, most of them descending in the Indian canoes. Three days after their return, the first detachment of seekers came in. They reported that they had followed the Indians closely, but that the latter had escaped in their canoes.

Brady told a Mr. Sumerall that he once started out alone from Wheeling for the purpose of bringing in prisoners, not scalps. He was gone over two weeks and returned with five prisoners—an Indian and squaw, one boy and girl and a pappoose. He proceeded to two villages and secreted himself in a swamp. He saw this family enter into a cabin lying on the outskirts of the village, and that night he broke open the door, told them who he was and that if they made one murmur he would slay them all. The warrior had heard of Brady and knew he would do as he said.

Brady told them if they would go peaceably with him, he would take them safely. He made the squaw carry the pappoose and drove the whole before him, traveling only by night. He was, as he expected to be, pursued, but he had selected his resting places so that he could reach them by wading up or down a stream to them, and as "water leaves no trail," he thus threw his pursuers off the track. Sumerall described to a Mr. Wadsworth the position of the two villages so accurately, that several years after the latter was traveling through that part of Ohio, and identified them as Greentown and Jerometown, between Mansfield and Wooster.

"Brady's Leap" Over the Cuyahoga River.

Brady's famed leap of twenty-five odd feet has been by many considered a myth of romance, and by others has been located on Slippery Rock Creek, or in Beaver county, Pa., but we have received so much detailed information about this asserted *leap*, that we not only feel certain it *did* take place, but that it was made by Brady over the Cuyahoga river.

General L. V. Bierce, the aged and honored antiquarian of Akron, Ohio, writes us that there can be no doubt whatever not only as to the fact, but also as to the exact locality where it occurred. The place, he writes, has ever since borne the name of "Brady's Leap." The little lake in which he afterwards concealed himself, also bears to this day the name of Brady's Lake. The tradition of his fight with the savages on the south shore of that same lake, has been confirmed by skulls and a sword having been found there; and, moreover, he heard the story narrated by John Jacobs, Henry Stough and John Haymaker, all friends of Brady, and who asserted they had it from his own mouth. Haymaker and Wadsworth both measured the stream where the leap was made, and found it twenty-five feet across and some thirty feet above the water. Brady jumped from the west to the east side and caught the bushes on the steep, rocky cliff, slipping down some three or four feet before he recovered himself.

But let us briefly and in substance narrate the story as told by Brady himself to Sumerall and by him to F. Wadsworth. There is a small lake in Portage county, Ohio, which still retains the name of Brady's Lake, and on the south side of which Brady had a severe battle. He had collected a company of twenty for a scout in the Sandusky country, but was waylaid by a much superior force at this lake, and his whole company cut off but himself and one more. Many years after, Wadsworth and Haymaker hunted up the precise locality, and by scraping away the earth and leaves, found many skulls and human bones and a basket-hilted sword.

At another time—the same occasion, according to some, when he threw either the chief's squaw or her child upon the fire built for himself— Brady was hotly pursued from Sandusky for about a hundred miles. When he arrived near the Cuyahoga, (which stream he intended crossing at the "Standing Stone,") he found he was headed on all sides. He reached the stream at the rocky gorge where the contracted current rushes through, as it were, a narrow fissure in the rocks. Finding himself thus hemmed in, Brady summoned all his energies for the mighty leap, and, as stated, caught by the bushes on the other side. When the pursuing savages saw the flying jump, they stood astonished, and then set up a terrific yell, three or four of them firing at him and wounding him in the leg.

Very soon he found the Indians had crossed the river at the "Standing Stone," and were again in hot pursuit. When he arrived at the lake, finding the savages rapidly gaining on him, and his wound greatly troubling him, he concluded that unless he could secrete himself somewhere, he was gone. Plunging into the water, he made his way to a place that was covered with lily pads or pond lilies. Fortunately he found that he could keep his face under water by breathing through the hollow stem of a weed. The Indians were not long after him. Following his bloody trail, they tracked him into the water and made minute search for him, but concluding that—severely wounded as he was— he had preferred drowning himself to losing his life and scalp at their hands, they finally gave up the search. Brady heard the Indians hunting around all that day and part of the night, and then made good his escape.

But Judge Moses Hampton, of Pittsburgh, gives us still other information, gathered not only from a personal visit to the locality of the leap, but from details derived from his father over fifty years ago. He writes us that the place where Brady leaped is at the Franklin Mills, Portage county, Ohio, within two miles of the Pittsburgh and Cleveland Railroad. While there he was informed that the distance leaped was twenty-seven feet six inches. After the search for Brady had been abandoned by the Indians, they returned to make a more careful survey of the spot of this extraordinary leap.

"After carefully contemplating the whole scene," continues the Judge, "and being unwilling to admit (and this is a well-known trait of Indian character) that any white man can excel an Indian in feats of activity, they gradually came to the conclusion that he was not a man, but a turkey, and flew across, saying, 'he no man, he turkey; he flew,' and in order to commemorate that fact, they carved on a rock close by a rude representation of a turkey's foot. This remained an object of curiosity to hundreds till the Summer of '56, when, being at the place, and finding the rock was about to be quarried, I obtained permission to have that part of the rock containing the carving of this turkey's foot cut out, which I brought home, and until recently held in my possession."

BRADY'S TRIAL—MARRIAGE TO DRUSILLA SWEARINGEN—HIS DEATH.

At one time Brady had to stand a trial at Pittsburgh for the killing, in time of peace, of a gang of redskins. It was proved by him that these savages had been on a plundering and scalping raid among the Chartiers settlements, and that he, selecting some of his tried followers, had made a rapid pursuit, and waylaid them at the Ohio river crossing near Beaver, thus justifying the attack as nothing but a swift punishment for flagrant acts of hostilities on the part of the savages. The trial created great excitement at the time, and was ably argued. Public sentiment—which had been lately greatly excited by savage marauds—was overwhelmingly in favor of Brady, and he was triumphantly acquitted.

One of the minor incidents of the trial may be noticed, as exhibiting an Indian's idea of the paramount claims of friendship. Guyasutha, the famed Mingo Chief, was one of the witnesses for Brady, and swore very extravagantly in his favor—in fact, far more than Brady wanted. After the session was over, the bystanders gathered about the chief and twitted him considerably for his reckless swearing. Drawing himself up with great dignity, and striking his brawny breast, the old chief gave this significant reply, "Why me no swear vely hard? Guyasutha vely big friend to Captain Blady."

Of Brady's private and social life it is very difficult to gather reliable particulars. About *all* these old Indian fighters there was so much of mystery and romance, and the feats attributed to them come to us with such changes of locality and incident, that it is hard to sift the true from the false. We have tried, in every instance, to get as near *facts* as possible, rejecting all that is doubtful or improbable. Lyman C. Draper, who is excellent authority, writes us that Brady married, about the year 1786, Miss Drusilla Swearingen, daughter of Captain Van Swearingen—" Indian Van," he was called on the border —a gallant officer in General Morgan's Rifle Corps. Drusilla was a very gentle and beautiful lady, and was sent East for her education. After the Revolution Captain Swearingen forted and settled where Wellsburg, West Va., now stands.

It is a tradition that the gentle Drusilla was first wooed by Dr. Bradford, of Whiskey Insurrection notoriety, but Brady returned from a long trip to Kentucky just in time to secure the coveted prize. Her father objected at first to his daughter's marrying Brady, on account of his roving and dangerous scout's life, but afterwards gave his consent. There was some foundation for this objection, for we have learned that the fond and lovely wife suffered untold miseries when her reckless husband was absent on distant scouts longer than the time agreed on for return. Dr. Darby once witnessed the meeting between husband and wife on such an occasion and states it as having been very affecting.

The exact time of Captain Brady's death we have not yet been able to fix definitely. It was probably somewhere near the year 1800. Joseph Quigley, who lived in the Chartiers settlement, which Brady made his headquarters during a large portion of his bachelor life, says that he frequently saw Brady at his father's house, and that he looked much older than he really was. He walked quite lame from the wound received in his leg at the time he leaped the Cuyahoga river. He was also then pretty deaf, which he attributed to lying so long in the lake where he was chased after he made his famous leap. Quigley says that it was John Dillow and a man by the name of Stoup or Sprott, who were with Brady on the Indian excursion terminated by the leap, and that when he approached the lake he swam out to a log, surrounded by pond lilies and secreted himself beneath, but kept his face just above water.

Brady spent the last years of his life at West Liberty, West Va., where he died. "After life's fitful fever he sleeps well." He left two sons, both now dead. His wife subsequently married again, moved to Tyler county, Va., and lived to a good old age.

ANDY POE'S FAMOUS FIGHT WITH BIGFOOT

The Only Reliable Account Ever Yet Published.

The narrations of the famous combat between the brothers Poe and Bigfoot are very much mixed up in the old border books, Doddridge and those who follow him substituting the name of Adam for that of Andy, while others have made the date of the occurrence 1782, instead of 1781. The subjoined detailed narrative of the desperate fight, is from the pen of Simpson R. Poe, of Ravenna, O., who is a grandson of Andrew Poe, and who possesses the very tomahawk which Bigfoot wielded in the sanguinary encounter. We have every reason to believe this account the only correct one.

Andrew Poe was born in Frederick county, Maryland, September 30th, 1742. His father, George Poe, possessed a large property in that county, but died when Andrew was fourteen years of age. Soon after Andrew became of age, finding he would get none of his father's estate, he left his mother and brother, with whom he had still lived, and came to Pittsburgh, Pa., and worked in that neighborhood for several years until he acquired a little property. He then, in company with two young men, went to Harmon's Creek, in Washington county, Pa., (then Virginia,) where each of them selected for himself a tract of land, and commenced making the first improvements in that part, and pursued their labors undisturbed for several years. Adam Poe was six years younger than Andrew. When he became of age Andrew returned to Maryland and induced him to come to Harmon's Creek, and Adam also took up a farm, and their little settlement increased to ten or twelve families. Adam Poe was married in 1778, and Andrew in 1780.

The Indians became very troublesome about this time. This little settlement was about twelve miles back from the Ohio river. The Indians very often came across the river into the settlement in small parties, and killed a number of the inhabitants. Such as were active on foot went in small scouting parties into the Indian settlements to learn their strength and retaliate their injuries. Andrew Poe went frequently on those excursions, as he was of a daring spirit and inured to all the perils of the woods. At one time, in the Spring of 1781, whilst Andrew Poe, Robert Wallace and Robert Kennedy were on a scout in the Indian settlement, a party of Indians came into their neighborhood and killed the wife and child (about a year old) of Robert Wallace, who lived nearest neighbor to Andrew Poe. The same year, in the month of June, a party of Indians, seven in number, came into the settlement, and about midnight broke into the house of William Jackson, a man of about sixty years of age; he being alone in the house, they took him prisoner.

They next tried to break into another house, where were several men, but failing to get in, they made off with Jackson. These men immediately gave the alarm; the whole settlement was collected, and it was found that Jackson was missing. They made preparations for following the Indians as soon as it was light enough to see their trail, which was very visible in the thick and high growth of herbage. Twelve of their number, mounted on horseback, pursued at the greatest possible speed until they reached the top of the river hill, which was about twelve miles. There they hitched their horses, as the hill was steep, and traveled on foot. When they arrived at the bottom of the hill, near to the river, the trail turned down the river, and in crossing a little rivulet that put into the river, Andrew observed that where the Indians had stepped into the water it was still riley, and cautioned the men to keep quiet; that the Indians were very near and would hear them and kill the prisoner, as the men were making considerable noise with their feet by running.

After several fruitless efforts to quiet them, he left the company, turning off square to the right, went to the bank of the river, and looking down, about twelve feet below him he saw two Indians standing about half bent, with their guns in their hands, looking down the river in the direction of the noise. He observed that one was a very large man. The thought struck him that he would shoot the big one and take the other prisoner. Accordingly, he squatted down in the weeds, they not having observed him. He crept up to the brow of the bank, put his gun through the weeds, took deliberate aim at the big Indian, who was three feet in advance of the other; but his gun missed fire. When the gun snapped, they both yelled, "Woh! Woh!!"

Poe immediately drew his head back, and the Indians did not see him. By this time the other men had overtaken the other five Indians with the prisoner, who were about one hundred yards lower down the river, and had begun to fire, which drew the attention of these two. Andrew cocked his gun and crept to the very edge of the bank, and again leveled his gun at the big Indian, but again it missed fire. He dropped the piece and sprang instantly on them. They, on wheeling about at the snap of his gun, were brought side by side, but had not time even to raise their guns before Andrew was upon them. He threw his weight on the big Indian, catching each of them around the

Andrew Poe's Famous Combat with Big Foot.
—See page 445.

neck. His weight coming on them so suddenly, threw them both down.

Bigfoot fell on his back, Andrew fell with his left side on him and his left arm around his neck. The little Indian fell rather behind Andrew, whose right arm was around his neck. Their guns both fell. One of them laid within reach of Andrew, who observed that it was cocked. The Indians had a raft fastened to the shore close by where they were standing, the river being very high. Their tomahawks and shot pouches, with their knives, were on the raft. Andrew's knife was in the scabbard attached to his shot pouch, which was pressed between him and Bigfoot. He got a slight hold of the handle and was trying to draw it out to dispatch Bigfoot, who, observing it, caught his hand and spoke in his own tongue very vehemently to the other, who was struggling hard to get loose.

Andrew made several efforts to get his knife, but in vain. At last he jerked with all his might. Bigfoot instantly let his hand go, and Andrew, not having a good hold of the handle, and the knife coming out unexpectedly easy in consequence of Bigfoot's instantly loosing his grasp, it flew out of Andrew's hand, and the little Indian drew his head from under his arm, his grasp being slackened by the act of drawing the knife. Bigfoot instantly threw his long arms around Andrew's body and hugged him like a bear, whilst the little Indian sprang to the raft, which was about six feet off, and brought a tomahawk and struck at Andrew's head, who was still lying on his side on Bigfoot, he holding him fast. Andrew threw up his foot as the stroke came, and hit the Indian on the wrist with the toe of his shoe, and the tomahawk flew into the river.

Bigfoot yelled at the little Indian furiously, who sprang to the raft and got the other tomahawk, and, after making several motions, struck at Andrew's head, who threw up his right arm and received the blow on his wrist, which cut off one bone of it and the cords of three of his fingers, disabling all the fingers of his right hand but the fore finger. Andrew immediately threw his hand over his head when he was struck, and the tomahawk, catching in the sinews of his arm, drew it out of the Indian's hand, and it flew over his head. After the stroke was given, Bigfoot let got his hold, and Andrew immediately sprang up. As he rose he seized the gun, which lay by his head, with his left hand, and it being already cocked, he shot the lesser Indian through the body.

But scarcely had he done so when Bigfoot arose, and, placing one hand on his collar and the other on his hip, he threw him into the river. Andrew threw his left hand back, caught the Indian by his buckskin breech-clout, and brought him along into the stream. The water being deep, they both went under. Then a desperate effort was made by each to drown the other, and sometimes one was under the water, sometimes the other, and sometimes both.

The Two Make a Desperate Effort to Drown Each Other.

In the struggle they were carried about thirty yards out into the river. Poe at length seized the tuft of hair on the scalp of the Indian, by which he held his head under water until he supposed him drowned. But he himself was sinking; not being able to do much with his right hand, he threw it on the back of Bigfoot's neck, who was under water, and swam with his left hand, to recruit himself a little. But Bigfoot had only been "possuming," and got from under Andrew's arm and swam for shore with all his speed. Poe followed him as fast as he could, but having only one hand to swim with, he could not catch him.

As soon as Bigfoot got out of the water, the gun being uncocked, he went to cock it and disabled the lock. He then threw it down and picked up the empty gun with which Andrew had shot the other Indian, and went to the raft for the shot pouch and powder horn, and commenced loading. In the meantime, as soon as Bigfoot reached the spot where both guns and tomahawk lay, Andrew swam back into the river and called for his brother Adam, who was with the other party.

Adam came running on the bank where Andrew had jumped off, stopped, began to load his gun, as he had discharged it at the other Indians. Andrew continued swimming away from them, with nothing but his face out of the water, still hurrying Adam to load quickly. The race between the two in loading was about equal, but the Indian drew the ramrod too hastily and it slipped out of his hands and fell a little distance from him. He quickly caught it up and rammed down his bullet. This little delay gave Poe the advantage, so that just as Bigfoot raised his gun to shoot Andrew, Adam's ball entered the breast of the savage, and he fell forward on his face upon the very margin of the river.

Adam, now alarmed for his brother, who was scarcely able to swim, jumped into the river to assist him to shore, but Andrew, thinking more of the honor of securing the big Indian's scalp as a trophy than of his own safety, called loudly upon his brother to leave him alone and scalp Bigfoot. Adam, however, refused to obey, and insisted upon saving the living before attending to the dead. Bigfoot, in the meantime, had succeeded in reaching the deep water before he expired, and his body was borne off by the waves without being stripped of the ornament and pride of an Indian warrior.

An unfortunate occurrence took place during this conflict. Just as Adam arrived at the top of the bank for the relief of his brother, the balance of his party, hearing the hallooing of Andrew, came running up the bank, and seeing him in the river, mistook him for a wounded Indian, and three of them fired at him, one of them wounding him dangerously. The ball entered his right shoulder near the junction with the neck, behind the collar bone and close to it; passing through his body, the ball came out at his left side, between the first rib and the hench bone.

During the contest between Andrew Poe and the two Indians, the rest of the party followed the Indian trail to the river, where the other five Indians were with the prisoner, Jackson. They had a large raft, and were preparing to cross the river. Jackson seeing the men coming as soon as the Indians did, ran to them. One of the Indians having a tomahawk ran after him and struck him on the back, making but a slight wound. The men fired on the Indians, who returned the fire and plunged into the river. They did not capture any of the Indians, but being badly wounded only one of them got across the river, and he was shot through the hand.

The Indians firing at our men, wounded but one of them. He was shot slightly through the side, but the ball cut his lungs, and he died in about an hour. His name was Cherry. The party took the dead man, Cherry, and Andrew Poe up the river hill to the horses, and then took them on horseback home. The locality on the Ohio river where this struggle occurred is in Virginia, nearly opposite the mouth of Little Yellow Creek. Andrew Poe recovered of his wounds and lived many years after his memorable conflict, but he never forgot the tremendous "hug" he sustained in the arms of Bigfoot. The smaller of the two Indians was a giant compared even with him.

Poe's Fight with a Young Bull—A Revenge Thwarted.

Thus far Poe's grandson. The old chroniclers state that Bigfoot had five brothers, all distinguished for their size and power. Andy Poe was a man of remarkable power and activity, and lived a long life of daring adventure. When advanced in years, and at the request of his friends, he used to fight over again his famous battle with Bigfoot, and those who saw him thus engaged, describe the scene as the most thrilling they ever beheld. The old man would enter thoroughly into the spirit of the combat, and, with dilated pupil; tense, rigid muscle, and almost choked with frothing rage, would go over each throe and struggle of that desperate conflict. These pantomime exhibitions were so painfully violent and furious that the old hunter would be as much exhausted by them as if they were actually real. Mr. F. Wadsworth states that Andy Poe was a very old man when he knew him, but would even then become very much excited when going over his hunting stories. "One evening, after telling a good many, he put his hand on my shoulder and said: 'Mr. Wadsworth, no man ever took more satisfaction in hunting deer, bear, wolves and buffalo than I have, but the greatest enjoyment I ever took was in hunting Indians.'"

As serving well to illustrate the power and obstinate determination of the man, we may relate a well-authenticated incident of Andrew's old age. Among his cattle was a fierce and vicious young bull, who endangered all who approached him. Poe was in the habit of visiting his stock yard regularly, until he supposed the bull knew him well. On one occasion he was suddenly attacked by the refractory brute, receiving a severe gash from one of its horns. So exasperated did this singularly bold man become, that he went at once to the cabin, armed himself with his trusty old tomahawk—his most familiar companion in times long past—and, despite the entreaties of his family, returned to the yard, and, driving all the cattle out but the bull, he faced it with his menacing scowl, like a Spanish matador, and laid hold of his right horn. The infuriated beast reared and plunged and gored, filling the air with its awful lows and bellows. No use. Poe held on like grim Death, at every moment bringing down with his right arm the pipe end of the tomahawk on the brute's skull. In this manner, and with hammer-headed obstinacy, he repeated his blows, until finally the vanquished animal sank dead at his feet.

Rev. Finley, M. E. missionary among the Wyandots, states that so deeply was the loss of Bigfoot felt by the Wyandots that, determined on revenge, they some time afterwards sent Rohn-yen-ness, a noted chief, to Poe's cabin to kill him. Andrew, not suspecting the design, received and entertained the chief with such kindness that he was completely disarmed. Knowing, however, that his tribe had selected him as avenger, he, after many conflicts with himself, rose from his bed, knife in hand, to execute the bloody deed. But the more he tried the worse he felt, and finally slunk back to his blanket, and next morning stole away. He said afterwards to Finley that the more he thought the less he could do, and was convinced it was the work of the Great Spirit. This noble chief afterwards became an humble and sincere Christian.

COL. CRAWFORD'S EXPEDITION AGAINST SANDUSKY.

Disastrous Defeat and Retreat—Crawford's Awful Tortures.

> Though of the past, from no carved shrines
> Canvas or deathless lyres, we learn;
> Yet arbored trees and shadowy pines
> Are hung with legends wild and stern.
> In deep, dark glen—on mountain side,
> Are graves whence stately pines have sprung;
> Naught telling how the victim died,
> Save faint tradition's faltering tongue.—*Street*.

We have alluded to the greatly demoralized state of the Virginia and Pennsylvania frontiers after the Moravian Massacre of March, 1782. The reds were earlier abroad that year than usual, and their numerous ruthless murders and scalpings so exasperated the borders that a savage and rancorous feeling sprang up, one horrible result of which had been the bloody butchery of a whole innocent community.

This, of course, failed to mend matters—such godless and barbarous measures never do. On the contrary, they grew much worse. The frightful tidings of the brutal slaughter were swiftly conveyed by fleet runners into every wigwam in Ohio, and the hate and rage of the savages became intensely bitter and vengeful. Their fierce and pitiless scalping parties filled the woods and crowded the trails towards those who had even given *them* a lesson in savagery. The entire border now became so alarmed, that numbers abandoned their homes and fled from the exposed frontier. The only salvation, all urged, was the immediate destruction of Sandusky, which—dominated from Detroit—was the swarming hive of all the vagabondizing gangs of marauding scalpers.

The clamor for a hostile expedition grew so hot and general, that the National Government, although not able then to spare any troops for one, agreed to give its official sanction. The County Lieutenants, therefore, conferred with General Irvine, of Fort Pitt; equipments and ammunition were furnished, and the orders went out for a secret assemblage of mounted volunteers at Mingo Bottom, on the Ohio, three miles below the present town of Steubenville, on or about the 20th of May.

All was now bustle and busy preparation. It was General Irvine's opinion that it would be rash in the highest degree to penetrate so far into hostile territory with less than three hundred men, but every glade and valley from Old Redstone to Fort Henry was now aroused, and as the time approached, it was seen that that number would be exceeded.

How many tender partings went with that motley assemblage! The enterprise was full of risk and peril. Many of the volunteers had made their wills. The usual style of leaving home, was to take down the loaded rifle from the buck's antlers above the mantel, examine the flint, see that the pouches were filled with patches and bullets, walk out of the rude log-cabin door, mount horse, discharge rifle, and immediately ride off without once looking behind or saying a word. The times were "terribly out of joint," and there was no time for these young Hotspurs to "play with mammets or to tilt with lips."

Every cluster of cabins, every sequestered valley had contributed its quota, and all these little streams of excited humanity now trended their various and devious ways towards Mingo Bottom. On that broad and fertile plateau, surrounded by the dense and solemn woods, into whose profound depths and solitudes they were about to plunge, they exchanged greetings, and fired off noisy *feus de joie*. They comprised the very pick and flower of the yeomanry from the rugged hills and wild glens of Western Pennsylvania—all volunteers, and most of them young and of the free, sturdy and obstinate Scotch-Irish stock. Not alone *three hundred*, which was Irvine's minimum, but no less than *four hundred and eighty,* mounted on the very best and fleetest horses of the border. Of this eager and noisy muster, about two-thirds were from Washington and the rest from Westmoreland county.

What a picturesque assemblage of stalwart, sinewy, loose-jointed men it was, to be sure, with their horns and pouches strapped to their brawny breasts; all accoutred in leggins, moccasins and fringed hunting shirts, belted at the waist. On the right side hung the keen tomahawk; on the left, the scalping knife. The long, heavy rifle, void of all show, but gotten up for use and range, was the faithful familiar of all. Scarce one there that could not bark a squirrel or decapitate a turkey from the loftiest tree. Strapped to each rustic saddle was the tow-cloth, or cowhide knapsack, crammed with indispensables for the journey. From the pommel hung the canteen and the supply of flour and bacon. The saddle blanket was to serve for bed at night.

A canvass for officers was the first business after all had gathered. If any there felt any apprehensions of the future, none did he exhibit. The whiskey flowed freely. The hoppled horses quietly munched the lush herbage under the huge sycamores, which there grew to an enormous size. Here one group played at cards; another engaged at rifle shooting; while another still was busy discussing the chances of the enterprise and who ought to be chosen to lead them. At the election that followed, Colonel William Crawford was elected over Colonel David Williamson—the leader of the late Gnadenhutten massacre expedition—

by a vote of two hundred and thirty-five against two hundred and thirty.

It is part of the secret history of the expedition, that General Irvine, and the whole Fort Pitt influence, was thrown in favor of the successful candidate. However much the Moravian massacre may have been approved, or at least excused, on the border, it had been universally condemned east of the mountains. Its bloody details had created among all classes a feeling of horror and indignation, and it was thought wise to restrain this officially-authorized expedition from any like damnable atrocity. There was still a remnant of the Christian Indians in the Sandusky country, whither they were going, that was to be saved from any further outrage and savagery.

The border histories of the day, following the wake of Withers, Doddridge and Heckewelder, do not hesitate to affirm that the destruction of the Moravian Indians, who had escaped the late massacre, was the sole end and aim of this expedition, but without going into details to prove our conviction, we can safely and most positively affirm that all reliable evidence points directly contrary. However much some of the rude and tempestuous borderers who made part of that muster, might desire another pillaging and slaughtering raid, nothing of that kind could be attempted, the popular Colonel Crawford being leader. His election was cheerfully submitted to by all present; his defeated competitor taking the second position. Major John Rose, a gallant gentleman and *protege* of General Irvine, was sent to act as *aide* to Crawford, while Dr. John Knight was detailed as surgeon.

Thus the whole enterprise was put under government auspices. While the noisy throng are loosing their rude bridles of skin and getting ready for the woods, let us say a few words of Colonel William Crawford, the able and gentlemanly leader of the troop.

Who Colonel Crawford Was—A Fight with Morgan.

Colonel William Crawford was one of the most notable men of the Pennsylvania border. Like his early and intimate friend, Washington, he commenced life as a surveyor, and it was while on a professional excursion in the Shenandoah Valley that Washington first made his acquaintance. Crawford's mother was a woman of unusual energy and physical strength, and by her second marriage with Richard Stephenson, had a troop of boys remarkable for their size and strength. There are many stories told of the athletic sports and trials of strength between Washington and the Stephenson and Crawford boys. In running and jumping with them, Washington was generally the victor, but in wrestling it was often his fate to be worsted.

In '55 he served as ensign at the disastrous battle of Braddocks Fields, and, for his gallantry, was soon after promoted to a lieutenancy, serving for some time on the harassed frontier, and acquiring great skill as an Indian fighter. In General Forbes' expedition against Fort Duquesne, he recruited and commanded a company under Washington. In connection with the marching of this company, we may relate one of the stories of the time. When all ready to move his command to join Washington, there was an urgent need of transportation, and a wagoner having stopped at the encampment to feed his team, Crawford told him he would have to impress him and his wagon into the public service. The teamster—a sturdy, stalwart, double-fisted yeoman—was much averse to this violent procedure, and after sullenly surveying Crawford's men, as if concluding on the uselessness of resistance, he observed to Crawford that it was a hard thing to have himself and property forced into service; that every man ought to have a fair chance, and offering, as he was but one against a number, to decide the matter by a contest with him or any one of the company—if beaten, he was to join them, but if victorious, he was to be allowed to go his way.

This proposition exactly accorded with the rude customs of the border, and the challenge of the teamster was at once gladly accepted, Crawford himself—noted, as stated, for his strength and agility—claiming the honor of handling him. Both now began to strip for the contest, the men quickly forming a ring about, when a strapping, powerful young stranger, who had lately joined the company, drew Crawford aside and most earnestly urged him to trust the struggle to him. "Captain," said he, coolly, "you must let *me* fight that fellow; he'll be sure to whip you, and it will never do to have the whole company whipped." The men around were so impressed with the confident and determined manner of their companion, as well as by the promising strength of his lithe and sinewy frame, that they persuaded their Captain to retire in his favor, and the contest began.

The huge wagoner, peeled to the buff and evidently an adept in pugilistic struggles, rushed briskly to the encounter, but the youthful stranger met him promptly half way; sprang upon him with the agility and fierceness of a catamount, and poured upon his luckless antagonist such a rain of fast and furious blows that the combat was as short as it was decisive. The teamster was very speedily vanquished, and eagerly proclaimed his willingness to go along with the company. The victor over the powerful wagoner was Daniel Morgan, afterwards General of the Riflemen of the Revolution.

After the evacuation of Fort Duquesne, Crawford remained in the Virginia service and chiefly engaged in frontier duty for several years. In 1767 he started on a horseback exploring expedition across the mountains, and was so pleased with the Youghiogheny Valley, that he resolved to locate on a spot on the river known in Braddock's expedition as "Stewart's Crossings," but now as Connellsville, Fayette county, Pa. He immediately set to work erecting his lonely cabin, clearing the howling wilderness around and trading with the Indians. In a year or two afterwards, his half-brother Hugh joined him, and both spent some years in clearing extensive tracts of land.

The intimate relations between Crawford and Washington were never disturbed. They corresponded constantly, took an occasional excursion together, and the former selected and located some fine tracts of land for Washington. At the breaking out of the disputes between Virginia and Pennsylvania as to the boundary lines of the respective States, Crawford took quite a prominent part, as he did also afterwards in the Revolutionary war. He was sent out, in 1778, by Washington, to take command on the frontier and for many years did most excellent service, becoming noted as a very able and efficient Indian fighter—cool, brave and a perfect woodsman.

After the capture of Cornwallis, deeming the war to be virtually over, he only thought of spending the rest of his days in the bosom of his large family. His children were all married and lived about him. His daughter Sallie, wife of William Harrison, was a beautiful woman, being considered the belle of the West. When, in '82, the expedition was being raised against Sandusky, he was often consulted and gradually all eyes turned towards him as its most fitting leader, but, although he warmly favored the enterprise, he positively refused to command it. But his beloved son John, his nephew William, and his son-in-law Harrison, having all volunteered, he was induced to say, that if elected to the command he would serve. He made his will, put his house in order, took a tender leave of his beloved family, mounted his horse and, having had a long interview with General Irvine at Fort Pitt, he left for Mingo Bottom, being, as stated, elected, on May 24th, to command the expedition, with Colonel Williamson as his second, Major Rose as his *aide-de-camp*, and Jonathan Zane and John Slover as guides. He was then about fifty years of age, of a very fine and attractive person, in the full vigor of life, and esteemed and respected by all.

Cavalcade Sets Out—Struggle About "Battle Island."

The formidable cavalcade, numbering no less than four hundred and eighty men—the very flower of the border, and mounted on the best and fleetest horses—moved early the next morning over the river bluff, and were immediately enshrouded in the vast wilderness. The fourth evening they encamped amid the deserted ruins of New Schœnbrun, the upper village of the Moravians, feeding their horses from the ungathered crops of the previous year.

Here they routed up and pursued two savages, who, however, escaped. All hope of secrecy was now abandoned, and nothing remained but to press on with all possible vigor. Five days later they reached the Sandusky near the present town of Crestline. Not an Indian seen since leaving the Muskingum! Was this a propitious or an ominous sign? Soon after, according to the statements of Zane and Slover, the two guides, they were approaching the Wyandot town, but strange that no signs of Indian occupation could be seen. Further on an opening in the woods is discovered. It is the town they seek. The horses are spurred into a rapid trot.

To the utter amazement and consternation of all, every hut was found deserted—nothing but a dreary solitude all around. The guides looked at the leaders with blank dismay in their faces. They had not the slightest suspicion that the year before, the Half King Pomoacon had moved his town some eight miles lower down the Sandusky. A halt was called at once, and a council of officers anxiously deliberated over the perplexing situation. It was the opinion of both Zane and Crawford that a return to the Ohio should be immediately made, as the absence of Indians and other suspicious signs made it highly probable that the savages were withdrawing before them and concentrating their forces. It was finally concluded that the troops should move forward that day but no longer.

The company of light horse rushed rapidly forward and soon reached a beautiful woody island in the midst of a prairie, which seemed to invite them out of the fierce heats of the June sun. They pause and rest, but finally strike out again into the open. All at once they suddenly come in view of the enemy running directly towards them. Aha! Shaken up at last! Listen to those yells and whoops! The skulking copperheads! A fleet horseman flies to the rear to apprise Crawford, and all at once is bustle and animation.

We may explain here what not a single soul of that expedition then knew. Instead of their movement being kept secret it was closely watched by a sleepless foe from the very first moment of its inception. Ever since the Gnadenhutten massacre, watchful Indian spies had been kept all along the border. The news of the present movement had been carried by fleet runners to the various allied tribes; and their towns were working like hives of angry bees. Not, however, until the Muskingum was passed, could the savages determine where the dread blow was to fall. Runners were then at once dispatched to Detroit for immediate aid. The tocsin of alarm was sounded in all the towns of the Shawnees on Mad river, the Delawares on the Tymochtee, and the Hurons on the Sandusky. The squaws and children were quickly hurried to a safe place of retreat, and all the braves commenced to paint and plume for the war path.

It was, then, the combined Delaware force of Pipe and Wingenund, amounting to two hundred, that Crawford's videttes had encountered. These were just waiting for four hundred Wyandots, under their great war chief, Shaus-sho-toh. Together they already outnumbered Crawford's troops, but this was by no means the whole. The news of the discovery of redskins was received by the grumbling Americans with the most lively satisfaction. They leaped to their horses, hurriedly looked to their weapons, rapidly fell into line and spurred briskly forward.

Now the superior genius of Major John Rose first began to exhibit itself. As the opposing forces drew near to the dread conflict, his keen, dark eyes flashed with excitement; his demeanor was calm, cool and confident. As he scoured along on his blooded mare from point to point, carrying the orders of the commander, his intrepidity and fine martial appearance attracted all eyes and won all hearts. The foe was now seen directly in front, taking possession of the grove on the prairie so lately abandoned by the light horse. A quick, forward movement, attended with hot, rapid firing, soon drove the enemy out again into the open. The savages then attempted to occupy a skirt of woods on the right flank, but were at once prevented by Major Leet's command.

The renegade, Captain Elliott, who now made his appearance as commander-in-chief, ordered The Pipe and his Delawares to flank to the right, and attack Crawford in the rear. This manœuvre was executed boldly and skillfully, nearly proving fatal to the Americans. The action now became general, and the firing was hot, close and continued, but the Americans maintained their position. The enemy skulked much behind the tall grass, and could only be picked off by sharpshooting. Big Captain Johnny, a huge Indian chief, near seven foot high and of frightful ugliness, was very conspicuous in this struggle; so, also, was Simon Girty, who, seated on a white horse of power ful stride, could both be seen and heard in different parts of the field, cheering his Indians to the encounter.

At dark the enemy's fire slackened, and Crawford's force was much encouraged. They did not, until long afterwards, know that *their* safety lay in forcing the fight, Elliott's and Girty's in delay. At length the foe drew off for the night, leaving Crawford in possession of the grove about which the battle had raged, and known in history as "Battle Island." The day had been sultry, and the volunteers suffered dreadfully from thirst. No prisoners were taken on either side, but quite a number of the Americans had been killed or wounded.

Both parties lay on their arms the whole night, kindling large fires in front, and then retiring some distance to the rear, in order to prevent night surprises.

BATTLE RENEWED THE NEXT DAY—CRAWFORD FORCED TO RETREAT.

Early the next day the battle was renewed, but only at long shot, and so continued during the whole day, but Crawford's position was plainly growing worse and more untenable each hour, while that of the enemy was just contrariwise. Crawford wished to compel closer and more decisive fighting, but his men were exhausted by the heat and thirst, or sickened by bad water, and it was finally concluded to lay by and then attempt a night attack.

A wonderful and disastrous change, however, soon set in. Then confidence soon turned to doubt, and doubt to dismay. Towards evening an outlying sentinel discovered a troop of horse approaching on a brisk trot in the direction of the Wyandots. They were Butler's British Rangers, and we *now* know were from Detroit, although none of Crawford's men knew then, if they did ever, *where* they were from. That British aid could come from Detroit, or from any other point, was never so much as dreamed of by any. It was now supposed they must have descended from Maumee or Sandusky Bay.

The tidings came to the Americans with startling and stunning force. A council of war was called at once. Even while they were deliberating, a large reinforcement of Shawnees from Mad river, about two hundred strong, was observed moving along in full view on their flank, and taking position with the Delawares, so that the trail our scouts followed ran along between two hostile camps. All over the prairie, too, small squads of the enemy could be seen pouring in from various directions. Matters began to look desperate. British cavalry, with a cloud of yelling savages on one side, and a strong force of Shawnees on the other! They were clearly outnumbered, two to one, and every hour was adding to their inferiority.

A retreat that night was instantly and unanimously resolved upon. It was commenced at nine o'clock, in four divisions. The dead were hastily buried, and litters were prepared for the dangerously wounded. Meanwhile the desultory firing was continued. The loud, hoarse voice of Girty was frequently heard in various directions, directing and locating his different forces, and it became at once patent to the very dullest comprehension that he was preparing for an overwhelming and irresistible attack the next day.

At dark the outposts were withdrawn as quietly as possible, and the whole body was put in motion. Unfortunately, the enemy early discovered the movement, and at once opened a hot fire. Many became panicky, and the retreat grew confused and precipitate. It is a delicate matter for even trained veterans to retire in face of a superior and victorious army. With raw volunteers an orderly withdrawal is almost impossible. Great wonder, dark as was the night, that this hasty retreat did not degenerate into an utter rout; but, thanks to the officers, some order was preserved.

A great blessing was it that the enemy was also in confusion and some alarm. They were not so sure that a retreat was intended, and were fearful of a feint or a night attack, a style of fighting that redmen never indulge in if it is possible to avoid. Unfortunately, a number of horses now became hopelessly bogged in a swamp, and had to be abandoned. The rear suffered severely, while many parties became detached from the main body and straggled off, blindly groping their way through the black, tangled woods. Only about three hundred were found together next morning.

The unpleasant discovery was now made that Colonel Crawford, the commander, was missing, with his son, son-in-law and nephew; also Slover, the guide, and Dr. Knight, the surgeon. None had heard of them, and knew not whether killed, wounded or straggling. Colonel Williamson now took command and, aided constantly and most efficiently by Major Rose, strove to bring order out of confusion.

It would require a volume to relate the various adventures and vicissitudes, or the sad and cruel fate that befell individuals and groups of stragglers. Some of them are intensely exciting and interesting. We can only follow the main body, which marched steadily and rapidly along all that day. The British cavalry and a body of mounted Indians hovered in their rear, but did little damage. That afternoon, as they were nearing the woods which bounded the Sandusky Plains on the east, the enemy began to press hard on their rear, and undertook a rapid flank movement on either side, with the design of cutting off all retreat, or of forcing a disastrous combat on the plain, before the shelter of the woods could be secured.

Our resolute little force was driven to bay just at the entrance of the forest, and doggedly faced about, their pursuers—all mounted, but with no artillery—overlapping them on both sides, and painfully superior both in number and equipments.

Williamson and Rose exerted themselves to the utmost to organize a spirited and efficient defence. The latter, especially, flew from rank to rank, cheering and encouraging all by his skill, his coolness and his intrepidity. "It is not too much to say," writes Butterfield, in his admirable and exhaustive account of Crawford's Expedition, "that the undaunted young foreigner was the *good angel* of the American forces." "Stand to your ranks, boys!" were his inspiring words sounding along the lines; "stand to your ranks! take steady aim! fire low! and don't throw away a single shot! Remember! everything depends upon your steadiness."

The enemy attacked vigorously in front, flank and rear, but in less than an hour were forced to give way, and were driven off at every point. The battle over, a driving storm swept along with unusual fury, wetting all the arms and drenching the troops to the skin. They continued the retreat, the enemy rallying their scattered force and following hard after.

Their firing became at last so galling that a complete panic would have resulted had it not been for the almost superhuman efforts of Major Rose, who enjoined upon the wavering lines that they must keep rank or not a soul of them would ever reach home. Order was at length restored, every now and then the front company filing to the left and taking position in the rear, thus giving each company its turn in covering the retreat.

Next morning, however, the enemy reappeared and hung for awhile in the rear, capturing and tomahawking two of the scouts; but just then, fortunately, the pursuit was abandoned. The last hostile shot was fired near where Crestline, O., now stands. Neither savage nor ranger was afterwards seen during the retreat; but many stragglers found their way back to the lines, and were received with welcome hurrahs.

The Muskingum was recrossed on the 10th, and Mingo Bottom was reached on the 13th, where some of the missing had arrived before them. They immediately recrossed the Ohio and dispersed to their several homes. Parties or single stragglers came in for days afterwards. The total loss in killed, wounded and missing, it has since been discovered, was less than seventy

Colonel Williamson, in his official report to General Irvine at Fort Pitt, writes thus of his aid, the gallant Major Rose: "I must acknowledge myself ever obliged to Major Rose for his assistance, both in the field of action and in the camp. His character is estimable, and his bravery cannot be outdone." General Irvine, too, in his letter to Crawford's widow, says: "After the defeat, Williamson and others informed me that it was owing, in a great degree, to the bravery and good conduct of Major Rose that the retreat was so well effected."

Thus ended this twenty days' campaign in the western wilds. The total failure of the expedition created incredible alarm and dismay along the whole border, which was now left more defenceless than ever, and for months after was exposed to merciless marauds and scalping forays

Colonel Crawford's Capture and Thrilling Adventures.

And where all this time was Colonel William Crawford, the courteous gentleman, the brave and gallant partisan officer, the daring defender of the West, and the trusted, life-long friend of Washington? Dr. Knight, in his thrilling account of his own escape, says he had not gone over a quarter of a mile in the general retreat before he heard Crawford calling out of the dark and confusion for his son, John; his nephew, William; his son-in-law, Major Harrison, and on his friend, Major Rose. Knight told him he thought they were all in front, and promised to stand by him. They both waited and called for the absent men until all the troops had passed, when the Colonel said his horse had given out, and he wished some of his best friends to stay by him.

By this time they were near the marsh, where they saw some volunteers vainly struggling to disengage their horses from the oozy bog. Crawford, Knight and two others, now changed their route to the north for a couple of miles, and then east, directing their course by the north star. They traveled all night, crossing the Sandusky. By daylight Crawford's horse gave out and was abandoned. That afternoon they fell in with Captain Biggs and Lieutenant Ashley—the latter severely wounded—and went into camp. The next day they were quietly thridding their way through the matted woods, when several Indians started up within a few feet of Knight and Crawford.

As only three were first discerned, Knight sprang behind a black oak and was taking aim when the Colonel called twice to him not to fire. One of the savages then ran up and took Crawford's hand, and another, whom Knight had formerly often seen, ran up to him, calling him Doctor. The party had fallen into an ambuscade of Delawares,

Wingenund's camp being only half a mile off. Captain Biggs had fired at the Indians and missed; but all succeeded, for the present, in escaping but Knight and Crawford, who were taken to the Indian camp. The scalps of Biggs and Ashley were brought in soon after.

As may well be supposed, the rejoicings of the savages at their late decisive victory had been immense. The allied forces retired to the Half King's town to celebrate the triumph with all sorts of dances, orgies and ceremonies. The British horse were compelled to retire to Detroit immediately, but the Indian women and children came out from their hiding places, and the festivities were kept up for some time. Among the spoils were numerous horses, guns, saddles, lashing-ropes, etc.

The first excitement over, a runner was sent to bring Crawford and Knight on to Pipe's town on the Tymochtee. Their doom was already sealed, but they were kept in total ignorance of their fate. As before stated, the burning and torture of prisoners was an obsolete custom among the Wyandots, and the Delawares did not dare to so put them to death without permission from Pomoacon. To obtain this the crafty Pipe resorted to a ruse. A runner, with a belt of wampum, was dispatched to the Half King with a message to the effect that they had a cherished project to accomplish and did not wish him to interfere, and that they would consider the return of the wampum as equivalent to his pledged word. The Half King was puzzled. He narrowly questioned the messenger, who feigned ignorance. Finally, supposing it must be some war expedition against the border which the Delawares wished to undertake, he returned the belt to the messenger with these words: "Say to my nephews they have my pledge!"

This was poor Crawford's death warrant. On June 10th he and Knight, with nine other prisoners, were all marched off on the trail to the Half King's town. Crawford had been told that Simon Girty— who had scarcely reached Detroit, from a border raid, before news of Crawford's expedition and Pomoacon's earnest appeal for immediate aid summoned him away again—was at the Half King's town. Girty was an old acquaintance of Crawford—some say a rejected suitor of one of his daughters—and at the latter's appeal he was conducted, under charge of two warriors, to interview the renegade. The rest continued on.

Crawford saw Girty that night; very little is known of the conference, but a Christian Indian, Tom Galloway by name, asserts that he heard the whole talk, and that Crawford had made to Girty an earnest appeal for his life, offering him a thousand dollars if he succeeded; and that Girty promised he would do all he could for him.

This being reported to Pipe and Wingenund, only made them more determined on his speedy death.

Girty also told the Colonel that Major Harrison, his son-in-law, and young William Crawford, his nephew, were prisoners to the Shawnees, but had been pardoned by them. True as to their capture, but false as to the pardon. The prisoners at the Half King's town, soon after Crawford's departure, were tomahawked and their heads stuck upon poles. It is certain they were not tortured to death.

Knight and his fellow prisoners meanwhile had been taken on to Old Town, and securely guarded during the night. Next day Pipe and Wingenund approached them, the former with his own hands painting all their faces black, a sure sign of intended death. Crawford soon after came up, and now saw the two redoubtable Delaware war chiefs for the first time. They both came forward and greeted him as an old acquaintance, Pipe telling him, in his blandest and oiliest manner, that he would have him *shaved* (adopted), but at the same time he *painted him black!*

The whole party now started for Pomoacon's town, the two chiefs keeping Knight and Crawford in the rear. They soon had the inexpressible horror of seeing, at intervals of half a mile apart, the dead, scalped bodies of four of their fellow prisoners. To add to their alarm and dismay, they now diverged off into a trail leading from Pomoacon's hut directly to Pipe's town. Their very last hope now died in their sad hearts.

On the Little Tymochtee, where there was an Indian hamlet, they overtook the other five prisoners, and all were ordered to sit on the ground. Here a lot of squaws and children fell on the five prisoners with incredible fury, and tomahawked and scalped them all. One hideous old hag cut off the head of John McKinly, and kicked it about over the grass. The boys came up to where the horror-stricken Knight and Crawford were sitting apart, and frequently dashed the gory and reeking scalps into their very faces.

Again they were driven forward, and were soon met by Simon Girty and several prominent Indians, all mounted. Girty well knowing what fate had been decided for Crawford, had ridden across the plains to Pipe's town—let us hope to save him, if possible.

Those who contend that Girty was nothing but a wild beast, assert that he never interfered or intended to interfere; that he not only consented to Crawford's death, but took a fiendish delight in witnessing it. Others, having quite as good means of information, strongly assert that he did all he could for Crawford, but that that was not much.

The Delawares were obstinately bent on making the "Big Captain," as they styled Crawford, a victim and an example. The late horrible massacre of so many of their tribe on the Muskingum had rendered them absolutely envenomed and pitiless, and it is probable that no one— not even Pomoacon himself—could have saved Crawford. Girty was an adopted Wyandot, and any strong or persevering effort on his part to defraud the zealous and infuriated Delawares of their revenge would not only have subjected him to insult, but to personal injury.

Joseph McCutcheon, in an article on Girty in the *American Pioneer*, asserts that he gathered from the Wyandots themselves that Girty offered a large sum of money to Pipe for Crawford, which the chief received as a great insult, promptly replying :

"Sir, do you think I am a squaw? If you say one word more on the subject, I will make a stake for you and burn you along with the White Chief."

Girty, knowing the Indian character, retired in silence.

McCutcheon also asserts that Girty had sent runners to Mohican Creek and Lower Sandusky, where there were some white traders, to come immediately and buy Crawford off. The traders came, but were too late, Crawford being then in the midst of his tortures.

Be all this as it may, if any efforts were made in Crawford's behalf, they were totally ineffectual. As the two prisoners moved along, almost every Indian they met struck them with their fists or with sticks. Girty asked Knight if he was the doctor; Knight said yes, and extended his hand ; upon which Girty called him a ——— rascal, and bid him begone, and afterwards told him he was to go to the Shawnees towns.

Colonel Crawford's Awful and Protracted Tortures.

We now approach the sad end of this mournful, cruel tragedy. The other prisoners were dispatched promptly and without ceremony, but for the "Big Captain" a more dreadful, appalling fate was reserved. All the devilish and excruciating tortures which ever entered into savage head to conceive were to be visited on the distinguished leader of the ill-starred expedition.

Almost within sight of Pipe's town, and amid a yelling, infuriated crowd of over one hundred braves, squaws and boys, a brisk fire was kindled. It was late on the afternoon of Tuesday, June 11th, 1782. There were the two Delaware war chiefs, Pipe and Wingenund ; Simon Girty, and Captain Elliott, in the uniform of a British officer, stood near. Dr. Knight was also a horrified and unwilling spectator of the awful scene.

He and Crawford, stripped entirely naked and painted black, were first ordered to sit down, when all at once the savages fell upon them and belabored them most unmercifully. Meanwhile a long stake had been firmly planted, to which the poor Colonel was fastened by a rope just long enough to allow him to either sit down or take two or three turns around. The wretched victim, seeing all these frightful preparations and the scowling, distorted visages of the yelling and leaping demons about him, called to Girty, and asked if the savages intended burning him. Girty answered "yes;" to which Crawford said he would strive to bear it all with fortitude. Pipe, who, of all present, seemed the most savage and implacable, made one of his ardent, stirring harangues, exciting his motley audience to a perfect fury.

Heckewelder relates that when Wingenund afterwards came to Detroit, he was severely censured for not saving the life of his old acquaintance, Colonel Crawford. He listened calmly, and then said to Heckewelder: "These men talk like fools," and then, turning to his accusers, he said, in English: "If King George himself had been on the spot, with all his ships laden with treasures, he could not have ransomed my friend, nor saved his life from the rage of a justly exasperated multitude." He never after would allude to the torture, but was full of grief, and felt greatly hurt at those who censured him; for he contended that the Gnadenhutten massacre was a wanton and most atrocious insult to his nation, and that the blood of those innocent Christians, so inhumanly butchered, called aloud for vengeance.

Another circumstance Heckewelder asserts was much against the prisoner. It was reported that the Indian spies, on examining the camp at Mingo Bottom, after the expedition left, found on the peeled trees these words, written with coal: "No quarters to be given to an Indian, whether man, woman or child!" If such rumors were circulated among the savages, they must have been done for effect, or were after-thoughts designed to excuse these atrocious tortures. There is not a tittle of evidence going to prove any such ferocious bravado, although doubtless a large proportion of the volunteers were the same Indian haters who were out on the Williamson raid.

Heckewelder also gives a highly interesting account of the conversation alleged to have occurred just before the commencement of the tortures, between Wingenund and Crawford, in which the former solemnly asserted that by Crawford's making himself an accomplice of the execrable miscreant Williamson, it was out of his power or that of any of his friends to save him.

Upon Crawford's most solemn assurance that both he and all good men not only condemned that atrocious slaughter, but that he was put at the head of this expedition expressly to prevent any excesses of that kind, and that it was not undertaken, as the Indians asserted, against the remnant of the Christian Indians, but for a purely military purpose, the chief said the Indians could not be made to believe such a story; that if Williamson had been taken, he (Wingenund) and his friends might have effected something; but since that savage murderer had run off, no man would dare to interfere; that the blood of the slaughtered, the relatives of those massacred, and that the whole nation cried aloud for revenge.

Heckewelder thus concludes: "I have been assured by respectable Indians that at the close of this conversation, which was related to me by Wingenund, as well as by others, both he and Crawford burst into a flood of tears; they then took an affectionate leave of each other, and the chief immediately *hid himself in the bushes*, as the Indians express it, or retired to a solitary spot. He never afterwards spoke of the fate of his unfortunate friend without strong emotions of grief, which I have several times witnessed." Whether this conversation actually occurred; whether it was the coinage of Heckewelder or of Wingenund—and each presumption has its adherents—must, at this late day, be left entirely to conjecture and the probabilities of the case. Certain it is, the cruel tortures went on.

The men now took up their guns and shot powder into Crawford's naked body from his feet up to his neck, to the number of full seventy loads. They then crowded in on him, and must have cut off his ears, since Dr. Knight saw the blood running in streams from both sides of his head. The circle of fire rose from small hickory poles, and was placed several yards from the stake, so that the poor sufferer had not, like the blessed martyrs of old, the consolation of a speedy, if a horrible death, but by a hellish refinement of cruelty his tortures were designedly prolonged. It would not serve the purposes of these incarnate fiends to have the victim become too soon insensate; they must gall and sting, beat and harass, rack and worry him by slow installments. Happy was the savage who could wreak upon the wretched sufferer one pang or agony more exquisite or excruciating than the last! who could wring from his poor humanity a more profound groan, or who could give his shrinking nerves or quivering flesh one added torment.

As Crawford began his weary rounds about the post, the yelling fiends would take up the blazing fagots and apply them to his shrinking, powder-scorched body. The squaws, more pitiless, if possible, than the men, gathered up the glowing embers on broad peelings of bark and cast them over his trembling body. Oh, it was horrible—most horrible. No escape from these merciless devils; their leering, hideous faces presented on all sides, and very soon the writhing martyr walked solely on a bed of scorching coals.

CRAWFORD'S LAST MOMENTS—"HE GIVES UP THE GHOST"

In the very midst of these awful orgies, Crawford called upon Girty again and again to shoot him and end his misery. Girty, it is said, replied he had no gun. He would not have dared to shoot even had he been so disposed. He soon after came up to Knight, and bade him prepare for the same death. He then observed that the prisoners had told him that if he were captured by the Americans they would not hurt him. He did not believe it, but was anxious to know the Doctor's opinion on the subject. He, at the same time, railed against Colonel John Gibson, of Fort Pitt, as one of his most hated enemies, and much more to the same purpose.

The unhappy Doctor was so distressed at the poignant and excruciating torments inflicted right before his very eyes upon his friend, and by the near prospect of a similar awful fate, that, he says in his "Narrative," he scarcely heard, much less answered.

Crawford was now nearly exhausted by his long-continued sufferings. His flesh was becoming callous, his nerves dulled by excess of pain. He bore all with heroic fortitude, uttering no cries, but calling in low, sad tones on a merciful God to have pity on him and give him surcease of suffering.

For nearly two hours longer he suffered every variety of inhuman torture. Devils in hell could devise no more or no worse. At last, being almost spent, and his dull, deadened nerves no longer responding to any kind of torment, he lay down on his fiery bed.

The end was near at last. The immortal spirit was about taking flight. The savages must hasten if they would inflict the last horrible anguish. One rushed in, and with his keen blade drew around the horrid circle, and pulled off the bleeding scalp of gray hairs. In vain! He had escaped them!

No, not even yet! A hideous old hag—with tigerish heart—had just then an infernal inspiration. She hastily screeched herself up to the insensate victim and threw a bark of burning embers on the raw, throbbing, palpitating brain.

A pitiful groan announced the success of the monstrous device. The fleeting soul was thus cruelly summoned back. The blind and staggering victim once more raised himself on his feet—once more began his weary round.

30

Burning sticks were again applied, but in vain, for the flesh had now utterly lost all feeling.

Dr. Knight was not to have the consolation of witnessing his chief's final triumph through death over his merciless foes, but was led away from the dreadful scene. As he was driven along the next morning he passed the cursed spot. He saw the charred remains of his beloved commander lying among the embers, almost burned to ashes.

It was long a tradition among the Indians that Crawford breathed his last just at sunset, and that, after his death, his body was heaped upon the fagots and so consumed, amid the delighted whoops and leapings of his tormentors. It was a veritable "dance of death."

The touching, harrowing details of this awful death, as published by Dr. Knight, was a terrible shock to the whole country. On the border there was universal gloom, and a low, sullen muttering of revengeful wrath. Crawford was such a prominent, popular leader, that the "deep damnation of his taking off" was almost a national calamity. No one felt it more keenly than Washington himself, who wrote as follows: "It is with the greatest sorrow and concern that I have learned the melancholy tidings of Colonel Crawford's death. He was known to me as an officer of much care and prudence, brave, active and experienced. The manner of his death was shocking; and I have this day communicated to Congress such papers as I have regarding it."

But the dolor and anguish of the sad and desolate widow, Hannah Crawford, as she sat watching and waiting in her lonely cabin on the Youghiogheny, who can describe! She had parted from her husband with a heavy, heavy heart. As one after another of the expedition straggled back, how tearfully did she question! how anxiously did she yearn for some tidings! Missed at the commencement of the retreat, with her only and idolized son, her nephew and her son-in-law, was all she could learn. Gone, all gone at one fell swoop! After three weeks of dread and intolerable suspense, she heard of her husband's death. Still later drifted to her the sickening details. It were better for her future peace had his loss forever remained an unfathomable mystery.

"I well recollect," says Uriah Springer, "when I was a little boy, my grandmother Crawford took me behind her on horseback, rode across the Youghiogheny, and turned into the woods, when we both alighted by an old moss-covered white-oak log. 'Here,' she said, as she sat down upon the log, and cried as though her heart would break —'here I parted with your grandfather!'"

That tradition, current in Western Pennsylvania, that Simon Girty aspired to the hand of one of Crawford's daughters, but was denied, is one of the many unauthentic and untraceable rumors afloat concerning the mysterious Girty. Sallie Crawford, who married the lamented Major Harrison, an officer of capacity and prominence, also lost in this expedition, was, as stated, a far-famed belle, and considered the most beautiful young lady in all that district.

DR. KNIGHT'S ESCAPE—SLOVER'S CAPTURE AND ADVENTURES.

The miraculous escapes of Dr. Knight and John Slover from the Indians are replete with adventure and interest. We wish we had room for fuller sketches. The former, after Crawford's torture and death, spent the night at Pipe's house and started early next morning for the Shawnee towns on Mad river, some forty miles distant. His only guard was on horseback, who, after having once more painted his prisoner black, drove the Doctor before him. He was a large, rough-looking, but very friendly savage, and Knight soon began to ingratiate himself.

That night the gallant Doctor attempted many times to untie himself, but the Indian was wary and scarce closed his eyes. At daybreak he untied his captive and arose to mend the fire, and the wood-gnats being very annoying, Knight asked him if he would make a big smoke behind him. The savage said "yes." The little Doctor soon picked up a short dog-wood fork, the only stick he could find near, and slipping up behind his guide he smote him on the head with all his force. The amazed redskin was so stunned that he fell head foremost into the fire, but soon sprang up and ran off, howling in a most frightful manner.

Knight seized the fellow's gun and ran after him some distance to shoot, but he had pulled back the lock so violently as to break it, and soon gave up the chase. He then took the Indian's effects and struck straight through the pathless woods for home. He changed his route several times to avoid all Indian trails and parties. His gun could not be mended and he had finally to throw it away. He was nearly starved, and had neither food nor gun to shoot any. He came across plenty of wild unripe gooseberries, but having his jaw nearly broken by a tomahawk blow, could not chew. He managed, however, to sustain life on the juice of a weed which he knew to be nourishing. Not being able to kindle a fire, the gnats and mosquitoes nearly devoured him. He soon, too, got bewildered in a vast swampy district, but still kept straggling east. Game was very plenty, including elk, deer and bear, but none for him. Save young nettles, the juice of herbs, a few wild berries, and two young blackbirds and a terrapin, which he devoured raw, he had no food. When all this strange food disagreed with his stomach he would chew wild ginger.

On the twentieth evening of his long and solitary wanderings, he struck Fort McIntosh, at the mouth of Big Beaver, and on the next day reached Fort Pitt, greatly to the astonishment of all and to the huge delight of General Irvine, with whom he was a great favorite. He remained at Fort Pitt till the close of the war and afterwards moved to Kentucky

The adventures of Slover, the guide, were much more varied and exciting. He had lived among the Miami and Shawnees from his early boyhood, and could talk their languages. When the retreat commenced he, James Paull, Young and five others, became mired in the cranberry swamp. After floundering about for a long time they finally emerged, only to plunge into another morass, where they had to wait daylight. They now struck an east trail and had nearly reached the Muskingum, when they were ambushed by a Shawnee party, who had tracked them all the way from the plains. Two were killed by the first fire. James Paull, notwithstanding a very bad burnt foot, bounded off and made good his escape. Slover and the other two were made prisoners.

Singular to relate, one of the Shawnees, who had aided in Slover's capture when a boy, now recognized him, calling him by his Indian name of Mannucothe, and reproached him severely for leading a party against them. The other prisoners were now mounted on horses and started off for Mad river, which they reached in three days. Up to this point they had been treated kindly, but now all they met glowered upon them in the most savage manner. The people of the first Shawnee village assaulted them with clubs and tomahawks. One of the captives was here painted black, but the savages forbade Slover from telling him what it meant

A runner having been sent to Wappatomica, the whole population swarmed out to give them a hot reception with guns, clubs and hatchets. All three were ordered to run the gauntlet. If they could reach the council house, three hundred yards distant, they would be safe. The poor fellow who was painted black was made the chief target. Men, women and children beat and fired loads of powder at him as he ran naked, amid shoutings and beating of drums. He managed, however, to reach the council house door, though in a pitiable plight. He was slashed with tomahawks, his body singed all over, and holes burnt into his flesh with the wadding.

He now thought himself safe. Fatal mistake! He was dragged back to another terrible beating and to a most cruel death. Slover saw his body lying by the council house, horribly mutilated and disfigured. He also saw and recognized three other dead bodies, all black, bloody and powder-burnt. They were all that remained of Major Harrison, Crawford's son-in-law; William Crawford, his nephew, and Major John McClelland, who had been fourth officer in command. The next day the limbs and heads were stuck on poles, and the corpses given to the dogs. Slover's surviving companion was sent off to another town to be executed, while he himself was, that evening, brought into the log council house and carefully interrogated as to the state of the country, the progress of the war, and the movements on the border. He spoke three Indian tongues, and had the satisfaction of informing them of Cornwallis' capture

The next day Captain Matthew Elliott and James Girty, Simon's brother, were present. The former assured the Indians that Slover had lied about Cornwallis. James Girty, a bad, drunken, violent bully, now had the audacity to publicly assert that, when he had asked Slover how he would like to live again among the Shawnees, he had answered that he would soon take a scalp and run off. It began to look black for poor Slover. This grand council lasted fifteen days. The third day Alexander McKee commenced to attend. He was grandly arrayed in a gold-laced uniform, but did not speak to the captive. Slover was not tied, and could have escaped, but had no moccasins. Each night he was invited to the war dance, which lasted almost till morning, but would take no part in the revels.

Dr. Knight's guard now arrived, with a wound four inches long on his head, and a truly marvelous story of a long and desperate struggle he had with the Doctor, whom he represented as a large, powerful man, but whose fingers he had cut off, and to whom he had given two terrible knife thrusts, which he was sure would prove fatal. Slover told the Indians that the Doctor was a small, weak man, at which they were greatly amused. The next day arrived the long-expected message and belt of wampum from De Peyster, of Detroit, the conclusion well expressing the general tenor: "Take no more prisoners, my children, of any sort —man, woman or child."

At a grand council held shortly after, at which eight tribes were fully represented, it was decided that no more prisoners should be taken, and that in case any tribe so did, the other tribes should seize said captives and put them to death; also, that war expeditions should be made against Fort Henry, the Ohio Falls, (Louisville,) and the Kentucky settlements. At another council his death by fire was resolved upon, and at the same time twelve prisoners, just arrived from Kentucky, were put to death.

Next day George Girty, an adopted Delaware and another brother of Simon, surrounded Slover's cabin with about forty followers, bound him, put a rope about his neck, stripped him naked, *painted him black*, and took him about five miles off. Here he was beaten and shamefully abused, dragged to Mack-a-chack and bound to the stake, which was in a part of the council house not yet roofed. Three piles of wood about this torture stake were fired, and the torments were about commencing, when a sudden storm arose, the rain descended in a flood and drowned out the fire. The superstitious savages stood silent and aghast.

A brief respite at least was secured! The captive was untied and seated on the ground, while wild leapings and frantic dances, punctuated with blows, kicks and tomahawk cuts, were continued until eleven at night. A chief by the name of Half Moon then asked Slover if he was sleepy. Yes, he was. The savages wishing a whole day's frolic with him on the morrow, he was graciously allowed to retire to a block-house under charge of three ferocious, forbidding-looking warriors.

Poor Slover was bound with extraordinary precautions. His arms were tied so tight, at wrists and elbows, that the thongs were buried in the flesh. The strip about his neck, just long enough for him to lie down, was fastened to a beam of the house. The three warriors now began to taunt and harass him. Now, if ever, an escape was to be attempted. Death, no matter how quick or by what means, was far better than a whole day's tortures. The sick and sore, but still undaunted captive feigned sleep. Would his cruel persecutors never close their eyes! Two now stretched themselves for rest, but the third lit his pipe and recommenced his mocking taunts. Slover obstinately kept his mouth closed.

SLOVER ESCAPES AND, NAKED, RIDES MADLY FOR LIFE.

At last—most joyful spectacle!—the third laid down and soon began to snore. No music sweeter to poor Slover, whose heart was beating like a muffled drum. Not an instant to lose, and well he knew it! The heavy beads of sweat which gathered on his clammy brow were witnesses not only of the intensity of his feelings, but of the violent and extraordinary exertions to free his arms. They were so benumbed as to be without feeling. He laid himself over on his right side, and with his fingers, which were still manageable, and after a violent and prolonged effort, he succeeded in slipping the cord from his left arm over elbow and wrist.

One of the guards now got up to stir the fire. Slover lay dead as a stone, sure it was all over with him; but the sleepy savage soon lay down again, and work was renewed. The arms free, the next attempt was made on the thong about his neck. It was thick as his thumb, and tough as iron, being made of buffalo hide. The wretched man tugged and tugged. It remained firm. He contrived to get it between his teeth, and gnawed it in a perfect frenzy of despair. It budged not a finger's breadth. It was a hard and cruel fate, but he had to give it up. The first gray lights of dawn were beginning to penetrate the gloomy apartment. He sank back in an agony of hopeless despair.

No! He would make yet one more effort. He inserted his hands between the thong and his neck, and pulled and pushed with almost superhuman strength. Oh, joy supreme! it yields! it yields! and he is free at last. It was a noose, with several knots tied over it. The sudden reaction almost makes him faint. One quick look at the sleepers about him, one cautious lift over their bodies, a few cat-like steps, and he stands under the still, shining stars, free as the fresh air which fanned and caressed his throbbing brow.

He now glided hurriedly through the town and reached a cornfield. He nearly stumbled over a squaw and her children, lying asleep under a tree. Making a circle about them, he reached the edge of the woods. Here he stopped to untie his arm, which was swollen and discolored from the tight ligature. He felt better at once, and having observed a number of horses feeding in a glade as he passed, he ventured to catch one. He was as naked as the day he was born. Picking up an old quilt for a saddle, and using his own hide bonds for a bridle, he managed to mount the horse he caught, and was off and away.

That was truly a ride for life. Slover's jaws were set, his teeth were clenched, his eyes were fixed steadily to the east, and digging his naked heels into the flanks of his horse—which, happily for him, proved very fleet and staunch—he scurried along through open wood and past grassy level.

—" Over bank, bush and scaur;
' They a nave fleet steeds that follow,' quoth young Lochinvar."

The sun was but little over quarter high ere he reached the Scioto, fully fifty miles off. Smoking hot, and bathed in sweat, the gallant steed breasted that forest stream, and cluttered up the thither bank. On! on they go! No pause! no rest! His exasperated pursuers, mounted on their fleetest horses, were pressing hard in the rear. It was a killing pace, but a saving race.

By noon his gallant steed began to flag; now it breathes hard and fast; now its eyes look staring and glassy; and now at three o'clock it sinks to rise no more. No time to waste, even on a gallant horse like that—faithful to the death. The naked rider at once springs to his feet and runs as fast as hope and fear can drive him. Neither did he cease his efforts with the dark, but pressed on, ever on, until ten o'clock, when, becoming extremely sick and faint, he sank down for a little rest.

By midnight he was up and away again, thridding his weary way by moonlight. At the first streak of coming day he forsook a trail he had found and followed all night, and plunged boldly into the trackless wilderness. As he walked he endeavored, with his old Indian habits, to conceal his trail, pushing back the weeds or bushes his tread may have disturbed. He left no more trace than a bird. All that day he forged steadily and uninterruptedly ahead, and the second night had the happiness of resting by the waters of the Muskingum. A marvelous journey, and accomplished with wonderful pluck and endurance!

Think, reader, what a fearful undertaking it must have been to run naked through a wild, pathless, tangled forest, with vine, bush, briar and thorn tree, stretching after to detain him! Nothing but his ragged saddle cloth to protect him! The nettles stung his feet; the briars and thorns pierced his bleeding limbs; the vines and low trees scraped his back, and the gnats and mosquitoes so tormented him that he found no peace by day or rest by night. So intolerable was the nuisance that he was obliged to carry a bundle of leafy branches to keep them off.

The first food he took was a few berries on the third day; but he felt more weak than hungry. He now reached and swam the Muskingum, and for the first time began to breathe securely. The next day he followed the Stillwater valley, and the night after lay but a few miles from Fort Henry. In his published statement, Slover asserts he did not sleep one wink the whole time, so annoying and blood-thirsty were the swarms of gnats and mosquitoes.

He had now earned a rest. He reached the Ohio by Indian Wheeling Creek, opposite the island, and descrying a man on it, he hailed him, but so strange and savage was his appearance that he had great difficulty in making him come to his relief. The surprise his appearance caused at Fort Henry, and the hospitable welcome he received there, can more readily be imagined than described.

THE MYSTERIOUS MAJOR JOHN ROSE—WHO WAS HE?

There can be little question but that the officer calling himself Major John Rose, was the life and soul of the Crawford expedition, and —Crawford, its leader, being lost—the fact that the retreat was not far more disastrous than it was, was mainly due to the Major's coolness and masterful skill. There was ever a mystery about Rose which has only lately been solved and made public. It makes a very pretty little episode of American history.

As stated, Major Rose was ever an inscrutable enigma. Every one who came in contact with him knew from the character of his face and his broken accent, that he must be a foreigner and that John Rose was but an assumed name. Everything about him betrayed the well-bred foreign gentleman, and it was thought that he must be a man of good family—probably a nobleman in disguise, but the Major so well kept his secret that even his patron, General Irvine, knew nothing definite about him until he re-embarked for Europe. Here he was, on a distant outpost, contentedly filling his daily routine of duties, and doing it, too, well and thoroughly.

Neat in his attire, courteous in his manner, quick to conceive and prompt to execute, and withal, a thorough and exact business man, he was everybody's favorite, but an especial *protege* of General Irvine.

All that even General Irvine then knew of him was that early in our Revolutionary struggle, a young foreigner, speaking the French and German languages, and giving his name as John Rose, sought a commission in the Continental army. Of himself and previous history he maintained an obstinate silence. Failing in his wishes, he then took a brief course of surgery, first serving as surgeon's mate, but, on his showing quickness and ability, he finally received a surgeon's appointment in the Seventh Pennsylvania Regiment, but soon attracting the attention of General Irvine, he succeeded in gaining both the esteem and affection of that able officer.

In 1780, on account of a feeling of jealousy excited among some of the American officers towards the young foreigner, he left that regiment, volunteered as a surgeon in the navy, was taken prisoner to New York and exchanged the same year; returned to Irvine's command as ensign, and was finally appointed his *aide*, with the rank of lieutenant, and taken into the General's family, where he immediately became a great favorite. On General Irvine's coming West, Rose accompanied him, and it is but faint praise to say that in every position in which he was placed, he did his full duty, with credit to himself and satisfaction to all with whom he was connected.

When the Crawford expedition was set on foot, General Irvine detailed his favorite officer to accompany it, and we have seen how well he did his whole duty. From Mingo Bottom he returned to Fort Pitt, remaining there until the Revolutionary war was fully over. He then went East, and served for a time as Secretary of the Council of Censors, and was afterwards engaged in adjusting General Irvine's accounts with the government at Philadelphia. This done to the General's complete satisfaction, the Major wrote him that he expected to leave for Europe the next week, but would write again before he sailed.

He Writes Irvine that He is a Russian Baron.

This good-bye letter came in due time, and in it the Major returned heartfelt thanks for the kind and generous treatment he had ever received from General Irvine and family, and expressed regret that he had so long kept an important secret from his benefactor. He then disclosed the interesting fact that his name was not John Rose, but Gustavus H. De Rosenthal, a Baron of the Empire of Russia. He had left Russia because of having killed, within the precincts of the Emperor's palace, a nobleman, in a duel brought on by a blow which his antagonist had given to an aged uncle in his presence. He had then fled to England, and thence to the United States, taking service in the Continental army, and finding his way to Fort Pitt in the manner already detailed. Through the mediation of his family, the Emperor Alexander had at last pardoned him, and graciously permitted his return, and now he was about embarking for Amsterdam.

By the kindness of Dr. William A. Irvine, of Warren county, Pennsylvania, and grandson of General Irvine, of Fort Pitt, we have had the pleasure of inspecting a series of highly interesting letters received by the Irvine family from Baron de Rosenthal, then advanced to the dignity of Grand Marshal of Livonia. These letters are mainly dated at Revel, Russia, and abound in expressions of the warmest affection and gratitude to General Irvine for his kind and generous treatment of him. He seemed to be anxious for the "Eagle and Order of Cincinnati," to which he was entitled, and adds, " the first man himself " (meaning the Emperor) "has been asking about it, and desires I should wear it."

In one, of date March 1st, 1823, he writes about the value of a tract of land in Venango county, Pennsylvania, granted by the State of

Pennsylvania, in consideration of his valuable services, and has not yet given up hope of making a trip to America.

Very lately we have, by the merest accident, learned that a power of attorney had been received in Venango county, so late as 1859, from the heirs of Sir Gustav Heinrich de Rosenthal, Captain of the Knighthood of the Province of Esthonia in Russia, with authority to sell and convey these lands, which of late years have become quite valuable.

Baron de Rosenthal, in his first letter, dated August 4th, 1806, announces that out of five children but three then lived, and of these the oldest daughter was married, the youngest daughter was at boarding-school at St. Petersburg, and his son was studying law at Moskwa.

The Baron de Rosenthal died in 1830, and so the name of this brave and patriotic Russian must be added to those of Lafayette, Steuben, Pulaski, De Kalb, and the galaxy of noble foreigners who made haste to peril their lives in our Revolutionary struggle.

Chapter VII

General George Rogers Clark.

The Hannibal of the West—His Heroic Deeds.

> The forest aisles are full of story;
> Here many a one of old renown,
> First sought the meteor-light of glory,
> And 'mid its transient flush went down.

One of the most remarkable men this country ever produced was George Rogers Clark. Americans have not yet learned to appreciate the force and power of his character, or the great importance of his conquests. Why such a hero never found scope and opportunity for his undoubted military talents, backed by an extraordinary sagacity and intrepidity, is one of the mysteries of the past. "When," said Joseph Davies, in one of his finest orations, "I contemplate the character of George Rogers Clark, I feel as did Moses when he drew near the *burning bush*, that I ought to put the shoes from off my feet, for the place whereon I stand is holy ground."

It is scarcely too much to say that but for him the valleys of the Lower Ohio and Upper Mississippi would not have belonged to the United States at the close of the Revolution. When, therefore, that prescient conqueror ran up the stars and stripes over the English fortifications of Kaskaskia, Illinois, and Vincennes, Indiana, he virtually added the whole of the vast and magnificent territory dominated from those centres, to his beloved country.

General Clark was born in Albemarle county, Va., in 1752, and like Washington and many of the most prominent and influential actors in the old times that "tried men's souls," was a land surveyor. He commanded a company in Dunmore's war, and in 1775, drawn thither by a love of adventure and probably by a forecast of its glorious future, he drifted to Kentucky and remained there until Fall, familiarizing himself with the character of the people and the resources of the country. Young as he was, his commanding talents must at once have inspired confidence. He was one of the few whom all are prompt to recognize as a *born* leader, and we find him temporarily placed in command of the irregular militia of Kentucky. He returned East to make preparations for a permanent residence in the West, and revisited Kentucky in the Spring of 1776.

His second appearance there, as related by General Ray, is interesting. "I had come down to where I now live (about four miles north of Harrodsburg) to turn some horses into the range. I had killed a small blue-wing duck that was feeding in our spring, and had roasted it nicely on the brow of the hill, near our house. After having taken it off to cool, I was much surprised on being suddenly arrested by a fine soldierly-looking man, who exclaimed, ' How do you do, my little fellow? What's your name? Ain't you afraid of being in the woods by yourself?' On satisfying his inquiries, I invited the traveler to partake of my duck, which he did without leaving me a bone to pick, his appetite was so keen." After satisfying Clark's appetite, Ray inquired of the stranger his own name and his business in that remote region. "My name is Clark," he answered, "and I have come out to see what you brave fellows are doing in Kentucky, and to lend you a helping hand if necessary." General Ray, then but a boy of sixteen, conducted Clark to Harrodsburg.

He almost immediately proved that he had a sagacity and comprehensiveness far beyond the ordinary pioneer. He was not merely content like the average run of western adventurers with planting, hunting or battling with Indians. The Revolution was now in full progress, and his patriotic soul was fired with lofty views—affairs of state and far-reaching schemes of daring emprise. His reflections and self-communings taught him at once the importance of a more thorough, organized and extensive system of public defence and military operations. He speedily, therefore, suggested to the Kentucky settlers the importance of a general convention in order to form a closer and more definite connection with Virginia. The proposed assembly was held at Harrodsburg, and Clark and Jones were chosen members of the Assembly of Virginia, of which State Kentucky was then considered an appanage, if not an integral part. Clark's earnest desire was to negotiate with Virginia, and should it refuse to recognize Kentucky as within its jurisdiction and under its immediate protection, then he proposed to offer lands to attract settlers and establish an independent State.

On Clark's arrival in Virginia, the Legislature stood adjourned, but he at once waited on Governor Henry, and stated plainly the objects of his journey making application for five hundred weight of gunpowder. But the Kentuckians had not yet been recognized as Virginians. and the Council could only offer to *lend* the gunpowder as to friends and not *give* it to them as to fellow-citizens having just claims upon the parent State. At the same time they required Clark to be personally responsible for the powder and the expense of conveying it West.

This would not suit Clark and he declined; representing that British agents were employing every means to engage Indians in the war; that the frontier people might be exterminated for want of the means of defence, and that then the fury of the savages would burst like a tempest over Virginia itself. The Council remained deaf and inexorable, and declared they could do no more. Clark promptly and peremptorily wrote declining to accept the powder on the conditions named, intimating his design of applying elsewhere, and significantly added: "*That a country which was not worth defending was not worth claiming.*"

On receipt of this pregnant letter the Council recalled Clark to their presence and gave him an order for the transmission of the powder to Pittsburgh, to be then delivered to him, or order, for the use of Kentucky. At the Fall session of the Legislature he obtained a full recognition of the County of Kentucky and thus became the founder of that Commonwealth.

Clark now proceeded to Fort Pitt and with seven boatmen embarked with the so much needed powder. At that time the whole country swarmed with hostile bands of savages, and the greatest caution was exercised. They were hotly pursued the whole way, but succeeded in making good their landing at Limestone, Kentucky, and in securely caching their cargo at different places in the woods.

Character of the Border Warfare of that Day.

Clark now began to be looked up to as a brave, intrepid and able commander, and one of the master spirits of the time. We cannot enter into details—exciting and interesting as they were—of the many adventurous excursions he successfully headed, but shall proceed at once to notice the scheme which he had so much at heart. He had entered into the hazardous forest life of the borderer with as much zest and vigor as the very best of them all. Appareled in hunting shirt and moccasins, with rifle and tomahawk in hand, he had fought the wily savage, hand to hand and foot to foot; but he plainly had an ambition far beyond mere bushwhacking and forest ranging, stirring and exciting as the life had proved. His genius soared to a broader sweep, and his eager and aspiring soul brooded over masterful schemes of which his followers never dreamed.

With that practical and far-reaching sagacity which rendered him so conspicuous above his fellows, he saw plainly that the borderers were playing a losing game, and exhausting themselves in petty skirmishes and desperate combats without making any single serious impression upon their swarming adversaries. He early saw the paramount necessity of "carrying the war into Africa"—of making it felt by the savages *at home;* by the destruction of their crops, their towns and all the "habitations of cruelty." His motto was, "never suffer an incursion from Indians without retaliating by a return incursion into the very heart of their own territory."

Looking farther and more deeply he at once recognized the undoubted fact that all the savage forays and smitings of the border had their *inspiration* from the British posts and forts which stretched from Ontario to the Mississippi. These were the parent fountains whence all the little runs and rills of invasion proceeded. It was from the British that arms, provisions, ammunition, and "bloody instructions" emanated. Why not strike at the root of the matter by wresting these central posts from his country's foes! Thus only could Kentucky enjoy permanent rest and peace within all her broad borders.

The war in Kentucky had hitherto been a mere border war, conducted in the spasmodic and desultory manner incident to that kind of hostilities. Nearly all the military operations of the period resembled more the predatory exploits of those sturdy cattle-lifters and stark moss-troopers of the Scottish Highlands. The intrepid backwoodsman would sharpen his hunting knife, shoulder his unerring rifle, fill his pouch with pone or parched corn, and thus equipped, would start for a fighting frolic in the Indian country, without beat of drum or other note of warning. Arrived on hostile soil, his roving eye was on the alert; his step grew stealthy as the panther's. With padded feet he would creep up to the neighborhood of some Indian hamlet and lie in ambush until opportunity offered to steal a horse or shoot its owner. All this was promotive of desperate combats and countless deeds of personal valor and strange adventure, but it settled nothing. Neither Virginia nor the General Government—engaged in a gigantic struggle with all Britain's power—could lend any systematic aid.

Clark pondered over all this; saw where the error lay; sought earnestly to correct it, and kept looking with his "mind's eye" ever to Detroit, Kaskaskia and Vincennes. It was with plans fully matured and with his whole soul strongly imbued with the ambition of reducing these posts, that, in the Summer of '78, he dispatched two spies to reconnoitre. They brought back reports both assuring and alarming. Assuring, because the forts were represented as negligently guarded, and the French about them were more inclined to the American than to the British side. Alarming, because there was great activity among the garrisons, and no effort was spared in promoting and fitting out Indian raids and marauds against the Kentucky border. Clark hastened to submit his plan of the reduction of these forts to the Virginia Executive. He asked small aid, and his plans were approved by both Governor and Council. He received two sets of instructions—one public, the other secret. Twelve hundred pounds were advanced, orders issued at Fort Pitt for boats, arms and ammunition, and a force of four companies rigidly selected from Virginia and Kentucky, was soon assembled at the Falls of the Ohio, afterwards Louisville.

General Clark's Secret Advance on Kaskaskia.

All being in readiness, the intrepid and adventurous little band embarked in boats down the Ohio. At the mouth of the Tennessee river they learned from a party of hunters, but recently arrived from Kaskaskia, that the garrison there was commanded by one M. Rocheblave; that the militia were maintained in a high state of discipline; that spies were stationed on the Mississippi river, and that a sharp lookout was kept for the Kentuckians. They learned further that the fort which commanded the old French town was without a regular garrison, and that the military defences were kept up merely as a matter of form. The hunters thought the place might easily be taken by surprise, and they were accepted as guides. The boats were dropped down to old Fort Massac, about forty miles from the Ohio mouth, and concealed in a creek on the Illinois side, and now the fearless little army took up its wilderness march through ponds, cypress-swamps, and over deep and muddy streams. Game was scarce, and to send out hunting parties would expose them to discovery. Drinking water was scarce, and in the prairies the wearied men were beaten upon with a fierce July sun. On the third day the guide became bewildered. The intolerant Kentuckians became suspicious and demanded his death. The poor fellow begged that he might go a little further under a guard. In a short time he joyfully exclaimed: "I know that point of timber," and pointed out the direction of Kaskaskia. It was on the 4th of July—not then a day of note—that this unflinching band of invaders, with garments soiled and travel-stained, and with beards of three weeks' growth, secreted themselves near to the town, but on the other side of Kaskaskia river.

That night Clark sent forward his spies, put his impatient command in motion, divided it into two parts, one of which was ordered to cross the river, while Colonel Clark himself should take possession of the fort. Kaskaskia contained about two hundred and fifty houses, and its inhabitants were French, who had heard the most exaggerated reports of the fierceness and cruelty of the bloody "Long Knives" of Virginia. Both divisions met with success. The unsuspecting little village was entered at either extreme; its quiet streets were filled with furious yells, and it was proclaimed, in French, that all should keep their houses on pain of instant death. In a moment the panic-stricken men, women and children were screaming in the greatest distress, "The Long Knives! the Long Knives!"

In the meantime Clark had broken into the fort and secured Rocheblave and his little garrison, but his papers, &c., had been concealed or destroyed by his wife. The victory was complete, though not a drop of blood had been shed. Observing the great dread the simple inhabitants entertained for those they had been taught to believe little less than savages, Clark determined, for wise ends, to play upon their fears, and ordered his wild Virginia troops to rush through the streets with yells and whoopings after the Indian fashion. Clark had determined to win all the French inhabitants to the American side, so, taking possession of the house of Monsieur Cerre, the richest and most influential citizen, he prevented all intercourse between his own men and the frightened citizens, and treated all those who came to beg protection with the greatest rigor and harshness. The wretched and trembling citizens were for five days kept thus in a state of consternation. The troops were then moved to the outskirts, and the citizens permitted to walk the streets again.

Clark now ordered the chief of them to be thrown in irons, without assigning reasons or permitting a word of defence. After a strategic delay, M. Gibault, the revered priest of the parish, obtained leave, with five or six of the chief citizens, to wait deferentially upon the cruel and ferocious Kentucky commander. The priest now, in the most submissive tone and posture, remarked that the inhabitants expected to be separated, perhaps never to meet again, and begged, as a great favor, that they might assemble in their church, offer up prayers to God, and take a long leave of each other. Colonel Clark observed, with apparent indifference, that Americans did not trouble themselves about the religion of others, but left every man to worship God in his own way; they might meet in the church if they would, but on no account must a single person leave the town. The conference was abruptly terminated and the deputation dismissed.

Colonel Clark's Policy at Kaskaskia—Singular Scenes.

The whole population now assembled in their church, mournfully chanted their prayers, and tearfully bade each other farewell. The priest and deputation then returned to Clark's lodgings and thanked him for the favor granted; they were willing to submit to the loss of their property, as the fate of war, but begged they might not be separated from their families, and that enough clothes and provisions might be allowed, sufficient, at least, for their necessities.

Clark, seeing that their fears had been raised to the pitch required, thus abruptly addressed them: "Who do you take me to be? Do you think we are savages, and that we intend to massacre you all? Do you think Americans will strip women and children and take the very bread out of their mouths? My countrymen never make war upon the innocent. It was to protect our own wives and children that we penetrated into this wilderness, to subdue these British posts, whence the savages are supplied with arms and ammunition to murder us. We do not war against Frenchmen. The King of France, your former master, is now our ally. His ships and soldiers are now fighting for the Americans. The French are our firm friends. Go and enjoy your religion, and worship where and when you please. Retain your property, and please inform all your citizens for me that they must dismiss all alarm and conduct themselves as usual. We are your friends instead of enemies, and came to deliver you from the British."

The total reaction of feeling occasioned by this timely and politic speech may be imagined. The deputation could scarce believe their own ears. The joyful news soon spread; the bells rang a merry peal; the streets were decorated with flowers and banners; the people again assembled in the church and sang a *Te Deum*, and the most uproarious joy prevailed throughout the whole night. All now cheerfully acknowledged Colonel Clark as commandant of the country, and several Kaskaskia gentlemen even accompanied Major Bowman's detachment—who were all mounted on French ponies—to surprise the post of Cahokia (opposite the city of St. Louis). The plan was entirely successful, and the post was secured without a wound or a drop of blood.

Colonel Clark now turned his attention to Vincennes, situate on the Wabash, fully satisfied that until that important point was reduced, he had really gained little or nothing. His uneasiness was great and his situation critical. His force was too small to garrison Kaskaskia and Cahokia and leave sufficient men to reduce Vincennes by open assault. M. Gibault was consulted and agreed, the British commandant at Vincennes having gone to Detroit, to bring the people of that post over to the views of the Americans. This project was completely successful, and in a few days the American flag was raised over that fort, too, and Captain Helm appointed to the command. Gibault and party, with several gentlemen from Vincennes, returned to Kaskaskia and reported all working charmingly. Clark was somewhat at a loss how now to act —as his instructions were vague and general, and the period of his men's enlistment had now expired, the objects being fully accomplished. To abandon the country now would be to lose all that was gained, and so the commander, always fertile in expedients, opened a new enlistment and even issued commissions to French officers to command home guards. He then established garrisons and at length was free to turn his whole attention to the surrounding Indian tribes.

The whole narrative concerning his negotiations with the Indian chiefs is replete with interest, but, in a brief and summary sketch like this, gives us no room for details. It was in this wild and dangerous diplomacy that Clark's peculiar talents showed illustriously. He thoroughly understood the Indian character in all its strength and weakness, and managed them with a masterful adroitness. He knew exactly when to be stern and inflexible, and when to be mild and conciliating. The tact and dexterous address with which he played upon their fears, their passions and their hopes and ambitions, was truly wonderful.

BIG GATE WON OVER—SOME CHIEFS THROWN INTO IRONS.

The chief of greatest command and influence at that time was known as Big Gate, or by the Indians as "The Grand Door to the Wabash," because nothing could be done by the Indian confederacy of that region without his approbation.

A grand "talk" was soon arranged with him by Captain Helm. These Indians had been under British pay and influence, and had done no small amount of mischief along the border. Clark, in his journal, states that he always thought it a mistaken notion, that soft speeches were best for Indians; he had carefully studied the French and Spanish modes of dealing with savages, and they exactly comported with his own. Under his instructions Big Gate was won over by Captain Helm. Letters were sent with belts of wampum to other chiefs of influence, "giving," as Clark writes, "harsh language to supply the want of men."

They were invited to lay down the tomahawk, but if they did not choose that, to fight for the English openly and like *men*, but they would soon see their Great Father, as they called him, given to the dogs to eat. If, however, they would give their hands to the Big Knives, they must give their hearts also. This bold language won the pompous chiefs. They replied that the Americans must be *men* or they would never have spoken as they did; that they liked such people; that the English were base liars, and that they had as much reason to fight them as the Americans had. This last clause had reference to an artful exposition of the cause of the war between the Americans and English, illustrated and made plain to their understandings by means of a fable. It did more service, quaintly writes Clark, than could have done a regiment of men.

Amazing numbers of the Indians soon flocked into Cahokia to hear what the Big Knives had to say. They came from regions five hundred miles distant, and represented Chippewas, Ottawas, Pottawattamies, Sacks, Foxes, Maumies, and a number of distant and powerful tribes living about the lakes and the upper Mississippi, and who all had known very little about the Americans, but had been put under the influence of the French posts and, after, the British posts. Clark confesses that he was under much apprehension " among such a number of devils and it proved to be just, for the second night a party of Puans, or Meadow Indians, endeavored to force the guards off my lodgings and to bear me off, but were happily made prisoners. The town took alarm and was immediately under arms, which convinced the savages that the French were in our interest."

Following out his principles—never to court Indians; never to load them with presents; never to seem to fear them, though always to show respect to courage and ability, and to speak in the most direct and honest manner possible, he waited for the assembled chiefs to make the first advances and offers for peace. But first, regarding the chiefs who had been at the head of the movement to break into his quarters, he ordered them to be put in irons. They alleged in excuse that they had no ill design, but only wished to know whether the French would take part with the Americans or not. This treatment of some of the principal chiefs produced much excitement among the rest. The captured chiefs submissively desired an interview with Clark, but were refused. They then made interest with the other chiefs for a conference, but Clark strengthened his guards and sent them word that he believed they were all a set of villains and were on the English side; that they were welcome to abide by the side they had espoused, but that he was a man and a warrior, did not care who were friends or foes, and would have nothing more to say to any of them. The whole town was much alarmed at this bold and arrogant course, and, indeed, considering the mere handful of men Clark had, many of his command having gone home, it does look like a rash presumption and over confidence on his part, but it had its effect, and at once.

To show the Indians that he disregarded them, Clark remained in his lodgings in the town about a hundred yards from the fort and seemingly without a guard, although he had taken the precaution to conceal a party of fifty picked men in an adjoining parlor and to keep the garrison under arms. There was a great pow-wowing among the savages during the whole night, but instead of showing the slightest anxiety Clark invited a number of the gay French ladies and gents of the town and danced nearly the whole night.

In the morning the Colonel summoned the different nations to a grand council, first releasing the incarcerated chiefs and admitting them, too, to seats. After the pompous ceremonies were over, Clark promptly produced a bloody or war belt of wampum and made them a plain, strong, and uncommonly bold and effective speech, in which he told them that he knew they were on the British side; that he did not blame them for it, but wished them to fight like brave men; that he scorned to take any mean advantage of the British by asking any of their allies to desert them; that there were none but Americans who would not have put them to death for their late bad behavior, but that he cared not for them and they were at perfect liberty to do as they pleased and go where they pleased, but they must behave like *men*; that he would have them escorted out of the village and they should not do any mischief for three days: after that he would fight them. If they did not want all their women and children to be massacred, they must instantly leave off killing those of the whites; that there was the war belt to take or leave as it pleased them, and it would soon be seen which party would make it the most bloody. Clark then said that it was customary among brave warriors to treat their enemies well; that, therefore, he should give them provisions and rum while they stayed, but that by their late behavior he could not deem them brave men, therefore, he did not care how soon they cleared off.

Extraordinary Scenes at a Grand Indian Council.

Clark says he watched the swarthy faces of the assembly keenly and narrowly while these bold and haughty words were spoken and that the whole, finding their hostile designs well known, looked like a pack of convicted criminals.

The principal chiefs now arose and made many submissive and explanatory excuses, alleging that they were persuaded to take up the hatchet by the English, but they now believed the Americans to be men and warriors, and would like to take them by the hand and treat them as brothers, and they hoped their blindness would be excused and their women and children spared.

Clark replied that he was instructed by the great men among the Big Knifes not to *ask* peace from *any* people, but to openly offer them peace or war; that as the English could no longer fight the Americans, it was most likely the young warriors of the Big Knives would grow into squaws unless they could find some one else to fight. He then offered the two belts—one red for war, the other white for peace, when they gladly took the latter. Clark then said that he would not treat with the late invaders of his lodgings *at all*, and would not smoke the pipe of peace, even with *them*, until they had consulted all their warriors, &c.

The chiefs now interceded for their guilty friends, but Clark remained obdurate, and was, he writes, "pleased to see them all sit trembling, as persons frightened at the apprehension of the worst fate. When they had tried their eloquence again to no purpose, they pitched on two young men to be put to death as an atonement for the rest, hoping that would pacify me. It would have amazed you to have seen how submissively those two young men presented themselves for death, advancing into the middle of the floor, sitting down by each other, and covering their heads with their blankets to receive the tomahawk. Peace was what I wanted with them, if I got it on my own terms, but this stroke prejudiced me in their favor, and for a few moments I was so agitated that I don't doubt but that I should, without reflection, have killed the first man that would have offered to have hurt them."

So much for Clark, but this dramatic scene, as well as Clark's treatment of the Meadow Indians, is given in more detail by others. We quote: When the American commander ordered the irons of the chiefs who had attempted to abduct him to be stricken off, he thus scornfully addressed them: "Everybody thinks you ought to die for your treacherous attempt upon my life. I had determined to inflict death upon you for your base attempt, but on considering the meanness of watching a bear and catching him asleep, I have found out that you are not warriors, only old women, and too mean to be killed by the Big Knife. But as you ought to be punished for putting on the breech-clothes of men, they shall be taken from you; plenty of provisions—since squaws know not how to hunt—shall be given for your journey home, and during your stay you shall be treated in every respect like squaws." The Colonel turned away to others, but his cutting words stirred the offenders to the very cores of their proud, though humbled hearts. They took counsel together, and presently a chief came forward with a belt and pipe, which, with proper words, he laid upon the table. With flashing eye and curling lip, the American said he didn't wish to hear *them*, and lifting a sword which lay before him, he shattered the offered pipe, with the biting expression that "he did not treat with women."

The bewildered Meadow Indians then asked the intercession of other red men, but the only reply vouchsafed from Clark was: "The Big Knife has made no war upon these people; they are of a kind that we shoot like wolves which we meet in the woods lest they eat the deer."

All this wrought more and more upon the offending tribe; again they took counsel, and then two young men came forward, and, covering their heads with blankets, sat down before the impenetrable commander; then two chiefs arose, and stating that these two young warriors offered their lives for the misdoings of their guilty brethren, again they presented the pipe of peace. Silence reigned in the assembly while the fate of the proffered victims hung in suspense. All watched the countenance of the American leader, who could scarce master the emotion which the incident excited. Still all sat noiseless—nothing heard but the deep breathing of those whose lives thus hung by a thread.

Presently, he upon whom all depended arose and approaching the young men, he bade them be uncovered and to stand up. They sprang to their feet. "I am glad to find," said Clark, warmly, "that there are men among all nations. With you, who alone are fit to be chiefs of your tribe, I am willing to treat; through *you*, I am willing to grant peace to your brothers; I take you by the hands as chiefs, worthy of being such."

Here, again, the fearless generosity of Clark proved perfectly successful, and while the tribe in question became the allies of America, the fame of this occurrence, which spread far and wide through the northwest, made the name of the white commander everywhere respected.

Gov. Hamilton Retakes Vincennes—Clark in Great Peril.

In October a detachment, under Lieutenant Bailey, proceeded from Kaskaskia, and one under Captain Helm, from Vincennes, to Ouiatenon, on the upper Wabash, and took the post with about forty men. The whole British power in Detroit and Canada was very much agitated at the reports of these American successes, and the very injurious influence they were having among the confederated tribes, hitherto so active in their own employ.

Henry Hamilton, the British Governor of Detroit, accordingly assembled a large force and appeared before Vincennes on December 15th, 1778. The French people made no effort to defend the place. The

Two victims are offered to appease Gen. Clark.
SEE PAGE 488.

gallant Captain Helm and a Mr. Henry were the only Americans in the fort. The latter had a cannon well charged, placed in the open gateway, while the commandant, Helm, stood by it manfully with a lighted match. When the British Governor Hamilton approached with his troops within hailing distance, Helm cried out, with a stentorian voice: "Halt!" This show of resistance caused the doughty English officer to stop and demand a surrender of the garrison. Helm exclaimed, with an oath, "No man shall enter here until I know the terms." Hamilton responded, "You shall have all the honors of war," and so the fort was duly given up, its *one officer and one private* receiving the customary marks of respect for their brave defence.

A part of Hamilton's force was now promptly dispatched against the border settlements on the Ohio river. Captain Helm was detained as prisoner and the French inhabitants were disarmed. Colonel Clark's position now became perilous in the extreme. Bands of depredators commenced to appear in the Illinois country. He had heard that General McIntosh had left Fort Pitt with a large force against Detroit, and presumed all the British forces would cluster about it for its defence. But McIntosh was much like the far-famed French king who "first marched up the hill and then—marched down again." His showy promenade amounted to nothing, and his ignominious retreat left the British free for an effort to recover their *prestige* among the savages so rudely disturbed by the Kentucky leader.

While quietly waiting, therefore, to hear daily news of Detroit's capture by McIntosh, Clark suddenly learned that Hamilton was marching towards Illinois. Supposing Kaskaskia to be his object, Bowman was at once ordered to evacuate Cahokia and meet him at Kaskaskia. The number of his men was so ridiculously small and his position so remote and the probability of speedy assistance so hopeless, that he scarce dared expect to maintain his post, but he did all he could, even burning down some houses to perfect his defences. For many days, hearing no further news, did Clark remain in the most anxious state of suspense. His situation was, indeed, desperate.

On the last day of January, 1779, however, light broke in upon his troubled mind. A Spanish merchant arrived straight from Vincennes and informed the astonished Kentuckian of its recapture by Hamilton, as also that he had sent away nearly all his Indians on different war parties. Almost any other than Clark would have been in utter despair at the impotence of his present situation, but the thought of losing the country so lately and so valorously conquered, was much worse than death to him, and the resolution at once leaped to his heroic soul to march directly against Vincennes.

As he writes in his quaint and oddly-spelt diary, "I would have bound myself seven years a slave to have had five hundred troops," but he had no five, but only two hundred. It was the dead of Winter. The march would be horrible, lying straight through what were called "the drowned lands" of Illinois. But still this dauntless and unquailing man never faltered for one moment, but conducted himself so gaily and confidently, that he not only inspired every man of his little band, but also the French citizens of the town, with his own lofty courage and hopefulness. He had a strong batteaux, or row galley, mounting two four-pounders and four large swivels, immediately prepared and equipped. This, with one company of forty-six men, was put in charge of Lieutenant Rogers, with specific instructions to go up the Wabash within ten leagues of Vincennes and lay there until further orders.

The Strangest and Most Daring March on Record.

On the 7th of February, having added to his own Spartan band two companies of Kaskaskia volunteers, the indomitable Clark, at the head of only one hundred and seventy men, set out on his desperate expedition of over two hundred miles, through a country almost all flooded and impassable at that inclement season. It looked like "a forlorn hope," indeed, but the secret of the invincible Kentuckian's whole life lies in the sentence written at that time in his report to Governor Henry: "I cannot account for it, but I still had inward assurance of success, and never could, when weighing every circumstance, doubt it."

It was just this calm and imperturbable confidence, when environed by perils that would have completely paralyzed or overwhelmed a common soul, which proclaimed the inborn grit and greatness of the man. In fact, Hamilton had wholly undervalued and misunderstood his opponent's character. Instead of sitting down content in the recaptured Vincennes and wasting his strength and opportunities in petty raids and harassing forays which ended in nothing, he should have advanced directly on Clark and driven him from Kaskaskia and afterwards from the whole country. Clark appreciated the situation far better, when he pithily exclaimed: "I knew if I did not take Hamilton that he would take me."

We wish we could give the details of that extraordinary expedition. It has, for daring, obstinacy, endurance and unflinching valor, no parallel in history. It deserves to be immortalized. The Winter was unusually wet and the streams all high. It was rain, mud, swamp and water almost the whole way. Clark's greatest care was to direct and inspirit his men. After incredible hardships, this peerless band of heroes arrived at "the two Wabashes" on the 13th, which, although, in ordinary times, three miles asunder, now made but *one stream*, spread out like an impassable lake. The water was generally three feet deep, and in many places four or five. The distance through this wide waste of water to the nearest high grounds, was *full five miles*. This, truly, as Clark writes in his report—which is as remarkable for its grammar as for its orthography—"would have been enough to have stopped any set of men that was not in the same temper that we was. If I was sensible that you would let no person see this relation, I would give you a detail of our sufferings for four days in crossing these waters, and the manner it was done, as I am sure that *you* would credit it, although almost incredible."

When Clark saw his soldiers gazing with blank dismay at this broad expanse of waters before them, he said but little, but his "actions spoke louder than words." Stepping briskly to the front, he was the very first to plunge in. The right chord had been struck, and, echoing the cheering cry of their trusted leader, the whole body of men who had just before stood shrinking and hesitating on the brink, followed their leader. It was a desperate undertaking—almost too much for human endurance. The march became slower and more toilsome. The shout and song soon died away, and nothing could be heard on all sides but the splash, splash, splash of panting and struggling men.

The course was by no means over a bottom of smooth sand or of graded shells and pebbles, but over mud holes, sunken logs or brush, and unknown depressions, where a single misstep would submerge one to the neck, or a stumble cover him with the turbid waters. Here some swam or paddled; there others held up against the current by projecting timber while they recovered strength or breath. There was an Irish drummer of the party, who possessed an uncommon talent for singing comic Irish songs. He was kept by Clark hard at that work, and served greatly to enliven the drooping spirits of the amphibious command. Another little drummer caused much amusement by floating over the deeper places straddled across his drum.

The progress was still on—slowly and painfully on. At length a small island was reached that afforded a little rest. It would not do, however, to remain there long, so Clark again led the way with a shout, but his example did not so much thrill and magnetize as before. Many were so exhausted and hesitating that it was with the greatest difficulty they kept along at all.

More Marching Through Deep Waters—Clark's Stratagems.

At last the eastern shore was reached, and, on the 17th, the lowlands of the Embarrass river, that enters the Wabash on the west, a little below Vincennes, was reached. It was now nine miles from the fort, which stood on the east side of the Wabash; and every foot of the desolate way was covered with deep water, and there were no provisions. Here was a terrible outlook? They could not afford to wait for the boat. We will let Clark, himself, tell the end of the whole wonderful story:

"This last day's march (February 21st) through the water was far superior to anything the Frenchmen had any idea of. A canoe was sent off and returned without finding that we could pass. I went in her myself, and sounded the water, and found it up to my neck. I returned but slowly to the troop, giving myself time to think. Every eye was fixed on me. I unfortunately spoke in a serious manner to one of the officers: the whole were alarmed without knowing what I said. I viewed their confusion for about a minute—whispered to those near me to do as I did—immediately put some water in my hand, poured on powder, blackened my face, gave the war whoop, and marched into the water without saying a word.

"The party gazed, fell in one after another without saying a word, like a flock of sheep. I ordered those near me to give a favorite song. It soon passed through the line, and the whole went on cheerfully. I now intended to have them transported across the deepest part of the water, but when about waist deep one of the men informed me that he thought he felt a path. We examined and found it so, and concluded it kept on the highest ground, which it did, and by taking pains to follow it, got to the sugar camp without the least difficulty, where there was about half an acre of dry ground.

"The Frenchmen whom we had taken on the river appeared uneasy, and begged that they might go in the two canoes into town that night; that it was impossible we could march from that place till the waters fell. Some of the officers thought it might be done. I would not suffer it. I never could well account for my obstinacy, but something seemed to tell me that it should not be done, and it was *not* done. This was the coldest night we had. The ice in the morning, near the shores, was three-quarters of an inch thick.

"A little after sunrise I lectured the whole. What I said I forget, but concluded by informing them that passing the plain, then in full view, and reaching the opposite woods, would put an end to their fatigues, and I immediately stepped into the water without waiting for any reply. A huzza took place. As we generally marched through the water in a line, before the third entered I halted, and calling to Major Bowman, ordered him to fall in the rear with twenty-five men, and *put to death* any man who refused to march, as we wished no such among us. The whole gave a cry of approbation, and in we went.*

" This was the most trying time of all. I generally kept fifteen or twenty of the strongest men next myself, and judged from my own feelings what must be those of others. Getting about the middle of the plain, the water about mid-deep, I found myself sensibly failing, and as there were no trees or bushes for the men to support themselves by, I feared that many of the weak would be drowned. I ordered the canoes to make the land, discharge their loading, and ply backward and forward to pick up the men. To encourage the party, I sent some of the strongest men forward with orders when they got to a certain distance to pass the word back that the water was getting shallow, and when getting near the woods to cry out—*Land! Land!*

" This stratagem had the desired effect. The men, thus encouraged, exerted themselves almost beyond their abilities—the weak holding by the stronger. The water *never* got shallow, but continued deepening. Getting to the woods where the men expected to land, the water was up to my shoulders, but gaining the woods was of great consequence; all the low and weakly men hung to the trees or floated on the old logs until they were taken off by the canoes. The strong and tall got on shore and built fires. Many would reach shore and fall with their bodies half in the water, not being able to support themselves without it.

" This was a delightful, dry spot of ground of about ten acres. We soon found that fires answered no purpose, but that two strong men, taking a weaker one by the arms, was the only way to recover him, and being a beautiful day, it did. Fortunately, a canoe of Indian squaws and children was coming up to town. Our canoes gave chase and took it, aboard of which was nearly half a quarter of buffalo, some corn, tallow, kettles, &c. This was a grand prize. Broth was immediately

---

*Without food, benumbed with cold, up to their waists in water, covered with broken ice, Clark's troops at one time mutinied and refused to march. All his persuasions had no effect on the half-starved, half-frozen soldiers. In one of his companies was a small boy who acted as drummer. In the same company was a sergeant, standing six feet two and devoted to his leader. Clark now mounted the little drummer on the shoulders of the stalwart sergeant and gave orders to plunge into the half-frozen water. He did so, the little drummer beating his *charge* from his lofty perch, while Clark, sword in hand, followed, giving the command, as he thrust aside the floating ice—' Forward !" Elated and amused with the scene, the men promptly obeyed, holding their rifles above their heads.—*Law's Vincennes, p.* 32.

made and served out to the most weakly. Most got a little, but many gave their share to the weakly, jocosely saying something cheering to their comrades.

"Crossing now a narrow, deep lake in the canoes, we came to a copse of timber called Warrior's Island; we were now in full view of town and fort—not a shrub between us, at two miles distance. Every man feasted his eyes and forgot he had suffered. It was now we had to display our abilities. The plain between us and the town was not a perfect level. The sunken grounds were covered with water, full of ducks. We observed several out on horseback shooting them and sent out many of our active young Frenchmen to decoy and take one prisoner, which they did. Learned that the British had that evening completed the wall of the fort and that there were a good many Indians in town; our situation was now truly critical; no possibility of retreat in case of defeat, and in full view of a town with upwards of six hundred men in it— troops, Indians and inhabitants.

"We were now in the situation that I had labored to get ourselves in. The idea of being made prisoner was foreign to almost every man, as they expected nothing but torture. We knew that nothing but the most daring conduct would insure success. I knew that a number of the inhabitants wished us well; that the Grand Chief, Tobacco's son, had openly declared himself a friend to the Big Knives. I therefore wrote and sent the following placard:

"*To the inhabitants of Post Vincennes:*

"GENTLEMEN—Being now within two miles of your village, with my army, determined to take your fort this night, and not being willing to surprise you, I take this method to request such as are true citizens to remain still in your houses. Those, if any there be, that are friends to the King, will instantly repair to the fort, join the "hair-buyer General, and fight like men. If any such do not go, and are found afterwards, they may depend on severe punishment. On the contrary, those who are true friends to liberty, may depend on being well treated, and I once more request them to keep out of the streets. Every one I find in arms on my arrival, I shall treat as an enemy.

"G. R. CLARK."

"A little before sunset we moved and displayed ourselves in full view of the town. Crowds gazing at us. We were plunging ourselves into certain destruction or success. There was no midway thought of."

What an extraordinary march! How simple and graphic the narrative describing it! We scarce know which to wonder at most, the commander who could inspire all his men—and many of them, too, gay, delicate and nerveless Frenchmen—with such spirit and endurance; or the men themselves who, environed with such appalling perils, would implicitly obey the orders and follow the lead of a man who must have appeared but little else than a rash and crack-brained zealot. But the sequel was quite as marvelous as the preface, and we are lost in astonishment at Clark's brilliant and unrecking valor. Truly, considering his desperate situation and the smallness of his following, his impudence was almost sublime. But rashness and audacity frequently attain magnificent results, where a halting prudence would fall pusillanimously by the way, and so it proved in this most notable instance.

OTHER STRATAGEMS—KENTUCKY SHARP-SHOOTING—FORT ASSAULTED.

Clark now spoke a few stern words to his men inculcating the absolute necessity of implicit obedience and received assurances that they would follow him to death. The astute and crafty commander now resorted to a stratagem worthy of his genius. All the colors, amounting to ten or twelve pair, which would denote a large force, were displayed to the very best advantage, and as the low, water-covered plain they were traversing was not a perfect level, but had frequent risings of eight or ten feet, running in an oblique direction to the town, advantage was taken of one of these, by marching and counter-marching through the water under or behind it, which prevented any count of the men. The colors, however, being fixed conspicuously on long poles made a brave and deceptive showing, and as several French duck hunters with their horses had just been captured, Clark's officers now mounted on these horses and rode to and fro rapidly, the more to deceive the enemy. "In this manner," says Clark, "we moved and directed our march in such a way as to suffer it to be dark before we had advanced more than half way to the town. We then suddenly altered our direction, crossed ponds where they could not have suspected us, and about eight o'clock gained the heights back of the town."

Clark immediately followed up his success with his usual promptness and boldness. The strongest posts of the town were seized and a noisy firing was commenced. The enemy in the fort were so astounded that they could not believe the noise was from an enemy, but credited it to some drunken Indians, until one of their men was wounded through a port hole. A large number of British Indians made haste to escape. A hundred others declared in favor of the strangers, and marched with Clark to attack the fort. That singular and self-confident character thanked the chief, told him the two parties might become mixed and requested him to rest quiet until the morning.*

---

* Butler's History of Kentucky gives an amusing incident of this siege. Captain Helm, the old commandant and then a prisoner, was at the time of the sudden attack playing at piquet with Governor Hamilton in the fort. One of Clark's men requested leave to shoot at Helm's headquarters so soon as they were discovered, to knock down the clay or mortar into his apple-toddy, which he was sure the Captain, from his well-known foundness for that liquor would have on his hearth. It is added that when the gallant but bibulous Captain heard the bullets rattling about the chimney, he sprang up, swore it must be Clark's men, who would make the whole of them prisoners, though the d—d rascals had no business to spoil his toddy.

Clark had made himself familiar with all the defences and their failings, and knowing that the fort cannon were on the upper floors of strong block-houses, and that the ports had been so badly planned and fashioned that they could not fire at low range, he snugged his best marksmen close under the walls. Here they were safe. The cannon did no execution except to the town buildings, which they much shattered. The musketry, too, employed in the dark against trained woodsmen covered by houses, palings, river banks and what not, was equally ineffectual, while the Kentuckians' unerring rifles searched out every vulnerable spot. In fact, those skilled riflemen finding the true direction, would pour in such volleys when the embrasures were open, that the British had quite a number of their gunners wounded and could no longer stand to their pieces.

The impudent Big Knives, too, would stand quite near the port holes, but out of reach of all missiles, and chaff and abuse the enemy in order to so exasperate them that they would open their ports and fire their cannon. But as soon as one was opened, fifty Kentucky rifles would be leveled at it on the instant, and if the British had stood to their artillery, every gunner would have been killed during the night, as the best marksmen lay well covered within thirty yards of the walls.

"Sometimes," says Clark, "an irregular fire, as hot as possible, was kept up from different directions for a few minutes, and then only a continual scattering fire at the ports, as usual; and a great noise and laughter immediately commenced in different parts of the town by the reserved parties, as if they had only fired on the fort for a few minutes for amusement, and as if those continually firing at the fort were being regularly relieved. Conduct similar to this kept the garrison constantly alarmed."

Thus did the wily and subtle American continue to befool and bamboozle the General, who from the scalp bounties he was constantly offering, was known on the border as the "British hair-buyer," until he was well worked into the belief that he must have the whole of Kentucky at his doors.

The time was now ripe for a change of tactics, which came in the shape of a summons to Hamilton for surrender. It was declined, but Hamilton's true feeling peeped out in a question to Helm. "Is he a merciful man?" quoth the Governor. The attack was now renewed with greater vigor than ever, Clark concluding to listen to no terms until in possession of the fort. Helm now cautioned the English soldiers not to look through the loopholes, for these Virginia riflemen, he said, would shoot their very eyes out. Indeed, seven having been actually shot in this manner, Hamilton then was induced to send out a flag proposing a truce of three days and a conference. The American was nonplused to get at the meaning of the demand for so long a truce, but finally sent word that he would agree to no other terms than a complete surrender of the garrison at discretion, and that if Hamilton desired a conference they could meet at the church.

MAJ. HAY TREMBLES—A CURIOUS INCIDENT—THE FORT SURRENDERS.

They met and the conference began. Hamilton agreed to surrender if certain conditions were granted. Clark deliberately rejected the whole, making quite a haughty speech as if he were already in possession, and concluded by assuring the Governor that his troops were impatient to get at all Indian partisan leaders, and to storm the works, and in that case they would all be cut off to a man. Not being able to agree they were parting, when Hamilton turned and asked politely if Clark would be so kind as to give him his reasons for granting no better terms. This was the kind of business Clark was good at, and be sure his ability to take the place whenever he wished, was amplitudinously set forth.

On Clark's concluding, Major Hay remarked, "And pray, sir, who is it that you call 'Indian partisans?'" "Sir," replied Clark sternly, "I take Major Hay to be one of the principal." "I never saw a man in the moment of execution," writes Clark, "so struck as he appeared to be—pale, trembling and scarce able to stand. Hamilton blushed and was much affected at his behavior."

Clark returned to his quarters and said he would reconsider and let Hamilton know the result. While all this was going on, an Indian scalping party, who had been to the Ohio, were seen returning. Captain Williams, with a proper party, went out to meet them. The savages, who mistook the whites for their own friends, continued to advance with all the parade of successful warriors. Williams' men, outraged at this unseemly exultation, fired at once, killing two, wounding three and taking six prisoners, one of whom proved to be white. The Indians were brought openly before the fort gates; there tomahawked in full sight of the garrison and their carcasses thrown into the river. This was done by Clark to show the numerous Indians around that Hamilton could give them none of his boasted protection, and to incense them against him for not exerting himself more in their behalf.*

---

*Clark mentions rather an odd incident in connection with these savages. An old French gentleman was a Lieutenant in one of the Kaskaskia companies, and when Clark ordered the white man who had been captured with this scalping party to be put to death, Lieutenant St. Croix stood by with drawn sword, so that he should not escape. The wretch, on seeing the tomahawk raised to give the fatal stroke, lifted his eyes and cried to the old Frenchman, "Oh, father, save me!" He *was his own son*, painted and disguised as a savage. The agitation and behavior of the two recognizing each other at such a critical moment, may be imagined. At the earnest solicitation of the father, the young man's life was spared on certain conditions.

On the 24th, the two commanders agreed on conditions, and the garrison capitulated as prisoners of war. The American flag floated over Fort Sackville, and thirteen guns boomed forth the victory. By this conquest were obtained seventy-nine white prisoners and $50,000 worth of stores. It was a masterful stroke, boldly and skillfully executed. Not only were the vast British-Indian combinations against the western border completely broken up, by which numbers of fighting men were allowed to join our eastern armies, but the whole northwestern country remained ever after in peaceable possession of the Americans; otherwise it would most probably have belonged to Britain at the peace. Governor Hamilton was sent to Richmond, Virginia, and his men to Detroit, on parole. The former was fettered and thrust in jail on account of his abominable policy in urging savages to *greater* savageries by offering large bounties for scalps, but none for prisoners. This policy naturally resulted in horrible, wholesale butcheries, for the Indians would actually drive their captives within sight of the British forts, and there butcher them for the hair bounty. Through the interference of Washington, Hamilton was afterwards released, his harsh and rigorous treatment not being in accordance with the terms of surrender.

Clark Wants Detroit—His Many Disappointments and Death.

There is but little doubt that had Clark now had as many men as were starving or idling in some of the western forts, he could easily have added the crown to his invaluable conquests by the capture of Detroit itself. This was now his daily dream and his most cherished ambition. He sent urgent appeals to Kentucky for more men. With this sole end in view, he returned to Kaskaskia. He was only now twenty-seven years of age, and his whole soul was fired with the enterprise. "If I had but three hundred men available," he wrote to Jefferson, "I would have attempted it." He was doomed to disappointment, however, and while preparing to set off with even two hundred at his command, he was advised by Governor Henry to wait until he could have a regiment. The auspicious time never came again.

He was soon after presented with a second-handed sword by the Assembly of Virginia. *It* arrived safely, but the additional men never. "Hope deferred maketh the heart sick," and, finally, Clark proceeded to the Falls of the Ohio, where Louisville was soon after built. In 1780 he constructed Fort Jefferson, on the Mississippi, and led an important expedition against the Ohio Indians. He then repaired to Richmond to press forward his Detroit scheme. His views were approved, but before he could get a suitable command, came the traitor Benedict Arnold, ruthlessly carrying fire and sword into the heart of the State. Clark took temporary command with Baron Steuben. He was now raised to the rank of Brigadier General, and spent many months in raising a force of two thousand men, which was to rendezvous at Louisville.

But insuperable difficulties arose and he was obliged to content himself with small commands and defensive operations. This was the turning point in Clark's life. The decadence of his fame and influence had now commenced. In 1782, after the disastrous battle of the Blue Licks, he led an expedition of a thousand mounted men against the Ohio Indians. The results were petty, as the Indians would not stand. In '86, a new army of a thousand was raised against the Wabash Indians, and Clark was given the lead. The expedition proved unfortunate, the men mutinous and was abandoned. Several years after he accepted a Major General's commission from Genet, in the French service, designing to lead a secret expedition against the Spanish on the Mississippi, but a revolution soon occurred in France and the project was abandoned.

Clark's military reputation now suffered an eclipse from which it never emerged. He lost much of his popularity and henceforth lived obscure and neglected. While yet in middle age, he disappeared almost completely from public life, a soured, disappointed and decrepid man. For a long time he had suffered from rheumatism, that fell foe of the early pioneers. This was followed by paralysis of which he finally died, in 1817, at his residence near Louisville.

Clark was never married, but although he left no descendants to hand down his name to posterity, he will never be forgotten by his grateful countrymen.

"THE WAR BELT—A LEGEND OF NORTH BEND."

Under this alluring title, Judge Hall, of Cincinnati, gives in his Romance of Western History a very glowing and amplified account of a treaty held by commissioners duly appointed—Generals George Rogers Clark, Richard Butler and Samuel Parsons—with the Shawnees. In all these treaty transactions General Clark is described as playing the most prominent *role*. But we will first condense Hall's relation and then correct some of his errors.

For several days previous to that appointed for the holding of the council, parties of Indian warriors were seen arriving and erecting temporary lodges near the fort of North Bend, at the outlet of the fertile Miami Valley. The number of Indians was much greater than necessary or expected, and they seemed anything but pacific. Irritated by recent events and puffed up by delusive promises of British support, they wore an offended and insolent air. Their glances were vindictive and their thirst for vengeance scarce concealed. The fort was a very slight work and the situation of the garrison very precarious. Both parties held separate councils the day previous. That of the Indians was declamatory and boisterous. Deeming their enemy too weak to offer much opposition, they had decided on their course and declaimed noisily on their wrongs.

The American commissioners sat with gloomy forebodings. To meet the excited savages in council would be to place themselves at their mercy; yet to break up negotiations would be tantamount to a declaration of war. Then Hall follows with an elaborate eulogy on Clark, as the master spirit of the occasion, at the expense of his colleagues. Clark, he says, treated the idea of danger with ridicule, and insisted, calmly and even playfully, that the negotiations should proceed. This is as though his colleagues had wished to postpone it. An apartment was prepared as a council room, and at the appointed hour the doors were thrown open.

"At the head of the table sat Clark, a soldier-like and majestic man, whose complexion, hair and all indicated a sanguinary temperament. His brow was high and capacious; his features manly and prominent, and his expression, ordinarily cheerful and agreeable, was now grave almost to sternness. Clark's reputation for courage and firmness was widely known and well appreciated by the chiefs and warriors. On his right sat General Richard Butler, a brave officer of the Revolution, who soon after fell in St. Clair's disastrous battle. On his left sat General Parsons, and around sat or stood officers, soldiers, secretaries, interpreters, &c.

"An Indian council is one of the most imposing spectacles in savage life. The chiefs and sages, the leaders and orators, occupy the most conspicuous seats; behind them are ranged the younger braves, and still further in the rear appear the women and youth as spectators. All are attentive, and their silence is impressive. The great pipe, gaudily adorned with paint and feathers, is passed from mouth to mouth. Whatever jealousy or party spirit may exist is carefully excluded from this dignified assemblage. It was an alarming evidence now of the temper prevailing, that the usual decorum and propriety were wanting. The customary formalities were forgotten or neglected, and an insulting levity took their place. The chiefs and braves stalked haughtily in and seated themselves promiscuously on the floor. An air of insolence marked their movements, and showed a design either to dictate terms or fix a quarrel. A dead silence of distrust and watchfulness, but not of respect, rested over the assembly."

The commissioners, without appearing to notice the ominous behavior of the Indians, opened the council in due form. The pipe was lighted and passed. General Clark explained the purpose for which the treaty was ordered with unembarrassed air and the tone of one accustomed to command; he stated they had come, authorized by their Great Father to offer the Shawnees peace, and asked some of their wise men to speak.

"A chief arose, drew up his tall person to its full height, and assuming a haughty attitude, threw his eye contemptuously over the commissioners and their small retinue, and then, stalking up to the table, threw upon it two belts of wampum of different colors—the *war* and the *peace* belt. 'We come here,' he exclaimed, 'to offer you two pieces of wampum; they are of different colors; you know what they mean; you can take which you like,' and, turning upon his heel, he resumed his seat. The chiefs drew themselves up, knowing they had offered an insult to which it would be hard to submit, but which they supposed he dare not resent.

"The pipe was laid aside and those fierce, wild men gazed intently on Clark. He sat undisturbed and apparently careless, until the chief who had thrown the belts on the table had taken his seat, then, with a small cane which he held in his hand he reached, as if playfully, towards the war belt, entangled the end of his stick in it, drew it towards him, and with a twitch of the cane *threw the belt into the midst of the chiefs*. The effect was electric. Every man in council, of each party, sprang to his feet; the savages with a loud *Ugh* of astonishment—the Americans in expectation of a hopeless conflict. Every hand grasped a weapon. Clark alone was unawed. The expression of his countenance changed to a ferocious sternness and his eye flashed, but otherwise he was unmoved. A bitter smile was perceptible upon his compressed lips as he gazed upon that savage band as they stood like a pack of wolves at bay, ready to rush upon him whenever one bolder than the rest should commence the attack. Raising now his arm and waving his hand towards the door, he exclaimed: '*Dogs! you may go!*'

"The Indians hesitated for a moment, and then rushed tumultuously out of the council room. The cool contempt with which their first insult was thrown back in their teeth surprised them, and they were foiled by the self-possession of *one man*. They quailed before a coolness they could not comprehend, and therefore feared to assail."

All this is very fine and picturesque, and has been widely published, but it is not true history. We are safe in stating that no such scene—exactly as the one described—occurred, and that in the scene, just as striking, which *did* occur, Clark was *not*, but Butler *was*, the chief actor. Mr. Hall seems to have amplified a much briefer article—describing the same dramatic spectacle—which was first published in the *Encyclopædia Americana*, and which, for the impressiveness of the scene depicted, enjoyed a wide currency. Clark would have been just the very man to do such an act as he is represented to have done, and he has earned glory enough without there being any necessity for his admirers adding one leaf to his chaplet of honor at the expense of his equally-gallant co-commissioner, General Richard Butler, one of the bravest old flints of the Revolution—an officer who was styled by General Lee "the renowned second and rival of Morgan at Saratoga;" who was Wayne's second at the brilliant dash at Stony Point, and who sealed his devotion to his country with his blood, a few years after, at St. Clair's disastrous defeat.

Butler kept a regular private diary of all the proceedings at this treaty, and his account is plain, modest, direct and unpretending. Clark, of course, had no part in his being made to figure as the hero of this striking scene. He died in 1817, and the *Encyclopædia* account first appeared in 1830. Let us now find out from Butler's unpretending journal what really did occur. The General's reputation as a man of the very highest honor and the very strictest veracity, would at once forbid the thought that he could basely concoct a lie, and that, too in his own private journal, intended for no eye but his own, and which has never yet seen the light, except in the *Olden Time*, published by Neville B. Craig, of Pittsburgh.

By this we learn that it was the Indians who first offered the *black* or war belt, and that it was General Butler who offered them in return the option of a *black* or *white* belt, just as Clark himself did at Kaskaskia several years before to the Indian chiefs assembled there. We also learn that the Delawares and Wyandots, too, were interested in this treaty, and quite numerously represented, for of the whole four hundred and forty-eight Indians—men, women and children—the Wyandots had eighty-three, the Delawares had forty-seven, while the Shawnees had three hundred and eighteen.

At this grand council, Kekewepellethe, the head Captain of the Shawnees, *did* make a most insolent speech, and at the end threw down a *black* or war belt. He said in effect, curtly and fiercely, that they would *not* give hostages, as required, for the return of all the white flesh in their hands; that it was not their custom; that they were Shawnees and when they said a thing they stood to it, and as for dividing their lands, God gave them the lands; they did not understand measuring out lands, as it was *all* theirs. As for the goods for their women and children, the whites might keep them or give them to other tribes, as they would have none of them.

The commissioners conferred a short time on this arrogant speech, and resolved they would bate no jot of their demands, "Whereupon," writes Butler, in his diary, "*I* (not Clark) addressed them in this short manner." We need not give the whole speech, but it was quite as crisp and double-shotted as the imperious chief's, and said, in effect, that the chief's speech was not only unwise and ungrateful, but flagrantly false; that they *had* granted hostages before, both to Bouquet and Dunmore; that they had proved false and perfidious to all their solemn pledges, and that they could no longer be believed, but were cruel and barbarous murderers. Butler (not Clark) concluded nearly as follows:

"You joined the British King against us. We have overcome him; he has cast you off and given us your country, and Congress, in bounty and mercy, offer you peace and a country. We have told you our terms and these we will not alter. They are just and liberal. We *now* tell you if you are so unwise as to adhere to what you have said and to refuse these terms, you may depart in peace; you shall have provisions to take you to your towns and no man shall touch you for eight days, but after that, we shall consider ourselves free from all ties of protection, and you may depend the United States will protect their citizens and distress your obstinate nation. It rests now with you. Peace or war is in your power. Make your choice like *men*. We tell you plainly that this country belongs to the United States—their blood has defended it and will protect it. You should be thankful for its forgiveness and offers of kindness instead of the sentiments which this black string imparts and the manner you have delivered it. We shall not receive it or any other from you in any such way."

"I then took it up," adds Butler, "and dashed it on the table. We then left them, and threw down a black and a white string. In the afternoon the Shawnees sent a message requesting a council; on which we went in. Kekewepellethe then arose and spoke as follows: 'Brothers, the thirteen fires—we feel sorry that a mistake has caused you to be displeased at us this morning. You must have misunderstood us. We told you yesterday that three of our men were to go off immediately to collect your flesh and blood. We had also appointed persons to remain with you till this is performed; they are here, and shall stay with you. Brethren, our people are sensible of the truths you have told them. You have everything in your power; we, therefore, hope that you will take pity on our women and children. Brothers, everything shall be as you wish; we came here to do that which is good, and we agree to all you have proposed, and hope, in future, we shall both enjoy peace and be secure.'" (A *white* string.)

Butler's speech, doubtless agreed to and possibly, in part, suggested by Clark, had settled the whole matter. Mark the contrast between this meek and submissive piping and the haughty and defiant trumpet tones of the same morning! "'Twas Hyperion to a Satyr." The council broke up, and a satisfactory treaty was made the very next day. Butler modestly writes: "It was worthy of observation to see the different degrees of agitation which appeared in the young Indians at the delivery of Kekewepellethe's speech. They appeared raised and ready for war. On the speech I spoke, they appeared rather distressed and chagrined at the contrast of the speeches."

JAMES HARROD, PIONEER HUNTER AND INDIAN-KILLER.

This gamy and noble-spirited pioneer is honored by being the builder of the first log-cabin and the founder of the first settlement in Kentucky. When Boone was sent, in '74, by Governor Dunmore to warn the surveyors at the Falls of the Ohio that an Indian war had broken out, he found the hunter and his company settled at Harrodstown.

So little is known of Harrod's youth, that history does not even name whence he came nor when he migrated. We only know that he went to Kentucky even prior to Boone; was most probably a Virginian; went back to that State, and returned to Kentucky in 1774; fought under Colonel Lewis at the Battle of Point Pleasant, and that next year he settled, as stated, on the site of the present town of Harrodsburg. But the name of the young hunter soon became familiar along the border. He was associated with Boone in many a feat of self-denying hardihood and generous chivalry. He was tall, brave, simple and modest—had read no book but that of Nature; knew no art but wood-craft; hated nothing on earth but an Indian and a pole-cat, and never said: "Boys, you do it," but "Boys, come on!" His rifle was the longest, the heaviest and the surest; his calm, frank eye was never at fault to mark the distant game, to meet the gaze of a deadly foe, or smile back truth to a friend. Such were his habits of incessant activity, and so great his coolness and self-reliance, that he never had to wait for companions in his longest and most dangerous expeditions.

Harrod would often be gone for weeks and even months together—no one knew whither or for what end. During these absences his industry was untiring; all the game killed was cured and stored, Indian fashion, beyond the reach of wild beasts. His knowledge of Indians and their ways was such that he would often continue hunting when he knew they were in the same range. The proud hunter would not give way, but took his chances with the red foe. On one such occasion, he perceived a group of several deer feeding in a small glade in the forest, near the Kentucky river. He had cautiously approached them, and was kneeling behind a tree and raising his rifle for a shot, when the buck of the herd suddenly lifted its head and uttered the peculiar shrill whistle which indicates that it has either seen or smelt danger.

Harrod was too skilled a woodsman not to know that there was another foe present besides himself. He held his breath, when, at the sharp crack of a rifle from the opposite side of the glade, the startled buck leaped into the air and fell dead. The report of Harrod's rifle followed so instantly that it seemed a mere echo, or rather a prolongation of the same sound. A nobler quarry had bitten the dust, for the unerring ball of the borderer had reached the heart of a Shawnee chief, who had leaned forward from his covert to fire. Harrod had known for several days that an Indian hunting party was in the neighborhood.

At another time his unwary game was nearly played upon himself. He was out upon a buffalo trail leading to the Blue Licks, and he had wounded a tough, surly old bull, that had left the herd and stood at bay in the recesses of a thick wood. The wounded animal was very fierce and dangerous, and the hunter had to approach it cautiously. While in the very act of firing, he caught a glimpse of a warrior taking aim at himself from behind a tree. He fired and the warrior fired, the former dropping instantly to the ground as if killed. He laid perfectly dead, while the savage, after stopping to load his rifle—an invariable habit with them before leaving cover—now approached—warily enough, leaping from tree to tree—to take his scalp. Seeing that the body was perfectly still, the Indian sprang forward, knife in hand, but as he stooped to grasp the scalp-lock, the long and powerful arms of Harrod were locked about him as those from a devil-fish, and with the tightening coil of a boa constrictor, the warrior was crushed in his herculean hug, and writhed helpless on the ground beneath him.

The Shawnees had made several attacks on Boone's settlement, he being absent at the Licks with a great portion of the men of the station, making salt. Prowling parties of Indians had at this time killed their cattle, driven their hunting parties and so shortened their supplies that the little garrison was reduced to great straits. At this juncture Harrod returned from one of his long tramps. He proposed to some of the men that they should accompany him to one of his nearest depots of meat. The risk was so great that none dared venture, so Harrod started out alone. He found game very shy and as there were plenty of "Indian sign" about, he concluded to get the first meat he could find.

He now noted a small herd of deer moving as if lately startled, and he advanced very circumspectly, and soon saw the prints of moccasins on the trail of the deer. He had progressed but a short distance when the sudden whistle of a deer, followed instantly by the cracks of two rifles, warned him it was time for business. The Indians saw him and treed, and while he was peeping cautiously forth for a shot, a rifle ball from the right whizzed through the heavy mass of black hair that fell over his shoulders, stinging his neck sharply as it grazed past. He crouched in a jiffy, and all was still as death for some time, the two savages being on the left and the new one on the right.

Harrod then concluded to play the cap game—a stale trick enough, but now effectual. Placing his famous wolf-skin cap on the muzzle of his rifle, he, after some prefatory manœuvering among the shrubs to show that he was getting restless, slowly and hesitatingly raised the cap. The ring of three rifles was almost simultaneous, and before the echoes had died away, that from Harrod followed, and the death-shriek of a warrior proclaimed the success of the venture. Another long quiet! The cap was elevated again, but this time only drew one fire, but enough! for it disclosed the exact position of his foes. In less than a minute, the savage who had fired, exposed part of his body in sending home his wiper. Harrod shot him through the heart.

The other Indian commenced a retreat, and got off, but not before carrying away a lump of the "pale-face's" lead. Harrod proceeded at his leisure to dress the two deer his foes had killed, and that night entered the station loaded down with meat.

Harrod Idolized by All—He Nurses a Wounded Indian.

Harrod's cabin soon became the nucleus of a station; whither hunters, surveyors, speculators and emigrants flocked for shelter and protection. Harrod's knowledge and good-will were at the service of all. He shouldered his axe and helped the new comers to run up a cabin. If they were out of meat, Harrod some how found it out, and was off to the woods and soon a fine deer or bear, or the haunches of a buffalo, were at their disposal. If the stranger's horses had strayed in the range, Harrod's frank and pleasant voice would be heard, "Halloo, Jones! no ploughing to-day? Nothing wrong, I hope?" "Well, yes—the old beast's been gone these five days—can't find him down thar in the canebrake—been lost myself two days in looking arter him, and I've jest about give it up." "Never mind, Jones, you'll get used to tha' range soon—that horse of your'n is a blood bay, ain't he?" "Yes, snip down the nose and left hind foot white, bad collar-mark on the shoulders." "Ah, yes; good morning, Jones," and a few hours after Jones' horse, with his snip on his nose, is quietly fastened to Jones' fence, and Harrod walks in.

News comes to the station that the savages have attacked the house of a settler five miles off and murdered all the family but two daughters, whom they have hurried off as captives. The war cry of Harrod is instantly heard, "Come, boys! come, boys! we must catch those rascals. We can't spare our girls." The swift and tireless pursuit, the wary approach to camp, the night attack, the short, fierce struggle, the rescue and the victorious return would then follow. Harrod liked most to go alone, for he said companions complained of hardships and dangers when the fun was just commencing with him, but when by himself he knew exactly what he could and what he would do. The Indians, on account of this extraordinary love for solitary adventure, had christened him the "Lone Long Knife," and greatly dreaded his mysterious prowess.

Once, when discovered by a young warrior, right in the centre of the Indian village, he struck him to the earth with his huge fist, and leaped for the forest, followed by a gang of redskins. But they had a man before them swifter and more tireless than themselves. By the time he had reached the Miami, ten miles off, there were only three who followed. Harrod swam the river without hesitation, being fired at while climbing the opposite bank. He now took a tree, and, removing the water-proof cover of deer's bladder from his rifle lock, quietly waited. After hesitating a moment, the three pursuers plunged in. Harrod waited until they approached the shore, when, at the ominous crack of his rifle, the foremost sank. The other two paused, then turned to go back, but before they could get out of range, he wounded a second desperately, who gave himself up to the current, and was swept down out of sight. The third, by a series of rapid dives, like those of a wary loon, succeeded in baffling the white hunter's aim, and at last swam out of range.

The hunter paused to rest, and some hour or so afterwards, while wandering along the bank, Harrod saw upon a pile of driftwood, which had collected at the mouth of one of the small runs, some living object, which he at first took for a large turtle glistening in the sun as he drew his unwieldy body up on the logs to bask. He approached nearer and stopped to gaze. Imagine his surprise on seeing a stalwart Indian drag his body slowly from the water and finally seat himself upon the logs. He had lost his gun, and now endeavored to stifle with moss and leaves the bleeding from a severe bullet wound in his shoulder. Harrod knew that it was the second savage he had shot. Here was a trial and a test of the man! The foe was wounded and helpless; to shoot the poor wretch he could not now; to leave him there to die would be still more cruel. His big heart melted, and, stealthily making a wide circuit, he crept silently upon the warrior from behind. A large tree stood close to the drift, which, being gained, Harrod laid down his gun, then suddenly stepping into full view, raised his empty hands to show he was unarmed.

"*Ugh!*" grunted the astounded warrior, making a sudden movement, as if to plunge into the water again. Harrod placed his hand upon his heart, spoke a few words in the Shawnee tongue, when the young Indian paused and looked for a moment earnestly into his late opponent's face, and bowed his head in token of submission. Harrod now examined his wound, helped him to the bank, tore his own shirt and bound up the wounds with healing, cooling herbs, and then, to crown all his benevolent efforts, when he found the Indian unable to walk, threw him across his own broad shoulders and bore him to a cave near by which he used as one of his deposits for game. The entrance was small and covered with brambles and vines, but as one entered, it opened out and presented a smooth floor, with beautiful and fantastically-shaped stalactites pendent from the rocky roof. At the farther extremity of this rocky chamber a clear, pure stream of sparkling water poured into a smooth, round basin, worn into the solid limestone, and finding exit through a dark hole in the wall.

The Indian was all eyes as he was gently laid down upon the floor, and in this strange and secluded hiding place, as the story goes, Harrod watched and waited on his wounded foe. His interest in the young warrior grew by tending him. He brought him meat and cooling fruits; washed and dressed his wounds, and carefully and tenderly nursed him back to health and strength. When the young savage grew sufficiently able to journey, Harrod gave him a supply of provisions, and, pointing towards the North, bade him return to his people and tell them how the hated Long Knife treated his wounded foe. Nothing was ever heard directly from this warrior again, but Boone, who about this time was, with his salt makers, taken prisoner by the Shawnees, always attributed the kind treatment he and his men received to the good offices of this grateful savage.

The popularity of Harrod now grew very great. He was a true leader, and was soon after elected Colonel, married a Kentucky girl, and was universally idolized, but he modestly shrank from all honors. Not all the comforts of a happy home, or the endearments of a growing family, however, could win him from his absorbing passion for long, solitary hunting rambles. From one of these he never returned. Whether he met his fate by some "moving accident by flood or field;" by some casualty of the hunt, or in some deadly and desperate conflict with his swarthy foes, none ever knew, but all, from their knowledge of his unquailing intrepidity, felt absolutely certain that in whatever shape death came, it was met bravely and unflinchingly.

COMBAT AND ESCAPE OF PETER KENNEDY.

About the year 1781, a band of Indians came into Hardin county, Kentucky, and after committing numerous depredations and killing some women and children, were pursued by the whites. During the pursuit a portion of the Indians, who were on stolen horses, took a southerly direction so as to strike the Ohio about where Brandenburg is now situated; while the other party, who were on foot, attempted to cross the Ohio at the mouth of Salt river. The whites pursued each party, the larger portion following the trail of the horses—the smaller, the foot party. Among the latter was the hero of this sketch, Peter Kennedy.

Young Kennedy was noted for his fleetness of foot, strength of body and intrepidity. He was selected as their leader. They pursued the Indians to within a mile of the river, the savages awaiting them in ambush.

The enemy were ten in number, the whites six. As they were led on by their daring leader in an effort to overtake them before they could reach the river, all of his comrades were shot down and he was left to contend single-handed with ten fierce and savage Indians. This was odds calculated to make the bravest tremble; but young Kennedy was determined to sell his life as dearly as possible. With one bound he reached a tree, and awaited his opportunity to wreak vengeance upon the savage foe. The redskins, with their usual wariness, kept their cover; but at last one more impatient than the remainder showed his head from behind his tree. As quick as thought Kennedy buried a rifle ball in his forehead and instantly turned to flee; but no sooner did he abandon his cover than nine deadly rifles were leveled at him and instantly fired, and with the fire a simultaneous whoop of triumph, for the brave Kennedy fell, pierced through the right hip with a ball. Disabled by the wound, and unable to make further resistance, he was taken prisoner and immediately borne off to the Wabash, where the tribe of the victorious party belonged.

The wound of Kennedy was severe, and the pain which he suffered from it, was greatly aggravated by the rapid movement of the Indians. The arrival of the party was hailed with the usual demonstrations of Indian triumph; but Kennedy, owing to his feeble and suffering condition, was treated with kindness. His wound gradually healed, and as he again found himself a well man, he felt an irrepressible desire for freedom. He determined to make his escape, but how to effect it was the question. In this state of suspense he remained for two years; well knowing that, however kindly the Indians might treat a prisoner when *first* captured, an unsuccessful attempt to escape would be followed by the infliction of death, and that, too, by the *stake*. But still Kennedy was willing to run this risk to regain that most inestimable of gifts—freedom. The vigilance of the Indians ultimately relaxed, and Kennedy seized the opportunity, and made good his escape to the Kentucky side of the Ohio.

Hitherto Kennedy had rapidly pressed forward without rest or nourishment, for he knew the character of the savages, and anticipated a rapid pursuit. Hungry and exhausted, he was tempted to shoot a deer which crossed his path, from which he cut a steak, cooked it, and had nearly completed his meal, when he heard the shrill crack of an Indian rifle, and felt that he was again wounded, but fortunately not disabled. He grasped his gun and bounded forward in the direction of Gooden's station, distant nearly thirty miles. Fortunately he was acquainted with the locality, which aided him greatly in his flight. The chase soon became intensely exciting. The fierce whoop of the Indians was met with a shout of defiance from Kennedy. For a few minutes, at the outset of the chase, the Indians appeared to gain on him; but he redoubled his efforts, and gradually widened the distance between the pursuers and himself.

But there was no abatement of effort on either side—both the pursuers and pursued put forth all their energies. The yell of the savages as the distance widened, became fainter and fainter—Kennedy had descended in safety the tall cliff on the Rolling Fork, and found himself, as the Indians reached the summit, a mile in advance.

Here the loud yell of the savages reverberated along the valleys of that stream, but so far from damping, infused new energy into the flight of Kennedy. The race continued, Kennedy still widening the interval, to within a short distance of Gooden's station, when the Indians, in despair gave up the chase. Kennedy arrived safely at the station, but in an exhausted state. His tale was soon told. The men instantly grasped their rifles, and under the direction of Kennedy, sallied forth to encounter the savages. The scene was now changed. The pursuers became the pursued. The Indians, exhausted by their long-continued chase, were speedily overtaken, and not one returned to their tribe to tell of the fruitless pursuit of Kennedy! Kennedy lived in Hardin county to a very old age and left a numerous and respectable progeny.

AN ADVENTURE OF BOONE, RELATED BY HIMSELF.

Audubon, the distinguished naturalist and one of Nature's truest noblemen—as fond of hunting and the free, unshackled life of the wilderness as Boone himself—passed some little time with the famous Kentucky pioneer at his home in Missouri, and relates the following extraordinary incident. We quote: Colonel Boone happened to spend a night with me, under the same roof, more than twenty years ago. We had returned from a shooting excursion, in the course of which his extraordinary skill in the use of the rifle had been fully displayed. On retiring to the room appropriated to that remarkable individual and myself, I felt anxious to know more of his exploits and adventures than I did, and accordingly took the liberty of proposing numerous questions to him. The stature and general appearance of this wanderer of the western forests approached the gigantic. His chest was broad and prominent; his muscular powers displayed themselves in every limb: his countenance gave indication of great courage, enterprise and perseverance, and when he spoke, the very motion of his lips conveyed the impression of truth. I undressed, while he merely took off his hunting shirt and arranged a few folds of blankets on the floor, choosing rather to lie there, as he observed, than on the softest bed. When we had both disposed of ourselves, each after his own fashion, he related to me the following account of his powers of memory:

"I was once," said he, "hunting on the banks of the Green river. We Virginians had for some time been waging a war of intrusion upon the savages, and I, among the rest, rambled through the woods in pursuit of their race as I now would follow the tracks of any venomous animal. The Indians outwitted me one dark night, and I was as suddenly as unexpectedly made a prisoner by them. The trick had been managed with great skill, for no sooner had I extinguished my fire and laid me down in full security, as I thought, than I felt myself seized by an indistinguishable number of hands, and was immediately pinioned fast. To have resisted would have been useless and dangerous, and I suffered myself to be removed to their camp, a few miles distant, without uttering one word of complaint. You are, doubtless, aware that this was the best policy, since it proved to the Indians at once that I was born and bred as fearless of death as any of themselves.

" When we reached the camp, great rejoicings were exhibited. The squaws and pappooses appeared particularly delighted to see me, and I was assured, by very unequivocal words and gestures, that on the morrow the mortal enemy of the redskins would cease to live. I never opened my lips, but was busy contriving some scheme which might enable me to give the rascals the slip before dawn. The women immediately fell a searching about my hunting shirt for whatever they might think valuable, and, fortunately for me, soon found my flask of strong whiskey. A terrific grin was exhibited on their murderous countenances, while my heart throbbed with joy at the anticipation of their intoxication. The crew immediately began to beat their stomachs and sing, as they passed the bottle from mouth to mouth.

"How often did I wish the flask ten times the size and filled with aquafortis! I observed that the squaws drank more freely than the warriors, and again my heart was depressed, when, all at once, the report of a gun was heard at a distance. The Indians all jumped to their feet. The singing and drinking were both brought to a stand, and I saw, with inexpressible joy, the men walk off to some distance and talk to their squaws. I knew that they were consulting about me, and foresaw that the warriors would go to see what the gun meant. I expected that the squaws would be left to guard me, and it was just so. They returned, while the men took up their guns and marched off. The squaws sat down again, and in less than five minutes had my bottle up to their ugly mouths, gurgling down their throats the remains of the whiskey.

"With what pleasure did I see them becoming more and more drunk, until the liquor took such hold of them that it was quite impossible for these women to be of any more service. They tumbled down, rolled about, and began to snore. Then I, having no other chance of freeing myself from the cords that fastened me, rolled over and over towards the fire, and, after a short time, succeeded in burning them asunder. I rose on my feet, stretched my stiffened sinews, snatched up my rifle, and, for once in *my* life, spared that of the Indians. I now recollect how desirous I once or twice felt to lay open the skulls* of the wretches with my tomahawk, but when I again thought upon killing beings unprepared and unable to defend themselves, it looked like murder without need, and I gave up that idea.

"But, sir, I determined to mark the spot, and, walking to a thrifty ash sapling, I cut out of it three large chips, and ran off. I soon reached the river, crossed it, and threw myself deep into the canebrake, imitating the tracks of an Indian with my feet. It is now nearly twenty years since that happened, and more than five since I left the white settlements, which I probably might never have visited again had I not been called on as a witness in a law suit pending in Kentucky, and which I really believe would never have been settled had I not come forward and established the beginning of a certain boundary line.

"'This is the story, sir: Mr. —— moved from Virginia to Kentucky, having a large tract of land granted him in the new State. He laid claim to a certain parcel of land adjoining Green river, and as chance would have it, took for one of his corners the very ash tree on which I had made my mark and finished his survey of some thousands of acres, beginning, as it is expressed in the deed, 'at an ash marked by three distinct notches of the tomahawk.' The tree had grown much and the bark had covered the marks. Mr. —— had heard from some one all that I have already told you, and thinking I might remember the spot, but which was no longer discoverable, wrote for me to come and try at least to find the place or tree. All expenses were to be paid me and not caring much about going back to Kentucky, I started and met Mr. ——.

"After some conversation, the affair with the Indians came to my recollection. I considered for a while and began to think that after all I could find the very spot as well as the tree if it was yet standing. We mounted our horses and off we went to the Green river bottoms. After some difficulties, for you must be aware, sir, that great changes had taken place in those woods, I found at last the spot where I had crossed the river, and, waiting for the moon to rise, made for the course in which I thought the ash tree grew. On approaching the place, I felt exactly as if the Indians were there still and I a prisoner among them. We camped near what I conceived to be the spot and waited the return of day.

"At the rising of the sun I was on foot, and after a good deal of musing thought that an ash tree then in sight must be the very one on which I had made my mark. I felt as if there could be no doubt of it and mentioned my thought to Mr. ——. 'Well, Colonel Boone,' said he, 'if you think so I hope it may prove true, but we must have some witnesses. Do you stay here and I will go and bring some of the settlers whom I know.' I agreed and he trotted off, and I, to pass the time, rambled about to see if a deer was still living in the land. But, ah! sir, what a wonderful difference thirty years makes in a country! Why, at the time when I was caught by the Indians, you could not have walked out in any direction for more than a mile without shooting a buck or bear. There were then thousands of buffalo on the hills of Kentucky; the land looked as if it never would become poor, and to hunt in those days was a pleasure indeed. But when left to myself on the banks of Green river, I dare say, for the last time in my life, a few signs only of deer were to be seen, and as to a deer itself, I saw none.

"Mr. —— returned, accompanied by three gentlemen. They looked upon me as if I had been Washington himself and walked to the ash tree, which I now called my own, as if in quest of a long-lost treasure. I took an axe from one of them and cut a few chips off the bark. Still no signs were to be seen. So I cut again until I thought it was time to be cautious, and I scraped and worked away with my butcher knife, until I *did* come to where my tomahawk had left an impression in the wood. We now went regularly to work and scraped at the tree with care until *three hacks, as plain as any three notches ever were,* could be seen. Mr. ——— and the other gentlemen were astonished, and I must allow I was as much surprised as pleased myself. I made affidavit of this remarkable occurrence in presence of these gentlemen, and Mr. ——— gained his cause. I left Green river forever and came to where we now are, and, sir, I wish you good night."

CHAPTER VIII.

THE TWO SIEGES OF FORT HENRY (WHEELING.)

> The mothers of our forest land,
> Their bosoms pillowed *men;*
> And proud were they by such to stand,
> In hamlet, fort or glen:
> To load the sure old rifle,
> To run the leaden ball,
> To watch a battling husband's place,
> And fill it should he fall.

Fort Henry, surrounded by the Zane settlements, endured two memorable sieges from British-Indian forces, one in 1777 (known all along the border as the "bloody year of the three sevens,") and again in the Fall of 1782. One glance at the map will clearly reveal why Virginia and Pennsylvania always suffered so much and in common, from savage incursions. At Yellow Creek, the Ohio takes a direct southern trend for nearly one hundred miles. All west of the Ohio was wilderness and Indian country, with the chief towns on the Mad, Scioto, Sandusky and Muskingum rivers. East of the Ohio lay a belt of settlements all the way from Fort Pitt to the Kanawha, with more sparsely scattered communities lying back along the various creek valleys.

At that time this district was called Augusta county, and was claimed and considered as part of Virginia. Some of it—a narrow strip running north and south, directly east of the Ohio—is now the Virginia "Pan-Handle;" the rest is now Pennsylvania. When the confederated Indians of Ohio, therefore, wanted to make a foray, all they had to do was to set their faces towards the rising sun until they came to white settlements, which, as stated, extended south and southwesterly for over three hundred miles.

In August, 1777, General Hand, of Fort Pitt, received secret information from Isaac Zane—who, with his Indian wife, lived at the Mack-a-chack towns of Mad river—that the Northwestern Confederacy, backed by the British, were making vigorous preparations to strike a terrible blow upon some of the settlements on the Ohio. As it was uncertain exactly where this blow was to fall, the whole frontier was warned by Hand, and especially Wheeling, the most probable objective point. The settlers at the mouth of Wheeling Creek, therefore, (numbering some thirty families,) betook themselves to Fort Henry, and kept out their scouts so as to be duly warned of all hostile approaches. Fort Henry, of which, elsewhere, we give a small but faithful representation, was built in '74, on a commanding bluff overlooking the Ohio on the east, and the broad "bottom" of Wheeling Creek on the south. It was a parallelogram in shape, its outer wall being a stockade of white-oak pickets about seventeen feet high, and supported by bastions on each corner—the commandant's house, storehouse, cabins, &c., being within. The Captain's house was two stories high, with the top adapted so as to work one small cannon. No regular garrison was ever maintained at Fort Henry, but its protection depended on the rifles of the settlement about.

Colonel Ebenezer Zane's cabin and outhouses stood at a little distance from the stockade, and between it and the high wooded hill. The grounds were cleared all around so as to prevent ambushes and concealment, and to give full sweep for the one small gun and the defenders' rifles. Of course the bastions and stockade were pierced with loop or port holes to facilitate firing under cover. A rude affair enough was this fort, but suited to the times, and perfectly impregnable to all Indian enemies unless having artillery. All border defences were of the same rough but substantial nature, and none were ever taken unless captured by treachery, the absence of male defenders, or by firing the roof, &c., from the outside. A well-served cannon or two would have knocked any of them into smithereens in very short order.

On August 31st Captain Joseph Ogle, who had been out with a company of fifteen on a scout all around, returned to Fort Henry and reported no cause for danger—not a hostile red to be seen, and no sign of any. The savages, however, under command of a crafty leader, suspecting that their movements might be watched, abandoned all the beaten trails; broke up into small parties, and scattered through the woods. Thus it happened that, without discovery, they all concentrated at Bogg's Island, (two miles below Wheeling Creek,) and there crossing the Ohio, proceeded, under cover of night, to the "bottom" of Wheeling Creek, right under the fort. The hostile array consisted of near four hundred Mingoes, Shawnees and Wyandots, well supplied with arms, ammunition, &c., by Hamilton, the "British hair-buyer" and Governor of Canada. All the border books and the oldest settlers of Wheeling have asserted, most positively, that this formidable force was under command of Simon Girty, the notorious renegade, but this is such an obvious error that we marvel how it ever could have obtained currency, or how it could so long have maintained an undisturbed place in history without refutation. It is *utterly impossible* that Simon Girty could have been there as its head, because the official records at Fort Pitt show that he was then at *that* post and serving in the patriot ranks, and also that he did not desert from Fort Pitt until the Spring of the following year, 1778. The Moravian records confirm this, as Girty, Elliott, McKee and other minor deserters arrived at the Muskingum in February, 1778. If, therefore, this beleaguering force was commanded by a Girty at all, it must have been by George or James Girty, who were then living among the savages, the former being a leader of some influence. Whoever the leader was, however, he was a crafty man, as his manner of approach shows. He now disposed of his men in two lines across the creek "bottom," concealing them among the corn and high weeds.

Mason's and Ogle's Commands Cut to Pieces.

Early on the morning of September 1st, a white and a negro were out to catch horses and had not far advanced before they were fired on by a party of six savages in ambush. Boyd was killed, but the negro was permitted to return, doubtless to mislead the whites as to the number of the foe and to decoy them to their swift destruction. Captain Samuel Mason, who had the preceding evening brought his company to the fort, now sallied out with fourteen men to shake up the impudent murderers. He soon routed up the six savages and fired on them.

On the crack of the rifles the entire swarming army arose, and with horrid, blood-curdling yells rushed upon the little band. Mason at once ordered a retreat, cutting his own way through the Indian line, but most of his gallant command were hacked to pieces. Only two escaped by hiding beneath the brush and fallen timber. William Shepherd, son of Colonel David Shepherd, fort commandant, had gained Indian Spring, where now the Wheeling market house stands, when, his feet being entangled in a grape vine, he fell and was immediately dispatched with a huge war club.

A dense river fog hung over the bottom at the time and those inside the fort could neither see the effect of this disastrous conflict nor guess at the number of the foe. Captain Joseph Ogle, with a dozen trained scouts, now, with singular fatuity, sallied out to the relief of their hardpressed friends. The fierce and discordant yells of the multitudinous savages and the shrieks of the assaulted party might, it seems, have suggested prudence, but fearlessly and unfalteringly they advanced to cover the retreat of their friends and were at once beset by the screeching, murdering demons, and all but the Captain and Sergeant Ogle, Martin Wetzel and one other, were killed. In making his escape Captain Ogle secreted himself amid a cluster of tall weeds in a fence corner. While there crouched, two plumed warriors seated themselves on the fence directly above him. One of them seemed badly wounded and cried piteously with pain. Ogle saw the blood streaming down his leg and fearing discovery, kept his finger on his rifle's trigger so that he could fire on the instant, but fortunately he was unseen and the savages soon moved off.

The loss of so many of the very best men of that district was a sad blow to the little garrison—those who fell were men of iron nerve, indomitable courage and devoted patriotism. Scarcely had the groans of the wounded and dying been quieted, before the yelling savages, flourishing the many reeking scalps, crowded about the fort and demanded an immediate surrender. They advanced in two divisions, with drum, fife and British colors—the right being distributed among the cabins on the bluff which stood between the fort and the high hill back, and the left being defiled beneath and under cover of the river bank, close under the fort. Their leader, whoever he was, shouted out aloud Hamilton's proclamation and offered protection in case of a surrender; if not, an immediate and indiscriminate massacre.

What was to be done! The little garrison now numbered only ten or twelve men and boys. Two-thirds of their original number, and the very best and bravest among them, had been lost. Surely they might have been excused for making, then, the best terms they could; but no, this heroic little Spartan band resolved to hold out against this overwhelming army. Colonel Shepherd at once replied: "Sir, we have consulted our wives and children, and *all* have resolved to perish at their posts rather than place themselves under the protection of such savages with *you* at their head." The leader attempted a reply, but a shot from the fort put a stop to further words.

Business now commenced in earnest. A tremendous rush by a large body of Indians was at once made. They attempted to force the gates and to try the strength of the pickets by a united effort. Failing to make any impression, and suffering from the unerring fire from the port holes, the reds were drawn off a few yards and a general fire was commenced on the port holes. An unintermittent hail of bullets was kept up during most of the day and part of the night, but without any sensible effect. About noon a temporary withdrawal took place, and the heroic and exhausted little garrison prepared for renewed resistance.

To each was assigned his or her post. Of the women, some were required to run bullets, others to get ready the ammunition, and others yet to cool and hand up the guns. Two of them actually took their position at the port holes, dealing death to many a dusky warrior. About three P. M. the Indians returned to the attack with redoubled fury, half their number distributing themselves among the cabins, behind fallen trees, &c., while the other half advanced along the base of the hill south of the fort and commenced a vigorous fire. This was to draw the few and overworked defenders to that quarter, while now a strong and united rush was made from the cabins on the bluff, and a tremendous effort made to force an entrance with heavy timber, but all failed, and a number of the most daring warriors were picked off by sharpshooters. Several similar attempts were made during the afternoon, but all were alike futile. Maddened and chagrined by these repeated discomfitures, the savages sullenly withdrew to their coverts until night. Just before their retirement, Basil Duke, Colonel Shepherd's son-in-law, who had been stationed at Beech Bottom Block-house, rode rapidly up to the fort, and had almost succeeded in gaining entrance, but was, unfortunately, shot dead in full view of the garrison he had so gallantly attempted to aid.

About nine, the savages reappeared, making the night hideous with their demoniac yells and the heavens lurid and sulphurous with their discharges of musketry. All lights in the fort had been carefully extinguished, and thus seeing well their foes while they themselves remained unseen, many a stalwart warrior was made to bite the sod before the unerring aim of the practiced marksmen of the border. Repeated attempts were made during that night of horror to storm, as well as to fire, the fort, but all signally failed through the heroism and sleepless vigilance of those within. Night passed only to bring another renewal of the attack. But the assaulters begin now to despair of success. Savages do not take well to such slow work. They would rather operate by stealth in small parties and creep upon such places as can be easily taken, or where the inmates can be ambushed and lured to destruction with but little loss to themselves, and so, after killing all the cattle, and firing almost all the buildings outside of the fort, including those of Colonel Zane, they were preparing for one last final effort, when a relief party of fourteen from Holliday's Fort, under Colonel Andrew Swearengen, landed secretly under the river bank from a pirogue, and succeeded in making an undiscovered entrance.

Happy and timely relief to the feeble and overtasked little band of defenders! Shortly after, Major Samuel McColloch, at the head of forty gallant mounted men from Short Creek, put in an appearance, and made an impetuous rush for the great gate, which was joyfully thrown open to admit them. The enemy made a counter rush to cut them off. All, however, succeeded in making good their entrance but the Major himself, who, delaying outside until every man of his command should enter, was surrounded and obliged to fly for his life. His mad ride for life; his extraordinary leap on horseback over Wheeling hill, and his fortunate escape, we have related elsewhere.

If the enemy could not overcome the feeble little garrison of ten men and boys, what chance had they now when so powerfully reinforced? They at once "accepted the situation," and after firing a few additional shots at the staunch little fort, "they folded their tents, like the Arabs, and quietly stole away." It has been conjectured that the enemy lost in this protracted attack from forty to fifty killed and wounded. The loss of the whites, in sallies, &c., has already been stated. Not a single person, however, was killed within the fort, and only one slightly wounded. This siege was followed, about three weeks after, by the

Deplorable Ambuscade of Foreman's Party.

Captain William Foreman, a brave and meritorious officer, but totally unfit for Indian warfare, organized a volunteer company in Hampshire county, Va., and came west to Wheeling, in the Fall of '77, to help fight the savages. After the withdrawal of the Indians from the siege of Wheeling, just related, the impression was general that they had returned to their towns.

On September 26th, a smoke was noticed at Wheeling, in the direction of Grave Creek, some twelve miles below, which caused an apprehension that the Indians might be burning the stockade and houses of Mr. Tomlinson. In order to ascertain this fact, and afford protection if any were necessary, Captain Foreman with his company, and a few experienced scouts, were dispatched by Colonel Shepherd for this purpose.

The party proceeded without interruption to Grave Creek, and found all safe. Remaining over night, they started early on the following morning to return. When they had reached the lower end of Grave Creek Narrows, some of the more experienced frontiermen suggested the expediency of leaving the river bottom, and returning by way of the ridge. The commander, however, hooted at the idea of so much caution, and ordered the party to proceed. The order was obeyed by his own men, including several of the volunteer scouts, but some declined to go with him, and one of these was a man named Lynn, whose great experience as a spy, added to his sagacity and judgment, should at least have rendered his opinions entitled to weight. His apprehensions were, that the Indians, if lurking about, had watched the movements of the party, and would most likely attack them at some point on the river. He said that, in all probability, they had been on the opposite side of the river and noticed the party go down; that they had crossed during the night, and most probably were at that time lying in ambush for their return. How fearfully were his apprehensions realized!

During the interchange of opinions between Foreman and Lynn, a man, Robert Harkness, a relative of Mr. Tomlinson, sat on a log near the parties, and often said that the controversy at times ran high. Foreman, who prided himself on being a thoroughly disciplined officer, was not disposed to yield to the suggestions of a rough backwoodsman. Lynn, on the other hand, convinced of the fatal error which the other seemed determined to commit, could not but remonstrate with all the power of persuasion at his command. Finally, when the order to march was given, Lynn, with some six or eight others, struck up the hill side, while Foreman with his company pursued the path along the base.

Nothing of importance occurred until the party reached the extreme upper end of the Narrows. Just where the bottom begins to widen, those in front had their attention drawn to a display of Indian trinkets, beads, bands, &c., strewn in profusion along the path. With a natural curiosity but a great lack of sagacity, the entire party gathered about those who had picked up the articles of decoy, and whilst thus standing in a compact group, looking at the beads, &c., two lines of Indians stretched across the path, one above and the other below, and a large body of them simultaneously arose from beneath the bank, and opened upon the devoted party a most deadly and destructive fire. The river hill rises at this point with great boldness, presenting an almost insurmountable barrier. Still, those of the party who escaped the first discharge, attempted to rush up the acclivity, and some with success. But the savages pursued and killed several.

At the first fire Captain Foreman and most of his party, including his two sons, fell dead. The loss is supposed to have been about twenty, including the Captain. When Lynn and his party heard the guns, they rushed down the side of the hill, hallooing as though they were five times as numerous. This had the effect of restraining the savages in pursuit, and perhaps saved the lives of many.

Of those who escaped up the hill were Robert Harkness and John Collins. The former, in pulling himself up by a sapling, had the bark knocked into his face with a ball from an Indian's gun. Collins was shot through the left thigh, breaking the bone and completely disabling him. Lynn and his companions carried him to a spring, said to have been just over the hill, and throwing together their supply of provisions, left him in a sheltered position, promising to send a messenger on the following day with a horse. Those who were so fortunate as to escape this terrible affair, made their way in safety to Wheeling. Collins, the wounded man, was taken off on horseback the second night, and the rest were buried in one grave.

THE SECOND SIEGE OF WHEELING IN 1782.

The Fort Henry settlement had another hostile visitation from about a hundred savages in '81, but having received due warning of the affair from Fort Pitt, but little harm was done. After destroying Colonel Zane's house and all other property they could, they departed as mysteriously as they came.

It was widely different, however, the next year. On the 11th of September, a body of three hundred Indians and a company of fifty British, known as the "Queen's Rangers," led by Captain Pratt, marched boldly up to the fort and peremptorily demanded an immediate surrender. It is said the whole body was under command of George Girty, but this is manifestly an error. *Simon* Girty himself, it is much more probable, was the chief. Girty promised all who would give up "the best protection King George could afford," but his summons was only scouted and he himself jeered at by the dauntless little garrison.

Girty delayed his attack till night. All was bustle and activity within the fort. The women were busy running bullets, securing children and making ready for the expected wounded, while the men, armed with knife, spear, rifle and tomahawk, made ready for an obstinate defence. The fighting strength, men and boys, did not exceed eighteen, all told, while the women and children were about forty.

Shortly before the enemy appeared, a pirogue loaded with cannon ball from Fort Pitt, designed for Louisville, had arrived at Wheeling, and a Mr. Sullivan, who was in charge, being a shrewd and experienced soldier, well versed in Indian cunning, was selected, with Silas Zane, to manage the siege. The regular commandant, Captain Boggs, had, on the first intimation of an enemy, ridden off to the nearest forts for succor.

At sundown Girty made his second and last summons, swearing if surrender was delayed, that the fort would be stormed and every soul massacred. He was answered with shouts of defiance; the defenders said they remembered too well the fate of Colonel Crawford to give up to him and be butchered like dogs. Girty replied that their doom was sealed, as he had just taken their express messenger and all hope of succor might as well be given up. "What kind of a looking man was he?" shouted Sullivan. "A fine, smart, active young fellow," answered the outlaw chief. "*That's* a cursed lie," snapped out Sullivan, "for he was an old, gray-headed man."

Girty, finding all attempts to intimidate vain, led on his motley army and attempted to carry the fort by storm. He made some furious dashes, but the gates and stockades were too strong. The small French cannon, mounted on the second story of the Captain's house, was thought to be a *dummy* or "Quaker Gun," and this, because at the 1777 siege the besieged had then no real cannon, but *did* mount a wooden one. The besiegers mocked at this piece and dared the garrison to shoot it off. They were soon accommodated, for just when the whole white and red mob were pressing up in dense columns, the little "bull dog" was fired, cutting a wide passage through the ranks of the affrighted savages. Captain Pratt, who had heard real guns before, now shouted out to his swarthy companions, "Stand back! Stand back! By —— there's no wood about that!" and there wasn't.

The enemy gave way at the first fire, but Girty told off his force in two small parties and attacked at different points; now attempting to storm it; now to fire it, and now to destroy its defenders through the port holes. The siege was thus vigorously kept up the whole night, and a terrible night it was to the plucky but exhausted little garrison, who had no moments' rest. One of the bastions having given way, but two now were occupied, and these by turn. The women during all this trying time, proved themselves heroines indeed. They stood at their posts like soldiers of a dozen campaigns, cooling and loading the rifles for the men. No timid shrieks escaped them; no maidenly fears caused them to shrink from their self-imposed task.

A WOODEN MONSTER—BETTY ZANE'S "GUNPOWDER EXPLOIT."

At an early hour the savages descried the pirogue with the cannon ball, and a happy thought possessed them. Why not rig up a cannon and utilize all these missiles! No sooner thought than they set to work. Procuring a stout log of sufficient size and length, these simple-minded men secretly split it open in the woods, hollowed it out, and then fastened it securely together again with chains and bars from Reikart's blacksmith shop, which stood outside the walls. The impromptu piece was then heavily charged with ball and powder, and first announcing that their cannon had at length arrived, the torch was applied, when whiz! boom! chebang! the whole contraption blew up, carrying with it a half-dozen gaping savages, who had clustered about to witness the discharge. A wooden gun was not tried again.

During the night a large number of Indians posted themselves in the loft of a house which stood thirty or forty yards north of the fort, and amused themselves by dancing and yelling, making night hideous with their discordant revelry. Thinking to dislodge them, several ineffectual attempts were made with grape shot, but that failing, full-sized ball were fired, which cut off a sleeper, and let the whole mass down together. The cannon was fired some sixteen times during the first night, and must have done considerable execution.

It will be remembered that Colonel Ebenezer Zane's cabin and outhouses stood outside and to the north of the fort. His property had been burned in the 1777 siege, and very much damaged at the Indian visitation of the year before, and he resolved that if Indians came again, he would defend his property to the last. To this end, he had fortified it, so as to make it at least bullet-proof and very dangerous of approach. In the house with him were now several members of his family, including his young and beautiful sister Betty, and a black servant by the name of Sam. So effectually had they defended Zane's property, that it was, as yet, safe, but they had run out of powder, and none to be had except from the fort.

It was now that an event occurred much celebrated in border chronicles, and which goes by the name of "Betty Zane's Gunpowder Exploit." It has been told in various ways: the credit has been given to different persons, and the event attributed to different years. The common version, taken originally from Doddridge and Withers, is that the stock of gunpowder in the fort having been exhausted, it was determined to send for a keg of powder known to be in the house of Ebenezer Zane, about sixty yards distant from the fort. The Colonel explained the necessity to his men, and unwilling to order men on so hazardous an expedition, inquired if any would volunteer. Three or four young men promptly stepped forward for the desperate service. Zane said the weak state of the garrison would not allow of the absence of more than one, and a discussion now ensued as to who was to be the one. At this crisis, Elizabeth, a young, lively and spirited sister of the Colonel's, who had been carefully educated at Philadelphia, and had lately returned home, stepped boldly forward and desired that *she* might be allowed to execute the service. The proposition appeared at first so extravagant that it at once met with a peremptory refusal, but she earnestly renewed and pressed the request, and all the remonstrances of her relatives failed to dissuade her. Her main argument was that the garrison was very weak; that none of the defenders could be spared; that she was as fleet as any of them, and that if it were her doom to fall, her loss would not be felt.

Her petition was at length granted, and the gate opened for her to pass out. The opening of the gate arrested the attention of several Indians straggling or lurking about, and their eyes were fastened upon the young girl as she bounded across the interval, but the contemptuous expression of "squaw! squaw!" arose, and she was allowed to pass without special hindrance. When she reappeared, however, with the powder in her arms, the savages, suspecting by this time the nature of her hazardous errand, rushed tumultuously after her, elevated their pieces and fired a volley at the fearless young girl as she ran like a deer across the exposed green and bounded into the arms of those who stood ready to receive her. All, happily, flew wide of the mark, and the heroic Betty Zane had the honor of saving the garrison.

That some such event as the above really happened admits of no question, but as to who did the deed, or whether or not there were *two* gunpowder exploits, is a serious matter of doubt. All the old books and the original pioneers gave the credit of the exploit to Betty Zane. The chief error, however, in the old versions of the affair, lay in stating that the powder was wanted at the fort, and that it was obtained from Zane's house. The fact is directly contrary, and far more in accordance with probability. The powder was exhausted at Zane's house on account of its prolonged defence, and a messenger was obliged, as would be natural, to go to the fort for a new supply.

To this day, at Wheeling, there exists doubt and controversy as to who performed the "Gunpowder Exploit." Kiernan, Withers and De Hass all give the credit of the feat to Elizabeth Zane, but the latter admits that the more he prosecuted his inquiries, the more the mystery thickened. The counter claim is made by the famous Mrs. Cruger, *nee* Lydia Boggs, on behalf of Molly Scott. She is a very important witness; one entirely reliable, and had unusual opportunities of knowing, since she was the daughter of Captain Boggs, the commandant at the time, and helped to serve the powder.

Mrs. Cruger, so late as 1849, made an affidavit in relation to the siege of 1782, which states, in effect, that there were three hundred Indians and fifty British soldiers, known as the Queen's Rangers, all under command of the renegade Girty; that, during a temporary withdrawal of the foe, those within the fort observed a female leaving Colonel Zane's house and making for the southern gate. She entered in safety, and "that person was none other than Molly Scott, and the object of her mission was to procure powder for those who defended Zane's dwelling. The undersigned was then in her seventeenth year; saw McHy Scott enter the fort; assisted her in getting the powder; saw her leave, and avers, *most positively*, that she, and she alone, accomplished the feat referred to." She swears, further, that as her father had left for aid at the commencement of the attack, her mother directed her, Lydia, as being the oldest child at home, to go with Molly Scott to the storehouse and give her what ammunition she wanted; that she "assisted said Molly Scott in placing the powder in her apron," and that Elizabeth Zane, whom she knew as a woman brave, generous and single-hearted, was at that time at the residence of her father, near Washington, Pa. Mrs. Cruger states, further, that at the time, the achievement was not considered extraordinary; that those were times when woman's heart was nerved to "do or die," and that more than one within that little stockade would have unhesitatingly done the same thing, if needed.

This affidavit, coming from a reliable living authority, and one personally assisting in the famed "exploit," would seem to settle the question so far as the siege of 1782 is concerned. We leave the matter for readers to decide, merely adding the following, from De Hass: "The proof in favor of Elizabeth Zane is most abundant. It is barely probable there may have been *two* gunpowder incidents. One of the parties may have carried powder at the first, and the other at the second. This seems the only way in which the conflicting claims can be reconciled."

The enemy made more than twenty attempts to fire the stockade by heaping bundles of hemp against the walls and setting fire to them; but, fortunately, the hemp was wet and would not burn readily. Dry wood and other combustibles succeeded no better. Night now closed in, and the attack was maintained without intermission until daybreak. Lydia Boggs (afterwards Mrs. General Cruger) was an inmate of the fort during the whole siege, and was constantly employed in moulding bullets and serving out ammunition. She says that the pickets were so decayed in places, they could not have withstood a united pressure from the foe, and that during this night many, at one corner, where the hottest fire had been kept up, gave way and fell; but, fortunately, the mishap was concealed from the enemy by a heavy growth of peach trees on the outside; also, that just before day, some one who was seen stealthily approaching the sally gate, was fired upon and wounded. The piteous cries from the wound and fright, induced the besieged to let him in, and he proved to be a negro, who asserted he was a deserter, and who gave much information of the enemy, true or false. Thinking he was only a spy or decoy, the intruder was handcuffed and committed to Lydia's care, who stood ready to tomahawk him in case he attempted an escape.

Shortly after sunrise the next day the enemy, despairing of success, commenced killing all the cattle, burning cabins, &c. Very soon a long, peculiar whoop from an Indian spy, who had been sent out to watch the approach of any relief party, was understood by the well-trained hunters in the fort to mean a signal for retreat. Scarcely had the echoes of his shrill voice ceased among the Ohio hills before the entire hostile array moved rapidly to the river, and so the long and trying siege was over. In less than an hour, Captains Boggs, Swearengen and Williamson rode up with seventy mounted men, and great was the rejoicing of the gallant but exhausted little garrison.

After raising the siege, a large division of the enemy marched against Rice's Fort, on Buffalo Creek. The savages surrounded the fort and demanded a surrender, crying "Give up! give up! too many Injun! Injun too big! no kill!" But the defenders shouted bravely back, "come on, you cowards! Show us your yellow hides, and we'll make holes in them for you!" This, however, was only a game of *bluff*, for the whole garrison consisted of only six, the rest having gone over the mountains to buy powder. The savages now set fire to a barn, and by its light kept up a constant fire until morning, when, finding the little fort prepared for defence, they decamped, having lost four warriors— three killed by the very first fire from the port holes.

THE NORTHWESTERN CAMPAIGN.

The surrender, in October, 1781, of Lord Cornwallis' army to the French-American forces at Yorktown, was generally deemed the finish of our Revolutionary war, but it was really only "the beginning of the end." It is true that in November of the next year provisional articles of peace had been signed at Paris; that on the 20th of January following an armistice followed; that on April 19th, 1783, peace was proclaimed to our armies, and that, on the 3d of September, a definite treaty was concluded; yet still, for many years to come, hostilities were virtually kept up between the outposts of the two nations. On the pretext that the provisions of the treaty of peace were not complied with by the United States, the British still held on to their forts in the North and Northwest, and continued to hold them down to 1796.

Meanwhile, hostilities with the Indians were, with smaller and greater intervals and violence, still kept up. In 1782, as stated, occurred the massacre of the Moravians, which unhallowed atrocity was followed by Crawford's expedition and defeat, the invasion of Kentucky and the battle of Blue Licks, the second siege of Wheeling and the burning of Hannastown, Pennsylvania. For several years afterwards the Indians, led by tory renegades like Girty, Elliott and McKee, and instigated and supplied by the British from their forts on the Maumee and Detroit, kept up their harassing depredations. In 1787 the northwest territory had been organized, and General Arthur St. Clair appointed Governor. For three years the seat of this territorial government was located at Marietta—the first American settlement made in Ohio—but in 1790 Governor St. Clair, with the officers of the infant government, descended the Ohio and located at Fort Washington, then growing into the town of Cincinnati.

The troubles with the western tribes, meanwhile, had grown so grave and their depredations had became so grievous and harassing as to demand the most serious notice of our government. Then commenced what is known in our history as the Northwestern Campaign, embracing the three separate expeditions of General Harmar, in 1790, of General St. Clair, in '91, and of Mad Anthony Wagne, in '94, his victory at the battle of the Fallen Timbers, forever crushing the power and bursting asunder the coherence of the Indian Confederacy.

EXPEDITION OF GENERAL HARMAR AGAINST THE MIAMI TOWNS.

On the last day of September, 1790, General Harmar left Fort Washington with a raw, undisciplined and badly-equipped force of fourteen hundred men, consisting of three hundred regulars, and the rest Kentucky and Pennsylvania militia. His object was the Miami villages. He had many brave and experienced fighters under him, but the command, as a whole, lacked compactness, was ill-assorted and all proper *esprit du corps* prevented by jealousies and dissensions. The country was rough, swampy, and in many places almost impassable, so that seventeen days were consumed before the main body could come within striking distance of the enemy. In the meantime, the great scarcity of provisions rendered it necessary for the General to sweep the forest with numerous small detachments, and as the woods swarmed with roving bands of Indians, most of these parties were cut off.

At length, the main body, considerably reduced by this petty warfare, came within a few miles of their towns. Here the General ordered Captain Armstrong, at the head of thirty regulars, and Colonel Hardin, of Kentucky, with several hundred militia, to advance and reconnoitre. In the execution of this order they suddenly found themselves in the presence of a superior number of Indians, who suddenly arose from the bushes and opened a heavy fire upon them. The militia instantly gave way; while the regulars, accustomed to more orderly movements, attempted a regular retreat. The enemy rushed upon them, tomahawk in hand, and completely surrounded them. The regulars attempted to open a passage with the bayonet, but in vain. They were all destroyed, with the exception of their Captain and one Lieutenant.

Captain Armstrong was remarkably stout and active, and succeeded in breaking through the enemy's line, although not without receiving several severe wounds. Finding himself hard pressed, he plunged into a deep and miry swamp, where he lay concealed during the whole night, within two hundred yards of the Indian camp, and witnessed the dances and joyous festivity with which they celebrated their victory. The Lieutenant (Hartshorn) escaped by accidentally stumbling over a log and falling into a pit, where he lay concealed by the rank grass which grew around him. The loss of the militia was very trifling. Notwithstanding this severe check, Harmar advanced with the main body upon their villages, which he found deserted and in flames, the

Indians having fired them with their own hands. Here he found several hundred acres of corn, which was completely destroyed. He then advanced upon the adjoining villages, which he found deserted and burned as the first had been. Having destroyed all the corn which he found, the army commenced its retreat from the Indian country, supposing the enemy sufficiently intimidated.

After marching about ten miles on the homeward route, General Harmar received information which induced him to suppose that a body of Indians had returned and taken possession of the village which he had just left. He detached, therefore, eighty regular troops, under the orders of Major Wyllys, and nearly the whole of his militia, under Colonel Hardin, with orders to return to the village and destroy such of the enemy as presented themselves. The detachment accordingly counter-marched and proceeded, with all possible dispatch, to the appointed spot, fearful only that the enemy might hear of their movement and escape before they could come up. The militia, in loose order, took the advance; the regulars, moving in a hollow square, brought up the rear. Upon the plain in front of the town, a number of Indians were seen, between whom and the militia a sharp action commenced. After a few rounds, with considerable effect upon both sides, the savages fled in disorder, and were eagerly and impetuously pursued by the militia, who, in the ardor of the chase, were drawn into the woods to a considerable distance from the regulars.

Suddenly, from the opposite quarter, several hundred Indians appeared, rushing with loud yells upon the unsupported regulars. Major Wyllys, who was a brave and experienced officer, formed his men in a square, and endeavored to gain a more favorable spot of ground, but was prevented by the desperate impetuosity with which the enemy assailed him. Unchecked by the murderous fire which was poured upon them from the different sides of the square, they rushed in masses up to the points of the bayonets, hurled their tomahawks with fatal accuracy, and putting aside the bayonets with their hands, or clogging them with their bodies, they were quickly mingled with the troops, and handled their long knives with destructive effect. In two minutes the bloody struggle was over. Major Wyllys fell, together with seventy-three privates and one Lieutenant. One Captain, one Ensign, and seven privates— three of whom were wounded—were the sole survivors of this short but desperate encounter.

The Indian loss was nearly equal, as they sustained several heavy fires which the closeness of their masses rendered very destructive, and as they rushed upon the bayonets of the troops with the most astonishing disregard to their own safety. Their object was to overwhelm the regulars before the militia could return to their support, and it was as boldly executed as it had been finely conceived. In a short time the militia returned from the pursuit of the flying party, which had decoyed them to a distance; but it was now too late to retrieve the fortune of the day. After some sharp skirmishing, they effected their retreat to the main body, with the loss of one hundred and eight killed and twenty-eight wounded. This dreadful slaughter so reduced the strength and spirits of Harmar's army that he was happy in being permitted to retreat unmolested, having totally failed in accomplishing the objects of the expedition, and, by obstinately persevering in the ruinous plan of acting in detachments, having thrown away the lives of more than half of his regular force. This abortive expedition served only to encourage the enemy and to give additional rancor to their incursions.

The Singular Adventure of Jackson Johonnet.

Among Harmar's soldiers was a gay young fellow from Connecticut, Jackson Johonnet by name, who, being entrapped by a Boston recruiting officer, enlisted in a company for the West, and soon found himself descending the Ohio from Pittsburgh in a flatboat. On the tenth day of the march, Johonnet, who had conceived the idea that war was but a succession of battles and triumphs, accompanied by gay music, splendid uniforms and showy parades, awoke from his dream. Hard marching, terrible work, gnawing hunger and constant exposure were his daily portion, but still he conducted himself so well that, having been promoted to the rank of sergeant, he was sent out on an exploring expedition at the head of ten men. Being all about as accomplished as himself in Indian warfare, they were quickly decoyed into an ambush, made prisoners, bound and secured, and driven before their captors like a herd of bullocks, in long marches, without a morsel of food.

On the second day George Aikens, an Irishman, was unable to endure his sufferings any longer, and sunk under his pack in the middle of the path. They instantly scalped him as he lay, and, stripping him naked, pricked him with their knives in the most sensitive parts of the body until they had aroused him to a consciousness of his situation, when they tortured him to death in the usual manner.

The march then recommenced, and the wretched prisoners, faint and famished as they were, were so shocked at the fate of their companion, that they bore up for eight days under all their sufferings. On the ninth, however, they reached a small village, where crowds of both sexes came out to meet them, with shrieks and yells which filled them with terror. Here they were compelled, as usual, to run the gauntlet, and as they were much worn down by hunger and fatigue, four of the party, viz: Durgee, Forsythe, Deloy, and Benton, all of New England, were unable to reach the council house, but fainted in the midst of the course. The boys and squaws instantly fell upon them, and put them to death by torture.

Here they remained in close confinement and upon very scanty diet for several days, in the course of which the news of Harmar's defeat arrived. Piles of scalps, together with canteens, sashes, military hats, etc., were brought into the village, and several white women and children were taken through the town on their way to the villages farther west. At the same time, four more of his companions were led off to the western villages, and never heard of afterwards. Himself and a corporal, named Sackville, were now the only survivors. They remained in close confinement two weeks longer. Their rations were barely sufficient to sustain life, and upon the receipt of any unpleasant intelligence, they were taken out, whipped severely, and compelled to run the gauntlet.

At length, on the fourteenth night of their confinement, they determined to make an effort to escape. Sackville had concealed a sharp penknife in a secret pocket, which the Indians had been unable to discover. They were guarded by four warriors and one old hag of seventy, whose temper was as crooked as her person. The prisoners having been securely bound, the warriors lay down about midnight to sleep, ordering the old squaw to sit up during the rest of the night. Their guns stood in the corner of the hut, and their tomahawks, as usual, were attached to their sides. Their hopes of escape were founded upon the probability of eluding the vigilance of the hag, cutting their cords, and either avoiding or destroying their guard. The snoring of the warriors quickly announced them asleep, and the old squaw hung in a drowsy attitude over the fire. Sackville cautiously cut his own cords, and, after a few minutes' delay, succeeded in performing the same office for Jackson.

But their work was scarcely begun yet. It was absolutely necessary that the old squaw should fall asleep, or be *silenced in some other way*, before they could either leave the hut or attack the sleeping warriors. They waited impatiently for half an hour, but perceiving that, although occasionally dozing, she would rouse herself at short intervals and regard them suspiciously, they exchanged looks of intelligence (being afraid even to whisper) and prepared for the decisive effort. Jackson suddenly sprang up as silently as possible, and grasping the old woman by the throat, drew her head back with violence, when Sackville, who had watched his movements attentively, instantly cut her throat from ear to ear. A short, gurgling moan was the only sound which escaped her, as the violence with which Jackson grasped her throat effectually prevented her speaking.

The sleepers were not awakened, although they appeared somewhat disturbed at the noise; and the two adventurers, seizing each a rifle, struck at the same moment with such fury as to disable two of their enemies. The other two instantly sprang to their feet, but before they could draw their tomahawks, or give the alarm, they were prostrated by the blows of the white men, who attacked them at the moment that they had gained their feet. Their enemies, although stunned, were not yet dead. They drew their tomahawks from their sides, therefore, and striking each Indian repeatedly upon the head, completed the work by piercing the heart of each with his own scalping knife. Selecting two rifles from the corner, together with their usual appendages, and taking such provisions as the hut afforded, they left the village as rapidly as possible, and, fervently invoking the protection of heaven, committed themselves to the wilderness.

Neither of them were good woodsmen, nor were either of them expert hunters. They attempted a southeastern course, however, as nearly as they could ascertain it, but were much embarrassed by the frequent recurrence of impassable bogs, which compelled them to change their course, and greatly retarded their progress. Knowing that the pursuit would be keen and persevering, they resorted to every method of baffling their enemies. They waded down many streams, and occasionally surmounted rocky precipices, which, under other circumstances, nothing could have induced them to attempt. Their sufferings from hunger were excessive, as they were so indifferently skilled in hunting as to be unable to kill a sufficient quantity of game, although the woods abounded with deer, beaver and buffalo.

AN ASSAULT UPON A QUARTETTE OF SAVAGES—DESPERATE COMBAT.

On the fourth day, about ten o'clock, they came to a fine spring, where they halted and determined to prepare their breakfast. Before kindling a fire, however, Sackville, either upon some vague suspicion of the proximity of an enemy, or from some other cause, thought proper to ascend an adjoining hillock and reconnoitre the ground around the spring. No measure was ever more providential. Jackson presently beheld him returning cautiously and silently to the spring, and being satisfied from his manner that danger was at hand, he held his rifle in readiness for action at a moment's warning. Sackville presently rejoined him with a countenance in which anxiety and resolution were strikingly blended. Jackson eagerly inquired the cause of his alarm. His companion, in a low voice, replied that they were within one hundred yards of four Indian warriors, who were reposing upon the bank of the little rivulet on the other side of the hillock; that they were about kindling a fire in order to prepare their breakfast, and that two white men lay bound hand and foot within twenty feet of them.

He added that the whites were evidently prisoners, exposed to the same dreadful fate which *they* had just escaped; and concluded by declaring that, if Jackson would stand by him faithfully, he was determined to rescue them or perish in the attempt. Jackson gave him his hand and expressed his readiness to accompany him. Sackville then looked carefully to the priming of his gun, loosened his knife in the sheath, and desired Jackson to follow him, without making the slightest noise.

They, accordingly, moved in a stooping posture up a small and bushy ravine, which conducted them to the top of the gentle hill. When near the summit, they threw themselves flat upon the ground, and crawled into a thick cluster of whortleberry bushes, from which they had a fair view of the enemy. The Indians had not changed their position, but one of the white men was sitting up, and displayed the countenance of a young man, apparently about twenty-five, pale, haggard and exhausted. Two Indians, with uplifted tomahawks, sat within three feet of him. One lay at full length upon the ground, while the remaining one was in the act of lighting a fire.

Sackville cocked his gun, and in a low voice directed Jackson to fire at one of the guards, who, from the quantity of beads and silver about his head, appeared to be a chief, while he selected the other guard for a mark. Each presented at the same moment, took a steady aim, and fired. Both Indians fell—the chief shot dead, the other mortally wounded. The other two Indians squatted in the grass like terrified partridges when the hawk hovers over them, and lay still and motionless. Sackville and Jackson reloaded their guns as rapidly as possible, and shifted their position a few paces in order to obtain a better view of the enemy. In the meantime, the two Indians cautiously elevated their heads above the grass, and glanced rapidly around in order to observe from what quarter the fatal shots were discharged. The thin wreaths of smoke which curled above the bushes where our adventurers lay, betrayed their hiding place to the enemy. Before they could take advantage of it, however, they were ready to fire again, and this second volley proved fatal to one of their enemies, who lay without motion, but the other was only slightly wounded, and endeavored to reach the bushes upon the opposite site of the brook.

Sackville and Jackson now sprang to their feet and rushed upon him, but the desperate savage shot Sackville through the heart, as he advanced, and flourished his tomahawk so menacingly at Jackson, that he was compelled to pause and reload his gun. The savage seized this opportunity to grasp the two rifles belonging to the Indians who had been first killed, and Jackson, in consequence, was compelled to retreat to the friendly shelter of the bushes, which he had too hastily abandoned. At this instant the two prisoners, having burst the cords which confined them, sprang to their feet and ran towards the bushes for protection. Before they could reach them, however, the Indian shot one dead, and fired his last gun at the other, but without effect. Jackson having loaded again, fired upon their desperate enemy and wounded him in the neck, from which he could see the blood spouting in a stream. Nothing daunted, the Indian rapidly reloaded his gun and again fired without effect.

The prisoner who had escaped now seized Sackville's gun, and he and Johonnet, having reloaded, once more left the bushes and advanced upon their wounded enemy. The savage, although much exhausted from loss of blood, sat up at their approach, and, flourishing a tomahawk in each hand, seemed at least determined to die game. Johonnet was anxious to take him alive, but was prevented by his companion, who, leveling his gun as he advanced, shot his adversary through the head, and thus put an end to the conflict. It was a melancholy victory to the survivors. Johonnet had lost his gallant comrade, and the rescued white man had to lament the death of his fellow captive. The last Indian had certainly inflicted a heavy penalty upon his enemies, and died amply revenged. The rescued prisoner proved to be George Sexton, of Newport, Rhode Island, a private in Harmar's army.

Fortunately for Johonnet, his new comrade was an excellent woodsman, and very readily informed his deliverer of their present situation, and of the proper course to steer. He said, that in company with three others, he had been taken by a party of Wabash Indians, in the neighborhood of Fort Jefferson; that two of his comrades having sunk under their sufferings, had been tomahawked and scalped upon the spot; that himself and his dead companion had been in hourly expectation of a similar fate, and concluded with the warmest expressions of gratitude for the gallantry with which he had been rescued. So lively, indeed, was his sense of obligation, that he would not permit Jackson to carry his own baggage, nor would he suffer him to watch more than three hours in the twenty-four. On the following day they fortunately fell in with a small detachment from Fort Jefferson, by which they were safely conducted to the fort.

THE DISASTROUS DEFEAT OF GENERAL ST. CLAIR.

> Fought eye to eye and hand to hand,
>   Alas! t'was but to die!
> In vain the rifle's deadly flash
> Scorch'd eagle plume and wampum sash,
>   The hatchet hissed on high;
> And down they fell in crimson heaps,
> Like the ripe corn the sickle reaps.

The ignominious failure of Harmar's expedition made a deep and very unpleasant impression upon the whole country. The depredations of the Indians, by consequence, became more flagrant and intolerable than ever. The delegates from Western Virginia memorialized the State for some protection to their exposed line of frontier nearly four hundred miles long. A demand for a new and larger expedition grew so strong and general, that in March, '91, Congress passed an Act for another regiment and for further protection of the frontiers, and President Washington appointed General St. Clair Commander-in-Chief, and authorized a new expedition of no less than three thousand men. In the meantime, two smaller and preliminary expeditions were dispatched *immediately*, one of eight hundred Kentuckians, under General Charles Scott, against the Wea towns on the Wabash and another of about six hundred, under Colonel Wilkinson, to destroy the towns on the Eel river; both were destructive and exasperating, but accomplished nothing definite. The burning of towns, crops and the captivity of their women and children only made the savages more desperate, and the chiefs, Little Turtle, Miami; Blue Jacket, Shawnee, and Buckongahelas, Delaware, were busy forming a new and strong Indian Confederacy.

General Arthur St. Clair was, as stated, Governor of the Northwestern Territory, and had generally ranked high as an officer of courage and patriotism, but had been more uniformly unfortunate than any other officer in the American service. He had commanded at Ticonderoga, in the Spring of 1777, and had conducted one of the most disastrous retreats which occurred during the Revolutionary war. Notwithstanding his repeated misfortunes, he still commanded the respect of his brother officers, and the undiminished confidence of Washington. He was now selected as the person most capable of restoring the American affairs in the Northwest, and was placed at the head of a regular force, amounting to near fifteen hundred men, well furnished with artillery, and was empowered to call out such reinforcements of militia as might be necessary. Cincinnati, as usual, was the place of rendezvous.

In October, 1791, an army was assembled at that place, greatly superior, in numbers, officers and equipments, to any which had yet appeared in the West. The regular force was composed of three complete regiments of infantry, two companies of artillery and one of cavalry. The militia, who joined him at Fort Washington, amounted to upwards of six hundred men, most of whom had long been accustomed to Indian warfare. The General commenced his march from Cincinnati, and on the 12th of October arrived at Fort Jefferson without material loss, although not without having sustained much inconvenience from scarcity of provisions. The Kentucky Rangers, amounting to upwards of two hundred men, had encountered several small parties of Indians, but no serious affair had as yet taken place. Shortly after leaving Fort Jefferson one of the militia regiments, with their usual disregard to discipline, determined that it was inexpedient to proceed farther, and, detaching themselves from the main body, returned rapidly to the fort, on their way home. This ill-timed mutiny not only discouraged the remainder, but compelled the General to detach the first regiment in pursuit of them; if not to bring them back, at least to prevent them from injuring the stores collected at the fort for the use of the army. With the remainder of the troops, amounting in all to about twelve hundred men, he, sick and suffering, continued his march to the great Miami villages, toiling along at the slow rate of about seven miles a day and the troops deserting by fifties.

On the evening of the 3d of November he encamped, now only about fourteen hundred strong, upon a very commanding piece of ground on the bank of a tributary of the Wabash, where he determined to throw up some slight works, for the purpose of protecting their knapsacks and baggage, having to move upon the Miami villages, supposed to be within twelve miles, as soon as the first regiment should join them. The remainder of the evening was employed in concerting the plan of the proposed works with Major Ferguson of the engineers; and when the sentries were posted at night, everything was as quiet as could have been desired. The troops were encamped in two lines, with an interval of seventy yards between them, which was all that the nature of the ground would permit. The battalions of Majors Butler, Clark and Patterson composed the front line, the whole under the orders of Major General Richard Butler, an officer of great bravery and merited reputation. The front of the line was covered by a creek, its right flank by the river and its left by a strong corps of infantry. The second line was composed of the battalions ot Majors Gaither and Bedinger, and the second regiment under the command of Lieutenant Colonel Darke. This line, like the other, was secured upon one flank by the river and upon the other by the cavalry and pickets. The night passed away without serious alarm. The sentinels were vigilant and the officers upon the alert.

BUTLER KILLED—WATERLOO DEFEAT AND DISASTROUS RETREAT.

A few hours before day St. Clair caused the reveille to be beaten, and the troops to be paraded under arms, as was the custom each day. In this situation they continued until daylight, when they were dismissed to their tents. Some were endeavoring to snatch a few minutes' sleep, others were preparing for the expected march, when suddenly the report of a rifle was heard from the militia, a few hundred yards in front, which was quickly followed by a sharp, irregular volley in the same direction. The drums instantly beat to arms, the officers flew in every direction, and in two minutes the troops were formed in order of battle. Presently the militia rushed into camp in the utmost disorder, closely pursued by swarms of Indians, who, in many places, were mingled with them and were cutting them down with their tomahawks.

Major Butler's battalion received the first shock, and was thrown into disorder by the tumultuous flight of the militia, who, in their eagerness to escape, bore down everything before them. Here Major General Butler had stationed himself, and here St. Clair directed his attention, in order to remedy the confusion which began to spread rapidly through the whole line. The Indians pressed forward with great audacity, and many of them were mingled with the troops before their progress could be checked. Major General Butler was wounded at the first fire, and before his wound could be dressed, an Indian, who had penetrated the ranks of the regiment, ran up to the spot where he lay and tomahawked him before his attendants could interpose. The desperate savage was instantly killed. By great exertions, Butler's battalion was restored to order, and the heavy and sustained fire of the first line compelled the enemy to pause and shelter themselves.

This interval, however, endured but for a moment. An invisible but tremendous fire quickly opened upon the whole front of the encampment, which rapidly extended to the rear, and encompassed the troops on both sides. St. Clair, who at that time was worn down by a fever and unable to mount his horse, nevertheless, as is universally admitted, exerted himself with a courage and presence of mind worthy of a better fate. He instantly directed his litter to the right of the rear line, where the great weight of fire fell, and where the slaughter, particularly of the officers, was terrible. Here Darke commanded, an officer who nad been trained to hard service during the Revolutionary war, and who was now gallantly exerting himself to check the consternation which was evidently beginning to prevail. St. Clair ordered him to make a rapid charge with the bayonet, and rouse the enemy from their covert.

The order was instantly obeyed, and, at first, apparently with great effect. Swarms of dusky bodies arose from the high grass and fled before the regiment, with every mark of consternation; but as the troops were unable to overtake them, they quickly recovered their courage, and kept up so fatal a retreating fire that the exhausted regulars were compelled in their turn to give way. This charge, however, relieved that particular point for some time; but the weight of the fire was transferred to the centre of the first line, where it threatened to annihilate everything within its range. There, in turn, the unfortunate General was borne by his attendants, and ordered a second appeal to the bayonet. This second charge was made with the same impetuosity as at first, and with the same momentary success. But the attack was instantly shifted to another point, where the same charge was made and the same result followed. The Indians would retire before them, still keeping up a most fatal fire, and the Continentals were uniformly compelled to retire in turn. St. Clair brought up the artillery, in order to sweep the bushes with grape; but the horses and artillerymen were destroyed by the terrible fire of the enemy before any effect could be produced. They were instantly manned afresh from the infantry and again swept of defenders.

A Prodigious Slaughter and a Disgraceful Rout.

The slaughter had now become prodigious. Four-fifths of the officers and one-half of the men were either killed or wounded. The ground was covered with bodies, and the little ravine which led to the river was running with blood. The fire of the enemy had not in the least slackened, and the troops were falling in heaps before it in every part of the camp. To have attempted to have maintained his position longer could only have led to the total destruction of his force, without the possibility of annoying the enemy, who never showed themselves unless when charged, and whose numbers (to judge from the weight and extent of the fire) must have greatly exceeded his own.

The men were evidently much disheartened; but the officers, who were chiefly veterans of the Revolution, still maintained a firm countenance, and exerted themselves with unavailing heroism to the last. Under these circumstances, St. Clair determined to save the lives of the survivors, if possible, and for that purpose collected the remnants of several battalions into one corps, at the head of which he ordered Lieutenant Colonel Darke to make an impetuous charge upon the enemy, in order to open a passage for the remainder of the army. Darke executed his orders with great spirit, and drove the Indians before him to the distance of a quarter of a mile. The remainder of the army instantly rushed through the opening in order to gain the road, Major Clark, with the remnant of his battalion, bringing up the rear and endeavoring to keep the Indians in check.

The retreat soon degenerated into a total rout, the greater part of the men throwing away their arms and accoutrements even long after the pursuit had terminated. Officers who strove to arrest the panic only sacrificed themselves. Clark, the leader of the rear guard, soon fell in this dangerous service, and his corps was totally disorganized. Officers and soldiers were now mingled without the slightest regard to discipline, and "devil take the hindmost" was the order of the day. The pursuit at first was keen; but, as at Braddock's defeat, the temptation afforded by the plunder of the camp, soon brought them back, and the wearied, wounded and disheartened fugitives were permitted to retire from the field unmolested. The rout continued as far as Fort Jefferson, twenty-nine miles from the scene of battle. The action lasted more than three hours, during the whole of which time the fire was heavy and incessant.

The loss, in proportion to the number engaged, was enormous, and unparalleled, except in the affair of Braddock. Sixty-eight officers were killed upon the spot and twenty-eight wounded. Out of nine hundred privates who went into the action, five hundred and fifty were left dead upon the field, and many of the survivors were wounded. General St. Clair was untouched, although eight balls passed through his hat and clothes, and several horses were killed under him. He was placed by a few friends upon an exhausted pack-horse that could not be pricked out of a walk, and in this condition followed in the rear of the troops.

The Indian loss was reported by themselves at fifty-eight killed and wounded, which was probably not underrated, as they were never visible after the first attack until charged with the bayonet. At Fort Jefferson the fugitives were joined by the first regiment, who, as noticed above, had been detached in pursuit of the deserters. Here a council of war was called, which terminated in the unanimous opinion that the junction with the first regiment did not justify an attempt upon the enemy in the present condition of affairs, and that the army should return to Fort Washington without delay. This was accordingly done; and thus closed the second campaign against the Indians.

The unfortunate General was, as usual, assailed from all points of the country. He was called a coward, a traitor and an imbecile. All the misfortunes of his life, and they were many and bitter, were paraded in dread array against him. His plan of battle was torn to pieces by newspaper critics and carpet knights who "had never set a squadron in the field," and all the bitter ingredients which go to fill the cup of the unsuccessful General was drained to the very dregs. "Nothing is so successful as success." Aware of the public odium, St. Clair demanded a court, but it was denied. He offered to resign, but was not allowed. It seems as if Washington alone stood by him.

It is now deemed that St. Clair was no coward; that his position was well chosen; that he conducted the battle after the surprise, not only with courage but with ability, and that he made repeated and desperate charges which failed because he was outnumbered, and because his foes were brave, impetuous and admirably led. But misfortune had marked St. Clair for its own. He never recovered from this disastrous blow. His whole subsequent life was but a long struggle with poverty and wretchedness, and when, in his penury and old age, he appealed to Congress for a pension, he was stigmatized as a "pauper," and his claim was almost indignantly scouted and rejected.

Benjamin Van Cleve, who fought as a volunteer in this terrible engagement, says that the enemy's fire was tremendous; that he saw one savage running off with a whole keg of powder, and that thirty officers and soldiers were lying scalped about the artillery. The ground was literally covered with dead and dying men. He saw a Lt. Morgan, an *aide* to General Butler, start on a run with six or eight men, and he started to run with them, but suddenly they broke right in among the savages, who were so taken back, thinking it was an attack, that they opened to right and left, and two hundred thus got through them and no shot fired.

WILLIAM KENNAN, THE RANGER, AND HIS RACE FOR LIFE.

William Kennan, of Fleming county, at that time a young man of eighteen, was attached to the corps of rangers who accompanied the regular force. He had long been remarkable for strength and activity. In the course of the march from Fort Washington, he had repeated opportunities of testing his astonishing powers in that respect, and was universally admitted to be the swiftest runner of the light corps. On the evening preceding the action his corps had been advanced, as already observed, a few hundred yards in front of the first line of infantry, in order to give seasonable notice of the enemy's approach.

Just as day was dawning he observed about thirty Indians within one hundred yards of the guard fire, advancing cautiously towards the spot where he stood, together with about twenty rangers, the rest being considerably in the rear.

Supposing it to be a mere scouting party, as usual, and not superior in number to the rangers, he sprang forward a few paces in order to shelter himself in a spot of peculiarly rank grass, and firing with a quick aim upon the foremost Indian, he instantly fell flat upon his face, and proceeded with all possible rapidity to reload his gun, not doubting for a moment but that the rangers would maintain their position and support him. The Indians, however, rushed forward in such overwhelming masses, that the rangers were compelled to fly with precipitation, leaving young Kennan in total ignorance of his danger. Fortunately, the Captain of his company had observed him when he threw himself in the grass, and suddenly shouted aloud, " Run, Kennan! or you are a dead man!" He instantly sprang to his feet, and beheld Indians within ten feet of him, while his company was already more than one hundred yards in front.

Not a moment was to be lost. He darted off with every muscle strained to its utmost, and was pursued by a dozen of the enemy with loud yells. He at first pressed straight forward to the usual fording place in the creek which ran between the rangers and the main army, but several Indians, who had passed him before he arose from the grass, threw themselves in the way, and completely cut him off from the rest. By the most powerful exertions he had thrown the whole body of pursuers behind him, with the exception of one young chief (probably Messhawa) who displayed a swiftness and perseverance equal to his own. In the circuit which Kennan was obliged to take, the race continued for more than four hundred yards. The distance between them was about eighteen feet, which Kennan could not increase nor his adversary diminish. Each, for the time, put his whole soul in the race.

Kennan, as far as he was able, kept his eye upon the motions of his pursuer, lest he should throw the tomahawk, which he held aloft in a menacing attitude, and at length, finding that no other Indian was immediately at hand, he determined to try the mettle of his pursuer in a different manner, and felt for his tomahawk in order to turn at bay. It had escaped from its sheath, however, while he lay in the grass, and his hair had almost lifted the cap from his head when he saw himself totally disarmed. As he had slackened his pace for a moment, the Indian was almost within reach of him when he recommenced the race, but the idea of being without arms lent wings to his flight, and for the first time he saw himself gaining ground. He had watched the motions of his pursuer too closely, however, to pay proper attention to the nature of the ground before him, and he suddenly found himself in front of a large tree which had been blown down, and upon which brush and other impediments lay to the height of eight or nine feet.

The Indian (who, heretofore, had not uttered the slightest sound) now gave a short, quick yell, as if secure of his victim. Kennan had not a moment to deliberate. He must clear the impediment at a leap or perish. Putting his whole soul into the effort, he bounded into the air with a power which astonished himself, and clearing limbs, brush and everything else, alighted in perfect safety upon the other side. A loud yell of astonishment burst from the band of pursuers, not one of whom had the hardihood to attempt the same feat. Kennan, as may be readily imagined, had no leisure to enjoy his triumph, but dashing into the bed of the creek (upon the edge of which his feat had been performed) where the high banks would shield him from the fire of the enemy, he ran up the stream until a convenient place offered for crossing, and rejoined the rangers in the rear of the encampment, panting from the fatigue of exertions which have seldom been surpassed. No breathing time was allowed him, however. The attack instantly commenced, and, as we have already observed, was maintained for three hours with unabated fury.

When the retreat commenced Kennan was attached to Major Clark's battalion, and had the dangerous service of protecting the rear. This corps quickly lost its commander, and was completely disorganized. Kennan was among the hindmost when the flight commenced, but exerting those same powers which had saved him in the morning, he quickly gained the front, passing several horsemen in the flight. Here he beheld a private of his own company, an intimate acquaintance, lying upon the ground, with his thigh broken, and in tones of the most piercing distress, imploring each horseman who hurried by to take him up behind him. As soon as he beheld Kennan coming up on foot, he stretched out his arms, and called upon him to save him. Notwithstanding the imminent peril of the moment, his friend could not reject so passionate an appeal, but seizing him in his arms, he placed him upon his back, and ran in that manner for several hundred yards. Horseman after horseman passed them, all of whom refused to relieve him of his burden.

At length the enemy was gaining upon him so fast that Kennan saw their death certain, unless he relinquished his burden. He, accordingly, told his friend that he had used every possible exertion to save his life, but in vain; that he must relax his hold around his neck, or they would both perish. The unhappy wretch, heedless of every remonstrance, still clung convulsively to his back, and impeded his exertions until the foremost of the enemy (armed with tomahawks alone) were within twenty yards of them. Kennan then drew his knife from its sheath and cut the fingers of his companion, thus compelling him to relinquish his hold. The unhappy man rolled upon the ground in utter helplessness, and Kennan beheld him tomahawked before he had gone thirty yards. Relieved from his burden he darted forward with an activity which once more brought him to the van. Here, again, he was compelled to neglect his own safety in order to attend to that of others.

Kennan Saves Madison—Lieutenant Colonel Darke's Escape.

Governor Madison, of Kentucky, who afterwards commanded the corps which defended themselves so honorably at Raisin, a man who united the most amiable temper to the most unconquerable courage, was at that time a subaltern in St. Clair's army, and being a man of infirm constitution was totally exhausted by the exertions of the morning, and was now sitting down calmly upon a log, awaiting the approach of his enemies. Kennan hastily accosted him, and inquired the cause of his delay. Madison, pointing to a wound which had bled profusely, replied that he was unable to walk further, and had no horse. Kennan instantly ran back to a spot where he had seen an exhausted horse grazing, caught him without difficulty, and, having assisted Madison to mount, walked by his side until they were out of danger. Fortunately, the pursuit soon ceased, as the plunder of the camp presented irresistible attractions to the enemy. The friendship thus formed between these two young men, endured without interruption through life. Mr. Kennan never entirely recovered from the immense exertions which he was compelled to make during this unfortunate expedition. He settled in Fleming county, and continued for many years a leading member of the Baptist Church. He died in 1827.

A party of Chickasaws were on their march to join St. Clair, but did not arrive in time to share in the action. One warrior of that nation alone was present, and displayed the most admirable address and activity. He positively refused to stand in the ranks with the soldiers, declaring that the "Shawnees would shoot him down like a wild pigeon," but took refuge behind a log a few yards in front of Butler's battalion, and discharged his rifle eleven times at the enemy with unerring accuracy. He could not be persuaded, however, to forego the pleasure of scalping each Indian as he fell, and in performing this agreeable office, he at length was shot down by the enemy, and scalped in turn.

The leader of the Indian army in this bloody engagement was a chief of the Missassago tribe, known by the name of the " Little Turtle." Notwithstanding his name, he was at least six feet high, strong, muscular, and remarkably dignified in his appearance. He was forty years of age, had seen much service, and had accompanied Burgoyne in his disastrous invasion. His aspect was harsh, sour and forbidding, and his person, during the action, was arrayed in the very extremity of Indian foppery, having at least twenty dollars' worth of silver depending from his nose and ears. The plan of attack was conceived by him alone, in opposition to the opinion of almost every other chief. Notwithstanding his ability, however, he was said to have been unpopular among the Indians, probably in consequence of those very abilities.

Many veteran officers of inferior rank, who had served with distinction throughout the Revolutionary war, were destined to perish in this unhappy action. Among them was the gallant and unrewarded Captain Kirkwood, of the old Delaware line, so often and so honorably mentioned in Lee's Memoirs. The State of Delaware having had but one regiment on Continental establishment, and that regiment having been reduced to a company at Camden, it was impossible for Kirkwood to be promoted without a violation of the ordinary rules by which commissions were regulated. He, accordingly, had the mortification of beholding junior officers daily mounting above him in the scale of rank, while he himself, however meritorious, was compelled to remain in his present condition, on account of the small force which his native State could bring into the field.

Notwithstanding this constant source of mortification, he fought with distinguished gallantry throughout the war, and was personally engaged in the battles of Camden, Guilford, Hobkirks, Ninety-six and Eutaw, the hottest and bloodiest which occurred during the Revolution. At the peace of 1783 he retired, with a broken fortune but a high reputation for courage, honor and probity, and upon the reappearance of war in the Northwest, he hastened once more to the scene of action, and submitted, without reluctance, to the command of officers who had been boys while he was fighting those severe battles in the South. He fell in a brave attempt to repel the enemy with the bayonet, and thus closed a career as honorable as it was unrewarded.

Lieutenant Colonel Darke's escape was almost miraculous. Possessed of a tall, striking figure, in full uniform, and superbly mounted, he headed three desperate charges against the enemy, in each of which he was a conspicuous mark. His clothes were cut in many places, but he escaped with only a slight flesh wound. In the last charge, Ensign Wilson, a youth of seventeen, was shot through the heart, and fell a few paces in the rear of the regiment, which was then rather rapidly returning to its original position. An Indian, attracted by his rich uniform, sprang up from the grass and rushed forward to scalp him. Darke, who was at that time in the rear of his regiment, suddenly faced about, dashed at the Indian on horseback and cleft his skull with his broadsword, drawing upon himself by the act a rapid discharge of more than a dozen rifles. He rejoined his regiment, however, in safety, being compelled to leave the body of young Wilson to the enemy. On the evening of the 8th of November the broken remains of the army arrived at Fort Washington, and were placed in Winter quarters.

"MAD ANTHONY WAYNE" TRIES IT AND WINS.

Two commanders had now been tested and failed. The whole country, burning under the disgrace of Harmar's and St. Clair's defeats, clamored for a third expedition. But who should be the leader? This was the theme of general discussion. Many, who had made noble records during the Revolution, sought the position. Washington had been very severely censured for his appointment of an old, infirm, and, above all, an unlucky General like St. Clair, and it behooved him now to make a careful selection.

The choice at last seemed to narrow down to General Wayne and General Henry Lee, the famous and intrepid partisan leader, whose brilliant dashes and daring achievements during the late war, were the themes of every tongue. Lee had many warm admirers, and it cannot be denied that he possessed peculiar qualifications for an enterprise of "such pith and moment." Washington also favored him, and it is asserted that nothing but the discontent which would be occasioned among old army Generals by the appointment of so young an officer, prevented his obtaining the coveted position.

But, finally, "Mad Anthony Wayne," to whom this objection could not apply, and who was equally brave, dashing and successful, was chosen. His remarkable capture of Stony Point—which General Lee, of Virginia, although personally no friend to him, declared to be not only the most brilliant achievement of the Revolutionary war, but of any war—had rendered him very popular. He never enjoyed the reputation of being a very skillful planner or a prudent commander, but as a bold, prompt executive officer, with that kind of magnetic force about him best calculated to win the confidence and maintain the spirit of his men, he was incomparable, and undoubtedly "a head and shoulders" above all others. He seemed to be of opinion that the whole art of war was embraced in his own favorite command: "Charge the d——d rascals with the bayonet."

Nearly a year elapsed after St. Clair's defeat before Wayne's appointment, and even a longer period was next spent in gathering together and drilling a proper force. General Wayne determined to avoid the fault which had so much embarrassed his predecessors, and prepared his command with great care. He arrived at Pittsburgh early in June, 1792, having been furnished with instructions from President Washington, in which it was emphatically stated "*that another defeat would be irredeemably ruinous to the reputation of the Government.*"

The force was to consist of five thousand men, carefully chosen and thoroughly drilled, to be called "The Legion of the United States." With ardent zeal and unwearied patience, Wayne commenced to gather his command. The very name of Indian was now such a dread, that many of the troops were completely demoralized and deserted by the score. At length, however, energy and indomitable will prevailed; order and discipline were introduced; the troops were daily drilled and manœuvred; bad or incapable material was weeded out; firing at a mark was ordered as a daily practice, and rivalry and a spirit of emulation was fostered between different divisions, so that a military pride and confidence and a commendable *esprit du corps* was soon engendered.

No branch of the service was overlooked. The scouts especially were selected with exceeding care from the bravest and most experienced hunters of the border. The artillery was in constant service. The dragoons were taught to practice with, and to rely upon, the broadsword, and to make furious and impetuous charges as the best means of safety, as well as the most important aids to success. The men were taught to charge in open order, and each to rely on himself. To crown all, this legion, about December, '92, was taken to a beautiful plain overlooking the Ohio and about twenty miles below Pittsburgh—to this day called Legionville—and there a Winter camp was made, and in addition to the daily drills and manœuvres, movements *en masse*, skirmishes and sham battles were indulged in.

All this care and wisdom had, of course, its natural effect, and when, upon the 13th of April, 1793, Wayne broke up his camp and embarked his legion for Cincinnati, he had an army fit to cope with any force the enemy dare bring in opposition. Reinforcements of regular troops were constantly arriving, and, in addition, mounted militia from Kentucky. It was so late in the season, however, before all the various forces could be collected, and all the necessary supplies procured, that he judged it prudent to defer any offensive movement until the Spring.

During the Winter, Wayne remained at a fort which he had built upon a western fork of the Little Miami, and to which he had given the name of Greenville. By detachments from the regular troops he was enabled to sweep the country lying between him and the Miami villages, and having taken possession of the ground upon which St. Clair was defeated, he erected a small fort upon it, to which he gave the name of Recovery. His orders were positive to endeavor, if possible, to procure peace upon reasonable terms without resorting to force, and he accordingly opened several conferences with the hostile tribes during the Winter.

"LEGION" READY—BATTLE OF "FALLEN TIMBERS."

Many of their chiefs visited him in his camp, and examined his troops, artillery and equipments with great attention, and from time to time made ample professions of a disposition to bury the hatchet; but nothing definite could be drawn from them. As the Spring approached, the visits of the Indians became more rare, and their professions of friendship waxed fainter. In February, they threw aside the mask at once, and made a bold effort to carry the distant outpost at Fort Recovery by a *coup-de-force*. In this, however, they were frustrated by the vigilance and energy of the garrison; and finding that Wayne was neither to be surprised nor deceived, they employed themselves in collecting their utmost strength, with a determination to abide the brunt of battle.

In the Spring the General called upon the Governor of Kentucky for a detachment of mounted men, who repaired with great alacrity to his standard in two brigades, under Todd and Barbee, the whole commanded by Major General Scott, amounting to more than fifteen hundred men accustomed to Indian warfare. The regular force, including cavalry and artillery, amounted to about two thousand, so that the General found himself at the head of three thousand men, well provided with everything, in high spirits, and eager for battle. The Indian force did not exceed two thousand, and was known to have assembled in the neighborhood of the British fort at the rapids of the Miami.

It was late in July before Wayne was ready to march from Greenville, and, from the nature of the country as well as the necessity of guarding against surprise, his progress was slow but sure. On the 19th of August, when within a day's march of the enemy's position, he determined to send a messenger, charged with the last offer of peace and friendship which he intended to make. For this dangerous and apparently useless office, he selected a private volunteer named Miller, who had formerly been taken by the Indians, and lived for many years upon the banks of the Miami. Miller, however, was reluctant to go, and said they would roast him alive. Wayne, however, answered that he would hold ten Indians as hostages for his safety, and if anything happened him would sacrifice the whole of them. With this assurance Miller went to the Indian camp. As soon as they beheld him approaching, they ran out to him with loud yells, brandishing their tomahawks, and crying out, in their own language, "Kill the runaway!" Miller, who well understood their language, instantly addressed them with great earnestness, and in a few words made known the cause of his visit, and the guarantee which Wayne held for his safe return. To the first part of the intelligence they listened with supreme contempt. A long conference ensued, in which many chiefs spoke, but nothing could be determined upon.

On the next day Miller was ordered to return to Wayne with some evasive message, intending to amuse him until they could devise some means of recovering their friends. He accordingly left them with great readiness, and was returning with all possible dispatch, when he met the General in full march upon the enemy, having become tired of waiting for the return of his messenger.

The General received the report of Miller without delaying his march for a moment, which was continued in order of battle until he arrived within view of the enemy. The regular force formed the centre column, one brigade of mounted volunteers moved upon the left under General Barbee, the other brought up the rear under General Todd. The right flank was covered by the river, and Major Price, with a selected corps of mounted volunteers, was advanced about five miles in front, with orders to feel the enemy's position, and then fall back upon the main body. About noon the advanced corps received so heavy a fire from a concealed enemy, as to compel it to retire with precipitation. The heads of the columns quickly reached the hostile ground, and had a view of the enemy. The ground for miles was covered with a thick growth of timber, which rendered the operation of cavalry extremely difficult. The Indians occupied a thick wood in front, where an immense number of trees had been blown down by a hurricane, the branches of which were interlocked in such a manner as greatly to impede the exertions of the regulars.

The enemy were formed in three parallel lines, at right angles to the river, and displayed a front of more than two miles. Wayne rode forward to reconnoitre their positions, and perceiving, from the weight and extent of the fire, that they were in full force, he instantly made dispositions for the attack. The whole of the mounted volunteers were ordered to make a circuit, for the purpose of turning the right flank of the Indians; the cavalry were ordered to move up under cover of the river bank, and, if possible, turn their left; while the regular infantry were formed in a thick wood in front of the "Fallen Timber," with orders, as soon as the signal was given, to rush forward at full speed, without firing a shot, arousing the enemy from their covert at the point of the bayonet, and *then* to deliver a close fire upon their backs, pressing them so closely as not to permit them to reload their guns. All these orders were executed with precision. The mounted volunteers moved off rapidly to occupy the designated ground, while the first line of infantry was formed under the eye of the commander for the perilous charge in front.

As soon as time had been given for the arrival of the several corps upon their respective points, the order was given to advance, and the infantry, rushing through a tremendous fire of rifles, and overleaping every impediment, hastened to close with their concealed enemy and maintain the struggle on equal terms. Although their loss in this desperate charge was by no means inconsiderable, yet the effect was decisive. The enemy rose and fled before them more than two miles, with considerable loss, as, owing to the orders of Wayne, they were nearly as much exposed as the regulars. Such was the rapidity of the advance, and the precipitation of the retreat, that only a small part of the volunteers could get up in time to share in the action, although there can be no question that their presence and threatening movement contributed equally with the impetuous charge of the infantry to the success of the day.

The Enemy Routed and Driven Under British Guns.

The broken remains of the Indian army were pursued under the guns of the British fort, and so keen was the ardor of Wayne's men, and so strong their resentment against the English, that it was with the utmost difficulty they could be restrained from storming it upon the spot. As it was, many of the Kentucky troops advanced within gunshot, and insulted the garrison with a select volley of oaths and epithets, which must have given the British Commandant a high idea of backwoods gentility. He instantly wrote an indignant letter to General Wayne, complaining of the outrage, and demanding by what authority he trespassed upon the sacred precincts of a British garrison? Now, "Mad Anthony" was the last man in the world to be dragooned into politeness, and he replied in terms little short of those employed by the Kentuckians, and satisfactorily informed Captain Campbell, the British Commandant, that his only chance of safety was silence and civility. After some sharp messages on both sides, the war of the pen ceased, and the destruction of property began. Houses, stores, cornfields, orchards, were soon wrapped in flames or leveled with the earth. The dwelling house and store of Colonel McKee, the Indian agent, shared the fate of the rest.

All this was performed before the face of Captain Campbell, who was compelled to look on in silence, and without any effort to prevent it. There remains not the least question *now* that the Indians were not only encouraged in their acts of hostility by the English *traders*, but were actually supplied with arms, ammunition and provisions, by order of the English Commandant at Detroit, Colonel England.* There remains a correspondence between this gentleman and McKee, in which urgent demands are made for fresh supplies of *ammunition*, and the approach of "the enemy" (as they called Wayne) is mentioned with great anxiety. After the battle of the Rapids, he writes that the Indians are much discouraged, and that "*it will require great efforts to induce them to remain in a body.*" Had Wayne been positively informed of this circumstance, he would scarcely have restrained his men from a more energetic expression of indignation.

The Indian force being completely dispersed, their cornfields cut up and their houses destroyed, Wayne drew off from the neighborhood of the British post, and in order to hold the Indians permanently in check, he erected a fort at the junction of the Auglaize and Miami, in the very heart of the Indian country, to which he gave the appropriate name of Defiance. As this was connected with Fort Washington by various intermediate fortifications, it could not fail completely to overawe the enemy, who, in a very short time, urgently and unanimously demanded peace.

No victory could have been better timed than that of Wayne. The various tribes of Indians throughout the whole of the United States, en-

---

* This gentleman was remarkable for his immense height and enormous quantity of flesh. After his return from America, the waggish Prince of Wales, who was himself no pigmy, became desirous of seeing him. Colonel England was one day pointed out to him by Sheridan, as he was in the act of dismounting from his horse. The Prince regarded him with marked attention for several minutes, and then turning to Sheridan, said with a laugh, "Colonel England, hey! By Jove! you should have said *Great Britain!*"

couraged by the repeated disasters of our armies in the Northwest, had become very unsteady and menacing in their intercourse wth the whites. The Creeks and Cherokees, in the South, were already in arms, while the Oneidas, Tuscaroras, &c., in the North, were evidently preparing for hostilities. The shock of the victory at the Rapids, however, was felt in all quarters. The southern Indians instantly demanded peace; the Oneidas, conscious of their evil intentions and fearful of the consequences, became suddenly affectionate, even to servility; and within a few months after the victory, all the frontiers enjoyed the most profound peace. The treaty of Greenville which followed, brought lasting peace and subjection. Wayne reported his loss at thirty-three killed and one hundred wounded. The Indian loss could not be ascertained, but was supposed to exceed that of the Americans. This, however, is very doubtful, as they gave way immediately, and were not so much exposed as the Continentals.

The Battle of the Fallen Timbers, therefore, although a mere skirmish in reality, must be judged by its effects. Had not Wayne taken such infinite pains to lead forth a compact, confident and well-drilled force, the battle would probably have been as much *larger* as its results might have been different.

One circumstance attending their flight is remarkable and deserves to be inserted. Three Indians, being hard pressed by the cavalry upon one side and the infantry upon the other, plunged into the river and attempted to swim to the opposite shore. A runaway negro, who had attached himself to the American army, was concealed in the bushes on the opposite bank, and perceiving three Indians approaching nearer than in his opinion was consistent with the security of his hiding-place, he collected courage enough to level his rifle at the foremost, as he was swimming, and shot him through the head. The other two Indians instantly halted in the water, and attempted to drag the body of their companion ashore. The negro, in the meantime, reloaded his gun and shot another dead upon the spot. The survivor then seized hold of both bodies, and attempted, with a fidelity which seems astonishing, to bring them both to land. The negro having had leisure to reload a second time, and firing from his covert upon the surviving Indian, wounded him mortally while struggling with the dead bodies. He then ventured to approach them, and from the striking resemblance of their features, as well as their devoted attachment, they were supposed to have been brothers. After scalping them he permitted their bodies to float down the stream.

CAPTAIN WILLIAM WELLS AND ROBERT McCLELLAN.

Two Most Daring Rangers—Their Thrilling Exploits.

The body of scouts and rangers employed by General Wayne embraced some of the most daring and famous woodsmen and Indian trackers that could be found on the borders. It is to this reason chiefly that may be ascribed his easy victory. The Indian scouting parties found him always ready—armed at every point. He could not be surprised—not even approached without a struggle. At length the savages, with whom surprise is half the battle, became completely discouraged and demoralized. They said: "No use fighting that man, his eye never shut." They used to call Wayne, when he was at Fort Washington, General Chebang, which means *to-morrow;* because, they said, he was always promising them gifts to-morrow, but never gave any. Now they called him General All-eye. He had, indeed, learned much from the failures of other Generals.

Captain Ephraim Kibby, a bold and intrepid scout from near Cincinnati, commanded the principal part of the spies. The most active sub-division was commanded by Captain William Wells, who had been taken prisoner when a youth, and who had grown to manhood with the Indians, under the name of Black Snake, and was, by consequence, well versed in all their wiles and stratagems. He became quite an influential man among the Indians and married a sister of the celebrated chief, Little Turtle. He had fought Harmar and St. Clair by the side of his dusky brother-in-law, but he seems to have been ever visited with dim memories of his childhood home, of parents, brothers and playmates, and to have been harassed with the thought that among the slain of those he was fighting against, may have been his own blood kindred. The approach of Wayne's army had stirred anew these heart memories and he resolved to part from the Indians, which he did in this open and honorable manner. Taking with him the great war chief, Little Turtle, to a secluded spot on the banks of the Maumee, Wells said to him: "I now leave your nation for my own people; we have long been friends. We are friends yet until the sun reaches that height, (which he indicated). From that time we are enemies. Then if you wish to kill me, you may. If I want to kill you, I may." At the appointed hour, crossing the river, Wells plunged into the forest and struck the trail of Wayne's army. He had a long interview with Wayne and being desperately brave, knowing well the Indian country and language, received a position of trust, and ever after remained faithful to the Americans. Two of Wells' daughters by Little Turtle's sister were educated in Kentucky, and became ladies of refinement and exemplary piety. He afterwards married another sister of Little Turtle, by whom he had one daughter.

John McDonald, of Ohio, was attached to Kibby's Rangers, and gives very interesting details of some of the principal scouts and of their daring exploits. He was intimately acquainted with the facts and persons of whom he treats, and is said to be perfectly reliable. We quote: Attached to Captain Wells' command were the following: Robert M'Clellan (whose name has been since immortalized by the graphic pen of Washington Irving, in his "Astoria,") was one of the most athletic and active men on foot that has appeared on this globe. On the grand parade at Fort Greenville, where the ground was very little inclined, to show his activity, he leaped over a road wagon with the cover stretched over; the wagon and bows were eight and a half feet high.

Next was Henry Miller. He and a younger brother, named Christopher, had been made captives by the Indians when young, and adopted into an Indian family. Henry Miller lived with them till he was about twenty-four years of age; and although he had adopted all their manners and customs, he, at that age, began to think of returning to his relatives among the whites. The longer he reflected on the subject, the stronger his resolution grew to make an attempt to leave the Indians. He communicated his intention to his brother Christopher, and used every reason he was capable of, to induce his brother to accompany him in his flight. All his arguments were ineffectual. Christopher was young when made captive—he was now a good hunter, an expert woodsman, and, in the full sense of the word, a free and independent Indian. Henry Miller set off alone through the woods, and arrived safe among his friends in Kentucky. Captain Wells was well acquainted with Miller during his captivity, and knew that he possessed that firm intrepidity which would render him a valuable companion in time of need. To these were added a Mr. Hickman, and Mr. Thorp, who were men of tried worth in Indian warfare.

Captain Wells and his four companions were confidential and privileged gentlemen in camp, who were only called upon to do duty upon very particular and interesting occasions. They were permitted a *carte blanche* among the horses of the dragoons, and, when upon duty, went well mounted; whilst the spies commanded by Captain Kibby went on foot, and were kept constantly on the alert, scouring the country in every direction.

SINGULAR MANNER BY WHICH HENRY MILLER REGAINED HIS BROTHER.

The headquarters of the army being at Fort Greenville, in the month of June, General Wayne dispatched Captain Wells and his company, with orders to bring into camp an Indian as a prisoner, in order that he could interrogate him as to the future intentions of the enemy. Captain Wells proceeded with cautious steps through the Indian country. He crossed the river St. Mary, and thence to the river Auglaize, without meeting any straggling party of Indians. In passing up the Auglaize they discovered a smoke; they then dismounted, tied their horses and proceeded cautiously to reconnoitre the enemy. They found three Indians camped on a high, open piece of ground, clear of brush or any underwood. As it was open woods, they found it would be difficult to approach the camp without being discovered.

While they were reconnoitering, they saw, not very distant from the camp, a tree which had lately fallen. They returned and went round the camp, so as to get the top of the fallen tree between them and the Indians. The tree-top, being full of leaves, would serve as a shelter to screen them from observation. They went forward upon their hands and knees, with the noiseless movements of the cat, till they reached the tree-top. They were now within seventy or eighty yards of the camp. The Indians were sitting or standing about the fire, roasting their venison, laughing and making other merry antics, little dreaming that death was about stealing a march upon them.

Arrived at the fallen tree, their purpose of attack was soon settled; they determined to kill two of the enemy, and make the third prisoner. McClellan, who, it will be remembered, was almost as swift on foot as a deer of the forest, was to catch the Indian, while to Wells and Miller was confided the duty of shooting the other two. One of them was to shoot the one on the right, the other the one on the left. Their rifles were in prime order, the muzzles of their guns were placed on the log of the fallen tree, the sights were aimed for the Indians' hearts—whiz went the balls and both Indians fell. Before the smoke of the burnt powder had risen six feet, McClellan was running at full stretch, with tomahawk in hand, for the Indian.

The Indian bounded off at the top of his speed, and made down the river; but by continuing in that direction, he discovered that McClellan would head him. He turned his course and made for the river. The river here had a bluff bank, about twenty feet high. When he came to the bank he sprang down into the river, the bottom of which was a soft mud, into which he sunk to the middle. While he was endeavoring to extricate himself out of the mud, McClellan came to the top of the high bank, and, without hesitation, sprang upon him, as he was wallowing in the mire. The Indian drew his knife—McClellan raised his tomahawk, told him to throw down his knife, or he would kill him instantly. He threw down his knife and surrendered without any further effort at resistance.

By the time the scuffle had ceased in the mire, Wells and his companions came to the bank, and discovered McClellan and the Indian quietly sticking in the mire. As their prisoner was now secure, they did not think it prudent to take the fearful leap the others had done. They selected a place where the bank was less precipitous, went down and dragged the captive out of the mud, and tied him. He was very sulky, and refused to speak either Indian or English. Some of the party went back for their horses, whilst others washed the mud and paint from the prisoner. When washed, he turned out to be a white man, but still refused to speak, or give any account of himself. The party scalped the two Indians whom they had shot, and then set off with their prisoner for headquarters.

While on their return to Fort Greenville, Henry Miller began to admit the idea that it was possible their prisoner was his brother Christopher, whom he had left with the Indians some years previous. Under this impression he rode alongside of him, and called him by his Indian name. At the sound of his name he started and stared round, and eagerly inquired how he came to know his name. The mystery was soon explained—their prisoner was indeed Christopher Miller! A mysterious providence appeared to have placed Christopher Miller in a situation in the camp by which his life was preserved. Had he been standing on the right or left, he would inevitably have been killed.

Captain Wells arrived safely with his prisoner at Fort Greenville. He was placed in the guard house, where General Wayne frequently interrogated him as to what he knew of the future intentions of the Indians. Captain Wells and Henry Miller were almost constantly with Christopher in the guard house, urging him to leave off the thought of living longer with the Indians, and to join his relatives among the whites. Christopher for some time was reserved and sulky, but at length became more cheerful, and agreed, if they would release him from confinement, that he would remain with the whites. Captain Wells and Henry Miller solicited General Wayne for Christopher's liberty. General Wayne could scarcely deny such pleaders any request they could make, and without hesitation ordered Christopher Miller to be set at liberty; remarking, that should he deceive them and return to the enemy, they would be but one the stronger. Christopher was set at liberty, and appeared pleased with his change of situation. He was mounted on a fine horse, and otherwise well equipped for war. He joined the company with Captain Wells and his brother, and fought bravely against the Indians during the continuance of the war. He was true to his word, and upon every occasion proved himself an intrepid and daring soldier.

As soon as Captain Wells and company had rested themselves and recruited their horses, they were anxious for another *bout* with the redmen. Time, without action, was irksome to such stirring spirits. Early in July they left Greenville; their company was then strengthened by the addition of Christopher Miller; their orders were to bring in prisoners. They pushed through the country, always dressed and painted in Indian style; they passed on, crossing the river St. Mary, and then through the country near to the river Auglaize, where they met a single Indian, and called to him to surrender. This man, notwithstanding that the whites were six against one, refused to surrender. He leveled his rifle, and as the whites were approaching him on horseback, he fired, but missed his mark, and then took to his heels to effect his escape. The undergrowth of brush was so very thick that he gained upon his pursuers. McClellan and Christopher Miller dismounted, and McClellan soon overhauled him. The Indian, finding himself overtaken by his pursuers, turned around and made a blow at McClellan with his rifle, which was parried. As McClellan's intention was not to kill, he kept him at bay till Christopher Miller came up, when they closed in upon him and made him prisoner, without receiving any injury. They turned about for headquarters, and arrived safely at Fort Greenville. Their prisoner was reputed to be a Pottawattamie chief, whose courage and prowess were scarcely equaled. As Christopher Miller had performed his part on this occasion to the entire satisfaction of the brave spirits with whom he acted, he had, as he merited, their entire confidence.

I have selected only a few of the acts performed by Captain Wells and his enterprising followers, to show what kind of men they were. History, in no age of the world, furnishes so many instances of repeated acts of bravery as were performed by the frontiermen of Western Pennsylvania, Western Virginia and Kentucky; yet these acts of apparent desperation were so frequently repeated by numbers, that they were scarcely noticed at the time as being any other than the common occurrence of the day. I have no doubt that, during General Wayne's campaign, Captain Wells, and the few men he commanded, brought in not less than twenty prisoners, and killed more than an equal number. Desperate as they were in combat, that bravery was only a part of their merit, as demonstrated by the following circumstance:

On one of Captain Wells' peregrinations through the Indian country, as he came to the bank of the river St. Mary, he discovered a family of Indians coming up the river in a canoe. He dismounted and concealed his men near the bank of the river, while he went himself to the bank, in open view, and called to the Indians to come over. As he was dressed in Indian style, and spoke to them in their own language, the Indians, not expecting an enemy in that part of the country, without any suspicion of danger, went across the river. The moment the canoe struck the shore, Wells heard the cocks of his comrades' rifles cry, "click, click," as they prepared to shoot the Indians; but who should be in the canoe but his Indian father and mother, with their children! As his comrades were coming forward with their rifles cocked, ready to pour in the deadly storm upon the devoted Indians, Wells called upon them to hold their hands and desist. He then informed them who those Indians were, and solemnly declared that the man who would attempt to injure one of them would receive a ball in his head. He said to his men "that that family had fed him when he was hungry, clothed him when he was naked, and kindly nursed him when sick, and in every respect were as kind and affectionate to him as they were to their own children."

This short, pathetic speech found its way to the sympathetic hearts of his leather-hunting-shirt comrades. Those hardy soldiers approved of the motives of Captain Wells' lenity to the enemy. They threw down their rifles and tomahawks, went to the canoe and shook hands with the trembling Indians in the most friendly manner. Captain Wells assured them they had nothing to fear from him; and after talking with them to dispel their fears, he said "that General Wayne was approaching with an overwhelming force; that the best thing the Indians could do was to make peace; that the white men did not wish to continue the war. He urged his Indian father for the future to keep out of the reach of danger." He then bade them farewell: they appeared grateful for his clemency. They then pushed off their canoe, and went down the river as fast as they could propel her.

The Five Rangers Recklessly Enter a Hostile Camp.

Early in the month of August, when the main army had arrived at the place subsequently designated as Fort Defiance, General Wayne wished to be informed of the intentions of the enemy. For this purpose Captain Wells was again dispatched to bring in another prisoner. The distance from Fort Defiance to the British fort, at the mouth of the

Maumee river, was only forty-five miles, and he would not have to travel far before he would find Indians. As his object was to bring in a prisoner, it became necessary for him to keep out of the way of large parties, and endeavor to fall in with some stragglers, who might be easily subdued and captured.

They went cautiously down the river Maumee till they came opposite the site on which Fort Meigs was erected by General Harrison, in 1813. This was two miles above the British fort, then called Fort Campbell. On the west bank of the Maumee was an Indian village. Wells and his party rode into the village, as if they had just come from the British fort. Being dressed and painted in complete Indian style, they rode through the village, occasionally stopping and talking to the Indians in their own language. No suspicion of who they were was excited, the enemy believing them to be Indians from a distance coming to take a part in the battle which they all knew was shortly to be fought. After they had passed the village some distance, they fell in with an Indian man and woman on horseback, who were returning to the town from hunting. This man and woman were made captives without resistance. They then set off for Fort Defiance.

As they were rapidly proceeding up the Maumee river, a little after dark, they came near a large encampment of Indians, who were merrily amusing themselves around their camp fires. Their prisoners were ordered to be silent, under pain of instant death. They went round the camp with their prisoners, till they got about half a mile above it, where they halted to consult on their future operations. After consultation they concluded to gag and tie their prisoners, and ride back to the Indian camp and give them a rally, in which each should kill his Indian. They deliberately got down, gagged and fastened their prisoners to trees, rode boldly into the Indian encampment and halted, with their rifles lying across the pommels of their saddles. They inquired when last they had heard of General Wayne and the movements of his army; how soon and where it was expected the battle would be fought.

The Indians who were standing around Wells and his desperadoes were very communicative, answering all their interrogatories without suspecting any deceit in their visitors. At length an Indian, who was sitting some distance from them, said, in an undertone, in another tongue, to some who were near him, that he suspected that these strangers had some mischief in their heads. Wells overheard what he said, and immediately gave the preconcerted signal, and each fired his rifle into the body of an Indian, at not more than six feet distance. The Indian who had suspected them, the moment he made the remark, and a number of others, rose up with their rifles in their hands, but not before Wells and his party had each shot an Indian.

As soon as Wells and his party fired, they put spurs to their horses, lying with their breasts on the horses' necks, so as to lessen the mark for the enemy to fire at. They had not got out of the light of the camp fire before the Indians shot at them. As McClellan lay close on his horse's neck he was shot, the ball passing under his shoulder blade, and coming out at the top of his shoulder. Captain Wells was shot through the arm on which he carried his rifle; the arm was broken and his trusty rifle fell. The rest of the party and their horses received no injury.

After having performed this act of military supererogation, they rode at full speed to where their captives were confined, mounted them on horses, and set off for Fort Defiance. Captain Wells and McClellan were severely wounded; and to Fort Defiance, a distance of about thirty miles, they had to travel before they could rest or receive the aid of a surgeon. As their march would be slow and painful, one of the party was dispatched at full speed to Fort Defiance, for a guard and a surgeon. As soon as Captain Wells' messenger arrived at Fort Defiance, with the tidings of the wounds and perilous situation of these heroic and faithful spies, very great sympathy was manifested in the minds of all. General Wayne's feeling for the suffering soldier was at all times quick and sensitive; we can then imagine how intense was his solicitude, when informed of the sufferings and perils of his confidential and chosen band. Without a moment's delay, he dispatched a surgeon, and a company of the swiftest dragoons, to meet, assist and guard these brave fellows to headquarters. Suffice to say, they arrived safely in camp, and the wounded recovered in due course of time.

As the battle was fought and a brilliant victory won a few days after this affair took place, Captain Wells and his daring comrades were not engaged in any further acts of hostility till the war with the Indians was auspiciously concluded by a lasting treaty of peace. A new and happy era was about dawning on the West. A cruel and exterminating war, of nearly fifty years' continuance, was closed by a general peace with the redmen of the forest.

What became of Thorp, Hickman, and the two Millers, I have never learned; but, if alive, they probably reside in some smoky cabin in the far and distant West, unknown and unhonored. The last I heard of the brave, hardy and active McClellan, he had just returned to St. Louis, in 1812, from an expedition across the Rocky Mountains. He had been to the Pacific Ocean, at the mouth of the Columbia river. The fate of the brave and lamented Captain Wells was sealed during the war of 1812, near Fort Dearborn, at the mouth of the Chicago river, where he was slain in an unequal combat, sixty-four whites attacked by upwards of four hundred Indian warriors. Then fell as bold a spirit as ever shouldered a rifle or wielded a tomahawk.

MORE ABOUT McCLELLAN—RESCUED BY A GIRL.

Such a remarkably daring and marvelously agile scout as McClellan deserves a somewhat more lengthy notice than McDonald has given him, and fortunately we are enabled to supplement his relation from other sources. John, William and Robert McClellan were sons of a pioneer living in Cumberland county, Pa., and were early schooled in all the arts of woodcraft and inured to all the hardships of frontier life; when mere boys they followed the business of pack-horse drivers, continuing in that business for several years after the Revolution. In 1790, Robert's reckless and restless disposition and personal prowess led him to seek adventures farther west, and he served as spy or ranger at Fort Gower, on the Hock-hocking, O., and soon made a name for himself, having many singular adventures; one of these we condense from Rev. James B. Finley's autobiography.

At the Hock-hocking block-house it was learned that the Indians were gathering in numbers at a large town situate where now stands Lancaster, O., for the purpose of striking some terrible blow upon the border. Two of the most skilled and fearless of the spies, White and McClellan, dauntless spirits that never quailed at any danger, and as tameless and unconquerable as Lybian lions, were sent out to watch the savages and report. They continued their march until they reached a remarkable prominence, now known by the name of Mount Pleasant, the western termination of which is a perpendicular cliff some hundreds of feet high. When this lofty point was gained, a fine outlook was enjoyed, and every movement of the Indians in the valley below could be distinctly seen. They thence witnessed for many days their dances, sports, and the constant arrival of new war parties. They dare not kindle a fire or shoot game, depending for food on the jerk and parched corn they brought with them, and for drink on rain water found in hollows of the rocks. In a short time, however, their store was exhausted and McClellan and White must abandon their post or seek a new supply. The former being the oldest and most experienced, started out with rifle in hand and two canteens slung accoss his shoulders, and cautiously descending to the prairie, he reached the river, and turning a bold spur of a hill, found a very bountiful spring. He filled his canteens and returned safely.

It was now determined to have a fresh supply of this delicious water daily, and the duty was performed alternately. One day after White had filled his canteens and was just about retiring, the light sound of footsteps caught his ear and upon turning he saw two squaws within a few feet of him. The elder of them, on sighting the white scout, stood petrified for a moment and then gave out a shrill and far-reaching Indian yell. White knew his peril on the instant. If the alarm should reach the Indian town, death to him and McClellan was inevitable. Self-preservation demanded that he should sacrifice the squaws, so, with his usual promptness, he sprang upon his victims and grasping the throat of each, leaped with them into the river. He thrust the head of the eldest under the water, but while essaying to do the same to the younger, he met with powerful resistance, and during the sharp struggle with this active and resolute athlete, to his astonishment she addressed him in good English.

Releasing her at once, she informed him that she had been taken captive with her brother below Wheeling; had been a prisoner for ten years, and that her brother had succeeded in making his escape on the second night. By this time the elder squaw had been drowned and floated off with the current. White now directed the girl to follow him. They had scarce made half way back to the mount when the alarm cry was heard. It was supposed that a party of savages had struck the stream below where the squaw's body was floating past. White and the girl succeeded in regaining McClellan, and almost immediately after Indians could be seen scattering in every direction, and a party of some twenty warriors making for the mount. Their swarthy foes were now observed gliding from tree to tree and from rock to rock till their position was surrounded, except on the west perpendicular side, and all hope of escape was cut off. Nothing was left to the scouts but to sell their lives as dearly as possible, and the girl was advised to make her escape and tell the Indians she was forcibly taken prisoner. But, to their astonishment, she replied, "No! death to me, in the company of my own people, is a thousand times sweeter than captivity with slavery. Furnish me with a gun, and I will show you I can fight as well as die. I leave not this place, and should either of you escape, you can carry the tidings of my death to my relations."

Remonstrance proved fruitless. The scouts now matured their plan of defence, and commenced firing in front, where, from the very narrow backbone of the hill or mount, the savages had to advance in single file and without any covert. Beyond this neck the warriors availed themselves of rocks and trees, but, in passing from one to the other, they must expose themselves for a moment, which was enough for such unerring marksmen.

A new danger now threatened. The watchful foe were preparing, also, to attack them in flank, which could be done only in one way—by reaching an isolated rock lying in one of the ravines on the southern hillside, and which dominated the scouts' position. There could then be no escape, and the scouts saw the hopelessness of their situation. Nothing could avert their fate but a brave companion and a far-reaching rifle. Soon McClellan saw a swarthy figure crouching along a ledge of rock and preparing to spring from a covert so near to the fatal rock that a bound or two would reach it. But a small portion of the Indian's body was exposed, but McClellan resolved to risk all rather than have him reach the rock.

So, coolly raising his rifle to his face and shading the sight with his hand, he drew a sure and careful bead. He touched the trigger with his finger; the hammer came down, but, in place of the timely spark of fire, the flint broke into many pieces. While hurriedly adjusting another flint, but keeping his eye constantly on the fascinating spot, he saw the fearless savage stretching every muscle for the leap; with the agility of a crouched panther, he made the spring, but instead of reaching the rock, he gave a most appalling yell, and his dark body fell, rolling down into the valley below.

He had evidently received a death blow from some unknown hand. A hundred voices, from a hundred anxious onlookers, re-echoed the terrible shout. But it would not do to give up the important enterprise with only one failure, so another "brave" was soon seen advancing to take the place of the former. At the same time the attack in front was renewed with increased fury, so as to require the undivided attention of both spies to save their position. With despair McClellan saw the second warrior in the very act of leaping. The spring was made, and, turning a complete somersault, *his* corpse, also, rolled down the hill. Again some mysterious agent had interposed in their behalf. This second misadventure cast dismay into the ranks of the assailants, and they shortly after withdrew to concert some new plan of attack.

Now, for the first time, they had opportunity to look about for their female companion. She was gone—killed, perhaps, or escaped to her former friends. They were not left long to conjecture. The fair maid was soon seen emerging from a rock with a rifle in her hand, and the mystery was soon cleared up.

During the heat of the fight she had seen a warrior fall who had advanced some distance before the rest, and she formed the quick resolve of getting his gun and ammunition. Crouching down beneath the underbrush, she slowly crawled to his body and succeeded in gaining his rifle. Her keen and practiced eye had early noticed the fatal rock, as also the attempt to reach it. Hers had been the hand by which the two warriors had fallen, the latter being the most blood-thirsty of the Shawnees and the leader of the very company which had killed her mother and sister, and taken her and her brother prisoners.

Darkness, deep and gloomy, soon shrouded the whole scene. It was determined to use the girl's knowledge of localities to effect their escape. Should they stumble across foes, they hoped much from her knowledge of the Indian tongue. Scarcely had they descended half way down, before a low *whist!* from the girl warned them of danger. The spies sank silently to earth and awaited the signal from her to move on again. For a quarter of an hour she did not return, and their suspense grew intolerable. At length she appeared, telling them she had succeeded in removing two sentinels who were awaiting their descent on the only practicable route.

The journey was noiselessly resumed, and the spies followed their intrepid leader for a half mile in the profoundest silence, when the sudden bark of a dog near at hand apprised them of danger. The almost simultaneous click of the scouts' rifles was heard by the girl, who informed them they were now in the midst of the Indian camps, and their lives depended on utter silence and closely following in her footsteps.

A moment after the girl was accosted by a squaw from an opening in her wigwam; she replied in the Shawnee tongue and pressed on without stopping. Now she pauses, and assures her companions that the village is cleared and that the greatest danger is passed. She knew that every pass from the mountain was carefully watched by foes, and adopted the hazardous adventure of passing through the centre of the village during the absence of the men. A course direct for the Ohio was now steered, and after three days' travel the block-house was reached. Their escape saved the station for the present, and the rescued girl was restored to her friends, proving to be the sister of the intrepid Corneal Washburn, long known as the renowned spy of Simon Kenton's Kentuckians.

James McBride says, that McClellan was a man of the most extraordinary activity. Many marvelous stories are related of his athletic exploits. While at Fort Hamilton, he would frequently leap over the tallest horse without apparent exertion. In the town of Lexington, Ky., when passing along a narrow sidewalk with Matthew Heuston, a yoke of oxen happened to be drawn up on the sidewalk and instead of walking around them, as did his companion, he, without a moment's hesitation, leaped over both at a bound. We have already stated, that when with the army at Greenville, at a special trial of soldiers and teamsters, he leaped over a wagon with a covered top—a height of eight feet and a half.

McClellan's Adventures, as Recorded by Washington Irving.

After General Wayne had made peace and disbanded the army, Robert McClellan made his home with his brother William, at Hamilton, Ohio, spending most of his time on long hunting rambles. In '99 he drifted to New Orleans, and was long ill of the yellow fever, and then went East to secure a pension, but it being much smaller than he thought he had a right to expect, his proud spirit spurned it altogether. General James O'Hara, the enterprising merchant of Pittsburgh, hearing much of McClellan and his services, engaged him at Carlisle, and, by care and diligence, he soon became a good scribe and careful accountant.

In 1801 McClellan went to St. Louis on business connected with the commissary department, and retiring from the service, commenced trading furs with the Indians. He made many long trading expeditions up the Missouri. In 1808 he entered into partnership with Ramsay Crooks, and Washington Irving gives an interesting account of one of his adventures with a large band of Sioux, excited to hostility against them by rival French traders. In 1810 a party of Sioux broke up one of his trading establishments while he was away hunting. But they did not know the fiery and resolute spirit they had to deal with. On his return, he went boldly among them and demanded restoration, and actually compelled a return of all the goods that had not as yet been carried off —about $500 worth. It was while dispirited by a constant run of ill luck, that he was admitted as partner by Astor's Fur Company—the leader of which, Mr. Hunt, had often heard of, and tried to secure him —to accompany them as guide and hunter to the far distant Pacific.

At this time he wrote home to his brother William: "Six days ago I arrived at this place from my establishment, two hundred miles above on the Missouri. My mare is with you at Hamilton, having two colts. I wish you to give one to brother John, the other to your son James, and the mare to your wife. If I possessed anything more but *my gun*, I would throw it into the river or give it away, as I intend to begin the world anew to-morrow."

At that time the expedition to the mouth of the Columbia river was like going to the end of the world.

Frequent mention is made of McClellan in Irving's Astoria; in fact, the distinguished author has therein immortalized the scout. He thus describes his hero: "McClellan was a remarkable man. He had been a partisan under General Wayne, and had distinguished himself by his fiery spirit and reckless daring, and most marvelous stories were told of his exploits. His frame was meagre but muscular, showing strength, activity and iron firmness. His eyes were dark, deep-set and piercing. He was reckless, fearless, but of impetuous and sometimes ungovernable temper."

We need not mention all the adventures and vicissitudes he passed through on that long and perilous excursion, lasting several years, but will only condense one passage from Irving's charming book, to show the obstinacy and fearless, independent spirit of the man.

When Mr. Reed determined to make an expedition to the States, McClellan, who was very decided and self-willed, concluded to go with it. The expedition had terrible times with the Indians, and was completely broken up. Robert Stuart afterwards started, with four trusty, well-tried men as guides and hunters. McClellan again determined to join the return party, and set out from Astoria on the 28th of June, 1812. After ascending the Columbia for ninety miles, one of the hunters became insane, and had to be sent back in charge of Indians. The remaining six went up the river slowly and painfully for six hundred miles, and, on July 31st, struck off, on horseback, for the overland journey.

They soon found themselves approaching the fatal region of the Snake river, and had not long proceeded on those craggy wastes and wilds, ere they found themselves among baked and naked hills, without water, a burning sky above and a parched desert beneath. Their sufferings from thirst became intense. They toiled and struggled on and on, and on September 12th, were surrounded with insolent and hostile Crow Indians, who dogged the party for six days, and finally succeeded in stealing and driving off every horse they had. They were now on foot, in a barren wilderness, having a journey of two thousand miles before them, and the danger of starvation imminent. Their adventures were exceedingly perilous and interesting, but we must hurry on.

They soon built some rafts and embarked on Mad river, and kept along for six days longer, when a landing was effected and preparations made to resume the journey on foot. Each had a pack of about twenty pounds of jerked meat. Their march was slow and toilsome, along the base of a mountain. Discovering Indian sign, however, a consultation was held, and it was thought prudent, in order to avoid wandering parties of Indians, to strike directly across the mountains.

This counsel was indignantly derided by McClellan as pusillanimous. Impatient and hot-headed at all times, he was now made more irascible by the fatigues of the journey and the condition of his feet, which were chafed and sore. He could not endure facing a lofty and craggy mountain, and swore he would rather cope with all the Blackfeet in the country.

He was overruled, however, and the party began to ascend, striving, with the ardor of young men, who should be first up. McClellan, who was double the age of most of his companions, soon began to lose breath and fall in the rear. It now became his turn, too, to carry the old beaver trap. Piqued and irritated, he suddenly came to a halt, swore he would not carry it any further, and jerked it halfway down the hill. He was offered, in place of it, a package of dried meat, but this he scornfully threw upon the ground. They might carry it, he said, who needed it, but for his part, he could provide his daily food with his rifle. He concluded by turning directly off from the party and keeping along the skirt of the mountain, leaving those, he said, to climb rocks who were afraid of Indians.

McClellan Alone in a Desert—Reduced to Starvation.

In vain the rashness of his course was pointed out to him, and the dangers to which he exposed himself. He rejected such counsels as craven. He turned a deaf ear to every remonstrance, and kept on his willful and solitary way.

Strange instance of perverseness in this odd character thus to fling himself off amid those savage wilds, where not only solitude must have been insupportably dismal, but where every step was full of peril. McClellan, however, was a man of peculiar temper, ungovernable in his will, of a courage that absolutely knew no fear and somewhat, too, of a braggart spirit, that took special pride in doing desperate and hairbrained things. Stuart and his party pursued their course. When on the mountain they could descry McClellan pushing his own solitary route.

Ten days after they encamped on a small stream where they met traces of McClellan, who was still keeping ahead of them through those desolate mountains. They found the embers of the fire by which he had slept and the remains of a wolf on which he had supped. He had fared better than they, for they had nothing to eat. The next night the famishing wanderers perceived a large smoke to the southeast, and such was their dread of starvation that they joyfully forged ahead, thinking it an Indian encampment.

Le Claire, a Canadian, was dispatched to reconnoitre, while they lay down supperless to sleep. Next day they saw Le Claire approaching, with no news except from that strange wanderer McClellan. It was his encampment which had taken fire while he was absent fishing. He, too, was in a forlorn condition, and had wandered twelve days with scarce anything to eat. He had been ill, wayworn, sick at heart, yet still he kept on, but now his strength and stubbornness were both exhausted, and he said he would wait at his camp until the rest came up.

When they reached the spot, they found the old scout lying on a parcel of withered grass, wasted to a skeleton and so feeble that he could scarcely raise his head to speak. They had no food for him, but they urged him to rise and go with them. He shook his head. It was all in vain. He argued he might as well stay and die where he was. At length they got him on his legs, carried his rifle and effects and cheered and aided him forward.

They proceeded about seventeen miles and were preparing to lie down to sleep when Le Claire, gaunt and wild with hunger, approached Stuart, gun in hand, and urged that it was vain to go further without food, and proposed that lots should be cast and one should die to save the rest, and adding, as an inducement for Stuart to assent, that he, as leader, should be exempt from the lot. Stuart was shocked, and attempted to reason with the man, but in vain. At length, snatching up his rifle, he threatened to shoot him if he ever proposed such a thing again. The man was cowed, begged pardon and promised never to so offend again.

We need not follow them on their mournful route. They traveled on thus until the 2d of November, when they came to a river bottom, covered with a thick growth of willow and trees for fuel and shelter, and plenty of game about. Here they made their Winter camp, and in the course of only two days, killed thirty-two buffalo, and the next day fifteen more from a herd which tramped right through their encampment. They now built a comfortable cabin, and new clothes were made from the deer skins so abundantly brought in. They made the mountains echo with their rifles, and in two days more, killed twenty-eight big-horns and black-tailed deer.

The party now commenced to live like fighting cocks, and enjoyed their repose for several weeks, when, alas! (*sic gloria transit mundi*) one morning, at daybreak, they were startled by a savage yelp, and peeping out, they beheld several Indian warriors among the trees, all armed and painted for war. McClellan was just at home in an Indian scrimmage. He had taken his gun apart the evening before, and while now putting it together with all haste, he proposed they should break out the clay from between the logs of their cabin, so as to be able to fire at the intruders. Not a word was uttered by the rest, but all silently slung their horns and pouches and prepared for battle.

Stuart thought best, however, to first try the effect of a parley, so, holding his rifle in one hand and extending the other to him who looked as if he were leader, he boldly advanced. The Indian chief took the proffered hand, and all his men did the same. It now appeared they were a war party of Arapahoes in pursuit of a band of Crows. This party of twenty-three remained two whole days, being liberally feasted by the whites, but no sooner had they gone when the luckless travelers held council. On one side of them were their old enemies, the Crows, and on the other the Arapahoes, no less dangerous freebooters. The security of their cabin was at an end, and with it all their dreams of a quiet and cosey Winter. It was reluctantly concluded to abandon their princely quarters and to turn out upon the plains again, now covered with snow.

For fourteen days they struggled on. The snow lay fifteen inches deep. No game, but miserable, broken-down bull buffalo. At length they came to an immense plain, with no vestige of timber or living animal. Here their hearts failed them. The river on which they were, they judged to be the Platte, but to go on at that season was dangerous in the extreme. It was at length concluded to retrace their last three days' journey of seventy-seven miles to a place where they had observed both timber and abundance of game. They reached the spot. Herds of buffalo were scattered about the neighboring prairie, and a shed was put up and plenty of game killed.

They were fortunate in this encampment, for the Winter passed without anything to molest. They shaped two large canoes, and, as Spring opened, prepared to embark. They tried navigation, but the water was too shallow, and they had to go afoot again. Their future travels, though interesting, had nothing very remarkable about them. They struck the Missouri, embarked on its rapid and turbid bosom, and on April 30th, having been ten months making their toilsome and perilous return expedition, they arrived safely at St. Louis.

Their return created quite a sensation, as it was the first news from Hunt's party in his adventurous expedition across the Rocky Mountains. But so many hardships and privations had broken down the iron constitution of the once agile and hardy scout. He never recovered from that extraordinary series of wilderness tramps. He settled at Cape Girardeau, but the decline of his health was so rapid that he died towards the end of 1814, aged over fifty.

Chapter IX.

A SERIES OF THRILLING EVENTS.

ADVENTURES OF MAY, JOHNSTON, FLINN AND SKYLES.

> In vain ! the tide of life flows on,
> On the daring hunters' track,
> And not the Indians' high emprise
> Can turn the current back.—*Julian.*

Mr. John May, a gentleman of Virginia and surveyor of Kentucky lands, had become so extensively involved in business as to require the aid of a clerk. In 1789 he employed Charles Johnston, a young man scarcely twenty years of age. Johnston accompanied his employer to Kentucky in the Summer of '89; returned to Virginia in the Autumn of the same year, and in February, 1790, it became necessary to return to Kentucky, in order to complete the business which had been left unfinished on the former trip. Heretofore they had traveled by land, but on the present occasion, May determined to descend the Great Kanawha and Ohio by water.

They, accordingly, traveled by the usual route to Green Briar court house, where the town of Lewisburg has since been built, and from thence crossed the wilderness which lay between that point and the Great Kanawha. After suffering much from the weather, which was intensely cold, they at length reached Kelly's station upon the Kanawha, from which point May proposed to embark. Having purchased a boat, such as was then used for the navigation of the western waters, they embarked in company with Mr. Jacob Skyles, a gentleman of Virginia, who had at that time a stock of dry goods intended for Lexington, and without any accident, in the course of a few days, they arrived at Point Pleasant. Here there was an accession to their number of three persons, a man named Flinn and two sisters of the name of Fleming. Flinn was a hardy borderer, accustomed from his youth to all the dangers of the frontiers, and the two Misses Fleming were women of low station. They were all natives of Pittsburgh and were on their way to Kentucky.

At Point Pleasant they learned that roving bands of Indians were constantly hovering upon either bank of the Ohio, and were in the habit of decoying boats ashore under various pretences, and murdering or taking captives all who were on board; so that, upon leaving, they determined that no considerations should induce them to approach either shore, but, steeling their hearts against every entreaty, they would resolutely keep the middle of the current and leave distressed individuals to shift for themselves. The Spring freshet was at its height at the time of their embarkation, and their boat was wafted rapidly down the stream. There was no occasion to use the side oars, and it was only necessary for one to watch at the steering oar, in order to keep the boat in the current.

On the morning of the 20th, when near the junction of the Scioto, they were awakened at daylight by Flinn, whose turn it was to watch, and informed that danger was at hand. All sprang to their feet, and hastened upon deck. The cause of Flinn's alarm was quickly evident. Far down the river a smoke was seen, ascending in thick wreaths above the trees, and floating in thinner masses over the bed of the river. They perceived that it could only proceed from a large fire. As the boat drifted on, it became evident that the fire was upon the Ohio shore, and it was determined to put over to the opposite side. Before this could be done, however, two white men ran down upon the beach, and clasping their hands in the most earnest manner, implored the crew to take them on board. They declared that they had been taken by a party of Indians in Kennedy's Bottom, a few days before—had been conducted across the Ohio, and had just effected their escape. They added, that the enemy was in close pursuit of them, and that their death was certain, unless admitted on board.

Resolute in their purpose, on no account to leave the middle of the stream, and strongly suspecting the suppliants of treachery, the party paid no attention to their entreaties, but steadily pursued their course down the river, and were soon considerably ahead of them. The two white men now ran down the bank, in a line parallel with the course of the boat, and their entreaties were changed into the most piercing cries and lamentations upon perceiving the obstinacy with which their request was disregarded. The obduracy of the crew soon began to relax. Flinn and the two females, accustomed from their youth to undervalue danger from the Indians, earnestly insisted upon going ashore and relieving the white men, and even the incredulity of May began to yield. May called to them from the deck of the boat, where he stood, and demanded the cause of the large fire, the smoke of which had caused so much alarm. The white men positively denied that there was any fire near them.

This falsehood was so palpable, that May's former suspicion returned with additional force, and he positively insisted upon continuing their course without paying the slightest attention to the request of the men.

This resolution was firmly seconded by Johnston and Skyles, and as vehemently opposed by Flinn and the Misses Fleming. Flinn urged that the men gave every evidence of real distress which could be required, and recounted, too, many particular circumstances attending their capture and escape, to give color to the suspicion that their story was invented for the occasion, and added that it would be a burning shame to them and theirs forever, if they should permit two countrymen to fall a sacrifice to the savages when so slight a risk on their part would suffice to relieve them. He acknowledged that they had lied in relation to the fire, but declared himself satisfied that it was only because they were fearful of acknowledging the truth, lest the crew should suspect that Indians were concealed in the vicinity. The controversy became warm, and during its progress the boat drifted so far below the men, that they appeared to relinquish their pursuit in despair.

At this time Flinn made a second proposal, which, according to his method of reasoning, could be carried into effect without the slightest risk to any one but himself. They were now more than a mile below the pursuers. He proposed that May should only touch the hostile shore long enough to permit him to jump out. That it was impossible for Indians (even admitting that they were at hand) to arrive in time to arrest the boat, and even should any appear, they could immediately put off from shore and abandon him to his fate. That he was confident of being able to outrun the red devils, if they saw him first, and was equally confident of being able to see them as soon as they could see him. May remonstrated against so unnecessary an exposure—but Flinn was inflexible, and, in an evil hour, the boat was directed to the shore. They quickly discovered, what ought to have been known before, that they could not float as swiftly after leaving the current as while borne long by it, and they were nearly double the time in making the shore that they had calculated upon. When within reach Flinn leaped fearlessly upon the hostile bank, and the boat grated upon the sand. At that moment five or six savages ran up out of breath, from the adjoining woods, and seizing Flinn, began to fire upon the boat's crew. Johnston and Skyles sprung to their arms, in order to return the fire, while May, seizing an oar, attempted to regain the current. Fresh Indians arrived, however, in such rapid succession, that the beach was quickly crowded by them, and May called out to his companions to cease firing and come to the oars. This was done, but it was too late.

Decoy Successful and the Boat Captured by Savages.

The river was very high, and their clumsy and unwieldy boat had become entangled in the boughs of the trees which hung over the water, so that after the most desperate efforts to get her off, they were compelled to relinquish the attempt in despair. During the whole of this time the Indians were pouring a heavy fire into the boat, at a distance not exceeding ten paces. Their horses, of which they had a great number on board, had broken their halters, and, mad with terror, were plunging so furiously as to expose them to a danger scarcely less dreadful than that which menaced them from shore. In addition to this, none of them had ever beheld a hostile Indian before, (with the exception of May,) and the furious gestures and appalling yells of the enemy struck a terror to their hearts which almost deprived them of their faculties. Seeing it impossible to extricate themselves, they all lay down upon their faces, in such parts of the boat as would best protect them from the horses, and awaited in passive helplessness the approach of the conquerors. The enemy, however, still declined boarding, and contented themselves with pouring in an incessant fire, by which all the horses were killed, and which at length began to grow fatal to the crew. One of the females received a ball in her mouth, which had passed immediately over Johnston's head, and almost instantly expired. Skyles, immediately afterwards, was severely wounded in both shoulders, the ball striking the right shoulder blade and ranging transversely along his back. The fire seemed to grow hotter every moment, when, at length, May arose and waved his night cap above his head as a signal of surrender. He instantly received a ball in the middle of the forehead and fell perfectly dead by the side of Johnston, covering him with his blood.

Now, at last, the enemy ventured to board. Throwing themselves into the water, with their tomahawks in their hands, a dozen or twenty swam to the boat and began to climb the sides. Johnston stood ready to do the honors of the boat, and, presenting his hand to each Indian in succession, he helped them over the side to the number of twenty. Nothing could *appear* more cordial than the meeting. Each Indian shook him by the hand, with the usual salutation of "How de do," in passable English, while Johnston encountered every visitor with an affectionate squeeze and a forced smile in which terror struggled with civility. The Indians then passed on to Skyles and the surviving Miss Fleming, where the demonstrations of mutual joy were not quite so lively. Skyles was writhing under a painful wound, and the girl was sitting by the dead body of her sister. Having shaken hands with all their captives the Indians proceeded to scalp the dead, which was done with great coolness, and the reeking scalps were stretched and prepared upon hoops for the usual process of drying, immediately before the eyes of the survivors.

The boat was then drawn ashore, and its contents examined with great greediness. Poor Skyles, in addition to the pain of his wounds, was compelled to witness the total destruction of his property by the hand of these greedy spoilers, who tossed his silks, cambric and broadcloth into the dirt with the most reckless indifference. At length they stumbled upon a keg of whiskey. The prize was eagerly seized and everything else abandoned. The Indian who had found it carried it ashore, and was followed by the rest with tumultuous delight. A large fire nearly fifty feet long was kindled, and victors and vanquished indiscriminately huddled around it. As yet no attempt had been made to strip the prisoners, but, unfortunately, Johnston was handsomely dressed in a broadcloth surtout, red vest, fine ruffled shirt and a new pair of boots. The Indians began to eye him attentively, and at length one of them, whose name he afterwards learned was Chick-a-tommo, a Shawnee chief, came up to him, and gave the skirt of his coat two or three hard pulls, accompanied by several gestures which were not to be mistaken. Johnston stripped off his coat, and very politely handed it to him. His red waistcoat was now exposed to full view and attracted great attention. Chick-a-tommo said, "Ugh! you big Cappatair!" Johnston hastily assured him that he was mistaken, that he was no officer, nor had any connection with military affairs whatever.

The Indian then drew himself up, pointed with his finger to his own breast, and exclaimed, "Me Cappatain! all dese," pointing to his men, "my sogers!" The red waistcoat accompanied the surtout, and Johnston quickly stood shivering in his shirt and pantaloons. An old Indian then came up to him, and placing one hand upon his own shirt (a greasy, filthy garment, which had not, probably, been washed for six months) and the other upon Johnston's ruffles, cried out, in English, "Swap! Swap!" at the same time giving the ruffles a gentle pull with his dirty fingers. Johnston, conquering his disgust at the proposal, was about to comply, and had drawn his shirt over his head, when it was violently pulled back by another Indian, whose name, he afterwards learned, was Tom Lewis. His new ally then reproached the other Indian severely for wishing to take the shirt from a prisoner's back in such cold weather, and directly afterwards threw his own blanket over Johnston's shoulders. The action was accompanied by a look so full of compassion and kindness, that Johnston, who had expected far different treatment, was perfectly astonished. He now saw that native kindness of heart and generosity of feeling were by no means rare even among savages.

The two white men who had decoyed them ashore, and whose names where Devine and Thomas, now appeared, and took their seats by the side of the captives. Sensible of the reproach to which they had exposed themselves, they hastened to offer an excuse for their conduct. They declared that they really *had* been taken in Kennedy's Bottom a few days before, and that the Indians had compelled them, by threats of instant death in case of refusal, to act as they had done. They concluded by some common-place expressions of regret for the calamity which they had occasioned, and declared that their own misery was aggravated at beholding that of their countrymen! In short, words were cheap with them, and they showered them out in profusion. But Johnston and Skyles' sufferings had been and still were too severe to permit their resentment to be appeased by such light atonement. Their suspicions of the existence of willful and malignant treachery on the part of the white men, (at least one of them,) were confirmed by the report of a negro, who quickly made his appearance, and, as it appeared, had been taken in Kentucky a few days before. He declared that Thomas had been extremely averse to having any share in the treachery, but had been overruled by Devine, who alone had planned, and was most active in the execution of the project, having received a promise from the Indians that, in case of success, his own liberty should be restored to him. This report has been amply confirmed by subsequent testimony.

In a few minutes, six squaws, most of them very old, together with two white children, a girl and a boy, came down to the fire, and seated themselves. The children had lately been taken from Kentucky. Skyles' wound now became excessively painful, and Flinn, who, in the course of his adventurous life, had picked up some knowledge of surgery, was permitted to examine it. He soon found it necessary to make an incision, which was done very neatly with a razor. An old squaw then washed the wound, and having caught the bloody water in a tin cup, presented it to Skyles, and requested him to drink it, assuring him that it would greatly accelerate the cure. He thought it most prudent to comply.

During the whole of this time, the Indians remained silently smoking or lounging around the fire. No sentinels were posted in order to prevent a surprise, but each man's gun stood immediately behind him, with the breech resting upon the ground, and the barrel supported against a small pole, placed horizontally upon two forks. Upon the slightest alarm, every man could have laid his hand upon his own gun. Their captors were composed of small detachments from several tribes. Much the greater portion belonged to the Shawnees, but there were several Delawares, Wyandots and a few wandering Cherokees. After smoking, they proceeded to the division of their prisoners. Flinn was given to a Shawnee warrior; Skyles to an old, crabbed, ferocious Indian of the same tribe, whose temper was sufficiently expressed in his countenance, while Johnston was assigned to a young Shawnee chief, whom he represented as possessed of a disposition which would have done him honor in any age or in any nation.

His name was Messhawa, and he had just reached the age of manhood. His person was tall, and expressive rather of action than strength; his air was noble, and his countenance mild, open and peculiarly prepossessing. He evidently possessed great influence among those of his own tribe, which, as the sequel will show, he exerted with great activity on the side of humanity. The surviving Miss Fleming was given to the Cherokees, while the Wyandots and the Delawares were not allowed to share in the distribution. No dissatisfaction, however, was expressed. The division had been proclaimed by an old chief in a loud voice, and a brief guttural monosyllable announced their concurrence. After the distribution of their captives, Flinn, Devine and Thomas were ordered to prepare four additional oars for the boat which they had taken, as they had determined to man it, and assail such other boats as should be encountered during their stay on the Ohio. These and several other preparations occupied the rest of the day.

Canoe Captured and Six Killed—Exciting Chase and Repulse.

On the next morning the Indians arose early, and prepared for an encounter, expecting, as usual, that boats would be passing. They dressed their scalp tufts and painted their faces in the most approved manner before a pocket glass which each carried with him, grimacing and frowning in order to drill their features to the expression of the most terrific passions. About ten o'clock a canoe containing six men was seen, slowly and laboriously ascending the river upon the Kentucky shore. All the prisoners were immediately ordered to descend the bank to the water's edge and decoy the canoe within reach of the Indian guns. Johnston, with whatever reluctance, was compelled to accompany the rest. Devine on this, as on the former occasion, was peculiarly active and ingenious in stratagems. He invented a lamentable story of their canoe having been overset and of their starving condition, destitute as they were of either guns or axes. It was with agony that Johnston beheld the canoe put off from the Kentucky shore, and move rapidly towards them, struggling with the powerful current, which bore them so far below them that they could not distinguish the repeated signs which Johnston made, warning them to keep off. The Indians perceiving how far the canoe was driven below them, ran rapidly down the river, under cover of the woods, and concealed themselves among the willows, which grew in thick clusters upon the bank. The unsuspecting canoemen soon drew near, and when within sixty yards, received a heavy fire which killed every man on board. Some fell into the river, and overset the canoe, which drifted rapidly down the current, as did the bodies of the slain. The Indians sprang into the water, and dragging them ashore, tomahawked two of them who gave some signs of life, and scalped the whole.

Scarcely had this been done when a more splendid booty appeared in view. It happened that Captain Thomas Marshall, of the Virginia artillery, with several other gentlemen, were descending the Ohio, having embarked only one day later than May. They had three boats, weakly manned but heavily ladened with horses and dry goods, intended for Lexington. About twelve o'clock, on the second day of Johnston's captivity, the little flotilla appeared about a mile above the point where the Indians stood. Instantly all was bustle and activity. The additional oars were fixed to the boat, the savages sprang on board, and the prisoners were compelled to station themselves at the oars, and were threatened with death unless they used their utmost exertions to bring them alongside of the enemy. The three boats came down very rapidly, and were soon immediately opposite their enemy. The Indians opened a heavy fire upon them, and stimulated their rowers to their utmost efforts. The boats became quickly aware of their danger, and a warm contest of skill and strength took place. There was an interval of one hundred yards between each of the three boats in view. The hindmost was for a time in great danger. Having but one pair of oars, and being weakly manned, she was unable to compete with the Indian boat, which greatly outnumbered her both in oars and men.

The Indians quickly came within rifle shot, and swept the deck with an incessant fire, which rendered it extremely dangerous for any of the crew to show themselves. Captain Marshall was on board the hindmost boat, and maintained his position at the steering oar in defiance of the shower of balls which flew around him. He stood in his shirt sleeves, with a red silk handkerchief bound around his head, which afforded a fair mark to the enemy, and steered the boat with equal steadiness and skill, while the crew below relieved each other at the oars. The enemy lost ground from two circumstances. In their eagerness to overtake the whites they had left the current, and attempted to cut across the river from point to point, in order to shorten the distance. In doing so, however, they lost the force of the current, and quickly found themselves dropping astern.

In addition to this, the whites conducted themselves with great coolness and dexterity. The second boat waited for the hindmost, and received her crew on board, abandoning the goods and horses, without scruple, to the enemy. Being now more strongly manned, she shot rapidly ahead, and quickly overtook the foremost boat, which, in like manner, received her crew on board, abandoning the cargo as before, and, having six pair of oars and being powerfully manned, she was soon beyond the reach of the enemy's shot The chase lasted more than an hour. For the first half hour the fate of the hindmost boat hung in mournful suspense, and Johnston, with agony, looked forward to the probability of its capture. The prisoners were compelled to labor hard at the oars, but they took care never to pull together, and by every means in their power endeavored to favor the escape of their friends.

At length the Indians abandoned the pursuit and turned their whole attention to the boats which had been deserted. The booty surpassed their most sanguine expectations. Several fine horses were on board, and flour and chocolate in profusion. Another keg of whiskey was found and excited the same immoderate joy as at first. It was unanimously determined to regale themselves in a regular feast, and preparations were made to carry their resolution into effect. A large kettle of chocolate and sugar, of which the sugar formed the greater part, was set upon the fire, which an old squaw stirred with a dirty stick. Johnston was promoted on the spot to the rank of cook, and received orders to bake a number of flour cakes in the fire. A deer skin, which had served for a saddle blanket, and was most disgustingly stained by having been applied to a horse's sore back, was given him as a tray, and being repeatedly ordered to "make haste," he entered upon his new office with great zeal.

By mixing a large portion of sugar with some dumplings, which he boiled in chocolate, he so delighted the palates of the Indians, that they were enthusiastic in their praises, and announced their intention of keeping him in his present capacity as long as he remained with them. The two kegs, which had been carefully guarded, were now produced, and the mirth began to border on the "fast and furious." A select band, as usual, remained sober, in order to maintain order and guard against surprise, but the prisoners were invited to get drunk with their red brothers. Johnston and Skyles declined the invitation, but Flinn, without waiting to be asked twice, joined the revelers, and soon became as drunk as any of them. In this situation he entered into a hot dispute with an Indian, which, after much abuse on both sides, terminated in blows, and his antagonist received a sad battering. Several of his tribe drew their knives and rushed upon Flinn with fury, but were restrained amid peals of laughter by the others, who declared that Flinn had proved himself a man, and should have fair play.

In the meantime, Johnston and Skyles had been bound and removed to a convenient distance from the drinking party, with the double design of saving their lives, and guarding escape. While lying in this manner, and totally unable to help themselves, they beheld, with terror, one of the revelers staggering towards them, with a drawn knife in his hand, and muttering a profusion of drunken curses. He stopped within a few paces of them, and harangued them with great vehemence for nearly a minute, until he had worked himself up into a state of insane fury, when suddenly uttering a startling yell, he sprang upon the prostrate body of Skyles and seizing him by the hair endeavored to scalp him. Fortunately he was too much intoxicated to exert his usual dexterity, and before he had succeeded in his design, the guard ran up at full speed and seizing him by the shoulders, hurled him violently backwards to the distance of several yards. The drunken beast rolled upon the ground, and with difficulty recovering his feet, staggered off, muttering curses against the white man, the guard, himself, and the whole world. Skyles had only felt the point of the knife, but had given up his scalp for lost, and rubbed the crown of his head several times with feverish apprehension, before he could be satisfied that his scalp was still safe.

Johnston Bothered by a Cow—The Game of "Nosey."

No other incident occurred during the night, and on the following morning the Indians separated. Those to whom Flinn belonged remained at the river, in expectation of intercepting other boats, while Johnston's party struck through the wilderness, in a steady direction, for their towns. During their first day's march he afforded much amusement to his captors. In the boat abandoned by Captain Marshall, they found a milch cow, haltered in the usual manner. Upon leaving the river, they committed her to the care of Johnston, requiring him to lead her by the halter. Being totally unaccustomed to this method of traveling, she proved very refractory and perplexed him exceedingly. When he took one side of a tree, she regularly chose the other. Whenever he attempted to lead her, she planted her feet firmly before her, and refused to move a step. When he strove to drive her, she ran off into the bushes, dragging him after her, to the no small injury of his person and dress. The Indians were in a roar of laughter throughout the whole day, and appeared highly to enjoy his perplexity.

At night they arrived at a small encampment, where they had left their women and children. Here, to his great joy, Johnston was relieved of his charge, and saw her slaughtered with the utmost gratification. At night, he suffered severely by the absence of the benevolent Messhawa, to whose charge, as we have already stated, he had been committed. The Indians were apprehensive of pursuit, and directed Messhawa, at the head of several warriors, up to the rear, to give them seasonable warning of any attempt on the part of the whites to regain their prisoners. In his absence, he had been committed to an Indian of very different character. While his new master was engaged in tying his hands, as usual, for the night, he ventured to complain that the cords were drawn too tight, and gave him unnecessary pain. The Indian flew into a passion, exclaiming, "D—— your soul!" and drew the cord with all the violence of which he was capable, until it was completely buried in the flesh. Johnston, in consequence, did not sleep for a moment, but passed the whole night in exquisite torture. In the morning Messhawa came up, and finding his prisoner in a high fever, and his hands excessively swollen, cut the cords, and exchanged some high words with the other Indian upon the subject.

The march was quickly recommenced, and Johnston could not avoid congratulating himself every moment upon his good fortune in having Messhawa for his guide. Skyles' master seemed to take pleasure in tormenting him. In addition to an enormous quantity of baggage, he compelled him to carry his rifle, by which his raw wound was perpetually irritated and prevented from healing. Messhawa permitted Johnston to share his own mess on all occasions, while the savages to whom Skyles belonged would scarcely permit him to eat a dozen mouthfuls a day, and never without embittering his meat with curses and blows. In a few days they arrived at the Scioto river, which, from the recent rains, was too high to admit of being forded. The Indians were immediately employed in constructing a raft, and it was necessary to carry one very large log several hundred yards. Two Indians, with a handspike, supported the lighter end, while the butt was very charitably bestowed upon Johnston alone. Not daring to murmur, he exerted his utmost strength, and aided by several Indians, with some difficulty, succeeded in placing the enormous burden upon his shoulder. He quickly found, however, that the weight was beyond his strength, and wishing to give his two companions in front warning of his inability to support it, he called to them in English to "take care!" They did not understand him, however, and continued to support it, when, finding himself in danger of being crushed to death, he dropped the log so suddenly that both Indians were knocked down, and lay for a time without sense or motion. They soon sprang up, however, and drawing their tomahawks, would instantly have relieved Johnston of all his troubles had not the other Indians, amid peals of laughter, restrained them, and compelled them to vent their spleen in curses, which were showered upon "Ketepels," as he was called, for the space of an hour, with great fury.

After crossing the Scioto, the Indians displayed a disposition to loiter and throw away time, but little in unison with Johnston's feelings, who was anxious to reach their towns as speedily as possible, flattering himself with the hope that some benevolent trader would purchase him of the Indians and restore him to liberty. They amused themselves at a game called "Nosey," with a pack of cards which had been found in one of the abandoned boats. The pack is equally divided between two of them, and by some process, which Johnston did not understand, each endeavored to get all the cards into his own possession. The winner had a right to ten fillips at his adversary's nose, which the latter was required to sustain with inflexible gravity, as the winner was entitled to ten additional fillips for every smile which he succeeded in forcing from him. At this game they would be engaged for a whole day, with the keenest interest, the bystanders looking on with a delight scarcely inferior to that of the gamblers themselves, and laughing immoderately when the penalty was exacted.

When gaming, they were usually kind to the prisoners, but this ray of sunshine was frequently very suddenly overcast. Johnston ventured to ask an old Shawnee chief how far they would be forced to travel before reaching his village. The old man very good-naturedly informed him by drawing a diagram upon the sand with a stick, pointing out the situation of the Ohio river, of the Scioto, and of the various Indian villages, and pointing to the sun, he waved his hand once for every day which they would employ in the journey. Johnston then ventured to ask "how many inhabitants his village contained?" The old man replied that the Shawnees had once been a great nation, but (and here his eyes flashed fire, and he worked himself into a furious passion) the "Long Knives" had killed nearly the whole of his nation. "However," continued he, "so long as there is a Shawnee alive, we will *fight! fight! fight!* When no Shawnee—then no fight."

The prisoners were also in great danger whenever the Indians passed through a forest which had been surveyed, and where the marks of the axe on the trees were evident. They would halt upon coming to such a tree, and, after a few minutes' silence, would utter the most terrible yells, striking the trees with their hatchets and cursing the prisoners with a fierceness which caused them often to abandon all hopes of life. On one occasion they passed suddenly from the most ferocious state of excitement to the opposite extreme of merriment at a slight disaster which befell Johnston. They were often compelled to ford creeks, but upon one occasion they attempted to pass upon a log. The morning was bitterly cold and frosty, and the log having been barked was consequently very slippery. In passing upon this bridge Johnston's foot slipped, and he fell into the cold water with an outcry so sudden and shrill that the whole party, which the instant before had been inflamed with rage, burst at once into loud laughter, which, at intervals, was maintained for several miles. Sometimes they amused themselves by compelling their prisoners to dance, causing them to pronounce, in a tone bordering on music, the words, "Mom-ne-kah! He-kah-hah! Was-sat-oo! Hos-ses-kah!" and this monotonous and fatiguing exercise was occasionally relieved by the more exciting one of springing over a large fire when the blaze was at its highest, in which they could only escape injury by the greatest activity.

The painful journey had now lasted nearly a month, and the Indian towns were yet at a great distance. Hitherto, Skyles and Johnston had remained together, but, by the whimsical fancy of their captors, they were now separated. Skyles was borne off to the Miami towns, while Johnston was destined for Sandusky. A few days after this separation, Johnston's party fell in with a Wyandot and a negro man, who, having run away from Kentucky, had been taken up by the Wyandot, and retained as an assistant in a very lucrative trade which he was at that time carrying on with the Indians of the interior. He was in the habit of purchasing whiskey, powder, blankets, &c., at Detroit, generally upon credit, packing them upon horses into the interior, and exchanging them at a profit of nearly a thousand per cent. for furs and hides. This casual rencontre in the wilderness was followed by great demonstrations of joy on both sides. The trader produced his rum, the Shawnees their merchandise, and a very brisk exchange ensued. Johnston's boots, for which he had paid eight dollars in Virginia, were gladly given for a pint of rum, and other articles were sold at a proportionate price.

Johnston, as before, was removed from the immediate neighborhood of the travelers and committed to the care of two sober Indians, with strict injunctions to prevent his escape. They, accordingly, bound him securely, and passing the ends of the cord under their own bodies, lay down to sleep, one upon each side of their prisoner. At midnight Johnston was awakened by a heavy rain, although his guides slept on with most enviable composure. Unable to extricate himself, and fearful of awakening them, he was endeavoring to submit with patience, when the negro appeared and very courteously invited him to take shelter in his tent, which stood within fifty yards of the spot where he lay. Johnston was beginning to explain to his black friend the impossibility of moving without the consent of his guards, when they suddenly sprang to their feet, and seizing the negro by the throat, and at the same time grasping Johnston's collar, they uttered the alarm halloo in the most piercing tones. The whole band of drunken Indians instantly repeated the cry, and ran up, tomahawk in hand, and with the most ferocious gestures. Johnston gave himself up for lost, and the negro looked white with terror, but their enemies conducted themselves with more discretion than, from their drunken condition, could have been anticipated.

They seized Johnston, bore him off a few paces into the woods, and questioned him closely as to the conference between himself and the negro. He replied by simply and clearly stating the truth. They then grappled the negro, and, menacing him with their knives, threatened to take his scalp on the spot if he did not tell the truth. His story agreed exactly with Johnston's, and the Indians became satisfied that no plot had been concerted. The incident, however, had completely sobered them, and for several hours the rum cask gave way to the dancing ring, which was formed in front of the negro's tent, where Johnston had been permitted, after the alarm subsided, to take shelter from the rain. He quickly fell asleep, but was grievously tormented by the nightmare. He dreamed that he was drowning in the middle of a creek which he had crossed on the morning, and his respiration became so painful and laborious that he at length awoke. The song and the dance were still going on around him, and the cause of his unpleasant dream was quickly manifest. A huge Indian had very composedly seated himself upon his breast, and was smoking a long pipe and contemplating the dancers, apparently very well satisfied with his seat. Johnston turned himself upon his side and threw the Indian off. He did not appear to relish the change of place much, but soon settled himself and continued to smoke with uninterrupted gravity.

The Two Children Saved by the Young Chief, Messhawa.

At daylight a new scene presented itself. The warriors painted themselves in the most frightful colors, and performed a war dance, with the usual accompaniments. A stake, painted in alternate stripes of black and vermilion, was fixed in the ground, and the dancers moved in rapid but measured evolutions around it. They recounted, with great energy, the wrongs they had received from the whites. Their lands had been taken from them—their corn cut up—their villages burnt—their friends slaughtered—every injury which they had received was dwelt upon, until their passions had become inflamed beyond all control. Suddenly Chick-a-tommo darted from the circle of dancers, and with eyes flashing fire, ran up to the spot where Johnston was sitting, calmly contemplating the spectacle before him. When within reach he struck him a furious blow with his fist, and was preparing to repeat it when Johnston seized him by the arms, and hastily demanded the cause of such unprovoked violence. Chick-a-tommo, grinding his teeth with rage, shouted, "Sit down! sit down!" Johnston obeyed, and the Indian, perceiving the two white children within ten steps of him, snatched up a tomahawk, and advanced upon them with a quick step and a determined look.

The terrified little creatures instantly arose from the log on which they were sitting and fled into the woods, uttering the most piercing screams, while their pursuer rapidly gained upon them, with his tomahawk uplifted. The girl, being the youngest, was soon overtaken, and would have been tomahawked, had not Messhawa bounded like a deer to her relief. He arrived barely in time to arrest the uplifted tomahawk of Chick-a-tommo, after which he seized him by the collar and hurled him violently backward to the distance of several paces. Snatching up the child in his arms, he then ran after the brother, intending to secure him likewise from the fury of his companion, but the boy, misconstruing his intention, continued his flight with such rapidity, and doubled several times with such address, that the chase was prolonged to the distance of several hundred yards. At length Messhawa succeeded in taking him. The boy, thinking himself lost, uttered a wild cry, which was echoed by his sister, but both were instantly calmed. Messhawa took them in his arms, spoke to them kindly and soon convinced them that they had nothing to fear from him. He quickly reappeared, leading them gently by the hand, and soothing them in the Indian language, until they both clung to him closely for protection. No other incident disturbed the progress of the ceremonies, nor did Chick-a-tommo appear to resent the violent interference of Messhawa.

Their rum was not yet exhausted, and after the conclusion of the war dance, they returned to it with renewed vigor. A lame Mingo, on a solitary hunting excursion, soon joined them, and, with drunken hospitality, was pressed and in some degree compelled to get drunk with them. They soon became very affectionate and the Mingo, taking advantage of the momentary generosity produced by the rum, ventured to ask that Johnston might be given to him for a particular purpose, which he explained to them. He said that he had lately killed a warrior of the Wyandot tribe, whose widow had clamorously demanded that he (the Mingo) should either procure her another husband or lay down his own life as the penalty for the slain Wyandot. He added that he was too poor to procure her another husband, unless he should take that honorable office upon himself, for which he had but small inclination, the squaw in question being well stricken in years, tolerably crooked, and withal a most terrible scold, and that he must submit to the other alternative and lay down his life, unless the Shawnees would have compassion upon him and give him Johnston, who (he said) being young and handsome, would doubtless be acceptable to the squaw aforesaid, and console her faithful heart for the loss of her former husband.

He urged his suit with so much earnestness that the Shawnees relented, and assured him that Johnston should be delivered into his hands. This was accordingly done, without the slightest regard to the prisoner's inclination, and within an hour the whole party took leave of him, shaking him heartily by the hand and congratulating him upon his approaching happiness, telling him that there was a fine squaw waiting for him at the Wyandot town. Johnston would have liked the adoption better without the appendage of the bride, but thinking that if she were one of the furies, her society would be preferable to the stake and hot irons, he determined to make the best of his condition, and wear his shackles as easily as possible, until an opportunity offered of effecting his escape. His new master, after lingering around the late encampment until late in the day, at length shouldered his wallet and moved off by the same route which the Shawnees had taken. By noon on the following day they came up with them, when a curious scene ensued. As soon as the Shawnees had become sober they repented their late liberality, and determined to reclaim their prisoner; the Mingo stoutly demurred, and a long argument took place, accompanied by animated gestures and not a few oaths on both sides. At length Messhawa put an end to the wrangling by seizing a horse by the halter and ordering Johnston instantly to mount. He then sprang upon another, and applying the lash smartly to both horses, he quickly bore the prisoner beyond the sound of the Mingo's voice. An hour's ride brought them to Upper Sandusky, where Messhawa dismounted and awaited the arrival of Chick-a-tommo. He quickly appeared, accompanied by his party and followed by the discontented Mingo. The latter regarded Johnston from time to time with so earnest a countenance, and appeared so desirous of approaching him, that the latter became alarmed lest, in the rage of disappointment, he should inflict upon the prisoner the vengeance which he dared not indulge against the Shawnees. But his fears were quickly relieved. The Mingo dogged him so faithfully that he at length came upon him while alone, and approaching him with a good-natured smile presented a small pamphlet which Johnston had dropped on the preceding day. Having done this, he shook him by the hand, and immediately left the village.

At Sandusky Johnston became acquainted with M. Duchouquet, a French trader, who had for several years resided among the Indians, and was extensively engaged in the fur trade. To him he recounted his adventures, and earnestly solicited his good offices in delivering him from the Indians. Duchouquet promptly assured him that every exertion should be used for that purpose, and lost no time in redeeming his pledge. That evening he spoke to Chick-a-tommo, and offered a liberal ransom for the prisoner, but his efforts were fruitless. The Shawnee chief did not object to the price, but declared that no sum should induce them to give him up, until they had first taken him to their towns. This answer was quickly reported to Johnston, and filled him with despair. But as the Shawnee party were engaged in another drinking bout, he entreated Duchouquet to seize the favorable moment, when their hearts were mellowed with rum, and repeat his offer. The Frenchman complied, and was again peremptorily refused. Johnston now desired him to inquire of Chick-a-tommo the name of the town to which he was to be taken, and the fate which was in reserve for him upon his arrival there.

To the first question Chick-a-tommo promptly replied, that the prisoner was to be carried to the Miami villages, but to the second he gave no satisfactory answer, being probably ignorant himself upon the subject. The mention of the Miami villages completely extinguished every spark of hope which still existed in Johnston's breast, as those towns had heretofore been the grave of every white prisoner who had visited them. He had also heard that the Indians carefully concealed from their victims the fate which awaited them, either from some instinctive feelings of compassion, or, more probably, from policy, in order to prevent the desperate efforts to escape which were usual with prisoners who were informed of their destiny. Under these circumstances he gloomily abandoned himself to despair, and lay down in helpless expectation of his fate. But no sooner had he abandoned the case, than fortune, as usual, put in her oar, and displayed that capricious but omnipotent power for which she has so long and so deservedly been celebrated. The same Wyandot trader, who had encountered them in the wilderness, now again appeared at Sandusky, with several horses laden with kegs of rum, and in the course of two days completely stripped them of every skin, blanket and article of merchandise which had escaped his rapacity before.

On the morning of the third day Chick-a-tommo and his party awoke as from a dream, and found themselves poor, destitute, ragged and hungry, without the means of supplying any of their wants. Ashamed to return to their village in this condition, after having sent before them so magnificent a description of their wealth, they determined to return to the Ohio, in hopes of again replenishing their purses at the expense of emigrants. They accordingly appeared, of their own accord, before Duchouquet, and declared, that as the scalp of their prisoner would be transported more easily than his person, they had determined to burn him on that evening—but, if he still wished to purchase him, they would forego the expected entertainment for his sake, and let him have the prisoner upon good terms. Duchouquet eagerly accepted the offer, and counted down six hundred silver broaches, the ordinary price of a prisoner. The Indians lost no time in delivering him into the trader's hands, and, having taken an affectionate leave of him, they again set out for the Ohio.

Johnston's gratification may easily be conceived, but on the following day his apprehensions returned with renewed vigor. To his great surprise, Chick-a-tommo and his party again made their appearance at Sandusky, having abandoned their contemplated trip to the Ohio, and loitered about the village for several days, without any visible cause for such capricious conduct. Johnston, recollecting their former whimsical bargain with the Mingo, was apprehensive that the same scene was to be repeated, and, resolving not to be taken alive, he armed himself and awaited calmly their determination. His suspicions, however, were entirely groundless. They passed him several times without the slightest notice, and at length set off in earnest for Detroit, leaving him at full liberty with his friend Duchouquet.

Flinn Endures Torture—Wonderful Escape of Skyles.

On the evening of their departure a Delaware arrived from the Miami villages, with the heart rending intelligence that his unfortunate companion, Flinn, had been burned at the stake a few days before.

The savage declared that he himself had been present at the spectacle, had assisted in torturing him, and had afterwards eaten a portion of his flesh, which he declared "was sweeter than bear's meat." The intelligence was fully confirmed on the following day by a Canadian trader, who had just left the Miami towns. He stated that Flinn had been taken to their villages, and at first had entertained strong hopes of being adopted, as his bold, frank and fearless character had made considerable impression upon his enemies. But the arrival of some wild chiefs from the extreme northern tribes, most of whom were cannibals, had completely changed his prospects. A wild council was held, in which the most terrible sentiments with regard to the whites were uttered. The custom of adopting prisoners was indignantly reprobated, as frivolous and absurd, and the resolution proclaimed that henceforth no quarter should be given to any age, sex or condition. Flinn was accordingly seized and fastened to the stake. The trader was one of the spectators. Flinn quickly observed him, and asked if he was not ashamed to witness the distress of a fellow creature in that manner, without making some effort to relieve him, upon which he immediately ran to the village and brought out several kegs of rum, which he offered as a ransom for the prisoner.

The Indians, who, by this time, were in a terrible rage, rejected the offer with fierceness, and split the heads of the kegs with their tomahawks, suffering the liquor to flow unheeded upon the ground. The disappointed trader again returned to the village, and brought out six hundred silver broaches. They in turn were rejected, with additional fury, and not without a threat of treating him in the same manner if he again interfered. The trader, finding every effort vain, communicated his ill success to Flinn, who heard him with composure, and barely replied, "Then all I have to say is, *God have mercy upon my soul!*" The scene of torture then commenced, amid whoops and yells, which struck terror to the heart of the trader, but which the prisoner bore with the most heroic fortitude. Not a groan escaped him. He walked calmly around the stake for several hours, until his flesh was roasted and the fire had burned down. An old squaw then approached in order to rekindle it, but Flinn, watching his opportunity, gave her so furious a kick in the breast that she fell back totally insensible, and for several minutes was entirely unable to take any further share in the ceremony. The warriors then bored his ankles, and passing thongs through the sinews, confined them closely to the stake, so that he was unable afterwards to offer the same resistance. His sufferings continued for many hours, until they were at length terminated by the tomahawk.

Within a few days he also heard of Skyles. After leaving Johnston, this gentleman had been conducted to one of the towns on the Miami of the Lake, near the scene of Flinn's execution, where, as usual, he was compelled to run the gauntlet. The Indian boys were his chief tormentors. One of the little urchins displayed particular address and dexterity in his infernal art. He provided himself with a stout switch taken from a thorn tree, upon which one of the largest thorns had been permitted to remain. As Skyles passed him, he drove the keen instrument up to the head in his naked back. The switch was completely wrested from his grasp, and was borne by Skyles, sticking in his back, to the end of his painful career. He continued in the hands of the same crabbed master, who had taken such pleasure in tormenting him upon the march through the wilderness, but had found means to make himself so acceptable to his squaw, that his time was rendered more agreeable than he could have anticipated. He carried water for her, gathered her wood, and soothed her sullen temper by a thousand little artifices, so that her husband, who stood in some awe of his helpmate, was compelled to abate somewhat of his churlishness.

He at length reaped the fruit of his civilities. The squaw returned one evening alone to the wigwam, and informed Skyles, in confidence, that his death had been determined on in council, and that the following day had been appointed for his execution. He at first doubted the truth of this startling intelligence, and retiring to rest as usual, feigned to be asleep, but listened attentively to the conversation of the old squaw with her daughter, a young girl of fifteen. His doubts were quickly dispelled. His approaching execution was the subject of conversation between them, and their language soon became warm. The old lady insisted upon it that he was a good man, and ought to be saved, while the girl exulted at the idea of witnessing his agonies, declaring, repeatedly, that the "white people were all devils," and ought to be put to death. At length they ceased wrangling, and composed themselves to rest. Skyles immediately arose, took down his master's rifle, shot bag and corn pouch, and stepping lightly over the bodies of the family, quickly gained the woods, and bent his steps to the banks of the Miami river. Without an instant's delay he plunged into the stream and swam to the opposite side. In so doing, however, he completely ruined his rifle, and was compelled to throw it away. Retaining the wallet of parched corn, he directed his steps to the southward, intending, if possible, to strike the settlements in Kentucky, but so poor a woodsman was he, that after a hard march of six hours, he again stumbled upon the Miami, within one hundred yards of the spot where he had crossed it before.

While anxiously meditating upon the best means of avoiding the dangers which surrounded him, he heard the tinkle of a bell within a few hundred yards of the spot where he stood, and hastily directing his steps towards it, he saw a horse grazing quietly upon the rank grass of the bottom. Instantly mounting him, he again attempted to move in a southern direction, but was compelled, by the thickness of the wood and the quantity of fallen timber, to change his course so frequently that he again became bewildered, and, abandoning his horse, determined to prosecute his journey on foot. Daylight found him in a deep forest, without a path to direct him, without the means of procuring food, and without the slightest knowledge of any of those signs by which an experienced woodsman is enabled to direct his course through a trackless wilderness with such unerring certainty. Fearful of stumbling unawares upon some Indian town, he lay concealed all day, and at night recommenced his journey. But fresh perplexities awaited him at every step. He was constantly encountering either a small village or a solitary wigwam, from which he was frequently chased by the Indian dogs, with such loud and furious barking, that he more than once considered detection inevitable.

In this manner he wandered through the woods for several days, until, faint with hunger, he determined, at all risks, to enter an Indian village, and either procure food or perish in the attempt. Having adopted this resolution, he no longer loitered on the way, but throwing himself boldly upon the first path which presented itself, he followed it at a brisk and steady pace, careless to what it might lead. About four o'clock in the afternoon he came so suddenly upon a village that it was impossible to retreat without exposing himself to detection, and as he considered it madness to enter it in daylight, he concealed himself among some old logs until nightfall, when he sallied out like an owl or a wolf in search of something to allay the piercing pangs of hunger. Nothing could be picked up upon the skirts of the village, as neither roasting ears nor garden fruit were in season, and it became necessary to enter the town or perish of hunger. Fortunately, the embers of a decayed fire lay near him, in which he found a sufficient quantity of coal with which to black his face and hands, and having completely disguised himself in this manner, he boldly marched into the hostile town, to take such fate as it should please heaven to send. He fortunately had with him the remnant of a blanket, which he disposed about his person in the usual Indian manner, and imitating at the same time their straggling gait, he kept the middle of the street and passed unquestioned by squaw or warrior.

Fortunately for him, the streets were almost entirely deserted, and, as he afterwards learned, most of the warriors were absent. Security, however, was not his present object so much as food, which indeed had now become indispensable. Yet how was he to obtain it? He would not have hesitated to steal, had he known where to look for the larders; nor to beg, had he not known that he would have been greeted with the tomahawk. While slowly marching through the village and ruminating upon some feasible plan of satisfying his wants, he saw light in a wigwam at some distance, which gave it the appearance of a trader's booth. Cautiously approaching, he satisfied himself of the truth of his conjecture. A white man was behind the counter, dealing out various articles to several squaws who stood around him. After some hesitation, Skyles entered the shop and in bad English asked for rum. The trader regarded him carelessly, and without appearing surprised at either his dress or manner, replied that he had no rum in the house, but would go and bring him some, if he would wait a few moments. So saying, he leaped carelessly over the counter and left the shop. Skyles instantly followed him, and stopping him in the street briefly recounted the story, and, throwing himself upon his mercy, earnestly implored his assistance.

The trader appeared much astonished, and visibly hesitated. Quickly recovering himself, however, he assured Skyles that he would use every effort to save him, although in doing so he himself would incur great risk. He then informed him that a band of Shawnees had appeared at the village on that very morning in keen pursuit of a prisoner, who (they said) had escaped a few days before, and whom they supposed to be still in the neighborhood, from the zigzag manner in which he had traveled. Many of the warriors of the town were at that moment assisting the Shawnees in hunting for him. He added that they might be expected to return in the morning, in which case, if discovered, his death would be certain. Skyles listened in great alarm to his account of the danger which surrounded him. If he left the village, he could scarcely expect to escape the numerous bands who were ranging the forests in search of him. If he remained where he was, the danger was still more imminent. Under these circumstances he earnestly requested the advice of the trader as to the best means of avoiding his enemies. The man replied that he must instantly leave the village, as keen eyes would be upon him in the morning, and his design would be penetrated. That he must conceal himself in a hazel thicket, which he pointed out to him, where in a short time he would join him with food, where they could arrange some feasible plan of escape. They then separated, the trader returning to his shop and Skyles repairing to the friendly thicket.

Here within a few minutes he was joined by his friend, who informed him that he saw but one possible mode of escape. That it would be impossible for him either to remain where he was or to attempt to reach the white settlements through the woods, but he declared that if he was diligent and active, he might overtake a boat which had left them that morning for Lake Erie, and offered him his own skiff for that purpose. He added, that the boat was ladened with furs, and was commanded by an English Captain, who would gladly receive him on board. Skyles eagerly embraced the offer, and they proceeded without a moment's delay to the river shore, where a handsome skiff with two oars lay in readiness for the water. Having taken an affectionate leave of the trader, Skyles put off from shore, and quickly gaining the current, rowed until daylight with the zeal of a man who knew the value of life and liberty. His greatest apprehension was, that his flight would be discovered in time to prevent his reaching the boat, and at every rustling of the bushes on the bank of the river, or at every cry of the owl which arose from the deep forest around him, the blood would rush back to his heart and he would fancy that his enemies were upon him.

At length, between dawn and sunrise, he beheld the boat which he had pursued so eagerly only a few hundred yards in front, drifting slowly and calmly down the stream. He redoubled his exertions, and in half an hour was within hailing distance. He called aloud for them to halt, but no answer was returned. Upon coming alongside, he was unable to see a single man on board. Supposing the crew asleep, he mounted the side of the vessel, and saw the man at the helm enjoying a very comfortable nap, with the most enviable disregard to the dangers which might await him on the waters of Lake Erie, which were then in sight. The helmsman started up, rubbed his eyes, looked around him, and, after saluting his visitor, observed that "he had almost fallen asleep." Skyles agreed with him, and anxiously inquired for the Captain. The latter soon made his appearance, in a woolen night cap, and the negotiation commenced. The Captain asked who he was, and what was the cause of so early a visit? Skyles was fearful of committing himself by a premature disclosure of his real character, and replied that he was an adventurer who had been looking out for land upon the Auglaize, but that he had been driven from the country by the apprehension of outrage from the Indians, who had lately become unusually incensed against the whites. The Captain coolly replied, that he had heard of one white man having been burned a few days before, at one of the Miami villages, and had understood that another had avoided the same fate only by running away into the woods, where, unless retaken, it was supposed he would perish, as he had shown himself a miserable woodsman, and as numerous parties were in search of him.

After a moment's hesitation, Skyles frankly acknowledged himself to
38

be that fugitive, and threw himself at once upon their mercy. The English Captain heard him apparently without surprise, and granted his request without hesitation. All was done with the utmost *sang froid.* In a short time they arrived at Detroit, where, to his no small astonishment, he beheld Chick-a-tommo, Messhawa and their party, who had just arrived from Sandusky, after the sale of Johnston. Carefully avoiding them, he lay close in the house of a trader till the following day, when another large party arrived in pursuit of him, (having traced him down the river to Lake Erie,) and paraded the streets for several days, uttering loud complaints against those who had robbed them of their prisoner. Poor Skyles entertained the most painful apprehensions for several days, but was at length relieved by their departure. As soon as possible he obtained a passage to Montreal, and returned in safety to the United States.

MISS FLEMING'S SAD PLIGHT—RESCUED BY KING CRANE.

In noticing the fate of the companions of Johnston's captivity, we are naturally led to say something of the only female of the party. The reader cannot have forgotten that one of the Misses Fleming was killed on the Ohio, and that the other became a prisoner, and was assigned to the Cherokees. Johnston had been much surprised at the levity of her conduct when first taken. Instead of appearing dejected at the dreadful death of her sister and the still more terrible fate of her friends, she never appeared more lively or better reconciled to her fate than while her captors lingered upon the banks of the Ohio. Upon the breaking up of the party, the Cherokees conducted their prisoner toward the Miami villages, and Johnston saw nothing more of her until after his own liberation. While he remained at the house of M Duchouquet, the small party of Cherokees to whom she belonged suddenly made their appearance in the village, in a condition so tattered and dilapidated as to satisfy every one that all their booty had been wasted with their usual improvidence.

Miss Fleming's appearance, particularly, had been entirely changed. All the levity which had astonished Johnston so much on the banks of the Ohio was completely gone. Her dress was tattered, her cheeks sunken, her eyes discolored by weeping, and her whole manner expressive of the most heartfelt wretchedness. Johnston addressed her with kindness, and inquired the cause of so great a change, but she only replied by wringing her hands and bursting into tears. Her master quickly summoned her away, and on the morning of her arrival she was compelled to leave the village and accompany them to Lower Sam-dusky. Within a few days Johnston, in company with his friend Duchouquet, followed them to that place, partly upon business and partly with the hope of effecting her liberation. He found the town thronged with Indians of various tribes, and there, for the first time, he learned that his friend Skyles had effected his escape. Upon inquiring for the Cherokees, he learned that they were encamped with their prisoner within a quarter of a mile of the town, holding themselves aloof from the rest and evincing the most jealous watchfulness over their prisoner. Johnston applied to the traders of Sandusky for their good offices, and, as usual, the request was promptly complied with. They went out in a body to the Cherokee camp, accompanied by a white man named Whittaker, who had been taken from Virginia when a child, and had been completely naturalized among the Indians.

This Whittaker was personally known to Miss Fleming, having often visited Pittsburgh, where her father kept a small tavern much frequented by Indians and traders. As soon as she beheld him, therefore, she ran up to the spot where he stood and, bursting into tears, implored him to save her from the cruel fate which she had no doubt awaited her. He engaged very zealously in her service, and finding that all the offers of the traders were rejected with determined obstinacy, he returned to Detroit and solicited the intercession of an old chief known among the whites by the name of "Old King Crane," assuring him (a lie which we can scarcely blame) that the woman was his sister. King Crane listened with gravity to the appeal of Whittaker, acknowledged the propriety of interfering in the case of so near a relative, and very calmly walked out to the Cherokee camp in order to try the efficacy of his own eloquence in behalf of the white squaw. He found her master, however, perfectly inexorable. The argument gradually waxed warm, till at length the Cherokees became enraged and told the old man that it was a disgrace to a chief like him to put himself upon a level with "white people," and that they looked upon him as no better than "dirt."

At this insupportable insult, King Crane became exasperated in turn, and a very edifying scene ensued, in which each bespattered the other with a profusion of abuse for several minutes, until the Old King recollected himself sufficiently to draw off for the present and concert measures for obtaining redress. He returned to the village in a towering passion and announced his determination to collect his young men and rescue the white squaw by force, and if the Cherokees dared to resist, he swore that he would take their scalps upon the spot. Whittaker applauded his doughty resolution, but warned him of the necessity of dispatch, as the Cherokees, alarmed at the idea of losing their prisoner,

might be tempted to put her to death without further delay. This advice was acknowledged to be of weight, and before daylight on the
following morning King Crane assembled his young men and advanced
cautiously upon the Cherokee encampment.

He found all but the miserable prisoner buried in sleep. *She* had
been stripped naked, her body painted black, and in this condition had
been bound to a stake, around which hickory poles had already been
collected and every other disposition made for burning her alive at
daylight. She was moaning in a low tone as her deliverers approached,
and was so much exhausted as not to be aware of their approach until
King Crane had actually cut the cords which bound her with his knife.
He then ordered his young men to assist her in putting on her clothes,
which they obeyed with the most stoical indifference. As soon as her
toilet had been completed the King awakened her masters and informed
them that the squaw was *his!* that if they submitted quietly, it was
well!—if not, his young men and himself were ready for them. The
Cherokees, as may readily be imagined, protested loudly against such
unrighteous proceedings, but what could words avail against tomahawks
and superior numbers? They finally expressed their willingness to resign the squaw, but hoped that King Crane would not be such a
"beast" as to refuse them the ransom which he had offered them on
the preceding day! The King replied coolly that he had the squaw
now in his own hands, and would serve them right if he refused to pay
a single broach, but that he disdained to receive anything at their
hands without paying an equivalent, and would give them six hundred
broaches. He then returned to Lower Sandusky, accompanied by the
liberated prisoner. She was then painted as a squaw by Whittaker and
sent off, under the care of two trusty Indians, to Pittsburgh, where she
arrived in safety in the course of the following week.

The remainder of Johnston's narrative is easily dispatched. He
quickly embarked in a boat laden with fur to Detroit, and after remaining there a few days, took passage to Montreal, and continued his
journey thence to New York. There he had an interview with President Washington, who, having been informed of his escape, sent for
him, in order to make a number of inquiries as to the strength of the
tribes through which he had passed, the force and condition of the
British garrisons, and the degree of countenance which they had
afforded to the hostile Indians. Having given all the information of
which he was possessed, he was dismissed with great kindness, and in
the course of the following week found himself in the bosom of his
family.

As the reader may probably take some interest in the fate of the

Indians whom we have mentioned, we are enabled to add something upon that subject. Chick-a-tommo was killed at the decisive battle of the "Fallen Timber," where the united force of the northwestern tribes was defeated by General Wayne. Messhawa fought at the same place, but escaped, and afterwards became a devoted follower of the celebrated Tecumseh. He fought at Tippecanoe, Raisin, and finally at the River Thames, where it was supposed he was killed. King Crane lived to a great age, was present at St. Clair's defeat and at the "Fallen Timber," but finally became reconciled to the Americans and fought under Harrison at Thames. Whittaker, the white man, was in St. Clair's defeat and afterwards with the Indians against Wayne. Tom Lewis fought against the Americans in all the northwestern battles until the final peace in 1796, and then was one of the deputation who came on to Washington City, where Johnston saw him in '97. He afterwards rose to the rank of chief among the Shawnees, but having an incurable propensity to rum and thieving, he was degraded from his rank, and removed, with a band of his countrymen, to the country west of the Mississippi.

ADVENTURES OF WARD, CALVIN AND KENTON.

In the month of April, 1792, a number of horses belonging to Captain Luther Calvin, of Mason county, Ky., were stolen by the Indians; and, as usual, a strong party volunteered to go in pursuit of the enemy and recover the property. The party consisted of thirty-seven men, commanded by Captains Calvin and Kenton, and was composed chiefly of young farmers, most of whom had never yet met an enemy. They rendezvoused upon the Kentucky shore, immediately opposite Ripley, and crossing the river in a small ferry boat, pursued the trail for five or six miles with great energy. Here, however, a specimen of the usual caprice and uncertainty attending the motions of militia, was given. One of the party, whose voice had been loud and resolute while on the Kentucky shore, all at once managed to discover that the enterprise was rash, ill advised, and if prosecuted, would certainly prove disastrous. A keen debate ensued, in which young Spencer Calvin, then a lad of eighteen, openly accused the gentleman alluded to of cowardice, and even threatened to take the measure of his shoulders, with a ramrod, on the spot. By the prompt interference of Kenton and the elder Calvin, the young man's wrath was appeased for the time, and all those who preferred safety to honor, were invited instantly to return. The permission was promptly accepted, and no less than fifteen men, headed by the recreant already mentioned, turned their horses' heads and recrossed the river. The remainder, consisting chiefly of experienced warriors, continued the pursuit.

The trail led them down on the Miami, and about noon, on the second day, they heard a bell in front, apparently from a horse grazing. Cautiously approaching it, they quickly beheld a solitary Indian, mounted on horseback, and leisurely advancing towards them. A few of their best marksmen fired upon him and brought him to the ground. After a short consultation, it was then determined to follow his back trail, and ascertain whether there were more in the neighborhood. A small, active, resolute woodsman, named McIntyre, accompanied by three others, was pushed on in advance, in order to give them early notice of the enemy's appearance, while the main body followed at a more leisurely pace. Within an hour McIntyre returned, and reported that they were then within a short distance of a large party of Indians, supposed to be greatly superior to their own; that they were encamped in a bottom upon the borders of a creek, and were amusing themselves, apparently awaiting the arrival of the Indian whom they had just killed, as they would occasionally halloo loudly, and then laugh immoderately, supposing, probably, that their comrade had lost his way.

This intelligence fell like a shower-bath upon the spirits of the party, who, thinking it more prudent to put a greater interval between themselves and the enemy, set spur to their horses and galloped back in the direction from which they had come. Such was the panic, that one of the footmen, a huge, hulking fellow, six feet high, in his zeal for his own safety, sprang up behind Captain Calvin, (who was then mounted upon Captain Ward's horse, the Captain having dismounted in order to accommodate him,) and nothing short of a threat to blow his brains out, could induce him to dismount. In this orderly manner they scampered through the woods for several miles, when, in obedience to the orders of Kenton and Calvin, they halted, and prepared for resistance in case (as was probable) the enemy had discovered them, and were engaged in the pursuit. Kenton and Calvin were engaged apart in earnest consultation. It was proposed that a number of saplings should be cut down and a temporary breastwork erected, and while the propriety of these measures were under discussion, the men were left to themselves.

Captain Ward, as we have already observed, was then very young, and perfectly raw. He had been in the habit of looking up to *one man* as a perfect Hector, having always heard him represented in his own neighborhood as a man of undoubted courage, and a perfect Anthropophagus among the Indians. When they halted, therefore, he naturally looked around for his friend, hoping to read safety, courage and assurance of success in that countenance, usually so ruddy and confident. But, alas! the gallant warrior was wofully chop-fallen. There had generally been a ruddy tinge upon the tip of his nose, which some ascribed to the effervescence of a fiery valor, while others, more maliciously inclined, attributed it to fumes of brandy. Even this burning beacon had been quenched, and had assumed a livid, ashy hue, still deeper, if possible, than that of his lips. Captain Ward, thinking that the danger must be appalling which could dampen the ardor of a man like this Bombastes, became grievously frightened himself, and the contagion seemed spreading rapidly, when Kenton and Calvin rejoined them, and speaking in a cheerful, confident tone, completely reanimated their spirits.

Finding themselves not pursued by the enemy, as they had expected, it was determined that they should remain in their present position until night, when a rapid attack was to be made, in two divisions, upon the Indian camp, under the impression that the darkness of the night, and the surprise of the enemy, might give them an advantage which they could scarcely hope for in daylight. Accordingly, everything remaining quiet, at dusk they again mounted and advanced rapidly, but in profound silence, upon the Indian camp. It was ascertained that the horses which the enemy had stolen were grazing in a rich bottom below their camp. As they were advancing to the attack, therefore, Calvin detached his son, with several halters which he had borrowed from the men, to regain their own horses, and be prepared to carry them off in case the enemy should overpower them. The attack was then made in two divisions. Calvin conducted the upper and Kenton the lower party. The wood was thick, but the moon shone out clearly, and enabled them to distinguish objects with sufficient precision. Calvin's party came first in contact with the enemy.

They had advanced within thirty yards of a large fire in front of a number of tents, without having seen a single Indian, when a dog, which had been watching them for several minutes, sprang forward to meet them, baying loudly. Presently an Indian appeared, approaching cautiously towards them, and occasionally speaking to the dog in the Indian tongue. This sight was too tempting to be borne, and Calvin heard the click of a dozen rifles in rapid succession, as his party cocked them in order to fire. The Indian was too close to permit him to speak, but turning to his men he earnestly waved his hand as a warning to be quiet. Then cautiously raising his own rifle, he fired with a steady aim just as the Indian had reached the fire and stood fairly exposed to its light. The report of the rifle broke the stillness of the night, and their ears were soon deafened by the yells of the enemy. The Indian at whom Calvin had fired fell forward into the burning pile of fagots, and by his struggling to extricate himself, scattered the brands so much as almost to extinguish the light. Several dusky forms glanced rapidly before them for a moment, which drew a volley from his men, but with what effect could not be ascertained. Calvin, having discharged his piece, turned so rapidly as to strike the end of his ramrod against a tree behind him, and drive it into its sheath with such violence, that he was unable to extricate it for several minutes, and finally fractured two of his teeth in the effort.

A heavy fire now commenced from the Indian camp, which was returned with equal spirit by the whites, but without much effect on either side. Trees were barked very plentifully, dogs bayed, the Indians yelled, the whites shouted, the squaws screamed, and a prodigious uproar was maintained for about fifteen minutes, when it was reported to Calvin that Kenton's party had been overpowered and was in full retreat. It was not necessary to give orders for a similar movement. No sooner had the intelligence been received than the Kentuckians of the upper division broke their ranks and every man attempted to save himself as he best could. They soon overtook the lower division, and a hot scramble took place for horses. One called upon another to wait for him until he could catch his horse, which had broken his bridle, but no attention was paid to the request. Some fled upon their own horses, others mounted those of their friends. "First come, first served," seemed to be the order of the night, and a sad confusion of property took place, in consequence of which, to their great terror, a few were compelled to return on foot. The flight was originally caused by the panic of one individual. As the lower division moved up to the attack most of the men appeared to advance with alacrity.

Captain Ward, however, happened to be stationed next to McIntyre, who was a practiced woodsman and peculiarly expert marksman. Heretofore he had always been foremost in every danger, and had become celebrated for the address, activity and boldness with which he had acquitted himself. As they were ascending the gentle acclivity upon which the Indian camp stood, however, he appeared much dejected, and spoke despondingly of their enterprise. He declared that it had been revealed to him in a dream, on the preceding night, that their efforts would be vain, and that he himself was destined to perish. That he was determined to fight, as long as any man of the party stood his ground, but if the whites were wise, they would instantly abandon the attempt upon the enemy, and recross the Ohio as rapidly as possible. These observations made but little impression upon Ward, but seemed to take deep root in the mind of the gentleman whose pale face had alarmed the company at the breastwork. The action quickly commenced, and at the first fire from the Indians, Barre, a young Kentuckian, was shot by ———'s side. This circumstance completed the overthrow of his courage, which had declined visibly since the first encounter in the morning, and elevating his voice to its shrillest notes, he shouted aloud, "Boys! it wont do for us to be here—Barre is killed and the Indians are crossing the creek!"

Bonaparte has said, that there is a critical period in every battle, when the bravest men will eagerly seize an excuse to run away. The remark is doubly true in regard to militia. No sooner had this speech been uttered by one who had never yet been charged with cowardice, than the rout instantly took place, and all order was disregarded. Fortunately, the enemy were equally frightened, and probably would have fled themselves, had the whites given them time. No pursuit took place for several hours, nor did they then pursue the trail of the main body of fugitives. But it unfortunately happened that McIntyre, instead of accompanying the rest, turned off from the main route, and returned to the breastwork, where some flour and venison had been left. The Indians quickly became aware of the circumstance, and following with rapidity, overtook, tomahawked and scalped him, while engaged in preparing breakfast on the following morning. Thus was his dream verified. The prediction in this case, as in many others, probably produced its own accomplishment by confounding his mind and depriving him of his ordinary alertness and intelligence. He certainly provoked his fate by his own extraordinary rashness.

WARD FINDS A LOST BROTHER—WARD, BAKER AND KENTON.

It is somewhat remarkable, that a brother of Captain Ward's was in the Indian camp at the moment when it was attacked. He had been taken by the Indians in 1758, being at that time only three years old, had been adopted as a member of the Shawnee tribe and had married an Indian woman, by whom he had several children, all of whom, together with their mother, were then in camp. Captain Ward has informed the writer of this narrative, that a few seconds before the firing began, while he stood within rifle shot of the encampment, an Indian girl, apparently fifteen years of age, attracted his attention. She stood for an instant in an attitude of alarm in front of one of the tents, and gazing intently upon the spot where he stood. Not immediately perceiving that it was a female, he raised his gun, and was upon the point of firing, when her open bosom announced her sex, and her peculiarly light complexion caused him to doubt for a moment whether she could be an Indian by birth. He afterwards ascertained that she was his brother's child.

It appears still more remarkable, that exactly one year afterwards, John Ward, the adopted Indian, should have been opposed to another one of his brothers, Captain James Ward, of Mason, in a night skirmish somewhat resembling that which we have just detailed. Captain James Ward, together with Kenton, Baker and about thirty others, while engaged in pursuit of some stolen horses, fell upon a fresh trail of Indians, that crossed the road which they were then pursuing. Instantly abandoning their former object, they followed the fresh trail with great eagerness, and a short time after dark arrived at an encampment. Having carefully reconnoitered it, they determined to remain quiet until daylight, and then fall upon the enemy, as before, in two divisions, one to be commanded by Kenton and the other by Baker.

Everything remained quiet until four o'clock in the morning, when Baker moved at the head of his party, in order to take the appointed position, (which was very advantageous, and in conjunction with Kenton's, completely surrounded the enemy,) while Kenton remained stationary, awaiting the signal of attack. By some mistake, Baker moved in a false direction, and, to the surprise of both parties, instead of enclosing the Indian camp, he fell directly upon it. A heavy firing and the usual yelling quickly announced the fact to Kenton, who moved hastily up to the assistance of his friends. It was still perfectly dark, and the firing was of course at random.

Baker, in whose fiery character courage predominated over everything else, lost all patience at the restraint under which they lay, and urged strenuously that they should rush upon the enemy and decide the affair at once with the tomahawk; but Kenton, whom repeated misfortunes had rendered extremely cautious, opposed it so vehemently that it was not done. One of their men had fallen, and they could hear one of the enemy, apparently not more than thirty yards from them, groan deeply, and occasionally converse with his companions in the Indian tongue. The wounded man was the unfortunate John Ward, whose hard fate it was to fight against the whites in a battle in which his own father was killed; to encounter two of his brothers in the field, and, finally, to fall mortally wounded in a night skirmish, when his brother was opposed to him and was within hearing of his groans. His father perished in the long battle at the "Point," as it was called, near the mouth of the Kanawha. The whole force of the Shawnees was assembled at that point, and John Ward was then nineteen years of age, so that there can be but little doubt of his having been present.

A DESPERATE ATTACK ON CAPT. WM. HUBBELL'S BOAT.

In the year 1791, while the Indians were yet troublesome, especially on the banks of the Ohio, Captain William Hubbell, who had previously emigrated to Kentucky from the State of Vermont, and who, after having fixed his family in the neighborhood of Frankfort, then a frontier settlement, had been compelled to go to the eastward on business, was a second time on his way to that country. On one of the tributary streams of the Monongahela he procured a flat-bottomed boat and embarked, in company with Mr. Daniel Light and Mr. William Plascut and his family, consisting of a wife and eight children, destined for Limestone, Kentucky. On their progress down the Ohio river, and soon after passing Pittsburgh, they saw evident traces of Indians along the banks, and there is every reason to believe that a boat which they overtook, and which, through carelessness, was suffered to run aground on an island, became a prey to these merciless savages. Though Captain Hubbell and his party stopped some time for it in a lower part of the river, it did not arrive, and has never, to their knowledge, been heard of since.

Before they reached the mouth of the Great Kanawha, they had, by several successive additions, increased their number to twenty, consisting of nine men, three women and eight children. The men, besides those mentioned above, were one John Stoner, an Irishman and a Dutchman, whose names are not recollected, Messrs. Ray and Tucker, and a Mr. Kilpatrick, whose two daughters also were of the party. Information received at Gallipolis confirmed the expectation, which appearances previously raised, of a serious conflict with a large body of Indians; and as Captain Hubbell had been regularly appointed commander of the boat, every possible preparation was made for a formidable and successful resistance of the anticipated attack. The nine men were divided into three watches for the night, which were alternately to continue awake, and be on the lookout for two hours at a time. The arms on board, which consisted principally of old muskets, much out of order, were collected, loaded and put in the best possible condition for service.

About sunset on that day, the 23d of March, 1791, our party overtook a fleet of six boats descending the river in company, and intended to have continued with them, but as their passengers seemed to be more disposed to dancing than fighting, and as, soon after dark, notwithstanding the remonstrances of Captain Hubbell, they commenced fiddling and dancing instead of preparing their arms, and taking the necessary rest preparatory to battle, it was wisely considered more hazardous to be in such company than to be alone. It was, therefore, determined to proceed rapidly forward by the aid of the oars, and to leave those thoughtless fellow travelers behind. One of the boats, however, belonging to the fleet, commanded by a Captain Greathouse, adopted the same plan, and for a while kept up with Captain Hubbell, but all its crew at length falling asleep, that boat also ceased to be propelled by the oars, and Captain Hubbell and his party proceeded steadily forward *alone*. Early in the night a canoe was dimly seen floating down the river, in which were probably Indians reconnoitering, and other evident indications were observed of the neighborhood and hostile intentions of a formidable party of savages.

It was now agreed that should the attack, as was probable, be deferred till morning, every man should be up before the dawn, in order to make as great a show as possible of numbers and of strength; and that, whenever the action should take place, the women and children should lie down on the cabin floor, and be protected as well as they could by the trunks and other baggage, which might be placed around them. In this perilous situation they continued during the night, and the Captain, who had not slept more than one hour since he left Pittsburgh, was too deeply impressed with the imminent danger which surrounded him to obtain any rest at that time.

Just as daylight began to appear in the East, and before the men were up and at their posts agreeably to arrangement, a voice at some distance below them, in a plaintive tone, repeatedly solicited them to come on shore, as there were some white people who wished to obtain a passage in their boat. This the Captain very naturally and correctly concluded to be an Indian artifice, and its only effect was to rouse the men, and place every one on his guard. The voice of entreaty was soon changed into the language of indignation and insult, and the sound of distant paddles announced the approach of the savage foe. At length three Indian canoes were seen through the mist of the morning rapidly advancing. With the utmost coolness the Captain and his comrades prepared to receive them. The chairs, tables and other incumbrances were thrown into the river, in order to clear the deck for action. Every man took his position, and was ordered not to fire till the savages had approached so near that (to use the words of Captain Hubbell,) "the flash from the guns might singe their eye-brows;" and a special caution was given, that the men should fire successively, so that there might be no interval. On the arrival of the canoes, they were found to contain about twenty-five or thirty Indians each.

As soon as they had approached within the reach of musket shot, a general fire was given from one of them, which wounded Mr. Tucker through the hip so severely that his leg hung only by the flesh, and shot Mr. Light just below his ribs. The three canoes placed themselves at the bow, stern and on the right side of the boat, so that they had an opportunity of raking in every direction. The fire now commenced from the boat, and had a powerful effect in checking the confidence and fury of the Indians. The Captain, after firing his own gun, took up that of one of the wounded men, raised it to his shoulder, and was about to discharge it, when a ball came and took away the lock; he coolly turned round, seized a brand of fire from the kettle which served for a caboose, and applying it to the pan, discharged the piece with effect. A very regular and constant fire was now kept up on both sides. The Captain was just in the act of raising his gun a third time, when a ball passed through his right arm, and for a moment disabled him. Scarcely had he recovered from the shock, and reacquired the use of his hand, which had been suddenly *drawn up* by the wound, when he observed the Indians in one of the canoes just about to board the boat in its bow, where the horses were placed belonging to the party. So near had they approached, that some of them had actually seized with their hands the side of the boat.

Severely wounded as he was, he caught up a pair of horsemen s pistols and rushed forward to repel the attempt at boarding. On his approach the Indians fell back, and he discharged a pistol with effect at the foremost man. After firing the second pistol he found himself without arms, and was compelled to retreat; but stepping back upon a pile of small wood which had been prepared for burning in the kettle, the thought struck him that it might be made use of in repelling the foe, and he continued for some time to strike them with it so forcibly and actively, that they were unable to enter the boat, and at length he wounded one of them so severely that with a yell they suddenly gave way. All the canoes then discontinued the contest, and directed their course to Captain Greathouse's boat, which was in sight. Here a striking contrast was exhibited to the firmness and intrepidity which had been displayed. Instead of resisting the attack, the people on board of this boat retired to the cabin in dismay. The Indians entered it without opposition, and rowed it to the shore, where they killed the Captain and a lad of about fourteen years of age. The women they placed in the centre of their canoes, and, manning them with fresh hands, again pursued Captain Hubbell and party. A melancholy alternative now presented itself to these brave but almost desponding men, either to fall a prey to the savages themselves, or to run the risk of shooting the women, who had been placed in the canoes in the hope of deriving protection from their presence. But "self-preservation is the first law of nature," and the Captain very justly remarked, there would not be much humanity in preserving their lives at such a sacrifice, merely that they might become victims of savage cruelty at some subsequent period.

Second Attack and Obstinate Resistance—A Brave Boy.

There were now but four men left on board of Captain Hubbell's boat capable of defending it, and the Captain himself was severely wounded in two places. The second attack, however, was resisted with almost incredible firmness and vigor. Whenever the Indians would rise to fire, their opponents would commonly give them the first shot, which, in almost every instance, would prove fatal. Notwithstanding the disparity of numbers, and the exhausted condition of the defenders of the boat, the Indians at length appeared to despair of success, and the canoes successively retired to the shore. Just as the last one was departing, Captain Hubbell called to the Indian who was standing in the stern, and on his turning round discharged his piece at him. When the smoke, which for a moment obstructed the vision, was dissipated, he was seen lying on his back, and appeared to be severely, perhaps mortally, wounded.

Unfortunately the boat now drifted near to the shore, where the Indians were collected, and a large concourse, probably between four and five hundred, were soon rushing down on the bank. Ray and Plascut, the only men remaining unhurt, were placed at the oars, and, as the boat was not more than twenty yards from shore, it was deemed prudent for all to lie down in as safe a position as possible, and attempt to push forward with the utmost practicable rapidity. While they continued in this situation, nine balls were shot into one oar and ten in the other, without wounding the rowers, who were hidden from view, and protected by the sides of the boat and the blankets in its stern. During this dreadful exposure to the fire of the savages, which continued about twenty minutes, Mr. Kilpatrick observed a particular Indian, whom he thought a favorable mark for his rifle, and, notwithstanding the solemn warning of Captain Hubbell, rose to shoot him. He immediately received a ball in his mouth, which passed out at the back part of his head, and was almost at the same moment shot through the heart. He fell among the horses that about the same time were killed, and presented, to his afflicted daughters and fellow travelers, who were witnesses of the awful occurrence, a spectacle of horror which we need not further attempt to describe.

The boat was now providentially and suddenly carried out into the middle of the stream, and taken by the current beyond the reach of the enemy's balls. Our little band, reduced as they were in numbers, wounded, afflicted and almost exhausted by fatigue, were still unsubdued in spirit, and being assembled in all their strength, men, women and children, with an appearance of triumph gave three hearty cheers, calling to the Indians to come on again if they were fond of the sport.

Thus ended this awful conflict, in which out of nine men two only escaped unhurt. Tucker and Kilpatrick were killed on the spot, Stoner was mortally wounded and died on his arrival at Limestone, and all the rest, excepting Ray and Plascut, were severely wounded. The women and children were all uninjured, excepting a little son of Mr. Plascut, who, after the battle was over, came to the Captain, and, with great coolness, requested him to take a ball out of his head. On examination it appeared that a bullet which had passed through the side of the boat, had penetrated the forehead of this little hero, and remained under the skin. The Captain took it out, and the youth, observing, "*that is not all*," raised his arm, and exhibited a piece of bone at the point of his elbow, which had been shot off, and hung only by the skin. His mother exclaimed, "Why did you not tell me of this?" "Because," he coolly replied, " the Captain directed us to be silent during the action, and I thought you would be likely to make a noise if I told you."

The boat made the best of its way down the river, and the object was to reach Limestone that night. The Captain's arm had bled profusely, and he was compelled to close the sleeve of his coat, in order to retain the blood and stop its effusion. In this situation, tormented by excruciating pain, and faint through loss of blood, he was under the necessity of steering the boat with the left arm till about ten o'clock that night, when he was relieved by Mr. William Brooks, who resided on the bank of the river, and who was induced by the calls of the suffering party to come out to their assistance. By his aid and that of some other persons who were in the same manner brought to their relief, they were enabled to reach Limestone about twelve o'clock that night.

Immediately on the arrival of Mr. Brooks, Captain Hubbell, relieved from labor and responsibility, sunk under the weight of pain and fatigue, and became for a while totally insensible. When the boat reached Limestone, he found himself unable to walk, and was obliged to be carried up to the tavern. Here he had his wound dressed, and continued for several days, until he acquired sufficient strength to proceed homewards.

On the arrival of the party at Limestone, they found a considerable force of armed men about to march against the same Indians, from whose attack they had so severely suffered. They now learned that, the Sunday preceding, the same party of savages had cut off a detachment of men ascending the Ohio from Fort Washington, at the mouth of Licking river, and had killed with their tomahawks, without firing a gun, twenty-one out of twenty-two men, of which the detachment consisted.

Crowds of people, as might be expected, came to view the boat which had been the scene of so much heroism and such horrid carnage, and to visit the resolute little band by whom it had been so gallantly and perseveringly defended. On examination it was found that the sides of the boat were literally filled with bullets and with bullet holes. There was scarcely a space of two feet square in the part above the water which had not either a ball remaining in it, or a hole through which a ball had passed. Some persons, who had the curiosity to count the number of holes in the blankets which were hung up as curtains in the stern of the boat, affirmed that in the space of five feet square there were one hundred and twenty-two. Four horses out of five were killed, and the escape of the fifth amidst such a shower of balls appears almost miraculous.

The day after the arrival of Captain Hubbell and his companions the five remaining boats, which they had passed on the night preceding the battle, reached Limestone. Those on board remarked that during the action they distinctly saw the flashes, but could not hear the reports of the guns. The Indians, it appears, had met with too formidable a resistance from a single boat to attack a fleet, and suffered them to pass unmolested; and since that time, it is believed, no boat has been assailed by Indians on the Ohio.

The force which marched out to disperse this formidable body of savages, discovered several Indians dead on the shore near the scene of action. They also found the bodies of Captain Greathouse and several others, men, women and children, who had been on board of his boat. Most of them appeared to have been *whipped to death*, as they were found stripped, tied to trees, and marked with the appearance of lashes, and large rods, which seemed to have been worn with use, were observed lying near them.

A SAVAGE BOAT ATTACK AND A TERRIBLE COMBAT.

In May, 1788, a flatboat loaded with kettles, intended for the manufacture of salt at Bullitt's Lick, Ky., left Louisville with thirteen persons, twelve armed men and one woman, on board. The boat and cargo were owned by Henry Crist and Solomon Spears; and the company consisted of Crist, Spears, Christian Crepps, Thomas Floyd, Joseph Boyce, Evans Moore, an Irishman named Fossett, and five others, and a woman, whose name is not preserved. The intention of the party was to descend the Ohio, which was then very high, to the mouth of Salt river, not far below, and then ascend the latter river, the current of which was entirely deadened by back water from the Ohio, to a place near the licks, called Mud Garrison, which was a temporary fortification, constructed of two rows of slight stockades, and the space between filled with mud and gravel from the bank of the river hard by. The works inclosed a space of about half an acre, and stood about midway between Bullitt's Lick and the falls of Salt river, where Shepherdsville, Ky., now stands. These works were then occupied by the families of the salt makers, and those who hunted to supply them with food and acted also as an advanced guard to give notice of the approach of any considerable body of men.

On the 25th of May the boat entered Salt river, and the hands commenced working her up with sweep-oars. There was no current one way or the other. While on the Ohio, the great breadth of the river secured them against any sudden attack, but when they came into Salt river they were within reach of the Indian rifle from either shore. It became necessary, therefore, to send out scouts to apprise them of any danger ahead. In the evening of the first day, Crist and Floyd went ashore to reconnoitre the bank ahead of the boat. Late in the evening they discovered a fresh trail, but for want of light they could not make out the number of Indians. They remained out all night, but made no further discoveries. In the morning, as they were returning down the river towards the boat, they heard a number of guns, which they believed to be Indians killing game for breakfast. They hastened back to the boat and communicated what they had heard and seen.

They pulled on up the river until eight o'clock, and arrived at a point eight miles below the mouth of the Rolling Fork, where they drew into shore on the north side of the river, intending to land and cook their breakfast. As they drew into shore, they heard the gobbling of turkeys (as they supposed) on the bank where they were going to land, and as the boat touched, Fossett and another sprang ashore, with their guns in their hands, to shoot turkeys. They were cautioned of their danger, but disregarding the admonition, hastily ascended the bank. Their companions in the boat had barely lost sight of them when they heard a volley of rifles discharged all at once on the bank immediately above, succeeded by a yell of savages so terrific as to induce a belief that the woods were filled with Indians. This attack, so sudden and violent, took the boat's company by surprise; and they had barely time to seize their rifles and place themselves in a posture of defence when Fossett and his companion came dashing down the bank, hotly pursued by a large body of Indians.

Crist stood in the bow of the boat, with his rifle in his hand. At the first sight of the enemy he brought his gun to his face, but instantly perceived that the object of his aim was a white man, and a sudden thought flashed across his mind that the enemy was a company of surveyors that he knew to be then in the woods, and that the attack was made in sport, &c., let his gun down, and at the same time his white foeman sank out of sight behind the bank. But the firing had commenced in good earnest on both sides. Crist again brought his rifle to his face, and as he did so the white man's head was rising over the bank with his gun also presented. Crist got the fire on him, and at the crack of his rifle the white man fell forward dead. Fossett's hunting companion plunged into the water and got in safely at the bow of the boat; but Fossett's arm was broken by the first fire on the hill. The boat, owing to the high water, did not touch the land, and he got into the river further towards the stern and swam round, with his gun in his left hand, and was taken safely into the stern.

So intent were the Indians on the pursuit of their prey that many of them ran to the water's edge, struck and shot at Fossett and his companion while getting into the boat, and some even seized the boat and attempted to draw it nearer the shore. In this attempt many of the Indians perished; some were shot dead as they approached the boat; others were killed in the river, and it required the most stubborn resistance and determined valor to keep them from carrying the boat by assault. Repulsed in their efforts to board the boat, the savages withdrew higher up the bank, and, taking their stations behind trees, commenced a regular and galling fire, which was returned with the spirit of brave men rendered desperate by the certain knowledge that no quarter would be given, and that it was an issue of victory or death to every soul on board.

The boat had a log chain for a cable, and when she was first brought ashore the chain was thrown around a small tree that stood on the water's edge, and the hook run through one of the links. This had been done before the first fire was made upon Fossett on shore. The kettles in the boat had been ranked up along the sides, leaving an open gangway through the middle of the boat from bow to stern. Unfortunately, the bow lay to shore, so that the guns of the Indians raked the whole length of the gangway, and their fire was constant and destructive. Spears, and several others of the brave men, had already fallen, some killed and others mortally wounded. From the commencement of the battle many efforts had been made to disengage the boat from the shore, all of which had failed. The hope was that if they could once loose the cable, the boat would drift out of the reach of the enemy's guns, but any attempt to do this by hand would expose the person to certain destruction.

Fossett's right arm was broken, and he could no longer handle his rifle. He got a pole and, placing himself low down in the bow of the boat, commenced punching at the hook in the chain, but the point of the hook was turned from him, and all his efforts seemed only to drive it further into the link. He at length discovered where a small limb had been cut from the pole and left a knot about an inch long; this knot, after a number of efforts, he placed against the point of the hook, and, jerking the pole suddenly towards him, threw the hook out of the link. The chain fell and the boat drifted slowly out from the bank, and by means of an oar worked overhead, was brought into the middle of the river with her side to the shore, which protected them from the fire of the Indians. The battle had now lasted upwards of an hour. The odds against the crew were at least ten to one. The fire had been very destructive on both sides, and a great many Indians had been killed; but if the boat had remained much longer at the shore, it was manifest that there would have been none of the crew left to tell the tale of their disaster.

The survivors had now time to look round upon the havoc that had been made of their little band. Five of their companions lay dead in the gangway; Spears, Floyd, Fossett and Boyce were wounded; Crepps, Crist and Moore remained unhurt. It was evident that Spears' wound was mortal, and that he could survive but a few moments. He urged the survivors to run the boat to the opposite side of the river and save themselves by immediate flight, and leave him to his fate. Crepps and Crist positively refused

But the boat was gradually nearing the southern shore of the river. At this time the Indians, to the number of forty or fifty, were seen crossing the river above, at a few hundred yards' distance, some on logs and some swimming and carrying their rifles over their heads. The escape of the boat was now hopeless, as there was a large body of Indians on each side of the river. If the boat had been carried immediately to the opposite side of the river as soon as her cable was loosed, the survivors might have escaped; but to such minds and hearts the idea of leaving their dying friends to the mercy of the Indian tomahawk was insupportable. The boat at length touched the southern shore; a hasty preparation was made to bury the wounded in the woods; Floyd, Fossett and Boyce got to land and sought concealment in the thickets. Crepps and Crist turned to their suffering friend, Spears, but death had kindly stepped in and cut short the savage triumph. The woman now remained. They offered to assist her to shore, that she might take her chance of escape in the woods; but the danger of her position, and the scenes of blood and death around her, had overpowered her senses, and no entreaty or remonstrance could prevail with her to move. She sat with her face buried in her hands, and no effort could make her sensible that there was any hope of escape.

A Very Obstinate Defence and a Barren Victory.

The Indians had gained the south side of the river, and were yelling like bloodhounds as they ran down towards the boat, which they now looked upon as their certain prey. Crepps and Crist seized a rifle apiece and ascended the river bank; at the top of the hill they met the savages, and charged them with a shout. Crepps fired upon them, but Crist, in his haste, had taken up Fossett's gun, which had got wet as he swam with it to the boat on the opposite side—it missed fire. At this time Moore passed them and escaped. The Indians, when charged by Crepps and Crist, fell back into a ravine that put into the river immediately above them. Crist and Crepps again commenced their flight. The Indians rallied and rose from the ravine, and fired a volley at them as they fled. Crepps received a ball in his left side; a bullet struck Crist's heel and completely crushed the bones of his foot. They parted and met no more. The Indians, intent on plunder, did not pursue them, but rushed into the boat. Crist heard one long, agonizing shriek from the unfortunate woman, and the wild shouts of the savages, as they possessed themselves of the spoils of a costly but barren victory.

Crepps, in the course of the next day, arrived in the neighborhood of Long Lick, and, being unable to travel farther, laid down in the woods to die. Moore alone escaped unhurt, and brought in the tidings of the defeat of the boat. The country was at once roused. Crepps was found and brought in, but died about the time he reached home. Crist described Crepps as a tall, fair-haired, handsome man; kind, brave and enterprising, and possessed of all those high and striking qualities that gave the heroic stamp to that hardy race of pioneers among whom he had lived and died. He had been the lion of the fight. By exposing himself to the most imminent peril, he inspirited his companions with his own contempt of danger. He and Crist had stood over Fossett, and kept the Indians treed while he disengaged the cable; and his coolness during the long, bloody struggle of the day had won the admiration of Crist himself—than whom a more dauntless man had never contended with mortal foe. Crepps left a young wife and one son, then an infant. His wife was *enceinte* at the time of his death— the posthumous child was a daughter, and is the wife of the Hon. Charles A. Wickliffe, of Kentucky. The son died shortly after he arrived at man's estate.

Crist was so disabled by the wound that he could not walk. The bones of his heel were crushed. He crept into a thicket and laid down. His wound bled profusely. He could not remain there long. His feet were now of no use to him. He bound his moccasins on his knees, and commenced his journey. Piece by piece, his hat hunting shirt and vest were consumed to shield his hands against the rugged rocks which lay in his way. He crawled on all day up the river, and at night crossed over to the north side upon a log that he rolled down the bank. He concealed himself in a thicket and tried to sleep—but pain and exhaustion and loss of blood had driven sleep from his eyes. His foot and leg were much swollen and inflamed. Guided by the stars, he crept on again. Between midnight and day he came in sight of a camp fire and heard the barking of a dog. A number of Indians rose up from around the fire, and he crept softly away from the light. He laid down and remained quiet for some time. When all was still again, he resumed his slow and painful journey. He crawled into a small branch, and kept on down it for some distance upon the rocks, that he might leave no trace behind him.

At daylight he ascended an eminence of considerable height to ascertain, if possible, where he was, and how to shape his future course; but all around was wilderness. He was aiming to reach Bullitt's Lick, now about eight miles distant, and his progress was not half a mile an hour. He toiled on all day. Night came on—the second night of his painful journey. Since leaving the small branch the night before, he had found no water—since the day before the battle, he had not tasted food. Worn down with hunger, want of sleep, acute pain and raging thirst, he laid himself down to die. But his sufferings were not to end here—guided again by the stars, he struggled on. Every rag that he could interpose between the rugged stones and his bleeding hands and knee (for he could now use but one) was worn away. The morning came—the morning of the third day; it brought him but little hope; but the indomitable spirit within him disdained to yield, and during the day he made what progress he could. As the evening drew on he became aware that he was in the vicinity of Bullitt's Lick; but he could go no further; nature had made her last effort, and he laid himself down and prayed that death would speedily end his sufferings.

When darkness came on, from where he lay he could see the hundred fires of the furnaces at the licks all glowing; and he even fancied he could see the dusky forms of the firemen as they passed to and fro around the pits, but they were more than half a mile off, and how was he to reach them? He had not eaten a morsel in four days; he had been drained of almost his last drop of blood; the wounded leg had become so stiff and swollen that for the last two days and nights he had dragged it after him; the flesh was worn from his knee and from the palms of his hands. Relief was in his sight, but to reach it was impossible. Suddenly he heard the tramp of a horse's feet approaching him, and hope sprang up once more in his breast. The sound came nearer and still more near. A path ran near the place where he lay; a man on horseback approached within a few rods of him; he mustered his remaining strength and hailed him, but to his utter surprise and dismay, the horseman turned suddenly and galloped off towards the licks.

Despair now seized him. To die alone of hunger and thirst, in sight of hundreds and of plenty, seemed to him the last dregs of the bitterest cup that fate could offer to mortal lips. O! that he could have fallen by the side of his friend in the proud battle! That he could have met the Indian tomahawk and died in the strength of his manhood, and not have been doomed to linger out his life in days and nights of pain and agony, and to die by piecemeal in childish despair. While these thoughts were passing in his mind, the horseman (a negro) regained the licks and alarmed the people there with the intelligence that the Indians were approaching. On being interrogated, all the account he could give was that some person had called to him in the woods, a half mile off, and called him by the wrong name. It was manifest it was not Indians, and forthwith a number of men set out, guided by the negro to the place. Crist's hopes again revived, when he heard voices and saw lights approaching. They came near and hailed. Crist knew the voice, and called to the man by name. This removed all doubt, and they approached the spot where he lay. A sad and mournful sight was before them. A man that had left them a few days before, in the bloom of youth, health and buoyant spirits, now lay stretched upon the earth, a worn and mangled skeleton, unable to lift a hand to bid them welcome. They bore him home; the ball was extracted, but his recovery was slow and doubtful. It was a year before he was a man again.

The woman in the boat was carried a prisoner to Canada. Ten years afterwards, Crist met her again in Kentucky. She had been redeemed by an Indian trader, and brought into Wayne's camp on the Maumee, and restored to her friends. She informed Crist that the body of Indians which made the attack on the boat numbered over one hundred and twenty, of whom about thirty were killed in the engagement. The account was confirmed by Indians whom Crist met with afterwards, and who had been in the battle. They told Crist that the boat's crew fought more like devils than men, and if they had taken one of them prisoner, they would have roasted him alive. Crist was afterwards a member of the Kentucky Legislature, and, in 1808, was a member of Congress. He died at his residence in Bullitt county, in August, 1844, aged eighty years.

A FIERCE COMBAT BY THREE KENTUCKIANS.

In the Spring of 1784 three young Kentuckians, Davis, Caffree and McClure, pursued a party of southern Indians, who had stolen horses from Lincoln county, and finding it impossible to overtake them, they determined to go on to the nearest Indian settlement and make reprisals —horse stealing being at that time a very fashionable amusement and much practiced on both sides. After traveling several days they came within a few miles of an Indian town near the Tennessee river, called Chicamauga. Here they fell in with three Indians. Finding themselves equal in point of numbers, the two parties made signs of peace, shook hands and agreed to travel together. Each, however, was evidently suspicious of the other. The Indians walked on one side of the road and the whites upon the other, watching each other attentively.

At length the Indians spoke together in tones so low and earnest, that the whites became satisfied of their treacherous intentions, and determined to anticipate them. Caffree being a very powerful man, proposed that he himself should seize one Indian, while Davis and McClure should shoot the other two. The plan was a bad one, but was unfortunately adopted. Caffree sprang boldly upon the nearest Indian, grasped his throat firmly, hurled him to the ground, and drawing a cord from his pocket attempted to tie him. At the same instant Davis and McClure attempted to perform their respective parts. McClure killed his man, but Davis' gun missed fire. All three, *i. e.*, the two white men and the Indian at whom Davis had flashed, immediately took trees and prepared for a skirmish, while Caffree remained upon the ground with the captured Indian—both exposed to the fire of the others. In a few seconds the savage at whom Davis had flashed, shot Caffree as he lay upon the ground and gave him a mortal wound, and was instantly shot in turn by McClure, who had reloaded his gun. Caffree becoming very weak, called upon Davis to come and assist him in tying the Indian, and directly afterwards expired. As Davis was running up to the assistance of his friend, the Indian, now released by the death of his captor, sprang to his feet, and seizing Caffree's rifle, presented it menacingly at Davis, whose gun was not in order for service, and who ran off into the forest, closely pursued by the Indian. McClure hastily reloaded his gun, and taking up the rifle which Davis had dropped, followed them for some distance into the forest, making all those signals which had been concerted between them in case of separation. All, however, was vain; he saw nothing more of Davis, nor could he ever afterwards learn his fate. As he never returned to Kentucky, however, he probably perished.

McClure, finding himself alone in the enemy's country and surrounded by dead bodies, thought it prudent to abandon the object of the expedition and return to Kentucky. He accordingly retraced his steps, still bearing Davis' rifle in addition to his own. He had scarcely marched a mile before he saw advancing from the opposite direction an Indian warrior, riding a horse with a bell around its neck, and accompanied by a boy on foot. Dropping one of the rifles, which might have created suspicion, McClure advanced with an air of confidence, extending his hand and making other signs of peace. The opposite party appeared frankly to receive his overtures, and, dismounting, seated himself upon a log, and drawing out his pipe, gave a few puffs himself and then handed it to McClure.

In a few minutes another bell was heard, at the distance of half a mile, and a second party of Indians appeared upon horseback. The Indian with McClure now coolly informed him by signs that when the horsemen arrived, he (McClure) was to be bound and carried off as a prisoner with his feet tied under the horse's belly. In order to explain it more fully, the Indian got astride of the log and locked his legs together underneath it. McClure, internally thanking the fellow for his excess of candor, determined to disappoint him, and while his enemy was busily engaged in riding the log, and mimicking the actions of a prisoner, he very quietly blew his brains out and ran off into the woods. The Indian boy instantly mounted the belled horse and rode off in an opposite direction.

McClure was fiercely pursued by several small Indian dogs, that frequently ran between his legs and threw him down. After falling five or six times, his eyes became full of dust and he was totally blind. Despairing of escape, he doggedly lay upon his face, expecting every instant to feel the edge of the tomahawk. To his astonishment, however, no enemy appeared, and even the Indian dogs, after tugging at him for a few minutes, and completely stripping him of his breeches, left him to continue his journey unmolested. Finding everything quiet, in a few moments he arose, and taking up his gun, continued his march to Kentucky. He reached home in safety, and in 1820 was still alive. This communication is from his own lips, and may be relied upon as correct.

THOMAS MARSHALL HAILED BY JAMES GIRTY.

In the course of the next year many families came down the Ohio in boats, landed at Maysville, and continued their route by land, in such parts of the country as pleased them. Out of a number of incidents which attended the passage of boats down the river, I shall select two, as worthy of being mentioned. Colonel Thomas Marshall, formerly commander of the Third Virginia Regiment on continental establishment, and subsequently holding the same rank in the Virginia artillery, embarked, with a numerous family, on board of a flat-bottomed boat, and descended the Ohio without any incident worthy of notice until he had passed the mouth of the Kanawha. Here, about ten o'clock at night, he was hailed from the northern shore by a man who spoke good English, and quickly announced himself as James Girty, the brother of Simon, both of whom have been repeatedly mentioned. The boat dropped slowly down within one hundred and fifty yards of the shore, and Girty, making a corresponding movement on the beach, the conference was kept up for several minutes. He began by mentioning his name, and inquired that of the master of the boat.

Having been satisfied upon this head, he assured him that he knew him well, respected him highly, etc., and concluded with some rather extraordinary remarks. "He had been posted there," he said, "by the order of his brother Simon, to warn all boats of the danger of permitting themselves to be decoyed ashore. The Indians had become jealous of him, and he had lost that influence which he formerly held among them. He deeply regretted the injury which he had inflicted upon his countrymen, and wished to be restored to their society. In order to convince them of the sincerity of his regard, he had directed him to warn all boats of the snares spread for them. Every effort would be made to draw passengers ashore. White men would appear on the bank, and children would be heard to supplicate for mercy. But," continued he, "do you keep the middle of the river, and steel your heart against every mournful application which you may receive." The Colonel thanked him for his intelligence, and continued his course.

CAPTAIN JAMES WARD AND THE FAT DUTCHMAN.

About the same time Captain James Ward, until late years a highly respectable citizen of Mason county, Ky., was descending the Ohio, under circumstances which rendered a *rencontre* with the Indians peculiarly to be dreaded. He, together with half a dozen others, one of them his nephew, embarked in a crazy boat, about forty-five feet long and eight feet wide, with no other bulwark than a single pine plank above each gunwale. The boat was much encumbered with baggage, and seven horses were on board. Having seen no enemy for several days, they had become secure and careless and permitted the boat to drift within fifty yards of the Ohio shore. Suddenly several hundred Indians showed themselves on the bank, and running down boldly to the water's edge, opened a heavy fire upon the boat. The astonishment of the crew may be conceived.

Captain Ward and his nephew were at the oars when the enemy appeared, and the Captain, knowing that their safety depended upon their ability to regain the middle of the river, kept his seat firmly and exerted his utmost powers at the oar; but his nephew started up at sight of the enemy, seized his rifle, and was in the act of leveling it, when he received a ball in the breast and fell dead in the bottom of the boat. Unfortunately, his oar fell into the river, and the Captain, having no one to pull against him, rather urged the boat nearer to the hostile shore than otherwise. He quickly seized a plank, however, and giving his own oar to another of the crew, he took the station which his nephew had held, and, unhurt by the shower of bullets which flew around him, continued to exert himself until the boat had reached a more respectable distance. He then for the first time looked around him, in order to observe the condition of the crew.

His nephew lay in his blood, perfectly lifeless; the horses had been all killed or mortally wounded. Some had fallen overboard; others were struggling violently, and causing their frail bark to dip water so abundantly as to excite the most serious apprehensions. But the crew presented the most singular spectacle. A Captain, who had served with reputation in the Continental army, seemed now totally bereft of his faculties. He lay upon his back in the bottom of the boat, with hands uplifted, and a countenance in which terror was personified, exclaiming, in a tone of despair, "Oh, Lord! Oh, Lord!" A Dutchman, whose weight might amount to about three hundred pounds, was anxiously engaged in endeavoring to find shelter for his bulky person, which, from the lowness of the gunwales, was a very difficult undertaking. In spite of his utmost efforts a portion of his posterial luxuriance appeared above the gunwale, and afforded a mark to the enemy which brought a constant shower of balls around it.

In vain he shifted his position. The hump still appeared, and the balls still flew around it, until the Dutchman, losing all patience, raised his head above the gunwale, and, in a tone of querulous remonstrance, called out, "Oh, now! quit tat tamned nonsense tere, will you?" Not a shot was fired from the boat. At one time, after they had partly regained the current, Captain Ward attempted to bring his rifle to bear upon them, but so violent was the agitation of the boat from the furious struggles of the horses, that he could not steady his piece within twenty yards of the enemy, and, quickly laying it aside, returned to the oar.

The Indians followed them down the river for more than an hour, but, having no canoes, they did not attempt to board; and as the boat was at length transferred to the opposite side of the river, they finally abandoned the pursuit and disappeared. None of the crew, save the young man already mentioned, were hurt, although the Dutchman's seat of honor served as a target for the space of an hour, and the Continental Captain was deeply mortified at the sudden, and, as he said, "unaccountable" panic which had seized him. Captain Ward himself was protected by a post, which had been fastened to the gunwale, and behind which he sat while rowing.

EXCITING NARRATIVE OF MAJOR VAN CAMPEN.

Moses Van Campen and his brother Jacobus, or "Cobus Van Camp," as he was called, were famous in the border wars along the Susquehanna. Moses was a bold, daring scout or spy, and was engaged by Sullivan on his expedition through the Six Nations' country, when, in return for the massacre of Wyoming and other enormities, it was determined to retaliate by ravaging the Indian country. From Major Van Campen's petition to Congress for a pension, (which, we may add, was speedily granted, so conspicuous were his courage and services,) we quote the following account of a desperate fight with Indians:

On the return of the army I was taken with the camp fever, and was removed to the fort which I had built in '78, where my father was still living. In the course of the Winter I recovered my health, and my father's house having been burnt in '78, by the party which attacked the before-mentioned fort, my father requested me to go with him and a younger brother to our farm, about four miles distant, to make preparations for building another, and raising some grain. But little apprehension was entertained of molestation from the Indians this season, as they had been so completely routed the year before. We left the fort about the last of March, 1780, accompanied by my uncle and his son, about twelve years old, and one Peter Pence. We had been on our farm about four or five days when, on the morning of the 30th of March, we were surprised by a party of ten Indians. My father was lunged through with a war spear, his throat was cut and he was scalped, while my brother was tomahawked, scalped and thrown into the fire before my eyes. While I was struggling with a warrior, the fellow who had killed my father drew his spear from his body and made a violent thrust at me. I shrank from the spear; the savage who had hold of me turned it with his hand so that it only penetrated my vest and shirt. They were then satisfied with taking me prisoner, as they had the same morning taken my uncle's little son and Pence, though they killed my uncle. The same party, before they reached us, had touched on the lower settlements of Wyoming, and killed a Mr. Upson, and took a boy prisoner of the name of Rodgers.

We were now marched off up Fishing Creek, and in the afternoon of the same day we came to Huntingdon, where the Indians found four white men at a sugar camp, who fortunately discovered the Indians and fled to a house; the Indians only fired on them and wounded a Captain

Ranson, when they continued their course till night. Having encamped
and made their fire, we, the prisoners, were tied and well secured, five
Indians lying on one side of us and five on the other; in the morning
they pursued their course, and, leaving the waters of Fishing Creek,
touched the head waters of Hemlock Creek, where they found one
Abraham Pike, his wife and child. Pike was made prisoner, but his
wife and child they painted, and told *Joggo squaw*, go home. They continued their course that day, and encamped the same night in the same
manner as the previous. It came into my mind that sometimes individuals performed wonderful actions and surmounted the greatest
dangers. I then decided that these fellows must die; and thought of the
plan to dispatch them. The next day I had an opportunity to communicate my plan to my fellow prisoners; they treated it as a visionary
scheme for three men to attempt to dispatch ten Indians. I spread before them the advantages that three men would have over ten when
asleep; that we would be the first prisoners that would be taken
into their towns and villages after our army had destroyed their corn;
that we should be tied to the stake and suffer a cruel death; we had now
an inch of ground to fight on, and if we failed it would only be death,
and we might as well die one way as another.

That day passed away, and having encamped for the night, we lay as
before. In the morning we came to the river, and saw their canoes;
they had descended the river and run their canoes up on Little Tunk-
hannock Creek, so called; they crossed the river and set their canoes
adrift. I renewed my suggestion to my companions to dispatch them
that night, and urged they must decide the question. They agreed to
make the trial; but how shall we do it, was the question. Disarm them,
and each take a tomahawk and come to close work at once. There are
three of us; plant our blows with judgment and three times three will
make nine, and the tenth one we can kill at our leisure. They agreed
to disarm them, and after that one take possession of the guns and
fire, at the one side of the four, and the other two take tomahawks on
the other side and dispatch them. I observed that would be a very uncertain way; the first shot fired would give the alarm; they would
discover it to be the prisoners, and might defeat us. I had to yield to
their plan. Peter Pence was chosen to fire the guns, Pike and myself
to tomahawk. We cut and carried plenty of wood to give them a
good fire; the prisoners were tied and laid in their places; after I was
laid down, one of them had occasion to use his knife; he dropped it
at my feet; I turned my foot over it and concealed it; they all lay
down and fell asleep.

About midnight I got up and found them in sound sleep. I slipped to Pence, who rose; I cut him loose and handed him the knife; he did the same for me, and I in turn took the knife and cut Pike loose; in a minute's time we disarmed them.

Pence now took his station at the guns. Pike and myself, with our tomahawks, took our stations; I was to tomahawk three on the right wing, and Pike two on the left. That moment Pike's two awoke, and were getting up; here Pike proved a coward, and laid down. It was a critical moment. I saw there was no time to be lost; their heads turned up fair; I dispatched them in a moment, and turned to my lot, as per agreement, and as I was about to dispatch the last on my side of the fire, Pence shot and did good execution; there was only one at the off wing that his ball did not reach; his name was Mohawke, a stout, bold, daring fellow. In the alarm he jumped off about three rods from the fire; he saw it was the prisoners that made the attack, and, giving the war whoop, he darted to take possession of the guns; I was as quick to prevent him; the contest was then between him and myself. As I raised my tomahawk he turned quick to jump from me; I followed him and struck at him, but, missing his head, my tomahawk struck his shoulder, or rather the back of his neck; he pitched forward and fell; at the same time my foot slipped, and I fell by his side; we clinched; his arm was naked; he caught me round my neck; at the same time I caught him with my left arm around the body and gave him a close hug, at the same time feeling for his knife, but could not reach it.

In our scuffle my tomahawk dropped out. My head was under the wounded shoulder, and almost suffocated me with his blood. I made a violent spring and broke from his hold; we both rose at the same time, and he ran; it took me some time to clear the blood from my eyes; my tomahawk got covered up and I could not find it in time to overtake him; he was the only one of the party that escaped. Pike was powerless. I always have had a reverence for Christian devotion. Pike was trying to pray, and Pence swearing at him, charging him with cowardice, and saying it was no time to pray—he ought to fight; we were masters of the ground, and in possession of all their guns, blankets, match coats, &c. I then turned my attention to scalping them, and recovering the scalps of my father, brother, and others, I strung them all on my belt for safe keeping. We kept our ground till morning, and built a raft, it being near the bank of the river where they had encamped, about fifteen miles below Tioga Point; we got all our plunder on it and set sail for Wyoming, the nearest settlement. Our raft gave way, when we made for land, and we lost considerable property, though we saved our guns and ammunition, and took to land; we reached Wyalusing late in the afternoon.

Came to the Narrows; discovered a smoke below, and a raft lying at the shore, by which we were certain that a party of Indians had passed us in the course of the day, and had halted for the night. There was no alternative for us but to rout them or go over the mountain; the snow on the north side of the hill was deep; we knew, from the appearance of the raft, that the party must be small; we had two rifles each; my only fear was of Pike's cowardice. To know the worst of it, we agreed that I should ascertain their number and give the signal for the attack; I crept down the side of the hill, so near as to see their fires and packs, but saw no Indians. I concluded they had gone hunting for meat, and that this was a good opportunity for us to make off with their raft to the opposite side of the river. I gave the signal; they came and threw their packs on to the raft, which was made of small, dry pine timber; with poles and paddles we drove her briskly across the river, and had got nearly out of reach of shore when two of them came in; they fired, but their shots did no injury. We soon got under cover of an island, and went several miles; we had waded deep creeks through the day; the night was cold; we landed on an island and found a sink hole, in which we made our fire; after warming we were alarmed by a cracking in the crust; Pike supposed the Indians had got on to the island, and was calling for quarters; to keep him quiet we threatened him with his life; the stepping grew plainer, and seemed coming directly to the fire; I kept watch, and soon a noble raccoon came under the light. I shot the raccoon, when Pike jumped up and called out, "Quarters, gentlemen! quarters, gentlemen!" I took my game by the leg and threw it down to the fire. "Here, you cowardly rascal," I cried, "skin that and give us a roast for supper." The next night we reached Wyoming, and there was much joy at seeing us.

Chapter X.

THE FRIGHTFUL MASSACRE OF WYOMING.

> A scream! 'tis but the panther's—naught
>   Breaks the calm sunshine there.
> A thicket stirs! a deer has sought
>   From sight a closer lair.
> Again upon the grass they droop,
> Then bursts the well-known whoop on whoop;
>   Shrill, deafening on the ear.
> And onward, from their ambush deep,
> Like wolves the savage warriors leap.—*Street.*

One of the most dreadful and memorable atrocities recorded in American history was the awful massacre of Wyoming, made more illustrious by affording the theme for Campbell's Gertrude of Wyoming. It happened in 1778. The valley of Wyoming, situate in Luzerne county, Pennsylvania, was, and is yet, one of the richest and most beautiful in the country. It was early settled by a happy, contented and patriotic population, but was greatly exposed to incursions from the powerful Six Nations, then under malign tory influence.

Nearly all the able-bodied men of Wyoming fit to bear arms had been called away into the Continental army. The settlement consisted of eight townships, each five miles square, beautifully situated on either side of the Susquehanna, and had increased so rapidly that they were enabled to send a thousand men to serve in the armies of their country. To provide against the dangers of their defenceless situation, four forts had been erected to cover them from savage irruptions; but they had also the misfortune to have among them some very bitter royalists, and the two parties of whigs and tories were actuated by feelings of the most rancorous animosity. It was to be expected that these tories, many of whom had fled to join Johnson and Brant, of the Mohawk valley, would bring down vengeance upon a settlement which had evinced such ardent spirit in the cause of liberty.

Late in June, therefore, a large body of tories and savages, numbering eleven hundred, under the lead of that notorious royalist, Colonel

John Butler, descended the Susquehanna, and appeared before Jenkins' Fort, at the head of the valley. The invasion had not altogether been unexpected. For several weeks previous small parties of strange Indians had come and gone, professing friendship with their lips but acting in the most secret and treacherous manner. Colonel Zebulon Butler at once took alarm, and wrote to Congress and Washington, presenting his fears and the reasons for them, but nothing was done.

Jenkins' Fort was obliged to capitulate, and Wintermoot's followed suit. There were several more stockade forts at Wyoming, but with no other means of defence than the small arms fired through loop holes. In all Wyoming valley there was but one cannon—a four-pounder, without balls, and simply maintained at the Wilkesbarre Fort as an alarm gun. Almost all the defenders took refuge in Forty Fort. They only numbered about four hundred men and boys. Many of the men were gray-headed—some of them grandfathers. By invitation, Colonel Zebulon Butler placed himself at the head of this force, and prepared to make defence as best he could.

History does not furnish an instance of more gallant devotion than they exhibited. On July 3d they marched out, very rashly and unwisely, it must be confessed, to meet the enemy, Colonel Butler commanding the right wing and Colonel Dennison the left. Opposed to Zebulon Butler was John Butler, with his own tory rangers, in full uniform, and a detachment of Sir John Johnson's Royal Greens. Opposed to Dennison were the Indians, chiefly Senecas, seven hundred strong, led on by Gi-en-gwah-toh. Until very lately, the celebrated Mohawk Chief, Brant, has been credited with the leadership of the hostile savages on this expedition, but it has been proved by incontestable evidence that he was *not*. He himself always denied it most vehemently, and so convinced the poet Campbell, who had given him such a bad eminence in his Gertrude of Wyoming, that in the preface to the next edition, he did Brant a tardy justice.

The engagement commenced in the afternoon, and for some time was fought with great spirit, but the overwhelming force of the enemy soon enabled them not only to outflank their opponents, but actually to gain their rear. The men falling rapidly on all sides, Colonel Dennison gave the order to fall back to obtain a better position. Some misunderstood the order as a retreat, and great confusion ensued. The practiced enemy sprang forward at once; raised a horrid yell along their whole ranks and rushed in among the retiring columns with spear and tomahawk.

When the left was thrown into confusion, Colonel Zebulon Butler threw himself in front and rode in between the two lines. "Don't

The Frightful Massacre of Wyoming.

leave me, my children," he appealed to them, "the victory will be ours." It was too late! The battle was lost! Indeed, it should never have been fought. It has even been considered a blunder, for what could four hundred do against eleven hundred, well posted and confident of victory.

Now followed a most dreadful massacre and the most heart-rending scenes. The brave but overpowered defenders were slaughtered without mercy, principally in flight and after having surrendered. The plain, the river and the island of Monockonock were the principal scenes of this atrocious massacre. Sixteen men, placed in a ring around a rock, called to this day Queen Esther's Rock, were held by stout Indians while they were, one by one, slaughtered by the knife or tomahawk, it is said, of Catharine Montour, generally known by the name of Queen Esther, but this is very positively denied. In another similar ring, nine persons were murdered in the same way. Many were shot in the river, or hunted out and slain in their hiding places on Monockonock island. But a small proportion of the men who went into battle survived.

The survivors took refuge in Wilkesbarre and Forty forts. Mr. Hollenback, who had swum the river naked, amid a shower of balls, came rushing into the former fort with the dread cry, "all is lost!" when the inmates fled to the mountains and down the river. Their sufferings were extreme. Colonel Zebulon Butler and the soldiers who had escaped the battle, understanding that no quarter was to be given, were among the refugees. Colonel Dennison, with a large number of the refugees from the battle, threw themselves into Forty Fort, and next day succeeded in getting terms from the tory Butler. The current historical accounts of the Wyoming battle and massacre were very much exaggerated, and especially of Butler's ferocity and the indiscriminate massacre which followed the surrender of the forts. *Not a life of all those under Dennison's charge was lost.* It was horrible enough, but not so bad as represented. A general scene of ruthless devastation now occurred throughout the valley. The houses and grounds of the tories alone escaped rapine and ruin. Such of the cattle as were not killed had their tongues cut out. Fire, sword and scalping knife, all were employed. This one attack made one hundred and fifty widows and six hundred orphans in that once peaceful and beautiful valley, while families were swept out of existence or driven to protracted sufferings by flight.

Of the Gore family, out of seven who went into battle, but one escaped. From the farm of Mr. Weeks seven males went to battle—not one escaped. The survivors fled to the mountains or down the valley, but their sufferings from fright, hunger and hurried traveling were extreme. In one party of a hundred, there was but one man.

The chief part of the invading army was led off by Butler in a few days, but parties of Indians continued in the valley for some time, until from every part of the compass fire after fire arose, and all who could get away fled. Every pathway was thronged with women and children, old men and boys. The following Sunday twenty Indians came to Mr. Weeks' house, and ordered breakfast and for him to clear out. "All my sons have fallen," said the old man, "and here I am left with fourteen grandchildren, all young and helpless." No use; he had to go. After breakfast an Indian leader wheeled a rocking chair into the middle of the road, sat himself down and complacently rocked himself. The rest afterwards followed his example, and thus rocked themselves into such good humor that they allowed Weeks a pair of oxen and a wagon to carry the family off.

When Forty Fort capitulated, Butler, as he entered, saw Sergeant Boyd, a late English deserter from the British, who was a good drill sergeant, and had been employed training the men in the fort. "Boyd," said Butler, recognizing him, "go to that tree!" pointing to a pine not far outside. "I hope," replied the poor Sergeant, "that your honor will consider me a prisoner of war." "Go to that tree," repeated Butler, sternly. Boyd had to go, and was instantly shot down.

CATHARINE MONTOUR, ALIAS QUEEN ESTHER.

Tioga Point, Bradford county, Pa., near the New York State line and at the junction of the Tioga and the Susquehanna, was noted in the annals of Indian warfare as the site of an ancient Indian town and a place of rendezvous for parties passing up and down the two rivers. At this place stood the "castle" of the celebrated Queen Esther, who is said to have played such a cruel and pitiless *role* at the Wyoming massacre. Her permanent residence was at Catharine's Town, at the head of Seneca Lake.

Catharine Montour was a half-breed, who had been well educated in Canada. Her reputed father was one of the French Governors of that province, and she herself was a lady of comparative refinement. She was much caressed in Philadelphia, and mingled in the best society. She exercised a controlling influence among the Indians, and resided in this quarter while they were making their incursions upon the Wyoming settlements. It has been even suspected that she presided at the bloody sacrifice of the Wyoming prisoners after the battle; but Colonel Stone, who is good authority upon the history of the Six Nations, utterly discredits the suspicion. The plain upon which her mansion stood is called Queen Esther's Flat. Old Mr. Covenhoven, who still lives in Lycoming county, was one of Colonel Hartley's expedition to Tioga, just after the battle of Wyoming, for the purpose of burning the Moravian villages and the Indian town at Tioga. Mr. Covenhoven says, that he himself put the brand to Queen Esther's "castle." He describes it as a long, low edifice, constructed with logs set in the ground at intervals of ten feet, with horizontal hewn plank or puncheons neatly set into grooves in the posts. It was roofed or thatched, and had some sort of a porch or other ornament over the doorway.

FIERCE ATTACK AND ESCAPE OF HAMMOND AND THE BENNETTS.

Among the many exciting adventures attending the massacre, none exceeds in thrilling interest the story of the escape of Hammond and the Bennetts from their Indian captors. Lebbeus Hammond was one of two who bounded off and escaped from the slaughter about Queen Esther's Rock. He, with Thomas Bennett and son, a lad only fourteen years old, were surprised in the woods on the march, when the snow was waist deep, but the savages drove them on without rest. At night they were secured by slender poles laid across them, a redskin lying upon either end. Their fate was sure. Bennett had torn a button from his coat and wished to replace it. "Fool!" said one of the captors, "only one day more; you die at Wyalusing!" Then they told of the fate of a man named Boyd, whom they knew, and who had been captured not long before. They related that they had cut off his fingers and toes, one by one, and plucked out his eyes, but could not extract from him a cry or a groan. "Boyd brave man," they applaudingly said.

The prisoners were now left alone for a few minutes. "Hammond," said Bennett, "we must rise upon them to-night!" "It will be a perilous undertaking," replied Hammond, "but it may be our last chance. We may succeed, and if I'm to die, I'll sell my life as dearly as possible." That night the prisoners were secured as usual. Towards morning they were released from the poles and suffered to walk about a little. Soon the Indians, save one, who acted as guard, fell into a deep slumber. This one sat over the fire, roasting a deer's head and lazily picking out the dainty morsels.

Now or never was the time! Hammond worked his way quietly to where lay an axe. The boy stood near where the guns were stacked. Bennett gained a spear unperceived, and cautiously approaching the nodding guard, drove it through his body, throwing him over into the fire. Hammond, with his axe, dashed in the skull of the savage who had told him of Boyd's torture. A third blow buried the axe in the neck of another wretch who was attempting to rise.

Bennett, leaving the spear in the body of his first victim, seized a tomahawk and dealt murderous blows. The boy snapped three guns at the enemy, one after the other. Not one would go off. A stout Indian now rushed upon him, but the brave lad, clubbing a musket, buried the lock deep in the head of his opponent. Five of the seven Indians were actually now dead. The other two fled, one desperately wounded by the boy. Bennett flung his hatchet at the other, which struck him in the back, without, however, impeding his course. Bennett was an old hunter, and now led his gallant party over the ridges, carefully avoiding all Indian trails. They waded through the deep snow, swam several streams, only stopping to pick some wintergreen here and there, where the snow was drifted off, and reached their homes in three days.

The Indian who had been wounded by young Bennett, died in the woods. His companion, whom the elder Bennett had hit, while in flight, with his hatchet, was found lying insensible by a party of his tribe. Several years after a treaty was negotiated with the Indians; Hammond, who was present, saw an old savage with a crooked back walking about, whose face seemed familiar to him. He inquired the cause of his stooping. "A Yankee tomahawked me at Wyoming," was the sullen reply. It was Bennett's old target.

FRANCES SLOCUM, THE LOST SISTER.

Three or four months after the massacre, many of the settlers returned and commenced rebuilding their ruined homes, but savage incursions and murders continued. Near the present town of Wilkesbarre lived a family by the name of Slocum. While the males were absent one day in the fields, the house was surrounded by yelling Indians. There were in it a mother, a daughter about nine years of age, a son aged thirteen, a daughter aged five and a little boy aged two and a half. A young man and a boy by the name of Kingsley were present, grinding a knife. The first thing the Indians did was to shoot down the young man and scalp him with the knife he had in his hand. The nine year old sister took the little boy, two and a half years old, and ran out of the back door to go to the fort. The Indians chased her just enough to give her a desperate fright, and laughed heartily at the way she ran and dragged along her chubby little brother.

They then took the Kingsley boy and young Slocum, aged thirteen, and little Frances, aged five, and prepared to depart, but finding young Slocum lame, at the earnest entreaties of the mother, they left him. The mother's heart was crushed, and for years she could not speak of the scene without blinding tears. She saw a savage throw her little girl over his shoulder, and as her hair fell over her little face, with one hand she brushed it aside and the other she held out imploringly to her mother. The Indian then turned into the bushes, and that was the last scene that dwelt in the mother's memory. About a month after the redskins came again, murdered the aged grandfather and wounded the lame boy. The last child was born a few months after these tragedies.

The hopes, fears and yearnings of the stricken mother concerning the little toddling Frances can never be described. As the boys grew up and became men, they were very anxious to know the fate of their little fair-haired sister. They wrote letters, sent inquiries, made journeys through all the West and into the Canadas, if peradventure they might learn anything respecting her fate. Four of these long journeys were made in vain. A silence, deep as that of the deepest forest through which they wandered, hung over her fate, and that for sixty years.

Readers will now pass over fifty-eight years from the time of this captivity, and suppose themselves far in the wilderness, in the farthest part of Indiana. A very respectable agent of the United States is traveling there, and weary and belated, with a tired horse, he stops at an Indian wigwam for the night. He can speak the Indian language. The family are rich, for Indians have horses and skins in abundance. In the course of the evening he notices that the hair of the woman is light, and her skin, under her dress, is also white. She told him she was a white child, but had been carried away when a very small girl. She could only remember that her name was Slocum, that she lived in a little house on the banks of the Susquehanna, and how many there were in her father's family and the order of their ages. But the name of the town she could not remember. On reaching his home, the agent mentioned the story to his mother; she urged and pressed him to write and print the account. Accordingly he wrote and sent it to Lancaster, Pa., requesting that it might be published. By some unaccountable blunder, it lay in the office *two years* before it was printed. But in 1838 it was published. In a few days it fell into the hands of Mr. Slocum, of Wilkesbarre, who was the little two and a half years old boy, when Frances was taken. In a few days he was off to seek his sister, taking with him his oldest sister, (the one who aided him to escape,) writing a brother who lived in Ohio, and who was born after the captivity, to meet him and go ՝ th him.

After traveling more than three hundred miles through the wilderness, they reached the Indian country, the home of the Miami Indian. Nine miles from the nearest white, they found the little wigwam. "I shall know my sister," said the civilized sister, because she lost the nail of her first finger. You, brother, hammered it off in the blacksmith shop when she was four years old." They go into the cabin and find an Indian woman having the appearance of seventy-five. She is painted and jeweled off, and dressed like the Indians in all respects. Nothing but her hair and color of skin, would indicate her origin. They get an interpreter and begin to converse. She tells them where she was born, her name, &c., with the order of her father's family. "How came your nail gone?" said the oldest sister. "My oldest brother pounded it off when I was a little child, in the shop?" In a word, they were satisfied that this was Frances, their long-lost sister! They asked her what her Christian name was. She could not remember. Was it *Frances?* She smiled and said "yes." It was the first time she had heard it pronounced for sixty years! Here, then, they were met—two brothers and two sisters! They were all satisfied they were brothers and sisters. But what a contrast! The brothers were walking the cabin unable to speak; the oldest sister was weeping, but the poor Indian sat motionless and passionless—as indifferent as a spectator. There was no throbbing, no fine chords in her bosom to be touched.

When Mr. Slocum was giving this history, one said to him, "But could she not speak English!" "Not a word." "Did she know her age?" "No—had no idea of it." "But was she entirely ignorant?" "Sir, she didn't know when Sunday comes!" Her whole history might be told in a word. She lived with the Delawares, who carried her off, till grown up, and then married a Delaware. He either died or run away, and she then married a Miami Indian, a chief. She had two daughters, both of whom married and lived in the glory of an Indian cabin. Not one of the family could speak a word of English. They had horses in abundance, and when the Indian sister wanted to accompany her new relatives, she whipped out, bridled her horse, and then, *a la Turk,* mounted astride and was off. At night she threw a blanket down upon the floor, and at once was asleep.

The brothers and sister tried to persuade their lost sister to return with them, and, if she desired it, bring her children. They would transplant her again on the banks of the Susquehanna, and of their wealth make her home happy. But no. They had always been kind to her; and she had promised her late husband, on his deatn-bed, that she would never leave the Indians. And there they left her and hers, wild and darkened heathens, though they sprang from a pious race.

THE REVENGE OF COLONEL JOHN MOREDOCK.

Towards the end of the last century there lived at Vincennes, Indiana, a woman who had passed her whole life on the troubled border. She had been widowed several times by the savages, and on the death of her last husband, Moredock by name, determined to move still further west to better the chances for her growing sons. Joining a company who were proceeding to Illinois by way of the Mississippi, they proceeded in pirogues safely and pleasantly down the Ohio, and thence up the Mississippi, until they reached Grand Tower, almost within sight of their destination. Here, supposing themselves entirely safe from danger, the men carelessly leaped on shore to cordell the boats up against the swift current which rushed like a mill race around the base of a cliff. The women and children, about twenty in number, thoughtlessly followed.

While the whole party were thus joyfully strolling along between the cliff and the swift river, all at once, "like thunder from a clear sky," was heard the horrid, blood-curdling yell of savage onset, and a volley from rifles above them stretched half a dozen of their number on the ground, while, almost at the same moment, a mob of the painted demons appeared at each end of this fatal death-trap.

The scene of confusion which followed beggars all description. The brave and experienced borderers saw the desperate strait they were in, and for an instant stood appalled. But only for an instant! for in the next the pluck and wondrous courage of the iron-nerved and lion-hearted pioneers appeared, and with a shout of defiance they rushed to the encounter, giving yell for yell, blow for blow. It was a desperate but a hopeless conflict. They were, being half armed, huddled together like a flock of sheep, and encumbered with terror-stricken women and children—all cut down but one single survivor—John, the brave son of the widow Moredock.

He had fought like a tiger-cat until all hope was lost, and then, aided by the confusion and the cloud of smoke which hung over the murderous spot like a dense funeral pall, leaped into a cleft of the cliff that had caught his roving eye, and for the moment was safe. From this "coign of vantage" he had the unspeakable misery of witnessing a scene so horrid and terrible as to burn itself forever in his memory; turn his warm, young heart to stone, and engender that terrible thirst for revenge which was the ruling passion of all his after life, even after he had become a man of mark and held offices of trust in his adopted State.

Crouching there among the rocks and beholding the inhuman and barbarous savages mutilating the remains of mother, brothers and sisters, he took a solemn oath to devote his future life to a terrible revenge against the race, and to stay not his blood-red hand until every single fiend of that accursed band should give blood for blood.

How long he remained in that rocky cleft he could never tell. But while the savages were rifling the boats and securing their gory trophies, his heart hardened, his nerves became like steel, and after the Indians' departure, he stept stealthily down from his hiding place a *man:* stern, desperate and pitiless. Having ascertained that all his company were stone dead, and having buried the remains of his relatives, the lonely and desolate youth struck across the prairie to the nearest settlement on the Kaskaskia river, where he arrived next morning and told his fearful tale.

He found many sympathizers among the hardy, reckless borderers, and having announced his determination to avenge the massacre, he became at once the leader of a band of unquailing scouts, who never knew fear and never turned the back to foe. Staunch and tireless as a pack of bloodhounds, this select band of avengers ranged from the Des Moines to the Ohio. Now they were on the track of the murderers, and were almost in sight of them. Once they came up with the objects of their anxious quest on the banks of the Missouri, a hundred miles from the frontier, but as Moredock wished to utterly wipe out the devilish crew, instead of merely striking a partial blow, he refrained because the peculiar location of his foes' camp allowed of escape. His revenge was only postponed; the thirst for blood was inextinguishable.

Fortune at last favored Moredock. A short time afterwards he tracked the whole gang to the Mississippi, and found that they had all crossed to and encamped on an island. His resolve was soon fixed and declared to his fellows. He had taken the desperate determination of shutting up his own band on that narrow sand bar, cutting off all retreat, and there fighting it out to the death. Slowly and stealthily, therefore, the canoes were paddled to the island. Not a sound was heard. The flames of the camp fire had burned low, serving only to mark the position of the doomed gang.

Now all the canoes, their own as well as those of the Indians, were set adrift, and then, with bated breath and with rifle in hand and toma-

The Revenge of Colonel John Moredock.

hawk clenched tightly, the scouts, led by Moredock, with gleaming eye and compressed lips, glided silently nearer and nearer, making no more noise than would their own shadows. Were there none to warn the poor victims of the terrible fate approaching? None whatever. Two or three of the startled savages caught the rustle of a leaf, a breaking of a twig, and their glittering eyes roved around the walls of encircling darkness, and their acute, practiced ears were stretched forward in an attitude of intense watchfulness.

Now is the long delayed moment. A low cluck from the mouth of Moredock gives the signal, and half a dozen savages received in their bodies the unerring leaden messengers. But savages may be surprised, but do not easily become panic-stricken. They are ever on the lookout for just such surprises, and when one comes they know well what to do. One moment and they are on their feet; the next they turned sullenly to meet the unknown foe, which now, with hideous uproar and long bounds, leaped in upon them.

The conflict was long, fierce and obstinate, but the savages had been taken at a fearful disadvantage, and were compelled to retreat and fight their way to their boats. A cry of despairful rage went up as they found all means of escape removed, and grimly and sullenly they stood at bay, fighting with desperate courage until all were killed but three, who plunged boldly into the stream, and, aided by the darkness, succeeded in making good their escape.

No less than twenty-seven of the gang at the Grand Tower massacre were now still in death. Only three had escaped from the island slaughter, but while these lived John Moredock could not rest. His revenge was not entirely glutted till the last had paid blood for blood, but all this might require long time and weary wanderings. They must, therefore, perish by his own hand. Dismissing his faithful band, and having learned from one of the wounded savages the nearest probable resorts of those who had escaped, he commenced to track them along. Tireless and unswerving as the sleuth-hound, he followed his prey across rivers, over hills and around prairies. Had the wretches known that the avenger of blood was on their trail they would have put oceans between them and their deadly foe.

Relentlessly and without intermission did Moredock pursue his purpose. His passion, however, was as quiet as it was deep and absorbing. Few even of his acquaintance knew the motive for his long and ceaseless journeyings to and fro, from Green Bay to the Ohio, and often far across the Mississippi.

At length, after two years of restless wandering, he quietly arrived at Kaskaskia and settled down to a quiet life. His terrible task had been accomplished. The scalp of the very last of his family's ruthless murderers hung at his girdle.

But, alas! John Moredock could not rest. His absorbing passion had taken utter and entire possession of his being. Revenge had become the ruling mania of his life. Although he no longer devoted all his time and energies to Indian tracking and killing, his hatred for the whole red race never once relaxed. A redskin was to him what a red flag was to a bull. He married, had children, held many public offices in Illinois; was promoted to a Colonelcy, and died at the age of sixty; but he never spared the life of a redskin when in his power, or refrained from inflicting an injury on one when he could.

And yet this man was known to his own color as a mild, gentle, peaceable person, fond of domestic quiet and averse to strife. There were many like him on the western border, and from precisely the same cause.

THRILLING ADVENTURE OF AUDUBON, THE NATURALIST.

On my return from the Upper Mississippi, I found myself obliged to cross one of the wide prairies, which in that portion of the United States vary the appearance of the country. The weather was fine; all around me was as fresh and blooming as if it had just issued from the bosom of nature. My knapsack, my gun and my dog were all I had for baggage and company. But, although well moccasined, I moved slowly along, attracted by the brilliancy of the flowers and the gambols of the fawns around their dams, to all appearance as thoughtless of danger as I felt myself.

My march was of long duration. I saw the sun sink beneath the horizon long before I could perceive any appearance of woodland, and nothing in the shape of man had I met with that day. The track which I followed was only an old Indian trace; and as darkness overshadowed the prairie, I felt some desire to reach at least a copse, in which I might lie down to rest. The nighthawks were skimming over and around me, attracted by the buzzing wings of the beetles, which form their food, and the distant howling of wolves gave me some hope that I should soon arrive at the skirts of some woodland. I did so, and at almost the same instant, a fire-light attracting my eye, I moved towards it, full of confidence that it proceeded from the camp of some wandering Indians. I was mistaken. I discovered from its glare, that it was from the hearth of a small log cabin, and that a tall figure passed and repassed between it and me, as if busily engaged in household arrangements.

I reached the spot, and, presenting myself at the door, asked the tall figure, which proved to be a woman, if I might take shelter under her roof during the night. Her voice was gruff, and her attire negligently thrown about her. She answered in the affirmative. I walked in, took a wooden stool and quietly seated myself by the fire. The next object that attracted my notice was a finely formed young Indian, resting his head between his hands, with his elbows on his knees. A long bow rested against the log wall near him, while a quantity of arrows and two or three raccoon skins lay at his feet. He moved not; he apparently breathed not. Accustomed to the habits of Indians, and knowing that they pay but little attention to the movements of civilized strangers, I addressed him in French, a language not unfrequently partially known to the people in that neighborhood. He raised his head, pointed to one of his eyes with his finger, and gave me a significant glance with the other. His face was covered with blood. The fact was, that an hour before this, as he was in the act of discharging an arrow at a raccoon in the top of a tree, the arrow had split upon the cord, and sprung back with such violence into his right eye as to destroy it forever.

Feeling hungry, I inquired what sort of fare I might expect. Such a thing as a bed was not to be seen, but many large untanned bear and buffalo hides lay piled in a corner. I drew a fine timepiece from my breast, and told the woman that it was late, and that I was fatigued. She had espied my watch, the richness of which seemed to operate upon her feelings with electric quickness. She told me that there was plenty of venison and jerked buffalo meat, and that on removing the ashes I should find a cake. But my watch had struck her fancy, and her curiosity had to be gratified by an immediate sight of it. I took off the gold chain that secured it from around my neck and handed it to her. She was all ecstacy, spoke of its beauty, asked me its value, and put the chain round her brawny neck, saying how happy the possession of such a watch would make her. Thoughtless, and as I fancied myself in so retired a spot, secure, I paid little attention to her talk or her movements. I helped my dog to a good supper of venison, and was not long in satisfying the demands of my own appetite. The Indian rose from his seat as if in extreme suffering. He passed and repassed me several times, and once pinched me on the side so violently that the pain nearly brought forth an exclamation of anger. I looked at him; his eye met mine; but his look was so forbidding that it struck a chill into the more nervous part of my system. He again seated himself, drew his butcher knife from its greasy scabbard, examined its edge as I would do that of a razor suspected dull, replaced it, and taking his tomahawk from his back, filled the pipe of it with tobacco, and sent me expressive glances whenever our hostess chanced to have her back towards us.

Never until that moment had my senses been wakened to the danger which I now suspected to be about me. I returned glance for glance to my companion, and rested well assured that whatever enemies I might have, he was not of their number. I asked the woman for my watch, wound it up, and, under pretence of wishing to see how the weather might probably be on the morning, took up my gun and walked out of the cabin. I slipped a ball into each barrel, scraped the edges of my flints, renewed the priming, and returning to the hut, gave a favorable account of my observations. I took a few bear skins, made a pallet of them, and calling my faithful dog to my side, lay down with my gun close to my body, and in a few minutes, to all appearance, was fast asleep.

A short time had elapsed when some voices were heard, and from the corners of my eyes I saw two athletic young men making their entrance, bearing a dead stag upon a pole. They disposed of their burden, and asking for whiskey, helped themselves freely to it. Observing me and the wounded Indian, they asked who I was, and why the devil that rascal (meaning the Indian, who, they knew, understood not a word of English) was in the house. The mother—for so she proved to be—bade them speak less loudly, made mention of my watch, and took them to a corner, where a conversation ensued, the purport of which it required little shrewdness in me to guess. I felt that he perceived danger in my situation. The Indian exchanged a last glance with me.

The young men had eaten and drunk themselves into such a condition, that I already looked upon them as *hors de combat;* and the frequent visits of the whiskey bottle to the ugly mouth of their dam, I hoped, would soon reduce her to a like state. Judge of my astonishment, when I saw this incarnate fiend take a large carving knife and go to the grindstone to whet its edge. I saw her pour the water on the turning machine, and watched her working away with the dangerous instrument, until the sweat covered every part of my body, in despite of my determination to defend myself to the last. Her task finished, she walked to her reeling sons and said, "There, that'll soon settle him! Boys, kill you—and then for the watch."

I turned, cocked my gun locks silently, touched my faithful companion, and lay ready to start up and shoot the first who might attempt my life. The moment was fast approaching, and that night might have been my last in this world, had not Providence made preparations for my rescue. All was ready. The infernal hag was advancing slowly, probably contemplating the best way of dispatching me, while her sons should be engaged with the Indian. I was several times on the eve of rising and shooting her on the spot, but she was not to be punished thus. The door suddenly opened, and there entered two stout travelers, each with a long rifle on his shoulder. I bounced up on my feet, and making them most heartily welcome, told them how well it was for me that they should arrive at that moment. The tale was told in a minute. The drunken sons were secured, and the woman, in spite of her defence and vociferations, shared the same fate. The Indian fairly danced for joy, and gave us to understand that as he could not sleep for pain, he would watch over us. You may suppose that we slept much less than we talked. The two strangers gave me an account of their once having been in a somewhat similar situation. Day came, fair and rosy, and with it the punishment of our captives.

They were now quite sober. Their feet were unbound, but their arms were still securely tied. We marched them into the woods off the road, and having used them as *Regulators* were wont to use such delinquents, we set fire to the cabin, gave all the skins and implements to the young Indian warrior, and proceeded, well pleased, towards the settlements.

Ogilvie's Adventure—One Contrary to the Above.

Mr. Ogilvie, once well known in Virginia as a supporter of the Godwinian philosophy, conceiving a vehement desire to see the western country, at that time newly settled, set off from Richmond for Lexington, in Kentucky. It was in the month of October, after a most lonely and wearisome day's ride that, a little before sunset, he came to a small cabin on the road, and fearing he should find no other opportunity of procuring refreshment for himself and his jaded horse, he stopped and inquired if he could be accommodated for the night. An old woman, the only person he saw, civilly answering him in the affirmative, he gladly alighted, and going in to a tolerable fire, enjoyed the luxury of rest, while his hostess was discharging the duties of hostler and cook. In no long time, she set before him a supper of comfortable but homely fare, of which having liberally partaken, and given divers significant nods, the old woman remarked, she "expected" he "chose bed," and pointing to one which stood in the corner of the room, immediately went into the yard a while to give him an opportunity of undressing.

Before he had been long in bed, and while he was congratulating himself on his good fortune, the latch of the door was drawn, and there entered a dark-looking man, of gigantic stature and form, with stiff, black hair, eyebrows and beard. He was apparently about eight and twenty, was dressed in a hunting shirt, which partly concealed a pair of dirty buckskin overalls, and he wore moccasins of the same material. Mr. Ogilvie thought he had never seen anything half so ferocious. As soon as this man entered the room, his mother, for so she proved to be, pointing to the bed, motioned him to make no noise; on which, with inaudible steps, he walked to the chimney, put up his gun on a rude rack provided for that and other arms, and sat softly down to the fire, then throwing a bright blaze around the room.

Our traveler, not liking the looks of the new comer and not caring to be teased by conversation, drew his head under the bed clothes, so that he could see what was passing without leaving his own face visible. The two soon entered into conversation, but in so low a voice that Mr. Ogilvie could not distinguish what was said. His powers of attention were wrought up to the most painful pitch of intensity. At length the man, looking toward the bed, made some remark to his mother, to which Mr. Ogilvie heard her reply, "No, I hardly think he's asleep yet;" and they again conversed in a low voice as before. After a short interval, while the man sat with his feet stretched out towards the fire, on which he was intently gazing, he was heard to say:

"Don't you think he's asleep now?"

"Stop," says she, "I'll go and see;" and moving near the bed, under the pretext of taking something from a small table, she approached so near as to see the face of our traveler, whose eyes were, indeed, closed, but who was anything but asleep.

On her return to the fire-place, she said, "Yes, he's asleep now."

On this the mountaineer, rising from his stool, reached up to the rack, and taking down with his right hand an old greasy cutlass, walked with the same noiseless step towards the traveler's bed, and stretching out the other hand, at the moment that Mr. Ogilvie was about to implore his pity, took down a venison ham, which hung on the wall near the head of the bed, walked softly back to the fire and began to slice some pieces for his supper, and Mr. Ogilvie, who lay more dead than alive, and whose romantic fancy heightened the terrors of all he saw, had the unspeakable gratification to find that these kind-hearted children of the forest had been talking low, and that the hungry hunter, who had eaten nothing since morning, had forborne making a noise, lest they should interrupt the slumbers of their way-worn guest. The next day Mr. Ogilvie, who was an enthusiast in physiognomy, discovered remarkable benevolence in the features of the hunter, which, by the false and deceitful glare of the fire light, had escaped him; and in his recital of this adventure, which furnished him with a favorite occasion of exercising his powers of declamation to great advantage in a matter of real life, he often declared that he had never taken a more refreshing night's rest, or made a more grateful repast, than he had done in this humble cabin.

OBSTINATE COMBAT OF HIGGINS, THE RANGER.

Thomas Higgins, a native Kentuckian, in the war of 1812, enlisted in a company of rangers, and was stationed, in the Summer of 1814, in a block-house or station eight miles south of Greenville, in what is now Bond county, Illinois. On the evening of the 30th of August, a small party of Indians having been seen prowling about the station, Lieutenant Journay with all his men, twelve only in number, sallied forth the next morning, just before daylight, in pursuit of them. They had not proceeded far on the border of the prairie before they were in an ambuscade of seventy or eighty savages. At the first fire the Lieutenant and three of his men were killed. Six fled to the fort under cover of the smoke. for the morning was sultry and the air being damp the smoke from the guns hung like a cloud over the scene; but Higgins remained behind, to have "one more pull at the enemy" and avenge the death of his companions.

He sprang behind a small elm, scarcely sufficient to protect his body, when, the smoke partly rising, discovered to him a number of Indians, upon which he fired and shot down the foremost one. Concealed still by the smoke, Higgins reloaded, mounted his horse and turned to fly, when a voice, apparently from the grass, hailed him with: "Tom, you won't leave me, will you?" He turned immediately around and seeing a fellow soldier by the name of Burgess lying on the ground wounded and gasping for breath, replied: "No, I'll not leave you—come along." "I can't come," said Burgess; "my leg is all mashed to pieces." Higgins dismounted, and taking up his friend, whose ankle had been broken, was about to lift him on his horse, when the animal taking fright, darted off in an instant, and left them both behind. "This is too bad," said Higgins; "but don't fear; you hop off on your three legs, and I'll stay behind between you and the Indians and keep them off. Get into the tallest grass and crawl as near the ground as possible." Burgess did so and escaped.

The smoke which had hitherto concealed Higgins now cleared away, and he resolved, if possible, to retreat. To follow the track of Burgess was most expedient. It would, however, endanger his friend. He determined, therefore, to venture boldly forward, and, if discovered, to secure his own safety by the rapidity of his flight. On leaving a small thicket, in which he had sought refuge, he discovered a tall, portly savage near by, and two others in a direction between him and the fort. He paused for a moment and thought if he could separate and fight them singly, his case was not so desperate. He started, therefore, for a little rivulet near, but found one of his limbs failing him—it having been struck by a ball in the first encounter, of which, till now, he was scarcely conscious. The largest Indian pressed close upon him, and Higgins turned round two or three times in order to fire.

The Indian halted and danced about to prevent his taking aim. He saw it was unsafe to fire at random, and perceiving two others approaching, knew he must be overpowered in a moment, unless he could dispose of the forward Indian first. He resolved, therefore, to halt and receive his fire. The Indian raised his rifle, and Higgins, watching his eye, turned suddenly, as his finger pressed the trigger, and received the ball in his thigh. He fell, but rose immediately and ran. The foremost Indian, now certain of his prey, loaded again, and with the other two pressed on They overtook him—he fell again, and as he rose the whole three fired, and he received all their balls. He now fell and rose a third time; and the Indians, throwing away their guns, advanced upon him with spears and knives. As he presented his gun at one or the other, each fell back. At last the largest Indian, supposing his gun to be empty from his fire having been thus reserved, advanced boldly to the charge. Higgins fired and the savage fell.

He had now four bullets in his body—an empty gun in his hand—two Indians unharmed as yet before him, and a whole tribe but a few yards distant. Any other man would have despaired. Not so with him. He had slain the most dangerous of the three, and having little to fear from the others, began to load his rifle. They raised a savage whoop and rushed to the encounter. A bloody conflict now ensued. The Indians stabbed him in several places. Their spears, however, were but thin poles, hastily prepared, and bent whenever they struck a rib or a muscle. The wounds they made were not, therefore, deep, though numerous.

At last one of them threw his tomahawk. It struck him upon the cheek, severed his ear, laid bare his skull to the back of his head, and stretched him upon the prairie. The Indians again rushed on; but Higgins, recovering his self-possession, kept them off with his feet and hands. Grasping, at length, one of their spears, the Indian, in attempting to pull it from him, raised Higgins up, who, taking his rifle, dashed out the brains of the nearest savage. In doing so, however, it broke —the barrel only remaining in his hand. The other Indian, who had, heretofore, fought with caution, came now manfully into the battle. His character as a warrior was in jeopardy. To have fled from a man thus wounded and disarmed, or to have suffered his victim to escape, would have tarnished his fame forever. Uttering, therefore, a terrific yell, he rushed on and attempted to stab the exhausted ranger, but the latter warded off his blow with one hand and brandished his rifle-barrel with the other. The Indian was as yet unharmed, and, under existing circumstances, by far the most powerful man. Higgins' courage, however, was unexhausted and inexhaustible. The savage, at last, began to retreat from the glare of his untamed eye, to the spot where he dropped his rifle. Higgins knew that if he recovered that his own case was desperate; throwing, therefore, his rifle-barrel aside, and drawing his hunting knife, he rushed upon his foe. A desperate strife ensued —deep gashes were inflicted on both sides. Higgins, fatigued and exhausted by the loss of blood, was no longer a match for the savage The latter succeeded in throwing his adversary from him, and went immediately in pursuit of his rifle. Higgins, at the same time, rose and sought for the gun of the other Indian. Both, therefore, bleeding and out of breath, were in search of arms to renew the combat.

The smoke had now passed away, and a large number of Indians were in view. Nothing, it would seem, could now save the gallant ranger. There was, however, an eye to pity and an arm to save—and that arm was a woman's! The little garrison had witnessed the whole combat. It consisted of but six men and one woman: that woman, however, was a host—a Mrs. Pursley. When she saw Higgins contending, single-handed, with a whole tribe of savages, she urged the rangers to attempt his rescue. The rangers objected, as the Indians were ten to one. Mrs. Pursley, therefore, snatched a rifle from her husband's hand, and declaring that "so fine a fellow as Tom Higgins should not be lost for want of help," mounted a horse and sallied forth to his rescue. The men, unwilling to be outdone by a woman, followed at full gallop, reaching the spot where Higgins fainted and fell before the Indians came up, and while the savage with whom he had been engaged was looking for his rifle, his friends lifted the wounded ranger up, and throwing him across a horse before one of the party, reached the fort in safety.

Higgins was insensible for several days, and his life was preserved by continual care. His friends extracted two of the balls from his thigh; two, however, yet remained, one of which gave him a good deal of pain.

Hearing, afterwards, that a physician had settled within a day's ride of him, he determined to go and see him. The physician asked him fifty dollars for the operation. This Higgins flatly refused, saying it was more than a half-year's pension. On reaching home he found the exercise of riding had made the ball discernible; he requested his wife, therefore, to hand him his razor. With her assistance he laid open his thigh until the edge of the razor touched the bullet, then, inserting his two thumbs into the gash, "he flirted it out," as he used to say, "without costing him a cent." The other ball yet remained; it gave him, however, but little pain, and he carried it with him to his grave. Higgins died in Fayette county, Illinois, a few years since. He was the most perfect specimen of a frontierman in his day, and was once assistant doorkeeper of the House of Representatives in Illinois. The facts above stated are familiar to many, to whom Higgins was personally known, and there is no doubt of their correctness.

COLTER'S FAMOUS RACE FOR LIFE.

On the arrival of the exploratory party of Lewis and Clark at the head waters of the Missouri, Colter, one of the guides, obtained permission for himself and another hunter by the name of Potts to remain awhile and hunt for beaver. Aware of the hostility of the Blackfoot Indians, one of whom had been killed by Lewis, they set their traps at night and took them up early in the morning, remaining concealed during the day.

They were examining their traps early one morning, in a creek which they were ascending in a canoe, when they suddenly heard a great noise resembling the tramp of animals; but they could not ascertain the fact, as the high, perpendicular banks on each side of the river impeded their view. Colter immediately pronounced it to be occasioned by Indians, and advised an instant retreat, but was accused of cowardice by Potts, who insisted the noise was occasioned by buffaloes, and they proceeded on. In a few minutes afterwards their doubts were removed by the appearance of about five or six hundred Indians on both sides of the creek, who beckoned them to come ashore. As retreat was now impossible, Colter turned the head of the canoe to the shore, and at the moment of its touching, an Indian seized the rifle belonging to Potts; but Colter, who was a remarkably strong man, immediately retook it and handed it to Potts, who remained in the canoe, and on receiving it pushed off into the creek. He had scarcely quitted the shore when an arrow was shot at him, and he cried out, "Colter, I am wounded." Colter remonstrated with him on the folly of attempting to escape, and urged him to come ashore. Instead of complying he instantly leveled his rifle at an Indian and shot him dead on the spot. This conduct, situated as he was, may appear to have been an act of madness, but it was doubtless the effect of sudden but sound enough reasoning; for if taken alive he must have expected to have been tortured to death, according to the Indian custom, and in this respect the Indians in this region excelled all others in the ingenuity they displayed in torturing their prisoners.* He was instantly pierced with arrows so numerous that, to use the language of Colter, " he was made a riddle of.'

They now seized Colter, stripped him entirely naked, and began to consult on the manner in which he should be put to death. They were first inclined to set him up as a mark to shoot at, but the chief interfered, and, seizing him by the shoulder, asked him if he could run fast. Colter, who had been some time among the Kee Katsa, or Crow Indians, had, in a considerable degree, acquired the Blackfoot language, and was also well acquainted with Indian customs. He knew that he had now to run for his life, with the dreadful odds of

---

* The Flathead Indians, who reside in Oregon, and the Blackfoot tribe, who hunt at the eastern base of the Rocky Mountains, are almost continually at war with each other. An English traveler, who remained a considerable time among the former, has given a description of the method of torturing their prisoners. A chief of the Blackfoot tribe having been taken captive in one of their wars, was condemned to death; and the Englishman repaired to camp to witness the frightful spectacle. The prisoner was fastened to a tree. The Flatheads, after heating an old gun-barrel red-hot, burnt with it, successively, his legs, thighs, stomach, cheeks and belly; and then cut the flesh around his nails, which they tore out; and afterwards cut off his fingers joint by joint. During this horrible torment the prisoner did not shrink in the least, nor testify the slightest emotion. Instead of crying for mercy and uttering groans, he endeavored to excite the barbarous ingenuity of his executioners by taunts and the most insulting reproaches. One of the Flatheads rushed upon him, and in an instant, with his knife, scooped out one of his eyes and clove his nose in two. But the poor fellow did not desist from his provocations. "I killed your brother," he cried. "I tore off the grey scalp of your father." The warrior to whom he spoke again rushed upon him and tore off his scalp, and was about to plunge a knife into his heart when the voice of his chief forbade him.

With his naked skull, his cloven nose, and the blood streaming from the socket of his eye, the intrepid Blackfoot offered a hideous spectacle, notwithstanding which, in this terrible condition, he continued to heap reproaches and outrageous insults upon his foes. " It was I," said he to the chief, " who took your wife prisoner! We tore out her eyes and tongue! We treated her like a dog! Forty of our young warriors"——He had not time to finish what he was going to say, for, at the mention of his wife, the fury of the chief broke through all bounds, and seizing his rifle he put an end at once to the insults which he, the prisoner, uttered, and the sufferings he endured. These cruelties were even surpassed by those that were exercised on the female prisoners; and it must be owned that the Flathead women showed a more fiendish barbarity than the men. The details of the tortures which they inflicted are too horrible to be described, save with a pen dipped in blood.

five or six hundred against him, and these armed Indians; he therefore cunningly replied that he was a very bad runner, although, in truth, he was considered by the hunters as remarkably swift.

The chief now commanded the party to remain stationary, and led Colter out on the prairie three or four hundred yards and released him, bidding him *to save himself if he could.* At that instant the war whoop sounded in the ears of poor Colter, who, urged with the hope of preserving life, ran with a speed at which he himself was surprised. He proceeded towards Jefferson's Fork, having to traverse a plain six miles in breadth, abounding with the prickly pear, on which he every instant was treading with his naked feet. He ran nearly half-way across the plain before he ventured to look over his shoulder, when he perceived that the Indians were very much scattered, and that he had gained ground to a considerable distance from the main body; but one Indian, who carried a spear, was much before all the rest, and not more than a hundred yards from him.

A faint gleam of hope now cheered the heart of Colter; he derived confidence from the belief that escape was within the bounds of possibility, but that confidence was nearly fatal to him, for he exerted himself to such a degree that the blood gushed from his nostrils, and soon almost covered the forepart of his body. He had now arrived within a mile of the river, when he distinctly heard the appalling sounds of footsteps behind him, and every instant expected to feel the spear of his pursuer. Again he turned his head and saw the savage not twenty yards from him. Determined, if possible, to avoid the expected blow, he suddenly stopped, turned around and spread out his arms. The Indian, surprised at the suddenness of the action, and perhaps at the bloody appearance of Colter, also attempted to stop; but, exhausted with running, he fell while attempting to throw his spear, which stuck in the ground and broke in his hand. Colter instantly snatched up the pointed part, with which he pinned him to the earth, and then continued his flight.

The foremost of the Indians, on arriving at the place, stopped until others came up to join them, and then gave a hideous yell. Every moment of this time was improved by Colter, who, although fainting and exhausted, succeeded in gaining the skirting of the cotton-wood trees on the borders of the Fork, to which he ran and plunged into the river. Fortunately for him, a little below this place was an island, against the upper point of which a raft of drift timber had lodged; he dived under the raft, and, after several efforts, got his head above water, among the trunks of trees covered over with smaller wood to the depth of several feet. Scarcely had he secured himself when the Indians arrived on the river, screeching and yelling, as Colter expressed it, "like so many devils."

They were frequently on the raft during the day, and were seen through the chinks by Colter, who was congratulating himself on his escape, until the idea arose that they might set the raft on fire. In horrible suspense he remained until night, when, hearing no more from the Indians, he dived from under the raft and swam silently down the river to a considerable distance, when he landed and traveled all night. Although happy in having escaped from the Indians, his situation was still dreadful; he was completely naked, under a burning sun; the soles of his feet were filled with the thorns of the prickly pear; he was hungry and had no means of killing game, although he saw abundance around him, and was at a great distance from the nearest settlement. Almost any man but an American hunter would have despaired under such circumstances. The fortitude of Colter remained unshaken. After seven days' sore travel, during which he had no other sustenance than the root known by naturalists under the name of *psoralea esculenta*, he at length arrived in safety at Lisa's Fort, on the Big Horn branch of the Roche Jaune or Yellow Stone river.

AN INDIAN'S SAGACITY AT TRAILING.

Heckewelder, in his Historical Account of the Indians, when speaking of their manner of surprising their enemies, relates a striking anecdote, by way of exemplification of the Indian's sagacity as well as veracity: "In the beginning," says he, "of the Summer of 1755, a most atrocious murder was unexpectedly committed by a party of Indians on fourteen white settlers, within five or six miles of Shamokin, Pa. The surviving whites, in their rage, determined to take their revenge by murdering a Delaware Indian who happened to be in those parts, and was far from thinking himself in danger. He was a great friend to the whites, was loved and esteemed by them, and in testimony of their regard, had received from them the name of *Luke Holland*, by which he was generally known. The Indian told the enraged settlers that the Delawares were not in any manner concerned in it, and that it was the act of some wicked Mingoes or Iroquois, whose custom it was to involve other nations in wars with each other by clandestinely committing murders, so that they might be laid to the charge of others than themselves.

But all his representations were vain; he could not convince exasperated men whose minds were fully bent upon revenge.

"At last, he offered that if they would give him a party to accompany him, he would go with them in quest of the murderers, and was sure he could discover them by the prints of their feet and other marks well known to him, by which he would convince them that the real perpetrators of the crime belonged to the Six Nations. His proposal was accepted; he marched at the head of a party of whites, and led them into the tracks. They soon found themselves in the most rocky parts of the mountain, where not one of those who accompanied him was able to discover a single track, nor would they believe that ever a man had trodden on this ground, as they had to jump over a number of crevices between the rocks, and in some instances to crawl over them. Now they began to believe that the Indian had led them across those rugged mountains in order to give the enemy time to escape, and threatened him with instant death the moment they should be fully convinced of the fraud. The Indian, true to his promise, would take pains to make them perceive that an enemy had passed along the places through which he was leading them; here he would show them that the moss on the rock had been trodden down by the weight of a human foot; there that it had been torn and dragged forward from its place: further, he would point out to them that pebbles or small stones on the rocks had been removed from their beds by the foot hitting against them; that dry sticks, by being trodden upon, were broken, and even that, in a particular place, an Indian's blanket had dragged over the rocks and removed or loosened the leaves lying there, so that they lay no more flat, as in other places; all which the Indian could perceive as he walked along, without ever stopping.

"At last, arriving at the foot of the mountain, on soft ground, where the tracks were deep, he found out the enemy were eight in number, and, from the freshness of the footprints, he concluded that they must be encamped at no great distance. This proved to be the exact truth, for, after gaining the eminence on the other side of the valley, the Indians were seen encamped, some having laid down to sleep, while others were drawing off their leggins for the same purpose, and the scalps they had taken were hanged up to dry. 'See!' said Luke Holland to his astonished companions, 'there is the enemy! not of my nation, but Mingoes, as I truly tell you. They are in our power; in less than half an hour they will all be fast asleep. We need not fire a gun, but go up and tomahawk them. We are nearly two to one, and need apprehend no danger. Come on, and you will now have your full revenge!' But the whites did not choose to follow the Indian's advice, and urged him to take them back by the nearest and best way, which he did, and when they arrived at home, late at night, they reported the number of the Iroquois to have been so great that they durst not venture to attack them."

BELL'S DEADLY CONFLICT WITH THREE SAVAGES.

Among the many achievements, says Loudon, against the Indians in our wars with them, few exceed that performed by Samuel Bell, formerly owner of the noted farm on the Stony Ridge, five miles below Carlisle, Pa., which was as follows: Some time after General Braddock's defeat, he and his brother James agreed to go into Sherman's valley to hunt for deer, and were to meet at Croghan's, now Sterret's Gap, on the Blue Mountain. By some means or other they did not meet, and Samuel slept all night in a cabin on Sherman's Creek. In the morning he had not traveled far before he spied three Indians, who at the same time saw him; they all fired at each other; he wounded one of the Indians, but received no damage, except through his clothes, by the balls; several shots were fired on both sides, for each took a tree. Bell took out his tomahawk and stuck it into the tree behind which he stood, so that should they approach he might be prepared; the tree was grazed with the Indians' balls, and he had thoughts of making his escape by flight, but on reflection had doubts of his being able to outrun them. After some time the two Indians took the wounded one and put him over a fence, and one took one course and the other another, taking a circuit so that Bell could no longer secure himself by the tree; but by trying to ensnare him they had to expose themselves, by which means he had the good fortune to shoot one of them dead; the other ran and took the dead Indian on his back, one leg over each shoulder. By this time Bell's gun was again loaded; he then ran after the Indian until he came within about four yards from him, fired, and shot through the dead Indian, and lodged his ball in the other, who dropped the dead man and ran off. On his return, coming past the fence where the wounded Indian was, he dispatched him, but did not know he had killed the third Indian until his bones were found afterwards.

WESTERN EMIGRATION—ODD SCENES—PACK-HORSES.

At the end of the Revolution there was no commerce, but little clothing and only wretched rag money, so depreciated that when one went to buy, the money would almost occupy more room than what it purchased. Hard as was the fate of the soldier while starving, freezing or fighting for independence, peace found him little better off. Many sank or became utterly vicious and worthless under their discouragement, but others migrated to the West as offering the only chance for a livelihood to them and theirs. The journey was long and full of perils. They generally came west by Braddock's road from Virginia, or by Bedford, Pa. Striking the Monongahela river at Redstone, now Brownsville, Pa., they would take boats to points along the Ohio.

Judge Wilkeson, of Buffalo, was one of a family of twenty who emigrated, in 1784, from Carlisle to Chartiers Creek, a few miles west of Fort Pitt, and gives a very instructive and entertaining account of the hardships and privations of emigrants. We select a few incidents. The paths across the mountains were so rough and impracticable, that pack-horses were the only means of transportation; on some were packed the stores and agricultural implements; on others the furniture, bedding and cooking utensils, and on others the women and children. Horses which carried small children were each provided with a pack-saddle and two large creels, made of hickory withes in the fashion of a crate, one over each side, in which were stowed clothes and bedding. In the centre of each would be also tucked a child or two, the top being well secured by lacing, so as to keep the youngsters in their places. The roads frequently were barely passable; sometimes lying along the brink of precipices; frequently overflown in places by swollen streams, all of which had to be forded; horses slipping, falling and carried away, both women and children being in great danger.

Sometimes the creels would break loose, the children falling to the ground and rolling off amid great confusion. Frequently mothers were separated for hours from their children, and long after the stopping places had been reached, would be obliged to gather them together, and then prepare the meals, thus losing the rest so much required, and then sleeping in the numbing, pinching cold, alongside of some icy stream.

Each family was supplied with one or more cows, and thus the family cavalcade would slowly pursue its rugged and devious way. Many hair-breadth escapes were continually occurring. The men were enured to hardships; it was the mothers and children who chiefly suffered. The Wilkeson family settled down on Chartiers Creek—the father exchanging a horse for a tract of two hundred acres. The new comers aided each other in erecting rude log cabins. The family thus enclosed, the timber was girdled for a clearing, and, as soon as possible, corn and vegetables were planted; the work of clearing and planting being done by the whole family, and extending into the night. Now came Indian attacks, wholly unlooked for, since it was supposed peace with Great Britain would secure peace with her Indian allies. Dreadful mistake! Savage marauds and incursions continued yet for many years. The very name of Indian chilled the blood of emigrants; but there they were, and it was too late to retreat. Murders, scalpings and captivities were frequent. Homes and cattle had to be watched closely. The frequent calls on the settlers to fight or pursue Indians, or take refuge in stations and block-houses, was a severe tax on their time and labor.

When horses were not stolen they would, tormented by flies, &c., run away, crossing rivers and taking a bee line for their old homes. Sometimes they would wander on one or two hundred miles before recovered. When the husband was thus absent, the family would be left alone in the woods, surrounded by wild beasts, or, far more horrible, the yelling, pitiless savages. Milk was the chief dependence for food. One cow was always provided with a bell, and the first duty of the woman in the morning was to listen for the sound of her cow-bell. While she was absent, her children, if small, were tied in bed to prevent their wandering, and to guard them from danger from fire, snakes, beasts, &c.

"A more intelligent, virtuous and resolute class of men," says Wilkeson, "never settled any country than the first settlers of Western Pennsylvania. The women were no less worthy. The times were at fault, not the people. Very many were professors of religion of the Seceder sect. It was common for families to ride from ten to fifteen miles to meeting. The young people walked, and in Summer carried their shoes and stockings, if they had any, in their hands, both going and returning. The meetings were held, even in Winter, in the open air. A grove was selected, a log pulpit erected, and logs ranged on a gentle incline rising from the pulpit, furnished seats. Among the men, ten were obliged to wear a blanket or coverlet for a coat, where one possessed that luxury. So great was the scarcity of clothing that when the first Court of Common Pleas was held at Catfish, now Washington, Pa., a certain highly-respectable citizen, whose presence was required, could not attend court without first borrowing a pair of leather breeches from a neighbor, who, lending them, had himself to stay at home.

"But little idea can now be formed of the ungrudging hospitality of the older pioneers. The increase of sheep was very slow, on account of wolves. Deerskin was invariably used for clothes by men and boys. The women had all to spin, and generally weave all the stuffs for the family. That they did not die from all their labors and anxieties was indeed a great marvel. To obtain salt and iron they had resort to the East. Winchester, Virginia, and Chambersburg, Pennsylvania, were the great salt depots. One man and some boys were chosen from each neighborhood to take charge of the horses. Each beast was provided with a pack-saddle, a halter, a lashing rope, to secure the load, and sufficient food for twenty days—the average duration of a trip—part of which was left on the mountain for a return supply. A substitute for cash was found in skins, furs and ginseng. After selecting a Captain, the cavalcade set out on its long and adventurous journey. The entire return journey had to be made on foot, yet, notwithstanding the fatigues and hazards of the trip, all the boys who were old enough competed with each other to be selected for these distant excursions. Not only salt, but all kinds of merchandise, were brought west on pack-horses down to 1790.

"In Kentucky pack-horseing was an important business down to 1795. The merchants provided as many horses and men as were required. The men were armed and organized, with officers and regulations of their own appointment. The expedition was conducted on strict military principles—the times and places for stopping settled by the officers, and sentries placed at night. These caravans would transport many tons of goods in safety, if the loads were well-balanced. About 1800 the packers were succeeded by the still greater lions of the day—keel-boatmen, of whom more anon."

Settlers in West Pennsylvania soon grew restless and excited by the glowing reports from Kentucky, and, as they do even to the present day, they sold out their improvements and migrated farther west. "Man never is, but always to be blest." The trade to New Orleans was like the trade East, attended with great hardships and hazards. The right bank of the Ohio, for hundreds of miles, was alive with hostile Indians. The voyage was performed in flatboats, and occupied from four to six months. Several neighbors united their means in building a boat and in getting up the voyage. Each put on board his own produce at his own risk, and one of the owners always accompanied the boat as Captain and Supercargo. A boat of ordinary size required about six hands. They returned home either by sea or more commonly through the wilderness, a distance of about two thousand miles. As they generally carried a large quantity of specie, and the road was infested with bold gangs of robbers waiting for them, large parties, numbering sometimes several hundred, were organized and armed. They were provided with mules to carry the specie and provisions, and those who preferred, or could afford it, rode mules or Indian ponies. Outlaws and fugitives from justice from the Eastern States infested this road, and many bloody encounters occurred. The first half of the journey was through a flat, unhealthy, agueish country, where there was bad water, and the spare mules were always loaded down with the sick. Many who survived an attack of fever to reach the healthy country of Tennessee, would stay there to recruit.

BOATING LIFE ON THE WESTERN WATERS.

> How oft in boyhood's joyous day,
> Unmindful of the lapsing hours,
> I've loitered on my homeward way,
> By wild Ohio's banks of flowers,
> While some lone boatman from the deck
> Poured his soft numbers to that tide,
> As if to charm from storm and wreck
> The boat where all his fortunes ride.
> Then, boatman, wind that horn again.—*Butler*.

Just previous to the beginning of the present century, after the settlements had become more dense on the Monongahela and on the Ohio, a new class sprang up in the West whose life was unique. This was the class of *boatmen*. These were a hardy, fearless set of men, who always kept just in advance of civilization and luxury. Many of them at first had been engaged in the border wars with the Indians; were bred from infancy amid dangers, and experienced in all the practices and arts in the life of a woodsman.

The boatmen were courageous, athletic, persevering, and patient of privations. They traversed, in their pirogues, barges or keels, the longest rivers; penetrated the most remote wilderness upon their watery routes, and kept up a trade and intercourse between the most distant points. Accustomed to every species of exposure and privation, they despised ease and luxury. Clothed in the costume of the wilderness, and armed in western style, they were always ready to exchange the labors of the oar for offensive or defensive war. Exposed to the double force of the direct and reflected rays of the sun upon the water, their complexion was swarthy, and often but little fairer than the Indians. Often, from an exposure of their bodies without shirts, their complexion, from the head to the waist, was the same.

Their toils, dangers and exposure; the moving accidents of their long and perilous voyages, were measurably hidden from the inhabitants who contemplated the boats floating by their dwellings on beautiful Spring mornings, when the verdant forest, the mild and delicious temperature of the air, the delightful azure of the sky, the fine bottom on the one hand and the rolling bluff on the other, the broad and smooth stream rolling calmly down the forest, and floating the boat gently forward, presented delightful images to the beholders. At such times there was no visible danger, or call for labor. The boat took care of itself; one of the hands scraped a violin, and others danced. Greetings, or rude defiances, or trials of art, or proffers of love to the girls on shore, or saucy messages were scattered between them and the spectators along the banks. The boat glided on until it disappeared behind a point of woods. At that moment the bugle, with which all boats were provided, struck up its notes in the distance, over the water. Those scenes and those notes, echoing from the bluffs of the beautiful Ohio, had a charm for the imagination which, although heard a thousand times, at all hours and in all positions, presented to even the most unromantic spectator the image of a tempting and charming youthful existence, that almost inspired in his breast the wish that he, too, were a boatman.

No wonder that the young, who were reared in the then remote regions of the West, on the banks of the great stream, with that restless curiosity which is fostered by solitude and silence, looked upon the severe and unremitting labor of agriculture as irksome and tasteless compared to such life, and that they embraced every opportunity, either openly or covertly, to devote themselves to an employment which seemed so full of romance to their youthful visions.

The boatmen, with their bodies naked to the waist, spent the long and tedious days traversing the "running board," and pushing with their whole force against their strong setting poles firmly fixed against the shoulder. Thus, with their heads suspended nearly to the track on the running board, they propelled their freighted barge up the long and tedious route of the river. After a hard day's toil, at night they took their "fillee" or ration of whiskey, swallowed their homely supper of meat half burned and bread half baked, and retiring to sleep, they stretched themselves upon the deck, without covering, under the canopy of heaven, or probably enveloped in a blanket, until the steersman's horn called them to their morning "fillee" and their toil.

Hard and fatiguing was the life of a boatman; yet it was rare that any of them ever changed his vocation. There was a charm in the excesses, in the frolics, and in the fightings which they anticipated at the end of the voyage, which cheered them on. Of weariness none would complain; but rising from his hard bed by the first dawn of day, and reanimated by his morning draught, he was prepared to hear and obey the wonted order, "Stand to your poles and set off!" The boatmen were masters of the winding horn and the fiddle, and as the boat moved off from her moorings, some, to cheer their labors, or to "scare off the devil and secure good luck," would wind the animating blast of the horn, which, mingling with the sweet music of the fiddle, and reverberating along the sounding shores, greeted the solitary dwellers on the banks with news from New Orleans.

Their athletic labors gave strength incredible to their muscles, which they were vain to exhibit, and fist-fighting was their pastime. He who could boast that he had never been whipped, was bound to fight whoever disputed his manhood. Keelboatmen and bargemen looked upon raftsmen and flatboatmen as their natural enemies, and a meeting was the prelude to a "battle-royal." They were great sticklers for "fair play," and whosoever was worsted in battle must abide the issue without assistance.

Their arrival in port was a general jubilee, where hundreds often met together for diversion and frolic. Their assemblages were often riotous and lawless to extremes, when the civil authorities were defied for days together. Had their numbers increased with the population of the West, they would have endangered the peace of the country; but the first steamboat that ascended the Ohio sounded their death-knell, and they have been buried in the tide, never more to rise.

MIKE FINK, THE "LAST OF THE KEELBOATMEN."

Mike Fink, usually called "the last of the boatmen," was a fair specimen of his race. Many curious anecdotes are related of him. He was born in Pittsburgh. In early youth his desire to become a boatman was a ruling passion, which soon had its gratification. He served on the Ohio and Mississippi rivers as a boatman, until thrown out of employment by the general use of steamboats. When the Ohio was too low for navigation he spent most of his time at shooting matches in the neighborhood of Pittsburgh, and soon became famous as the best shot in the country. On that account he was called *bang all*, and hence frequently excluded from participating in matches for beef; for which exclusion he claimed and obtained for his forbearance, the *fifth quarter* of beef, as the hide and tallow are called. His usual practice was to sell his fifth quarter to the tavern keeper for whiskey, with which he treated everybody present, partaking largely himself. He became fond of strong drink, and could partake of a gallon in twenty-four hours without the effect being perceivable.

Mike's weight was about one hundred and eighty pounds; height about five feet nine inches; countenance open; skin tanned by sun and rain; form broad and very muscular, and of herculean strength and great activity. His language was of the half-horse and half-alligator dialect of the then race of boatmen. He was also a wit, and on that account he gained the admiration and excited the fears of all the fraternity; for he usually enforced his wit with a sound drubbing, if any one dared to *dissent* by neglecting or refusing to laugh at his jokes ; for, as he used to say, he cracked his jokes on purpose to be laughed at in a good-humored way, and that no man should make light of them. As a consequence, Mike had always around him a chosen band of laughing philosophers. An eye bunged up, or a dilapidated nose or ear, was sure to win Mike's sympathy and favor, for he made proclamation: "I'm a Salt River Roarer! I'm chuck full of fight, and I love the wimin," &c.; and he did, for he had a sweetheart in every port. Among his chosen worshippers, who would fight their death for him, as they termed it, were Carpenter and Talbot. Each was a match for the other in prowess, in fight or skill in shooting, having each been under Mike's diligent training.

Mike, at one time, had a woman who passed for his wife; whether she was truly so, we do not know. But at any rate, the following anecdote is a rare instance of conjugal discipline. Some time in the latter part of Autumn, a few years after the close of the late war with Great Britain, several keelboats landed for the night near the mouth of the Muskingum, among which was that of Mike's. After making all fast, Mike was observed, just under the bank, scraping into a heap the dried beech leaves, which had been blown there during the day, having just fallen from the effects of the early Autumn frosts. To all questions as to what he was doing, he returned no answer, but continued at his work until he had piled them up as high as his head. He then separated them, making a sort of an oblong ring, in which he laid down, as if to ascertain whether it was a good bed or not. Getting up he sauntered on board, hunted up his rifle, made great preparations about his priming, and then called, in a very impressive manner, upon his wife to follow him. Both proceeded up to the pile of leaves, poor "*Peg*" in a terrible flutter, as she had discovered that Mike was in no very amiable humor.

"Get in there and lie down!" was the command to Peg, topped off with one of Mike's very choicest oaths. "Now, *Mr*. Fink"—she always mistered him when his blood was up—"what have I done, I don't know, I'm sure—"

" Get in there and lie down, or I'll shoot you !" with another oath, and drawing his rifle up to his shoulder. Poor Peg obeyed, and crawled into the leaf pile, and Mike covered her up with the combustibles. He then took a flour barrel and split the staves into fine pieces, and lighted them at the fire on board the boat, all the time watching the leaf pile, and swearing he would shoot Peg if she moved. So soon as the splinters began to blaze, he took them into his hand and deliberately set fire, in four different places, to the leaves that surrounded his wife. In an instant the whole mass was on fire, aided by a fresh wind which was blowing at the time, while Mike was quietly standing by enjoying the fun. Peg, through fear of Mike, stood it as long as she could; but it soon became too hot, and she made a run for the river, her hair and clothing all on fire. In a few seconds she reached the water and plunged in, rejoicing to know she had escaped both fire and rifle so well. "There," said Mike, "that'll larn you not to be lookin' at them fellers on t'other boat."

Mike first visited St. Louis as a keelboatman in 1814 or '15. Among his shooting feats, the following are related by eye witnesses: In ascending the Mississippi, above the Ohio, he saw a sow with a couple of pigs, about one hundred feet distant, on the bank. He declared, in boatman phrase, he wanted a pig, and took up his rifle to shoot one, but was requested not to do so. He, however, laid his rifle to his face, and as the boat glided along, under easy sail, he successively shot off the tail of each of them, close to the rump, without doing them any other harm. Being, on one occasion, on his boat at the St. Louis landing, he saw a negro standing on the river bank, gazing in wonder at the show about him. Mike took up his rifle and shot off the poor fellow's heel. He fell, badly wounded and crying *murder*. Mike was arrested and tried in the county court, and found guilty by a jury. His justification of the offence was that the fellow's heel projected too far behind, preventing him from wearing a *genteel boot*, and he wished to correct the defect. His particular friend, Carpenter, was also a great shot. Carpenter and Mike used to fill a tin cup with whiskey, and place it by turns on each other's heads and shoot at it with a rifle at the distance of seventy yards. It was always bored through, without injury to the one on whose head it was placed. This feat is too well authenticated to admit of question. It was often performed, and they liked the feat the better because it showed their confidence in each other.

In 1822, Mike and his two friends, Carpenter and Talbot, engaged, in St. Louis, with Henry and Ashley, to go up the Missouri with them, in the three-fold capacity of boatmen, trappers and hunters. The first year a company of about sixty ascended as high as the mouth of the Yellow Stone river, where they built a fort for the purposes of trade and security. From this place small detachments of men, ten or twelve in a company, were sent out to hunt and trap on the tributary streams of the Missouri and the Yellow Stone. When Winter set in, Mike and his company returned to a place near the mouth of the Yellow Stone; and preferring to remain out of the fort, they dug a hole or cave in the bluff bank of the river, in which they resided during the Winter, which proved a warm and commodious habitation, protecting them from the winds and the snows. Here Mike and his friend Carpenter had a deadly quarrel, supposed to have been caused by a rivalry in the good graces of a squaw. It was, for a while, smothered by the interposition of friends.

On the return of Spring the party revisited the fort, where Mike and Carpenter, over a cup of whiskey, revived the recollection of their past quarrel, but made a treaty of peace, which was to be solemnized by their usual trial of shooting the cup of whiskey off each other's heads. To determine who should have the first shot, Mike proposed that they should "sky (toss up) a copper," which was done, and resulted in Mike's favor. Carpenter seemed to be aware of Mike's unforgiving, treacherous disposition; but scorning to save his life by refusing to fulfill his contract, he prepared for death, and bequeathed his gun, shot pouch, powder horn, belt, pistols and wages to Talbot. Without changing a feature, Carpenter filled the cup with whiskey to the brim. Mike loaded, picked the flint and leveled his rifle at the head of Carpenter, at the distance of sixty yards. After drawing the bead, he took down his rifle from his face, and smilingly said:

"Hold your noddle steady, Carpenter! Don't spill the whiskey—I shall want some presently."

He again raised, cocked his piece, and in an instant, Carpenter fell and expired without a groan. Mike's ball had penetrated precisely through the centre of his head. He coolly set down his rifle, and applying the muzzle to his mouth, blew the smoke out of the touch hole, without saying a word, keeping his eye steadily on the fallen body of Carpenter. His first words were:

"Carpenter, have you spilt the whiskey?" He was then told he had killed him. "It is all an accident!" rejoined Mike, "for I took as fair *a bead* on the black spot on the cup, as ever I took on a squirrel's eye. How did it happen?" He then cursed the gun, the powder, the bullet, and, finally, himself.

This catastrophe, in a country where the strong arm of the law could not reach, passed off for an accident. Talbot determined to revenge the death of his friend. No opportunity offered for some months after, until one day Mike, in a fit of gasconading, declared that he had pur-

"*Hold your noddle steady, Carpenter, and don't spill the whiskey!*"
MIKE FINK, "LAST OF THE KEELBOATMEN."

—*See page* 658.

posely killed Carpenter, and was glad of it. Talbot instantly drew from his belt a pistol, bequeathed by Carpenter, and shot Mike through the heart; he fell and expired without a word. Talbot also went unpunished, as nobody had authority or inclination to call him to account. In truth, he was as ferocious and dangerous as the bear of the prairies, and soon after perished in attempting to swim a river.—*M. Neville.*

GAME AND "DEER DRIVES" OF THE OLDEN TIME.

"Deer Drives" were frequently gotten up in the western wilds by those who were not professed hunters, but who wished to enjoy the sport of killing game. A large tract of game land was surrounded by lines of men, with such intervals that each person could see or hear those next to him on either flank. The whole acted under command of a clever and experienced Captain and at least four subordinates, who were generally mounted. At a signal of horn or trumpet, every man advanced in line towards a common centre, preserving an equal distance from those on either hand, and making as great a din as possible. From the middle of each side of the exterior line a "blazed" line of trees was previously marked to the centre as a "guide," and one of the sub-officers proceeded along each "guide" as the hunt progressed.

About a half or three-quarters of a mile from the central point a ring of "blazed" trees was made, and a similar one at the ground of meeting, with a diameter at least equal to the greatest rifle ranges. On arriving at the first ring the advancing lines halted, till the Captain made a circuit and saw all the men equally distributed and every gap closed.

By this time a herd of deer might occasionally be seen careering in affright from one line to another. At the signal the ranks moved forward from the first to the second ring, which was generally drawn around the foot of an eminence, on the margin of an open lake or swamp. Here, if the "drive" had been successful, great numbers of turkeys could now be seen flying among the trees with great tumult; deer, in herds, sweeping around the ring under an incessant rambling fire, panting and exhausted. When thus hard pressed, it was difficult to detain them long within the ring. Becoming desperate and terror-stricken, they would make for the line at full speed. If the men were too numerous or resolute to escape through, they would take flying leaps over their heads, and over all the sticks, guns, pitchforks, &c., raised to beat them back. By a concert of the regular hunters, gaps were sometimes purposely left open to allow them a runway, when they would either be shot down in flight or kept for their own guns on a subsequent occasion. The wolf might now be seen skulking through the bushes, hoping to escape observation by concealment. An occasional panther would every now and then be beaten up. If bears were driven in, they would dash through the brush in a rage from one part of the field to the other, utterly regardless of the shower of bullets playing upon their thick hides. After all the game which had not escaped the lines had been mostly killed, a few good dogs and marksmen were sent in to scour the ground and rout out all that might be concealed or wounded. This over, they advanced again to the centre with a shout, dragging along the carcasses that had fallen, for the purpose of making a count and distribution. Sometimes at these circular hunts a grand feast or barbecue would close the sport.

At times the bear or panther would become so annoying and destructive in a certain region, that the whole community would turn out and surround a special swamp, canebrake or savage glen, and a regular clearance was made. At the close of one of these bear "drives" in Portage county, Ohio, the carcasses of no less than twenty-six bears were collected. Wolves were taken, with difficulty, in steel traps, but more readily in log pens, prepared like the roof of a house, shelving inwards on all sides, and containing the half-devoured carcass of a sheep or calf. The wolf easily clambered up the exterior side of the cabin and entered at the top, which was left open; but once fairly within it, he could neither escape nor throw it down. The wolves used to make sad havoc with the sheep, and also with the deer, which they chased in packs, but Bruin had a preference for pigs, and many a settler's cabin has been thrown, at nights, into violent excitement, by the sudden cries from the pig-pen. Bruin would spring suddenly upon his victim, grasp him in his strong fore legs, erect himself on his hind legs and walk off with his prey. A large bear would make his way, in this manner, through a thick wood, faster than a man on foot could follow. The dogs, however, would soon bring him to bay or force him to drop his porker. But, if undisturbed, the squeals and struggles of the hog would become weaker and weaker, and finally cease altogether. Sometimes the recovered pig would be so badly hurt as to require killing, and would then be used as bait, so that Bruin, the next night, would be "hoist by his own petard." Border Chronicles contain many exciting adventures with bears and wolves, and frequently their bold pursuers and slayers would be the pioneer boys or women. If a hog were only partly eaten by a bear, he would invariably return the next night for the balance, showing not a little sagacity in avoiding his fate. To catch nim, a heavy steel trap, with smooth jaws and a long drag-chain, was used, with iron claws at the extremity. It was not fastened, because the great strength of the animal would enable him to free himself, but as he ran, after being caught, the claws would catch in the brush, leaving a distinct trail. He was generally overtaken by the dogs within a mile or so, when, notwithstanding his shackles and wounds, the bear would make desperate fight, killing or lacerating valuable dogs, and perhaps, after all, requiring the rifle.

Turkeys were generally taken in square pens, made of lighter timber than wolf cabins, and covered at the top. They entered at an open door in the side, which was suspended by a string that led to a catch within, surrounded with grain. While engaged picking and scratching among the bait, the catch would be struck and down would come the door. A better way than the door, however, was to make a hole in the ground under one side of the pen, large enough for the turkeys to enter, a trail of bait being laid through this to the outside. The turkeys would then readily enter, but once inside and finding themselves confined, they would lift their heads, and, becoming dazed, would never have sense enough to find their way out by the same hole.

In pioneer times the country was much infested with rattlesnakes. There were two kinds, the large yellow and the smaller, but more irascible and venomous, black rattlesnake, which frequented low grounds. The poison of rattlesnakes never affected hogs, and, fortunately, these latter were very fond of snakes, and would entirely rid a piece of woods of them where they were allowed to range. Some hogs would show as much ardor and dexterity in the chase and killing of a rattlesnake as would a wolf in chase of a wounded or exhausted deer. Trailing them through the woods, either by sight or scent, they would rush at them with incredible swiftness and boldness, regardless of their fangs, and jumping on them repeatedly with their fore feet, would soon dispatch them.

There was little diminution of game in Ohio until 1820. To give a good illustration of a "deer drive," we learn from General L. V. Bierce, of Akron, Ohio, that one occurred in 1818, in the Western Reserve. Five miles square were marked off for the hunt, and a half mile square reserved into which to finally drive the game. The lines were formed by nine A. M. The horns sounded at ten from the different corners. When the half mile square line was reached, a halt was made to reform and close up the lines. The firing then commenced and continued three hours. A great many deer succeeded in breaking through, and turkeys were shot by the score. The grand result was one hundred and twenty deer, twenty-one bears and eighteen wolves.

CAPTAIN MINTER'S FAMOUS BEAR FIGHT.

Captain John Minter, of Kentucky, was a noted hunter. Soon after settling in Delaware county, Ohio, he had a famous bear fight, by which he came near losing his life. When hunting alone one day, he came across a very large bear and fired at him. The bear fell, and, reloading his piece, Minter, supposing him to be dead, advanced and touched his nose with the muzzle of his gun, when the bear instantly rose upon his hind legs to seize him. Minter fired again and cast his hatchet, only inflicting flesh wounds, however, which served but to increase the creature's rage. As the huge beast sprang forward to grasp him, he struck him with the rifle on the head with all his might, producing no other effect than shivering his gun to pieces. Too late now to escape! So Minter drew his big knife from its sheath and made a plunge at old Bruin's heart, but the cunning varmint, by one stroke of his paw, whirled the knife into the air, and enfolding its weaponless owner within his huge arms, both rolled to the ground.

A fearful struggle now ensued between the combatants; one fighting by instinct and the other guided by the dictates of reason. The former was wholly bent upon hugging his active adversary to death; while the latter aimed at presenting his body in such positions as would defeat those vise-like squeezes till he could loosen the grasp. Minter was full six feet high, of large frame and toughened muscles, and was noted for his litheness and agility. He needed it all. The woods were open, free from underbrush, and in those desperate throes and struggles the two rolled in all directions. Several times the hapless, gasping hunter thought the boa-constrictor hug of the bear would finish him, but by choking the brute with all his strength, he would compel him to release his hold to knock off his hands, when he would recover his breath and gain a better hold and position.

In this varying way the dreadful conflict was maintained for several hours, when, in a struggle more obstinate and protracted than usual, the contestants rolled towards where Minter's knife lay. This inspired the exhausted hunter with new strength and heart, but he had to make many ineffectual efforts before he could tumble the bear within reach of it. Finally, by a desperate lurch, he was enabled to clutch the welcome weapon, which, at every chance he had, he plunged to the hilt with all his remaining strength, till at last the horrid beast began, gradually, to relax his hold, and finally rolled over in the agonies of death. He was game to the very last.

The panting, recumbent hunter watched his last breath, for he could not rise from the ground. He finally was enabled to crawl to a log, where his eyes closed and his heart sickened at the scene. Not a rag was left him, and over his back, arms and legs the flesh was torn to the bones by the teeth and claws of the bear—in some places hanging in shreds. By crawling and walking, alternately, the poor fellow managed to reach home some time during the night, with no other covering, however, than a gore of blood from head to foot. Next morning his friends, who went out to survey the field of combat and bring in the trophy, said the surface was torn up for a full half acre. After several weeks Minter recovered, but he carried to his grave broad scars and long welts from a quarter to a half inch thick. He never coveted another bear fight, but gave up hunting and turned his attention to agriculture.

Bears in the old pioneer days were very thick and troublesome throughout Ohio and Kentucky, but very few were of the ferocity of the one Minter fought. In one of the circular drives held in Portage county, Ohio, a great haunt for bears, called "Perkins' Swamp," was embraced, and *no less than twenty-six* were brought to the centre and others reported. Mrs. John Austin, of Ashtabula county, once heard a bear out among her hogs and determined to spoil his sport. So hurrying her children up a ladder in case she should be the worsted party, she seized a rifle and rushing out saw the bear with one of the hogs in its forearms, striding off for the woods. Soon as it saw the woman, it dropped the squealing porker and faced her. Falling upon her knees to take steady aim, and resting her rifle on the fence, within six feet of his bearship, the intrepid woman let fly. Perhaps fortunately for her, the flint missed fire. Again and again she snapped the piece, but with the same result. The bear, after keeping his erect position some time, finally dropped on all fours and scrambled off into the woods.

Not long afterwards, the wives of two absent settlers occupied a cabin together and heard a dreadful noise from the pig-pen, which was near and in full sight of the house. They knew well from what the noise proceeded, and, upon looking out, could see the black intruder making an assault upon the swine. They attempted, by loud screams and by hurling firebrands, to frighten the animal off, but not succeeding, they took an unloaded rifle and having heard their husbands say it required just two fingers of powder, they poured liberally into the muzzle (the fingers, however, measured lengthwise instead of breadthwise,) and putting a ball on top, they boldly sallied out to the attack. One held the light while the other fired the gun.

Such another report from a tube of equal capacity sure was never heard! The females both fell prostrate and insensible, and the gun flew into the bushes. The bear may have been frightened to death, but no trace of him could be found. It was his last visit.

HOW MULDROW FOUND HIS NEXT NEIGHBOR.

Judge James Hall was once riding in Kentucky over a range of savage precipices called Muldrow's Hill, and came across a cluster of dilapidated log houses, and wondered to himself why any pioneer should ever have settled on such a bare and inhospitable tract, when he might have selected any of the rich plains and delightful valleys surrounding, and yet such a choice of location was not uncommon among the earliest settlers, reference being had to security from Indian hostilities. Muldrow, he learned from a resident of that region, settled there when not a single white man but himself was in that whole district, and resided there with his wife for an entire year without having seen the face of any other human being. His cabin being secure by its seclusion, he could safely range among all the neighboring hunting grounds.

He was thus wandering one day in search of game when he heard the barking of a dog, and supposing that an Indian was near, concealed himself. Presently a small dog came running along his track, with his nose to the ground as if pursuing his footsteps, and had nearly reached his hiding place, when it stopped, snuffed the air and uttered a low whine, as if to admonish its master that the object of pursuit was near at hand. In a few minutes the owner of the dog came stepping cautiously along, glancing his eyes jealously around, and uttering low signals to the dog. But the dog stood at fault, and the owner halted within a few yards of our hunter and fully exposed to view. The new comer was a tall, athletic man, completely armed with rifle, tomahawk and knife; but whether he was a white man or an Indian, could not be determined either by his complexion or dress. He wore a hunting shirt and leggins of dressed deerskin, and a hat from which the rim was entirely worn away and the crown elongated into the shape of a sugar loaf. The face, feet and hands, which were exposed, were of the tawny hue of the savage, but whether the color was natural, or the effect of exposure, could not be ascertained even by the keen eye of the hunter, and the features were so disguised by dirt and gunpowder, that their expression afforded no clue, by which the question could be decided, whether the individual was a friend or a foe.

There was but a moment for deliberation, and, after a hasty scrutiny, the pioneer, inclining to the opinion that the stranger was an Indian, cautiously drew up his rifle and took a deliberate aim; but the bare possibility that he might be pointing his weapon at the bosom of a countryman, induced him to pause. Again he raised his gun, and again hesitated; while his opponent, with his rifle half raised towards his face, and his finger on the trigger, looked eagerly around. Both stood motionless and silent; one searching for the object of his pursuit, the other in readiness to fire. At length the hunter, having resolved to delay no longer, cocked his rifle—the *click* reached the acute ear of his opponent, who instantly sprang behind a tree; the hunter imitated his example and they were now fairly opposed, each covered by a tree, from behind which he endeavored to get a shot at his adversary without exposing his own person. And now a series of stratagems ensued, each seeking to draw the fire of the other—until the stranger, becoming weary of suspense, called out, "Why don't you shoot, you tarnal cowardly varmint?" "Shoot, yourself, you bloody redskin!" retorted the other. "No more a redskin than yourself!" "Are you a white man?" "To be sure I am; are you?" "Yes; no mistake in me."

Whereupon, each being undeceived, they threw down their guns, rushed together, with open arms, and took a hearty hug. The hunter now learned that the stranger had been settled, with his family, about ten miles from him for several months past, and that they had often roamed over the same hunting grounds, each supposing himself the sole inhabitant of that region. On the following day the hunter saddled his horse and taking up his good wife behind him, carried her down to make a call upon her new neighbor, who, doubtless received the visit with far more sincere joy than usually attends such ceremonies.

A WILD WHITE MAN AND HIS STORY.

One morning, in Bourbon county, Kentucky, about the year 1785, a young man, of dark, wild and savage appearance, suddenly arose from a cluster of bushes and hailed the inmates of a cabin in a barbarous jargon that none could understand. He talked fast but uncouthly, making violent gestures, rolling his eyes and shrinking from contact with the neighbors, who were soon attracted. As several present understood Indian, they finally gathered that he had been captured while a child and adopted, but knew not who he was or whence he came.

A short time previously his Indian father and younger brother started with him for a war expedition into Kentucky. The hoot of an owl had twice alarmed the father, boding, as he said, death or captivity, and wished to return, but his two sons dissuaded him, and they had marched until in sight of the cabin he was now in. Suddenly the associations produced by the sight of the cabin, and other articles he had seen when a child, unlocked his memory, and the desire of rejoining his people so strongly seized his mind as to exclude every other idea. He had, therefore, concealed himself, and neglected to reply to all concerted signals, upon which the rest had made off, and he had approached the cabin.

The appearance of the young man was so wild and suspicious that his strange story was doubted, and many urged that he should be arrested as a spy or a decoy. Others, however, were inclined to believe, and asked, as a test of the truth of his narrative, whether he would conduct them to where the canoe was buried. To this the stranger objected most vehemently, declaring that although he had deserted his father and brother, yet they had been very kind to him and he would not betray them. This only increased suspicion, and it was at once demanded that he should lead them to the canoe. With obvious reluctance the young man complied. From twenty to thirty mounted men followed him to the Licking.

The stranger, probably in the hope of allowing his relations time to get off, said he would first conduct them to the spot where they had encamped when the scream of the owl alarmed his father, and where an iron kettle had been left concealed in a hollow tree. He was probably induced to do this from the hope of delaying the pursuit so long as to afford his friends an opportunity of crossing the river in safety. If such was his intention, no measure could have been more unfortunate. The whites approached the encampment in deep silence and quickly perceived two Indians, an old man and a boy, seated by the fire and busily employed in cooking some venison. The deserter became much agitated at the sight of them, and so earnestly implored his countrymen not to kill them, that it was agreed to surround the encampment and endeavor to secure them as prisoners. This was accordingly attempted, but so desperate was the resistance of the Indians that the whites were compelled to fire upon them, and the old man fell mortally wounded, while the boy, by an incredible display of address and activity, was enabled to escape.

The deserter beheld his father fall, and, throwing himself from his horse, ran up to the spot where the old man lay bleeding but still sensible, and, falling upon his body, besought his forgiveness for being the unwilling cause of his death, and wept bitterly. His father evidently recognized him, gave him his hand, but almost instantly expired. The white men now called upon him to conduct them at a gallop to the spot where the canoe was buried, expecting to reach it before the Indian boy and intercept him. The deserter in vain implored them to compassionate his feelings. He urged that he had already sufficiently demonstrated the truth of his former assertions at the expense of his father's life, and earnestly entreated them to permit his younger brother to escape. His companions, however, were inexorable. Nothing but the blood of the young Indian would satisfy them, and the deserter was again compelled to act as a guide.

Within two hours they reached the designated spot. The canoe was still there, and no track could be seen upon the sand, so that it was evident that their victim had not yet arrived. Hastily dismounting, they tied their horses and concealed themselves within close rifle shot of the canoe. Within ten minutes after their arrival the Indian appeared in sight, walking swiftly towards them. He went straight to the spot where the canoe had been buried, and was in the act of digging it up, when he received a dozen balls through his body, and, leaping high into the air, fell dead upon the sand. He was scalped and buried where he fell, without having seen his brother, and probably without having known the treachery by which he and his father had lost their lives. The deserter remained but a short time in Bourbon, and never regained his tranquillity of mind. He shortly afterwards disappeared, but whether to seek his relations in Virginia or Pennsylvania, or whether, disgusted by the ferocity of the whites, he returned to the Indians, has never yet been known. He was never heard of afterwards.

HOW MAJOR SMITH RECOVERED HIS SWEETHEART.

Among the adventurers whom Boone describes as having reinforced his little colony was a young gentleman named Smith, who had been a Major in the militia of Virginia, and who, in the absence of Boone, was once chosen to command the rude citadel, which contained all the wealth of this patriarchal band—their wives, their children and their herds. It held also an object particularly dear to this young soldier—a lady, the daughter of one of the settlers, to whom he had pledged his affections.

It came to pass, upon a certain day, that this young lady, with a female companion, strolled out along the banks of the Kentucky river.

Having rambled about for some time, they espied a canoe lying by the shore, and, in a frolic, stepped into it with the determination of visiting a neighbor on the opposite bank. It seems that they were not so well skilled in navigation as the *Lady of the Lake*, who "paddled her own canoe" very dexterously; for, instead of gliding to the point of destination, they were whirled about by the stream, and at length thrown on a sand bar, from which they were obliged to wade to the shore. Full of the mirth excited by their wild adventure, they hastily arranged their dresses, and were proceeding to climb the bank when three Indians, rushing from a neighboring covert, seized the fair wanderers and forced them away.

Their savage captors, evincing no sympathy for their distress, nor allowing them time for rest or reflection, hurried them along during the whole day by rugged and thorny paths. Their shoes were worn off by the rocks, their clothes torn and their feet and limbs lacerated and stained with blood. To heighten their misery, one of the savages began to make love to Miss ———, (the *intended* of Major S.,) and while goading her along with a pointed stick, promised, in recompense for her sufferings, to make her *his squaw*. This at once roused all the energies of her mind and called its powers into action. In the hope that her friends would soon pursue them, she broke the twigs as she passed along and delayed the party as much as possible by tardy and blundering steps. But why dwell on the heartless and unmanly cruelty of these savages? The day and the night passed, and another day of agony had nearly rolled over the heads of these afflicted females, when their conductors halted to cook a wild repast of buffalo meat.

The ladies were soon missed from the garrison. The natural courage and sagacity of Smith, now heightened by love, gave him the wings of the wind and the fierceness of the tiger. The light traces of female feet led him to the place of embarkation; the canoe was traced to the opposite shore; the deep print of the moccasin in the sand told the rest, and the agonized Smith, accompanied by a few of his best woodsmen, pursued " the spoil-encumbered foe."

The track once discovered, they kept it with that unerring sagacity so peculiar to our hunters. The bended grass, the disentangled briers and the compressed shrub, afforded the only but to them the certain indications of the route of the enemy. When they had sufficiently ascertained the general course of the retreat of the Indians, Smith quitted the trace, assuring his companions that they would fall in with them at the pass of a certain stream ahead, for which he now struck a direct course, thus gaining on the foe, who had taken the most difficult paths. Arrived at the stream, they traced its course until they discovered the water newly thrown upon the rocks. Smith, leaving his party, now crept forward upon his hands and feet, until he discovered one of the savages seated by a fire, and with deliberate aim shot him through the heart.

The women rushed towards their deliverer, and recognizing Smith, clung to him in the transport of newly-awakened joy and gratitude, while a second Indian sprang towards him with his tomahawk. Smith, disengaging himself from the ladies, aimed a blow at his antagonist with his rifle, which the savage avoided by springing aside, but, at the same moment, the latter received a mortal wound from another hand. The other and only remaining Indian fell in attempting to escape. Smith, with his interesting charge, returned in triumph to the fort, where his gallantry was finally repaid by the sweetest of all rewards—the girl herself.

JESSE HUGHES, THE MOUNTAIN HUNTER.

Jesse Hughes was one of the most daring, energetic and successful Indian hunters in the mountain region of Virginia, and was an adept with the rifle and tomahawk. A man of delicate frame but an iron constitution, he could endure more fatigue than any of his associates, and thus was enabled to remain abroad at all seasons without detriment. He averted many a threatened blow and saved the lives of numerous helpless settlers, and, consequently, his memory is still dear in the region which he helped to protect. The following incidents of his career De Hass derives from sources entitled to every credit:

About 1790, no Indian depredations having recently occurred in that vicinity, the inhabitants began to think that difficulties were finally at an end, when, one night, a man heard the fence of a small lot, in which he had a horse confined, fall, and, running out, he saw an Indian spring on the horse and dash off. The whole settlement was soon alarmed, and a company of twenty-five or thirty men raised, prepared to start at daylight. They went around the settlement, and found the trail of eight or ten horses, and they supposed there were about that many Indians. The Captain, who had been chosen before Hughes arrived called a halt and held a council to determine in what manner to pursue them. The Captain and a majority of the company were for following on their trail, but Hughes was opposed, and said he could take them to the place where the enemy would cross the Ohio, by a shorter way. But the Captain insisted on pursuing the trail.

Hughes then pointed out the danger of trailing the Indians, and insisted that they would waylay their trail, to find whether they were pursued or not, and would choose a situation where they could shoot two or three and set the rest at defiance, and thus out-travel them and make their escape. The commander found that Hughes was likely to get a majority for his plan, and that he (the Captain) would lose the honor of planning the expedition, and so he broke up the council by calling aloud to the men to follow him and let the cowards go home, and dashed off at full speed, the men all following.

Hughes knew the Captain's remark was intended for him, and felt the insult deeply, but followed on with the rest. They had not gone many miles until the trail led down a ravine, where the ridge on one side was very steep, with a ledge of rock for a considerable distance. On the top of this cliff lay two Indians in ambush, and when the company got opposite they made a noise of some kind that caused the men to stop; that instant two of the whites were shot and mortally wounded. They now found Hughes' prediction verified, for they had to ride so far around before they could get up the cliff, that the Indians, with ease, made their escape. They all now agreed that Hughes' plan was the best, and urged him to pilot them to the river where the Indians would cross. He agreed to do it, but was afraid the Indians, knowing they were pursued, would make a desperate push and get ahead. After leaving some of the company to take care of the wounded, they started for the Ohio and reached it the next day, but shortly after the Indians had crossed. The water was still muddy, and the rafts they had used in crossing were in sight, floating down close to the opposite shore. The men were now unanimous for returning home. Hughes soon got satisfaction for the insult the Captain had given him. He said he wanted now to find out who the cowards were; that if any of them would go, he would cross the river and scalp some of the Indians. They all refused. He then said if one man would go with him, he would undertake it. Hughes then said *he* would go and take one of their scalps or leave his own.

The company now started home, and Hughes went up the river three or four miles, keeping out of sight of it, for he expected the Indians were watching to see if they would cross. He then made a raft, crossed the river and encamped for the night. The next day he found their trail and pursued it very cautiously, and about ten miles from the Ohio found their camp. There was but one Indian in it; the rest were out hunting. The Indian left to keep camp, in order to pass away the time, got to playing the fiddle on some bones they had for the purpose. Hughes crept up and shot him, took his scalp, and made the best of his way home.

The following anecdote illustrates the great discernment and instantaneous arrangement of plans of this Virginia hunter. At a time of great danger from incursions of the Indians, when the citizens of the neighborhood were in a fort at Clarksburg, Hughes, one morning, observed a lad very intently fixing his gun. "Jim," said he, "what are you doing that for?" "I am going to shoot a turkey that I hear gobbling on the hillside," said Jim. "I hear no turkey," said the other. "Listen," said Jim: "There, didn't you hear it? Listen again." "Well," says Hughes, after hearing it repeatedly, "I'll go and kill it." "No, you won't," said the boy, "it is my turkey; I heard it first." "Well," said Hughes, "but you know I am the best shot. I'll go and kill it, and give you the turkey!" The lad demurred, but at length agreed. Hughes went out of the fort on the side that was furthest from the supposed turkey, and passing along the river, went up a ravine, and cautiously creeping through the bushes behind the spot, came in whence the cries issued, and, as he expected, espied a large Indian sitting on a chestnut stump surrounded by sprouts, gobbling, and watching if any one would come from the fort at his decoy. Hughes shot him before the Indian knew of his approach, took off the scalp and went into the fort, where Jim was waiting for his prize. "There now," says Jim, "you have let the turkey go. I would have killed it if I had gone." "No," says Hughes, "I didn't let it go;" and, taking out the scalp, threw it down. "There, take your turkey, Jim, I don't want it." The lad was overcome, and nearly fainted to think of the certain death he had escaped, purely by the keen perception of Jesse Hughes.

SAD DEATH OF CAPTAIN VAN BUSKIRK.

Early in June, 1792, occurred the last conflict on the upper Ohio, between an organized party of Virginians and Indians. In consequence of the numerous depredations on the settlements now embraced in Brooke and Hancock counties, it was determined to summarily chastise these marauders; and, accordingly, a party of men organized under the command of Captain Van Buskirk, an officer of tried courage and acknowledged efficiency. A party of Indians had committed sundry acts of violence, and it was believed they would endeavor to cross the Ohio, on their retreat, at some point near Mingo Bottom. Van Buskirk's party consisted of about forty experienced frontiermen, some of whom were veteran Indian hunters. The number of the enemy was known to be about thirty.

The whites crossed the river below the mouth of Cross Creek, and marched up the bottom, looking cautiously for the enemy's trail. They had discovered it along the run, but missing it, they concluded to take the ridge, hoping thus to cross it. Descending the ridge, and just as they gained the river, the Indians fired upon them, killing Captain Van Buskirk and wounding John Aidy.

The enemy were concealed in a ravine amidst a dense cluster of pawpaw bushes. The whites marched in single file, headed by their Captain, whose exposed situation will account for the fact that he was riddled with thirteen balls. The ambush quartered on their flank, and they were totally unsuspicious of it. The plan of the Indians was to permit the whites to advance in numbers along the line before firing upon them. This was done; but instead of each selecting his man, every gun was directed at the Captain, who fell with *thirteen* bullet-holes in his body. The whites and Indians instantly treed, and the contest lasted more than an hour. The Indians, however, were defeated, and retreated towards the Muskingum, with the loss of several killed; while the Virginians, with the exception of their Captain, had none killed, and but three wounded.

Captain Van Buskirk's wife was killed just eleven months previous to the death of her husband. They lived about three miles from West Liberty. She had been taken prisoner by the Indians, and on their march towards the river her ankle was sprained so that she could not walk without pain. Finding her an incumbrance, the wretches put her to death on the hill just above where Wellsville now stands. On the following day her body was discovered by a party who had gone out in pursuit.

MASSACRE OF THE PURDY FAMILY.

One of the boldest murders perpetrated in the neighborhood of Wheeling, in 1790, was that of the family of James Purdy, a worthy and industrious settler on the hill above Bedelion's mill. The family consisted of Mr. and Mrs. Purdy and their four children. The cabin in which they lived was unfinished; a blanket supplying the place of a door. But this was not deemed unsafe, as no Indians had appeared in the settlements for some months. Soon after dark four Indians stepped into the cabin, and, without uttering a word, commenced butchering the defenceless family. Two of them fell upon Purdy, who called to his wife for a knife, which she handed him; but he was then too much exhausted from the repeated blows of the tomahawk to use it, and the next moment sank lifeless to the floor. Mrs. Purdy was knocked down with a war club; one child was dashed against the doorway and its brains scattered over the room, while an interesting little boy, who was screaming with fright, was quieted by a blow from the tomahawk. The two remaining children, daughters, were then made prisoners, and after plundering the house, the Indians made a rapid retreat across the Ohio. The girls were released after ten years' captivity. Mrs. Purdy was only stunned by the blow with the war club, and falling near the door, crawled off and secreted herself while the Indians were eating.

MASSACRE OF THE TUSH FAMILY

The valley of Wheeling Creek, one of the most beautiful and productive in West Virginia, was the theatre of many a painful and bloody drama. Scarcely a quiet bend, or a surrounding hill, or a rippling tributary, that is not memorable as connected with the wars of the Indians. To one unacquainted with its tragic history, it would indeed be difficult to imagine that those clear waters were once tinged with the blood of helpless women and children, and those stern old hills ever echoed to the terrible whoop of the savage. Of those who settled at an early day in this region, was George Tush. His residence was about twelve miles from the river, and his family consisted of himself, wife and five children. During the year 1794 the settlements on Wheeling Creek had been almost entirely exempt from Indian visitation, and many of the inhabitants began to console themselves with the reflection that day was about to dawn upon their long night of terror.

On the evening of Saturday, September 6th, as George Tush was in the act of feeding his hogs, in a sty close to his cabin, he was fired upon by three savages, who had concealed themselves and waited until he should leave the house. A ball struck him transversely upon the breast, cutting a deep gash and inflicting a serious and painful wound, as it carried off a portion of the bone. It lodged in the shoulder blade. Tush, losing entirely his presence of mind, or, in all charitableness, we may allow that his pain deprived him of self-control, rushed madly by his own door, in direction of the forest, leaving his helpless family to the mercy of relentless savages. The next moment the Indians were in the house.

The mother was instantly made prisoner, and in powerless but quivering agony, compelled to witness the horrid butchery of her innocent children. In an instant the youngest-born was dashed against a tree, and the other four fell beneath the reeking tomahawk. Pillaging the house of such articles as they could carry off, a hurried retreat was made, lest the escaped husband should follow in pursuit. The feeble woman was brutally urged on before them. But, alas! the scenes which she had just witnessed, together with her own situation, rendered her movements both slow and painful. Fearing discovery, the wretches tomahawked their helpless victim and left her at a point about eight miles from the place of captivity. Her bleached remains were found some years afterwards by her husband while hunting.

Of the children tomahawked and scalped, one, a little girl of four years, recovered, and the infant, whose brains were supposed to have been dashed out, was found alive on the following day, lying upon its dead sisters and brothers. That child lives and became the wife of George Goodrich, residing near Shelbyville, Ind. The children had, a few days before, gathered a quantity of acorns, which, it is supposed, prevented the hogs disturbing the remains.

MASSACRE OF CAPTAIN THOMAS AND FAMILY.

On the night of the 5th of March, 1781, a party of Indians came to the house of Captain John Thomas, on Booth's Creek, one of the branches of the Monongahela. Captain Thomas was a man of much piety, and had regular family devotion. While thus engaged, surrounded by his wife and seven children, the Indians approached his cabin. The settlement had as yet felt no apprehension of Indian depredation, as the season was not sufficiently advanced to cause alarm. Anticipating no attack, Captain Thomas was therefore not prepared, and his house not so well secured as was his custom. He had just repeated the line of the hymn, "Go worship at Immanuel's feet," when the Indians approached and fired. The Christian father fell dead at the moment, and a band of savages, forcing the door, entered and commenced the work of death. Mrs. Thomas implored their mercy for herself and children; but, alas! the savage knows no mercy for feeble woman or helpless infancy. The tomahawk did its work until the mother and six children lay weltering in blood by the side of the slaughtered father. They then proceeded to scalp the fallen and plunder the house and then departed, taking with them one little boy as a prisoner.

Elizabeth Juggins was in the house at the time the Indians came, but as soon as she heard the report of the guns and saw Captain Thomas fall, she threw herself under the bed and escaped the observation of the savages. When they had left the house, fearing they might still be in the neighborhood, she remained where she was until she discovered the house was on fire. When she crawled forth from her asylum, Mrs. Thomas was still alive, though unable to move, and casting a pitying glance towards her murdered infant, asked that it might be handed to her. Upon seeing Miss Juggins about to leave the house, she exclaimed, "Oh, Betty, do not leave us!" Still anxious for her own safety, the girl rushed out, and taking refuge for the night between two logs, in the morning early spread the alarm. When the scene of the murder was visited, Mrs. Thomas was found in the yard, much mangled by the tomahawk and considerably torn by hogs—she had, perhaps in the death-struggle, thrown herself out at the door. The house, together with the remains of Captain Thomas and the children, was a heap of ashes.

AN ATTACK UPON KIRKWOOD'S CABIN.

Early in the Spring of 1790 a large body of Indians made an attack upon the settlement at the mouth of Indian Wheeling Creek, opposite Wheeling, Virginia. A block-house was in course of erection, but was not in condition to be occupied; the cabin of Captain Robert Kirkwood was used as a place of resort for the neighborhood. On this occasion Captain Joseph Biggs, who commanded a company of scouts, was in the cabin with fourteen of his men. About four o'clock in the morning Captain Biggs, feeling restless, arose and went out into the air. Returning, he closed the door, and, what was unusual, rolled a barrel of pork against it, in order to make it more secure. He had scarcely time to get into bed when the attack was commenced, and a furious assault made upon the door by means of rails, logs, &c.

The besieged placed themselves under the command of Captain Biggs, by whom the defence was maintained in a manner highly creditable to him as a brave and skillful officer. He ordered every particle of light to be extinguished, and so stationed his men as to fire upon the enemy from every direction. The night was clear and beautiful; the moon, being nearly full, gave those within great advantage over the enemy, as they were enabled, by the light, to shoot the savages whenever they presented themselves. Early in the engagement Captain Biggs received a serious wound, but, with the courage of a true soldier, concealed the nature of it until daylight. In noticing the movements of the enemy through one of the windows of the cabin, an Indian, who had slipped close under the side of the house, suddenly thrust his rifle through the window at which Captain Biggs was standing, and, discharging it, lodged the ball in the left arm of the Captain, just below the shoulder. The bone was badly fractured, and parts of it afterwards came away.

Foiled in their attempt to effect an entrance at the door, (which had been well secured by puncheons from the floor,) the savages determined to try the effect of fire, and, accordingly, hurled burning fagots upon the roof, which, in a few minutes, was enveloped in flames. But again they were unsuccessful, for the whites pushed the roof off the house. The Indians now became furious, and commenced piling brush against the side of the house and set it on fire. At one time the noble little band thought their fate was sealed, as the flames would often mount to the top of the walls. With perseverance and caution, however, they succeeded in extinguishing the fire. This they did first with water, milk, and such other liquids as could be commanded, and finally with sand from beneath the cabin floor. Early in the attack the mortar was removed from the chinks of the walls and the savages, having suffered severely from the steady aim of the scouts through these convenient port holes, retired behind the half-finished block-house.

Shortly after daybreak the boom of a cannon was heard echoing among the hills, which the besieged hailed as the harbinger of help. The firing had been heard at Wheeling, and the gun announced that assistance would soon be at hand. The savages, too, understood it, and without delay gathered up their wounded and disappeared in the forest. Five of the whites were severely wounded, one mortally. These were Captain Joseph Biggs, John Walker, Elijah Hedges, John Barrett and Joseph Van Metre. Walker was shot through the hip, causing his death early the next day. He was removed to the residence of Colonel Zane, Wheeling, where he died, and was buried with military honors. A coat belonging to some of the inmates, which had been suspended by the centre log and was left hanging after the roof had been thrown off, was found, on examination, to be completely riddled with bullets. The number of Indians was never fully ascertained, nor the extent of their killed and wounded. They were supposed to have been the same concerned in the engagement with Captain Van Buskirk's company at the mouth of Brush Run, an account of which has already been given.

A "PERFECT DEVIL" KILLS SEVEN INDIANS.

In 1758 an incident occurred near the present village of Petersburg, Va., which stands without a parallel in modern history. A man named Bingaman lived with his family in a cabin remote from any neighbors. He had been cautioned against the Indians; but, being a man of most determined resolution and herculean strength, he laughed at the idea of fear and said no cut-throat savages should ever drive him from his home. In the Fall of this year a party of eight Indians made a descent upon his cabin, late at night, while all his family were asleep. The household consisted of Bingaman, his wife, child and parents, who slept down stairs, and a hired man who slept above. Before Bingaman was aware of his danger the savages had forced the door and were in the house. Mrs. Bingaman, the younger, was shot through the left breast, but not dangerously wounded. Bingaman got his parents, wife and child beneath the bed, and then prepared for battle. The hired man was called down, but refused to come. The room was dark, and having discharged his gun, he commenced beating about at random with his heavy rifle. In this manner he fought with the desperation of a hero, and terribly did his blows tell upon the enemy. One after another he beat down before him, until, finally, of the eight but one remained, and he, terror-stricken, made from the house and escaped to tell his tribe that he had met with a man who was a "perfect devil." The intrepid Virginian had actually killed seven of his foes, which, certainly, is unexampled in the history of single-handed combat. During the fight the Indians frequently grappled their powerful antagonist, but were unable to keep him down, as early in the engagement he had pulled off his shirt. In the morning, when he found that his wife was wounded, he became so exasperated at the cowardice of the hired man that he would have killed him, had not Mrs. Bingaman interposed to save his life. Bingaman afterwards moved to Natchez, where his son Adam, who was a lad at the time of the fight, had previously moved, and there he (the elder) died.

Kerchieval gives another incident illustrative of the energy and courage of this man, which we give. A party of whites (of whom Bingaman was one) had started in pursuit of some retreating Indians. They were overtaken late at night, and the pursuing party dismounting; the Captain ordered Bingaman to remain with the horses whilst the rest made the attack. This he refused to do, and followed after the company. To make the destruction of the enemy more certain, it was deemed advisable to wait until daylight before they began the attack; but a young man, whose zeal overcame his discretion, fired into the group, upon which the Indians sprang to their feet and fled. Bingaman singled out a fellow of giant-like size, whom he pursued, throwing aside his rifle that his speed might not be retarded—passed several smaller Indians in the chase—came up with him, and, with a single blow of his hatchet, cleft his skull. When Bingaman returned to his battle ground, the Captain sternly observed, "I ordered you to stay and guard the horses." Bingaman as sternly replied, "You are a rascal, sir; you intended to disgrace me; and one more insolent word, and you shall share the fate of that Indian," pointing towards the Indian he had just slain. The Captain quailed under this stern menace and held his peace. He and Bingaman, a few days before, had a falling out. Several Indians fell in this affair, while the whites lost none of their party.

LEVI MORGAN'S STRATAGEM FOR HIS LIFE.

In 1787 the Indians again visited the settlement on Buffalo, Pa., and as Levi Morgan was engaged in skinning a wolf which he had just taken from his trap, he saw three of them—one riding a horse which he well knew, the other two walking near behind, coming towards him. On first looking in the direction they were coming, he recognized the horse and supposed the rider to be its owner—one of his near neighbors. A second glance discovered the mistake, and he seized his gun and sprang behind a large rock—the Indians at the same instant taking shelter by the side of a large tree. As soon as his body was obscured from their view, he turned, and seeing the Indians looking towards the farther end of the rock as if expecting him to make his appearance there, he fired and one of them fell. Instantly he had recourse to his powder horn to reload, but while engaged in skinning the wolf the stopper had fallen out and his powder was wasted. He then fled, and one of the savages took after him.

For some time he held to his gun, but finding his pursuer sensibly gaining on him he dropped it, under the hope that it would attract the attention of the Indian and give him a better chance of escape. The savage passed heedlessly by it. Morgan then threw his shot pouch and coat in the way, to tempt the Indian to a momentary delay. It was equally vain—his pursuer did not falter for an instant. He now had recourse to another expedient to save himself from captivity or death. Arriving at the summit of the hill up which he had directed his steps, he halted; and, as if some men were approaching from the other side, called aloud, "Come on! come on! here is one; make haste!" The Indian, not doubting that he was really calling to some men at hand, turned and retreated as precipitately as he had advanced; and when he heard Morgan exclaim, "Shoot quick or he will be out of reach," he seemed to redouble his exertions to gain that desirable distance. Pleased with the success of the artifice, Morgan hastened home, leaving his coat and gun to reward the savage for the deception practiced on him. At the treaty of Auglaize, Morgan met with the Indian who had given him this chase, and who still had his gun. After talking over the circumstance, rather more composedly than they had acted it, they agreed to test each other's speed in a friendly race. The Indian being beaten, rubbed his hams and said, "*Stiff, stiff; too old.*" "Well," said Morgan, " you got the gun by outrunning me then, and I should have it now for outrunning you;" and accordingly took it.

RIDDLED WITH BULLETS AND YET ESCAPES.

One of the most remarkable escapes upon record is that of Thomas Mills. The circumstances were these: On the thirtieth day of July, 1783, Mills and two other men, Henry Smith and Hambleton Kerr, started on a fishing excursion, up the river, from Wheeling. When near Glenn's Run, a party of Indians, who had watched the movements of the whites, fired upon them, killing Smith and wounding Mills in fourteen places. He had that many distinct bullet holes in him, and yet not one of them was mortal. Kerr escaped. Just before the attack, Mills and his companions had caught an enormous catfish (weighing eighty-seven pounds); and when the men were taken from the canoe, at Wheeling, their appearance was truly frightful; they were literally covered with blood and sand. Mills, attended by Rebecca Williams and Mrs. Ebenezer Zane, both skilled nurses, recovered from his wounds, and, as late as 1850, was living on the Ohio, near Shade river. He was, in his time, a most useful man on the frontier, possessing great experience as a hunter and scout.

Kerr was one of the most efficient spies west of the Ohio river. His father was killed near the mouth of Duck Creek, in the Summer of 1791. Two of his neighbors, who were passing down the river in a canoe on the Virginia side of the island, hearing the report of a gun, landed and passed over the island, where they saw two Indians going from the canoe in which Kerr lay with the struggle of death still upon him. This murder of his father greatly exasperated Hambleton, and thenceforward no Indian was safe who crossed his path. He settled at the mouth of a small stream now known as Kerr's Run, at the upper end of Pomeroy, Ohio.

A HANDSOME SQUAW MAKES LOVE TO BIGGS.

In the year 1788 William Biggs was a settler in West Illinois, and while riding not far from home, was taken prisoner by a party of Kickapoo Indians, one of whom was very bitter and ferocious, and tried several times to kill him. He, however, was prevented by the rest. When a halt was made for a meal, the party held a council to determine what they would do with this contumacious one, who, they said, was stubborn and a coward, and would kill their captive the first opportunity. They finally concluded they would kill their refractory Indian. Two started out in his company, and soon after Biggs heard the report of a gun. An old chief then told him that, according to their custom, this one, who would not obey commands, had been killed.

Biggs was made a Kickapoo and treated with marked kindness. He describes the character of the Illinois Indians as being entirely different from that of more eastern and northern tribes—milder, more amiable and much fonder of fun. A young squaw of the household took a great fancy for him, and was not slow to betray it. She very tenderly combed out the captive's hair, and then queued it with ribbons. The chief then gave him a regimental blue cloth coat, faced with buff, a fine beaver hat and a new ruffled shirt—all taken from officers they had killed—and made him put them on and strut across the ground; when "the funny Indian" said he was a pretty man and a big captain.

His humane captors carried their civility so far as to offer him a wife, which, on account of having one already, Biggs says he declined. The tawny lady, however—the same who had combed out his hair—did not conceal her partiality. We quote the love scene, as follows:

"When the Indians were about to take me to another village, she came up and stood at the door, but would not go in. I discovered the Indians laughing and plaguing her—she looked in a very ill humor; she did not want them to take me away. They immediately started from the cabin, and took a tolerably large path that led into the woods, in a pretty smart trot; the squaw started immediately after them; they would look back once in a while, and when they would see the squaw coming, they would whoop and laugh. When they got out of sight of the squaw, they stopped running and traveled in a moderate walk. When we got about three miles from the town, they stopped where a large tree had fallen by the path, and laid high off of the ground; they got up high on the log and looked back to see if the squaw was coming; when the squaw came up she stopped, and they began to plague her and laugh at her; they spoke English. They talked very provokingly to the squaw; she soon began to cry.

"On arriving at their destination that evening, he found her again posted at the door of the cabin at which he lodged, and her Indian friends making themselves merry at her constancy and want of success. The incorrigible white man, when reminded by his companions that he would be accepted if he chose to offer himself, parried the proposal by replying, 'I reckon not.'" He adds, "she stayed two days and three nights before she returned home; I never spoke a word to her while she was there. She was a very handsome girl, about eighteen years of age, a beautiful, full figure and finely featured, and very white for a squaw." It has been asserted that nothing is so uncertain as the female except the male.

CACASOTTE THROWS FOURTEEN ROBBERS OVERBOARD.

During the last part and the first part of the present century, the West was very much infested with fugitives from justice and lawless desperadoes. The intercourse between St. Louis and New Orleans was especially dangerous. Goods were carried by barges and keelboats, and as they were very richly laden, they were considered glorious prizes, and were laid in wait for by bands of robbers. A very large and desperate gang, commanded by Culbert and Majilbray, had their nest at Cottonwood Creek, where they carried on an extensive system of piracy.

In 1787 a richly-laden barge, belonging to Mr. Beausoliel, of St. Louis, was on her way from New Orleans and was carried by a stiff breeze safely past Cottonwood Creek. The baffled robbers immediately dispatched a company of men up the river for the purpose of heading. The manœuvre was effected in the course of two days, at an island which has since been called Beausoliel's island. The barge had just put ashore. The robbers boarded. The men were disarmed, guards were stationed in every part of the vessel, and she was soon under way. Mr. Beausoliel gave himself up to despair. This vessel would have shared the fate of many others that had preceded it, but for the heroic daring of a negro, who was one of the crew.

Cacasotte, the negro, was a man rather under the ordinary height, very slender in person but of uncommon strength and activity. The color of his skin and the curl of his hair alone, told that he was a negro, for the peculiar characteristics of his race had given place in him to what might be termed beauty. His forehead was finely moulded, his eyes small and sparkling as those of a serpent, his nose aquiline, his lips of a proper thickness; in fact, the whole appearance of the man, joined to his known character for shrewdness and courage, seemed to indicate an uncommon character. Cacasotte, as soon as the robbers had taken possession of the barge, danced, sang, laughed and soon induced his captors to believe that they had liberated him from irksome slavery, and that his actions were the ebullitions of pleasure. His constant attention to their smallest wants and wishes, too, won their confidence; and whilst they kept a watchful eye on the other prisoners, they permitted him to roam through the vessel unmolested and unwatched.

This was the state of things that the negro desired. He laid his plan before his master, who, after a great deal of hesitation, acceded to it. Cacasotte then spoke to two of the crew, likewise negroes, and engaged them in the conspiracy. Cacasotte was cook, and it was agreed between him and his fellow conspirators that the signal for dinner should be the signal for action. The hour of dinner at length arrived. The robbers assembled in considerable numbers on the deck, and stationed themselves at the bow and stern and along the sides, to prevent any rising of the men. Cacasotte went among them with the most unconcerned look and demeanor imaginable. As soon as he perceived that his comrades had taken the stations he had assigned them, he took his position at the bow of the boat, near one of the robbers, a stout, herculean man, who was armed cap-a-pie.

Everything being arranged to his satisfaction, Cacasotte gave the preconcerted signal, and immediately the robber near him was struggling in the water. With the speed of lightning he went from one robber to another, and in less than three minutes he had thrown fourteen of them overboard. Then, seizing an oar, he struck on the head those who attempted to save themselves by grappling the running boards, then shot, with the muskets that had been dropped on deck, those who swam away. In the meantime the other conspirators were not idle, but did great execution. The deck was soon cleared, and the robbers that remained below were too few in number to offer any resistance. Having got rid of his troublesome visitors, Mr. Beausoleil deemed it prudent to return to New Orleans, and after that the barges went in company and well armed with swivels.

Chapter XI.

PIONEER WOMEN—THEIR TRIALS AND HEROISM.

> The mothers of our forest land,
>   Stout-hearted dames were they;
> With nerve to wield the battle brand,
>   And join the border fray.
> Our rough land had no braver,
>   In its days of blood and strife,
> Aye, ready for severest toil,
>   Aye, free to peril life.

The history of our western border may well be deemed a record of woman's trials, privations and heroic deeds. We have already given numerous instances of all these. We have now to add a few more. How tender, shrinking women ever had the heart to expose themselves, as they did, to all the Protean perils of the savage wilderness, is the marvel of the present day. They seemed to be richly and peculiarly endowed to suit the times and the localities in which their lots were cast. We may be sure it was not for themselves that they thus cheerfully gave up home, society, and all the blessings of peace and quiet, to brave the savage wilds, to patiently endure its perils and privations, and to challenge the fierce assaults of wild beasts and of still wilder and more ferocious human foes. Ah, no: it was for those they loved. That solves the mystery.

> Man's love is of Man's life a part,
> 'Tis Woman's whole existence.

It was wonderful! The constant dread by day and the consuming care by night—even though women were ever environed by extraordinary hazards—was utterly unselfish. It was felt but for those most dear to them, and thus the sufferings of their soul might be termed the soul of their sufferings, since it was through the tender, devoted and unselfish woman's heart that the chiefest agonies were inflicted. Especially were their innocent and helpless children the objects of unceasing care and anxiety, for these seemed to be the peculiar objects of savage hate and malignancy, and were used by fiendish tormentors to wring and agonize a mother's or a sister's heart, and to stir it down to its deepest depths. But let us now group together only a few from the very many examples of the heroism and sufferings of pioneer women, and first we give

THE TOUCHING NARRATIVE OF MASSY HARBISON.

On the return of my husband from General St. Clair's defeat, and on his recovery from the wound he received in the battle, he was made a spy, and ordered to the woods on duty, about the 22d of March, 1792. The appointment of spies to watch the movements of the savages was so consonant with the desires and interests of the inhabitants, that the frontiers now resumed the appearance of quiet and confidence. Those who had for nearly a year been huddled together in the blockhouses, were scattered to their own habitations, and began the cultivation of their farms. The spies saw nothing to alarm them, or to induce them to apprehend danger, till the fatal morning of my captivity. They repeatedly came to our house to receive refreshments and to lodge.

On the 15th of May my husband, with Captain Guthrie and other spies, came home about dark and wanted supper; to procure which I requested one of the spies to accompany me to the spring and springhouse, and William Maxwell complied with my request. While he was at the spring and spring-house, we both distinctly heard a sound like the bleating of a lamb or fawn. This greatly alarmed us and induced us to make a hasty retreat into the house. Whether this was an Indian decoy, or a warning of what I was to pass through, I am unable to determine. But from this time and circumstance, I became considerably alarmed and entreated my husband to remove me to some more secure place from Indian cruelties. But Providence had designed that I should become a victim to their rage, and that mercy should be made manifest in my deliverance.

On the night of the 21st of May two of the spies, Mr. James Davis and Mr. Sutton, came to lodge at our house, and on the morning of the 22d, at daybreak, when the horn blew at the block-house, which was within sight of our house and distant about two hundred yards, the two men got up and went out. I was also awake, and saw the door open and thought, after I was taken prisoner, that the scouts had left it open. I intended to rise immediately, but having a child at the breast, and it being awakened, I lay with it at the breast to get it to sleep again, and accidentally fell asleep myself. The spies have since informed me that they returned to the house again, and found that I was sleeping;

that they softly fastened the door and went immediately to the blockhouse, and those who examined the house after the scene was over, say that both doors had the appearance of being broken open.

The first thing I knew from falling asleep, was the Indians pulling me out of bed by my feet. I then looked up and saw the house full of Indians, every one having his gun in his left hand and tomahawk in his right. Beholding the danger in which I was, I immediately jumped to the floor on my feet, with the young child in my arms. I then took a petticoat to put on, having on only the one in which I slept; but the Indians took it from me, and as many as I attempted to put on, they succeeded in taking from me, so that I had to go just as I had been in bed. While I was struggling with some of the savages for clothing, others of them went and took the children out of another bed, and immediately took the two feather beds to the door and emptied them.

The savages immediately began their work of plunder and devastation. What they were unable to carry with them, they destroyed. While they were at their work, I made to the door, and succeeded in getting out with one child in my arms and another by my side; but the other little boy was so much displeased by being so early disturbed in the morning, that he would not come to the door.

When I got out, I saw Mr. Wolf, one of the soldiers, going to the spring for water, and beheld two or three of the savages attempting to get between him and the block-house; but Mr. Wolf was unconscious of his danger, for the savages had not yet been discovered. I then gave a terrific scream, by which means Mr. Wolf discovered his danger and started to run for the block-house. Seven or eight of the Indians fired at him, but the only injury he received was a bullet in his arm, which broke it. He succeeded in making his escape to the block-house. When I raised the alarm, one of the Indians came up to me with his tomahawk as though about to take my life; a second came and placed his hand before my mouth and told me to hush, when a third came with a lifted tomahawk and attempted to give me a blow; but the first that came raised his tomahawk and averted the blow, and claimed me as his squaw.

The commissary, with his waiter, slept in the store-house near the block-house. And upon hearing the report of the guns, came to the door to see what was the matter, and beholding the danger he was in, made his escape to the block-house; but not without being discovered by the Indians, several of whom fired at him, and one of the bullets went through his handkerchief, which was tied about his head, and took off some of his hair. The handkerchief, with several bullet holes in it, he afterwards gave to me.

The waiter, on coming to the door, was met by the Indians, who fired upon him, and he received two bullets through the body and fell dead by the door. The savages then set up one of their tremendous and terrifying yells, and pushed forward and attempted to scalp the man they had killed; but they were prevented from executing their diabolical purpose by the heavy fire which was kept up through the port holes from the block-house.

In this scene of horror and alarm I began to meditate an escape, and for that purpose I attempted to direct the attention of the Indians from me and to fix it on the block-house, and thought if I could succeed in this I would retreat to a subterranean cave with which I was acquainted, which was in the run near where we were. For this purpose, I began to converse with some of those who were near me respecting the strength of the block-house, the number of men in it, &c., and being informed that there were forty men there, and that they were excellent marksmen, the savages immediately came to the determination to retreat, and for this purpose they ran to those who were besieging the block-house and brought them away.

They then began to flog me with their wiping sticks, and to order me along. Thus what I intended as the means of my escape, was the means of accelerating my departure in the hands of the savages. But it was no doubt ordered by a kind Providence for the preservation of the fort and the inhabitants in it; for when the savages gave up the attack and retreated, some of the men in the fort had the last load of ammunition in their guns, and there was no possibility of procuring more, for it was all fastened up in the store-house, which was inaccessible.

The Indians, when they had flogged me away with them, took my oldest boy, a lad about five years of age, along with them, for he was still at the door by my side. My middle little boy, who was about three years of age, had by this time obtained a situation by the fire in the house, and was crying bitterly to me not to go, and making sore complaints of the depredations of the savages. But these monsters were not willing to let the child remain behind them; they took him by the hand to drag him along with them, but he was so very unwilling to go, and made such a noise by crying, that they took him up by his feet and dashed his brains out against the threshold of the door. They then scalped and stabbed him, and left him for dead. When I witnessed this inhuman butchery of my own child, I gave a most indescribable and terrific scream, and felt a dimness come over my eyes, next to blindness, and my senses were nearly gone. The savages then gave me a blow across my head and face and brought me to my sight and recollection again. During the whole of this agonizing scene I kept my infant in my arms.

As soon as the murder was effected they marched me along to the top of the bank, about forty or sixty rods, and there they stopped and divided the plunder which they had taken from our house, and here I counted their number and found them to be thirty-two, two of whom were white men painted as Indians. Several of the Indians could speak English well. I knew several of them well, having seen them going up and down the Allegheny river. I knew two of them to be from the Seneca tribe of Indians, and two of them Munsees; for they had called at the shop to get their guns repaired, and I saw them there.

We went from this place about forty rods, and they then caught my uncle, John Currie's horses, and two of them, into whose custody I was put, started with me on the horses towards the mouth of the Kiskiminetas, and the rest of them went off towards Puckety. When they came to the bank that descended towards the Allegheny it was so very steep, and there appeared so much danger in descending it on horseback, that I threw myself off the horse, in opposition to the will and command of the savages.

My horse descended without falling, but the one on which the Indian rode who had my little boy, in descending, fell and rolled over repeatedly; and my little boy fell back over the horse, but was not materially injured; he was taken up by one of the Indians, and we got to the bank of the river, where they had secreted some bark canoes under the rocks, opposite the island that lies between the Kiskiminetas and Buffalo. They attempted, in vain, to make the horses take the river, and had to leave the horses behind them, and took us in one of the canoes to the point of the island and there left the canoe.

Here I beheld another hard scene, for as soon as we landed my little boy, who was still mourning and lamenting about his little brother, and who complained that he was injured by the fall in descending the bank, *was murdered.* One of the Indians ordered me along, probably that I should not see the horrid deed about to be perpetrated. The other then took his tomahawk from his side, and with this instrument of death killed and scalped him. When I beheld this second scene of inhuman butchery I fell to the ground senseless, with my infant in my arms, it being under and its little hands in the hair of my head. How long I remained in this state of insensibility I know not.

The first thing I remember was my raising my head from the ground and feeling myself exceedingly overcome with sleep. I cast my eyes around and saw the scalp of my dear little boy, fresh bleeding from his head, in the hand of one of the savages, and sunk down to the earth again upon my infant child. The first thing I remember, after witnessing this spectacle of woe, was the severe blows I was receiving from the hands of the savages, though at that time I was unconscious of the injury I was sustaining. After a severe castigation, they assisted me in getting up, and supported me when up. The scalp of my little boy was hid from my view, and in order to bring me to my senses again they took me back to the river and led me in knee-deep; this had its intended effect. But "the tender mercies of the wicked are cruel."

We now proceeded on our journey by crossing the island, and coming to a shallow place where we could wade out, and so arrive at the Indian side of the country. Here they pushed me in the river before them, and had to conduct me through it. The water was up to my breast, but I suspended my child above the water, and with the assistance of the savages, got safely out. Thence we rapidly proceeded forward, and came to Big Buffalo; here the stream was very rapid and the Indians had again to assist me. When we had crossed this creek, we made a straight course to the Connoquenessing Creek, the very place where Butler, Pa., now stands; and thence we traveled five or six miles to Little Buffalo, which we crossed.

I now felt weary of my life, and had a full determination to make the savages kill me, thinking that death would be exceedingly welcome when compared to the fatigue, cruelties and miseries I had the prospect of enduring. To have my purpose effected I stood still, one of the savages being before me, and the other walking behind me, and I took from off my shoulder a large powder horn they made me carry, in addition to my child, who was one year and four days old. I threw the horn on the ground, closed my eyes, and expected every moment to feel the deadly tomahawk. But to my surprise the Indian took it up, cursed me bitterly, and put it on my shoulder again. I took it off the second time, and threw it on the ground, and again closed my eyes, with the assurance I should meet death; but instead of this, the Indian again took up the horn, and with an indignant, frightful countenance, came and placed it on again. I took it off the third time, and was determined to effect it, and, therefore, threw it as far as I was able from me, over the rocks. The savage immediately went after it, while the one who had claimed me as his squaw, and who had stood and witnessed the transaction, came up to me and said: "Well done; you did right and are a good squaw, and the other is a lazy son of a gun; he may carry it himself."

The savages now changed their position, and the one who claimed me as his squaw, went behind. This movement, I believe, was to prevent the other from doing me any injury; and we went on till we struck the Connoquenessing at the Salt Lick, about two miles above Butler, where was an Indian camp, where we arrived a little before dark, having no refreshment during the day. The camp was made of stakes driven into the ground sloping, and covered with chestnut bark, and appeared sufficiently long for fifty men. The camp appeared to have been occupied for some time; it was very much trodden, and large beaten paths went out from it in different directions.

That night they took me about three hundred yards from the camp, up a run, into a large, dark bottom, where they cut the brush in a thicket and placed a blanket on the ground and permitted me to sit down with my child. They then pinioned my arms back, only with a little liberty, so that it was with difficulty that I managed my child. Here, in this dreary situation, without fire or refreshment, having an infant to take care of, and my arms bound behind me, and having a savage on each side of me, who had killed two of my dear children that day, I had to pass the first night of my captivity.

But the trials and tribulations of the day I had passed had so completely exhausted nature, that notwithstanding my unpleasant situation, and my determination to escape, if possible, I insensibly fell asleep, and repeatedly dreamed of my escape and safe arrival in Pittsburgh, and several things relating to the town, of which I knew nothing at the time; but found to be true when I arrived there. The first night passed away and I found no means of escape, for the savages kept watch the whole of the night, without any sleep.

In the morning one of them left us to watch the trail we had come, to see if any white people were pursuing us. During the absence of the Indian, the one that claimed and remained with me, and who was the murderer of my last boy, took from his bosom his scalp, and prepared a hoop and stretched the scalp upon it. Those mothers who have not seen the like done to one of the scalps of their own children, will be able to form but faint ideas of the feelings which then harrowed up my soul. I meditated revenge! While he was in the very act I attempted to take his tomahawk, which hung by his side and rested on the ground, and had nearly succeeded, and was, as I thought, about to give the fatal blow, when, alas! I was detected.

The savage felt me at his tomahawk handle, turned upon me, cursed me and told me I was a Yankee; thus insinuating he understood my intention, and to prevent me from doing so again, faced me. My excuse to him for handling his tomahawk was, that my child wanted to play with the handle of it. The savage who went upon the lookout in the morning came back about twelve o'clock, and had discovered no pursuers. Then the one who had been guarding me went out on the same errand. The savage who was now my guard began to examine me about the white people, the strength of the armies going against the Indians, &c.,

and boasted largely of their achievements in the preceding Fall, at the defeat of General St. Clair.

He then examined the plunder which he had brought from our house the day before. He found my pocket book and money among his plunder. There were ten dollars in silver and a half a guinea in gold in the book. During this day they gave me a piece of dried venison, about the bulk of an egg, and a piece about the same size the day we were marching, for my support and that of my child; but, owing to the blows I had received from them on the jaws, I was unable to eat a bit of it. I broke it up and gave it to the child.

The savage on the lookout returned about dark. This evening, (Monday, the 23d,) they moved me to another station in the same valley, and secured me as they did the preceding night. Thus I found myself the second night between two Indians, without fire or refreshment. During this night I was frequently asleep, notwithstanding my unpleasant situation, and as often dreamed of my arrival in Pittsburgh.

Early on the morning of the 24th a flock of mocking birds and robins hovered over us as we lay in our uncomfortable bed; and sang and said, at least to my imagination, that I was to get up and go off. As soon as day broke, one of the Indians went off again to watch the trail, as on the preceding day, and he who was left to take care of me appeared to be sleeping. When I perceived this I lay still and began to snore, as though asleep, and he also fell asleep. Then I concluded it was time to escape. I found it impossible to injure him for my child at the breast, as I could not effect anything without putting the child down, and then it would cry and give the alarm; so I contented myself with taking, from a pillow-case of plunder stolen from our house, a short gown, handkerchief and child's frock, and so made my escape; the sun then being about half an hour high.

I struck the Connoquenessing, and went down stream until about two o'clock in the afternoon, over rocks, precipices, thorns, briers, &c., with my bare feet and legs. I then discovered I was on the wrong course, and waited till the North star appeared. Marking out the direction for the next day, I collected a bed of leaves, laid down and slept, though my feet, being full of thorns, began to be exceeding painful, and I had nothing for self or babe to eat. The next morning I started early, nothing material occurring. Towards evening a gentle rain came on, and I began to prepare my leaf bed, setting the child down the while, who began to cry. Fearful of the consequences, I put him to the breast and he became quiet. I then listened and distinctly heard footsteps. The ground over which I had traveled was soft and my foot traces had been followed.

Greatly alarmed, I looked about for a place of safety, and providentially discovered a large tree which had fallen, into the top of which I crept. The darkness greatly assisted me and prevented detection. The savage who followed me had heard the cry of the child and came to the very spot where it had cried, and there he halted, put down his gun, and was at this time so near that I heard the wiping stick strike against his gun distinctly. My getting in under the tree and sheltering myself from the rain, and pressing my boy to my bosom, got him warm, and, most providentially, he fell asleep, and lay very still during that time of extreme danger. All was still and quiet, the savage was listening to hear again the cry. My own heart was the only thing I feared, and that beat so loud that I was apprehensive it would betray me. It is almost impossible to conceive the wonderful effect my situation produced upon my whole system.

After the savage had stood and listened with nearly the stillness of death for two hours, the sound of a bell and a cry like that of a night owl, signals which were given to him by his companions, induced him to answer, and after he had given a most horrid yell, which was calculated to harrow up my soul, he started and went off to join them. After his retreat, I concluded it unsafe to remain there till morning.

But by this time nature was so nearly exhausted that I found some difficulty in moving; yet, compelled by necessity, I threw my coat about my child and placed the end between my teeth, and with one arm and my teeth I carried him, and with the other groped my way between the trees and traveled on, as I supposed, a mile or two, and there sat down at the root of a tree till morning. The night was cold and wet, and thus terminated the fourth day and night's difficulties, trials and dangers!

The fifth day, wet, exhausted, hungry and wretched, I started from my resting place as soon as I could see my way, and on that morning struck the head waters of Pine Creek, which falls into the Allegheny about four miles above Pittsburgh; though I knew not then what waters they were; I crossed them, and on the opposite bank I found a path, and on it two moccasin tracks, fresh indented. This alarmed me; but as they were before me, and traveling in the same direction as I was, I concluded I could see them as soon as they could see me, and, therefore, I pressed on in that path for about three miles, when I came to where another branch emptied into the creek, where was a hunter's camp, where the two men, whose tracks I had before discovered and followed, had breakfasted and left the fire burning.

I became more alarmed, and determined to leave the path. I then crossed a ridge towards Squaw Run, and came upon a trail. Here I stopped and meditated what to do; and while I was thus musing, I saw three deer coming towards me at full speed; they turned to look at their pursuers; I looked, too, with all attention, and saw the flash and heard the report of a gun. I saw some dogs start after them, and began to look about for a shelter, and immediately made for a large log to hide myself. Providentially, I did not go clear to the log; for as I put my hand to the ground, to raise myself so that I might see who and where the hunters were, I saw a large heap of rattlesnakes, the top one being very large, and coiled up very near my face, and quite ready to bite me.

I again left my course, bearing to the left, and came upon the head waters of Squaw Run, and kept down the run the remainder of that day. It rained, and I was in a very deplorable situation; so cold and shivering were my limbs, that frequently, in opposition to all my struggles, I gave an involuntary groan. I suffered intensely from hunger, though my jaws were so far recovered that, wherever I could, I procured grapevines, and chewed them for a little sustenance. In the evening I came within one mile of the Allegheny river, though I was ignorant of it at the time; and there, at the root of a tree, through a most tremendous rain, I took up my fifth night's lodgings. In order to shelter my infant as much as possible, I placed him in my lap, and then leaned my head against the tree, and thus let the rain fall upon me.

On the sixth (that was the Sabbath) morning from my captivity, I found myself unable, for a very considerable time, to raise myself from the ground; and when I had once more, by hard struggling, got myself upon my feet and started, nature was so nearly exhausted and my spirits were so completely depressed, that my progress was amazingly slow and discouraging. In this almost helpless condition I had not gone far before I came to a path where there had been cattle traveling; I took it, under the impression that it would lead me to the abode of some white people, and in about a mile I came to an uninhabited cabin, and though I was in a river bottom, yet I knew not where I was nor yet on what river bank I had come.

Here I was seized with feelings of despair, went to the threshold of the cabin and concluded that I would enter and lie down and die, since death would have been an angel of mercy to me in such a miserable situation. Had it not been for the sufferings which my infant, who would survive me some time, must endure, I would have carried my determination into execution. Here I heard the sound of a cow bell, which imparted a gleam of hope to my desponding mind. I followed the sound till I came opposite the fort at the Six Mile island, where I saw three men on the opposite bank of the river.

My feelings then can be better imagined than described. I called to them, but they seemed unwilling to risk the danger of coming after me and asked who I was. I told them and they requested me to walk up the bank awhile that they might see if Indians were making a decoy of me, but I replied my feet were so sore I could not walk. Then one of them, James Closier, got into a canoe to fetch me over, while the other two stood with cocked rifles ready to fire on the Indians, provided they were using me as a decoy. When Mr. Closier came near and saw my haggard and dejected appearance, he exclaimed, " Who in the name of God are you ? " This man was one of my nearest neighbors, yet in six days I was so much altered that he did not know me, either by my voice or countenance.

When I landed on the inhabited side of the river, the people from the fort came running out to see me. They took the child from me, and now that I felt safe from all danger, I found myself unable to move or to assist myself in any degree, whereupon the people took me and carried me out of the boat to the house of Mr. Cortus.

Now that I felt secure from the cruelties of the barbarians, for the first time since my captivity, my feelings returned in all their poignancy and the tears flowed freely, imparting a happiness beyond what I ever experienced. When I was taken into the house, the heat of the fire and the smell of victuals, of both of which I had so long been deprived, caused me to faint. Some of the people attempted to restore me and some to put clothes on me, but their kindness would have killed me had it not been for the arrival of Major McCully, who then commanded along the river. When he understood my situation, and saw the provisions they were preparing for me, he was greatly alarmed; ordered me out of the house, away from the heat and smell; prohibited me taking anything but a very little whey of buttermilk, which he administered with his own hands. Through this judicious management, I was mercifully restored to my senses and gradually to health and strength.

Two of the females, Sarah Carter and Mary Ann Crozier, then began to take out the thorns from my feet and legs, which Mr. Felix Negley stood by and counted to the number of one hundred and fifty, though they were not all extracted at that time, for the next evening, at Pittsburgh, there were many more taken out. The flesh was mangled dreadfully, and the skin and flesh were hanging in pieces on my feet and legs. The wounds were not healed for a considerable time. Some of the thorns went through my feet and came out at the top. For two weeks I was unable to put my feet to the ground to walk. The next morning a young man, employed by the magistrates of Pittsburgh, came for me to go immediately to town to give in my deposition, that it might be published to the American people. Some of the men carried me into a canoe, and when I arrived I gave my deposition. As the intelligence spread, Pittsburgh, and the country for twenty miles around, was all in a state of commotion. The same evening my husband came to see me, and soon after I was taken back to Coe's Station. In the evening I gave an account of the murder of my boy on the island, and the next morning a scout went out and found the body and buried it, nine days after the murder.

DESPERATE ATTACK ON WIDOW SCRAGGS' CABINS.

On the night of the 11th of April, 1787, the house of a widow by the name of Scraggs, in Bourbon county, Kentucky, became the scene of a thrilling adventure. She occupied what is generally called a double cabin, in a lonely part of the county, one room of which was tenanted by the old lady herself, together with two grown sons and a widowed daughter, at that time suckling an infant, while the other was occupied by two unmarried daughters, from sixteen to twenty years of age, together with a little girl not more than half grown. The hour was eleven o'clock at night. One of the unmarried daughters was still busily engaged at the loom, but the other members of the family, with the exception of one of the sons, had retired to rest.

Some symptoms of an alarming nature had engaged the attention of the young man for an hour before anything of a decided character took place. The cry of owls was heard in the adjoining woods, answering each other in rather an unusual manner. The horses, which were enclosed as usual, in a pound near the house, were more than commonly excited, and, by repeated snorting and galloping, announced the presence of some object of terror. The young man was often upon the point of awakening his brother, but was as often restrained by the fear of incurring ridicule and the reproach of timidity, at that time an unpardonable blemish in the character of a Kentuckian. At length hasty steps were heard in the yard, and quickly afterwards several knocks at the door, accompanied by the usual exclamation, "who keeps house?" in very good English. The young man, supposing, from the language, that some benighted settlers were at the door, hastily arose and was advancing to withdraw the bar which secured it, when his mother, who had long lived upon the frontier and had probably detected the Indian tone in the demand for admission, sprang out of bed and ordered her son not to admit them, declaring that they were Indians.

She instantly awakened her other son, and the two young men, seizing their guns, which were always charged, prepared to repel the enemy. The Indians, finding it impossible to enter under their assumed characters, began to thunder at the door with great violence, but a single shot from a loophole compelled them to shift the attack to some less exposed point; and, unfortunately, they discovered the door of the other cabin, which contained the three daughters. The rifles of the brothers could not be brought to bear upon this point, and by means of several rails, taken from the yard fence, the door was forced from its hinges, and the three girls were at the mercy of the savages. One was immediately secured, but the eldest defended herself desperately with a knife which she had been using at the loom, and stabbed one of the Indians to the heart before she was tomahawked. In the meantime the little girl, who had been overlooked by the enemy in their eagerness to secure the others, ran out into the yard, and might have effected her escape had she taken advantage of the darkness and fled, but instead of that the terrified little creature ran around the house wringing her hands and crying out that her sisters were killed.

The brothers, unwilling to hear her cries without risking everything for her rescue, rushed to the door and were preparing to sally out to her assistance, when their mother threw herself before them and calmly declared that the child must be abandoned to her fate—that the sally would sacrifice the lives of all the rest without the slightest benefit to the little girl. Just then the child uttered a loud scream, followed by a faint moan, and all was again silent. Presently the crackling of flames was heard, accompanied by a triumphant yell from the Indians, announcing that they had set fire to that division of the house which had been occupied by the daughters, and of which they held undisputed possession.

The fire was quickly communicated to the rest of the building, and it became necessary to abandon it or perish in the flames. In the one case, there was a possibility that some might escape; in the other, their fate would be equally certain and terrible. The rapid approach of the flames cut short their momentary suspense. The door was thrown open, and the old lady, supported by her eldest son, attempted to cross the fence at one point, while the daughter, carrying her child in her arms, and attended by the younger of the brothers, ran in a different direction. The blazing roof shed a light over the yard but little inferior to that of day, and the savages were distinctly seen awaiting the approach of their victims. The old lady was permitted to reach the stile unmolested, but, in the act of crossing, received several balls in her breast and fell dead. Her son, providentially, remained unhurt, and, by extraordinary agility, effected his escape. The other party succeeded also in reaching the fence unhurt, but, in the act of crossing, were vigorously assailed by several Indians, who, throwing down their guns, rushed upon them with their tomahawks. The young man defended his sister gallantly, firing upon the enemy as they approached, and then wielding the butt of his rifle with a fury that drew their whole attention upon himself, and gave his sister an opportunity of effecting her escape. He quickly fell, however, under the tomahawk of his enemies, and was found, at daylight, scalped and mangled in a shocking manner. Of the whole family, consisting of eight persons when the attack commenced, only three escaped. Four were killed upon the spot, and one (the second daughter) carried off as a prisoner.

The neighborhood was quickly alarmed, and by daylight about thirty men were assembled, under the command of Colonel Edwards. A light snow had fallen during the latter part of the night, and the Indian trail could be pursued at a gallop. It led directly into the mountainous country bordering on Licking, and afforded evidences of great hurry and precipitation on the part of the fugitives. Unfortunately, a hound had been permitted to accompany the whites, and as the trail became fresh and the scent warm, she followed it with eagerness, baying loudly and giving the alarm to the Indians. The consequences of this imprudence were soon displayed. The enemy, finding the pursuit keen and perceiving that the strength of the prisoner began to fail, sunk their tomahawks in her head and left her, still warm and bleeding, upon the snow. As the whites came up, she retained strength enough to wave her hand in token of recognition, and appeared desirous of giving them some information with regard to the enemy, but her strength was too far gone. Her brother sprang from his horse and knelt by her side, endeavoring to stop the effusion of blood, but in vain. She gave him her hand, muttered some inarticulate words, and expired within two minutes after the arrival of the party.

The pursuit was renewed with additional ardor, and in twenty minutes the enemy were within view. They had taken possession of a steep, narrow ridge, and seemed desirous of magnifying their numbers in the eyes of the whites, as they ran rapidly from tree to tree, and maintained a steady yell in their most appalling tones. The pursuers, however, were too experienced to be deceived by so common an artifice, and being satisfied that the number of the enemy must be inferior to their own, they dismounted, tied their horses, and flanking out in such a manner as to enclose the enemy, ascended the ridge as rapidly as was consistent with a due regard to the shelter of their persons. The firing quickly commenced, and now, for the first time, they discovered that *only two Indians were opposed to them.* They had voluntarily sacrificed themselves for the safety of the main body, and had succeeded in delaying pursuit until their friends could reach the mountains. One of them was shot dead, and the other was badly wounded, as was evident from the blood upon his blanket, as well as that which filled his tracks in the snow for a considerable distance. The pursuit was recommenced, and urged keenly until night, when the trail entered a running stream and was lost. On the following morning the snow had melted, and every trace of the enemy was obliterated. This affair must be regarded as highly honorable to the skill, address and activity of the Indians, and the self-devotion of the rear guard is a lively instance of that magnanimity of which they are at times capable, and which is more remarkable in them from the extreme caution and tender regard for their own lives, which usually distinguishes their warriors.

MRS. MERRILL, THE TERRIBLE "LONG KNIFE SQUAW."

During the Summer the house of Mr. John Merrill, of Nelson county, Kentucky, was attacked by the Indians, and defended with singular address and good fortune. Merrill was alarmed by the barking of a dog about midnight, and upon opening the door, in order to ascertain the cause of the disturbance, he received the fire of six or seven Indians, by which his arm and thigh were both broken. He sank upon the floor and called upon his wife to shut the door. This had scarcely been done when it was violently assailed by the tomahawks of the enemy, and a large breach soon effected. Mrs. Merrill, however, being a perfect Amazon, both in strength and courage, guarded it with an axe, and successively killed or badly wounded four of the enemy as they attempted to force their way into the cabin. The Indians then ascended the roof and attempted to enter by way of the chimney, but here, again, they were met by the same determined enemy. Mrs. Merrill seized the only feather bed which the cabin afforded, and hastily ripping it open, poured its contents upon the fire. A furious blaze and stifling smoke ascended the chimney, and quickly brought down two of the enemy, who lay for a few moments at the mercy of the lady. Seizing the axe, she dispatched them, and was instantly afterwards summoned to the door, where the only remaining savage now appeared, endeavoring to effect an entrance while Mrs. Merrill was engaged at the chimney. He soon received a gash in the cheek which compelled him, with a loud yell, to relinquish his purpose and return hastily to Chillicothe, where, from the report of a prisoner, he gave an exaggerated account of the fierceness, strength and courage of the "long knife squaw!"

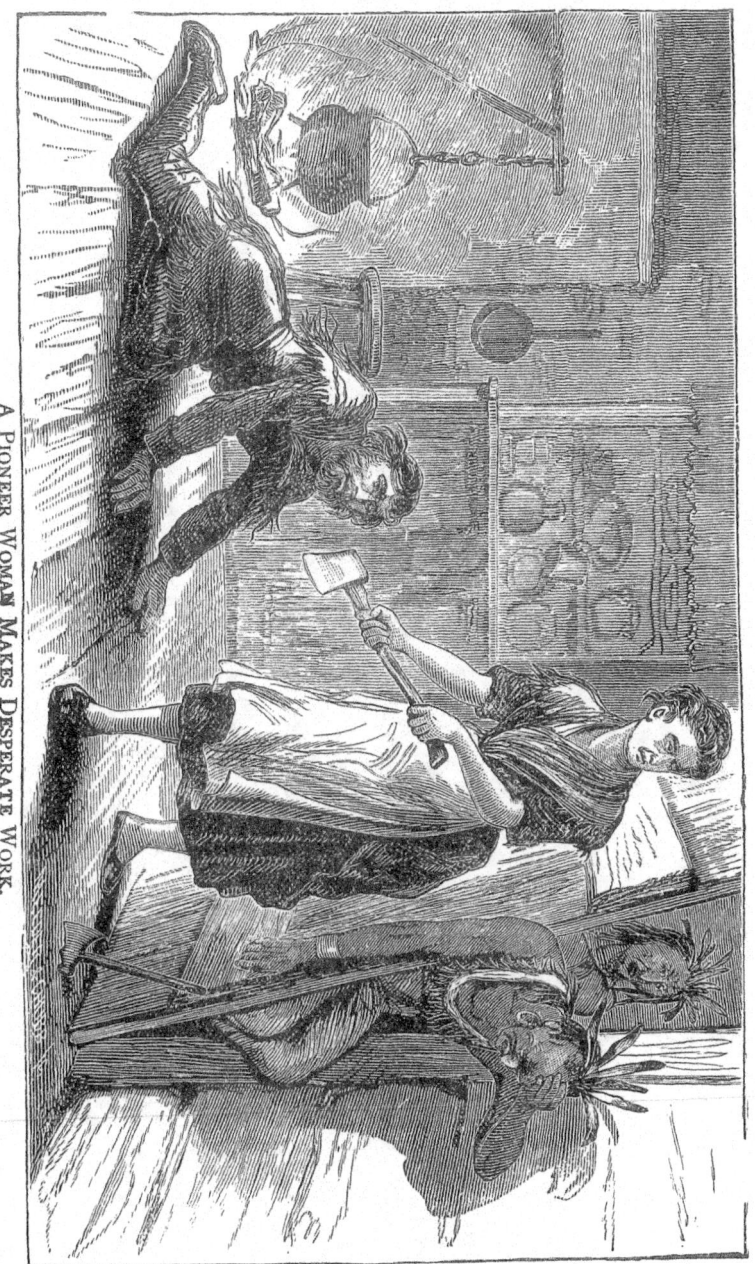

A Pioneer Woman Makes Desperate Work.
—See page 698.

MRS. WOODS AND THE LAME NEGRO.

In the Summer of 1792 a gentleman named Woods, imprudently removed from the neighborhood of a station, and, for the benefit of his stock, settled on a lonely heath near Beargrass, Ky. One morning he left his family, consisting of a wife, a daughter not yet grown and a lame negro man, and rode off to the nearest station, not expecting to return until night. Mrs. Woods, while engaged in her dairy, was alarmed at seeing several Indians rapidly approaching the house. She instantly screamed loudly in order to give the alarm, and ran with her utmost speed, in order to reach the house before them. In this she succeeded, but had not time to close the door until the foremost Indian had forced his way into the house. As soon as he entered, the lame negro grappled him and attempted to throw him upon the floor, but was himself hurled to the ground with violence, the Indian falling upon him.

Mrs. Woods was too busily engaged in keeping the door closed against the party without, to attend to the combatants, but the lame negro, holding the Indian in his arms, called to the young girl to cut his head off with a very sharp axe which lay under the bed. She attempted to obey, but struck with so trembling a hand that the blow was ineffectual. Repeating her efforts, under the direction of the negro, however, she at length wounded the Indian so badly, that the negro was enabled to arise and complete the execution. Elated with success, he then called to his mistress and told her to suffer another Indian to enter and they would kill them all one by one. While deliberating upon this proposal, however, a sharp firing was heard without, and the Indians quickly disappeared. A party of white men had seen them at a distance, and, having followed them cautiously, had now interposed, at a very critical moment, and rescued a helpless family from almost certain destruction.

FAMILY OF MRS. DAVIESS CAPTURED—A RESCUE.

Early one morning, in August of 1782, Samuel Daviess, a settler at Gilmer's Lick, Kentucky, having stepped a few paces from his cabin, was suddenly surprised by an Indian appearing between him and the door with an uplifted tomahawk, almost within striking distance; and, in a moment after, he perceived that four other Indians had just entered his dwelling. Being entirely unarmed, he made for an adjacent cornfield, closely pursued by the first Indian. He, however, eluded the savage, and ran with the utmost speed to the nearest station, five miles distant, and raised a party to pursue the enemy, whom it was ascertained, on visiting the cabin, had taken off the whole family captive. After going a few miles they heard the barking of a dog, which they knew was the family house dog, and which the Indians, for precaution's sake, were undertaking to kill. They now rushed impetuously forward, but were discovered by the two spies in the rear, who ran forward, knocked down the oldest boy, and, while scalping him, were fired at, but without effect. Mrs. Daviess, seeing the alarm and confusion, saved herself and babe by jumping into a sink hole. The Indians fled and the whole family were rescued. So soon as the boy had risen to his feet, the first words he spoke were, "Curse that Indian, he has got my scalp."

Mrs. Daviess related the following account of the manner in which the Indians had acted: A few minutes after her husband had opened the door and stepped out of the house, four Indians rushed in, while the fifth, as she afterwards found out, was in pursuit of her husband. Herself and children were in bed when the Indians entered the house. One of the Indians immediately made signs, by which she understood him to inquire how far it was to the next house. With an unusual presence of mind, knowing how important it would be to make the distance as far as possible, she raised both her hands, first counting the fingers of one, then of the other—making a distance of eight miles. The Indian then signed to her that she must rise: she immediately got up, and as soon as she could dress herself, commenced showing the Indians one article of clothing after another, which pleased them very much; and in that way delayed them at the house nearly two hours. In the meantime, the Indian who had been in pursuit of her husband returned, with his hands stained with pokeberries, which he held up, and with some violent gestures and waving of his tomahawk, attempted to induce the belief that the stain on his hands was the blood of her husband, and that he had killed him. She was enabled at once to discover the deception, and instead of producing any alarm on her part, she was satisfied that her husband had escaped uninjured. After the savages had plundered the house of everything that they could conveniently carry off with them, they started, taking Mrs. Daviess and her children, seven in number, as prisoners along with them. Some of the children were too young to travel as fast as the Indians wished, and discovering, as she believed, their intention to kill such of them as could not conveniently travel, she made the two oldest boys carry them on their back.

Mrs. Daviess was a woman of cool, deliberate courage, and accustomed to handle the gun so that she could shoot well, as many of the women were in the habit of doing in those days. She had contemplated, as a last resort, that if not rescued in the course of the day, when night came and the Indians had fallen asleep, she would rescue herself and children by killing as many of the Indians as she could—thinking that, in a night attack, as many of them as remained would most probably run off. Such an attempt would now seem a species of madness; but to those who were acquainted with Mrs. Daviess, little doubt was entertained that, if the attempt had been made, it would have proved successful.

Kentucky, in its early days, like most new countries, was occasionally troubled with men of abandoned character, who lived by stealing the property of others, and, after committing their depredations, retired to their hiding places, thereby eluding the operation of the law. One of these marauders, a man of desperate character, who had committed extensive thefts from Mr. Daviess, as well as from his neighbors, was pursued by Daviess and a party whose property he had taken, in order to bring him to justice. While the party were in pursuit, the suspected individual, not knowing any one was pursuing him, came to the house of Daviess, armed with his gun and tomahawk—no person being at home but Mrs. Daviess and her children. After he had stepped into the house, Mrs. Daviess asked him if he would drink something, and, having set a bottle of whiskey on the table, requested him to help himself. The fellow, not suspecting any danger, set his gun up by the door, and, while drinking, Mrs. Daviess picked up his gun, and placing herself in the door, had the gun cocked and leveled upon him by the time he turned round, and in a peremptory manner ordered him to take a seat or she would shoot him. Struck with terror and alarm, he asked what he had done. She told him he had stolen her husband's property, and that she intended to take care of him herself. In that condition she held him a prisoner until the party of men returned and took him into their possession.

In the year 1786, about twenty young persons of both sexes were in a field pulling flax, in the vicinity of a fort on Green river, Kentucky, when they were fired on by a party of Indians in ambush. They instantly retreated towards the fort, hotly pursued by the savages. Among them were two married women, who had gone out to make them a visit, one of whom had taken with her a young child about eighteen months old. The older of the two mothers, recollecting in her flight that the younger, a small and feeble woman, was burdened with her child, turned back in the face of the enemy, they firing and yelling hideously, took the child from its mother, and ran with it to the fort, nearly a quarter of a mile distant. During the chase she was twice shot at with rifles, when the enemy was so near that the powder burned her, and one arrow passed through her sleeve, but she escaped uninjured.

MURDER OF THE TWO MISSES CROW.

Next to the Tush murder, perhaps the most melancholy occurrence on Wheeling Creek was that of two sisters—the Misses Crow, which occurred in 1785. The parents of these girls lived about one mile above the mouth of Dunkard, or lower fork of the creek. According to the statement of a third sister, who was an eye witness to the horrid tragedy and herself almost a victim, the three left their parents' house for an evening walk along the deeply-shaded banks of that beautiful stream. Their walk extended over a mile and they were just turning back, when suddenly several Indians sprang from behind a ledge of rocks and seized all three of the sisters. With scarcely a moment's interruption, the savages led the captives a short distance up a small bank when a halt was called and a parley took place. It seems that some of the Indians were in favor of immediate slaughter, while others were disposed to carry them into permanent captivity.

Unfortunately, the arm of mercy was powerless. Without a moment's warning, a fierce-looking savage stepped from the group, with elevated tomahawk, and commenced the work of death. This Indian, in the language of the surviving sister, "Began to tomahawk one of my sisters—Susan by name. Susan dodged her head to one side, the tomahawk taking effect in her neck, cutting the jugular vein, the blood gushing out a yard's length. The Indian who held her hand jumped back to avoid the blood. The other Indian then began the work of death on my sister Mary.

"I gave a sudden jerk and got loose from the one that held me and ran with all speed, taking up a steep bank, but just as I caught hold of a bush to help myself up, the Indian fired and the ball passed through the clump of hair on my head, slightly breaking the skin. I gained the top in safety, the Indian taking round in order to meet me as I would strike the path that led homeward. But I ran right from home and hid myself in the bushes near the top of the hill. Presently I saw an Indian passing along the hill below me; I lay still until he was out of sight; I then made for home."

MRS. BOZARTH SLAYS THREE SAVAGE INTRUDERS.

On Dunkard Creek, now within the limits of Monongalia county, W. Va., lived a Mr. Bozarth, his wife and three children. The alarm which had caused the settlers to resort to Prickett's Fort, induced two or three families living convenient to Mr. Bozarth, to collect at his house. About the 1st of April, 1789, when but two men were in the house with Mrs. Bozarth, the children, who had been out playing, ran suddenly in, crying that "Indians were coming!"

In order to ascertain the true cause of this alarm, one of the men stepped to the door and was struck upon the breast with a rifle ball, which knocked him back into the house. A savage sprang in after him and attacked the other white man with all the fury of his nature. The man being unarmed called for a knife, but Mrs. Bozarth, not seeing one at the instant, picked up an axe and killed the savage on the spot.

While the courageous woman was thus engaged, a second Indian presented himself at the door, and, firing, killed the man who had been struggling with his companion. Quick as thought, the intrepid matron turned upon this new comer, and, at one blow, ripped open his abdomen, causing the savage to yell most lustily for help. Immediately, several of his companions rushed to the rescue, but the invincible woman was ready for them. The first who attempted to enter was struck upon the head and his skull cleft, making the third victim to the axe of this Virginia Amazon. The others, having drawn out the wounded savage and learning the strength of the house, attempted to force the door, but Mrs. Bozarth had so securely fastened it as to defy all their efforts. The savages then killed the children still in the yard and made off.

A DESPERATE ATTACK ON THE CUNNINGHAMS.

In the latter part of June, 1785, a small party of Indians visited the house of Edward Cunningham, an enterprising settler on Bingamon Creek, a branch of West Fork. Thomas Cunningham, the brother of Edward, lived in a house almost adjoining; the two families affording protection thus one to another. At the time spoken of, Edward and his family were in one cabin, and the wife of Thomas, with her four children, (her husband having gone East on a trading expedition,) were in the other. Both families were eating their dinners, when in stepped, before the astonished mother and children, a huge savage, with drawn knife and uplifted tomahawk. Conscious of his security with the mother and children, but fearing danger from Edward Cunningham, who had seen him enter, the savage quickly glanced around for some means of escape in an opposite direction. Edward watched the movements of the savage through an opening in the wall.

In the other house was a similar hole, (made to introduce light,) and through it the Indian fired, shouting the yell of victory. It was answered by Edward, who had seen the aim of the savage just in time to escape—the bark from the log close to his head was knocked off by the Indian's ball, and flew in his face. The Indian, seeing that he had missed his object, and observing an adze in the room, deliberately commenced cutting an aperture in the back wall, through which he might pass out without being exposed to a shot from the other building.

Another of the Indians came into the yard just after the firing of his companion, but observing Edward's gun pointing through the port hole, endeavored to retreat out of its range. Just as he was about to spring the fence, a ball struck him and he fell forward. It had, however, only fractured his thigh bone, and he was yet able to get over the fence and take shelter behind a quilt suspended on it, before Edward could again load his gun. Meantime the Indian in the house was engaged in cutting a hole through the wall, during which Mrs. Cunningham made no attempt to get out, well aware that it would only draw upon her head the fury of the savage; and that if she escaped this one, she would probably be killed by some of those who were watching outside. She knew, too, it would be impossible to take the children with her. She trusted in the hope that the one inside would withdraw without molesting any of them.

A few minutes served to convince her of the hopeless folly of trusting to an Indian's mercy. When the opening had been made sufficiently large, the savage raised his tomahawk, sunk it deep into the brain of one of the children, and, throwing the scarcely lifeless body into the back yard, ordered the mother to follow him. There was no alternative but death, and she obeyed his order, stepping over the dead body of one of her children, with an infant in her arms and two others screaming by her side.

When all were out, he scalped the murdered boy, and, setting fire to the house, retired to an eminence, where two of the savages were with their wounded companion—leaving the other two to watch the opening of Edward Cunningham's door, when the burning of the house should force the family from their shelter. They were disappointed in their expectation of that event by the exertions of Cunningham and his son. When the flame from the one house communicated to the roof of the other, they ascended to the loft, threw off the loose boards which covered it and extinguished the fire; the savages shooting at them all the while; their balls frequently striking close by.

Unable to force out the family of Edward Cunningham, and despairing of doing further injury, they beat a speedy retreat. Before leaving, however, the eldest son of Mrs. Thomas Cunningham was tomahawked and scalped in the presence of the shuddering mother. Her little daughter was served the same way; but to make the scene still more tragical, her head was dashed against a tree and her brains scattered about. The mother, during the whole of these bloody acts, stood motionless in grief, and in momentary awe of meeting a similar fate. But, alas! she was reserved for a different, and, to a sensitive woman, a far more dreadful fate. With her helpless babe, she was led from this scene of carnage. The savages carried their wounded companion upon a litter. Crossing the ridge they found a cave near Bingamon Creek, in which they secreted themselves until after night, when some of the party returned to Edward Cunningham's, but not finding any one at home, fired the house and made a hasty retreat towards their own country.

Mrs. Cunningham suffered untold mental and physical agonies during her march to the Indian towns. For ten days her only nourishment was the head of a wild turkey and a few paw-paws. After a long absence, she was returned to her husband through the intercession of Simon Girty, who first said she would be better there than at home; then that his saddle bags were too small to conceal her, but who finally ransomed her and sent her home. This one single act should redeem his memory from a multitude of sins.

After the savages had withdrawn, Cunningham went with his family into the woods, where they remained all night, there being no settlement nearer than ten miles. In the morning the alarm was given, and a company of men soon collected to go in pursuit of the Indians. When they came to Cunningham's they found both houses heaps of ashes. They buried the bones of the boy who was murdered in the house, with the bodies of his brother and little sister, who were killed in the field; but so cautiously had the savages conducted their retreat, that no traces of them could be discovered and the men returned to their homes.

Subsequently, a second party started in pursuit and traced them to the cave, but it was found the enemy had left the night previous, and all hope of effecting a successful pursuit was given over. After her return from captivity, Mrs. Cunningham stated that at the time of the search on the first day the Indians were in the cave, and that several times the whites approached so near that she could distinctly hear their voices; the savages standing with their guns ready to fire in the event of being discovered, and forcing her to keep the infant to her breast, lest its cry might indicate their place of concealment.

CAPTIVITY AND WANDERINGS OF MRS. FRANCES SCOTT.

Mr. Scott, a citizen of Washington county, Virginia, had his house attacked on Wednesday night, June 29th, 1785, and himself, with four children, butchered upon the spot.

Early in the evening a considerable body of Indians passed his house and encamped within a couple of miles. Himself and family had retired, with the exception of Mrs. Scott, who was in the act of undressing when the painted savages rushed in and commenced the work of death.

Mr. Scott being awake, jumped up, but was immediately fired at; he forced his way through the midst of the enemy and got out of the door, but fell. An Indian seized Mrs. Scott and ordered her to a particular spot and not to move. Others stabbed and cut the throats of the three younger children in their bed, and afterwards lifting them up, dashed them on the floor near the mother; the oldest, a beautiful girl of eight years, awoke, escaped out of bed, ran to her parent, and, with the most plaintive accents, cried, "O mama! mama! save me!" The mother, in the deepest anguish of spirit and with a flood of tears, entreated the savages to spare her child; but with a brutal fierceness they tomahawked and scalped her in the mother's arms.

Adjacent to Mr. Scott's dwelling house another family lived, of the name of Ball. The Indians attacked them at the same time; but the door being shut, the enemy fired into the house through an opening between two logs and killed a young lad. They then tried to force the door, but a surviving brother fired through and drove them off. The remaining part of the family ran out of the house and escaped. In Mr. Scott's house were four good rifles, well loaded, and a good deal of clothing and furniture; part of which belonged to people that had left it on their way to Kentucky. The Indians, being thirteen in number, loaded themselves with the plunder, then speedily made off and continued traveling all night. Next morning their chief allotted to each man his share, and detached nine of the party to steal horses from the inhabitants on Clinch river.

The eleventh day after Mrs. Scott's captivity, the four Indians who had her in charge stopped at a place of rendezvous to hunt. Three went out, and the chief, being an old man, was left to take care of the prisoner, who, by this time, expressed a willingness to proceed to the Indian towns, which seemed to have the desired effect of lessening her keeper's vigilance. In the daytime, as the old man was graining a deerskin, the captive, pondering on her situation and anxiously looking for an opportunity to make her escape, took the resolution, and went to the Indian carelessly, asked liberty to go a small distance to a stream of water to wash the blood off her apron, that had remained besmeared since the fatal night of the murder of her little daughter. He told her, in the English tongue, "Go along!" She then passed by him, his face being in a contrary direction from that she was going, and he very busy.

After getting to the water, she went on without delay towards a high, barren mountain, and traveled until late in the evening, when she came down into the valley in search of the track she had been taken along, hoping thereby to find the way back without risk of being lost and perishing with hunger in uninhabited parts. That night she made herself a bed with leaves, and the next day resumed her wanderings. Thus did that poor woman continue from day to day, and week to week, wandering in the trackless wilderness. Finally, on the 11th of August, she reached a settlement on Clinch river, known as New Garden.

Mrs. Scott related, that during her wanderings from the 10th of July to the 11th of August, she had no other subsistence but chewing and swallowing the juice of young cane, sassafras, and some plants she did not know the name of; that, on her journey, she saw buffalo, elk, deer and frequently bears and wolves, not one of which, although some passed very near, offered to do her the least harm. One day a bear came near her, with a young fawn in his mouth, and, on discovering her, he dropped his prey and ran off. Hunger prompted her to try and eat the flesh; but, on reflection, she desisted, thinking that the bear might return and devour her; besides she had an aversion to raw meat.

Mrs. Scott long continued in a low state of health, and remained inconsolable at the loss of her family, particularly bewailing the cruel death of her little daughter.

REBECCA BOONE, AND HOW DANIEL WON HER.

The first woman who went to Kentucky was Rebecca Boone, and a most noble, heroic and excellent wife and mother she was in every respect. Here is the way Daniel Boone is said to have won her. It will be remembered Boone's father lived on the Yadkin, N. C.

Daniel was once, when a young man, out on a "fire hunt," with what might be called a "boone companion." They had got into a heavily-timbered piece of "bottom," skirted by a small stream which bordered the plantation of a Mr. Morgan Bryan, (a very respectable farmer and head of a family,) the hunter's friend preceding him with the "fire pan," when all at once Boone quietly gave the concerted signal to stop— an indication that he had "shined the eyes" of a deer. Dismounting and tying his horse, he then crept cautiously forward—his rifle at a present—behind a covert of hazel and plum bushes, and, sure enough! there again were the two blue, liquid orbs turned full upon him.

Boone now raised his fatal rifle, but a mysterious something—only tender lovers can say what—arrested his arm and caused his hand to tremble—when off sprang the startled game with a bound and a rustle, and the ardent young hunter in hot chase after it. On! on! they go; when, lo and behold! a fence appears, over which the nimble deer vaulted in a strangely human sort of a way, while Boone, burdened with his rifle and hunting gear, clambered after as best he could. Another kind and differently spelled *deer* now takes possession of Boone's fancy, as he sees Bryan's house in the distance. "I will chase this pet deer to its covert," thinks he, and so, fighting his way through a score of snarling and scolding hounds, he knocked at the door, and was admitted and welcomed by farmer Bryan. The young hunter, panting from his recent exertions, had scarce time to throw his eyes about inquiringly, before a boy of ten, and a flushed and breathless girl of sixteen, with ruddy cheeks, flaxen hair and soft blue eyes, rushed into the room.

"Oh, father! father!" excitedly cried out young hopeful. "Sis was down to the creek to set my lines, and was chased by a 'painter' or something. She's too skeared to tell." The "painter" and "deer" were now engaged in exchanging glances, and apparently the eyes of *both* had been most effectually "shined," for, to make a long story short, that is how Rebecca Bryan became Rebecca Boone, and a most excellent wife she made.

"MAD ANN BAILEY," OF WEST VIRGINIA.

What a strange, wild, solitary life this woman led, as we find it living in border chronicles! It is said that "Hell hath no fury like a woman scorned." Neither hath it any like a woman wronged and thoroughly imbued with the spirit of vengeance. There was a wild, unnatural brightness in her sharp, gray eyes, and a mocking jeer in her loud, grating laugh. One could scarce help pitying while he shuddered to see a woman, who should be tender and affectionate, cherished and protected by the love of friends and children and surrounded with every care and comfort, so thoroughly unsexed; roaming alone the vast wilderness solitudes and exposed to all the spiteful elements. She was a veritable Meg Merriles—a thorough gypsy in look, habit and vagabondage.

Her maiden name was Hennis, and she was raised at Liverpool, emigrating to America with her husband, Richard Trotter, who was a volunteer in Dunmore's war of 1774, and fell fighting at the bloody Indian battle of Point Pleasant. From the period of his death she became possessed with a strange, savage spirit of revenge against the Indians. She was somewhat disordered in her intellect; forsook her sewing and spinning and commenced practicing with the rifle, casting the tomahawk, hunting the wild game of the forests, and riding about the country to every muster of scouts or hunters. She even discarded female attire, and differed little in appearance from the ordinary scout of the border. The rifle was her constant companion; she frequently carried off the prizes at the various shooting matches; spent most of her time scouring the woods, with no companion but a powerful black horse, which she called Liverpool, after her birthplace.

She was much esteemed by the people of West Virginia, having once performed an inestimable service for the beleaguered garrison of Charleston Fort by riding day and night, amid appalling perils, a distance of two hundred miles through the savage wilds and unbroken forests of West Virginia, and procuring a supply of powder from Camp Union (now Lewisburg). With a led horse weighted down with ammunition, she resolutely commenced her return; her trail followed by packs of ravenous wolves or still more dangerous redskins, sleeping by night amid the profound solitudes of the wilderness and on spreads of boughs raised high on stakes to protect her from venomous snakes or savage beasts; crossing raging torrents, breasting craggy heights; ever watching for Indian "sign," but ever avoiding Indian attacks, until she heroically delivered her powder and saved the fort. She afterwards took her place among the men in defending the place, and used to boast that she had fired many a shot at her foes.

Strange, that such an odd, rugged, intractable character should ever, even for a day, allow the soft passion of love to usurp the place of her fierce and cruel revenge! Stranger still, that any mortal man could be found who would be attracted by such a wild, stormy, riotous spirit. He must have "wooed her as the lion wooes *his* bride," where the mutual caresses and encounters of love pass amid savage roars and growls and rude buffetings. But a man did *woo*, and win her, too, and his name it was Bailey, and so she became Mrs. Ann Bailey.

Whether he ever "tamed this shrew" history sayeth not, but we read that her unquenchable spirit and audacity, in spite of her many eccentricities, greatly endeared her to the whole border. She engaged in the hunt of deer, bear and panther; was, during the Indian troubles, employed as fort messenger, and afterwards—mounted on her famed black hunter—used to visit many of the chief people of West Virginia, returning laden down with gifts.

THE BEAUTIFUL AND DASHING LOUISA ST. CLAIR.

In the Winter of 1790, the Governor of the Northwest Territory, General Arthur St. Clair, removed his family from his plantation at "Potts' Grove," in Westmoreland county, Pa., to Marietta, O. One of his daughters, Louisa, was long remembered as one of the most distinguished among the ladies of that day. In strength and elasticity of frame, blooming health, energy and fearlessness, she was the ideal of a soldier's daughter, extremely fond of adventure and frolic, and ready to draw amusement from everything around her. She was a fine equestrian, and would manage the most spirited horse with perfect ease and grace, dashing at full gallop through the open woodland surrounding the "Campus Martius," and leaping over logs or any obstacle in her way. She was also expert in skating, and was rivaled by few, if any, young men in the garrison, in the speed, dexterity and grace of movement with which she exercised herself in this accomplishment.

The elegance of her person, and her neat, well-fitting dress, were shown to great advantage in her rapid gyrations over the broad sheet of ice in the Muskingum, which, for a few days in Winter, offered a fine field, close to the garrison, for this healthful sport; and loud were the plaudits from young and old, from spectators of both sexes, called forth by the performance of the Governor's daughter. As a huntress she was equally distinguished, and might have served as a model for a Diana, in her rambles through the forest, had she been armed with a bow instead of a rifle, of which latter instrument she was perfect mistress, loading and firing with the accuracy of a backwoodsman, killing a squirrel on the top of the tallest tree, or cutting off the head of a partridge with wonderful precision. She was fond of roaming through the woods, and often went out alone into the forest near Marietta, fearless of the savages who often lurked in the vicinity. As active on foot as on horseback, she could walk several miles with the untiring rapidity of a practiced ranger.

Notwithstanding her possession of these unfeminine attainments, Miss St. Clair's refined manners would have rendered her the ornament of any drawing-room circle; she was beautiful in person, and had an intellect highly cultivated, having received a carefully finished education, under the best teachers in Philadelphia. Endowed by nature with a vigorous constitution and lively animal spirits, her powers, both of body and mind, had been strengthened by such athletic exercises, to the practice of which she had been encouraged from childhood by her father. He had spent the greater part of his life in camps, and was not disposed to fetter by conventional rules his daughter's rare spirit, so admirably suited to pioneer times and manners, however like an Amazon she may seem to the less independent critics of female manners at the present day. After the Indian war, Miss St. Clair returned to her early home in the romantic glens of Ligonier valley.

MRS. MASON KILLS ONE AND FRIGHTENS A SCORE.

In the beginning of 1794, a party of Indians killed George Mason, on Flat Creek, twelve miles from Knoxville, Tenn. In the night he heard a noise in his stable, and stepped out; was intercepted before he could return, by the savages, and fled, but was fired upon and wounded. He reached a cave, from which he was dragged out and murdered, and the Indians returned to the house to dispatch his wife and children. Mrs. Mason heard them talking as they approached, and hoped her neighbors, aroused by the firing, had come to her assistance. But perceiving that the conversation was neither in English nor German, she knew they were enemies. She had that very morning learned how to set the double trigger of a rifle. Fortunately the children were not awakened, and she took care not to disturb them. She had shut the door, barred it with benches and tables, and taking down her husband's well-charged rifle, placed herself directly opposite the opening which would be made by forcing the door. Her husband came not, and she was but too well convinced he had been slain. She was alone in darkness, and the yelling savages were pressing on the house. Pushing with great violence, they gradually opened the door wide enough to attempt an entrance, and the body of one was thrust into the opening and filled it, two or three more urging him forward. Mrs. Mason set the trigger of the rifle, put the muzzle near the body of the foremost and fired. The first Indian fell; the next uttered the scream of mortal agony. The intrepid woman observed profound silence, and the savages were led to believe that armed men were in the house. They withdrew, took three horses from the stable and set it on fire. It was afterwards ascertained that this high-minded woman had saved herself and children from the attack of over twenty assailants.

ESCAPE OF HANNAH DENNIS—MRS. CLENDENIN.

In 1761 a party of sixty Shawnees invaded the James river, Va., settlements and killed many, among others Joseph Dennis and child, and making prisoner his wife, Hannah. The Indians took her over the mountains and through the forests to the Chillicothe towns north of the Ohio. There she seemed to conform to their ways, painted and dressed herself and lived as a squaw. Added to this, she gained fame by attending to the sick, both as a nurse and a physician; and became so celebrated for her cures as to obtain from that superstitious people the reputation of being a necromancer, and the honor paid to a person supposed to have power with the Great Spirit.

In 1763 she left them, under the pretext of obtaining medicinal herbs, as she had often done before. Not returning at night, her object was suspected and she was pursued. To avoid leaving traces of her path, she crossed the Scioto three times, and was making her fourth crossing, forty miles below the towns, when she was discovered and fired upon without effect. But in the speed of her flight, she wounded her foot with a sharp stone, so as to be unable to proceed. The Indians had crossed the river, and were just behind her. She eluded their pursuit by hiding in a hollow sycamore log. They frequently stepped on the log that concealed her, and encamped near it for the night. Next morning they proceeded in their pursuit of her; and she started in another direction as fast as her lameness would permit, but was obliged to remain near that place three days. She then set off for the Ohio, over which she rafted herself, at the mouth of the Great Kanawha, on a drift log; traveling only by night, through fear of discovery, and subsisting only on roots, wild fruits and the river shell-fish, she reached the Green Briar, having passed forests, rivers and mountains for more than three hundred miles. Here she sank down exhausted and resigned herself to die, when, providentially, she was discovered by some of the people of that settlement, and hospitably treated at one of their habitations.

The settlement was made to suffer severely for this hospitable act. A party of fifty or sixty Shawnees, coming under the garb of friendship, suddenly fell upon the men, butchering every one of them, and made captives of the women and children. They next visited the Levels, where Archibald Clendenin had erected a rude block-house, and where were gathered quite a number of families—and were here again entertained with hospitality. Mr. Clendenin had just brought in three fine elk, upon which the savages feasted sumptuously. One of the inmates was a decrepid old woman, with an ulcerated limb; she undressed the member, and asked an Indian if he could cure it. "Yes," he replied, and immediately sunk his tomahawk into her head. This was the signal, and instantly every man in the house was put to death.

The cries of the women and children alarmed a man in the yard, who escaped and reported the circumstances to the settlement at Jackson's river. The people were loth to believe him, but were soon convinced, for the savages appeared, and many of the flying families were massacred without mercy. The prisoners were then marched off in the direction of the Ohio. Mrs. Clendenin proved herself in that trying moment a woman fit to be one of the mothers of the West. Indignant at the treachery and cowardly conduct of the wretches, she did not fail to abuse them from the chief down, in the most unmeasured manner. The savages, to intimidate her, would flap the bloody scalp of her dead husband against her face, and significantly twirl their tomahawks above her head, but still the courageous woman talked to them like one who felt her injuries and resolved to express the feeling. On the day after her captivity, she had an opportunity to escape, and giving her infant to a woman, slipped unobserved into a thicket. The child soon beginning to cry, one of the Indians inquired concerning the mother; but getting no satisfactory reply, swore he would "bring the cow to the calf," and taking the infant by the heels dashed out its brains against a tree. Mrs. Clendenin returned to her desolate home, and secured the remains of her husband from the rapacious jaws of the wild animals with which the woods abounded. It is stated that a black woman, in escaping from Clendenin's house, killed her own child to prevent its cries attracting the attention of the savages.

MRS. CUNNINGHAM ATTACKS TWO SAVAGES.

Early in 1778 an attack was made on a block-house in the country of the Upper Monongahela. The children allowed to play outside discovered Indians and, running in, gave the alarm. John Murphy stepped to the door, when one of the Indians, turning the corner of the house, fired at him. The ball took effect and Murphy fell into the house. The Indian springing in, was grappled by Harbert, and thrown on the floor. A shot from without wounded Harbert, yet he continued to maintain his advantage over the prostrate savage, striking him as effectually as he could with his tomahawk, when another gun was fired from without, the ball passing through his head. His antagonist then slipped out at the door, badly wounded in the encounter.

Just after the first Indian entered, an active young warrior, holding a tomahawk with a long spike at the end, came in. Edward Cunningham instantly drew up his gun, but it flashed, and they closed in doubtful strife. Both were active and athletic; each put forth his strength and strained every nerve to gain the ascendency. For a while the issue seemed doubtful. At length, by great exertion, Cunningham wrenched the tomahawk from the hand of the Indian, and buried the spike end to the handle in his back. Mrs. Cunningham closed the contest. Seeing her husband struggling with the savage, she struck at him with an axe. The edge wounding his face severely, he loosened his hold and made his way out of the house. The third Indian who had entered before the door was closed, presented an appearance almost as frightful as the object he had in view. He wore a cap made of the unshorn front of a buffalo, with the ears and horns still attached, and hanging loosely about his head. On entering the room this hideous monster aimed a blow with his tomahawk at Miss Reece, which inflicted a severe wound on her hand. The mother, seeing the uplifted weapon about to descend on her daughter, seized the monster by the horns; but his false head coming off, she did not succeed in changing the direction of the weapon. The father then caught hold of him; but, far inferior in strength, he was thrown on the floor, and would have been killed, but for the interference of Cunningham, who, having cleared the house of one Indian, wheeled and struck his tomahawk into the head of the other. During all this time the door was kept secure by the women. The Indians from without endeavored several times to force it, and would at one time have succeeded; but, just as it was yielding, the Indian who had been wounded by Cunningham and his wife, squeezed out, causing a momentary relaxation of their efforts, and enabling the women again to close it.

On the 11th of April some Indians visited the house of William Morgan, on Dunker's Bottom. They killed his mother and two or three others, and took the wife and her child prisoners. On their way home, coming near Prickett's Fort, they bound Mrs. Morgan to a bush, and went in quest of a horse for her to ride, leaving the child with her. She succeeded in untying, with her teeth, the bands which confined her, and wandered all that day and part of the next, before she came within sight of the fort. Here she was kindly treated and in a few days sent home.

HEROIC DEFENCE BY THE TWO WIDOWS COOK.

In 1791 two brothers, Jesse and Hosea Cook, and others, formed a settlement on the Elk Horn, at Innes' Bottom. In April, '92, an attack by about a hundred savages was made, and first upon the Cooks, who were out shearing sheep. The elder fell dead at once, but the younger reached his cabin and then expired. The two newly-made widows instantly secured the strong door. With them were three children—two white and one black. The savages shot at the door, but their balls failed to penetrate. They then tried to cut it down, but with no better success.

There was a rifle in the house, but no balls could be found. One of the women, in this extremity, found one ball, and placing it in her teeth, such was her excitement, actually bit it in two. With one half she instantly loaded her rifle. Peering cautiously through a crevice, she observed one savage seated on a log at a little distance off and fearing nothing. Taking quick aim she fired, when the astounded savage gave a loud yell, bounded into the air, and fell dead in his tracks. The infuriated savages now climbed to the roof of the cabin, and there kindled a fire. The flames began to crackle, but the resolution of the heroic females below was equal to the occasion. One instantly climbed to the loft, and the other handing her water, the fire was put out. Again and again was the roof fired. The water failing, the undaunted women broke eggs and threw the contents on the fire. The next recourse was the bloody waistcoat of the dead husband. Not enough! and now they used the contents of the chamber bucket, and at last quenched the flames. The savages then becoming frightened, descended.

Meanwhile a young man named McAndre had ridden off to give the alarm, and some of the Indians climbed neighboring trees and kept a sharp lookout. One of them from thence fired a ball into the cabin loft, which cut off a hank of yarn near Mrs. Cook's head, but that was all. A body of seventy-five hunters soon collected and made pursuit, but the main body of marauders had crossed the Ohio. The rest lingered and were attacked. The whites fired and the hindmost savage fell mortally wounded, but on one of the whites rushing his horse through the tall grass to the spot, the dying Indian raised his rifle and shot him through the heart. He then staggered to his feet, and was attempting to reach the nearest thicket, when he fell dead, pierced with twenty balls.

"THAT'S JOHN'S GUN!"—A WIDOW WON AT LAST.

At the disastrous battle of the Blue Licks there were a few reported slain who had been captured, and, after running the gauntlet, had been allowed to live. Among them was a certain husband, who, with eleven other captives, had been painted black as a signal of death. The whole twelve were stripped and placed on a log, the husband being at one extremity. The cruel savages now slaughtered eleven, one by one, but when they came to this one, though they drew their knives and tomahawks over him ready to strike, they paused and had an animated powwow, ending in sparing his life—why he never could find out.

For over a year his wife awaited his return, hopeful against all arguments to the contrary. She almost gave up at last, but, wooed by another, she postponed the day from time to time, declaring she could not shake off the belief that her husband would yet come back. Her friends reasoned on her folly; she reluctantly yielded, and the nuptial day was fixed. But, just before it dawned, the crack of a familiar rifle was heard near her lonely cabin. At the welcome sound she leaped out like a liberated fawn, ejaculating as she sprang, "That's John's gun!

That's John's gun!" It was John's gun, sure enough, and in an instant she was again in her beloved husband's arms. Nine years later, however, that same husband did really fall at St. Clair's defeat, and the same persevering lover renewed his suit and at last won the widow.

RUTH SEVIER MARRIES A SHAWNEE CHIEF.

Ruth Sparks was a famous character on the Tennessee border. She was the second daughter of General Sevier and the famous Catharine Sherrill. She was a girl of uncommon nerve and spirit. Without any regular schooling, she made rapid progress, having been gifted by nature with an active mind, a ready apprehension and great strength of purpose.

She was a great friend to the Indians, and learned not only the names of the chiefs but many of the warriors. She learned all she could from them of manners of living and domestic customs. Her father had been very kind to thirty of their race who had been taken and kept liberally by him. Ten of these had remained for three years at Sevier's residence. Ruth was greatly beloved by all of them. They taught her their language, and when they went back to their tribe were never tired of sounding her praises, predicting that "Chuckas Ruth make chief's wife some day," a prediction that was soon after amply verified.

Many instances are given of Ruth's spirit and courage. Once she gave notice of the approach of tories in time enough for her mother to have the most valuable of her effects removed to an old lime kiln. On another occasion, while bathing in the stream with some Indian girls, she saw enemies lurking near the banks and gave timely warning. Once, when crossing the same stream with an Indian girl, she was nearly drowned, and was rescued by two of the Cherokee captives above alluded to. She had learned in childhood to shoot well with a rifle, and was a far better shot than many of the hunters.

Among some children that were captured in Kentucky and carried to the Indian towns on the Scioto was a boy of about four. He was adopted by a head chief of the Shawnees, who had two sons of about the same age—the famous Tecumseh and his brother, the Prophet. The boy was called in adoption Shawtunte—a name changed after release to Richard Sparks. Shawtunte remained with the Indians until he was sixteen, becoming a thorough Indian. Some time before Wayne's victories he was exchanged and proceeded to Kentucky, and thence to the settlements on the Holston and Nolachucka. He soon managed to make the acquaintance of General Sevier, who was deeply interested in his history, and learned all he could about the northern Indians and his various adventures. His "moving accidents by flood and field." "These things to hear would *Ruth* seriously incline," and conceived quite an interest for the young chief.

General Sevier exerted his influence to procure an appointment for Shawtunte, and he soon obtained a Captain's commission and did service as a scout. He stood high as an officer and a gentleman. All this ended by his becoming deeply enamored of Ruth; and it is no wonder, for in symmetry of form and grace of attitude she was unrivaled. It was said of her, that "she never was the least awkward. She never sat, stood or walked but with a native ease and grace that was perfect, and she was always a figure for a painter." She had regular features, fair complexion, laughing blue eyes and an expressive mouth. She was, besides, frank, cheerful, sociable and a good talker.

Ruth returned the attachment, and the marriage came off, Richard not then knowing how to read or write. His charming bride became his teacher, and he soon made rapid progress. He was soon promoted to a Colonelcy in the United States Army, and, in 1801-2, was stationed at Fort Pickering, now Memphis. When Louisiana was purchased, Colonel Sparks took his regiment to New Orleans, his wife acting as his secretary, keeping his accounts, writing his reports, &c. During her residence there, some of the Choctaws—who knew her and had heard of Shawtunte's history—called almost daily at her house, bringing venison, ducks and turkeys. After residing South ten years Colonel Sparks resigned on account of ill health, and returned to Tennessee and thence to Staunton, where he died in 1815. His widow afterwards contracted a second marriage with a wealthy Mississippi planter, having a beautiful plantation near Port Gibson. She died in 1824, while on a visit to Kentucky. She never had any children, although extremely fond of them, and was an exemplary Christian.

THE "ISAAC AND REBECCA" OF WEST VIRGINIA.

Rebecca, the Jewess, was not, in her time, more celebrated for her skill and success in treating wounds than was Rebecca Williams all along the Ohio border. She very early in life became a widow, her husband having been killed, together with one of her uncles, by savages, in 1770. Her father was the first settler west of Fort Pitt, having located on Grave Creek, below Wheeling, even before the Zanes settled the latter place. Here she kept house for her two brothers, and would remain entirely alone for whole weeks in her cabin, while they were absent on hunting excursions. She never knew what fear was.

In 1774, immediately after the massacre of Logan's relatives at Baker's Station, she paid a visit to her sister, who had married Mr. Baker, and returned as she came, all alone, in a canoe, a distance of fifty miles. She "paddled her own canoe" till dark; made for the wilderness shore to wait for the moon to rise, and fastened it in a clump of willows, where she landed and waited. On stepping again into her canoe she happened to tread on something cold and soft, and, stooping down, discovered, to her horror, that it was a human body. The pale moonlight streamed upon the ghastly face of a dead savage, evidently not long killed. Rebecca recoiled at first, but uttered no scream, for in that was peril. She stepped over the corpse, entered her canoe and reached Grave Creek before morning.

The next Summer, while alone and kindling her fire in her cabin, she heard steps, and on turning about saw a gigantic savage standing close by. He shook his tomahawk threateningly, and motioned her to silence. He then looked around the cabin for plunder. Seeing her brother's rifle hanging over the fireplace, he seized it and went out. Rebecca showed no fear, but when he left hid in the corn till her brother's return.

The next year the youthful widow married Isaac Williams, a man after her own heart—a hunter and scout as absolutely devoid of fear as she was herself. On account of constant Indian marauds, they moved to near Redstone Fort, on the Monongahela, and after to Fort Henry. While there she and Mrs. Colonel Zane nursed Mills (whose case is mentioned elsewhere) back to perfect health. While spearing fish by moonlight, he received no less than fourteen bullet wounds. With warm fomentations and Indian herb applications, they not only cured every wound, but saved an arm and leg that were broken, and which all said must come off.

In consideration of her faithful services to them, her two brothers had given her four hundred acres of land just opposite the mouth of the Muskingum, where Marietta, the oldest settlement in Ohio, was located. To this point Isaac and Rebecca Williams removed and ever after lived, and, like Isaac and Rebecca of old, were given to hospitality and good deeds. In 1790 there happened a dreadful famine. Many of the new settlers were completely destitute. Old, mouldy corn went up to a fabulous price. Williams, however, had a large stock of good corn, with which he refused to speculate, but distributed to all who needed.

Chapter XII.

PLUCK AND SPIRIT OF THE BORDER BOYS.

> I ween you would have seen with joy
> The bearing of the gallant boy,
> When worthy of his noble sires
> His wet cheek glowed 'twixt fear and ire:
> He faced the bloodhound manfully,
> And held his little bat on high ;
> So fierce he struck, the dog, afraid,
> At cautious distance hoarsely bayed,
> But still in act to spring.

The above lines, by Walter Scott, fittingly portray the heir of Branksome—the gallant son of a bold border chief. Like father, like son, and the boys of the American border, having sires of extraordinary courage, and being environed from their very infancy with perils of uncommon character, were cool, bold, intrepid and fearless, frequently loving danger for the danger's sake.

> If a path were dangerous known,
> The danger's self was lure alone.

Wary as loons, and wild and hardy as young partridges, every sense was on the alert. Accustomed from the cradle to the most appalling perils, and to take amazing hazards ; liable to run athwart of lurking savages every day and in every woodland walk, familiarity bred contempt. Judge Hall mentions the characteristic incident of a pioneer woman who, on witnessing the quiet and peaceful death of a young man in his bed, declared it to be a " most beautiful sight." Appropriate enough for those who lived amid scenes of storm, violence and bloodshed, and who rarely witnessed a natural death. Border chronicles are full of incidents of youthful heroism, and subjoined are a few selections. They speak for themselves, and need no further comment from us.

REMARKABLE EXPLOIT OF THE JOHNSON BOYS.

No event of border history can exceed, for coolness and daring, the exploit of two little brothers, John and Henry Johnson—the former thirteen and the latter only eleven years of age. Their parents lived near the mouth of Short Creek, West Virginia. The facts of the case have been very much mixed up by local chroniclers, but we condense the veracious narrative of the tragedy, written for De Hass by Henry himself, who, in 1851, lived at Antioch, Ohio.

One day, in October, 1788, they went about a mile from the house to look for a hat which one of them had lost, and were sitting on a log by the roadside cracking nuts. They soon saw two men approaching, whom they took for two neighbors, but when the two came up they found "they were black." They sat still, and one said, "How do, brodder." John, the thirteen-year old, asked if they were Indians, and they said yes, and that the boys must go with them.

They took up their march, one of the savages in advance the other in the rear, and after traveling some distance, halted in a deep hollow. The two boys saw them whet their knives and heard them talk in their strange tongue, and thought they were about to be killed; but Henry states he felt no alarm, as he thought he would rather die than go with them, but was troubled that his parents would be fretting after them. John went up to the Indians, and, with great art, said his father was cross and made him work hard, and that he would rather be a hunter and live in the woods, all which seemed to please them, and they talked quite pleasantly. The two were Delawares—one a prominent chief—and they asked John many questions, and seemed well informed about the name and force of every border fort and station. They concluded by asking him if he knew the way home, and John, though knowing well, pointed the wrong way every time, which made them laugh.

They halted for the night about four miles from where they were first taken, and, as evening closed in, Henry became fretful, when John encouraged him by whispering that they must *kill their captors that night*. After they had selected a sleeping place and struck a fire, one of them reprimed his gun and went to an old stump to get some tinder wood. John then seized the gun and would have fired had not his brother taken hold of it and prevented, as the other might be close by, and told him if he would wait for night he would help. After supper they all sat down and talked for some time, the savages asking many questions, and stating that they never could catch his father's black horse that wore the bell. From this point we will quote from Henry's own narrative:

"We then went to bed on the naked ground, to rest and study out the best mode of attack. They put us between them, that they might be the better able to guard us. After a while one of the Indians, supposing we were asleep, got up and stretched himself on the other side of the fire, and soon began to snore. John, who had been watching every motion, found they were sound asleep. He whispered to me to get up, which we did as carefully as possible. John took the gun with which the Indian had struck fire, cocked it, and fixed it on a log in the direction of the head of one of the Indians. He then took a tomahawk and drew it over the head of the other Indian. At the word, I pulled the trigger and he struck at the same instant: the blow, falling too far back on the neck, only stunned the Indian. He attempted to spring to his feet, uttering most hideous yells, but my brother repeated the blows with such effect that the conflict became terrible, and somewhat doubtful.

"The Indian, however, was forced to yield to the blows he received on his head, and, in a short time, he lay quiet at our feet. The one that was shot never moved; and, fearing there were others close by, we hurried off, and took nothing with us but the gun I shot with. They had told us we would see Indians about to-morrow, so we thought that there was a camp of Indians close by; and fearing the report of the gun, the Indian hallooing, and I calling to John, might bring them upon us, we took our course towards the river, and, on going about three-fourths of a mile, came to a path which led to Carpenter's Fort. My brother here hung up his hat, that he might know where to take off to find the camp. We got to the fort a little before daybreak. We related our adventure and, the next day, a small party went out with my brother, and found the Indian that was tomahawked on the ground; the other had crawled off, and was not found till some time after. He was shot through, close by the ear."

A LAD KILLS A RED-CRESTED GOBBLER.

In Wood county, W. V., a man had a son, twelve years of age, who had been used to firing his father's gun, as most boys did in those days. He heard, he supposed, turkeys on or near the bank of the Ohio, and asked his father to let him take the gun and kill one. His father, knowing that the Indians frequently decoyed people by such noises, refused.

The Little Johnson Lads Kill their Captors.
—See page 700.

saying it was probably an Indian. When he had gone to work, the boy took the gun and paddled his canoe over the river, but had the precaution to land some distance from where he had heard the turkey all the morning, probably for fear of scaring the game, and perhaps a little afraid of Indians. The banks were steep, and the boy cautiously advanced to where he could see without being seen.

Watching a while for his game, he happened to see an Indian cautiously looking over a log, to notice where the boy had landed. The lad fixed his gun at a rest, watching the place where he had seen the Indian's head, and when it appeared again, fired and the Indian disappeared. The boy dropped the gun and ran for his canoe, which he paddled over the river as soon as possible. When he reached home, he said, "Mother, I have killed an Indian!" and the mother replied, "No, you have not." "Yes, I have," said the boy. The father coming in, he made the same report to him, and received the same reply; but he constantly affirmed it was even so; and, as the gun was left, a party took the boy over the river to find it and show the place where he shot the Indian, and, behold, his words were found verified. The ball had entered the head, where the boy affirmed he shot, between the eye and ear.

CAPTURE OF TWO BOYS AND THE PRICE PAID.

In the Spring of 1785 the Indians early reappeared in the neighborhood of Wheeling. One of their first acts, on Wheeling Creek, was the captivity of two boys, John Wetzel, Jr., and Frederick Erlewyne, the former about sixteen years of age and the latter a year or two younger. The boys had gone from the fort at Shepherd's for the purpose of catching horses. One of the stray animals was a mare with a young colt, belonging to Wetzel's sister, and she had offered the foal to John as a reward for finding the mare. While on this service they were captured by a party of four Indians, who, having come across the horses, had seized and secured them in a thicket, expecting the bells would attract the notice of their owners, so they could kill them.

The horse was ever a favorite object of plunder with the savages; as not only facilitating his own escape from pursuit, but also assisting him in carrying off the spoil. The boys, hearing the well-known tinkle of the bells, approached the spot where the Indians lay concealed, congratulating themselves on their good luck in so readily finding the strays, when they were immediately seized by the savages. John, in attempting to escape, was shot through the wrist. His companion hesitating to go with the Indians, and beginning to cry, they dispatched him with the tomahawk. John, who had once before been taken prisoner and escaped, made light of it, and went along cheerfully with his wounded arm.

The party struck the Ohio river early the following morning at a point near the mouth of Grave Creek, and just below the clearing of Mr. Tomlinson, who, with his family, was at that time in the fort at Wheeling. Here they found some hogs, and killing one of them, put it into a canoe they had stolen. Three of the Indians took possession of the canoe with their prisoner, while the other was busied in swimming the horses across the river. It so happened that Isaac Williams, Hambleton Kerr and Jacob, a Dutchman, had come down that morning from Wheeling to look after the cattle, &c., left at the deserted settlement. When near the mouth of Little Grave Creek, a mile above, they heard the report of a rifle. "Dod rot 'em," exclaimed Mr. Williams, "a Kantuck boat has landed at the creek, and they are shooting my hogs."

Quickening their pace, in a few minutes they were within a short distance of the creek, when they heard the loud snort of a horse. Kerr, being in the prime of life and younger than Mr. Williams, was several rods ahead and reached the bank first. As he looked into the creek, he saw three Indians standing in a canoe; one was in the stern, one in the bow and the other in the middle. At the feet of the latter lay four rifles and a dead hog; while a fourth Indian was swimming a horse, a few rods from shore. The one in the stern had his paddle in the edge of the water, in the act of turning and shoving the canoe from the mouth of the creek into the river. Before they were aware of his presence, Kerr drew up and shot the Indian in the stern, who instantly fell into the water. The crack of his rifle had scarcely ceased, when Mr. Williams came up and shot the one in the bow, who also fell overboard. Kerr dropped his rifle, and seizing that of the Dutchman, shot the remaining Indian. He fell over into the water, but still held on to the side of the canoe with one hand. So amazed was the last Indian at the fall of his companions, that he never offered to lift one of the rifles, which lay at his feet, in self-defence, but acted like one bereft of his senses.

By this time the canoe, impelled by the impetus given to it by the first Indian, had reached the current of the river, and was some rods below the mouth of the creek. Kerr instantly reloaded his gun, and seeing John Wetzel lying in the bottom of the canoe, raised it to his face as in the act of firing, when he cried out, "Don't shoot, I am a white man!" Kerr told him to knock loose the Indian's hand from the side of the canoe, and paddle to the shore. In reply he said his arm was broken, and he could not. The current, however, set it near some rocks not far from land, on which he jumped and waded out. Kerr now aimed his rifle at the Indian on horseback, who, by this time, had reached the middle of the river. The shot struck near him, splashing the water on his naked skin.

The Indian, seeing the fate of his companions, with the utmost bravery, slipped from the horse and swam for the canoe in which were the rifles of the four warriors. This was an act of necessity as well as of daring, for he well knew that he could not reach home without the means of killing game. He soon gained possession of the canoe unmolested, crossed with the arms to his own side of the Ohio, mounted the captive horse, which had swam to the Indian shore, and, with a yell of defiance, escaped into the woods. The canoe was turned adrift to spite his enemies, and was taken up near Maysville, Ky., with the dead hog still in it—the cause of all their misfortunes.

ADVENTURES OF FIVE KENTUCKY BOYS.

About four years after the untimely murder by Indians of the famous hunter and pioneer, Colonel William Linn, Colonel Pope, who lived near Louisville, had a tutor employed for his own sons, and was induced to receive also the sons of his neighbors. Among these were Colonel Linn's two boys, to whom Colonel Pope acted as guardian.

In February, 1785, five of these boys, the two Linns, Brashear, Wells and another, whose name is not recollected, went out one Saturday to hunt. The ages of these boys are not now known; they were little fellows, however, probably between the ages of nine and thirteen. They encamped for the night near the bank of the Ohio, at a place where a wide scope of bottom land was covered with heavy forest trees, and with ponds which were frequented by great numbers of swans, geese and ducks. A snow fell during the night, and in the morning they found themselves surrounded by a party of Indians, who had laid near them in ambush, and who captured them. Brashear, being a very fleet runner, attempted to escape, but was overtaken and secured with the rest. The elder Linn also attempted to run, but being stout and clumsy, and encumbered with some game which he had thrown over his shoulder, stumbled and fell, and was seized by a tawny warrior, who patted him on the back and called him, in the Indian tongue, "the little fat bear;" while Brashear, on account of his agility, received the name of the "buck elk."

The Indians, desiring to ascertain whether there was any unprotected house or settlement near that might be pillaged, asked the boys where they came from? The guarded reply was, "from Louisville." "You lie!" responded the savage; but the boys, mindful of their friends, even at a moment so distressing to themselves, kept their own counsel, and neither by word nor sign gave any indication that their assertion was not true. Their sagacity and firmness saved the family of Colonel Pope from destruction. The Indians retired with their young captives, who marched off with apparent indifference. Crossing the Ohio, they were taken to an Indian town in Northern Indiana, distant many days' journey; and on the way won the favor of their new masters by the patience with which they suffered captivity and fatigue, and the cheerful interest they appeared to take in the occurrences of the march.

At the Indian village the reception usually extended to prisoners awaited them. The women and children crowded around them with shouts of exultation, loaded them with reproaches, pelted them with dirt and stones, struck, pinched and heaped indignities upon them. But the gallant little fellows were probably prepared for these and greater cruelties, and found them no worse than they expected. For a while they submitted bravely; but at length the Linn blood became heated and the younger of the brothers, whose temper was quick, and who had frequently been cautioned by his companions to restrain his passions, losing all patience, singled out a tawny boy bigger than himself, who had struck him, and being left-handed, returned the blow in a way so unexpected that his foe, unable to parry it, was knocked down.

The warriors were delighted with an exploit so much to their taste, and applauded it with loud shouts and laughter. Another champion assailed the little hero, who, springing upon the juvenile savage with the ferocity of the panther, dealt him blows, kicks and scratches, with a vigor which surprised and delighted the spectators. The whole mass of boyhood became pugnacious; his companions joined with alacrity in the fight—Kentucky against the field. The heroic lads fought against odds, but displayed such prowess that they soon cleared the ring, and were rescued from further annoyance by their captors, who were particularly amused by the efficiency and odd effect of the left-handed blows of the younger Linn.

Such fine boys soon became favorites. Bold and bright-eyed, muscular and healthy, equal to the Indian boys in all athletic sports and superior to them in intelligence, they were readily adopted into the tribe and domesticated in families. Wells, however, fell to the lot of an Indian belonging to some distant town, whither he was taken, and thus separated from his comrades, saw them no more. He remained with the Indians all his life; married a sister of the celebrated chief Little Turtle, and became the father of a family. We have already sketched him at length. The other four adapted themselves so completely to their new mode of life, and seemed so well satisfied with the employments and sports of the savage youth; with fishing and hunting, wrestling, racing and riding Indian ponies, that all suspicion in regard to them was quieted, and they were allowed to roam about unregarded. They were "biding their time;" with a watchfulness that never slept they sought an opportunity to make their escape.

The hour of deliverance came at last. In the Autumn of their capture the warriors set out upon their annual hunt, roaming far off from home, in parties, and leaving their village in the care of the old men, the women and the children. The four boys found themselves one day at a camp, at some distance from the village, engaged in fishing, with no other companions but an old Indian and a squaw. A severe conflict of mind took place. The long-sought opportunity for escape was at hand; but they could regain their liberty only by the death of a woman and an old man, with whom they were associating as companions. To be the captives of a race in hostility with their countrymen, of a people they had been taught from infancy to fear and hate, and who had been the murderers of the father of two of them, was not to be tolerated. To leave their companions alive was to insure an early discovery of their flight, and a pursuit which must probably result in their capture and death. All their scruples yielded to a stern necessity; the bold resolve was taken; they killed the man and woman, and directed their steps homeward.

Pursuing the nearest course, with the unerring sagacity of Indians themselves, they struck for home through the wilderness. Traveling by night, and lying concealed during the day in coverts and hiding places, living upon wild fruits and nuts, and upon such small game as could be taken with the least noise and the least delay, and practicing all the cunning, the patience and the self-denial of the savage warrior, they reached the bank of the Ohio river, directly opposite to Louisville, after a journey of three weeks. Having no means of crossing the river, which here, at the head of the falls, is wide and rapid, they endeavored to attract the attention of the people at Louisville by firing their guns; but the Indians having lately been very troublesome, those who heard these signals, not understanding them, were unwilling to cross the river to ascertain their meaning.

The persevering boys then marched up the shore of the river nearly six miles, and at a place near the Six Mile island constructed a raft, with no tool to facilitate their labors but a knife. Even this frail and rough contrivance was not large enough to carry them all, and the elder Linn, who was an expert swimmer, plunged into the water and pushed the clumsy craft before him, while his companions paddled with all their might with poles. Thus they were wafted slowly and laboriously down and across the stream, until they were discovered from the town, and parties sent to their relief. About the same time the Indians who had been pursuing them reached the shore they had left, fired at them, and expressed their rage and disappointment by loud yells. Young Linn was nearly frozen by his immersion in the water, which, at that season, in the month of November, was very cold; but by the prompt and skillful remedies applied under the direction of his kind guardian, Colonel Pope, who had been driven by the Indians from his residence in the woods, and was now living in Louisville, he was recovered.

JONATHAN ALDER CAPTURED—HIS STRANGE RETURN.

In March, 1782, Jonathan Alder, a lad of nine years, while out near his father's home in West Virginia, with his brother David, hunting for a mare and her colt, was taken prisoner by a small party of Indians. His brother ran, but was pursued, and a spear pierced through his body. When finally taken, one caught him about the body while another pulled out the spear. Jonathan moved to him and asked him if he was much hurt, when the little fellow said he was, which were his last words. At that moment he turned pale and began to sink, and Jonathan was hurried on, but saw, soon after, one of the wretches coming up with his little brother's scalp in his bloody hand.

A Mrs. Martin, with a young child aged five, neighbors of the Alders, were taken at the same time, but finding the child burdensome, the savages soon killed and scalped it also. The last member of her family was thus destroyed, and the poor mother screamed out in an agony of grief. Upon this, one of the cruel savages caught her by the hair and, drawing the edge of his knife across her forehead, cried "scalp! scalp!" with the hope of stilling her cries. But, indifferent to life, she continued her screams, and then they procured some switches and whipped her until she was silent.

The next morning Jonathan, not having risen, through over-fatigue, saw, as his face was to the north, the shadow of a man's arm with an uplifted tomahawk. He turned about, and there stood an Indian ready for the fatal blow. Upon this the savage let down his arm and commenced feeling the boy's head. He afterwards told Alder it had been his intention to have killed him; but, as he turned, he looked so smiling that he could not strike, and on feeling his head and noticing that his hair was very black, the thought struck him that if he could only get him to his tribe, he would make of him a good Indian.

After crossing the Ohio they killed a bear, and remained four days to dry the meat for packing. He was now taken to a Shawnee village on Mad river, and forced to run the gauntlet formed by young children armed with switches. He was not hurt, and soon after was adopted into an Indian family.

His Indian mother washed him thoroughly with soap and water having herbs in it, and dressed him in leggins, moccasins and breechclout. Jonathan was at first very homesick. Everything was strange. He could not speak a word of Indian; their food disagreed with him, and for more than a month he used to go and sit under a big walnut and cry for hours. His father was a chief, Succohanos, his mother's name was Whinecheoh, and the daughters were called by the English names of Mary, Hannah and Sally. The parents were old people who had lost a son, and Alder was to take his place. They took pity on him, and did all possible to comfort him. His Indian sister, Sally, however, treated him like a slave, and when out of humor called him bad names.

Jonathan lived for a while with Mary, the wife of Colonel Lewis, a noted Shawnee chief. "In the Fall of the year," says he, "the Indians would generally collect at our camp, evenings, to talk over their hunting expeditions. I would sit up to listen, and frequently fall asleep. After the Indians left, Mary would fix my bed, and, with Colonel Lewis, would carefully take me up and carry me to it. On these occasions they would often say, supposing me to be asleep, 'poor little fellow, we have sat up too long for him and he has fallen asleep on the cold ground;' and then how softly they would lay me down and cover me up! Oh, never can I express the affection I had for these two persons."

Jonathan, with other lads, went into Mad river to bathe, and once came near drowning. He was taken out senseless and was some time in recovering. The boys, after bringing him to, gave him a silver buckle not to tell on them, and he did not. When Alder had learned the language he became more content, and said he would have lived very happily had it not been for several years of fever and ague. The chief food was game and hominy, with honey and sugar. When he was old enough, a musket was given him to learn to hunt. He used, at first, to follow the water courses and shoot mud turtles. Occasionally he killed a raccoon or a wild turkey, and received great praise from the Indians, who told him he would make a great hunter.

In the June after he was taken, occurred Crawford's defeat. He describes the anxiety of the squaws when the men had gone to battle, and their joy on the return of the spoil-laden victors. He defends Simon Girty from the charge of being the instigator of Crawford's tortures, and asserts that he could not possibly have saved Crawford's life, because he, Girty, had no influence among the Delawares. He was at the Mack-a-chack towns when they were destroyed by Logan in 1786; went to Kentucky on a horse-stealing expedition, and remained with the Indians until after Wayne's victory. He now lived on Big Darby, and, when white settlers first came there, he could scarcely speak one word of English. He was then about twenty-four years of age, fifteen of which had been passed with the Indians.

Alder married a squaw and began to farm like the whites. He kept horses, cows, hogs, &c.; sold milk and butter to the Indians, horses and pork to the whites, and soon began to accumulate property. He was shortly able to hire white laborers, but becoming dissatisfied with his squaw—a cross, peevish woman—he wished to wife among the whites and farm like them. He now made inquiries for his white relations, but was at a loss to know even what State he came from. While talking with a John Moore once, he told him he was captured somewhere near a place called Green Briar. Moore then asked him if he could recall the names of any of his old neighbors. After a little reflection, Alder said, "Yes, a family of Gulions lived close by us." Upon this Moore dropped his head, muttering to himself, "Gulion, Gulion," and then said, "Oh, yes; my father and I were out in that country and we stopped at their house one night; if your people are living 1 can find them."

Moore went to Wythe county, Va., and inquired for the Alder family, but they had moved. He advertised for them, stating where Jonathan was to be found and then returned. Alder now gave up all hope, but some time after he was at Franklinton, O., and was informed there was a letter at the post office for him. It was from his brother Paul, stating he had read the advertisement and that his mother and brothers were still alive. Alder now prepared to go back to Virginia, but first separated from his Indian wife, dividing the property equally; but she was very hard at a bargain, and he ended by giving her nearly all. She then claimed $200 more in silver, that he had saved. Alder says,

"I saw I could not get along without a fuss, and told her that if she would promise never to trouble me again she might have it."

Moore accompanied him to his brother's house. They arrived on horseback, pretending they were entire strangers, and inquired who lived there. "I had concluded," says Alder, "not to make myself known for some time, and eyed my brother very close but did not recollect his features. I had always thought I should have recognized my mother by a mole on her face. In the corner sat an old lady who I supposed was her, although I could not tell, for when I was taken her head was as black as a crow, and now it was almost perfectly white. Two young women were present, who eyed me very close, and I heard one of them whisper to the other, 'He looks very much like Mark,' (my brother.) I saw they were about to discover me, and accordingly turned my chair around to my brother and said, 'You say your name is Alder.' 'Yes,' he replied, 'my name is Paul Alder.' 'Well,' I rejoined, 'my name is Alder, too.' Now it is hardly necessary to describe my feelings at that time, but when I thus disclosed my name, he rose to shake hands with me, so overjoyed that he could scarcely utter a word, and my old mother ran, threw her arms around me, while tears rolled down her aged cheeks. The first words she spoke, after she grasped me in her arms, were, 'How you have grown! I am proud to own you for my son!' We passed the day in conversation. My brothers, Mark and John, were sent for, and we all had a happy time."

THE CAPTIVITY OF TWO LITTLE BROTHERS.

Dr. Denny, of Pittsburgh, persuaded the venerable James Lyon, of Beaver, Pa., then in his 71st year, to give a narrative of his boyish captivity among Indians, from which we condense, as follows: In 1782 his sister Mary lived on Turtle Creek, Pa., with his father, (the mother being dead,) and made for him and his brother Eli pin-hooks, with which they were busy fishing in the creek for minnows, when they heard a noise like the tramping of horses. Eli told James to go up the bank to see what it was. He ran up and, looking towards the house saw Indians jumping the fence and coming towards them, and had scarce time to halloo to Eli before the savages were upon them.

A large Indian, who had their father's bloody shirt and hunting frock on, and two scalps hanging to his girdle, caught James, while Eli ran up the opposite bank, striking the foremost Indian with his fishing rod. The enraged savage now pulled out his tomahawk when Eli grew quiet. James, too, had made a terrible hullabaloo when first seized by the Indian, but the sight of the brandished tomahawk quieted him also. The redskins seized the two boys and, lifting them almost off the ground, carried them to the hills above Dirty Camp, where they were joined by another party of Indians, with three stolen horses of Mr. Lyon. On the small black mare was a feather bed, on which Eli was seated in front and James behind him.

That evening they stole from a waste field they were passing a roan mare, and after a while one of the Indians climbed up a tree which was leaning against another, looked around and then motioned the lads to get off at once. They all then squatted for some time, till the danger, whatever it was, was past, and the direction was changed; the children being too young to tell what course they were traveling. They soon, however, struck a river, supposed to be the Allegheny, where all the horses were driven in to swim across; but the roan mare, proving refractory, was cruelly tomahawked, and the best of her cut into steaks and broiled. Some of it was handed to us; it was tough eating, but we were very hungry and glad to get it. They now examined the murdered Mr. Lyon's pocket book, and seemed specially pleased at the jingle of some gold guineas therein contained. The next day the river was crossed on a raft, the horses (all but Long's, which ran off and safely reached its old quarters,) having first been hunted up.

On that night, as well as the whole day after, a severe storm of rain and wind prevailed. A shelter was allowed James, but Eli was compelled to weather it outside. Both boys spent much of that night in tears over their forlorn situation. The next day their hair was all cut off, both lads resisting strenuously, which seemed mightily to please their captors. James' hair was unusually long and white, which procured him the name of O-pon-to-pos, or White-head. The first town they came to they were treated, before entering, with the horrid spectacle of their father's and sister's scalps stretched on small hoops and then suspended to long poles. The villagers came out to meet them, and escorted their party and the gory trophies in.

Among those who visited them was a white man, who took little James on his knee, caressed him and treated him so kindly that when he came to go the boy wanted to go with him, and could only be pacified by the promise that he would come and see him again, but that was the last he ever saw of him; he was told by his brother that the white man was Simon Girty. They soon reached a larger town, were put on two horses, and compelled again to run the gauntlet, an Indian pointing out to them the council house. Eli whipped his horse with a ramrod, and reached the house without a touch, but not so with

James, who was dragged off his horse by boys of about his own size, and severely kicked, cuffed and beaten, but finally succeeded in reaching his brother. There they remained several days, and then moved to White Woman's Creek, O., where James was adopted into a respectable Indian family.

We may mention two or three interesting incidents of this boy's captivity. He had a little Indian brother of about his own age and size, and a brother of his Indian father, badly crippled by a bear, used to set the two little ones to wrestle, which sometimes ended in a fight, when they would be parted. One time they both had knives, while husking corn, and when James had laid his knife down, his Indian brother slipped it away and put his own in its place. On making a dash for his own knife again he was severely cut, (the scar of which lasted during life,) for which his brother received a severe drubbing from the mother.

At another time their father brought in a deer, and after cutting off a steak, left his hunting knife on the ground. His little Indian brother had been amusing himself by getting splinters from the fire and burning James' naked hips. The white boy told him he would whip him if he did not desist, and on his continuing, James made at him, clinched and threw him, but, unfortunately, on the point of the knife, which entered above the little lad's hips, near the backbone, inflicting a severe wound. Seeing his Indian father reaching for his tomahawk, James ran down to the creek and hid under some rocks. It was in Winter, with much snow on the ground, and there the little fellow lay until night, when, feeling very cold, he crept out and saw his mother going for water. She made signs for him to come to her, and insisted on his going back to the camp, which he did, very much frightened, expecting he would be killed, or, at least, severely chastised. When he went in, however, no one had an angry word to say to him. He went up to where his little brother was lying in great pain, and being sincerely sorry for the accident, he was pardoned.

At another time he went to live with a sister who had married, who used him cruelly, striking him on the head with the back of a scalping knife so violently as to make it bleed profusely. Once, when she went to the creek to wash, she took hold of him and threw him into the creek, holding him under water until he would have been drowned, had not her husband just then returned from a hunt and witnessed the whole proceeding. His mother, coming that day to pay him a visit, noticed blood on his hair, and asked what did it. On being told she was exceedingly angry, and gave her daughter a terrible scolding, and took him home with her.

When told that, by treaty just made, he was to be sent back to his white relatives, James had to be coaxed to go, but on being informed he would again see his brother, consented, and was delivered up at Fort McIntosh, whence he reached his own old home safely. His sister Mary, who had not been killed, as the brothers supposed, told him of the agonies she endured when she missed them and saw moccasin prints in the mud. She ran at once and gave the alarm at Rayburn's garrison, and thus escaped herself. Lyon, in his narrative, neglects to state what became of his brother Eli, but it is presumed that he also was returned in safety to his friends.

FRANCIS DOWNING SAVED BY A BEAR.

In August, 1786, young Francis Downing was living in a fort, where, subsequently, some iron works were erected by Mr. Jacob Myers, which are now known by the name of Slate Creek works. About the 16th, a young man belonging to the fort called upon Downing, and requested his assistance in hunting for a horse which had strayed away on the preceding evening. Downing readily complied, and the two friends traversed the woods in every direction, until at length, towards evening, they found themselves in a wild valley, at a distance of six or seven miles from the fort. Here Downing became alarmed, and repeatedly assured his elder companion, (whose name was Yates,) that he heard sticks cracking behind them, and was confident that Indians were dogging them. Yates, being an experienced hunter, and from habit grown indifferent to the dangers of the woods, diverted himself freely at the expense of the lad, often inquiring at what price he rated his scalp, and offering to insure it for sixpence.

Downing, however, was not so easily satisfied. He observed that, in whatever direction they turned, the same ominous sound continued to haunt them, and as Yates still treated his fears with the most perfect indifference, he determined to take his measures upon his own responsibility. Gradually slackening his pace, he permitted Yates to advance twenty or thirty steps in front of him, and immediately after descending a gentle hill, he suddenly sprang aside and hid himself in a thick cluster of whortleberry bushes. Yates, who at that time was performing some woodland ditty to the full extent of his lungs, was too much pleased with his own voice to attend either to Downing or the Indians, and was quickly out of sight. Scarcely had he disappeared, when

Downing, to his unspeakable terror, beheld two savages put aside the stalks of a canebrake and look out cautiously in the direction which Yates had taken. Fearful that they had seen him step aside, he determined to fire upon them and trust to his heels for safety, but so unsteady was his hand, that in raising his gun to his shoulder it went off before he had taken aim. He lost no time in following its example, and after having run fifty yards, he met Yates, who, alarmed at the report, was hastily retracing his steps.

It was not necessary to inquire what was the matter. The enemy were in full view, pressing forward with great rapidity, and "devil take the hindmost" was the order of the day. Yates would not outstrip Downing, but ran by his side, although in so doing he risked both of their lives. The Indians were well acquainted with the country, and soon took a path that diverged from the one which the whites followed at one point and rejoined it at another, bearing the same relation to it that the string does to the bow. The two paths were at no point distant from each other more than one hundred yards, so that Yates and Downing could easily see the enemy gaining rapidly upon them. They reached the point of reunion first, however, and quickly came to a deep gully, which it was necessary to cross or retrace their steps. Yates cleared it without difficulty, but Downing, being much exhausted, fell short, falling with his breast against the opposite brink, rebounded with violence, and fell at full length on the bottom.

The Indians crossed the ditch a few yards below him, and, eager for the capture of Yates, continued the pursuit, without appearing to notice Downing. The latter, who at first had given himself up for lost, quickly recovered his strength, and began to walk slowly along the ditch, fearing to leave it lest the enemy should see him. As he advanced, however, the ditch became more shallow, until at length it ceased to protect him at all. Looking around cautiously, he saw one of the Indians returning, apparently in quest of him. Unfortunately, he had neglected to reload his gun while in the ditch, and, as the Indian instantly advanced upon him, he had no resource but flight. Throwing away his gun, which was now useless, he plied his legs manfully in ascending a long ridge which stretched before him, but the Indian gained upon him so rapidly that he lost all hope of escape. Coming, at length, to a large poplar which had been blown up by the roots, he ran along the body of the tree upon one side, while the Indian followed it upon the other, doubtless expecting to intercept him at the root.

But here the supreme dominion of fortune was manifested. It happened that a large she bear was suckling her cubs in a bed she had made at the root of the tree, and as the Indian reached that point first, she instantly sprang upon him and a prodigious uproar took place. The Indian yelled and stabbed with his knife, the bear growled and saluted him with one of her most endearing "hugs;" while Downing, fervently wishing her success, ran off through the woods, without waiting to see the end of the struggle. Downing reached the fort in safety, and found Yates reposing after a hot chase, having eluded his pursuers and gained the fort two hours before him. On the next morning they collected a party and returned to the poplar tree, but no traces either of the Indian or bear were to be found. They both probably escaped with their lives, although not without injury.

NARRATIVE OF JOHN BRICKELL'S CAPTIVITY.

We condense from the *American Pioneer*, long out of print, John Brickell's interesting narrative of his four and a half years' captivity among the Delawares. He was born in 1781, near Uniontown, Pa., and in 1791, when but ten years old, and while clearing out a fence row, was taken prisoner by an Indian, who took his axe. He had always been intimate with the Indians, who had constantly frequented the neighborhood, and did not feel afraid. So he was not alarmed, but went with the redman willingly. When he came, however, to a couple of logs, between which his companion had lain all night, he became suspicious and attempted to run, but was thrown down on his face and tied.

After going a little distance they fell in with a son of George Girty— a brother of the notorious Simon Girty—who told him that white people had killed Indians and now they were retaliating, and that if he would go peaceably, they would make an Indian of him; but if not, they would kill and scalp him. They then went to the Big Beaver; crossed on a raft, and Girty and he took a new direction. Young Brickell felt very bitter against Girty, and thought, if a good chance offered, he would kill him. They soon made a fire, Girty tying the lad to a sapling; but Brickell untied himself and laid down by the fire, and Girty, coming back, asked him what he had untied himself for. He answered he was cold. "Then you no run away?" "No," Brickell replied, upon which his companion said there were Indians close by, and he was afraid they would find the boy.

At the camp he saw many Indians who had been often at his father's. They treated him very kindly and gave him food. His captor now took him towards Sandusky; met two warriors on the way and got drunk with them, when one of the savages fell upon the boy and beat him so unmercifully that he ran into the woods and hid behind a log. They soon missed him and searched for him with torches, calling out, "White man! white man!" but Brickell lay still, and when the warriors left he went into camp again. At the Seneca town he had to run the gauntlet, and was bruised from head to foot, but a chief came up, threw the rest off of him, and led him through the lines with such rapidity that his feet scarce touched ground. Those who were the worst at the beating were now the kindest, and did all they could to cure him up but he was over two months getting well. His impression was that the Indian who rescued him was Captain Pipe himself.

His owner took himself a wife at the Seneca towns, and all then traveled on to the Maumee towns and the Auglaize, where he was adopted into the family of Whingroy Pooshies, or Big Cat, one of the best of the Delaware chiefs. He was treated exactly as one of the family, his employment being mostly hunting. They had a comfortable log cabin and seven acres of corn to cultivate. They slept on skins stretched on raised platforms, the men pulling off all but their breech-clouts and using the clothes for pillows. Brickell became a thorough Indian boy, adopting their clothes, customs, &c. He says the Delawares were excellent at raising children, never whipping and scarcely ever scolding them, but exacting order and obedience. A dozen might be in one cabin, of all ages, and scarcely any noise at all. They spent much time training their children in their ideas of right and virtue. Honesty, bravery and hospitality were their cardinal virtues, and the young were taught to honor and revere the aged, especially their parents.

When St. Clair's army was reported to be advancing, all the squaws and children were moved down the Maumee to await the result of the battle. After the Indian victory, the Indians came home laden down with spoils; Big Cat's share of the booty being two fine horses, four elegant tents, clothing in abundance, axes, guns, &c. There was much joy among them. Soon after he and another lad went hunting and came across a skeleton stripped of flesh, which his companion said had been eaten by the Chippewa Indians who were at the battle, and he called them brutes to so use their prisoners.

Two Touching Incidents of Indian Generosity.

Brickell soon came across some whites captured at St. Clair's defeat, when one of them, Isaac Patton, told him that as a certain Isaac Choat was sitting, after his capture, in a very melancholy mood, his owner asked him what made him look so sorry. Choat answered, because he could not help it, as he kept thinking of his wife and children and how they would get along without him. The Indian looked around and said, "I have a squaw and two children, and I would be sorry, too, if I were taken prisoner and carried away from them." He then arose, and, putting his hand on Choat's head, said, "Choat, you shall not stay away from them. I will let you go; but I will not turn you out alone for fear other Indians may catch you; I will go with you." This he actually did, accompanying him as far as the Muskingum, and there left him, telling him to go home to his family.

On one of Brickell's annual visits to the Rapids he saw Jane Dick, one of his own neighbors. She suddenly became missing, and great but unavailing search was made for her. He learned afterwards, that her husband had hired Alexander McKee's black cook to steal her away, which he did by taking her aboard a small vessel in a canoe and headed her up in an empty hogshead, where she remained until a day after the vessel sailed. The cook told Brickell it was part of the plan to steal him away also, but that he was watched so close they dare not venture it. At this time, indeed, the lad, who appears to have been a great favorite, was watched very closely. They would not let him sleep alone, or even go to draw water.

In June, 1794, two Indians and a boy, besides himself, started out on a hunt. They had been out about two months, and, on returning, found all the towns evacuated. Next morning an Indian runner came down the river giving the alarm whoop, and they were told to run for their lives as the whites were coming. "We scattered," says Brickell, "like a flock of partridges, leaving our breakfast cooking on the fire. The Kentucky riflemen saw our smoke and just missed me as I passed them through the corn. They took the whole of our two months' work, jerk, skins and all."

"Two or three days after we arrived at the Rapids, Wayne's spies came right into our camp boldly and fired on the Indians. Their names were Miller, McClellan, May, Wells, Mahaffy, and another whose name I forget. Miller was wounded; May was chased to the smooth, rocky bed of the river, where his horse fell and he was made prisoner. They knew him, as he had formerly been a prisoner and ran away, and took him back to camp. They said, 'We know you—you speak Indian language—you not content to live with us; to-morrow we take you to that burr-oak; we will tie you up, make a mark on your breast, and will try what Indian can shoot nearest.' This they did, riddling his body with bullets. Thus ended poor May."

Next day was Wayne's battle of Fallen Timbers. Brickell was out hunting and met some Indians on the retreat, who told him they had been badly whipped. Many of the Delawares were killed and wounded. Among the former was the Indian who captured May, and who was much missed, as he was the only gunsmith among the Indians. The Indians now had a terrible time. The British did not half support them. All their dogs and cattle died, and they were nearly starved, and very bitter against the British, who had goaded them on to hostilities. They then went and made peace with the Americans, and had an exchange of prisoners, but as there was no Indian to give up for Brickell, he continued, and in the Spring all went to Fort Defiance; and now follows a scene very creditable to the Indian character. We quote:

"On the same day Big Cat told me I must go over to the fort. The children hung around me crying, and asked me if I was going to leave them. I told them I did not know. When we got over, and were seated with the officers, Big Cat told me to stand up, which I did. He then rose and addressed me in about these words: 'My son, there are men the same color as yourself. There may be some of your kin there, or your kin may be a great way off from you. You have lived a long time with us. I call on you to say if I have not been a father to you.' I said, 'You have used me as well as a father could a son.' He said, 'I am glad you say so. You have lived long with me; you have hunted for me, but our treaty says you must be free. If you choose to go with the people of your own color, I have no right to say a word; but if you choose to stay with me, your people have no right to speak. Now reflect on it and take your choice, and tell us as soon as you make up your mind.'

"I was silent a few minutes, in which time it seemed as if I thought of almost everything. I thought of the children I had just left crying; I thought of the Indians I was attached to, and I thought of my own people, and this latter thought predominated, and I said, 'I will go with my kin.' The old man then said, 'I have raised you; I have taught you to hunt; you are a good hunter; you have been better to me than my own sons. I am now getting old and cannot hunt. I thought you would be a support to my age. I leaned on you as a staff; now it is broken. You are going to leave me and I have no right to say a word, but I am ruined.' He then sank back, in tears, to his seat. I heartily joined him in his tears; parted with him, and have never seen nor heard of him since."

ADVENTURES OF YOUNG JAMES RAY.

We have already quoted from James Ray, (afterwards General Ray,) how, when but a youth of seventeen, he first became acquainted with George Rogers Clark. From all accounts Ray must have been a very daring and spirited youth. We select the following incidents relating to him:

In March, 1777, while he, his brother William, William Coomes and Thomas Shores were engaged in clearing some land about four miles from Harrodstown, Ky., they were attacked by a very large party of savages, under the command of the celebrated chief Blackfish. The Indians were attracted to the place by the sound of the axes, and rushing upon the choppers, killed William Ray and took Shores prisoner; Coomes hiding in the brush. James Ray being uninjured by the discharge of rifles, fled rapidly in the direction of the fort at Harrodstown. Several of the swiftest Indian runners pursued him, but such was the white lad's fleetness and activity, that he distanced them all and reached the fort in safety. His remarkable speed elicited the admiration of the Indians—most excellent judges of that power—and Blackfish himself remarked to Boone, when he was a captive, that some Kan-tuck boy at Harrodstown had outrun all his best warriors.

This swiftness was a fortunate circumstance for the fort, as it enabled the garrison to prepare for an attack. The militia was organized, ammunition prepared, water and provisions procured, and all put in readiness for an attack. The hot-headed McGary openly charged Harrod with having been wanting in precaution, and were about to shoot at each other, when McGary's wife rushed in and turned aside the rifle of her husband, when Harrod immediately withdrew his. McGary instantly insisted that a party of thirty should be immediately dispatched in search of Coomes, Shores and Ray. Harrod and Rogers Clark opposed the measure as imprudent.

At length, however, McGary's passion prevailed, and thirty mounted men were placed under him, and moved with great rapidity. Near an abandoned encampment they discovered the mangled remains of William Ray, who was McGary's son-in-law, at sight of which McGary turned pale and was near falling from his horse. When the body was first sighted, one of the men shouted out: "See there! They have killed poor Coomes!" Coomes, who had hitherto lurked in his hiding place, now sallied forth, exclaiming, "No, by gob, they haven't killed him, Coomes is safe yet!" The party having buried Ray and rescued Coomes, returned in sadness to the fort.

A few days after the Indians approached the fort, first firing a cabin on the east side of the place. The garrison, supposing the fire to be the result of an accident, rushed out to quench the flames. The artful Indians, having succeeded in their decoy, instantly attempted to intercept their return to the fort. The whites retreated, keeping up a random fire, until they reached a grove on the hill, where the Harrodsburg Court House was afterwards built. Each man now taking his tree, the Indians were compelled to retire, one white being killed and four Indians —one of whom afterwards died—being wounded.

Some time after the Indians collected in great numbers about Harrodstown, in order, it was thought, to prevent any corn from being raised. In this period of peril and distress, James Ray, at that time but seventeen, rendered himself an object of general favor by his coolness, enterprise and intrepidity. He often arose before day, and left the fort on an old horse—the only one left by the Indians, of forty brought to the country by Major McGary—in order to procure food for the garrison. Proceeding cautiously to Salt river, (generally riding in the water, or in the bed of some small stream, in order to conceal his route,) when sufficiently out of hearing, he would kill his load of game and bring it in to the suffering inhabitants after nightfall. Older and more experienced hunters, in similar hazardous enterprises, were killed by the Indians.

During the same year, while Ray and a man named McConnell were shooting at a mark near the fort, the latter was suddenly shot down by the Indians. Ray instantly glanced his eye in the direction of the shot, and perceiving the enemy, raised his rifle to avenge the death of his friend, when he was suddenly attacked by a large body of Indians, who had crept near him. His powers as a runner were again called into requisition, and Ray bounded towards the fort, distant a hundred and fifty yards, with the speed of an antelope, amidst showers of bullets from the savages. But when he approached the gates of the fort he found them closed, and the garrison too much under the influence of their fears to open them for his admittance.

Ray Four Hours Under Fire—Clark Compliments Ray.

In this critical situation, pursued by the savages and refused shelter by his friends, Ray threw himself flat upon the ground, behind a stump just large enough to protect his body. Here, within seven steps of the fort wall, in sight of his mother, he lay for four hours, while the Indians kept up an incessant fire, the balls often striking and tearing up the ground on either side of him. At last, becoming somewhat impatient, he called out to the garrison, "For God's sake, dig a hole under the cabin wall, and take me in." Strange as may have appeared the suggestion, it was immediately carried out, and the noble young hunter was speedily within the shelter of the fort and in the arms of his friends.

During the Fall of this year, (1777,) in order to make up the deficiency arising from having raised no corn, the people of the fort determined to make a turnip patch about two hundred yards northwest of the station. While clearing the ground, an Indian was shot at by the guard and the men retired. The next day the cattle were perceived to be disturbed, and snuffing the air about a small field in the furthest corner, that had been allowed to grow up in very high weeds. The presence of concealed Indians was instantly suspected, so sure were the cattle to betray their vicinity, either from the sight of the Indians themselves or from the smell of paint upon their persons. The indication prompted Major George Rogers Clark to turn the ambuscade upon the enemy. For this purpose some men were still kept at work in the turnip patch nearest the fort, and, in order to prevent suspicion by the Indians of any movement from within, they occasionally hallooed to their companions to come out to their work, while Clark, with a party of the garrison, sallied out of the fort with great secrecy, and, making a circuit, came up in the rear of the Indians as they lay concealed in the weeds.

A volley was discharged at the concealed foe, and four of their number killed—one by Clark and another by Ray. The Indians instantly retreated, and were pursued by the whites about four hundred yards down the creek, where they came upon the remains of a deserted Indian encampment, of sufficient extent for the accommodation of five or six hundred warriors. From this camp the enemy had issued during the preceding Summer to assail the stations, which they had kept in a state of constant alarm, and had destroyed the greater portion of their horses and cattle. The Indians had now abandoned their position, and the party which had just been pursued was supposed to be the remnant of the Indian force which had occupied the encampment. Major Clark complimented James Ray with the gun of the Indian which he had shot, and which was the first he had ever killed.

HOW READILY CAPTIVE BOYS BECOME INDIANIZED.

Frederick Lee, with a brother-in-law and a few families, settled on the Green Briar, a branch of the Kanawha. In time of peace a large party of savages encamped on Lee's place for several days, appearing to be on one continuous frolic. Mr. Lee, however, was anxious, and did all he could to propitiate them, killing a fine hog, supplying them with bread, &c. It all availed nothing. When the time came for the blow he was the first to fall. He had a large family, several daughters grown, and one married, with her first child at her breast. Several savages one day entered the cabin and tomahawked old Mr. Lee and his son-in-law, and made prisoners of the rest. The blood of the father fell on the head and face of his little son, who was then seated on his lap. The Indians, intending to spare the boy and fearful he might be hurt, carried him to the creek and washed him. While this tragedy was enacting, many neighboring families were sharing the same fate.

All now started out for the Indian towns. There were several women along, all with babes at the breast. Mrs. Johnson, one of the daughters, who gives the narrative, says that her sister pressed her babe to her breast and bore her long march with fortitude, hoping the child would be saved. The day before the Indian town was reached, however, all the babes were pitilessly murdered, and their bodies left in the woods to be devoured. After this Mrs. Johnson said her sister wished to die, and did all she could to provoke the Indians to kill her, and made several attempts on their lives. She lived, however, to marry afterwards.

Soon after getting to the Indian towns the women were put to hard drudgery and the boys allowed to run wild with the Indian lads: to shoot with bow and arrow, dabble in the water, &c. They were kept prisoners some ten years, and after peace was declared, found their way home. The boys, and especially the younger ones, had become so completely Indian that they had to be forced away: a close watch had to be kept on them, and, notwithstanding all, John Lee made his escape on the third night, evaded all pursuit, made his way back to the Indians, and was two years longer with them before his relatives could get him away. They, however, said that they never undertook such a task as breaking in those wild Indian boys, and especially John. It was utterly impossible to keep clothes on them. In the Summer it was useless to attempt it, at least any more than shirts, for the strongest tow or hemp linen shirt, with the strongest kind of fastenings at the collar and wristband, would, in an hour's time, be torn off and thrown away, and they would be found swimming like wild ducks in the river, or rolling naked on the sand beaches, and in their melancholy moments they would often be heard to exclaim, in tones of real distress, "Oh, my Innies, my Innies," (meaning Indians). It took a number of years to root out this attachment, and indeed some of the boys carried their woodland habits and costumes to the grave.

TWO LADS SAVE THE LIFE OF A GIRL.

In 1776 the settlements along the West Virginia and North Carolina border had notification of a large force of Cherokees coming upon them. It was anxiously debated which were best; to await the enemy's coming in the crazy fort, or to march out boldly and meet them in the woods. The latter resolve prevailed, and a sharp contest ensued, when the savages disappeared like magic, leaving eleven or twelve dead behind. Alexander Moore, a strong, athletic man, grappled with a cunning savage of about his own size and strength, and being hard pressed, William King ran up to Moore's relief, but the Indian adroitly kept Moore in such a position that King could not shoot him without first shooting his friend. The savage had a large knife at his belt, for the possession of which both struggled, but at length Moore drew it and plunged it into the Indian's bosom, when King finished him by shooting him through the head.

Shortly after two parties, supposing hostilities over for the present, went out to visit their farms, and were both violently attacked in full hearing of the fort, and causing indescribable confusion. The men in the fort sallied out, but the savages quickly retired. One incident deserves mention. A lad by name of William Casey had a sister, a beautiful little girl, along with the party in the field, and as he was running for his life, he discovered the Indians in close pursuit of his sister. At that moment his eyes fell upon another lad of about his own age by name of Robert Hasold, and he shouted to him to come and help him save Nancy. Hasold obeyed, and although there were five Indians in pursuit, (some say seven,) the lads rushed between them and the girl, and by dexterously managing to fire alternately, still keeping one gun loaded when the other was discharged, they so galled the pursuers that they were glad to give up the chase.

SILAS HART'S SON AVENGES HIS FATHER.

In September, 1782, a marauding band of savages appeared in Hardin county, Ky., and committed many depredations. Silas Hart, named "Sharp Eye" by the Indians, on account of his skill and penetration as a fighter, pursued them with a chosen few, Hart shooting their chief. Vengeance was denounced by the tribe against Sharp Eye and his family, and some time after, another gang, led by the brother of the slain chief, appeared again in Hardin county. Hart was the very first upon their trail, but was unable to overtake them. The savages now worked back on the trail of the whites. Hart arrived home about dark and slept soundly after his chase. Next morning, just as his family were seating themselves for breakfast, the savages appeared and the chief's brother shot Hart dead.

The scout's son, a brave lad of only twelve years, the instant he saw his father fall, grasped his rifle, and, before the savage could enter the door, sent a ball through his heart. The Indians now rushed on in a body, but the first who entered received from the hands of the gallant lad a hunting knife in his breast, driven to the hilt. The contest, however, was too unequal. He, and his mother and sister, were overpowered and carried to the Wabash. The sister, unable on account of feebleness to keep up, was soon dispatched. The mother and son were intended for a more terrible sacrifice. All the horrid preparations were made, but an influential squaw interfered and saved the boy's life, while a chief, who wished the mother as a wife, interfered in her behalf. Both were ultimately redeemed by traders and returned home. Mrs. Hart subsequently married a Mr. Countryman, and the boy migrated to Missouri.

GEORGE BOZARTH'S RUSE AND ESCAPE.

The last incursion of savages in Northwestern Virginia happened in 1794. A murderous band appeared on Leading Creek. Expresses were sent all about to warn the people, but they had been so long exempt from savage marauds, that a false security was engendered. Among other careless settlers, John Bozarth, with his sons, George and John, were busy in a field drawing grain to the barn, when the agonizing shrieks of those at the house rent the air, and they hastened to ascertain the cause.

The elasticity of youth enabled George to approach the house some few paces in advance of his father, but the practiced eye of the old gentleman first discovered an Indian, only a small distance from his son, and with his gun raised to fire upon him. With parental solicitude he exclaimed, "Take care, George, an Indian is going to shoot you!" George was then too near the savage to think of escaping by flight. He looked at him steadily, and when he supposed the fatal aim was taken and the finger just pressing the trigger, he fell, and the ball whistled by him. Not doubting but that the youth had fallen in death, the savage passed by him and pressed in pursuit of the father. Mr. Bozarth was yet springy and agile, and was enabled to keep ahead of his pursuer. Despairing of overtaking him, by reason of his great speed, the savage hurled a tomahawk at his head. It passed harmless by, and the old gentleman got safely off.

When George Bozarth fell as the Indian fired, he lay as if dead, and supposing the scalping knife would be next applied to his head, determined on seizing the savage by the legs as he would stoop over him, and endeavor to bring him to the ground, when he hoped to be able to gain the mastery over him. Seeing him pass on in pursuit of his father, he arose and took to flight also. On his way he overtook a younger brother, who had become alarmed and was hobbling slowly away on a sore foot. George gave him every aid in his power to facilitate his flight, until he discovered that another of the savages was pressing close upon them. Knowing that if he remained with his brother, both must inevitably perish, he was reluctantly forced to leave him to his fate. Proceeding on, he came up with his father, who, not doubting but he was killed when the savage fired at him, broke forth with the exclamation, "*Why, George, I thought you were dead!*" and manifested, even in that sorrowful moment, a joyful feeling at his mistake. The Indians who were at the house wrought their work of blood, killing two or three small children and took Mrs. Bozarth and two boys prisoners. With these they made their way to their towns, and arrived in time to surrender their captives to General Wayne.

TWO BOYS IN THE WOODS ALL WINTER.

In the Fall of 1803 Henry Perry, one of the first pioneers about Delhi, Ohio, after getting up his cabin in the woods, left his two little sons in it and returned to Philadelphia for the remainder of his family; but finding his wife sick, and afterwards falling sick himself, could not get West again until the following June. His two little boys, Levi and

Reuben, only eleven and nine years old, remained there alone eight months, fifteen miles from any white family and surrounded by savages, with no food but the rabbits they could trap or catch in hollow logs, the remains of one deer that the wolves drove and killed near their cabin, and a little corn meal that they occasionally obtained of Thomas Cellar by following down the "Indian Trail." The Winter was a severe one and their cabin was open, having neither daubing, fireplace nor chimney; they had no gun and were wholly unaccustomed to forest life, being fresh from Wales, and yet these little fellows not only struggled through the Winter but actually made a considerable clearing.

A BOY MADE TO SLAY SIX INDIANS.

In May, 1788, a man by the name of Kirk lived near Knoxville, Tenn. While he was absent, an Indian by the name of Slim Tom visited the family and was supplied with provisions. Having learned their defenceless condition, he soon after returned with a party, and the whole Kirk family—eleven in number—were brutally massacred. Kirk soon after returning, saw the dead bodies of his dear family lying in the yard, gave the alarm, and soon a band of several hundred men, under Colonel Sevier, were in pursuit, and ravaged several villages on the Hiwassee river. Abraham, a friendly Indian, who lived with his son on the Tennessee, had publicly declared that if the Indians went to war he would remain at his home and never quit it.

When the troops came to the south side, Hubbard, Colonel Sevier not then being present, sent for Abraham and his son to come over the river to the troops, and to bring with them the chief Tassel and other Indians that they might have a talk with them. They came over, all unsuspicious, and were put in a house, and young Kirk, the son of him whose family had been killed, was urged to go into the house and commence killing with the tomahawk. As soon as the first dropped dead, the others, six in number, foresaw their fate. Each cast his eyes to the ground, bowed his head, and one after the other stoically received the fatal tomahawk strike.

Colonel Sevier, on returning, was very indignant, and rebuked the savage tragedy, but was answered by Kirk—who was largely backed by the troops—that if Sevier had suffered from the murderous savages as he had, that he, too, would have acted the same way. Sevier, unable to punish the offender, was obliged to smother his resentment and overlook the flagitious deed. The Indians, however, exacted a terrible revenge, and for some time after ravaged that whole border.

ANECDOTES OF INDIANS.

—An Indian chief, on being asked whether his people were free, answered, "Why not, since I myself am free, although their king?"

—An Indian having been found frozen to death, an inquest of his countrymen was convened to determine by what means he came to such a death. Their verdict was, "Death from the freezing of a great quantity of water inside of him, which they were of opinion he had drunken for rum."

—A white man, meeting an Indian, accosted him as "brother." The red man, with a great expression of meaning in his countenance, inquired how they came to be brothers; the white man replied, "Oh, by way of Adam, I suppose." The Indian added, "Me thank him Great Spirit we no nearer brothers."

—About 1794 an officer presented a western chief with a medal, on one side of which President Washington was represented as armed with a sword, and on the other an Indian was seen in the act of burying the hatchet. The chief at once saw the wrong done his countrymen, and very wisely asked, "Why does not the President bury his sword, too?"

—An Ottawa chief, known to the French by the name of Whitejohn, was a great drunkard. Count Frontenac asked him what he thought brandy to be made of? He replied that it must be made of hearts and tongues. "For," said he, "when I have drunken plentifully of it, my heart is a thousand strong, and I can talk, too, with astonishing freedom and rapidity."

—A chief of the Five Nations, who fought on the side of the English in the French wars, chanced to meet, in battle, his own father, who was fighting on the side of the French. Just as he was about to deal a deadly blow on his head, he discovered who he was, and said to him, "You have once given me life, and now I give it to you. Let me meet you no more, for I have paid the debt I owed you."

—When any of the Indians come into our towns, our people are apt to crowd around them, gaze upon them and incommode them, when they desire to be private; this they esteem great rudeness, and the effect of the want of instruction in the rules of civility and good manners. "We have," say they, "as much curiosity as you, and when you come into our towns we wish for opportunities of looking at you; but for this purpose we hide ourselves behind bushes where you are to pass, and never intrude ourselves into your company."

—A missionary residing among a certain tribe of Indians, was one day, after he had been preaching to them, invited by their chief to visit his wigwam. After having been kindly entertained, and being about to depart, the chief took him by the hand and said, "I have very bad squaw. She had two little children. One she loved well, and the other she hated. In a cold night, when I was gone hunting in the woods, she shut it out of the wigwam and it froze to death. What must be done with her?" The missionary replied, "She must be hanged." "Ah!" said the chief, "Go, then, and hang your God, whom you make just like her."

—An Indian of the Kennebec tribe, remarkable for his good conduct, received a grant of land from the State, and fixed himself in a new township where a number of families were settled. Though not ill-treated, yet the common prejudice against Indians prevented any sympathy with him. This was shown at the death of his only child, when none of the people came near him. Shortly afterwards, he went to some of the inhabitants and said to them, "When white man's child die, Indian man be sorry—he help bury him. When my child die, no one speak to me—I make his grave alone. I can no live here." He gave up his farm, dug up the body of his child, and carried it with him two hundred miles through the forests, to join the Canada Indians.

—A certain clergyman had for his text on a time, "Vow, and pay the Lord thy vows." An Indian happened to be present, who stepped up to the priest, as soon as he had finished, and said to him, "Now, me vow me go home with you, Mr. Minister." The priest, having no language of evasion at command, said, "You must go, then." When he had arrived at the home of the minister, the Indian vowed again, saying, "Now, me vow me have supper." When this was finished, he said, "Me vow me stay all night." The priest, by this time thinking himself sufficiently taxed, replied, "It may be so, but I vow you shall go in the morning. The Indian, judging from the tone of his host that more vows would be useless, departed in the morning *sans ceremonie.*

—About the time Cornplanter left his nation to proceed on his mission to the hostile tribes, three of his people were traveling through a settlement upon the Genesee, when they stopped at a house to light their pipes. There happened to be several men within, one of whom killed the foremost Indian with an axe as he stooped to light his pipe. One of the others was badly wounded with the same weapon, while escaping from the house. They were not pursued, and the other, a boy, escaped unhurt. When Cornplanter learned what had happened, he charged his warriors to remain quiet, and not to seek revenge. He was only heard to say, "It is hard, when I and my people are trying to make peace for the whites, that we should receive such a reward. I can govern my young men and warriors better than the thirteen fires can theirs."

—An Indian came, one day, to a tavern in Sherman's Valley, Pa., called for a gill of whiskey and drank it, when there came another Indian in. He also called for a dram, but set it on the table without tasting. He then took the first savage outside and discoursed with him most seriously for some time. The first Indian then stripped himself naked and stretched himself on the floor. The other stood at the door, and when he was ready, he stepped forward with his knife and stabbed his companion, who was lying down, to the heart. The prostrate Indian received the stab quietly, leaped to his feet, drank the other whiskey off and dropped down dead. The white people made prisoner of the other Indian, and sent word to the heads of the nation. Two of them came, saw the Indian homicide, and then told the whites to let him go, as he had done right. The cause of the killing was a mystery. The dead man had probably broken some tribal law, and cheerfully submitted to the penalty.

—In a time of Indian troubles, an Indian visited the house of Governor Jenks, of Rhode Island, when the Governor took occasion to request him that if any strange Indian should come to his wigwam, to let him know it, which the Indian promised to do; but, to secure his fidelity, the Governor told him that when he should give him such information he would give him a mug of flip. Some time after, the Indian came again: "Well, Mr. Gubenor, a strange Indian come to my house last night." "Ah!" says the Governor, "and what did he say?" "He no speak," replied the Indian. "What! not speak at all?" added the Governor. "No, he no speak at all." "That certainly looks suspicious," said His Excellency, and inquired if he were still there, and being told that he was, ordered the promised mug of flip. When this was disposed of, and the Indian was about to depart, he mildly said, "Mr. Gubenor, my squaw have child last night;" and thus the Governor's alarm was suddenly changed into disappointment, and the strange Indian into a new-born pappoose.

—A white trader sold a quantity of powder to an Indian, and imposed upon him by making him believe that it was a grain which grew like wheat, by sowing it upon the ground. He was greatly elated by the prospect of not only raising his own powder, but of being able to supply others, and thereby becoming immensely rich. Having prepared his ground with great care, he sowed his powder with the utmost exactness in the Spring. Month after month passed away, but his powder did not even sprout, and Winter came before he was satisfied that he had been deceived. He said nothing; but some time after when the white trader had forgotten the trick, the same Indian succeeded in getting credit of him to a large amount. The time set for payment having expired, he sought out the Indian at his residence and demanded payment for his goods. The Indian heard his demand with great complaisance; then looking him shrewdly in the eye, said, "Me pay you when my powder grow." This was enough. The guilty white man quickly retraced his steps, satisfied, we apprehend, to balance his account with the chagrin he had received.

—An Indian came into Bethlehem, Penn'a., to dispose of his peltry. "Well, Thomas," said a trader who happened to be there, to him, "I believe you have turned Moravian." "Moravian!" answered the Indian, "what makes you think so?" "Because," replied the trader, "you used to come to us to sell your skins and peltry; and now you trade them away to the Moravians." "So!" rejoined the Indian, "now I understand you well, and I know what you mean to say. Now, hear me. See, my friend! when I come to this place with my skins and peltry to trade, the people are kind; they give me plenty of good victuals to eat, and pay me in money or whatever I want, and no one says a word to me about drinking rum, neither do I ask for it! When I come to your place with my peltry, all call to me, 'Come, Thomas! here's rum; drink heartily, drink! it will not hurt you!' All this is done for the purpose of cheating me. When you have obtained from me all you want, you call me a drunken dog, and kick me out of the room."

—An aged Indian, who, for many years, had spent much time among the white people, both in Pennsylvania and New Jersey, one day, about the year 1770, observed that the Indians had not only a much easier way of getting a wife than the whites, but also a more certain way of getting a good one. "For," said he, in broken English, "white man court—court—may be one whole year! may be two years before he marry: Well, may be then he get very good wife—but may be not—may be very cross! Well, now, suppose cross! scold so soon as get awake in morning! scold all day! scold until sleep!—all one—he must keep him—white people have law forbidding throw away wife if he be ever so cross—must keep him always! Well, how does Indian do? Indian, when he see industrious squaw, he go to him, place his two forefingers close aside each other, make two like one—then look squaw in the face —see him smile—this is all—he say, yes!—so he take him home—no danger he be cross! No, no—squaw know too well what Indian do if he cross! throw him away and take another! Squaw love to eat meat —no husband no meat. Squaw do everything to please husband, he do everything to please squaw—live happy."

—An Indian well known as Sam Hide, was notorious for his lying and his propensity for cider, which he obtained by traveling through the country and begging it from door to door. At one time he happened to be in a part of the country where cider was very hard to get; but Sam was determined to have it, if he could obtain it by lying. Being not far from the house of an acquaintance, who he knew had cider—but he was well satisfied that in the ordinary way of begging he could not get it—he set his wits to work, and soon contrived a way to obtain his desire. On arriving at the house of the gentleman, instead of asking for cider he inquired for the man of the house, whom, on appearing, Sam requested to go aside with him, as he had something important to communicate. When they were alone, Sam told him that he had that morning shot a fine deer, and if he would give him a crown he would tell him where it was. The gentleman declined, but offered half a crown. Finally, Sam said, as he had walked a great distance that morning, and was very dry, for half a crown and a mug of cider he would tell him This was agreed upon, and the price paid. Then Sam pointed out the place in this manner. He said to his friend, "You know of such a meadow?" describing it. "Yes." "You know a big ash tree, with a big top, by the little brook?" "Yes." "Well, under that tree lies the deer." This was satisfactory and Sam departed. It is scarcely necessary to say the meadow was found and the tree, but no deer. The duped man was greatly enraged, but as Sam was out of his reach, he had to go home contented. Some years afterwards he happened to fall in with the Indian, and immediately began to rally him for deceiving him so, and demanded back his money, and pay for his cider and trouble. "Why," said Sam, "would you find fault if Indian told truth half the time?" "No." "Well," says Sam, "you find him meadow?" "Yes." "You find him tree?" "Yes." "What for, then, you find fault with Sam Hide when he told you two truth to one lie." Sam heard no more from the farmer. In all the wars with the Indians, during his lifetime, Hide fought on the side of the English, and was a brave soldier. He was a great jester and passed as an uncommon wit. He died in Dedham, January 15, 1732, at the age of one hundred and five years.

www.ingramcontent.com/pod-product-compliance
Lightning Source LLC
Chambersburg PA
CBHW052107010526
44111CB00036B/1491